The

DICTIONARY

of Family

Psychology

and *Family*

Therapy

Second Edition

The
DICTIONARY
of *Family*
Psychology
and *Family*
Therapy
Second Edition

S. Richard Sauber
Luciano L'Abate
Gerald R. Weeks
William L. Buchanan

SAGE Publications
International Educational and Professional Publisher
Newbury Park   London   New Delhi

For information address:

SAGE Publications, Inc.
2455 Teller Road
Newbury Park, California 91320

SAGE Publications Ltd.
6 Bonhill Street
London EC2A 4PU
United Kingdom

SAGE Publications India Pvt. Ltd.
M-32 Market
Greater Kailash I
New Delhi 110 048 India

Printed in the United States of America

Library of Congress Cataloging-in-Publication Data

Main entry under title:

The dictionary of family psychology and family therapy / S. Richard
    Sauber . . . [et al.].—2nd ed.
        p.   cm.
    Includes bibliographical references.
    ISBN 0-8039-5332-1.—ISBN 0-8039-5333-X (pbk.)
    1. Family psychotherapy—Dictionaries.   2. Family—Psychological
aspects—Dictionaries.   I. Sauber, S. Richard.
    RC488.5.D525   1993
    616.89′156′03—dc20   93-1588

JUN 2 6 1995

93   94   95   96   10   9   8   7   6   5   4   3   2   1

Sage Production Editor: Diane S. Foster

Contents

List of Tables and Figures

Foreword to the First Edition

Family Therapy: Basic Concepts and Terms is the first family therapy dictionary that goes beyond the scope of a glossary. The authors have struggled for years with the problem. The literature burgeons, the number of family therapists proliferates, and new practitioners want to know more and more about ideas that govern the field. The authors have responded to the demand with a dictionary that represents the way people understand the terminology. Rather than survey all of the involved originators, the authors have used the device of going back to the literature to define terms the way they were used by the originating writers.

I have written this Foreword to compliment the effort of those who have done this book, without becoming involved in all of the detail about me or anyone else. The authors are serious people who have done their best, whether old-timers agree or disagree. They have made an attempt to get beyond the maze of polarized personal opinions and to report the field as it exists today. They have made a contribution to the literature. The book is the best of its kind, to date. A copy of the book should be available to the entire profession, to the increasing number of family therapists, and to the hordes of students who hope to become family therapists.

It is difficult for me to write without some idea about the chaos and explosion in the family therapy field. Psychoanalysis, which began in the late 19th century, was the first of the psychological theories about human behavior. Its difference from medicine brought up the issue of nonmedical analysts. Psychoanalysis focused on the principle of psychopathology within the patient, which was treated in the analytic relationship. Poorly defined family ideas surfaced from time to time. Group therapy evolved in the 1930s. One can only guess why formal family research was delayed until the late 1940s and early 1950s. The research revealed a number of phenomena never previously reported in the literature. It gave voice to some smoldering ideas about family therapy that had existed in isolation. The research led to discussion about family therapy at a national meeting in March 1957.

I have been active in psychiatry since the mid 1940s and active in the family field since its beginning in the mid 1950s. The explosion of family therapy starting in 1957 began immediately after it became a recognized open subject. Ideas about therapy displaced previous ideas about history and more complex notions about theory. Dozens of new professional people from divergent theoretical backgrounds began performing "therapy." New therapists quickly became teachers. Each teacher taught succeeding groups of trainees, who, in turn, became practitioners and teachers. As concepts passed from one generation of students to the next, the ideas were amplified, simplified, and distorted to fit the prevailing orientation of the teacher.

The first professional journal, *Family Process,* appeared early in 1962. Societal facts played a part. Mental health legislation in the early 1960s was designed to make services available to the masses. Family therapists were employed in the increasing network of mental health centers. The idea of *systems* became a catchword that helped define family therapy as different. An increase occurred in the number of family institutes, where groups of teachers worked together for teaching and professional exchange. During the 1960s, the institutes began admitting those who had master's degrees in a discipline that dealt with human behavior. Psychiatry gradually moved away from its psychoanalytic orientation and toward a more biological drug orientation. A big change and new growth came in the late 1970s when the government agreed that family therapy was new and different and was qualified to be a discipline on its own, without responsibility to the other professions. All of this activity stimulated a rapid growth in the number of family therapists, family journals, and family meetings of all kinds. At the present time, the field is in a state of explosion that is without parallel in my professional experience. The rapid growth and the profusion of terminology have been a powerful force in the writing of this dictionary.

The authors have done a credible job in defining the multiple terms in use today. I believe that the rapid growth of past decades will continue into the foreseeable future. At some time in future years, we may even look back on the good old days of 1984 as they were defined by this unique book. I hope the authors will have the energy to publish successive volumes as new terms come into use.

My own interest is more theoretical than therapeutic. One can only wonder about what will be taking place a century from now. I believe there is a powerful theoretical potential in the basic family idea and that verifiable facts from the human family eventually may merge with other verifiable facts from other accepted sciences. The big hurdle comes from feelings that are not verifiable but that are still important to human experience. When feelings and imagination can be viewed as functional facts, they can contribute, rather than detract, from a final view of that part of man that is scientific. Brain research may help close the gap.

Murray Bowen, M.D.
The Family Center
Washington, DC

Foreword to the Second Edition

In their first edition dictionary of important terms and concepts and in the current revised and updated edition, the authors have provided an enormous service to all of those involved in the field of the family—theoreticians, researchers, clinicians, teachers, trainers, supervisors, and students. As the field has continued to expand exponentially with great rapidity since the first publication of this interesting dictionary in 1985, the need for a volume that pulls together and defines the major salient words, phrases, and concepts in the field has become even more acute.

This new volume provides a compact, handy reference for all family professionals because it simultaneously encompasses all schools of family theory and therapy, deftly citing and quoting the originators of the ideas, as well as other primary sources who have elaborated and refined the concepts. Many of the most prominent members of the first generation of family therapists who pioneered the field, such as Ackerman, Bowen, Bateson, Jackson, and Satir, are no longer with it; yet their seminal ideas live on, and a silent tribute is paid to their contributions in the terms included in this work. The authors also have incorporated cornerstone concepts from others of the grandparent generation, such as Bell, Boszormenyi-Nagy, Haley, Minuchin, Satir, Watzlawick, Weakland, Whitaker, and Wynne. Fortunately they also have done a thorough search of the literature that contains writings of second, third, and fourth generation family therapists, researchers, and clinicians (see Kaslow, 1991, for delineation of the generations), culling and then including what they deem to be the most significant and most used concepts. This concise compendium also acknowledges the contributions of colleagues in other countries, such as Howells and Stierlin. Thus the authors also herald the advent of the spread of family therapy into an international phenomenon in the 1970s and 1980s. This spread is reflected further in the expanded list of organizations involved in the family field that appears in the back of the book: both the International Family Therapy Association (IFTA), started in 1987, and the International Academy of Family Psychology, started in 1990.

I believe that this enlarged yet succinct dictionary rapidly will become an essential reference book for all engaged in the family field and that it provides the basis for a consensually agreed-upon conceptual terminology for the field. I plan to consult it whenever I encounter a term that is used in an ambiguous way and to study its contents directly to augment my own fund of knowledge.

It is a privilege to have been invited to write the foreword to this important book. and I congratulate the authors and Sage Publications on collaborating to produce this volume.

Florence Kaslow, Ph.D.
West Palm Beach, Florida

Preface

The current proliferation of books and viewpoints in the field of family psychology and family therapy demands that the professional have available a ready reference that contains many of the new terms that have been coined in the past three decades. This dictionary attempts to satisfy this need; the book has been long in the making. In the early 1970s, Roberta Golden (then a graduate student), at Luciano L'Abate's prompting, started a glossary of family sociology terms. This early glossary, which was stenciled, lay dormant but was made available to interested professionals. Among those who received it was Richard Sauber, who used it in his seminars at Brown University and found it helpful to students and professionals alike. Sauber eventually asked L'Abate to collaborate on a full-fledged dictionary. The project proved to be so massive that, several years later, Gerald Weeks was asked to join in the effort. After calls to our colleagues, we started to receive definitions and examples from friends, colleagues, and students. Eventually the number of terms grew beyond our expectations and our plans. Finally, however, a book was completed.

The first edition was published in 1985. Five years later, the field had grown. Family Psychology had established itself with its own Division (43) in the American Psychological Association and had its own journal, the *Journal of Family Psychology*. Thus it was time for a revision. William L. Buchanan was recruited, and the work began again, with many new terms added.

We see three major needs for a dictionary in the family psychology field: (a) as already noted, the need for a ready reference; (b) the need for a bibliographical source where the professional can find references for more information about a concept; and (c) the need for a summary of the many viewpoints and sources that have by now proliferated beyond the command of any one person. One cannot find under one cover the contributions that have mushroomed in family psychology in the past two decades. This dictionary thus attempts to condense into one volume many of the terms in the field and also to indicate the pragmatic use of each.

Acknowledgments

Writing a dictionary is probably the most difficult and tedious academic project that we have undertaken. Our work began in 1978. During our initial years of referencing, three major glossaries in the family therapy literature were available to us. These were the works of Roberta Golden at the Family Study Center of Georgia State University, the articles by Jules Riskin and Elaine E. Faunce, and a glossary by Michael J. Gerson and Marilyn Barsky published respectively in *Family Process* (1972) and the *American Journal of Family Therapy* (1979).

We also wish to acknowledge the following colleagues who personally contributed concepts to our dictionary: Daniel L. Araoz, Ben N. Ard, Jr., Joanna R. Baisden, Jeffrey J. Block, Arthur M. Bodin, Murray Bowen, Harman D. Burck, James W. Croake, Albert Ellis, Edmond F. Erwin, S. I. Greensdan, Florence Kaslow, Fortune V. Mannino, M. Livia Osborn, Daniel R. Panitz, Gerald R. Patterson, and the late Robert A. Ravich. Many others contributed definitions and are acknowledged with their contributed entries throughout the text.

A special thanks to Cathy and Frank Rowan, who spent several months scanning text into a file, editing, typing dictation, and being true perfectionists in getting this document ready for the publisher. Their hard work is greatly appreciated, and they deserve a special recognition for the endless hours of retyping.

Finally, we appreciate the contribution of the countless individuals, colleagues, friends, and students who helped us in this enormous task.

S. Richard Sauber, Ph.D.
Luciano L'Abate, Ph.D.
Gerald R. Weeks, Ph.D.
William L. Buchanan, Ph.D.

Introduction: About This Dictionary

The purpose of this dictionary is to introduce the reader to two relative newcomers in the field of psychology: family psychology and family therapy. We assume the reader to be a doctorate level teacher, researcher, or practitioner, or a graduate student in psychology, counseling, or marriage and family therapy. The previous edition of this dictionary (Sauber, L'Abate, & Weeks, 1985) focused mainly on family therapy. However, with the advent of the new APA Division 43 of Family Psychology during the same year of publication as the previous edition, it became necessary to expand the original number of terms to include those that are consistent and congenial with this emerging field. Despite the few courses, and even fewer curricula, currently available in family psychology, it is inevitable this field will acquire a substantive content matter of its own that will become the basis for specialized academic interest and course work. We hope this dictionary will facilitate the formation and development of such a new discipline, both academic and applied.

A question the reader may ask relates to the process of how the terms contained in this dictionary were selected and eventually included here. In the first edition, these terms were compiled by the first three authors (S. R. S., L. L., and G. W.) in their personal reading of the family therapy literature by selecting terms that were frequently cited and/or accepted in the literature. For the second edition, a fourth author was added (W. B.), and the dictionary was broadened to include family psychology. The four authors consider themselves to be family psychologists with strong academic interests who are also practitioners.

Collecting the terms for the dictionary was both a subjective and an objective process. The authors reviewed all of the major family psychology and family therapy journals (e.g., *Family Process, Journal of Family*

Psychology, American Journal of Family Therapy, Journal of Sex and Marital Therapy, Journal of Marital and Family Therapy) in search of terms. Textbooks also were reviewed, especially those that are considered to be handbooks, reviews, or introductions to the field. These texts rendered the basic terms in the field because the same content area was being covered and the same terms were chosen across texts as key concepts. In addition, the major theories in the field were given close attention to ensure inclusion of their terminology. In short, frequently cited terms and those from major theories were included on an objective basis. However, this field is rapidly growing, with new terms being generated at an astounding rate. Many terms were included on a subjective basis. Some were terms that the contributors agreed had sufficient merit for inclusion. These terms captured a concept particularly well or were believed to hold promise as interesting new concepts for the future development of the field. The editors agreed to err on the side of being overly inclusive.

In selecting and defining terms, no one theoretical perspective dominated our work. We included terms and concepts from all of the various schools of family psychology and family therapy. In any emerging field, terms often are transposed from other fields of study. Thus we included terms that did not necessarily fit any school of family psychology or family therapy, but were terms "borrowed" from other fields and frequently used by family psychologists and family therapists. The reader will notice terms from the literatures of clinical child psychology, family law, sex therapy, and others. Perhaps the best example of the need to be inclusive is the work of Milton Erickson. Erickson died before the founding of family psychology, wrote nothing about family psychology, and wrote very little about family therapy per se, yet his work has had a profound impact on the originators of several schools of family therapy. Thus terms used by Erickson are included when appropriate. Other terms, such as *attention deficit disorder* and *learning disability,* are included because these are the two most frequent problems in which families with preschool children seek the services of a psychologist. Everyone in the family is affected when a child has ADHD.

The "meaning" of a term, as we see it, is given by (a) its definition, (b) an example relevant to its usage, (c) an early source using the term, and, if relevant, (d) a recent source. Definitions were paraphrased from an early source or were arrived at by our personal understanding of how each term was used originally by its source, as we saw it and as we all agreed. Examples were taken generally from our personal clinical experience, a composite abstracted from many similar cases, or from an example cited by the source reference. Examples were used to illustrate the meaning or application of the term. Many terms did not need examples because they were clear in and of themselves or did not lend themselves to an example. Terms that referred to techniques usually were illustrated to demonstrate their application. As for the references, we could not always trace a term to its true, "original" source. Often too many people claim to be the actual wordsmiths, or no name is attached to a term that already has been accepted in the professional literature or jargon. Thus we cited "early" references, many of which were original sources using the terms; many others were not. We attempted also to locate where the term was used in a more current reference. Often terms change meanings or significance over time. By including a more recent reference, we hope that the reader, at whatever level of expertise, will be able to make a connection with a specific term encompassing a whole new literature that has entered in the field of psychology in the last generation. The selection of early and recent references, however, had to be a judgment call because we realized fully that many other references could have been cited as well.

S. Richard Sauber, Ph.D.
Luciano L'Abate, Ph.D.
Gerald R. Weeks, Ph.D.
William L. Buchanan, Ph.D.

abortive runaway   An attempt to run away from home that does not succeed. The child either returns home after a short period of time or contrives a situation in which he or she will be retrieved by parents or other authorities.

Stierlin, H. (1974). *Separating parents and adolescents: A perspective on running away, schizophrenia and waywardness.* New York: Quadrangle.

absence of involvement   A family in which members show no interest in each other except to share their instrumental functions.
   Example: A family may operate smoothly in their daily activities but not share any personal thoughts or feelings. See also **disengaged family.**

Epstein, N., & Bishop, D. (1981). Problem-centered systems therapy of the family. In A. S. Gurman & D. P. Kniskern (Eds.), *Handbook of family therapy* (pp. 444-482). New York: Brunner/Mazel.
Epstein, N., Bishop, D., & Levin, S. (1978). The McMaster model of family functioning. *Journal of Marriage and Family Counseling, 4,* 19-31.

absent member maneuver   A strategy used in systems therapy, especially the Milan model. The therapist assesses which members of the family should be present. If the family comes for the session missing a member, the family is told the session cannot take place without that person and no session is held. In the following session, the meaning of that person's absence is analyzed in-depth.

Prata, G. (1987). The absent family member maneuver at the first sessions of concentration. *Journal of Strategic and Systemic Therapies, 6,* 24-41.

ACA   See **adult child of an alcoholic.**

accelerated change   An immediate change in behavior in relation to one's spouse, produced through a planned strategy.

Example: The therapist gives a prescription aimed at reversing self- or other-defeating, repetitious, transactional patterns between the couple. The prescription stresses action, not interpretation.

Papp, P. (1976). Brief therapy with couples groups. In P. J. Guerin (Ed.), *Family therapy: Theory and practice* (pp. 350-363). New York: Gardner.

accession process   The addition of unwanted arrivals to the family, such as newborns, adopted children, and elderly parents.

Reiss, D. (1980). Pathways to assessing the family. In C. Hofling & I. Lewis (Eds.), *The family: Evaluation and treatment* (pp. 86-92). New York: Brunner/Mazel.

accommodation   A tactic in which the therapist makes personal adjustments in order to join with the family; a calculated move used to achieve a therapeutic alliance by appearing to be similar to the family. See **mimesis, joining,** and **maintenance.**

Example: The male therapist removes his coat and tie for a family that comes to the session in shirt sleeves.

Gerson, M., & Barsky, M. (1979). For the new family therapist: A glossary of terms. *American Journal of Family Therapy, 7,* 15-30.

Minuchin, S. (1974). *Families and family therapy.* Cambridge, MA: Harvard University Press.

accordion family   A type of family in which one parent is away for extended periods of time. The other parent then assumes the responsibilities of the missing parent (e.g., nurturing, organizing) until that parent returns.

Example: The husband works for an international corporation that requires him to reside for several months in foreign countries. His wife works out expected behaviors and family routines during her husband's absence.

Minuchin, S., & Fishman, H. (1981). *Family therapy techniques.* Cambridge, MA: Harvard University Press.

achievement sensitive families   Families that work competitively to master problems and whose members are optimistic about their own individual abilities. Such families have a negative view of people, with the parents bitter and angry at the children.

Example: The youngest of three brothers becomes a race car driver. His older brothers' success in school and eventually becoming doctors has engendered resentment on his part. He begins racing cars in high school despite his parents' objections and even their disapproval, which occur despite his winning many contests. He now receives more public recognition and attention than his brothers.

Reiss, D. (1981). *The family's construction of reality.* Cambridge, MA: Harvard University Press.

ACOA See **adult child of an alcoholic.**

acting "as if" An action-oriented intervention in which one or both partners are instructed to behave as they wish they could but believe they cannot at the present time.

Baruth, L. G., & Huber, C. H. (1984). *An introduction to marital theory and therapy.* Belmont, CA: Brooks/Cole.

acting out The enactment of unconscious tension in the form of disruptive behavior. The behavior is associated with poor frustration tolerance, poor reality testing, and a tendency toward repetition compulsion. Defined from a family systems perspective, acting out is symptom cultivated when a family is undergoing stress; it reflects back to cyclical, sequential patterns that may be referred to as *operating principles,* such as boundary dysfunction, systemic void, systemic intensity, and systemic rocking. In many cases, several of these principles may operate at once; in fact, one may lead to another.

Carter, E. A., & McGoldrick, M. (1980). The family life cycle and family therapy: An overview. In E. A. Carter & M. McGoldrick (Eds.), *The family life cycle* (pp. 3-20). New York: Gardner.

action learning A type of psychotherapy in which emphasis is placed on nonverbal exchanges and direct observation. Often, in this form of therapy, what the therapist does is much more important than what the therapist says; the model that the therapist provides is rapidly internalized and effective, in contrast to the slow process of change accompanying traditional psychotherapies.

Example: Rather than talk about assertiveness with a client, the therapist models and role-plays with the client, forcing interaction.

Skynner, A. C. R. (1976). *Systems of family and marital psychotherapy.* New York: Brunner/Mazel.

active listening A technique of listening to, reflecting comments from, and questioning clients to assist them in focusing and clarifying thoughts and feelings.

Example:

Therapist What do you want to tell your husband?

Client	I don't want to tell him anything.
Therapist	You say you don't want to tell him anything, but the way you just said that sounded like you're angry.
Client	Yes, I guess I didn't realize just how angry I was about it.

Here the therapist uses active listening to focus on the underlying feelings of anger. The therapist may reflect not only what is said but also how it is said.

Gordon, T. (1982). *P. E. T. in action.* New York: Bantam.

activity catharsis   The therapeutic release of feelings through activity or the acting out of conflicts, as opposed to the verbal catharsis of an analytic therapist.

Example: A man is angry at his father. Instead of yelling at his father, he beats a punching bag. Redirecting his emotions to activity instead of directly to his father relieves feelings of anger while avoiding a situation in which he would feel guilty.

Slavson, S. (1943). *An introduction to group therapy.* New York: Commonwealth Fund.

actuality therapy   A type of family therapy concerned with happenings in the present family. Psychic traumas arising within and outside the family are dealt with in the present, even though the problem may stem from some past event. Treatment at this level is oriented to restoring the individual to the pretrauma period.

Example: A mother's depression first occurred when her daughter married. The current depressive episode was triggered by a phone call from the daughter. The actuality therapist would be interested in the current family situation that produced the problem.

Howells, J. (1975). *Principles of family psychiatry.* New York: Brunner/Mazel.

actualizing family transactional patterns   Clarifying family interactions and hierarchies by the therapist asking the family to enact a common family scenario.

Example: The therapist asks the family to discuss the 15-year-old son staying out all night last Saturday. As they do this, an argument develops.

Minuchin, S. (1974). *Families and family therapy.* Cambridge, MA: Harvard University Press.

actualizing tendency   An inherent tendency to develop all of one's capacities in ways that serve to maintain or enhance the organism. The movement is toward more autonomy and away from control by others. The construct includes other concepts of motivation, such as need reduction, tension reduction, and drive reduction.

Example: A healthy, functioning family allows its members to develop ways of fulfilling individual potentials within and without the family context.

Horne, A. M., & Ohlson, M. M. (1982). *Family counseling and therapy.* Itasca, IL: F. E. Peacock.

Rogers, C. P. (1959). A theory of therapy, personality and interpersonal relationships, as developed in the client-centered framework. In S. Koch (Ed.), *Psychology: A study of a science: Vol. III. Formulations of the person and the social context* (pp. 184-256). New York: McGraw-Hill.

ADD See **attention deficit disorder.**

ADHD See **attention deficit hyperactivity disorder.**

adult child of an alcoholic (ACA or ACOA) An adult who grew up as a child in a home in which an adult was alcoholic. Because a parent was abusing substances, the parent was not able to provide the emotional and sometimes the physical needs of the child adequately. This lack resulted in the child growing up with inadequate personality development, which is manifest in a variety of ways. Adult children of alcoholics typically have many of the following: difficulty discerning what is normal behavior, difficulty following projects through, often lie, often are judgmental, often have difficulty having fun, often take themselves too seriously, often have difficulty with intimacy, often seek constant approval and affirmation, feel essentially different from other people, are either super-responsible or super-irresponsible, and show extreme loyalty even to people who do not deserve such loyalty.

Woititz, J. G. (1990). *Adult children of alcoholics* (Expanded ed.). Pompano Beach, FL: Health Communications.

adversary system A system that purports to help individuals resolve their differences through legal representation but is likely to prolong and intensify hostilities and cause psychopathological behavior.

Example: In divorce proceedings, litigants often are provided with weapons to use against one another that they may not have realized they possessed. A wife may be advised by her divorce attorney to request 90% of her husband's income and all of their marital property and to obstruct visitation with the children's father unless he pays her desired alimony and child support. Thus attorneys often contribute to an increasingly vicious cycle of vengeance. Disputes are unnecessarily prolonged, and the hardship on both parties is often greatly increased. The divorce proceedings may, in this way, cause greater psychological pain to the parties than the marriage that brought about the decision for divorce in the first place.

Gardner, R. A. (1989). *Family evaluation in child custody, mediation, arbitration, and litigation.* Cresskill, NJ: Creative Therapeutics.
Marlow, L., & Sauber, S. R. (1990). *Handbook of divorce mediation.* New York: Plenum.

advisory attorney   An attorney used in family mediation disputes. Although the role of impartial advisory attorney is relatively new, lawyers have demonstrated their ability to move from the role of advocate into impartial roles, such as that of judge or arbitrator, often serving with distinction in the impartial role.

The advisory attorney first appears when the mediator and the couple believe they have arrived at a working settlement or either party presents a legal question for which a legal explanation is indicated. The advisory attorney must refine this tentative agreement, as explained by the parties and the mediator, into a clearly worded legal agreement in a relatively short time. The agreement must be one that can be understood and followed by the parties in their ongoing relationship after divorce.

The attorney's knowledge, experience, and sensitivity in addressing the needs of the family's postdivorce relationships (including support, custody, and visitation) must equal the attorney's professional skill in dealing with property, legal questions, and tax saving options. The attorney's impartiality must be beyond question. With a thorough understanding of the settlement arrangements developed by the mediator and the parties, the attorney then must draft the final settlement document as a legal entity and present it to the parties, making sure that it conforms with their agreement reached by mutual discussion with the mediator.

Coogler, O. J. (1978). *Structured mediation in divorce settlement.* Lexington, MA: Lexington.
Marlow, L., & Sauber, S. R. (1990). *Handbook of divorce mediation.* New York: Plenum.

aesthetics   The art, as opposed to the pragmatics, of therapy. Aesthetics refers to holism, complexity, and the larger patterns that connect.

Keeney, B. P. (1983). *Aesthetics of change.* New York: Guilford.
Keeney, B. P., & Sprenkle, D. H. (1982). Ecosystemic epistemology: Critical implications for the aesthetics and pragmatics of family therapy. *Family Process, 21,* 1-19.

affect   The feelings, short and long term, expressed in the family. Affect comprises the expression of feelings, moods, and tones (the emotional statement of the family), the degree of irresolvable conflict in the family, and the judgment of the amount of empathy present.

Example: Family members who discharge their aggressive impulses toward one another and also toward outsiders can be characterized as a hostile family.

Beavers, W. R. (1977). *Psychotherapy and growth: A family systems perspective.* New York: Brunner/Mazel.

affect bridge   A hypnotic technique used to uncover the cause of problems. The individual is asked to reexperience the feeling in trance and then to work back to the first time the experience occurred.

Watkins, J. (1971). The affect bridge: A hypnotherapeutic technique. *International Journal of Clinical and Experimental Hypnosis, 19,* 10-12.
Zilbergeld, B., & Hammond, D. (1988). The use of hypnosis in treating sexual disorders. In S. Leiblum & R. Rosen (Eds.), *Sexual desire disorders* (pp. 192-223). New York: Guilford.

affective binding   The exploitation of dependency needs with emphasis on regressive gratification. This process results in a fostered dependency that binds the individual, usually a child, to the family system. See also **id binding.**

Example: A grown man visits his parents and begins to expect his mother to "wait on him hand and foot," to expect his father to pay for dinner, and so on.

Stierlin, H. (1974). *Separating parents and adolescents: A perspective on running away, schizophrenia and waywardness.* New York: Quadrangle.

affective disorder   A disorder of mood characterized by feelings of pervasive depression, meaninglessness, emptiness, expansiveness, elevation, or irritation—that is, major depression, bipolar disorder, dysthymia, and so on.

Example: A middle child suffers from alienation feelings, finding no special place in his family with male siblings one year older and one year younger than he.

American Psychiatric Association. (1987). *Diagnostic and statistical manual of mental disorders* (3rd ed., rev.). Washington, DC: Author.
Foley, V. (1974). *An introduction to family therapy.* New York: Grune & Stratton.
Singer, M., & Wynne, L. (1965). Thought disorders and family relations of schizophrenics, III. Methodology using projective techniques. *Archives of General Psychiatry, 12,* 187-200.

affective involvement   The degree to which a family shows interest in and values the activities of other family members. The degree of involvement may range from none to a fusion of feelings. See also **enmeshment** and **symbiosis.**

Example: A wife may be overinvolved with her husband to the extent that she cannot separate her feelings from his.

Barker, P. (1981). *Basic family therapy.* Baltimore: University Park Press.
Epstein, N. B., Bishop, D. S., & Levin, S. (1978). The McMaster model of family functioning. *Journal of Marriage and Family Counseling, 4,* 19-31.

A

affectivity-rationality   A dimension of couples' reactions, ranging from a primarily emotional to a primarily logical basis, in trying to resolve a conflict situation.

Example: On the one hand, a couple might approach a conflict rationally by talking about different alternatives. On the other hand, they could approach the conflict affectively by expressing their feelings.

Gerson, M., & Barsky, M. (1979). For the new family therapist: A glossary of terms. *American Journal of Family Therapy, 7,* 15-30.

Ryder, R., & Goodrich, D. (1966). Married couples' responses to disagreement. *Family Process, 5,* 30-42.

affective responsiveness   The ability of the family to respond to a range of stimuli with the appropriate quality and quantity of feelings. The affective responses include welfare feelings (e.g., love, tenderness, joy) and emergency feelings (e.g., fear, anger, depression).

Epstein, N. B., Bishop, D. S., & Levin, S. (1978). The McMaster model of family functioning. *Journal of Marriage and Family Counseling, 4,* 19-31.

affiliation   A psychological motive to be with other people or to belong to a group. Affiliation is one of the components of love.

Example: A woman may wish to get married in order to be accepted and belong to a group of women, all of whom are married.

Berscheid, E., & Walster, E. (1978). *Interpersonal attraction* (2nd ed.). Reading, MA: Addison-Wesley.

Rubin, Z. (1973). *Liking and loving: An invitation to social psychology.* New York: Holt, Rinehart & Winston.

affirmation of self   All statements made by a family member that pertain to that person's attributes and characteristics of behavior or to those of another family member. As a coding category, discrepancies between what the individual says about self and what others say about that person are recorded.

Example:

Mother   You are the laziest kid I know.

Son   I'm not lazy.

Gerson, M., & Barsky, M. (1979). For the new family therapist: A glossary of terms. *American Journal of Family Therapy, 7,* 15-30.

Lennard, H., & Bernstein, A. (1969). *Patterns in human interaction.* San Francisco: Jossey-Bass.

aftersession   An informal session, without a leader, that is held immediately after a therapy session. The session may last for an extended period of time and may involve the expression of sexual and hostile impulses.

A

Example: A family member may ask another member to go for coffee and then discuss that member's behavior in the family therapy.

Fried, E. (1971). Basic concepts in group psychotherapy. In H. Kaplan & B. Sadock (Eds.), *Comprehensive group psychotherapy* (pp. 47-71). Baltimore: Williams & Wilkins.

aggression Behavior intended to harm oneself or another. Dollard and Miller theorize that aggression is motivated by a desire to remove frustration caused by the blockage of goal-directed behavior. Thus infliction of injury terminates the aggressive sequence. Bach's theory that aggression arises in most individuals not only from their desire to remove frustration but also from their desire to influence each other promotes the maintenance of contact and fun and individual catharsis. Thus the primary function of aggression is the exchange of information and the change that it produces in an intimate relationship. Fighting furnishes information to the couple about where they stand with one another in their relationship, where they have been, and where they are going. Change or impact produced by the information is the terminal point of the fight. See also **battering** and **battered woman syndrome.**

Bach, G., & Goldberg, H. (1974). *Creative aggression.* Garden City, NY: Doubleday.
Dollard, J., & Miller, N. (1950). *Personality and psychotherapy.* New York: McGraw-Hill.

agreement A coding category that applies to all statements that contain an explicit agreement with the preceding statement.

Example: If two statements are positively evaluated, they are classified as being in explicit agreement.

Gerson, M., & Barsky, M. (1979). For the new family therapist: A glossary of terms. *American Journal of Family Therapy, 7,* 15-30.
Lennard, H., & Bernstein, A. (1969). *Patterns in human interaction.* San Francisco: Jossey-Bass.

AIDS anxiety A condition in which a person without AIDS may experience acute or chronic anxiety with panic attacks, agitated depression, obsessional thoughts about AIDS symptoms, and hypochondriacal symptoms that mimic AIDS symptoms.

Cochran, S., & Mays, N. (1989). Women and AIDS-related concerns. *American Psychologist, 44,* 529-535.

alignment The ways family members align with or split off from one another in efforts to maintain homeostasis. As an alignment in one part of the family develops, a split may emerge in another part. See also **alliance** and **coalition.**

Example: A father and son manifest empathic responses to each other. The mother, noting the two drawing close, intervenes with a remark designed to split the father from the son by inducing conflict and disagreement.

> **Father**   Maybe we could let you have the car (to Jim), say, once a week. Will you be willing to buy your own gas?
>
> **Jim**   Yeah, if I could have it next Saturday, I could earn enough.
>
> **Mother**   But if you let Jim have the car, you'd have to let Susan (daughter) have it too, and you know she can't be trusted.

The mother's comment diverts the father's attention from Jim to a potential area of conflict between the mother and Susan. Now Susan and father or Susan and mother become involved in new patterns of alignment. The son, meanwhile, has been split off from the family. He may attempt an alliance with his sister against one or both parents. In schizophrenic families, patterns of alignment and splitting off shift rapidly. Moreover, the specific meaning of the split or alignment is difficult to analyze. Overall, the process creates chaotic forms of relationships with confused and disassociated meanings.

Wynne, L. (1961). The study of intrafamilial alignments and splits in exploring family therapy. In N. W. Ackerman, F. L. Beatman, & S. N. Sherman. (Eds.), *Exploring the base of family therapy* (pp. 95-115). New York: Family Services Association.

alliance   A type of alignment in which two or more family members join together to cooperate on a task, often in opposition to another family member.

Example: A mother and older daughter may form an alliance to fulfill certain needs, such as discussing particular problems while leaving out other problems.

Minuchin, S. (1974). *Families and family therapy.* Cambridge, MA: Harvard University Press.
Wynne, L. (1961). The study of intrafamilial alignments and splits in exploratory family therapy. In N. W. Ackerman, F. L. Beatman, & S. N. Sherman (Eds.), *Exploring the base of family therapy* (pp. 95-115). New York: Family Services Association.

allocative discrepancy   A failure in role complementarity; one person questions another person's right to a role that that person has assumed.

Example: A mother is angry over the favoritism and attention the father gives to his oldest daughter. The mother accuses him of being seductive and not a typical American daddy. He denies that his behavior is inappropriate. In this situation, the father attempts to validate his ascribed role as father and his achieved role as husband, while his wife attempts to invalidate these roles.

Foley, V. (1974). *An introduction to family therapy.* New York: Grune & Stratton.
Spiegel, J. (1957). The resolution of role conflict within the family. *Psychiatry, 20,* 1-16.

alteration   A maneuver in which one person characterizes another person's behavior in terms of the effect that behavior has on the feelings of the first person.

Example: A child does something a parent does not like. The parent avoids commenting on the behavior directly but says, "You're breaking my heart."

Framo, J. (1965). Systematic research on family dynamics. In I. Boszormenyi-Nagy & J. Framo (Eds.), *Intensive family therapy: Theoretical and practical aspects* (pp. 407-462). New York: Harper & Row.

amourant   An ongoing relationship between two people in which there is no intention of a serious emotional commitment and the contact is primarily or exclusively for sexual purposes. The man is referred to as *amator* and the woman as *amatrix,* based on the Latin term for "lover."

Sauber, S. R. (1988). *It's all in the name: A language guide for the single, his friends, and her family.* Hollywood, FL: Frederick Fell.
Sauber, S. R., & Weinstein, C. (1986). Terminology for male/female relationships for the 1980s. *Australian Journal of Sex, Marriage, and the Family, 7,* 99-108.

amyl nitrite   A drug considered to be an aphrodisiac that affects the excitement phase of sexual response. The use of this drug may be extremely dangerous to an individual.

Kaplan, H. S. (1979). *Disorders of sexual desire.* New York: Brunner/Mazel.

analogic   Communication encoded to resemble the idea or meaning it represents (as opposed to **digital** in communication theory). Most non-verbal communication is held to be analogic. However, there are also verbal examples, such as onomatopoeic words (*tick-tock*). Analogic communication lacks the syntactical and logical precision of digital communication; it is the preferred code for representing feelings and relationships. Analogical communication is the process, as opposed to content, of a message. See also **digital.**

Examples: A child indicates her age by holding up three fingers; the quantity of fingers resembles the quantity of years being represented. Wrinkling the nose to indicate disgust, rejection, or disapproval resembles the act of smelling a disgusting odor. Embracing someone is an analogy to the idea of closeness or union that it conveys.

Bateson, G. (1987). *Steps to an ecology of mind.* New York: Ballantine.
Watzlawick, P., Beavin, J. H., & Jackson, D. D. (1967). *Pragmatics of human communication.* New York: Norton.

analogic communication   A class of messages in which each statement has multiple referents, in that it deals with resemblances of one thing to another thing. In analogic communication, each message refers to a context of other messages; the message can be expressed in a verbal statement, such as analogy or metaphor, or in action, such as by showing how something is by acting it out.

Example:

Wife   I called your hotel last night, but you weren't in.

Husband   I had to go out for a while. Did I mention that I was taking you out to your favorite restaurant tonight?

Wife   Now I know something is wrong here.

The husband's offer to take his wife out could represent several intentions. However, the wife interpreted his gesture within the context of their marital situation to mean that something was wrong.

Bateson, G., & Jackson, D. (Eds.). (1968). *Some varieties of pathogenic organization in communication, family, and marriage.* Palo Alto, CA: Science & Behavior Books.

Haley, J. (1987). *Problem-solving therapy* (2nd ed.). San Francisco: Jossey-Bass.

analysis of correlative meaning   A procedure used to interpret the Thematic Apperception Test (TAT) of families. Analysis of the stories to each card proceeds in three steps: first, reading all of the individually told stories to a given card as a collective family product; second, looking at each story to the card as an individual product of the storyteller; and third, examining pairs or grouping of stories to discern interpersonal relationships within the family. This method of analysis rests on the assumption that the meaning of an individual's stories is not exhausted by reference to the individual's own personality or stories. The assumption is, rather, that a part of the meaning of the individual's stories is discovered by reference to the stories of the other family members.

Handel, G. (1967). Analysis of correlative meaning: The TAT in the study of whole families. In G. Handel (Ed.), *The psychosocial interior of the family: A source book for the study of whole families* (pp. 104-124). Chicago: Aldine.

anarchistic family   Families that set high values on personal freedom. In such families, there are few rules, and little attention is paid to boundaries.

Example: The parents were raised in poor families and believe their children have to work for everything they want. Both parents are employed, and their two children are responsible for fixing their own food, cleaning their rooms, and earning spending money by baby-sitting, washing cars, and so on. One child spends most of her time with her best friend's family, eating in their home and watching television after school. The other child hangs out on the corner or at the sports center with other boys.

Hoffman, L. (1981). *Foundations of family therapy.* New York: Basic Books.

Kantor, D., & Lehr, W. (1975). *Inside the family: Toward a theory of family process.* San Francisco: Jossey-Bass.

anatomically correct doll   A doll that is anatomically correct sexually and that is used to interview children suspected of being victims of sexual abuse. Sexually anatomically correct (SAC) dolls are introduced to the suspected victim in an interview format. Most often the dolls are used to interview children ages 3 through 7 who have difficulty verbalizing and correctly identifying parts of the body.

White, S. (1986). Uses and abuses of sexually anatomically correct dolls. *Division of Child, Youth and Family Services Newsletter, 9,* 3, 6.

anatomically correct doll interview   An interview using sexually anatomically correct (SAC) dolls to determine whether a young child has been sexually molested. Approximately one third of all victims of incest are first abused prior to the age of 6. Standardized interviews using the SAC dolls have been established. Often at least four dolls are used: a male adult doll, a male child doll, a female adult doll, and a female child doll. Anatomically correct doll interviews often are videotaped and frequently are used in court proceedings if prosecution of the suspected molester occurs. For the interview to be valid, strict guidelines must be adhered to (see sources below).

Boat, B. W., & Everson, M. D. (1986). *Using anatomical dolls: Guidelines for interviewing young children in sexual abuse investigations.* Unpublished manuscript, University of North Carolina, Department of Psychiatry, Chapel Hill.

White, S., Strom, G., & Santilli, G. (1985). *Clinical protocol for interviewing preschoolers with sexually anatomically correct dolls.* Unpublished manuscript, Case Western Reserve University, School of Medicine, Cleveland Metropolitan General Hospital, Cleveland, OH.

androgyny   A situation in which two or more individuals do not perform tasks based on traditional sex roles, but rather share tasks on the basis of equality. Individuals thus have both masculine and feminine behavior and traits and act to have gender equality. Androgyny transcends cultural stereotypes and refers to an inner balance and wholeness that allows an individual to be both strong and gentle, logical and emotional, and comfortable with a full range of modes of being. An androgynous male is secure enough in his own masculinity to permit the feminine aspects of his personality to emerge; an androgynous female is secure enough to allow her masculine traits to blossom.

Example: A husband is responsible for cooking the meals, while his wife takes care of their car, because each possesses special skills in these respective areas. The husband is strong yet gentle; the wife is both warm and a rational decision maker.

Bern, S. (1974). The measurements of psychological androgyny. *Journal of Consulting and Clinical Psychology, 42,* 155-162.
Kaplan, A., & Sidney, M. (1980). *Psychology and sex roles: An androgynous perspective.* Boston: Little, Brown.
Singer, J. (1976). *Androgyny: Toward a new theory of sexuality.* Garden City, NY: Anchor/Doubleday.

anejaculatory orgasm   A normal orgastic experience without ejaculation. This disorder is caused by a failure to produce semen or by a blockage of the urethra. Anejaculation must be differentiated from retrograde ejaculation.

Kaplan, H. S. (1983). *The evaluation of sexual disorders.* New York: Brunner/Mazel.

anhedonia   This term literally means "without pleasure." In sex therapy, an individual with anhedonia experiences sexual activity without a feeling of pleasure or enjoyment. These individuals often have obsessive-compulsion personalities.

LoPiccolo, J., & Friedman, J. (1988). Broad-spectrum treatment of low sexual desire. In S. Leiblum & R. Rosen (Eds.), *Sexual desire disorders* (pp. 107-144). New York: Guilford.

antagonism   A state of negative expressiveness involving such concepts as conflict, hostility, disaffiliation, and angry rebelliousness and noncompliance.

Example: A sister teases her brother in order to receive attention from her mother.

Parsons, T., & Bales, R. (1955). *Family, socialization, and interaction process.* New York: Free Press.
Riskin, J., & Faunce, E. (1972). An evaluative review of family interaction research. *Family Process, 11,* 365-455.

antecedental therapy   Therapy directed toward the resolution of events that occurred in the past. The therapy may be conducted with the family of origin in discussing the effect the previous family had on the etiology of the problem.

Example: A woman presents with depression over her work and marital situation. The depression stemmed from the fact that, when her mother became more successful than her father, the father became angry and depressed, eventually finding a woman who would be dependent on him.

Howells, J. (1975). *Principles of family psychiatry.* New York: Brunner/Mazel.

antiandrogen therapy   A controversial procedure using antiandrogen (cyproterone acetate) that is advocated by some clinicians for the treatment of sexual offenders. The technique involves a dose-dependent, temporary, and therefore reversible, reduction in the target organ's (especially central nervous system's) sensitivity to circulating androgens. The result is diminution of erotic arousal, desire, libido, and activity by reducing testosterone levels.

Example: An antiandrogen drug is used in ease management of a heterosexual married man with a history of transvestism and homosexual incestuous pedophilia.

Barlow, D., & Wincze, J. (1980). Treatment of sexual deviations. In S. Leiblum & L. Pervin (Eds.), *Principles and practice of sex therapy* (pp. 367-376). New York: Guilford.

Laschet, U., & Laschet, L. (1975). Antiandrogen in the treatment of sexual deviation of men. *Journal of Steroid Biochemistry, 6,* 821-826.

anticipatory therapy   Therapy concerned with the resolution of events that could occur in the future. Special attention is given to ensuring the health of the children, who are the future of the family.

Example: A married woman becomes pregnant by accident. She stays in the marriage for the sake of the child, redirecting her hostility from her husband onto the child. Therapy could be useful to help the mother realize what she is doing so that she can be accepting of the child.

Howells, J. (1975). *Principles of family psychiatry.* New York: Brunner/Mazel.

anxiety cohesion   A patient's state of emotional helplessness and despair produced by the whole family's effort to deal with a conflict between frustrated dependency needs and the family ideal of independence, respectability, and avoidance of selfishness. In this situation, the family is integrated in a way that requires each member to give testimony to the family ideal, while suppressing individual needs. Anxiety cohesion is believed to play a role in the etiology of ulcerative colitis.

Example: A young man who lives at home is rejected covertly by both parents, who experience frustrated needs. The mother desires family solidarity, respectability, and social success. The father, fearing poverty and lack of security, compensates by overworking. At one level, the parents consider the son to be a burden, but they also want him to reflect the success of the family. This kind of family structure causes him to feel helpless and hopeless. He develops ulcerative colitis in trying to deal with the situation.

Titchner, J., Risking, J., & Emerson, R. (1960). The family in psychosomatic medicine. *Psychosomatic Medicine, 22,* 127-142.

A

anxiety induction   A flow of anxiety between persons, especially when there preexists a relationship charged with emotional tension.

Example: A father and son are in constant conflict. The father arrives home and starts complaining about his day at the office. The son reacts defensively. The son believes that his father is certain to attack him because of the father's emotional state.

Sullivan, H. (1948). The meaning of anxiety in psychiatry and life. *Psychiatry, 11,* 1-13.

Zuk, G., & Rubinstein, D. (1965). A review of concepts in the study and treatment of families of schizophrenics. In I. Boszormenyi-Nagy & J. Framo (Eds.), *Intensive family therapy: Theoretical and practical aspects* (pp. 1-32). New York: Harper & Row.

arbitration   A method involving a neutral third party to resolve a controversy. The arbitrator's role is unlike that of the mediator and conciliator. Arbitration may be used to resolve an impasse reached in mediation or in an alternative method of dispute resolution. When parties submit a controversy to an arbitrator, they agree to be bound by the decision the arbitrator renders. There is no appeal from an arbitrator's decision, and in most states it will be enforced by the courts.

Arbitration is an adversarial process when the parties are represented by legal counsel. Lawyers must use every lawful means of asserting their clients' interests. The parties also may present their own cases to the arbitrator without an attorney. It is considerably easier to do this in arbitration than it is in court. Even so, it is still an adversarial process because the parties, acting as advocates for themselves, compete with each other for a favorable decision by the arbitrator.

Arbitration offers the following advantages:

- It is private; only the parties, arbitrator, witnesses, and legal counsel (if any) may attend.
- Hearings are scheduled to meet the convenience of the arbitrator, parties, witnesses, and legal counsel.
- Hearings may be recessed when circumstances dictate and continued at another agreed-upon time.
- Hearings actually take place when scheduled.
- Only the issues submitted are considered by the arbitrator.
- The hearing takes place within a few days or weeks after the issues are submitted.
- The arbitrator has only one case to consider at a time.
- The arbitrator is selected by the parties.
- The outcomes are less dependent on the skill of legal counsel and technicalities.

Coogler, O. J. (1978). *Structured mediation in divorce settlement.* Lexington, MA: Lexington.

Marlow, L., & Sauber, S. R. (1990). *Handbook of divorce mediation.* New York: Plenum.

areta   The qualities a person ideally should possess, according to the values of that person's community. The qualities are not necessarily good for the person or are what that person likes, gets, or does. They are what the person ought to be and do, were it not for human frailty, weakness, or accidents of fate. They constitute the moral imperative of a spiritually unified person.

Example: A husband should not get angry with his wife, neither in front of friends nor in the privacy of their own home.

Goldschmidt, W. (1971). Areta-motivation and models for behavior. In I. Galdston (Ed.), *The interface between psychiatry and anthropology* (pp. 55-87). New York: Brunner/Mazel.

argument   A communicative interchange in which there is an expression of ideas and feelings but in which the partial or total conscious or unconscious purpose is to hurt the partner.
Example:

Husband   I wish you could find some nice things to say about your job for a change.
Wife   What! If it weren't for you, we wouldn't be stuck in this town and I would have a better job.

In this interchange, both partners are angry and make statements that hurt the other. The husband's hurtful remark is less direct; he negates his wife's feelings. The wife blames her husband for her situation.

Wahlroos, S. (1974). *Family communication: A guide to emotional health.* New York: Macmillan.

arm levitation   A sex hypnotherapy technique used to treat male vaso-congestive dysfunctions. The levitation of the arm (moving up into the air) is associated with penile erection.

Araoz, D. L. (1982). *Hypnosis and sex therapy.* New York: Brunner/Mazel.

ascribing noble intention   A strategy in which the therapist attributes noble motivations to even the most destructive behavior shown by individuals in the family.

Example: Every time the parents of an alcoholic son start talking about divorce, the son goes on a binge. The therapist may start by saying to the parents, "You're lucky to have a son willing to sacrifice himself for your sake."

Stanton, M. (1981). Strategic approaches to family therapy. In A. S. Gurman & D. P. Kniskern (Eds.), *Handbook of family therapy* (pp. 361-402). New York: Brunner/Mazel.
Stanton, M., & Todd, T. (1979). Structural family therapy with drug addicts. In E. Kaufman & P. Kaufman (Eds.), *The family therapy of drug and alcohol abuse* (pp. 55-69). New York: Gardner.

asexuality   A state in which sexual appetites fall on the low side of the normal distribution. Asexual persons are not bothered by the infrequency of their need for sex unless external circumstances exert pressure.

Kaplan, H. S. (1979). *Disorders of sexual desire.* New York: Brunner/Mazel.

assertiveness training   The training to develop the ability to be effectively assertive. The rights of self and others are emphasized. This training usually involves use of behavior therapy techniques, such as covert rehearsal, modeling, and role playing.

Example: A wife says in role-playing what she wants to tell her husband: "I resent your favoritism toward your daughter. You immediately take her side and avoid listening to our other children."

Alberti, R., & Emmons, M. (1974). *Your perfect right: A guide to assertive behavior.* San Luis Obispo, CA: Impact.

assessment   The act of defining, observing, and recording behavioral and stimulus events occurring in the family. Objectives and quantitative data are derived from behavioral observations.

Example: A husband records how many times he and his wife have expressed loving statements to one another by incident, date, time of occurrence, and who initiated the statements.

Patterson, G. (1971). *Families: Applications of social learning to family life.* Champaign, IL: Research Press.

attachment   An organizing concept that indexes a broad range of behavior extending across a wide developmental time span. If attachment is viewed, in part, as the formation of and investment in significant human relationships, it can be seen that these significant human relationships have many qualities—some positive, some negative, some anxious, some evoking sadness, some ambivalent, some happy, some formed on terror, and some formed on love. A reconsideration of attachment considers such terms as *the capacity of concern.* This capacity arises as a result of a transaction between a child and a parent who has the ability to give spontaneously the feeling of concern and understanding for the needs of the child. Attachments are not fully formed at the beginning. Relationships deepen and gain greater meaning as time passes, but the development of the capacity to form such relationships is an early developmental task. It has been said that our society allows adults to have multiple marriages but that children are reared to love and trust only their natural parents. Perhaps this phraseology is the key to the discussion of changes in attachment. Can children really be raised now to allow for multiple attachments? What if, indeed, we now consider the reality of children of divorce and remarriage who may be raised by many caregivers, children who need to relate to a large number of people and to have attachments and loyalties of many kinds to many different people. Ultimately children must achieve workable solutions to maintaining significant human relationships to many different people.

Huntington, D. S. (1982). Attachment loss and divorce: A reconsideration of the concepts. In J. C. Hansen & L. Messinger (Eds.), *Therapy with remarriage families* (pp. 17-28). Rockville, MD: Aspen.

attachment interactions Interactions that center around the establishing of affiliative bonds between individuals. In the absence of these types of interactions, sexual difficulties and dysfunctions may arise.

Bowlby, J. (1969). *Attachment and loss: Vol. 1. Attachment.* New York: Basic Books.
Verhulst, J., & Heiman, J. (1988). A systems perspective on sexual desire. In S. Leiblum & R. Rosen (Eds.), *Sexual desire disorders* (pp. 243-270). New York: Guilford.

attention A generic term used to designate a group of hypnotheoretical mechanisms that collectively serve this function. There are five basic types of attention, each of which may present its own problem (examples of problems are provided below):

divided attention The ability to divide one's attention so that one can complete two tasks simultaneously.
Example: The child has difficulty listening to a teacher while simultaneously taking notes.

focused attention The ability to keep one's attention focused on completing a particular task. Children who have difficulty with focused attention are described often as daydreaming and preoccupied with other activities instead of the assigned task. Focused attention refers to the intensity of the attentional process at any given moment.
Example: Instead of doing class work, the child stares out the window.

selective attention Distractibility; the ability not to be distracted by extraneous events. Children who have difficulty with selective attention are distracted easily by minor noises or movement in the classroom. They are unable to prioritize and select what is most important to pay attention to in their immediate environment.
Example: Although the teacher may be standing at the front of the room and speaking, the child is paying attention to the classmate next to him.

sustained attention Persistence; the ability to remain on task for a sufficient amount of time to satisfactorily complete a task. Sustained attention refers to the length of time one can have focused attention.

A

Example: The child is unable to complete 20 minutes worth of mathematics homework without getting off task.

vigilance   Wakefulness and readiness to respond. Normal vigilance is required for adequate attention.
Example: Instead of listening to the teacher, the child puts her head down on the desk and sleeps during class.

Barkley, R. A. (1990). *Attention deficit hyperactivity disorder: A handbook for diagnosis and treatment.* New York: Guilford.

Douglas, V. I. (1983). Attention and cognitive problems. In M. Rutter (Ed.), *Developmental neuropsychiatry* (pp. 280-329). New York: Guilford.

Goldstein, S., & Goldstein, M. (1990). *Managing attention disorders in children.* New York: John Wiley.

attention control strategies   An interactional domain defined operationally by participation rate, who speaks to whom, and statement length.
Example: The father talks the most. He is in control while he is talking. The mother and children defer to him as the head of the household.

Mishler, E., & Waxler, N. (1968). *Interaction in families: An experimental study of family processes and schizophrenia.* New York: John Wiley.

attention deficit disorder (ADD)   A disorder, first evidenced in childhood, in which the child has developmentally inappropriate attention and impulsivity. Most frequently, the child also has hyperactivity, although not always. As a result, there are two subtypes of ADD: *attention deficit disorder with hyperactivity* and *attention deficit disorder without hyperactivity.* The *DSM-III* term *attention deficit disorder* was replaced in *DSM-III-R* with the term *attention deficit hyperactivity disorder* due to a belief that hyperactivity is an essential, though secondary, aspect of the disorder. See also **attention deficit hyperactivity disorder.**

American Psychiatric Association. (1980). *Diagnostic and statistical manual of mental disorders* (3rd ed.). Washington, DC: Author.

attention deficit disorder, residual type (ADD-R)   The individual once met the criteria for attention deficit disorder with hyperactivity. However, signs of the hyperactivity are no longer present, but the attention deficit and impulsivity are still present. Adults who once were hyperactive as children often meet the criteria for attention deficit disorder, residual type. This term was in the *DSM-III* but is not in the *DSM-III-R.*

American Psychiatric Association. (1980). *Diagnostic and statistical manual of mental disorders* (3rd ed.). Washington, DC: Author.

Wender, P. H. (1987). *The hyperactive child, adolescent and adult.* New York: Oxford University Press.

attention deficit hyperactivity disorder (ADHD)   A disorder, beginning in early childhood, that includes inattention, hyperactivity, impulsivity, difficulty delaying gratification, and a deficit in rule-governed behavior. ADHD is one of the most commonly referred childhood disorders for mental health treatment. The deficit in attention typically manifests itself in one or more of the following types of attention: *vigilance, focused attention, sustained attention, selective attention,* and *divided attention.* The disorder is pervasive in nature and is not accounted for on the basis of gross neurological, sensory, or motor impairment or due to severe emotional disturbance. The disorder is viewed as a developmental deficiency in the regulation and maintenance of behavior by its consequences. Thus problems occur in inhibiting, initiating, or sustaining responses to task or stimuli, as well as in adhering to rules or instructions, particularly in situations where consequences for behavior are delayed, weak, or nonexistent. These deficiencies appear to be chronic in nature and although they may improve with maturation, the deficit appears to persist in comparison to same-age normal children. This disorder appears to have multiple etiologies, most of which are biological, rather than environmental. The disorder is six times more common in males than females, and approximately 3% to 5% of school-age children exhibit this disorder. ADHD children often fidget, squirm, have difficulty remaining seated, are easily distracted, have difficulty awaiting their turn, have difficulty following through on instructions from others, fail to finish chores, have difficulty sustaining attention, shift from one activity to another, talk excessively, have difficulty playing quietly, often interrupt others, often do not seem to listen, and often engage in physically dangerous activities without considering the possible consequences of their behavior.

American Psychiatric Association. (1987). *Diagnostic and statistical manual of mental disorders* (3rd ed., rev.). Washington, DC: Author.

Barkley, R. (1990). *Attention deficit hyperactivity disorder: A handbook for diagnosis and treatment.* New York: Guilford.

Goldstein, S., & Goldstein, M. (1990). *Managing attention disorders in children.* New York: John Wiley.

attraction   The tendency or predisposition to evaluate another person or a symbol of that person in a positive or negative way.

Example: A wife looks up to her husband and gives him special attention when he is dressed in a three-piece suit, ready for work.

Berscheid, E., & Walster, E. (1978). *Interpersonal attraction* (2nd ed.). Reading, MA: Addison-Wesley.

attributions   A "hypnotic" method of coercion and control of behavior—and ultimately identity—in which a family member is encouraged to be what is desired by telling the person that he or she has achieved this already.

Example: Parents may tell their son how he feels, or even may tell a third party in front of him what he feels. Such attributions are thought to be more powerful than orders.

Laing, R. (1969). *The divided self.* New York: Penguin.

autism   A tendency to be overly regulated by personal desires or needs in one's thinking or perceiving, at the expense of regulation by objective reality; a tendency to view the world as closer to one's wishes than it is objectively. The term also indicates the withdrawal from reality into a private world of thoughts and emotions not related to other individuals.

Example: An individual's daydreams may be self-centered and pure fantasy. In extreme cases, the schizophrenic's thinking is cut off from reality and represents the person's internal world.

English, H., & English, A. (1958). *A comprehensive dictionary of psychological and psychoanalytic terms.* New York: David McKay.
Knopf, I. (1979). *Childhood psychopathology: A developmental approach.* Englewood Cliffs, NJ: Prentice-Hall.

autonomous otherness   Disregard for the discrete individuality of family members. Other family members are not allowed to be independent others.

Example: A mother might say, "You're feeling cold, aren't you?" The overprotective mother may supersede the child's feelings by completing sentences for the child or by trying to express the child's innermost feelings.

Boszormenyi-Nagy, I. (1965). A theory of relationships: Experience and transaction. In I. Boszormenyi-Nagy & J. Framo (Eds.), *Intensive family therapy: Theoretical and practical aspects* (pp. 33-86). New York: Harper & Row.

autonomy   A condition of maximal independence and minimal restraint on one's actions. Autonomy seems to be essential to the development of a satisfactory ego identity because one must be permitted to consider oneself a separate person and to experience oneself as such in order to find an identity. Without such autonomy, it is likely that a child will be unable to solve the basic problems of separation from his or her family of orientation and will remain overdependent. See also **interdependency.**

Example: A teenager says to his father, "Thank you for offering to call your friends to get me a summer job, but I would rather try to get my own work, doing what I prefer."

Lewis, J. M., Beavers, W. R., Gossett, J. T., & Phillips, V. A. (1976). *No single thread: Psychological health in the family system.* New York: Brunner/Mazel.

Westley, W., & Epstein, N. (1969). *The silent majority.* San Francisco: Jossey-Bass.

autopoiesis An organizational characteristic of living systems to be self-creating and to produce structurally similar systems across generations.

Efran, J. S., Lukens, R. J., & Lukens, M. D. (1988). Constructivism: What's in it for you? *Family Therapy Networker, 12,* 27-35.

auxiliary ego In psychodrama, a therapist or assistant therapist who acts or speaks roles that are representative of an important figure in a patient's life. The therapist re-creates the patient's delusions, hallucinations, pleasurable wishes, or guilty feelings in order to concretize and intensify the patient's mental processes.

Example: During psychodrama, a therapist might role-play the patient's deceased wife to further the grieving process.

Moreno, J. (1971). Psychodrama. In H. Kaplan & B. Sadock (Eds.), *Comprehensive group psychotherapy* (pp. 460-500). Baltimore: Williams & Wilkins.

aversive stimulation A punishment procedure in which a painful or unpleasant event is presented, contingent on the emission of a behavior. Its major effect is to decelerate the behavior it follows.

Example: A 4-year-old child reaches toward an electrical outlet. The mother makes a painfully loud remark to keep the child's hands away. The probability that the child will reach for the outlet again has been reduced.

LeBow, M. (1972). Behavior modification for the family. In G. D. Erickson & T. P. Hogan (Eds.), *Family therapy: An introduction to theory and technique* (pp. 347-376). Belmont, CA: Wadsworth.

awareness The symbolic, although not necessarily verbal, representation of some portion of experience. The term is synonymous with *symbolization* and *consciousness*.

- Availability to awareness. When experience can be symbolized freely, without defensive denial and distortion.
- Accurate symbolization. Hypotheses implicit in awareness can be proved to be true by acting on them.
- Perception. A hypothesis or prognosis for action that comes into being in awareness when stimuli impinge on the person. *Perception* and *awareness* are synonymous terms; however, *perception* emphasizes the stimulus in the process, while *awareness* is the symbolizations and meanings that arise from internal stimuli, such as memory traces and visceral changes, and from external stimuli.

Rogers, C. P. (1959). A theory of therapy, personality and interpersonal relationships, as developed in the client-centered framework. In S. Koch (Ed), *Psychology: A study of a science: Vol. III. Formulations of the person and the social context* (pp. 184-256). New York: McGraw-Hill.

Thayer, L. (1982). A person-centered approach to family therapy. In A. M. Horne & M. M. Ohlsen (Eds.), *Family counseling and therapy* (pp. 175-213). Itasca, IL: F. E. Peacock.

babes-in-the-wood marriage   Marriage in which the participants have not successfully mastered a particular developmental level.

Skynner, A. C. R. (1976). *Systems of family and marital psychotherapy.* New York: Brunner/Mazel.

balanced ledger   A concept of health in a multiperson relationship or family (minimum two persons) as the balance of a long-range ethical ledger. The main dimensions are obligation, repayment, concern, and merit. Satisfactions for one member cannot be viewed without regard to the impact (justice) for others. Chronic imbalance is a pathological system.

Boszormenyi-Nagy, I., & Spark, G. L. (1973). *Invisible loyalties: Reciprocity in intergenerational family therapy.* New York: Harper & Row.

barbed messages   Messages that communicate hostility, usually through body language and tone of voice sarcasm, rather than by content of the verbal message.

Beck, A. T. (1988). *Love is never enough.* New York: Harper & Row.

bargaining   (1) The step-by-step process that enables a couple to communicate freely and clearly with one another. The process produces "quid pro quos" that permit each to satisfy unconscious needs and expectations of equality within the relationship. (2) The third stage of the dying process, in which the dying patient attempts to "make a deal" with God, the doctors, nurses, hospital staff, and so on. In exchange for getting better or living until some event has occurred, the patient promises to do something specific (e.g., "live a good life").

Jackson, D., & Lederer, W. (1968). *The mirages of marriage.* New York: Norton.

Kubler-Ross, E. (1969). *On death and dying.* New York: Macmillan.

Okun, B. F., & Rappaport, L. J. (1980). *Working with families: An introduction to family therapy.* Belmont, CA: Brooks/Cole.

B

basic assumption group   A group whose existence is based on basic needs, fears, or fantasies. Groups are said to function at two levels. At the manifest level, the group acts in ways that are conscious, rational, and constructive. However, from a deeper level, irrational fears and fantasies may rise to the surface. The reasons for the group's existence may include dependency needs, the need to find a sexual partner, or the need for security. Depending on the state of these basic reasons or assumptions, a leader must emerge to help fulfill the group's needs.

Example: A singles group may be formed without the overt intent of providing activities for its members. However, the hidden or latent needs of the group are to find sexual partners.

Bion, W. (1960). *Experience in groups.* New York: Basic Books.

BASIC ID profile   An acronym for an approach to assessment in multimodal therapy. The acronym refers to behavior, affect, sensation, imagery, cognition, interpersonal relationship, and drugs, including biological factors.

Example: In assessing a man for lack of sexual desire, the following was found:

Behavior: withdrawn

Affect: anxiety

Sensation: bodily tension

Imagery: vivid images of negative sexual experiences

Cognition: perfectionistic thoughts

Interpersonal relations: underassertive

Drugs/biological: nonspecific prostatitis

Lazarus, A. (1988). A multimodal perspective on problems of sexual desire. In S. Leiblum & R. Rosen (Eds.), *Sexual desire disorders* (pp. 145-167). New York: Guilford.

battered woman syndrome   A process of victimization when a woman, abused by her partner, stays in the relationship despite the abuse. Walker proposed three stages to this victimization process. In the first stage, the woman is confused and disbelieves and denies the violence. She is more likely to be aware of feeling embarrassed than angry. She does not express her feelings openly. She is hopeful the violence will be a one-time occurrence. She tries to please the partner, to "be a better wife," and continues to invest in the relationship. In the second stage, more incidents have occurred. The battered woman is afraid for herself and her children. She denies the extent of the violence and begins to blame herself for the violence. However, she begins to turns outside for help. At this point, she is likely to leave, only to return again. In the third stage, the battered woman feels passive and hopeless. She has internalized her anger and has turned it against herself. She feels worthless and like a failure. She considers suicide and/or homicide. Without therapeutic help, this syndrome can go on for decades.

Walker, L. E. (1979). *The battered woman.* New York: Harper & Row.
Walker, L. E. (1984). *The battered woman syndrome.* New York: Springer.

battering   Any act carried out with the intention of, or perceived as having the intention of, physically hurting another person. *Physical battering* refers to the use by a man or woman of his or her body or other objects to inflict physical damage or pain on the partner. This type of battering includes forced physical activity. Another, less apparent, category is *psychological battering,* which concerns the "intention" and "perceived intention" to do harm. Such battering is likely to include verbal or nonverbal threats of violence against a woman or a man, as well as her or his repeated humiliation and degradation. Another aspect of battering generally included in the category of psychological battering is *environmental abuse,* such as punching walls, throwing objects near the man or woman, and destroying pets or other belongings. See also **battered woman syndrome** and **aggression.**

Example: The wife was living with the constant sense of danger and expectation of violence, which led to her feelings of terror because of the way her husband treated her.

Edleson, J. L., Eisikobits, Z., & Guttman, N. E. (1985). Men who batter women. *Journal of Family Issues, 6,* 229-247.
Purdy, F., & Nickle, N. (1981). Practice principles for working with groups of men who batter. *Social Work With Groups, 4,* 111-122.

battle for initiative   The process of determining who controls a client's life, thereby enabling family members to take initiatives for new ways of relating.

Example: The father tells his mother in front of his wife that, from now on, the mother is excluded from discussions about disciplining the children.

Bernard, C., & Corrales, R. (1979). *The theory and technique of family therapy.* Springfield, IL: Charles C Thomas.

battle for structure   In the early stages of therapy, the conflict over who controls the context of therapy. The therapist should win this battle as soon as possible.

Example: During the initial phone contact, the therapist insists that the father attend the first session with his wife and son.

Bernard, C., & Corrales, R. (1979). *The theory and techniques of family therapy.* Springfield, IL: Charles C. Thomas.

Beavers model   Proposed by Beavers, the model defines healthy family functioning as a structured and flexible balance between the family's internal and external environments. See also **Beavers-Timberlawn Family Evaluation Scale.**

Lewis, J. M., Beavers, W. R., Gossett, J. T., & Phillips, V. A. (1976). *No single thread: Psychological health in the family system.* New York: Brunner/Mazel.

Beavers-Timberlawn Family Evaluation Scale   A scale, based on the Beavers model, that measures five constructs using 13 scales: (a) family structure (overt power, parent coalitions, closeness), (b) autonomy (self-disclosure, responsibility, invasiveness, permeability), (c) affect (expressiveness, mood and tone, conflict, empathy), (d) perception of reality (family mythology), and (e) task efficiency (goal-directed negotiations).

Lewis, J. M., Beavers, W. R., Gossett, J. T., & Phillips, V. A. (1976). *No single thread: Psychological health in the family system.* New York: Brunner/Mazel.

becoming alive   A sex hypnotherapy technique used to treat inadequate feelings of pleasure. The client is guided through a detailed process of awareness of bodily sensations, especially genital sensations.

Araoz, D. L. (1982). *Hypnosis and sex therapy.* New York: Brunner/Mazel.

behavioral approaches   Approaches that deal with learning, reinforcing, or extinguishing certain behaviors, irrespective of their original causes. Even relatively minor changes in the behavior of a family member or a dyad may bring about a significant alteration in the behavior and feelings of the other family members. Techniques of behavioral therapy include assertiveness training, operant conditioning, relaxation and desensitization, contingency reinforcement, and cognitive behavior modification. Family members can be used as co-therapists in various behavior modification exercises that are rehearsed initially in the therapist's office and are assigned for practice at home.

Hansen, J. C., & L'Abate, L. (1982). *Approaches to family therapy.* New York: Macmillan.

behavioral group therapy   Group therapy in which overt, observable behavior, especially symptomatic behavior, is emphasized, rather than thoughts and feelings. The objectives are changes in behavior, leading to the elimination of suffering and maladjustment. Conditioning and teaching techniques are used predominantly.

Lazarus, A. (1968). Behavior therapy in groups. In G. Gazda (Ed.), *Basic approaches to group psychotherapy and group counseling* (pp. 149-175). Springfield, IL: Charles C Thomas.

B

behavioral marital therapy Therapy that involves the training of couples in communication skills, contingency contracting, and the application of reinforcement principles to increase positive relationship behavior. A functional analysis of the client's presenting problem behaviors is conducted by continuous assessment of the identified target behaviors. See also **marital behavior modification.**

Example: The presenting complaint of the husband is secondary impotence. Data collected at home reveal that unsuccessful intercourse generally follows discussions "about the relationship." Husband and wife are taught communication skills and problem-solving techniques to be used at times that are not in close proximity to expressions of affection and intimacy. The result is that the husband is able to maintain erections when prior associations are not negative and tension producing, as their previous interactions had been.

Jacobson, N. (1978). A review of the research on the effectiveness of marital therapy. In T. Paolino & B. McCrady (Eds.), *Marriage and marital therapy* (pp. 395-444). New York: Brunner/Mazel.
Stuart, R. B. (1980). *Helping couples change: A social learning approach to marital therapy.* New York: Guilford.
Weiss, R. (1978). The conceptualization of marriage from a behavioral perspective. In T. Paolino & B. McCrady (Eds.), *Marriage and marital therapy* (pp. 165-239). New York: Brunner/Mazel.

behavioral units Standard units in which behavior appears. In all cultures, individuals learn to perform and shape their behavior into molds, or units, that make the behavior mutually recognizable and predictable. These units also have been called *structural units* or *behavioremes.*

Example: The acts of bathing a baby or attending a church service.

Pike, K. (1954). *Language, Part I.* Glendale, CA: Summer Institute of Linguistics.
Scheflen, A. (1972). Human communication: Behavioral programs and their integration in interaction. In G. D. Erickson & T. P. Hogan (Eds.), *Family therapy: An introduction to theory and technique* (pp. 86-102). Belmont, CA: Wadsworth.

behavior-change phase The second phase of working with a family in functional family therapy. During this phase, the therapist works toward changing specific patterns of interaction. The therapist works toward stressing skills to affect these changes.

Alexander, J. (1988). Phases of family therapy process: A framework for clinicians and researchers. In L. Wynne (Ed.), *The state of the art in family therapy and research: Controversies and recommendations* (pp. 175-187). New York: Family Process Press.

B

behavior control dimension   The pattern that a family adopts to handle behavior in physically dangerous situations—that is, those that involve the expression of psychological desires or interpersonal socializing behavior inside and outside the family. In meeting these needs, any of four style patterns may be used: rigid, flexible, laissez-faire, and chaotic.

Example: Regarding curfew:

1. Rigid: The child must be home at the prescribed time; no exceptions.
2. Flexible: The child is allowed to come home at different times, depending on the situation.
3. Laissez-faire: The child may come home whenever the child likes.
4. Chaotic: The parents set an arbitrary, different curfew each night the child goes out.

Epstein, N., & Bishop, D. (1981). Problem-centered systems therapy of the family. In A. S. Gurman & D. P. Kniskern (Eds.), *Handbook of family therapy* (pp. 444-482). New York: Brunner/Mazel.

behavior disorder   A disorder in which the sufferer has emotional pain, has no chronic psychotic symptoms, but experiences continuing difficulty in following the rules of behavior expected in the world beyond the family.

Example: A child who misbehaves in school may be manifesting a conduct disorder.

Beavers, W. R. (1977). *Psychotherapy and growth: A family systems perspective.* New York: Brunner/Mazel.

behavior exchange   A therapeutic contract between partners to change patterns of interaction using a two-winner, holistic bargaining approach; "You scratch my back, I'll scratch yours." See also **therapeutic contract.**

Stuart, R. B. (1980). *Helping couples change: A social learning approach to marital therapy.* New York: Guilford.

behavior modification   A therapeutic approach for ameliorating the socially relevant problems of people. The technique deals basically with objectively defined and observable behavior occurring as a function of antecedent and consequent environmental events. These events are the crucial independent variables that must be manipulated to produce critical changes in behavior. Behavior modification occurs in three stages: assessment, intervention, and evaluation.

Example: A point system is devised for children in the family in which points are earned for completion of chores. Points can be exchanged for privileges.

LeBow, M. (1972). Behavior modification for the family. In G. D. Erickson & T. P. Hogan (Eds.), *Family therapy: An introduction to theory and technique* (pp. 347-376). Belmont, CA: Wadsworth.

B

behavior rehearsal   A technique in which the patient is instructed to express personal feelings to the therapist, who assumes the role of an individual toward whom the patient has strong inhibited feelings.

Example: A woman may have difficulty asserting herself with her husband. The therapist may assume the role of the husband to give the client practice in saying no.

LeBow, M. (1972). Behavior modification for the family. In G. D. Erickson & T. P. Hogan (Eds.), *Family therapy: An introduction to theory and technique* (pp. 347-376). Belmont, CA: Wadsworth.
Wolpe, J. (1969). *The practice of behavior therapy.* Elmsford, NY: Pergamon.

behind-the-back technique   A technique, used in encounter groups, requiring that a patient sit with his or her back to the group after talking about himself or herself to the group. Members of the group then discuss the patient as if he or she were not present. Subsequently the patient turns around and participates in the group discussion.

Spotnitz, H. (1971). Comparison of different types of group psychotherapy. In H. Kaplan & B. Sadock (Eds.), *Comprehensive group psychotherapy* (pp. 72-103). Baltimore: Williams & Wilkins.

belongingness   The basic human need for affirmation and acceptance by significant others.

Example: A student during school graduation exercises looks toward his or her parents and experiences a sense of belongingness.

Maslow, A. (1954). *Motivation and personality.* New York: Harper & Row.

beneficial relationship   A relationship based on an egalitarian, co-partner type of relatedness ideology, emphasizing success through personal accomplishment, personal growth, and humanistic concern.

Example: The wife is a college graduate; the husband is a high school dropout. Both are successful in their own endeavors and respect each other's accomplishments, and they volunteer together to support a foundation for victims of trauma.

Weiss, R. (1978). The conceptualization of marriage from a behavioral perspective. In T. Paolino & B. McCrady (Eds.), *Marriage and marital therapy* (pp. 165-239). New York: Brunner/Mazel.

benevolent sabotage A strategic intervention in which parents admit impotence in controlling an adolescent's behavior; cease issuing rules, warnings, and punishments; but allow the natural consequences of the adolescent's behavior to "punish" him or her or to impose indirect punishments.

Example: A teenager stays out past curfew and comes home to find the doors locked and the locks changed.

Watzlawick, P., Weakland, J., & Fisch, R. (1974). *Change: Principles of problem formation and problem resolution.* New York: Norton.

benexperiential psychotherapy A type of psychotherapy in which the treatment is the use of a new, beneficial experience. The beneficial experience is, in effect, the therapy. Symptoms, as viewed from this perspective, are the result of malexperience—that is, adverse experience in the past, adverse experience in the present, or the interaction of both. In contrast to the adverse neurotic process, benexperiential psychotherapy uses an experience to the advantage of the individual or family psyche.

Example: The therapist emphasizes activities that the family enjoy doing together (e.g., picnics, field trips).

Howells, J. (1975). *Principles of family psychiatry.* New York: Brunner/Mazel.

best interests of the child A term that emphasizes the rights of children in custody cases. In awarding custody, parental rights traditionally have dominated decision making. For many years, the child, as property, belonged to the father. Then the mother was deemed the natural parent. Gradually, however, it was recognized that society's best interests were promoted when children were reared in a manner that best ensured their effectiveness as adult citizens. The "best interests of the child" became a dominant concern in awarding custody. In 1963, the Family Law Section of the American Bar Association stated that custody shall be awarded according to the best interests of the child. The Revised Uniform Marriage and Divorce Act, enacted as a model for state legislation, stipulates that the court shall determine custody in accordance with the best interests of the child. As laws change and place more emphasis on the child's well-being, it will be increasingly difficult for courts to award custody on the basis of parental gender.

Little, M. (1982). *Family break-up.* San Francisco: Jossey-Bass.

biased thinking A negative cognitive set that influences thinking about a spouse so that all behavior is seen in a negative light.

Beck, A. T. (1988). *Love is never enough.* New York: Harper & Row.

bilateral identity delineation   In a dialectical model of the person, a postulated need for a bilateral identity delineation, one that is directed simultaneously toward both good and bad objects. The basic assumption is a transactional, ego-structural theory of ambivalence. The ultimate motivation for seeing others as good and bad stems from primitive archetypes of good versus bad, life versus death, and so on.

Boszormenyi-Nagy, I. (1965). A theory of relationships: Experience and transaction. In I. Boszormenyi-Nagy & J. Framo (Eds.), *Intensive family therapy: Theoretical and practical aspects* (pp. 33-86). New York: Harper & Row.

bilateral sexual inadequacy   A relationship in which both partners are sexually dysfunctional. Masters and Johnson found that a substantial number of couples presented with dual dysfunction. This fact may reflect the general incidence of sexual dysfunction in the population, as well as unconscious motivation in individuals to select someone who is equally functional or dysfunctional.

Example: Stanley sought sex therapy because of his erectile problem. During the assessment, it was learned that his wife, Danuta, experienced pain during her few premarital encounters. On an unconscious level, she had selected Stanley as a way to avoid having to deal with her sexual problem.

Masters, W., & Johnson, V. (1970). *Human sexual inadequacy.* Boston: Little, Brown.

bilateral transference   Adaptation of some of the language, accents, or rhythm of the family and their use by the therapist as a metaphorical set.

Example: A wife found that she did not have enough experience to get the job she wanted. She thought she did have the experience, but the employer wanted someone with much more. The husband developed the metaphor of major versus minor league jobs. He said she still needed to play in the minor league before moving up. The therapist used this metaphor to help the wife see that both leagues were acceptable and that she really should be ready before moving up.

Whitaker, C., & Keith, D. (1981). Symbolic-experiential family therapy. In A. S. Gurman & D. P. Kniskern (Eds.), *Handbook of family therapy* (pp. 187-225). New York: Brunner/Mazel.

bilaterality   In family therapy, a sense of growth and change in both therapist and client.

Example: The therapist cites an illustration from the therapist's own family that is helpful both to the therapist and to the patient in treatment.

Bernard, C., & Corrales, R. (1979). *The theory and technique of family therapy.* Springfield, IL: Charles C Thomas.

Whitaker, C. (1970). *Marital and family therapy* [Cassette audiotapes]. Chicago: Instructional Dynamics.

bilocal residence   A rule of residence that allows a married couple the choice of living with either of the two parental families.

Example: A couple chooses to live with the wife's mother to have her assist with child care.

Zelditch, M. (1964). Cross-cultural analyses of family structure. In H. T. Christensen (Ed.), *Handbook of marriage and the family* (pp. 462-500). Chicago: Rand McNally.

binding   A mode in which the family is gripped by centripetal forces. The family's unspoken rule is that satisfactions and securities can be obtained only within the family, while the outside world looks hostile and forbidding. The parents delay their own developmental crises by keeping their children from leaving home.

Stierlin, H. (1974). *Separating parents and adolescents: A perspective on running away, schizophrenia and waywardness.* New York: Quadrangle.

binuclear   A family system with two households, whether or not the households have equal importance in the child's life experience. Relationships between family members in the binuclear system are determined by the type of relationship established between the biological parents (the former spouses). This situation gets complicated when both parents remarry and the binuclear family then becomes composed of two stepfamily households. Although binuclear families share some similarities with extended kin networks, the lack of socialized norms to guide the binuclear family's functioning results in undefined and ambiguous role expectations. The divorce process can be viewed as a series of transitions that mark the family's change from nuclearity to binuclearity. The reorganization of the nuclear family through divorce results frequently in the establishment of two households—maternal and paternal. After both spouses remarry, these two households become maternal and paternal stepfamily subsystems. These two interrelated households (or nuclei of the child's family of orientation), however, form one family system—a binuclear family system.

Ahrons, C. R. (1979). The binuclear family: Two households, one family. *Alternative Lifestyles, 2,* 499-515.

Ahrons, C. R., & Perlmutter, N. S. (1982). The relationship between former spouses: A fundamental subsystem in the remarriage family. In J. C. Hansen & L. Messinger (Eds.), *Therapy with remarriage families* (pp. 31-46). Rockville, MD: Aspen.

birth fantasy   A family sculpting technique developed by Satir. The client writes the fantasy of how his or her birth and that of his or her mother and father took place in preparation for family reconstruction.

Nerin, W. F. (1986). *Family reconstruction: Long day's journey into light.* New York: Norton.

birth father   The biological father of an offspring. The term is used in reference to adoption where it is assumed that the birth father voluntarily abdicated responsibility for the care and support of the child and thus lost his right to learn the child's identity, which would establish contact. Attitudes toward birth mothers who relinquish custody is more favorable, and they often are allowed access to their offspring. This permission is in disagreement to the principle of coterminous rights. Birth fathers are seen as a "Don Juan" or "phantom father," and this negative image is only beginning to change as fathers' groups organize and assert parental capability and legal rights.

   Examples: It was not a lack of parental feeling in his "consent" to adoption, but rather the predicament the birth father faced against his hostile, neurotic wife in her vicious custody battle for control of the vulnerable children. Or the birth father refused to marry his pregnant girlfriend, and the adoptive parents, in turn, had no interest in having him or the birth mother be given any identifying information on their child.

Deykin, E. Y., Patti, P., & Ryan, J. (1988). The fathers of adopted children: A study of the impact of the child surrender on birth fathers. *American Journal of Orthopsychiatry, 58,* 240-248.

birth order theory   Originally proposed by Alfred Adler is the theory that people develop personality characteristics and worldviews based on the perspective of a particular sibling position (oldest children are competitive, achievement-oriented; youngest children are creative, relaxed, disorganized).

Toman, W. (1969). *Family constellation.* New York: Springer.

black box concept   The idea that no ultimately verifiable intrapsychic hypotheses need be invoked in order to study communication. The observer limits observations to input-output relations. This concept has been extended to viewing symptoms as one kind of input into the family system, rather than as an expression of intrapsychic conflict. This term originally was used by B. F. Skinner and then was adapted by the communication school of family therapy.

Skinner, B. F. (1953). *Science and human behavior.* New York: Macmillan.
Watzlawick, P., Beavin, J. H., & Jackson, D. D. (1967). *Pragmatics of human communication.* New York: Norton.

blame technique   A method for generating family interaction that is part of the structured family interview. The interviewer and the family are seated around a table, with the father to the left of the interviewer, the mother to the father's left, and then the children in order of age. Each family member is handed a 3 × 5 index card and is asked to write down "the main fault of the person to the left of you." After doing this, they hand the cards back to the interviewer, who mixes them up and inserts two cards that say "too good" and "too weak." Then the interviewer reads the cards in random sequence and asks each family member, in turn, to whom the fault applies.

Watzlawick, P. (1966). A structured family interview. *Family Process, 5,* 256-271.

blamer   A pattern of family communication in which one member finds faults, or acts like a dictator. The blamer feels superior and is often very loud. The blamer is very critical of other people.

Satir, V. (1972). *Peoplemaking.* Palo Alto, CA: Science & Behavior Books.

blended family   A family in which at least one partner of the new couple has had children from a previous union or a household made up of a husband and his children from a previous marriage, a wife and her children from a previous marriage, and younger children born into the present union. In speaking of their children, parents in blended families often distinguish among them as "his," "hers," and "ours." The two major tasks to be accomplished are (a) The new partners have accepted each other as executives in the new family hierarchy, and (b) the children have accepted the new partner without experiencing many problems of care from unclear or dysfunctional boundaries.

When families are stuck, the problems in the process of blending can be characterized by the following three situations: (1) A family acts like an instant family when (a) the space of the absent parent is invaded, (b) forced blending occurs, and/or (c) the new woman takes over parental function for the father; (2) an adversarial relationship between the new partner and the child's other parent is established; and (3) the family hierarchy is reversed, with the new partner lower on the hierarchy than the child. Thus the problems of blending are those of boundaries and structure.

Isaacs, M. B. (1982). Facilitating family restructuring and re-linkage. In J. C. Hansen & L. Messinger (Eds.), *Therapy with remarriage families* (pp. 121-144). Rockville, MD: Aspen.

blended orgasm   A combination of the vulval orgasm and the uterine orgasm, one of three types of orgasms postulated by Singer and Singer. It is characterized by contractions of the orgasmic platform and is regarded as deeper than a vulval orgasm.

Singer, J., & Singer, I. (1978). Types of female orgasm. In J. LoPiccolo & L. LoPiccolo (Eds.), *Handbook of sex therapy* (pp. 175-186). New York: Plenum.

blind spots   Any area of a relationship that does not readily come into consciousness; for example, a man does not see the good things his wife does for him, but focuses only on the deficiencies.

B

Beck, A. T. (1988). *Love is never enough.* New York: Harper & Row.

blind walk   A technique that involves having one person take another on a walk while the second person keeps eyes closed. Particularly useful for couples with serious trust and dependence problems in their relationship.

Satir, V. (1983). *Conjoint family therapy* (3rd ed.). Palo Alto, CA: Science & Behavior Books.

blocking and soothing   A technique by which, when a conflict esca-lates to the point where milder strategies are unsuccessful, the mediator or therapist can disrupt the situation by interrupting assertively and blocking the ongoing dialogue, taking charge of the discussion, convert-ing the dialogue into a monologue, slowing down the pace, and turning the volume down to a calmer level. If this procedure is done skillfully, the mediator or therapist can continue to maintain sole control by using an almost trancelike monotonal monologue about anything that will keep the conflict quelled. This calm gives the couple time to cool off and relax, and it also creates an opportunity for later discussions to be more productive. Obviously, the more the mediator or therapist talks, the less opportunity the spouses have to talk. For some couples, this means less opportunity for conflict. In such cases, the mediator or therapist can allow the spouses to talk only insofar as the talk is productive. Periodically the mediator or therapist again can block the discussion and slow down the spouses until they are ready to continue their discussion in a calmer way.

Saposnek, D. T. (1983). Strategies in child custody mediation: A family systems approach. *Mediation Quarterly, 1,* 29-54.

body contact maneuver   Any technique that involves group mem-bers' touching one another and then speaking of the feelings aroused. This maneuver is used mainly by encounter groups but could be used with families in which taboos about body contact may be present.

Gottschalk, L., & Davidson, R. (1971). Sensitivity groups, encounter groups, training groups, marathon groups, and the laboratory movement. In H. Kaplan & B. Sadock (Eds.), *Comprehensive group psychotherapy* (pp. 422-459). Baltimore: Williams & Wilkins.

body language   The way a person's physical appearance, mannerisms, and gestures express that person's thinking. A person's body language may affirm a statement or may communicate a different kind of idea.

Example: A wife says she wants to go out, but she says it in a hostile tone, while turning her head away from her partner. Her verbal and nonverbal behaviors are incongruent.

Satir, V. (1972). *Peoplemaking*. Palo Alto, CA: Science & Behavior Books.

body trip   A sex hypnotherapy technique used to treat preorgasmia. The woman takes an imaginary trip through her genital area to find those special places that produce the most pleasurable sensations.

Araoz, D. L. (1982). *Hypnosis and sex therapy*. New York: Brunner/Mazel.

bonding   The linking of two or more persons in intimacy and love; usually refers to marriage or parent-child relationships.

Gleitman, H. (1981). *Psychology*. New York: Norton.
Harlow, H. (1958). The nature of love. *American Psychologist, 13,* 673-685.

borderline process   A style of interacting in the family that involves splitting, reciprocal projective identification, and children in triangles. This interaction usually exists for several generations in a particular family. See also **splitting, projective identification,** and **triangulation.**

Everett, C. A., Halperin, S., Volgy, S., & Wissler, A. (1989). *Treating the borderline family*. Boston: Allyn & Bacon.

boundaries   Invisible lines drawn within and among family members that form subsystems—for example, the lines within the individual self, the marital coalition, and the children. Part of the therapeutic task is to help the family define, redefine, or change the boundaries within the family. The therapist also helps the family either strengthen or loosen boundaries, depending on the family's situation—for example, when children are entering too much into the parents' domain. The therapist may help establish boundaries through either spatial or verbal techniques. Boundaries can be rigid, clear, or diffuse. Clear boundaries are considered to be healthful and functional. See also **clear boundaries, diffuse boundaries,** and **rigid boundaries.**

Example: A family living in a trailer has no inside doors except on the bathroom. To help define the parents' boundaries vis-à-vis the child's, doors are placed on the bedrooms.

Minuchin, S. (1974). *Families and family therapy*. Cambridge, MA: Harvard University Press.

boundary function/dysfunction Badly drawn or diffuse boundary lines among family subsystems. Boundaries are the invisible dividers that serve to define and structure the various generational and environmental subsystems within the overall family system—for example, child, marital, family of origin, and environmental subsystems. Each subsystem has its own set of tasks, responsibilities, and roles, which can be performed only when boundary formation allows for subsystemic autonomy and appropriate degrees of interdependence. Boundaries, therefore, must be defined clearly to prevent undue interference in meeting subsystemic demands and also must be permeable and sufficiently fluid to allow access and communication between subsystems and adaptability to developmental change. Diffusion leads to subsystemic "overload," whereby allocated positions and tasks are free-floating or inappropriately assigned. Structural therapy specific to boundary dysfunction involves the enactment and re-creation of healthier transactional patterns through altering communication patterns and marking boundaries vis-à-vis tasks that encourage a specific transaction.

Example: Acting out results when a child is more powerful than a parent or when a member of another subsystem (e.g., grandparent) usurps a parent's power.

Minuchin, S. (1974). *Families and family therapy.* Cambridge, MA: Harvard University Press.

boundary maintenance A homeostatic mechanism within a system that functions to restrict the input of matter/energy/information to an amount the system can cope with and that acts to restore equilibrium when the system has been disturbed.

Example: A family in the midst of a crisis attempts to protect itself from any new stresses or from dealing with input that would be even more disturbing.

Skynner, A. C. R. (1976). *Systems of family and marital psychotherapy.* New York: Brunner/Mazel.

bounding A mechanism by which families establish and maintain their territory with the larger community space by regulating both incoming and outgoing traffic. Members of the family decide what kinds of things are allowed to enter the family space and under what conditions, and what kinds of things are simply not permitted admission. Inevitably, bounding issues are issues of safety, of providing an enclosure for the protection of family members against external danger. A family demarcates a perimeter and defends its territory: "This is ours. We are safe here."

Example: A 10-year-old girl is told she may invite some of her friends over to the house, but not others. Similarly she is encouraged to go to ballet practice but is warned against ice skating on a local pond.

Kantor, D., & Lehr, W. (1975). *Inside the family: Toward a theory of family process.* San Francisco: Jossey-Bass.

Bowenian family therapy (multigenerational family therapy)

A complex, highly developed theory that emphasizes the understanding and treatment of intergenerational processes; it includes such concepts as the multigenerational transmission process, nuclear family emotional system, differentiation, triangulation, family projection process, and sibling position.

Bowen, M. (1978). *Family therapy in clinical practice.* New York: Jason Aronson.

breakaway guilt   Guilt over running away from home. The adolescent suffers mainly from unconscious guilt, which gives rise to either massive self-destruction or heroic atonement.

Example: Even though he hated his father for beating him, abusing his mother, and criticizing his baby sister, the runaway adolescent son believes he should have stayed at home to help protect his mother and sister. Because of this guilt, the son begins to use drugs.

Stierlin, H. (1974). *Separating parents and adolescents: A perspective on running away, schizophrenia and waywardness.* New York: Quadrangle.

brief therapy   A therapy whose goal is to accomplish as much as possible in as short a time as possible—for example, in 4 to 10 one-hour sessions. The therapist focuses on the main complaint, uses active techniques for promoting change, and searches for the minimal change required to resolve the problem.

Weakland, J., Fisch, R., Watzlawick, P., & Bodin, A. (1974). Brief therapy: Focused problem resolution. *Family Process, 13,* 141-168.

bug-in-the-ear technique   A supervision strategy in which the trainee and the supervisor are linked by a microphone, while the supervisor observes the therapy session through a one-way mirror. The supervisor is able to communicate suggestions and criticisms to the trainee at all times.

Okun, B. F., & Rappaport, L. J. (1980). *Working with families: An introduction to family therapy.* Belmont, CA: Brooks/Cole.

bull session A leaderless group session in a social setting. While not ostensibly therapeutic, bull sessions can have anxiety-relieving and insight-producing effects.

Example: A family meets before, during, or after dinner, and the members discuss their feelings about what is going on in the home.

B

Amaranto, E. (1971). Glossary. In H. Kaplan & B. Sadock (Eds.), *Comprehensive group psychotherapy* (pp. 823-871). Baltimore: Williams & Wilkins.

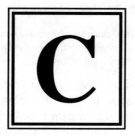

calibration Setting a system to operate within a defined range. For the family, calibration is the rule that governs limits of behavior.

Example: A family may develop a rule that their adolescent daughter should be home between 10:30 and 11:00 p.m. If the daughter were to come in later, she would disrupt the system's calibration.

Foley, V. (1974). *An introduction to family therapy.* New York: Grune & Stratton.
Watzlawick, P., Beavin, J. H., & Jackson, D. D. (1967). *Pragmatics of human communication.* New York: Norton.

call system The technique of calling on members of a family to disclose a specific issue.

Example: The therapist asks the older brother to tell his younger sister how he managed his curfew when his friends stayed out later during school nights.

Slavson, S. R. (1943). *An introduction to group therapy.* New York: Commonwealth Fund.

can't live with, can't live without syndrome A syndrome typifying marriages in which the mates use each other or the children as bad internal object representations. The real personalities of the family members become extinct. The mates respond to each other as a parent or a child. Children may be ignored, punished, or used to express marital hostility.

Example: A wife exclaims to her husband: "You are your father's son, in whatever you do, say, and think. You are a child who just wants me to mother you."

Dicks, H. (1964). Concepts of marital diagnosis and therapy as developed at the Tavistock Family Psychiatric Units, London, England. In E. M. Nash, L. Jessner, & D. W.

Abse (Eds.), *Marriage counseling in medical practice*. Chapel Hill: University of North Carolina Press.

Framo, J. (1965). Rationale and techniques of intensive family therapy. In I. Boszormenyi-Nagy & J. Framo (Eds.), *Intensive family therapy: Theoretical and practical aspects* (pp. 143-212). New York: Harper & Row.

caring days   Developed by Stuart, caring days is a technique in marital therapy in which each spouse makes a written list of positive, specific actions the partner can do to please the spouse. Behaviors done to please the other communicate "I love you." The couple agree to do a certain number of caring behaviors for the other, regardless of what the partner does or does not do and no matter how they feel about each other.

Examples: Bring me a cup of coffee in the morning; kiss me before you leave the house; compliment me on the way I look; hold my hand; walk the dog with me.

Stuart, R. B. (1980). *Helping couples change: A social learning approach to marital therapy*. New York: Guilford.

casual runaways   Runaways who experience little difficulty when they separate from their families. They appear tough and indifferent and are absorbed easily into the runaway culture. Their object relations are typically transient, shallow, and exploitive.

Example: Having reached her 17th birthday, a girl ran away with her girlfriend who already had joined a teenage prostitution group. The runaway never got along with her mother or with her father, who worked the evening shift. She was the only and unplanned child of a marriage later in life.

Stierlin, H. (1974). *Separating parents and adolescents: A perspective on running away, schizophrenia and waywardness*. New York: Quadrangle.

catalyst   An agent, process, or context that accelerates or facilitates changes in others. In chemistry, a catalyst itself is unaffected by the process. In the clinical training process, a catalyst is a person affected in discrete, continuing, and important ways by the new information, ideas, and processes that are developed.

Duhl, B. S. (1983). *From the inside out and other metaphors*. New York: Brunner/Mazel.

catalytic agent   A group member who stimulates others in the group to engage in verbal and nonverbal social activities.

Example: A group member keeps asking for each other person's opinion as therapeutic issues are raised.

Slavson, S. (1943). *An introduction to group therapy*. New York: Commonwealth Fund.

category difference questions   A class of circular questions used in the Milan model. Four types of questions fall into this class: (a) differences between persons; (b) differences between interpersonal relationships; (c) differences between perceptions, ideas, or beliefs; and (d) differences between actions and events.

Example: A person-oriented question is, "Who gets angrier when Mom and Dad have a fight over the son's grade?"

Tomm, K. (1985). Circular interviewing. In D. Campbell & R. Draper (Eds.), *Applications of systemic family therapy* (pp. 33-45). New York: Grune & Stratton.

category method   A technique used in structured interactional group psychotherapy in which group members are requested to rate other group members as to intelligence, appearance, and so on.

Example: Members might be asked to rate one another on their ability to be assertive.

Kaplan, H., & Sadock, B. (Eds.). (1971). *Comprehensive group psychotherapy.* Baltimore: Williams & Wilkins.

catharsis   The reduction of tension by telling one's troubles to someone else. Catharsis helps reduce purposeless vindictiveness and limits conflict by breaking the vicious cycle of attack and retaliation.

Example: A wife who tells her therapist about an affair her husband is having will feel less need covertly or overtly to attack and punish her husband.

Blood, R. (1969). Resolving family conflicts. In B. N. Ard & C. C. Ard (Eds.), *Handbook of marriage counseling* (pp. 329-341). Palo Alto, CA: Science & Behavior Books.

celebrant role   A role in which the therapist joins in a celebration with the family regarding what they have accomplished. Rather than having termination of therapy perceived as rejection, it is important to identify the termination process as a commencement or graduation.

Example: During the session, the mother may serve a cake she baked to celebrate the accomplishments that have taken place as a result of family therapy.

Bernard, C., & Corrales, R. (1979). *The theory and technique of family therapy.* Springfield, IL: Charles C Thomas.

Zuk, G. (1971). *Family therapy: A triadic-based approach.* New York: Behavioral Publications.

centering   A mechanism for developing, maintaining, and transmitting spatial guidelines to determine how traffic should flow within and across a family's borders. Every family generates such guidelines to organize the total space in which it lives. Centering includes the assessment of whether traffic flows in accordance with the guidelines or whether the guidelines should be modified to accommodate the traffic.

Example: A black family, anxious to safeguard its identity after moving into a white neighborhood, turns its dinner hour into an occasion for pinpointing the racial demands of its new community.

Kantor, D., & Lehr, W. (1975). *Inside the family: Toward a theory of family process.* San Francisco: Jossey-Bass.

C

central shared family group preoccupation   The sense of identity of the family group when the family is based on the binding around a shared preoccupation, rather than the sharing of life tasks.

Example: A family may be bound together around the avoidance of mourning a death or an impending separation, or they may focus all of their attention on the upcoming birthday of a child.

Cooklin, A. (1974). *Family preoccupation and role in conjoint therapy.* Paper presented to the Royal College of Psychiatrists, London.
Skynner, A. C. R. (1976). *Systems of family and marital psychotherapy.* New York: Brunner/Mazel.

central switchboard   A family member who acts as the official router of all discussions in a family session. Rather than allowing members to speak for themselves, the central switchboard member speaks for them. Another name for this member is *family spokesperson.* The term *central switchboard* has its origin in communications theory.

Gerson, M., & Barsky, M. (1979). For the new family therapist: A glossary of terms. *American Journal of Family Therapy, 7,* 15-30.
Minuchin, S. (1974). *Families and family therapy.* Cambridge, MA: Harvard University Press.

centrality   A situation in which the therapist directs all communications among family members toward the therapist.

Minuchin, S., & Fishman, H. (1981). *Family therapy techniques.* Cambridge, MA: Harvard University Press.

centralizing engagement   A situation in which the therapist discourages intrafamilial interaction by promoting transactions directly between the family as a whole or the members of the family and the therapist.

Example: A therapist may discuss good study habits with an adolescent, apart from family issues. The discussion could take place in the context of the family session or in an individual session.

Aponte, H., & van Deusen, J. (1981). Structural family therapy. In A. S. Gurman & D. P. Kniskern (Eds.), *Handbook of family therapy* (pp. 310-360). New York: Brunner/Mazel.

centrifugal conflict solution An approach to conflict resolution used by couples who openly admit their problems and look for satisfaction outside the marriage in such activities as careers and affairs.

Example: Alexander and Althea openly admit to having numerous marital problems. However, they stay together for the sake of their children. Alexander spends his evenings and weekends in his gun shop in the basement, and Althea devotes her time to selling real estate.

Stierlin, H. (1974). *Separating parents and adolescents: A perspective on running away, schizophrenia and waywardness.* New York: Quadrangle.

C

centrifugal family A family in which sources of gratification are viewed as existing essentially outside, not inside, the family. The parents and children in a noncohesive family look beyond the family orbit when frustrated; they feel considerable pressure to distance themselves and to seek peers as solace when family conflict is great. In this type of family, children are expelled from the family in such a way that premature separation frequently occurs, as in the case of sociopathic behavior by the children.

Example: Perlita finds greater comfort outside her home than inside it. She enjoys the shallow relationships that frequently end as quickly as they began. She gets in trouble with the juvenile justice authorities for sexually acting out and stealing.

Beavers, W. R. (1977). *Psychotherapy and growth: A family systems perspective.* New York: Brunner/Mazel.

centrifugal forces Forces in the family that push the members apart.

Stierlin, H. (1974). *Separating parents and adolescents: A perspective on running away, schizophrenia and waywardness.* New York: Quadrangle.

centripetal conflict solution An approach used by couples to resolve conflicts in which the couple deny they have any problems and present the facade of a happy couple to others.

Example: Although a couple argue continuously, they prefer to go everywhere together.

Stierlin, H. (1974). *Separating parents and adolescents: A perspective on running away, schizophrenia and waywardness.* New York: Quadrangle.

centripetal family A family that thinks family members hold greater promise for the fulfillment of crucial relationship needs than does the outside world. The world outside the family boundaries is perceived only dimly and appears frightening and threatening. Separation in such a family is, therefore, quite difficult. Characteristically the children lag behind their peers in their investment in people and institutions in the larger world. This style binds children to the family.

Example: Efforts to have children "close by" promote guilt; the acceptance of the status quo in parental coalitions usually involves dominant/submissive patterns.

Stierlin, H. (1974). *Separating parents and adolescents: A perspective on running away, schizophrenia and waywardness.* New York: Quadrangle.

centripetal forces   Forces in the family that keep the members together.

Stierlin, H. (1974). *Separating parents and adolescents: A perspective on running away, schizophrenia and waywardness.* New York: Quadrangle.

CERTS   A treatment approach for incest survivors that discusses the conditions for healthy sexual experience. These conditions are consent (C), equality (E), respect (R), trust (T), and safety (S).

Maltz, W., & Holman, B. (1987). *Incest and sexuality: A guide to understanding and healing.* Lexington, MA: Lexington.

changing the subject   A strategy used as a diversionary tactic when there is something to hide.

Example: The wife asks her daughter whether she has been completing her homework assignments for school at a time when the therapist is addressing the complaint of the daughter about feeling nagged, pressured, and harassed by her mother.

Zuk, G. (1971). *Family therapy: A triadic-based approach.* New York: Behavioral Publications.

channels of communication   A mechanism that defines "who speaks to whom." When channels of communication are blocked, needs cannot be fulfilled, problems cannot be solved, and goals cannot be achieved. Channels of communication normally exist between and among all family members.

Lennard, H., & Bernstein, A. (1969). *Patterns in human interaction.* San Francisco: Jossey-Bass.
Riskin, J., & Faunce, E. (1972). An evaluative review of family interaction research. *Family Process, 11,* 365-455.

chaotic family   A family characterized by disintegration, lack of structure, chronic psychosis and delinquency, and low commitment to the family unit.

Cuber, J., & Harroff, P. (1966). *Sex and the significant Americans.* New York: Penguin.
Glick, I. D., & Kessler, D. P. (1980). *Marital and family therapy* (2nd ed.). New York: Grune & Stratton.

charting Keeping an accurate record of a problem behavior.
Example: In a case of a paranoid jealous wife, the woman is asked to keep a record of her irrational accusations.

Katkins, S. (1978). Charting as a multi-purpose treatment intervention in family therapy. *Family Process, 17,* 465-468.

chemical castration The use of antiandrogenic agents such as estrogen, medroxyprogesterone, and cyproterone acetate to reduce sex drive in a male. Most of these drugs suppress androgen levels and are used to treat chronic sex offenders.

Seagraves, R. (1988). Drugs and desire. In S. Leiblum & R. Rosen (Eds.), *Sexual desire disorders* (pp. 313-347). New York: Guilford.

child abuse The degree to which a parent uses aversive, punitive, or inappropriate control strategies with his or her child. Thus child abuse is not necessarily a symptom of an underlying personality disorder, but rather is conceptualized as a hypertheoretical extreme of aversive control to which a parent will go during interactions with his or her child without exercising restraint. Child abuse is an extreme disturbance of child rearing. Child abuse appears to have three stages. In Stage 1, there is reduced tolerance for stress and a disinhibition of aggression. In Stage 2, there is poor management of acute crisis and provocation. In Stage 3, there are habitual patterns of arousal and aggression with family members. Thus child abuse can be conceptualized in terms of transitional stages from milder forms of child abuse to more harmful interaction over time.

Azar, S. T., & Wolfe, D. A. (1989). Child abuse and neglect. In E. J. Mash & R. A. Barkley (Eds.), *Treatment of childhood disorders* (pp. 451-489). New York: Guilford.

child and family psychiatry The psychiatric discipline in which, having accepted the child as the referred family member, the psychiatrist thereafter gives the rest of the family equal attention in assessments and moves to treating the family as a whole. The family itself is the focus of endeavor.
Example: "Johnny," says the therapist, "who else in your family uses bad language? . . . How about your mother and father?"

Howells, J. (1975). *Principles of family psychiatry.* New York: Brunner/Mazel.

child-centered family A family in which the parents give primary importance to the child's developmental needs and welfare. Although child centeredness may be functional at times, it is usually an expression of deviant family development. It often leads to deviant symptoms in the child and averts the resolution of marital difficulties.

Example: The wife states to her husband that she prefers to take her three children with her on their spring vacation, rather than to accept her mother's offer to baby-sit for the children while the parents go away alone.

Barragan, M. (1976). The child-centered family. In P. J. Guerin (Ed.), *Family therapy: Theory and practice* (pp. 232-248). New York: Gardner.

child custody   Legal responsibility for child support and development. In the adversary legal system, controversies over custody are common and frequently are used by parents as a tactic to gain financial leverage. But in marital mediation, controversies over custody are rare, and the major contentions center on visitation arrangements for the noncustodial parent. This experience tends to support what matrimonial lawyers have been saying, that most custody fights are really financial squabbles. The current trend toward shared support responsibility, as well as shared parenting, offers the hope that both parents can cooperate to provide a better and more supportive environment for the development of their children, even though the parents lead separate lives.

Example: In reaching agreement regarding custodial arrangements that reflect the "best interests of the child," the parties, according to current child custody guidelines, consider all relevant factors, including the following:

the wishes of each parent as to the custody of the child

the wishes of the child as to custodial arrangements

the interaction and interrelationship with the child's parent or parents, siblings, and any other person who may significantly affect the child's best interests

the child's adjustment to location of home, school, and community

the mental and physical health of all individuals involved

A parent's conduct that does not demonstrably affect that parent's relationship with the child, or in some other way can be shown to be contrary to the best interests of the child, shall not be considered.

Rights of the noncustodial parent or, in joint custody, the "nonresidential parent." Child custody guidelines further stipulate that the noncustodial or nonresidential parent of the child shall be entitled to reasonable visitation rights insofar as they do not adversely affect the child's education or physical health or significantly impair the child's emotional development. The noncustodial or nonresidential parent shall carry out visitation arrangements as a privilege and obligation of parenthood and must share parenting responsibility with the custodial parent. The noncustodial or nonresidential parent is entitled to participate in the child's development to the extent that that parent contributes meaningfully to the child's welfare and development.

Rights of the custodial parent or "residential parent in joint custody." The custodial parent may determine the child's upbringing, including education, health care, and religious training, except as otherwise agreed by the parties. The residential or custodial parent shall have the right to require that the nonresidential or noncustodial parent follow agreed-upon visitation rights with the children on a consistent and dependable basis.

C

Marlow, J., & Sauber, S. R. (1990). *Handbook of divorce mediation.* New York: Plenum.

childhood depression A mood disorder that manifests itself with a variety of symptoms. Depression will have five or more of the following symptoms during a 2-week period: depressed mood, loss of interest or pleasure, weight loss or weight gain, insomnia or hypersomnia, psychomotor agitation or retardation, fatigue and loss of energy, feelings of worthlessness or excessive guilt, diminished ability to concentrate or indecisiveness, and thoughts of suicidal ideation. However, developmental differences are associated with depression. Although there is a greater instance of depression in females than males in adults, this is not true for children. Depression is also less evident in children than adults. Depression in childhood has been viewed historically as "masked" or expressed in "depressive equivalents." Thus a depressed mood was not necessarily the major symptom of the depression in childhood. Rather, the depression was expressed by a variety of behavioral problems, such as temper tantrums, disobedience, running away, delinquency, phobias, somatic complaints, anxiety, or underachievement.

American Psychiatric Association. (1987). *Diagnostic and statistical manual of mental disorders* (3rd ed., rev.). Washington, DC: Author.
Kazdin, A. E. (1989). Childhood depression. In E. G. Mash & R. A. Barkley (Eds.), *Treatment of childhood disorders* (pp. 135-166). New York: Guilford.
Kovacs, M., & Beck, A. T. (1977). An empirical clinical approach towards a definition of childhood depression. In J. G. Schulterbrandt & A. Raskin (Eds.), *Depression in children: Diagnosis, treatment, and conceptual models* (pp. 1-25). New York: Raven.

childhood disorders The area of abnormal psychology that deals with assessment, classification, and epidemiology of childhood disorders. These disorders include problems produced by internalization (e.g., academic underachievement, anxiety, phobias, depression, somatization) and externalization (e.g., hyperactivity, impulsivity, acting out). From a family perspective, these disorders are the outcome of dysfunctional family or marital relationships, where physical, verbal, or sexual abuse and neglect are present.

Example: Helen and her family are referred by the family pediatrician for treatment of nightmares, phobias, and fears that are not responding to medication or to the advice by the referring physician. During the first interview with this family, consisting of two parents, Helen, age 9, and her older, well-functioning brother, age 14, it was found that the parents allowed Helen to sleep in their bed anytime she was fearful, thus reinforcing her fears and allowing her fears to control the household. It seemed as if the marital coalition was weak or unclear and that her older brother was receiving a great deal of attention from both parents for his athletic and academic achievements.

Nicol, A. R. (Ed.). (1985). *Longitudinal studies in child psychology and psychiatry.* New York: John Wiley.

Quay, H. C., & Werry, J. S. (Eds.). (1986). *Psychopathological disorders of childhood.* New York: John Wiley.

Steinhauer, P. D., & Rae-Grant, Q. (Eds.). (1983). *Psychological problems of the child in the family.* New York: Basic Books.

childlike family   A family characterized by spouses who have remained dependent on their own families or on the community because of inadequacy or immaturity.

Example: Whenever the wife has to make a decision, she asks her mother. The husband objects, but she accuses him of not respecting her mother's wisdom.

Cuber, J., & Harroff, P. (1966). *Sex and the significant Americans.* New York: Penguin.

Glick, I. D., & Kessler, D. P. (1980). *Marital and family therapy* (2nd ed.). New York: Grune & Stratton.

child sexual abuse accommodation syndrome   The syndrome includes five categories, two of which are preconditions to the occurrence of sexual abuse, and the remaining three categories are sequential contingencies that take on increased invariability and complexity: (a) secrecy; (b) helplessness; (c) entrapment and accommodation; (d) delayed, conflicted, and unconvincing disclosure; and (e) refraction.

Lusk, R., & Waterman, J. (1986). Effects of sexual abuse on children. In K. MacFarland & J. Waterman (Eds.), *Sexual abuse of young children* (pp. 101-118). New York: Guilford.

Summit, R. (1983). The child sexual abuse accommodation syndrome. *Child Abuse and Neglect, 7,* 177-193.

child snatching   The taking of a minor child without consent from the child's primary caregiver or custodial agent. Usually snatching involves parental kidnapping: One parent (or agent of the parent) absconds with the child without the permission of the other parent (or agent of that parent). Such snatching may be in violation of existing court-ordered child custody arrangements or may be done in anticipation of such court orders.

Example: Some states now routinely fingerprint children to provide identifying information on children who are vulnerable to snatching. Each child-snatching incident involves one or more of the following dimensions: motivation, planning, hostility, familial involvement, and agency involvement.

Palmer, C. E., & Noble, D. N. (1984). Child snatching: Motivations, mechanisms, and melodrama. *Journal of Family Issues, 5,* 27-46.

child support   A legal responsibility requiring that either parent or both parents, according to their ability to do so, accept the duty of support for a child of the marriage, or of marriage adoption as in the case of a stepchild, and contribute an amount reasonably necessary after considering all relevant factors. These factors include:

the financial resources of the child. For example, the child may have received an inheritance from a grandparent, uncle, or aunt that may contribute substantially toward the child's support.

the financial resources and needs of the residential or custodial parent. It is likely that both parents will have to use not only their income but also other resources to provide support for their minor children.

the financial resources and needs of the nonresidential or noncustodial parent. Obviously both parents must be able to meet their reasonable financial and emotional needs if they are to provide financial and other support for their children.

the standard of living established by the family prior to the dissolution of the marriage. Both parties must decide whether the maintenance of two households rather than one calls for a reduction in life-style.

the physical and emotional condition and the educational needs of the child. Certain children have unusual physical or emotional disabilities that call for medical or psychological treatment and perhaps special education.

Marlow, L., & Sauber, S. R. (1990). *Handbook of divorce mediation.* New York: Plenum.

child within   A term used in the addictions field, meaning the "real self," "true self," or "inner child." To recapture the child within, one must recover from whatever dysfunction one suffers: addictions, abuse, lack of spirituality, and so on. The child within is thought to be spontaneous, expansive, loving, giving, and communicating. The child within accepts feelings without judgment and fear. The child within is expressive, assertive, and creative. The false self is thought to be co-dependent, unauthentic, envious, critical, blaming, shaming, and perfectionistic.

Whitfield, C. L. (1987). *Healing the child within.* Deerfield Beach, FL: Health Communications.

child witness   When a child is a witness in a court, competence is the central issue. Thus reliability of children's memories, children as witnesses, children's ability to differentiate fact from fantasy, and the jurors' reaction to child witnesses are all issues. Data suggest that children can be competent and credible witnesses, but the data also suggest that special factors must be considered in questioning children; for example, suggestibility, semantics, social demand characteristics, developmental factors, and other situational factors may influence the accuracy of children's testimony. The current controversy is whether children should conform to the same standards that adults must conform to while testifying. For example, all witnesses must appear in court and meet face-to-face with the defendant. The underlying principle is that the witness will be more truthful in the presence of the accused. However, in the case of sex abuse cases, in which a child victim must face the molester, undue harm and retraumatization may occur for the child. Although some states have enacted legislation to shield young victim-witnesses from direct confrontations in courtroom testimony, a recent U.S. Supreme Court ruling has upheld the right to meet one's accuser face-to-face (*Coy v. Iowa*, 1988).

Koocher, G. P., & Keith-Spiegel, P. C. (1990). *Children, ethics, and the law*. Lincoln: University of Nebraska Press.

choreography   A family assessment and therapeutic technique that treats the physical arrangement of people in relation to one another while engaged in a transaction. This technique usually is used in families to project alliances, triangles, and emotional patterns outward, as in a silent motion picture.

Example: A family presented for treatment vaguely describes several problems. The family members are asked to visualize what happens when a specific problem occurs. They are asked to play out this scene silently. The process of acting it out helps reveal their emotions, as shown on their faces, and clarifies some of the patterns of transaction within the family.

Papp, P. (1976). Family choreography. In P. J. Guerin (Ed.), *Family therapy: Theory and practice* (pp. 465-479). New York: Gardner.

circular causality   Thinking that involves the feedback model of causality in which a circular process is involved. The so-called cause is really an effect of a prior cause. What is defined initially as an effect becomes the cause of yet a later event. In essence, the concept involves the notion of a vital interrelationship of system members. The pattern can be viewed as a perpetuation of family dysfunction. See also **linear causality.**

Example: An adolescent boy steals money from his mother and informs his father that his younger brother bought a new cassette tape, which he is hiding.

Watzlawick, P., Beavin, J. H., & Jackson, D. D. (1967). *Pragmatics of human communication.* New York: Norton.

circular epistemology A view of reality that one event does not directly cause another, as in linear epistemology. This model of causality is multicausal, multidetermined, and reciprocal.

Example: The child says, "They never let me leave the house." The parents reply, "We tried, but he always gets lost." The circle of events spirals as each accuses the other.

Hoffman, L. (1981). *Foundations of family therapy.* New York: Basic Books.

circular questioning A technique, commonly used in the Milan approach, for asking questions that address a difference or define a relationship. These include more/less, before/after, old hypothetical (e.g., "what if?") questions.

Example: A child is asked to rank the family members on who has been most upset by a problem.

Selvini Palazzoli, M., Boscolo, L., Cecchin, G., & Prata, G. (1980). Hypothesizing-circularity-neutrality: Three guidelines for the conductor of the session. *Family Process, 19,* 3-12.

circulatory-eliciting Information, provided by family members about relationships, which provides information about differences and change. To obtain this type of information, the therapist asks one member of the family to comment on the relationships of two other members in their presence. Questions are very specific and generate a multidimensional picture of who does what to whom, when, and how.

Tomm, K. (1985). Circular interviewing. In D. Campbell & R. Draper (Eds.), *Applications of systemic family therapy* (pp. 33-45). New York: Grune & Stratton.

clarity A quality of speech in which the words and the affective tone of voice match each other—that is, are congruent and make sense to the observer.

Example: A mother screams at her daughter, "I am angry when you disobey me by going into the medicine cabinet."

Riskin, J., & Faunce, E. (1972). An evaluative review of family interaction research. *Family Process, 11,* 365-455.

classification of bonds A system developed by Dicks that groups bonds at three levels: the public level, the personal norm level, and the unconscious forces level. Each level is based on the Freudian structural model: superego, ego, id.

Dicks, H. V. (1967). *Marital tensions.* London: Routledge & Kegan Paul.

Skynner, A. C. R. (1976). *Systems of family and marital psychotherapy.* New York: Brunner/Mazel.

C

clear boundaries   A definitive separation of subsystems within a system, allowing a subsystem to close ranks to deal in detail with an issue requiring a minimum of interference from other subsystems. The subsystems in a family constitute a hierarchy going from grandparents or parents and children. The absence of clear boundaries is associated with family pathology.

Example: In a family, the boundaries between mother and daughter become blurred. The daughter acts as a co-equal with the mother. She does not accept any limit setting appropriate to her status. A clear boundary is necessary for the mother and daughter to assume their roles.

Minuchin, S. (1974). *Families and family therapy.* Cambridge, MA: Harvard University Press.

clitoral adhesions   Adhesions that prevent the preorgastic rotation and retraction of the clitoris. The cure is a simple physical "freeing" procedure.

Kaplan, H. S. (1981). *The new sex therapy.* New York: Brunner/Mazel.

closed family system   A family system in which all participating members must be very cautious about what they say. The principal rule seems to be that everyone is supposed to have the same opinions, feelings, and desires—whether or not this is true. Honest self-expression is viewed as deviant, and differences are treated as dangerous.

Example: A mother tells her son, "Don't invite your friends over to the house. We have our own way of being together."

Satir, V. (1983). *Conjoint family therapy* (3rd ed.). Palo Alto, CA: Science & Behavior Books.

closed system   A self-contained system that does not have the property of equifinality and whose final state is determined by initial conditions. When a therapist thinks of a family as a closed system, specific topics might be focused on, rather than patterns of behavior and interactions. Closed systems are usually nonliving systems (physical phenomena).

Bertalanffy, L. von. (1974). General systems therapy and psychiatry. In S. Arieti (Ed.), *American handbook of psychiatry* (Vol. 1, 2nd ed., pp. 1095-1120). New York: Basic Books.

Watzlawick, P., Beavin, J. H., & Jackson, D. D. (1967). *Pragmatics of human communication.* New York: Norton.

closure   The family's tendency to suspend or apply order and connected concepts to raw sensory experience. Closure encompasses the notion of continuity of experience over short time spans. Reiss's "environment-sensitive" families tend to manifest a considerable amount of delayed or suspended closure; the problem is experienced as "out there." In contrast, "distance-sensitive" and "consensus-sensitive" families tend to desire early closure. In consensus-sensitive families, early or premature closure is used as a barricade against the outside world, whereas distance-sensitive families employ early closure to maintain isolated continuity and solidarity over time.

Reiss, D. (1981). *The family's construction of reality.* Cambridge, MA: Harvard University Press.

closure problems   Problems that arise from responses in the form of questions from disqualifying responses or from contradicting a response in the same speech.
   Example: A wife responds to her husband's question by saying, "What do you want me to do now?"

Riskin, J., & Faunce, E. (1972). An evaluative review of family interaction research. *Family Process, 11,* 365-455.
Singer, M., & Wynne, L. (1965). Thought disorders and family relations of schizophrenics: III. Methodology using projective techniques. *Archives of General Psychiatry, 12,* 187-200.

clue   An intervention designed to make the family aware that some behavior is likely to continue. Cluing is intended to build mutual support and momentum for carrying out later interventions.
   Example: A therapist says to a family, "I want each of you to observe what happens when Gunnar is with you and misbehaves. Notice when this happens and exactly what he does."

de Shazer, S. (1982). *Patterns of brief family therapy.* New York: Guilford.

coaching   A technique in which the therapist acts as an active, supportive agent in encouraging the client to make changes in the family. A therapist might use such coaching to help a client delve into his or her own family system.
   Example: The therapist suggests to the stepfather that he could practice saying several things and then say them to his wife's son when the son misbehaves.

Bowen, M. (1971). The use of family theory in clinical practice. In J. Haley (Ed.), *Changing families* (pp. 159-192). New York: Grune & Stratton.

coalition An alliance between specific members of a family. The following types of coalitions have been described by systems theorists:

- *Functional coalition:* A coalition in which the marital channel is the strongest pathway in the family, with all other channels open and about equal to each other in importance.

- *Schismatic coalition:* A coalition in which either (a) there is a relatively weak or absent marital coalition but strong alliances across the generations and sexes (between father and daughter or mother and son) or (b) the cross-generational ties are between father and son, mother and daughter, with a relative absence of other effective channels.

- *Skewed family coalition:* A coalition in which one family member is relatively isolated from the others, who form the coalition, or fairly cohesive unit.

- *Generation-gap coalition:* A coalition in which the marital unit and the offspring each form a fairly cohesive unit, with little or no interaction across generational lines.

- *Pseudodemocratic coalition:* A coalition in which all channels in the family seem to be of about equal importance, with the marital coalition and the parental role not particularly well differentiated.

- *Disengaged family (no coalition at all):* A family in which each member is cut off from every other member and expects very little sense of positive interaction or feeling of belonging to a family unit.

- *Enmeshed family (total coalition):* A family in which the coalition is tight between all members, and the actions, feelings, and thoughts of any member send shock waves through the whole family.

Glick, I. D., & Kessler, D. P. (1980). *Marital and family therapy* (2nd ed.). New York: Grune & Stratton.

Haley, J. (1963). *Strategies of psychotherapy.* New York: Grune & Stratton.

Minuchin, S. (1974). *Families and family therapy.* Cambridge, MA: Harvard University Press.

coalition game A situation in which there is switching of a two-party alliance with a third party on the outside; that is, two people, A and B, talk about a third, C; then A talks with C about B; and then B talks about A with C. A common coalition game is one in which there is a rigid, impenetrable boundary in the relationship of two people, as in a folie à deux, that does not allow others to come into it.

Example: A mother and a child have a coalition that keeps father out; that is, the mother and the child talk about the father. When the father and mother get together, they talk about the child. Then the father talks with the child about the mother.

Minuchin, S. (1974). *Families and family therapy.* Cambridge, MA: Harvard University Press.

co-dependence A term used by members in various anonymous groups and the lay public to refer to what originally was thought of as an addictive process that afflicts the significant other of a person who is chemically addicted. The person who is co-dependent is often considered to be a "caretaker," such that the addicted person is "enabled" to continue his or her addiction. Thus the co-dependent person sacrifices his or her own needs to fulfill the wants and needs of another person even though the other person's wants and needs are dysfunctional. More recently, the term has been used broadly to describe all caretaking behavior of a significant other to a person with any sort of addictive and/or psychological disorder. Because of his or her insecurities and dependency needs, the co-dependent individual protects another person from the natural and logical consequences of the other person's dysfunctional behavior. This protective behavior, often justified by "love and concern," perpetuates the dysfunctional behavior. The term *co-dependence* is used in a variety of ways by various people and thus has not been defined adequately for research purposes.

Example: A wife works a second job to earn enough money to pay the bills because her alcoholic husband spends large amounts of money on alcohol and thus cannot pay the bills himself.

Beattie, M. (1987). *Co-dependent no more.* New York: Harper/Hazeldon.
Schaef, A. W. (1986). *Co-dependence misunderstood—mistreated.* New York: Harper & Row.

coercion The general process of control by pain. The individual uses aversive behaviors as stimulus events in punishment and/or negative reinforcement arrangements.

Example: A child attempts to coerce his mother into buying him a candy bar in a store by having a temper tantrum or threatening to have one. The mother buys him some candy to turn off his tantrum, which reinforces his behavior.

Patterson, G. (1976). The aggressive child: Victim and architect of a coercive system. In E. Mash, L. Hamerlynck, & L. Handy (Eds.), *Behavior modification and families* (pp. 267-316). New York: Brunner/Mazel.
Patterson, G., & Reid, J. (1970). Reciprocity and coercion: Two facets of social systems. In C. Neuringer & J. Michael (Eds.), *Behavior modification in clinical psychology* (pp. 133-177). New York: Appleton-Century-Crofts.

coercive binder A person who coerces others, yet depicts self as well-meaning and caring. The more dependent and immature the bindee, the more fateful the violence of the binder.

Example: A father is hypercritical of his son in order to inure him to the perils of later life. The father depicts himself as being his son's savior.

Stierlin, H. (1974). *Separating parents and adolescents: A perspective on running away, schizophrenia and waywardness.* New York: Quadrangle.

co-evolution   (1) A biological term used to describe change as a result of the progressive interaction between organisms. (2) Applied to families, it describes the continual changes in family interactions across time and the changing therapeutic relationship between the therapist, family, and other systems.

Hoffman, L. (1982). A co-evolutionary framework for systemic family therapy. *Australian Journal of Family Therapy, 4,* 9-21.

cognitive behavior therapy   Derived from behavior therapy, cognitive behavior therapy is an integration of cognitive psychology, with an emphasis on how thinking affects behavior, and behavioral psychology, with an emphasis on empirically derived methods to modify specific behaviors. Cognitive behavior therapy focuses on thinking processes and teaching strategies in order to change behaviors. The cognitive behavior therapist collaborates with the patient to assess distorted thinking processes (e.g., expectations, self-statements, attributions) and to design new learning experiences to remediate the dysfunctional cognitions, behaviors, and affective patterns.

Kendall, P. C., & Braswell, L. (1985). *Cognitive-behavioral therapy for impulsive children.* New York: Guilford.

cognitive binding   A situation in which a parent interferes with the child's differentiated self-awareness and self-determination. The ability of the child to perceive and articulate personal feelings, needs, motives, and goals (as against those that others attribute to the child) is crucial in order for the child to cope without conflicts when separated.
   Example: A mother who rejects her child misdefines her behavior to the child as loving. For example, she may tell her child that the child cannot go to a dance because undesirable people would be there.

Stierlin, H. (1974). *Separating parents and adolescents: A perspective on running away, schizophrenia and waywardness.* New York: Quadrangle.

cognitive constructs   Verbal messages used to encourage clients to experience things in a different way.
   Example: A sister frequently answers questions the therapist directs to her brother. The therapist says to her, "You're helpful, aren't you? You take his memory." This cognitive construct indicates a need for separation and nonintrusion.

Minuchin, S., & Fishman, H. (1981). *Family therapy techniques.* Cambridge, MA: Harvard University Press.

cognitive distortion   A way of looking at reality that involves a significant degree of distortion. Types of distortions include overgeneralization, all-or-nothing thinking, magnifying the negative, and personalization. Cognitive distortions can have destructive effects in marital and family relationships.

Example: A couple was given a sex therapy homework assignment. They were 80% successful in carrying out the assignment. When they started to report their progress, they claimed they were totally unsuccessful. Both partners had magnified an aspect of the experience that had not worked.

Burns, D. (1980). *Feeling good: The new mood therapy.* New York: New American Library.

Hof, L. (1987). Evaluating the marital relationship of clients with sexual complaints. In G. Weeks & L. Hof (Eds.), *Integrating sex and marital therapy* (pp. 5-22). New York: Brunner/Mazel.

cognitive involvement   The degree to which a family system allows a topic to be discussed—for example, death.

Example: A mother tells her children not to talk about their father's drinking.

Lewis, J. M., Beavers, W. R., Gossett, J. T., & Phillips, V. A. (1976). *No single thread: Psychological health in the family system.* New York: Brunner/Mazel.

cognitive restructuring   A therapeutic intervention in which the therapist helps the patient modify a self-statement, attribution, viewpoint, or perception. See also **reframing.**

Examples: Seeing the glass as half-full instead of half-empty; viewing a negative behavior as an "opportunity for growth."

Davison, G. C. (1966). Differential relaxation and cognitive restructuring in therapy with a "paranoid schizophrenia" or "paranoid state." *Proceedings of the 74th Annual Convention of the American Psychological Association.* Washington, DC: American Psychological Association.

cognitive style   The characteristic way a person selects information, processes it, and communicates the outcome to others. When spouses have different cognitive styles, they arrive at different conclusions, making it difficult to resolve their differences through direct argumentation.

Example: A father thinks the mother should take care of the children when he comes home from work tired, and the mother thinks the children need time with their father and time away from her.

Sager, C. (1981). Couples therapy and marriage contracts. In A. S. Gurman & D. P. Kniskern (Eds.), *Handbook of family therapy* (pp. 25-32). New York: Brunner/Mazel.

cohabitation   A living-together-arrangement (LTA) in which two adult persons, usually of different genders, reside under marriagelike conditions in the same household without having confirmed their relationship through the rituals of marriage. The relationship is defined as involving the sharing of a bedroom at least four nights a week for at least three consecutive months, to differentiate it from a relationship involving merely a sexual partner's visitations.

Macklin, E. (1972). Heterosexual cohabitation among unmarried college students. *Family Coordinator, 11,* 463-472.

coherence   A congruent interdependence in functioning whereby all aspects of a family fit together.

Dell, P. (1982). Beyond homeostasis: Toward a concept of coherence. *Family Process, 21,* 21-41.

coherence factor   The relative consistency and continuity of a system's identity and relationship to the ecosystem as the system's structure evolves and modifies.
   Example: A family loses a member through death. On the one hand, the family may continue as a unit and define itself in the same way as before the death. On the other hand, the family may become incoherent. It could dissolve, and its members could acquire a new identity.

Aponte, H., & Van Deusen, J. (1981). Structural family therapy. In A. S. Gurman & D. P. Kniskern (Eds.), *Handbook of family therapy* (pp. 310-360). New York: Brunner/Mazel.

cohesion   Those forces, whether positive or negative, that hold together a relationship. Cohesion often is expressed in terms of commitment and the degree of intimacy in the interpersonal dimension.
   Example: The husband's attitude toward sexual exclusivity helps enhance his wife's feelings of love for him and helps her resist a temptation to become involved in an extramarital affair.

Waring, E. M., & Russell, L. (1982). Cognitive family therapy. In F. W. Kaslow (Ed.), *The international handbook of family therapy* (pp. 186-195). New York: Brunner/Mazel.

coital alignment technique   A technique of sexual intercourse used to facilitate female orgasm by maximizing clitoral stimulation. In this position, the male assumes a position on top and "rides high," or thrusts in a downward fashion while both partners attempt to emphasize pressure and counterpressure during pelvic movement.

Eichel, E., Eichel, Q., & Kule, S. (1988). The technique of coital alignment and its relation to female orgasmic response and simultaneous orgasm. *Journal of Sex and Marital Therapy, 14,* 129-141.

coital anxiety Anxiety, experienced by males during coitus, that can be traced to feelings of inadequacy, apprehension, or possibly a childhood fear.

Cooper, A. (1969). A clinical study of "coital anxiety" in male potency disorders. *Journal of Psychosomatic Research, 13,* 143.

Reckless, J., & Geigger, N. (1978). Impotence as a practical problem. In J. LoPiccolo & L. LoPiccolo (Eds.), *Handbook of sex therapy* (pp. 295-322). New York: Plenum.

collaborative marital therapy A therapeutic technique wherein each spouse is seen individually by separate therapists, who then collaborate. This therapy may be helpful in aiding a passive and withdrawn spouse to self-disclose. With this technique, clinicians may recognize distortions of reality and omission of facts, which often aids in the recognition of the patients' ego defenses.

Martin, P. A., & Bird, M. W. (1953). An approach to the psychotherapy of marriage partners: The stereoscopic technique. *Psychiatry, 16,* 123-127.

collaborative parent-child therapy A form of therapy in which the parent and the child are seen individually by different therapists, who then collaborate. This therapy is particularly beneficial to adolescent patients, who are often reluctant to self-disclose while under the parents' scrutiny. With this technique, the clinician need not rely entirely on information provided by one patient, information that often is distorted.

Johnson, A. M., & Fishback, D. (1944). Analysis of a disturbed adolescent girl and the collaborative psychiatric treatment of the mother. *American Journal of Orthopsychiatry, 14,* 195-203.

collaborative therapy The use of two therapists, each seeing a spouse separately and then consulting together.

Example: The husband is in the process of terminating an affair, and the wife is severely depressed. The spouses see separate therapists for their individual problems. The therapists consult with each other to obtain more complete pictures of their individual clients.

Greene, B., & Solomon, A. (1963). Marital disharmony: Concurrent psychoanalytic therapy of husband and wife by the same psychiatrist. *American Journal of Psychiatry, 17,* 443-450.

Prochaska, J., & Prochaska, J. (1978). Twentieth century trends in marriage and marital therapy. In T. Paolino & B. McCrady (Eds.), *Marriage and marital therapy* (pp. 1-24). New York: Brunner/Mazel.

collapsing time Locating a problem within the context of a trend, and marking this trend as "newsworthy" by encouraging family members to draw distinctions between the "state of affairs" at one point in time and the "state of affairs" at another point in time. Thus problems are seen to have a past, present, and future. The therapist describes these trends in such a way that, by implicating the past and predicting the future, time collapses on such trends.

White, M. (1986). Negative explanation, restraint, and double description: A template for family therapy. *Family Process, 25,* 169-184.

collective cognitive chaos   Bizarre, disruptive intrusions of so-called primary process thinking. Individual statements may appear sufficiently normal so that one would not ordinarily question the isolated statements. The overall transactional sequence, however, may be utterly disjoined and fragmented.

Example: A husband appears to be talking with his wife about how he feels about her attitude toward his going hunting on the weekend. She responds to him by talking about his attitude toward the children. Each continues a separate dialogue. Although each person makes sense, the interaction is disjointed.

Singer, M., & Wynne, L. (1963). Thought disorder and family relations of schizophrenics: I. A research strategy. *Archives of General Psychiatry, 9,* 191-198.
Wynne, L. (1965). Some indications and contraindications for exploratory family therapy. In I. Boszormenyi-Nagy & J. Framo (Eds.), *Intensive family therapy: Theoretical and practical aspects* (pp. 289-322). New York: Harper & Row.

collective pleasure principle   The assumption that if two or more people join forces to help each other avoid the pain of emotional growth, their escape from reality amounts to a shared venture, as though their regressive mental economy was guided by a collective pleasure principle. This principle requires the coordinated role playing of its adherents. The symbiotic goal of the relationship is usually unconscious.

Example: Two individuals marry to form a childlike relationship based on mutual dependency and the sharing of good times.

Boszormenyi-Nagy, I. (1965). A theory of relationships: Experience and transaction. In I. Boszormenyi-Nagy & J. Framo (Eds.), *Intensive family therapy: Theoretical and practical aspects* (pp. 33-86). New York: Harper & Row.

collusion   A form of defective communication that allows parts of a family system to exploit the whole system. Such a system operates according to private rules of morality. There may be competition between parents or siblings and hostility toward others, which can be talked about only with certain people; and two or more members of the family may collude to discuss these secrets. The end result may be the appearance of deviant symptomatic behavior.

Example: The father uses the adolescent daughter to express his dissatisfaction with the mother. The father and daughter share the secret of his covert hostilities toward the mother. The daughter then begins to act out to divert some of the hostility toward the mother.

MacGregor, R., Ritchie, A., Serrano, A., & Schuster, F. (1964). *Multiple impact therapy with families.* New York: McGraw-Hill.

color-matching test   A technique used to generate interaction. The test is designed to see how couples cope with differences through built-in deception. A husband and a wife are seated opposite each other, with an easel between them so that they are blocked from each other's view. Each spouse looks at a series of numbered, colored cards and is instructed to come up with the best possible match with a card that the tester holds up in view of both of them. A series of 20 trials is administered; for half of them, the correctly matched card is numbered differently for each spouse so that they must come to some agreement between themselves about the best possible match.

Goodrich, D., & Boomer, D. (1963). Experimental assessment of modes of conflict resolution. *Family Process, 2,* 15-24.

co-marital relationship   An intimate involvement, probably but not necessarily including sexual intimacy, that is an adjunct to an established dyadic marriage. Co-marital relations are distinguished from extramarital relations in that they are open and shared, rather than covert and unshared, and they are based on prior agreement within the dyadic relationship.

Constantine, L. L., Constantine, J. M., & Edelman, S. K. (1975). Counseling implications of alternative marriage styles. In A. S. Gurman & D. G. Rice (Eds.), *Couples in conflict* (pp. 124-134). New York: Jason Aronson.

combined marital therapy   A mix of conjoint (seeing both spouses together) and concurrent (seeing spouses separately) sessions that responds to changing needs and promotes adaptation to variable marital patterns.

Example: The husband feels inadequate and needs help in viewing himself as more capable; he accepts individual therapy and practices being more assertive to his wife in conjoint sessions. The wife is extremely critical of others, especially of her husband. She needs individual therapy to understand her inferiority complex and how she strives to be superior by making others feel less competent; conjoint sessions help her learn to allow and encourage her husband to be successful and do something right.

Greene, B., & Solomon, A. (1963). Marital disharmony: Concurrent psychoanalytic therapy of husband and wife by the same psychiatrist. *American Journal of Psychiatry, 17,* 433-450.

Prochaska, J., & Prochaska, J. (1978). Twentieth century trends in marriage and marital therapy. In T. Paolino & B. McCrady (Eds.), *Marriage and marital therapy* (pp. 1-24). New York: Brunner/Mazel.

command level   The aspect of a message that implies a directive. Each message conveys not only content and information (the report level) but also a directive to the receiver. The command level of a message may make a statement about the status of the two people communicating, about the meaning (e.g., playful or serious, general or specific) of the statement, or whether the nonverbal behavior should be given primary status. See also **report level.**

Haley, J. (1959). An interactional description of schizophrenia. *Psychiatry, 22,* 321-332.

Watzlawick, P., Beavin, J. H., & Jackson, D. D. (1967). *Pragmatics of human communication.* New York: Norton.

commitment   A standard that measures whether the family members take clear, definite stands (commit themselves to ideas, suggestions, and issues) and how they are asked to take such stands.

Example: Parents enforce bedtime schedules with their children regardless of the children's efforts to make excuses and manipulate the parents so that they can stay up later in the evening.

Riskin, J., & Faunce, E. (1968). *Family interaction sides scoring manual.* Unpublished manuscript.

Riskin, J., & Faunce, E. (1972). An evaluative review of family interaction research. *Family Process, 11,* 365-455.

communal marriage   A marriage in which, theoretically, there is sexual access by all members of a community to all persons (or a large specified subset) of the opposite sex in the community.

Constantine, L. L., & Constantine, J. M. (1971). Group and multilateral marriage: Definitional notes, glossary and annotated bibliography. *Family Process, 10,* 157-176.

communication   Nonverbal and verbal behavior in a social context. Communication includes all of those symbols and clues used by persons in giving and receiving meaning. The communication techniques that people use can be seen as reliable indicators of interpersonal functioning. A study of communication can help close the gap between inference and observation, as well as help document the relationship between patterns of communication and symptomatic behavior.

Satir, V. (1983). *Conjoint family therapy* (3rd ed.). Palo Alto, CA: Science & Behavior Books.

communication games A series of interactional techniques used to teach people to communicate more effectively and congruently by using eye and skin contact. It is very difficult to argue or deliver an incongruent message when one is talking to, touching, and looking at the listener.

Example: A couple first are asked to talk with one another while standing back to back at a distance. They then are asked to eyeball each other and to hold hands while trying to argue. The therapist helps the couple process what they learn from these exercises; for example, not looking at each other is a setup for miscommunication.

Satir, V. (1983). *Conjoint family therapy* (3rd ed.). Palo Alto, CA: Science & Behavior Books.

communication therapy An approach started by Jackson, fostered by the theoretical writing of Gregory Bateson, and developed more fully at the Palo Alto Mental Research Institute by Watzlawick and his associates (Levant, 1984). This approach has been elaborated and applied more directly by the Milano group (Hansen & L'Abate, 1982). Family communication processes have been incorporated into the basic theory underlying family therapy (Nichols, 1984). From studies of communication patterns in schizophrenic families, the following observations have been made:

- The family members do not affirm what they say; instead, they disqualify their own statements (e.g., smiling while saying something hurtful).
- Members do not confirm statements made by other family members; instead, they challenge the right of the other members to express themselves.
- Members do not assume the initiative, or leadership, in communication.
- Members do not permit overt alliances among other members.
- The mother is blamed for a communication breakdown but in ways that enable her to avoid accepting blame.

Because of ineffective communication, a family may be in a constant state of chaos and unreality. The confused, often contradictory, patterns of communication obscure, or mask, family problems, rather than facilitate their resolution. Studies of schizophrenic families have yielded important information about communication on two levels: (a) denotative (literal or overt content of message) and (b) metacommunicative (a covert message about the overt message).

Example: The denotative message may say, "I hate you," but the metacommunicative message says, "I wish I could love you" or "You hurt me."

Hansen, J. C., & L'Abate, L. (1982). *Approaches to family therapy.* New York: Macmillan.

Levant, R. F. (1984). *Family therapy: A comprehensive overview.* Englewood Cliffs, NJ: Prentice-Hall.

Nichols, M. P. (1984). *Family therapy: Concepts and methods.* New York: Gardner.

commuter marriage   A marriage of professional spouses who maintain separate residences in the service of dual careers. A commuter marriage distinguishes between household and family, the latter term denoting a kinship or relational concept. Because two-residence marriages are a financial drain, commuters tend to be highly committed professionals who view their work as "a central life interest."

Gerstel, N., & Gross, H. E. (1983). Commuter marriage: Couples who live apart. In E. Macklin & R. Rubin (Eds.), *Contemporary families and alternate lifestyles* (pp. 180-193). Beverly Hills, CA: Sage.

competition   A concept used in multiple family therapy to describe mechanisms of change. Competition between systems (families) or subsystems (individuals) produces change in the internal power distribution of the system faster than work with a single family can do. A threat to the status of a family or an individual stimulates competition, which leads, in turn, to productive interaction of the family members at an early stage in treatment.

Example: A young boy scratches sores produced by a skin condition. He is given several behavioral alternatives to reduce the scratching behavior. The family members are instructed to keep a record of his scratching so that the therapist can tell which family member is most helpful to the boy.

Laqueur, H. P. (1972). Mechanisms of change in multiple family therapy. In C. J. Sager & H. S. Kaplan (Eds.), *Progress in group and family therapy* (pp. 400-415). New York: Brunner/Mazel.

Laqueur, H. P. (1976). Multiple family therapy. In P. J. Guerin (Ed.), *Family therapy: Theory and practice* (pp. 405-416). New York: Gardner.

competitive marriage   A marriage in which each partner tries to inflict the most harm on the other to gain the most for self.

Example: Seiji constantly criticizes his wife, Yoko, for her lack of attention and affection. Consequently he feels justified in not acting in a loving way toward her and frequently goes out partying with his single friends.

Ravich, R., & Wyden, B. (1974). *Predictable pairing.* New York: Wyden.

complementarity   Serving to fill out, complete, or make perfect; mutually supplying each other's lack. *Complementarity* refers to the degree to which the needs and abilities of both spouses dovetail effectively, to the specific patterns of family role relations that provide satisfactions, avenues of solution of conflict, support for a needed self-image, and means of buttressing crucial forms of defenses against anxiety. Complementarity in family role relations may be further differentiated as being either positive or negative. *Positive complementarity* exists when the members of family pairs and triads experience mutual fulfillment of a need in a way that promotes positive emotional growth of the relationships of the interacting individuals. *Negative complementarity* in family relations signifies a buttressing of defenses against pathogenic anxiety but does not significantly foster positive emotional growth. Negative complementarity mainly neutralizes the destructive effects of conflict and anxiety and barricades family relationships and vulnerable family members against trends toward disorganization.

Examples: Positive complementarity: A wife and a husband who are faced with a long automobile trip that neither wishes to make alone decide to go together, to make it a pleasure trip instead of an anxiety-producing duty, and to cooperatively share the driving. *Negative complementarity:* A husband believes he must have financial responsibility to avoid becoming anxious, while his wife fears financial responsibility and becomes anxious and depressed if forced to assume control of fiscal matters; here the partners complement each other negatively: One wants control, the other eschews it.

Ackerman, N. W. (1958). *The psychodynamics of family life.* New York: Basic Books.
Sager, C. J. (1976). *Marriage contracts and couple therapy.* New York: Brunner/Mazel.
Winch, R. (1954). The theory of complementary need in mate selection: An analytic and descriptive study. *American Sociological Review, 19,* 241-249.

complementarity of roles A relationship in which each person automatically acts in conformity with the role that that person is expected to assume by the partner. When these expectations are violated, the result is tension, anxiety, and frustration.

Example: A husband acts passively to comply with the requests of his domineering wife.

Goodwin, H. M., & Mudd, E. H. (1969). Marriage counseling: Methods and goals. In B. N. Ard & C. C. Ard (Eds.), *Handbook of marriage counseling* (pp. 93-105). Palo Alto, CA: Science & Behavior Books.

complementary schismogenesis A tendency toward progressive change between individuals or groups of individuals. A cycle is established in which a change in one leads to a change in the others.

Example: In a marital relationship, one partner is more assertive than the other. The more assertive the first partner, the more the other submits, thereby forcing the assertive partner to be even more assertive.

Bateson, G. (1958). *Naven* (2nd ed.). Stanford, CA: Stanford University Press.
Bodin, A. (1981). The interactional view: Family therapy approaches of the Mental Research Institute. In A. S. Gurman & D. P. Kniskern (Eds.), *Handbook of family therapy* (pp. 267-309). New York: Brunner/Mazel.

compliance-based paradox   An intervention in which the client tries to obey a paradoxical prescription designed to bring an involuntary behavior under voluntary control by creating an ordeal for the patient.

Example: A woman who is a perfectionist at housecleaning is told to do more. The increased work makes her problem so aversive that she decides to give it up.

Rohrbaugh, M., Tennen, H., Press, S., & White, L. (1981). Compliance, defiance, and therapeutic paradox. *American Journal of Orthopsychiatry, 51,* 454-467.
Weeks, G., & L'Abate, L. (1982). *Paradoxical psychotherapy: Theory and practice with individuals, couples, and families.* New York: Brunner/Mazel.

compliment   An intervention designed to build a yes set for a family. A compliment consists of some positive statement with which all members of the family can agree.

Example: The therapist says to the parents: "I am impressed with all the fine details you've given me. It's clear you are loving parents who have tried to find ways to solve the problem."

de Shazer, S. (1982). *Patterns of brief family therapy.* New York: Guilford.

components in marital interaction   Four areas of interaction between spouses: (1) the things you know about yourself and those your mate knows about you, (2) the things your mate knows about you that you do not know about yourself, (3) the things you know about yourself that your mate does not know, and (4) the things about yourself that neither you nor your mate know.

Example: The marriage therapist knows that, at the beginning of the counseling, the "open" area is usually very small, otherwise the couple would be getting along better. As counseling proceeds successfully, Area 1 gets much larger as you and your partner really get to know each other. At the same time, the "hidden" area gets much smaller. You do not think you have to be as defensive. Later in counseling, Area 2, "blindness," gets smaller as you grow more honest with yourself. Gradually you gain the courage to face yourself, and you finally decrease the size of Area 4, the "unknown." You come to understand some of your unconscious motives and improve your ways of communicating. Permanent change in the marital relationship can occur at this stage. These components can be depicted graphically (see Figure 1).

Sauber, S. R. (1972). *An honest guide to marriage counseling.* West Palm Beach, FL: Mental Health Association Press.

	Known to you	Unknown to you
Known to spouse	1 Open Area freedom	2 Blind Area caution
Unknown to spouse	3 Hidden Area defensiveness	4 Unknown Area fear

Figure 1. Components in Marital Interaction

compression theory   The theory that dysfunctional families continually oscillate from intense fusion with the nuclear family to intense fusion with the family of origin.

Example: A young couple are normally inseparable until they have an argument. They then split and return to their respective families for support.

Stanton, M. (1981). Strategic approaches to family therapy. In A. S. Gurman & D. P. Kniskern (Eds.), *Handbook of family therapy* (pp. 361-402). New York: Brunner/Mazel.

compulsory relationship   A relationship in which two family members feel that an association is not voluntary, so neither can accept as valid any indication from the other about wanting to be together. Affectionate gestures are disqualified as requests that the person doing the gesturing not be turned out or left alone; the gestures are regarded as a kind of bribery.

Example: A mother indicates with some contempt that her husband is afraid to leave her because he cannot stand being alone. She suggests he is cruel to her because he is angry at being tied to her. She also rejects his affectionate overtures because she considers them to be only a kind of bribery to ensure his staying with her. She herself is unable to leave him even for a night, though he is drunk several nights a week and beats her regularly.

Haley, J. (1959). The family of the schizophrenic: A model system. *Journal of Nervous and Mental Disease, 129,* 357-374.
Haley, J. (1972). The family of the schizophrenic. In G. D. Erickson & T. P. Hogan (Eds.), *Family therapy: An introduction to theory and technique* (pp. 51-75). Belmont, CA: Wadsworth.

computer   A pattern in family communication in which one member deals with emotional issues in a very rational, calm, unemotional manner. A computer is correct, reasonable, and shows no feelings.

Satir, V. (1972). *Peoplemaking.* Palo Alto, CA: Science & Behavior Books.

conation   The ability to choose goals and to pursue them with energy, motivation, and drive.

Beavers, W. R. (1977). *Psychotherapy and growth: A family systems perspective.* New York: Brunner/Mazel.

conciliation   A technique often used in connection with mediation. The conciliator (a) offers options for the parties to consider, (b) points out the advantages and disadvantages of various options, and (c) encourages the parties to adopt an available option, rather than remain at an impasse. To some extent, the conciliator takes over the parties' responsibility for examining the issues and discovering options. Conciliation is thus a less desirable procedure than mediation and serves as an alternative to an impasse. It may be needed, not because the parties are unwilling to take responsibility, but because they often are inexperienced in dealing with much of the subject matter.

Coogler, O. J. (1978). *Structured mediation in divorce settlement.* Lexington, MA: Lexington.

concordance   The ratio of agreements to disagreements for an individual or the whole family.

Lennard, H., & Bernstein, A. (1969). *Patterns in human interaction.* San Francisco: Jossey-Bass.

concurrent marital therapy   Therapy in which both spouses are treated simultaneously either by the same therapist or by different therapists who communicate with each other.

Mittleman, B. (1944). The concurrent analysis of marital couples. *Psychoanalytic Quarterly, 13,* 479-491.
Prochaska, J., & Prochaska, J. (1978). Twentieth century trends in marriage and marital therapy. In T. Paolino & B. McCrady (Eds.), *Marriage and marital therapy* (pp. 1-24). New York: Brunner/Mazel.

concurrent processes   Interviews with different groupings of the family, conducted separately by the therapist during the same period of treatment.
   Example: A couple cannot sit together in the therapist's office without fighting. While continuing the sessions together, they also are seen for individual sessions to help reduce the level of anger.

Aponte, H., & van Deusen, J. (1981). Structural family therapy. In A. S. Gurman & D. P. Kniskern (Eds.), *Handbook of family therapy* (pp. 310-360). New York: Brunner/Mazel.

conduct disorder   A broad range of "acting out" behaviors exhibited by children that violate the basic rights of others. The behavior pattern is typically pervasive and is seen at home, at school, with peers, and in the community. Physical aggression is common. Overall, conduct disorder is the most frequently occurring child behavior disorder both in the clinic and in the general population. Boys typically are diagnosed more frequently than girls. A child is diagnosable as having conduct disorder when he or she has three of the following behaviors: has stolen, has run away from home overnight, often lies, has deliberately set fires, has been truant from school, has broken into someone else's home or car, has deliberately destroyed others' property, has been physically cruel to animals, has forced someone into sexual activity with him or her, has used a weapon in a fight, often initiates fights, and has been physically cruel to people. Children with conduct disorders typically are seen as disobedient, cruel, irritable, bragging, blaming others, attacking others, impulsive, argumentative, demanding, and prone to alcohol and drug abuse.

American Psychiatric Association. (1987). *Diagnostic and statistical manual of mental disorders* (3rd ed., rev.). Washington, DC: Author.

McMahon, R. J., & Wells, K. C. (1989). Conduct disorders. In E. J. Mash & R. A. Barkley (Eds.), *Treatment of childhood disorders* (pp. 73-132). New York: Guilford.

conductors Therapists who have aggressive, public, charismatic personalities and who have strong value systems that are imparted in the therapy session. Conductors exercise their active control in families in direct and obvious ways. They take the role of educators or "superparents" and openly and directly confront the family's pathological functioning. They may intervene persuasively and positively.

Example: A therapist takes charge of a family meeting and sees to it that most family business is transacted in a democratic atmosphere.

L'Abate, L. (1983). Styles in intimate relationships: The A-R-C model. *Personnel and Guidance Journal, 61,* 277-283.

Skynner, A. C. R. (1976). *Systems of family and marital psychotherapy.* New York: Brunner/Mazel.

confidentiality An ethical standard that protects patients from disclosure of information received in the context of a professional relationship without their consent. In most states, the parents or legal guardians of children under 18 years of age hold the rights of confidentiality. Thus parents sign releases of information, secure school and medical records, and authorize searches of children's property. Although a family psychologist is not legally obligated to seek permission of the child before disclosing confidential information, it is ethically mandatory to attempt to get such permission. This request should recognize the child's cognitive, social, and emotional development to levels with appropriate allowances. Thus the family psychologist should discuss appropriate "ground rules" for confidentiality in advance with the parents and child together.

Koocher, G. P., & Keith-Spiegel, P. C. (1990). *Children, ethics, and the law.* Lincoln: University of Nebraska Press.

Margolin, G. (1982). Ethical and legal considerations and marital and family therapy. *American Psychologist, 37*, 788-801.

configuration   One of three underlying dimensions used by Reiss to characterize the concept of *family constructs. Configuration* refers to the degree of complexity allowable in the experiences of family members. The configuration dimension varies from subtle, detailed, and highly structured to coarse, simple, or chaotic. Families that tend toward the former pole of the dimension reflect a sense of optimism and mastery when confronted with a novel or ambiguous social setting; events and people are construed as multifaceted, with relationships between family members conditional on many factors. Families that tend toward low configuration reflect a resistance to exploring novel or ambiguous environments; such families would be classed according to simple attributes, and the relationships between family members would be perceived as either incomprehensible or very stylized.

Reiss, D. (1981). *The family's construction of reality.* Cambridge, MA: Harvard University Press.

confirmation   The therapist responding sympathetically to family members (expressions of concern, sadness, anger, fear, rejection, etc.).

Minuchin, S. (1974). *Families and family therapy.* Cambridge, MA: Harvard University Press.

confirming   A process in which the therapist validates the reality of the holons (the component parts of the system) that he or she joins. The therapist acknowledges and rewards positive aspects and identifies stressful, difficult, or painful areas. In confirming the positive, the therapist becomes an important source of self-esteem. By acknowledging the negative, the therapist becomes a source of sensitivity and understanding. Confirming also may be a nonjudgmental appraisal of transactions between family members.

Minuchin, S., & Fishman, H. (1981). *Family therapy techniques.* Cambridge, MA: Harvard University Press.

conflict   Disruptions that, in abstract terms, are viewed as power struggles and, in simple operational terms, are regarded as interruptions or disagreements.

Example: A son tells his natural father that he prefers to spend time with his new stepfather.

Riskin, J., & Faunce, E. (1972). An evaluative review of family interaction research. *Family Process, 11,* 365-455.

conflict-habituated marriage A marriage characterized by severe conflicts but in which, unpleasant as it is, the partners are held together by a fear of separation. The spouses quarrel habitually, acknowledge their incompatibility, and accept tension as normal. Arguments are often over trivial matters.

Example: A husband and a wife in their later years acknowledge their incompatibility as they identify the wife's intellectual curiosity about life and social interests and the husband's lack of education and his preference to be alone and to exclude himself from knowledge-stimulating experiences. Their dissatisfaction is compounded by the wife's resentment of the excessive number of working hours the husband spends in his business and her hostility when he returns home after work exhausted from his long day.

Cuber, J., & Harroff, P. (1965). *The significant Americans.* New York: Random House.

conflict induction A technique of invoking conflict in a family when the family habitually avoids conflict. The family is then in a position of confronting the conflict, and the members develop new ways of managing and resolving the conflict.

Example: With a family that refuses to set clear limits with a child, the therapist encourages the family to "stand firm" with a child who is throwing a temper tantrum.

Minuchin, S. (1974). *Families and family therapy.* Cambridge, MA: Harvard University Press.

conflict negotiation A process in which thoughts, feelings, and a range of solutions are shared by family members in conflict as the members alternate roles of sender and receiver.

Bernard, C., & Corrales, R. (1979). *The theory and technique of family therapy.* Springfield, IL: Charles C Thomas.
Miller, S., Nunnally, E., & Wackman, D. (1975). *Alive and aware: Improving communications in relationships.* Minneapolis: Interpersonal Communications.

conflict resolution family therapy Therapy that presents the usual interaction framed as interpersonal problems and suggests that these problems have concrete solutions in the interpersonal realm. The tasks are structured clearly, deal with family situations, are focused on the here and now, and compel family members to search for solutions through interaction among themselves.

Example: A family council is established to meet weekly to review family chores: how each member is completing household responsibilities that that member has selected as contributions to the management of the home, and the consequences to the individual and the family when a member is unreliable.

Minuchin, S. (1965). Conflict-resolution family therapy. *Psychiatry, 28,* 278-286.
Minuchin, S. (1972). Conflict-resolution family therapy. In G. D. Erickson & T. P. Hogan (Eds.), *Family therapy: An introduction to theory and technique* (pp. 293-305). Belmont, CA: Wadsworth.

confusion technique   A technique, originated by Milton Erickson, that involves inducing a trance by overwhelming the person's conscious ability to make sense of what the hypnotist is saying or doing.

O'Hanlon, W. H., & Hexum, A. L. (1990). *An uncommon casebook: The complete clinical work of Milton H. Erickson, M.D.* New York: Norton.

congruent communication   Communication in which two or more messages are sent via different levels, but none of the messages seriously contradict any of the others.

Example: A husband says, "The dog is on the couch," in an irritable tone and in a context that tells his wife that he is irritated and why he is irritated.

Satir, V. (1983). *Conjoint family therapy* (3rd ed.). Palo Alto, CA: Science & Behavior Books.

conjoint family therapy   A therapeutic approach, devised by D. Jackson, in which the whole family is the therapeutic unit for treatment and the family members meet as a group with the therapist to change family interaction.

Jackson, D., & Weakland, J. (1961). Conjoint family therapy. *Psychiatry, 24,* 30-45.
Satir, V. (1983). *Conjoint family therapy* (3rd ed.). Palo Alto, CA: Science & Behavior Books.

conjoint marital therapy   A therapeutic model in which both marital partners are seen together by the same therapist or by co-therapists, one male and one female, and in which the problem is seen as an interactional one.

Jackson, D., & Weakland, J. (1961). Conjoint family therapy. *Psychiatry, 24,* 30-45.
Martin, P. (1976). *A marital therapy manual.* New York: Brunner/Mazel.

conjoint parent-child therapy   A technique in which parent and child are seen together by one therapist. Conjoint parent-child therapy allows the clinician to assess the parent's functioning, the child's functioning, and the parent-child relationship. Children aged 6 to 10 often react favorably to this technique.

Wertheim, E. S. (1959). A joint interview technique with mother and child. *Children, 6,* 23-29.

consanguine family A family joined on the basis of blood relationships so that several generations of offspring are included within one family unit.

Christensen, H. (1964). Development of the family field of study. In H. T. Christensen (Ed.), *Handbook of marriage and the family* (pp. 3-32). Chicago: Rand McNally.

consecration ceremonials Interactional behavior patterns, usually engaged in by all family members, that are often formalized and repetitive in nature. These ritual patterns define the family's image, exemplify its past history, and objectify its beliefs about itself.

Example: Three sons arm-wrestle with their father each time he returns home after a long absence, with their mother cheering them on. This ritual encompasses the family's sense of its tough past. The concern of the father not to hurt the boys, and, as they become men, their care not to hurt him, symbolize the family's compassion for the weak.

Reiss, D. (1981). *The family's construction of reality.* Cambridge, MA: Harvard University Press.

consensual experience theory A theory developed to explain, relate, and predict observations made simultaneously on both family interactions and the thinking and perception of individual members as these unfold together through time. Essentially the theory states that each family develops its own shared and distinctive view or explanation of its environment and of the patterns or principles that govern its members and events.

Example: A family moves to a new neighborhood. All of the family members see themselves as outsiders. They are suspicious of their neighbors, carefully protect their privacy, and make it a rule never to disclose personal information about themselves or the family.

Reiss, D. (1971). Intimacy and problem solving: An automated procedure for testing a theory of consensual experience in families. *Archives of General Psychiatry, 25,* 442-455.

consensual validation A method by which patients compare mental reactions to certain experiences while learning to understand, recognize, and feel more certain of their expressions of thought and feeling.

Example: A father who thinks he is socially inept learns from his family's reactions that he can handle interpersonal situations with skill, but his belief that he cannot prevents him from doing so.

Sullivan, H. S. (1953). *The interpersonal theory of psychiatry.* New York: Norton.

consensus-sensitive family A family in which the primary characteristic is the press toward agreement. Family members discard accurate information in favor of data that are consistent with the views of others. Consequently information is not evaluated by objective standards but according to its congruence with family myths. The outside world is viewed as unpredictable, which promotes agreement in the family as a needed source of security. The family members maintain a rigid boundary with an outside world that is rarely trusted. The members display little tolerance for feedback that contradicts their view of the world. As a result, verbal and nonverbal communications that are contrary to the family's consensus are rarely expressed.

Example: A father who has been unemployed for more than a year blames the union for his lack of work. Despite the evidence that his dismissal was due to repeated failure to perform his duties, no one in the family mentions this. They also fail to mention that he has lost jobs in the past, usually because of his drinking problem. Instead they nod agreement to his indictment of the union and even contribute their own examples of the injustices wrought on them by union staffers.

Reiss, D. (1981). *The family's construction of reality.* Cambridge, MA: Harvard University Press.

consent A legal term used for a patient to give permission to release information or to participate in research, therapy, and/or medical treatment. For children under age 18, it is usually the parents or legal guardian who must give consent. *Informed consent* indicates the participants are fully aware of all consequences of participation before they decide to proceed. Thus consent typically must be documented in a way that ensures the provisions for consent have been met; thus consent is usually a written document. Consent must be free from coercion and undue influences.

Koocher, G. P., & Keith-Spiegel, P. C. (1990). *Children, ethics, and the law.* Lincoln: University of Nebraska Press.

Margolin, G. (1982). Ethical and legal considerations and marital and family therapy. *American Psychologist, 37,* 788-801.

constricted family A family characterized by excessive restriction of a major aspect of family emotional life, such as expression of anger, negative affect, or ambivalence. These emotions become internalized into anxiety, depression, and somatic complaints. The presenting patient is often a passive, depressed child or young adult.

Example: A domineering mother resents anyone arguing with her and sets up family rules of compliance. Her son's manner of resisting her is to become sick and get out of family obligations.

Cuber, J., & Harroff, P. (1966). *Sex and the significant Americans.* New York: Penguin.
Glick, I. D., & Kessler, D. P. (1980). *Marital and family therapy* (2nd ed.). New York: Grune & Stratton.

constructive questions   Questions that lead toward goals and solutions. They are future oriented and are worded to support positive change and the creation of new solutions.

Examples: "How will you know he is listening (constructive individual)?" "How do you think he'll know that you know he is listening?"

Lipchik, E., & de Shazer, S. (1986). The purposeful interview. *Journal of Strategic and Systemic Therapies, 5,* 88-99.

constructivism   An epistemological position in which all knowledge of the world is the result of our own constructing, ordering, inventing, creating, and so on, and is not the result of discovering the world as it objectively exists. In therapy, this position holds that the therapist and client co-create new meaning for experience. This psychological position has been espoused most commonly by systems and strategic therapists.

Held, B. (1990). What's in a name? Some confusion and concerns about constructivism. *Journal of Marital and Family Therapy, 16,* 179-189.
Watzlawick, P. (Ed.). (1984). *The invented reality.* New York: Norton.

consulting break   A method of working with families that involves the use of a team that observes the therapist(s) and family from behind a one-way mirror. The therapist periodically leaves the treatment room to consult with the team. This procedure provides the team opportunities to design interventions.

de Shazer, S. (1982). *Patterns of brief family therapy.* New York: Guilford.

contact victimization   A reaction sometimes experienced by therapists working with incest survivors. The therapist begins to develop symptoms of posttraumatic stress disorder, such as fear, startle responses, and nightmares.

Courtois, C. (1988). *Healing the incest wound.* New York: Norton.

content   (1) The "report" aspect of a message that conveys information. The content of communication is different from the process of communication. Content is a matter of "what"; process is a matter of "how." (2) In family systems theory, the particular themes and concretized attributes of life that, joined together through time, give thematic meaning to the daily activities of a family and its members. *Content* refers to the psychological phenomena that are the substance of systems concepts, such as information and energy. The hopes, dreams, envies, loves, memories, and aspirations of people's daily lives make up the content of individual phenomenal experience. One may select for study a content theme (such as personal identity images, family ideals, or parental power), or one may postulate a human activity is about anything, such as the defense against forbidden impulses, the organization of mental operations into automatic response patterns, and so forth. But once the content theme has been selected, one needs to recognize that it, per se, is only of secondary importance, at least from a systems perspective. See also **process.**

Example: A mother speaks about how busy her day was and all of the activities that she had to accomplish.

Satir, V. (1983). *Conjoint family therapy* (3rd ed.). Palo Alto, CA: Science & Behavior Books.

Umbarger, C. C. (1984). *Structural family therapy.* New York: Grune & Stratton.

Watzlawick, P., Beavin, J. H., & Jackson, D. D. (1967). *Pragmatics of human communication.* New York: Norton.

content-context syndrome   A kind of marital relationship in which one partner pays attention to content only in verbal communications, both his or her own and others, and the other partner pays attention to nonverbal communications, both his or her own and others. The first partner is content oriented; the second is context oriented. In such a situation, there are bound to be communication gaps between the two.

Example: A wife listens carefully to what her husband says as he does home repairs and evening business work and they discuss family matters. The husband ignores his wife's "babbling" and responds only when she approaches him with nonverbal strokes of affection leading to sex or when, in anger, she stamps her foot to demand his attention.

Gerson, M., & Barsky, M. (1979). For the new family therapist: A glossary of terms. *American Journal of Family Therapy, 7,* 15-30.

Hogan, P. (1963). The content-context syndrome. *Newsletter, Society for Medical Psychoanalysts, 4,* 1-6.

context   The situation in which people are communicating, including both the physical situation and the stated premises about what sort of situation it is. The context in which a statement is made may disqualify the statement.

Example: A college student makes a sexual statement to her instructor in class, but the statement is disqualified due to the public nature of the situation.

Haley, J. (1972). The family of the schizophrenic. In G. D. Erickson & T. P. Hogan (Eds.), *Family therapy: An introduction to theory and technique* (pp. 51-75). Belmont, CA: Wadsworth.

context marker   A concept used in the Milan model to refer to an interaction in which one person defines the context for others.

Example: The therapist may act as the context marker by stating that he or she sees all of the actions in the family flowing from love. The meaning of the family's actions will have been altered if the therapist can use information and other people to validate this perspective.

Boscolo, L., Cecchin, G., Campbell, D., & Draper, R. (1988). Twenty more questions— Selections from a discussion between the Milan associates and the editors. In D. Campbell & R. Draper (Eds.), *Applications of systemic family therapy* (pp. 225-293). New York: Grune & Stratton.

C

contextual family therapy   Therapy in which family members are guided toward working on their own relational commitments and balances of fairness. The aim is to loosen the chains of invisible loyalty and legacy in such a way that each person can give up symptomatic behaviors and explore new options.

Example: A father has difficulty showing love to his son. The therapist asks him about how his own father showed affection toward him. The therapist also asks the father to see his own father's side in order to help open a multilateral perspective of fairness toward his son. In addition, the therapist may have the father open his relationship with his own father in order to balance the ledger.

Boszormenyi-Nagy, I., & Ulrich, D. (1981). Contextual family therapy. In A. S. Gurman & D. P. Kniskern (Eds.), *Handbook of family therapy* (pp. 159-186). New York: Brunner/Mazel.

contextual questions   A class of circular questions in the Milan model. These questions examine the relationships between meaning and action.

Example: The therapist might ask, "When you think your husband is trying to control you, what is he trying to accomplish?" This question gives the therapist information about the meaning given to a particular set of behaviors.

Tomm, K. (1985). Circular interviewing. In D. Campbell & R. Draper (Eds.), *Applications of systemic family therapy* (pp. 33-45). New York: Grune & Stratton.

contextual transference   The individual's or couple's transference to the therapist's capacity to provide safety and help. In sex therapy, the couple may not believe that the therapist can change their relational and/or sexual difficulties and ultimately will reject them.

Scharff, D. (1988). An object relations approach to inhibited sexual desire. In S. Leiblum & R. Rosen (Eds.), *Sexual desire disorders* (pp. 45-74). New York: Guilford.

contingencies of reinforcement   Situations in which, instead of rewarding maladaptive behavior with attention and concern, family members learn to give each other recognition and approval for desired behavior.

Example: When Tyrone completes his homework, Dad reinforces this study behavior by showing his interest and approval and by playing a game of Scrabble with him.

Liberman, R. (1970). Behavioral approaches to family and couple therapy. *American Journal of Orthopsychiatry, 40,* 106-118.
Liberman, R. (1972). Behavioral approaches to family and couple therapy. In G. D. Erickson & T. P. Hogan (Eds.), *Family therapy: An introduction to theory and technique* (pp. 120-134). Belmont, CA: Wadsworth.

C

contingency contracting   A specific, usually written schedule or contract describing the terms for the trading or exchange of behaviors and reinforcers between two or more individuals.

Example: A man's newly married wife joined him when he had weekend visitations with his children from a previous marriage. The husband then agreed to spend more time with his new in-laws.

Stuart, R. B. (1976). An operant interpersonal program for couples. In D. H. L. Olson (Ed.), *Treating relationships* (pp. 119-132). Lake Mills, IA: Graphic Publishing.

contingency management   A technique that involves assessing the way contingencies are being mismanaged and instructing change agents about the necessary modifications.

Example: A young boy with encopresis is being reinforced by his mother's attention. When this support is pointed out to the mother, who is the change agent, and she is instructed to reward certain toileting behaviors, the problem is ameliorated.

Homme, L., & Tosti, D. (1969). Contingency management and motivation. In D. Gelfand (Ed.), *Social learning in childhood: Readings in theory and application.* Belmont, CA: Brooks/Cole.
LeBow, M. (1972). Behavior modification for the family. In G. D. Erickson & T. P. Hogan (Eds.), *Family therapy: An introduction to theory and technique* (pp. 347-376). Belmont, CA: Wadsworth.

continuity   A coding category referring to messages that affect the continuation of communication in terms of facilitating or interfering responses—for example, pauses, silences, repetitions, and restatements of previous messages.

Example: A wife is not sure what she heard her husband say. She repeats what she thought she heard, which helps facilitate the communication.

Sojit, C. (1969). Dyadic interaction in a double bind situation. *Family Process, 8,* 235-260.

contract   See **therapeutic contract.**

contract marriage   A marital union, either legal or paralegal, that is identified by explicit written or spoken agreement outlining duties and privileges of the union's members. The contract may specify such items as who is responsible for domestic services, child care, and financial support and how many children the couple wish to have.

Belkin, G., & Goodman, N. (1980). *Marriage, family, and intimate relationships.* Chicago: Rand McNally.

Rolfe, D. (1977). Pre-marriage contracts: An aid to couples living with parents. *Family Coordinator, 26,* 281-285.

contradictory communication   A communication in which two or more messages are sent in a sequence via the same communication level but in opposition to each other.

Examples: A person says, "Come here," followed by "No, go away"; or a person pulls another person closer and then pushes that person away again.

Satir, V. (1983). *Conjoint family therapy* (3rd ed.). Palo Alto, CA: Science & Behavior Books.

control group   The family group that is compared to an experimental family group. Many types of control groups are analyzed in family interaction research—for example, "normal" controls, hospitalized psychiatric nonschizophrenic patients and their families, hospitalized nonpsychiatric patients and their families, nonhospitalized patients and their families, and families from differing social classes and structures.

Mishler, E., & Waxler, N. (1968). *Interaction in families: An experimental study of family processes and schizophrenia.* New York: John Wiley.

controlling-domineering messages   Messages that order, command, or forbid; challenge another's assertion; refuse to do something; contradict, protest, or deny; compare or compete; or brag or persist in a topic.

Example: A wife says to her husband, "You must visit my parents with me whether you like it or not."

McPherson, S. (1968). *A manual for multiple coding of family interaction.* Unpublished manuscript.

Riskin, J., & Faunce, E. (1972). An evaluative review of family interaction research. *Family Process, 11,* 365-455.

cooperating   A means of accommodation in a relationship. Each individual, couple, or family has a unique way of attempting to cooperate. The therapist's job is to identify that particular manner and then to cooperate with the family's way, thus promoting change. The concept of *cooperating* completely negates the traditional concept of *resistance.* Whatever the family members do is an expression of how they cooperate with the therapist.

de Shazer, S. (1982). *Patterns of brief family therapy.* New York: Guilford.

cooperative marriage   A marriage in which the partners take turns exercising power in a positive way.

Example: The husband makes decisions about money after consulting with his wife, and she makes social and domestic plans after asking her husband's opinion.

Ravich, R., & Wyden, B. (1974). *Predictable pairing.* New York: Wyden.

C

coordination   Family members' ability and willingness to develop similar problem solutions. Coordination also refers to the experience by all family members that they are, for the moment, in the same experiential universe, whose principles and patterns are equally true and equally relevant for all.

Example: All members of a family agree that the best way to deal with cleaning the house is for everyone to have assigned tasks that are to be fulfilled on a specified day of the week.

Reiss, D. (1981). *The family's construction of reality.* Cambridge, MA: Harvard University Press.

co-parental relationship   The relationship between former spouses. The relation of styles is varied and is formed on a continuum that ranges from *my former spouse as my best friend* to *my former spouse as my bitter enemy.* Interactions are generally child focused.

Ahrons, C. R., & Perlmutter, N. S. (1982). The relationship between former spouses: A fundamental subsystem in the remarriage family. In J. C. Hansen & L. Messinger (Eds.), *Therapy with remarriage families* (pp. 31-46). Rockville, MD: Aspen.

coping devices   Expedients that meet or attenuate the effect of an attacking agent and repair its damage. Coping involves defense, adaptation, and reparation. It is the price the organism must pay to preserve its integrity. The devices may be primitive (verbal hostility, withdrawal, anxiety) or directed (fantasy, unrealistic thought, perceptual distortions).

Example: A man suspects that his wife is having an affair. His mother is dying of cancer. Rather than deal with his suspicions regarding his wife while under such stress, he begins to distort his perceptions of himself and to tell himself that he is an overly jealous husband.

Howells, J. (1975). *Principles of family psychiatry.* New York: Brunner/Mazel.

coping patterns   The patterns used to respond to different kinds of influences to change behavior.

Example: Every time a wife asks her husband to make a specific change, he agrees but then acts as if nothing had been discussed.

Goldstein, M., Judd, L., Rodnick, E., Alkire, A., & Gould, E. (1968). A method for studying social influence and coping patterns within families of disturbed adolescents. *Journal of Nervous and Mental Disorders, 148,* 233-251.

Riskin, J., & Faunce, E. (1972). An evaluative review of family interaction research. *Family Process, 11,* 365-455.

cop-out The use of excuses for not engaging in potentially desirable behavior.

Example: A wife states that if she shows her husband any affection, he will only want to have sex with her.

Wahlroos, S. (1974). *Family communication: A guide to emotional health.* New York: Macmillan.

corporal punishment Spanking, used as a form of discipline or punishment for misbehavior. Although many states have banned corporal punishment in public schools, this is not true in all states. Many states still permit school administrators or teachers to administer physical punishment to promote discipline. Many psychologists view corporal punishment as a legally sanctioned form of child abuse. However, the U.S. Supreme Court has refused to consider school-administered corporal punishment as "cruel and unusual punishment." The common rationale cited by supporters of official corporal punishment tends to be, "It taught me a lesson when I was their age."

Koocher, G. P., & Keith-Spiegel, P. C. (1990). *Children, ethics, and the law.* Lincoln: University of Nebraska Press.

co-therapeutic modeling A process in which two therapists, each taking the point of view of one of the spouses, argue on behalf of their clients in front of the couple.

Example: The husband's therapist argues that he is dissatisfied with the marriage because he continually experiences criticism, no matter what efforts he makes to improve the relationship and please his wife. The wife's therapist points out that she sees her husband as only trying to placate her superficially to assuage his guilt in making a separation.

Lazarus, A. (1968). Behavior therapy and marriage counseling. *Journal of the American Society of Psychosomatic Dentistry and Medicine, 15,* 49-56.

LeBow, M. (1972). Behavior modification for the family. In G. D. Erickson & T. P. Hogan (Eds.), *Family therapy: An introduction to theory and technique* (pp. 347-376). Belmont, CA: Wadsworth.

co-therapy Therapy in which a male therapist and a female therapist work with a couple concerning sexual and identity issues in the marriage in order to represent each gender's point of view and to serve as couple-relationship role models and potential transference figures.

Gurman, A., & Kniskern, D. (1978). Research on marital and family therapy: Progress, perspective, and prospect. In S. Garfield & A. Bergin (Eds.), *Handbook of psychotherapy and behavior change* (pp. 817-901). New York: John Wiley.

counteraccusation   A primitive way of avoiding personal responsibility for solving a problem and of hurting another person in return.

Example: A wife says to her husband, "How long are you going to postpone fixing that fence?" The husband replies, "Look who's talking! What about you and your ironing? I don't even get to wear a clean shirt to the office!"

Wahlroos, S. (1974). *Family communication: A guide to emotional health.* New York: Macmillan.

counterparadox   A therapeutic double bind. In dysfunctional families, the identified patient receives the message from the rest of the family not to change (the family paradox). The therapist sends a message to the patient to change, which is counter to the family's paradox to the patient.

Selvini Palazzoli, M., Boscolo, L., Cecchin, G., & Prata, G. (1980). *Paradox and counterparadox: A new model in the therapy of the family in schizophrenic transaction.* New York: Jason Aronson.

countertransference   A process in which the therapist begins to experience feelings toward a family member that are reminiscent of feelings experienced in relation to a person in the therapist's past. The therapist may report this phenomenon to the family, and the family then may process any similar feelings on its part. The countertransference material then can become corrective feedback for the family.

Example: A hostile father in a family reminds the therapist of abuse that the therapist sustained as a child, causing the therapist to respond to the father with fear and hostility.

Bernard, C., & Corrales, R. (1979). *The theory and technique of family therapy.* Springfield. IL: Charles C Thomas.

covenant contracting   An intervention to help couples negotiate emotional and behavioral components of their relationship. Individual contracts are trileveled: (a) conscious and verbalized, (b) conscious but unspoken, and (c) beyond awareness. Their categories of expectation are based on (a) expectations of a relationship, (b) each individual's psychological needs, and (c) external problems resulting from the preceding two areas. The actual contract focuses on four sets of needs within the actual marriage: self, marriage, spouse, and children.

Example: A wife lists the following needs in her contract:

- Self: (1) I want to be more self-confident. (2) I want to exercise more.

- Marriage: (1) I want to do more things with my husband. (2) I want to talk more about feelings.
- Spouse: (1) I want my spouse to believe in me. (2) I want him to be proud of himself.
- Children: (1) I want my children to be responsible. (2) I want my children to enjoy learning.

L'Abate, L., & McHenry, S. (1983). *Handbook of marital interventions.* New York: Grune & Stratton.
Sager, C. J. (1976). *Marriage contracts and couple therapy.* New York: Brunner/Mazel.

C

covert sensitization A conditioning technique in which deviant sexual behavior is paired with noxious stimuli or an aversive event.

Example: A rapist is asked to imagine approaching a woman to rape her. He then is asked to shift from this image to one that is highly aversive to him, such as vomiting or seeing maggots on his victim.

Callahan, E., & Leitenberg, H. (1973). Aversion therapy for sexual deviation: Contingent shock and covert sensitization. *Journal of Abnormal Psychology, 21,* 60-73.
Walen, S., Hauserman, N., & Lavin, P. (1977). *Clinical guide to behavior therapy.* Baltimore: Williams & Wilkins.

covert sexual examination A diagnostic sex hypnotherapy technique in which the client is asked to stand naked in front of a full-sized, three-way mirror and to describe and evaluate every part of his or her body.

Araoz, D. L. (1982). *Hypnosis and sex therapy.* New York: Brunner/Mazel.

crazy-making A variety of techniques, all of which have one thing in common: to make one doubt one's sanity.

Example: A husband exercises complete control over his wife's behavior. When she points out his control, he says he is only taking care of her. In effect, he says it is for her sake that he monitors her behavior.

Bach, G., & Wyden, P. (1968). *The intimate enemy.* New York: William Morrow.

creating a crisis A situation in which the therapist deliberately creates or provokes a crisis situation to upset the family balance or homeostasis and to force the family to change.

Example: A family with an anorectic child might be forced into a direct confrontation by having the parents force the child to eat.

Gerson, M., & Barsky, M. (1979). For the new family therapist: A glossary of terms. *American Journal of Family Therapy, 7,* 15-30.
Jackson, D. (1968). The question of family homeostasis. In D. Jackson (Ed.), *Communication, family, and marriage* (pp. 1-11). Palo Alto, CA: Science & Behavior Books.

crisis An event or happening outside or inside the family unit that upsets the traditional ways of interacting, thus demanding change in the family system. In an adaptive approach to crises, any change is regulated carefully so that when the crises occur, the upset is minimal and a rapid return to the status quo is facilitated. Past experiences or future goals are used to solve the crises. In a maladaptive approach, no process for family interaction in crisis resolution is experienced. A crisis is handled by means of superimposed structures or fixed rules. If these structures are ineffective, a secondary crisis develops out of the family dysfunction.

Example: A wife suddenly announces to her husband that she is incapable of returning to the marriage and does not deserve his love. She admits having been sexually abused as a child and says she no longer wishes to be married. The wife's decision creates disruption and confusion. It can create an opportunity for individual and/or couple growth if pursued therapeutically, or it can lead to harm if the wife withdraws from the relationship and the husband becomes depressed, believing himself to be a failure in meeting his wife's needs.

Dodson, L., & Kurpuis, D. (1977). *Family counseling: A systems approach.* Muncie, IN: Accelerated Development.

crisis runaways Runaways who fall between unsuccessful nonrunaways and abortive runaways. Crisis runaways manage to leave home for a while but do not find refuge in the runaway culture. They either return home or allow their parents to rescue them.

Example: A young adolescent male is caught shoplifting and then is humiliated by his peers at school and is rejected by his parents. He runs away but returns after a week.

Stierlin, H. (1974). *Separating parents and adolescents: A perspective on running away, schizophrenia and waywardness.* New York: Quadrangle.

critical identity images The internal memory pictures that comprise one's preferred self and ideal family. The conceptions of "ideal self" and "ideal context," which each partner attempts to implement within an intimate relationship, result in a family system whose structure may be functional or dysfunctional.

Kantor, D., & Lehr, W. (1975). *Inside the family: Toward a theory of family process.* San Francisco: Jossey-Bass.
Okun, B. F., & Rappaport, L. J. (1980). *Working with families: An introduction to family therapy.* Belmont, CA: Brooks/Cole.

cross-confrontation The use of audiotapes and videotapes, letters, and poems containing unpleasant, emotionally charged material that is derived from one set of client families as stressor stimuli for another set of client families. The rationale underlying cross-confrontation is the need to assist people to perceive and understand that all feeling states are normal and that there are no abnormal fantasies.

Example: A family experiences difficulty grieving over the loss of a child. The therapist plays a tape from another family in which a breakthrough was made in dealing with a delayed grief reaction.

Paul, N. (1976). Cross-confrontation. In P. J. Guerin (Ed.), *Family therapy: Theory and practice* (pp. 520-529). New York: Gardner.

cross-generational conflict An inappropriate alliance between a parent and a child who side together against a third member of the family.

Example: A woman and her mother always resented the daughter's husband for not providing her with the better things in life to which she was accustomed.

Bowen, M. (1960). A family concept of schizophrenia. In D. D. Jackson (Ed.), *The etiology of schizophrenia* (pp. 346-372). New York: Basic Books.

cross-generational incest Sexual contact with a partner of a considerable age difference who is a parent, stepparent, in-law, grandparent, aunt, uncle, second cousin, or a quasi relative such as a guardian.

Courtois, C. (1988). *Healing the incest wound.* New York: Norton.

cross-generation coalition A triadic structure that causes distress in social systems. The presence of such a triangle is associated with violence, symptomatic behavior, and dissolution of the system. The triangle consists of (a) two persons of the same status (generations) and another from a different level, (b) two members on different levels uniting against the third person, or (c) two persons who have united in secret, with the third person excluded covertly.

Example: A mother feels lonely and bored in her marriage. She becomes dependent on her teenage son and begins to be overly permissive with him. The son takes advantage of the situation by becoming demanding, aggressive, and slack in school. The father attempts to discipline the son but finds his attempts covertly undermined by his wife.

Haley, J. (1977). Toward a theory of pathological systems. In P. Watzlawick & J. Weakland (Eds.), *The interactional view* (pp. 11-27). New York: Norton.
Hoffman, L. (1981). *Foundations of family therapy.* New York: Basic Books.

cross-monitoring A therapeutic exchange in which the person who is being spoken about is present and probably listening. Consequently the person can alter behavior because of the information.

MacGregor, R. (1962). Multiple impact psychotherapy with families. *Family Process, 1,* 15-19.

MacGregor, R. (1972). Multiple impact psychotherapy. In G. D. Erickson & T. P. Hogan (Eds.), *Family therapy: An introduction to theory and technique* (pp. 150-163). Belmont, CA: Wadsworth.

cross-transactions   Situations in which, when asked a question, the respondent becomes defensive, assumes a child's ego state, and responds as if accused by a parent, thereby breaking off congruent communication.

Example: A husband asks a question from the adult ego state: "Would you like to go out tonight?" His wife responds from the child ego state: "No, you must want to go out so you can be with your friends." This reply elicits a response from the husband's parent ego state: "You're being childish again."

Berne, E. (1967). *Games people play.* New York: Grove.

cryptic paradoxes   Messages used to create a state of confusion through the use of vague or ambiguous terms, undefined referents, contradictions, double meanings, and so on.

Example: The following statement is made to a couple: "Your relationship is very nicely complementary, but because you can only be what the other is not, you cannot really be yourself."

Weeks, G., & L'Abate, L. (1982). *Paradoxical psychotherapy: Theory and practice with individuals, couples, and families.* New York: Brunner/Mazel.

crystal ball syndrome   A situation in which a client believes he or she should know something but does not know and cannot ask. Furthermore the client assumes that the therapist should be able to guess what that client is thinking.

Example: A male patient has a sexual attraction toward his male therapist but denies his homosexual feelings. He is too uncomfortable to express his emotions but thinks the doctor will be able to "read his mind."

Satir, V. (1983). *Conjoint family therapy* (3rd ed.). Palo Alto, CA: Science & Behavior Books.

cybernetics   The study of common processes in systems, especially analysis of the flow of information in closed systems. The cybernetic model is important to family theorists because it introduces the idea of circular causality by way of the feedback loop. Cybernetics focuses on the interaction between the parts of the system and holistic patterns. *First-order cybernetics* assumes the system being observed is separate from the observer. *Second-order cybernetics* emphasizes the observer (therapist) as part of the system. See also **first-order cybernetics** and **second-order cybernetics.**

Example: A husband may be convinced that his wife's nagging (cause) makes him withdrawn (effect). She is equally likely to believe that his withdrawal causes her to nag.

Bateson, G. (1987). *Steps to an ecology of mind.* New York: Ballantine.
Nichols, M. P. (1984). *Family therapy: Concepts and methods.* New York: Gardner.
Weiner, N. (1954). *The human use of human beings: Cybernetics and society.* Garden City, NY: Doubleday.

C

cybernetics of cybernetics   A term acknowledging the fact that social cybernetics is actually second-order cybernetics. In therapy, this concept refers to the idea of the therapist becoming a part of the system being treated.

Foerster, H. von (1979). Cybernetics of cybernetics. In K. Krippendorff (Ed.), *Communication and control in society* (pp. 5-8). New York: Gordon & Breach.

cyclothymiosis   The cyclical nature of the mood changes of elation and depression. The condition is regarded as organic and endogenous.

Howells, J. (1975). *Principles of family psychiatry.* New York: Brunner/Mazel.

C

decision making The process used to make selections among alternatives based on an understanding of past experiences, the present situation, and future expectations. The components are (a) identifying the problem, (b) obtaining information and formulating possible courses of actions, (c) considering the consequences of each alternative, and (d) selecting a course of action. The content of a decision, the situation, and the personality of decision makers influence the arrangement of and the emphases within the components. The uses of the components are affected by the attitudes of the family members, the composition and resources of the family, the physical setting, and the power structure of the family. *Egalitarian decision making* refers to sharing among family members, in contrast to *autonomic decision making,* which is the delegation of decisions to individual family members according to specialization of areas. Strategies for decision making accord each family member a consensually agreed-upon measure of control over the form and content of the interaction.

Example: A husband who appears quite dominant in decision making may take cues from his wife's conversations that lead him to select a given alternative. Although he is dominant, his wife influences the outcome of the decision.

Nickell, P., Rice, A. S., & Tucker, S. P. (1976). *Management in family living* (5th ed.). New York: John Wiley.

defense The behavioral response of the organism to threat. The goal of defense is the maintenance of the current structure of the self. This goal is achieved by (a) the perceptual distortion of the experience in awareness to reduce the incongruity between the experience and the structure of the self or (b) the denial to awareness of the experience, thus denying any threat to the self. Thus an observed phenomenon that is significantly inconsistent with the concept of *self* cannot be directly and freely admitted to awareness. When an experience is even vaguely perceived as being incongruent with the self, the individual reacts with a distortion of the meaning of the experience.

Horne, A. M., & Ohlsen, M. M. (Eds.). (1982). *Family counseling and therapy.* Itasca, IL: F. E. Peacock.

Rogers, C. P. (1959). A theory of therapy, personality and interpersonal relationships, as developed in the client-centered framework. In S. Koch (Ed.), *Psychology: A study of a science, Vol. III. Formulations of the person and the social context* (pp. 184-256). New York: McGraw-Hill.

D

defiance-based paradoxes   Interventions based on the assumption that the client will defy or oppose the paradoxical directive, that by predicting something will happen, the therapist helps to make it not happen.

Example: A couple begin to have arguments after a few sessions of therapy. The therapist predicts more fights. This prediction challenges the couple to prove the therapist wrong.

Rohrbaugh, M., Tennen, H., Press, S., & White, L. (1981). Compliance, defiance, and therapeutic paradox. *American Journal of Orthopsychiatry, 51,* 454-467.

Weeks, G., & L'Abate, L. (1982). *Paradoxical psychotherapy: Theory and practice with individuals, couples, and families.* New York: Brunner/Mazel.

deficiency needs   Needs based on having been deprived of something necessary for emotional satisfaction, such as a need for love, respect, belonging, or security. The individual thus is motivated to fill the deficit.

Example: A woman raised solely by her divorced mother seeks relationships with older men.

Maslow, A. (1954). *Motivation and personality.* New York: Harper & Row.

degradation ceremonials   Interactional behavior patterns, engaged in by family members, whose primary function is to conceal aspects of the family's life that are considered to be frightening. Scapegoating is one form of degradation ceremonial. See also **scapegoating.**

Example: A family dealing with the father's heart trouble begins to accuse one child of constantly damaging things belonging to the child or to the family. This scapegoating allows family members to conceal their shared fears regarding the possible death of the father.

Reiss, D. (1981). *The family's construction of reality.* Cambridge, MA: Harvard University Press.

deindividuation   The sum total of transferences, misidentifications, generational reversals, and fusions resulting in implicit weakening of all family members' discrete ego boundaries and regression to an ego mass or ego fusion in the family. The members of the group do not notice or support the other group members as individuals.

Example: Mrs. Steinberg's ego boundaries shift back and forth among (a) identifying with her daughter's childish self, (b) identifying herself as her daughter Deborah's extension, and (c) identifying herself as her own mother's extension.

Boszormenyi-Nagy, I. (1965). Intensive family therapy as process. In I. Boszormenyi-Nagy & J. Framo (Eds.), *Intensive family therapy: Theoretical and practical aspects* (pp. 87-142). New York: Harper & Row.

delegated legacy obligation   An obligation that is paid only in the way an individual has been taught.

Example: A beaten child becomes a child-beating parent.

Stierlin, H. (1976). The dynamics of owning and disowning: Psychoanalytic and family perspectives. *Family Process, 15,* 277-288.

delegates   A child becomes a delegate when his or her parents subject the child to centrifugal and centripetal pressures. By making the child into a delegate, they send the child out, while at the same time holding on to him or her. The child becomes an extension of the parents' ambivalence.

Example: An adolescent daughter is encouraged to go out with her friends, but the parents restrict her social contacts to the ethnic neighborhood and request that she tell them where she has been and all about her friends' parents.

Stierlin, H. (1974). *Separating parents and adolescents: A perspective on running away, schizophrenia and waywardness.* New York: Quadrangle.

demystification   A technique by which the therapist counters mystification, which involves attribution (of negative traits that denote either "weakness" or "badness"), invalidation, and induction. To counter damaging attributions (attributions that such and such a person is weak or sick), the therapist must ensure that the family members learn to speak for their own feelings, needs, and interests.

Example: A mother who has constantly said, "Louise (her adolescent daughter) is always so depressed," "Louise is afraid of boyfriends," "Louise hates her teachers," and so on learns that Louise can speak for her own feelings, experiences, and interests. At the same time, the mother learns to speak for herself and hence learns to communicate "I feel depressed," "I need to be alone," "I am annoyed when Louise wears dirty blue jeans," or even, "I need Louise as a buffer between me and my husband."

Satir, V. (1983). *Conjoint family therapy* (3rd ed.). Palo Alto, CA: Science & Behavior Books.

denial   The invalidation of a previous statement or the contradiction of a previous statement's content (a subcategory of the disagreement code developed by Lennard and Bernstein).

Example:

Wife   Remember, you promised you would be home at 5:00 p.m. tomorrow.
Husband   I did not. I never used the word *promise.*

Lennard, H., & Bernstein, A. (1969). *Patterns in human interaction.* San Francisco: Jossey-Bass.

denial of sexuality   The repression of erotic impulses. Frequently sex is viewed as pornographic or dirty; the individual is taught as a youngster that sexual impulses are not acceptable and that sexuality is nasty, hostile, and immoral.

Example: A teenage girl refuses contraceptives because she denies herself as a sexual being; she has been told premarital sex is sinful and immoral.

Kaplan, H. S. (1974). *The new sex therapy.* New York: Brunner/Mazel.

denotative level   The literal content of a message.

Satir, V. (1983). *Conjoint family therapy* (3rd ed.). Palo Alto, CA: Science & Behavior Books.

dependence   A type of family system in which boundaries between individuals or family roles are distorted. In some cases, however, the boundaries still may be clearly articulated—for example, when one member is self-reliant and another is servile in an interdependent relationship. The first person may function in a problem-solving capacity, while the other person may focus continually on personal feelings and needs. This type of symbiotic relationship is seen dramatically in the hardworking wife and the alcoholic husband. There is often a shift of feelings and responsibility for behavior from one person to the other, exemplified by the statement, "She made me do it." For such symbiotic families, the goal in therapy is to help each person function independently, consistent with that person's developmental level. The aim is for each person to take responsibility for that person's own thoughts, feelings, and behaviors.

Erskine, R. G. (1982). Transactional analysis in family therapy. In A. M. Horne & M. M. Ohlsen (Eds.), *Family counseling and therapy* (pp. 245-275). Itasca, IL: F. E. Peacock.

dependency   Behavior characterized by overly frequent or intense attachment to another person. The attachment can be emotional, physical, or financial, depending on what one person needs to survive. The family life cycle can be characterized in terms of three major stages: (a) dependency; (b) independence, or denial of dependence, as in adolescence; and (c) interdependence-autonomous adulthood, with the recognition that all of us need to rely on others, just as others need to rely on us.

Example: The child needs to rely on a caretaker to survive. When the child grows into adulthood, however, he or she learns to become freer financially, to achieve greater physical distance, and to separate emotionally from the caretaker.

L'Abate, L. (1985). Descriptive and explanatory concepts in family therapy: Distance, defeats, and dependency. In L. L'Abate (Ed.), *Handbook of family psychology and therapy* (Vols. I & II, pp. 1218-1248). Pacific Grove, CA: Brooks Cole.

D

depersonalization   The process of not responding to feelings and of reducing another person to a thing. Depersonalization is employed by an insecure person when the other person becomes too tiresome or disturbing. The insecure person feels that any kind of relationship will be self-impoverishing.

Example: A husband gives his wife his paycheck and expects that she will provide meals, have sex with him when he requests, and take care of all of the needs and problems of the children. He, in turn, brings in the money and is entitled to go out socially to the neighborhood bar and to sports events with his male friends on weekends.

Laing, R. (1969). *The divided self.* New York: Penguin.

descent group   A larger type of family group based on parent-child genealogical relationships.

Zelditch, M. (1964). Cross-cultural analysis of family structure. In H. T. Christensen (Ed.), *Handbook of marriage and the family* (pp. 462-500). Chicago: Rand McNally.

designed experience   Exercises, simulations, and planned procedures that provide a common structure within which individuals interact. In the process, each person's creativity, meanings, and reflections come into play. Such experiential structures, coupled with cognitive generalizations and frameworks, aid people in learning "from the inside out." Abstract concepts can be drawn from commonly experienced simulations and explorations.

Example: The following exercise could be used in helping a large group of strangers get to know each other: Think of two nicknames or adjectives used to describe you as a child. One of these labels should be positive, the other negative. When you enter the conference room, go around the room and introduce yourself, using these two labels; do not explain the labels, just say something such as, "Hi, I'm beautiful and prissy."

Duhl, B. S. (1983). *From the inside out and other metaphors.* New York: Brunner/Mazel.

desire discrepancy   A discrepancy in sexual desire in a couple in which neither partner is overly excessive or deficient in sexual interest.

Leiblum, S., & Rosen, R. (1988). Introduction: Changing perspectives on sexual desire. In S. Leiblum & R. Rosen (Eds.), *Sexual desire disorders* (pp. 1-20). New York: Guilford.

detouring   A process by which two family members preserve their relationship by detouring incipient conflict through a third person. A conflict between parents is transformed into a conflict between either mother and child or father and child to maintain the illusion of a harmonious relationship between the parents, even at the expense of the child. This is a rigid form of triad in which the marital coalition or spouse subsystem is expressed by their unity to attack or protect, either way avoiding their own antagonisms.

Example: The husband goes to work but often leaves work during the day. The wife discovers this behavior and reprimands him for it. The child senses the tension between the parents and begins to play hooky from school to redirect the parents' conflict. The child is then highly scrutinized for being late to activities.

Minuchin, S. (1974). *Families and family therapy.* Cambridge, MA: Harvard University Press.

detouring-attacking coalition   A situation in which, although conflict exists, the parents handle it by uniting against the child, who is defined as "bad" or "the family problem." This pattern tends to produce behavior disorders, delinquency, and learning difficulties.

Example: Two spouses are having marital problems and are considering divorce. Their teenage son becomes argumentative, runs away from home, and acts out repeatedly. The parents "unite" temporarily to deal with their child's problem behavior.

Barragan, M. (1976). The child-centered family. In P. J. Guerin (Ed.), *Family therapy: Theory and practice* (pp. 232-248). New York: Gardner.
Minuchin, S. (1974). *Families and family therapy.* Cambridge, MA: Harvard University Press.
Umbarger, C. C. (1984). *Structural family therapy.* New York: Grune & Stratton.

detouring-supporting coalition   A coalition in which the parents mask their relationship differences by focusing on their child. The parents get together in overprotecting and being overly concerned with the child, whom they define as "weak" or "sick," rather than "bad." This pattern tends to produce shyness, insecurity, and psychosomatic disorders.

Examples: Two parents have an implicit rule never to express conflict openly; this rule results in covert hostility. Their daughter refuses to eat, forcing them to redirect their attention to her anorexia. Or when a husband becomes angry with his wife, she reminds him of their autistic child, who must never see them argue. She fears that the child would only withdraw further if subjected to parental disagreement and tension.

Minuchin, S. (1974). *Families and family therapy.* Cambridge, MA: Harvard University Press.

detriangulation The process of withdrawing from a role as buffer, go-between, or confounder in a disturbed family in which the members do not deal with each other on a one-to-one basis. Detriangulation reverses the process and permits the members to relate to one another on a person-to-person basis, responding rather than reacting.

Example: An older sister no longer finds it necessary to defend her effeminate younger brother when her father insists he play sports, stand up for himself when other students in the school pick on him, and act like a man. He is now able to try to take care of himself.

Bowen, M. (1971). The use of family theory in clinical practice. In J. Haley (Ed.), *Changing families* (pp. 159-192). New York: Grune & Stratton.
Gerson, M., & Barsky, M. (1979). For the new family therapist: A glossary of terms. *American Journal of Family Therapy, 7,* 15-30.

developmental arithmetic disorder The *DSM-III-R* term for learning disability in arithmetic. Arithmetic skills, as measured by standardized, individually administered tests, are markedly below the expected level, given the person's education and intelligence. The disorder significantly interferes with academic achievement or activities of daily living requiring arithmetic.

American Psychiatric Association. (1987). *Diagnostic and statistical manual of mental disorders* (3rd ed., rev.). Washington, DC: Author.

developmental expressive writing disorder The *DSM-III-R* term for learning disability in writing. Writing skills, as measured by standardized, individually administered tests, are markedly below the expected level, given the person's education and intelligence. The disorder significantly interferes with academic achievement or activities of daily living requiring the composition of written texts (spelling words and expressing thoughts in grammatically correct sentences in organized paragraphs).

American Psychiatric Association. (1987). *Diagnostic and statistical manual of mental disorders* (3rd ed., rev.). Washington, DC: Author.

D

developmental reading disorder   The *DSM-III-R* term for learning disability in reading. Reading achievement, as measured by standardized, individually administered tests, is markedly below the expected level, given the person's education and intelligence. The disturbance significantly interferes with academic achievement or activities of daily living requiring reading.

American Psychiatric Association. (1987). *Diagnostic and statistical manual of mental disorders* (3rd ed., rev.). Washington, DC: Author.

deviation amplification   A process by which stress is increased in a system to a point of crisis, resulting in the need to organize a new set of relational patterns. It is an increasing cycle of escalating behaviors such that the more one person does something, the more another person does something else. The term is contrasted with *deviation-counteracting*. In deviation amplification, there may be a drift, over time, toward increasing differentiation, which at some point loses its advantageous nature and stability. All processes of mutual casual relationships that amplify an insignificant event build up deviation and impact from the initial state. See also **runaway**.

Example: Many young people start living together, with the comfortable impression that they can always leave each other. Sooner or later, however, they find that time and habit have placed them in as binding a relationship as any marriage.

Hoffman, L. (1973). Deviation-amplifying processes in natural groups. In J. Haley (Ed.), *Changing families* (pp. 285-311). New York: Grune & Stratton.
Hoffman, L. (1981). *Foundations of family therapy.* New York: Basic Books.

devitalized marriage   A marriage that has lost its original zest, intimacy, and meaning. In this type of marriage, the couple do not express dissatisfaction overtly. The spouses may conduct separate lives in many areas but are joined together by legal and moral bonds and by children.

Example: The children have gone off to college, and the parents have little to share as husband and wife because most of their relationship was child oriented rather than couple focused.

Cuber, J., & Harroff, P. (1966). *Sex and the significant Americans.* New York: Penguin.
Glick, I. D., & Kessler, D. P. (1980). *Marital and family therapy* (2nd ed.). New York: Grune & Stratton.

dialectic metatheory   *Metatheory* is a theory about theories. A *dialectic metatheory* is an encompassing theory that helps us comprehend the dynamic relationships among systems. In family therapy, this theory is used to describe causal relationships, the interactive and constitutive nature of relationships, and the process of change.

Weeks, G. (1986). Individual-system dialectic. *American Journal of Family Therapy, 14,* 5-12.

differentiation   The degree of individuality one has vis-à-vis others, defined by a continuum of likeness (e.g., symbiosis, sameness, similarity, differentness, oppositeness, autism). An individual does not base his or her behavior on being like someone else or being different from someone else; rather, his or her behavior is autonomous.

> *Example:* A man in his 20s stops doing things the opposite of how his father did things ("I'm not going to be like him!") and, instead, makes decisions on a rational basis, appropriate to a given situation.

D

L'Abate, L. (1976). *Understanding and helping the individual in the family.* New York: Grune & Stratton.

differentiation of self   This concept is the cornerstone of Murray Bowen's theory of human relationships. People are defined according to the degree of fusion, or differentiation, between emotional and intellectual functioning. This characteristic is so universal that all people can be classified somewhere along the continuum. People at the low end of the continuum are not able to distinguish between feeling and intellectual processes. These "fused" people are dominated by their automatic emotional system. Consequently they are less flexible, less adaptable, and more emotionally dependent on those around them. These fused individuals are stressed more easily into dysfunction and have a difficult time recovering. People at the opposite end of the continuum are said to be differentiated. They are able to separate emotional and intellectual processes. They are more flexible, adaptable, and independent of others. The differentiated individual can cope effectively with the stresses of life, which results in a relatively problem-free existence. See also **undifferentiated family ego mass.**

> *Example:* An undifferentiated husband is not able to confront a marital problem without excessive reassurance, approval, and validation. Being very emotional and reactive, the husband has one crisis after another, unable to distinguish feelings from facts. When asked what he thinks, he responds with what he feels; when asked what he believes, he reports what others have told him. He finds it very difficult to take a stand and tries never to upset his wife.

Bowen, M. (1976). Theory in the practice of psychotherapy. In P. J. Guerin (Ed.), *Family therapy: Theory and practice* (pp. 42-90). New York: Gardner.

Differentiation-of-Self Scale   A clinical scale developed to convey the idea that people have different gradations of differentiation of self. The scale is divided into four parts, each with an accompanying profile.

Example: At the low level of differentiation, individuals live in a feeling-dominated world in which it is impossible to distinguish fact from feeling. Individuals at this level are relationship oriented and strive to win love and approval.

Bowen, M. (1976). Theory in the practice of psychotherapy. In P. J. Guerin (Ed.), *Family therapy: Theory and practice* (pp. 42-90). New York: Gardner.

D

differentness   How each person is innately different from every other person in the whole area of individuality. The concept relates to differences in such things as physical appearance, personality, preferences, and expectations. These differences may unite a couple or may create an irreconcilable division.

Example: A husband and wife have very different attitudes toward religion. The husband is religious, while his wife stresses the importance of religious values and goes to church.

Satir, V. (1983). *Conjoint family therapy* (3rd ed.). Palo Alto, CA: Science & Behavior Books.

diffuse boundaries   Highly permeable boundaries that allow an easy flow of communication between subsystems; this flow promotes enmeshment. See also **enmeshment.**

Example: A single mother and her teenage daughter discuss the sex life of the mother and her current male relationship.

Minuchin, S. (1974). *Families and family therapy.* Cambridge, MA: Harvard University Press.

digital   The arbitrary encoding of a message so that it bears little or no resemblance to what it represents, as opposed to "analogic" in communication theory. Verbal language is primarily digital: It is abstract, efficient, and precise, yet may be less credible than analogical (nonverbal) communication in relationships. Whenever a word is used to represent something, the relationship between the noun and the thing is always arbitrary. Digital communication is the content, as opposed to the process, of a message.

Example: The spoken words "I love you" represent a feeling. The words are arbitrary, and they may not represent the way the person really feels. The person's actions (analogic communication) convey the true feelings.

Bateson, G. (1987). *Steps to an ecology of mind.* New York: Ballantine.
Watzlawick, P., Beavin, J. H., & Jackson, D. D. (1967). *Pragmatics of human communication.* New York: Norton.

directive A therapeutic technique used to teach people how to behave differently while actively involving the therapist in the family system. The technique also provides the therapist with information regarding the functioning of the family system. The directive may consist of home-work assignments, paradoxical or linear tasks, or specific prescriptions and specifications of roles and activities for various family members.

Lange, A., & van der Hart, O. (1983). *Directive family therapy.* New York: Brunner/Mazel.

directiveness The therapist's ability to control the process of the family in and beyond the therapy session. It might include giving instruction, prompting members to speak, and giving feedback and support.

Example: A husband interrupts his wife before she has completed her thought. The therapist intervenes to direct the husband to stop and asks that the wife complete her thought; otherwise, she might have shut down as her typical response to his interruption.

Barton, C., & Alexander, J. (1981). Functional family therapy. In A. S. Gurman & D. P. Kniskern (Eds.), *Handbook of family therapy* (pp. 403-443). New York: Brunner/Mazel.

disaffirmation Contradictions contained in a message, including state-ments (a) erroneously indicating that the other person misunderstood, thereby contradicting one's previous message, (b) attributing one's own opinion to the other (although incongruent or contradictory with the previously stated opinion of the other), and (c) reframing the previous message of the other incongruently or in contradiction with the other's previous message.

Example:

Husband	I would like to go to the beach today.
Wife	OK.
Husband	I really have to work on the car today. It's not running right.
Wife	Does this mean you're not going?
Husband	I don't know.

Sojit, C. (1969). Dyadic interaction in a double bind situation. *Family Process, 8,* 235-260.

disagreement (1) Denial of a previous statement; (2) negative evalu-ation of a previous statement; (3) qualification of the content of a previous statement; (4) dismissal of a previous statement as irrelevant; (5) sarcasm in referring to a previous statement.

Example: The brother says to the child, "Put the paint back where you found it." The child responds, "This is where I found it."

Lennard, H., & Bernstein, A. (1969). *Patterns in human interaction.* San Francisco: Jossey-Bass.

Riskin, J., & Faunce, E. (1972). An evaluative review of family interaction research. *Family Process, 11,* 365-455.

disconfirmation   Communication, given in a family, that states, "I don't notice you, you're not here, you don't exist."

Selvini Palazzoli, M., Boscolo, L., Cecchin, G., & Prata, G. (1980). *Paradox and counterparadox: A new model in the therapy of the family in schizophrenic transaction.* New York: Jason Aronson.

discontinuity   A break in the sequence of interaction. In *topic discontinuity,* the previous statement is disregarded or there is implicit disagreement.

   Example: The husband says to the wife, "Did you get my clothes from the laundry?" The wife answers, "Mary called today. She wants us to go over to their place tonight."

Lennard, H., & Bernstein, A. (1969). *Patterns in human interaction.* San Francisco: Jossey-Bass.
Riskin, J., & Faunce E. (1972). An evaluative review of family interaction research. *Family Process, 11,* 365-455.

discussion   A communicative interaction in which an exchange of ideas and feelings occurs and in which the object is to reach greater understanding to solve a problem or simply to enjoy each other's company.

   Example: The family members expect that, at mealtime, they will share their experiences and learn what is happening in the family.

Wahlroos, S. (1974). *Family communication: A guide to emotional health.* New York: Macmillan.

disengaged family   An extreme family type in which each family member is cut off emotionally from the other. There is little interaction, exchange of feelings, or sense of belongingness. There is relative absence of connections, and relationships between family members are weak or nonexistent. The *enmeshed family,* by contrast, is characterized by a tight interlocking of its members. See also **absence of involvement** and **rigid boundaries.**

   Example: The father is involved with his work, the mother with church activities and various volunteer and charitable organizations. One child belongs to the Boy Scouts and is working on an Eagle Scout badge, while another child skips school and acts out in predelinquent ways.

Minuchin, S. (1974). *Families and family therapy.* Cambridge, MA: Harvard University Press.

disengaged subsystem   A family subsystem that has developed overly rigid boundaries around itself. Members of disengaged subsystems function autonomously without interdependence and lack feelings of loyalty, support, and belonging; they have lost the ability to function interdependently or to request support when needed.

Example: Two siblings form an enmeshed relationship in delinquency that is separate and apart from parental influence.

Minuchin, S. (1974). *Families and family therapy.* Cambridge, MA: Harvard University Press.

dismemberment crisis The loss of an individual member from a family through divorce, separation, or death (as opposed to a *crisis of accession,* meaning an addition to the group, e.g., parenthood).

Eliot, T. D. (1948). Handling family strains and shocks. In H. Becker & R. Hill (Eds.), *Family, marriage, and parenthood* (pp. 616-640). Lexington, MA: D. C. Heath.
Hoffman, L. (1981). *Foundations of family therapy.* New York: Basic Books.

disqualification A method of denying a relationship by denying one or more of the four conceptual elements of communication: (1) "I (2) am saying something (3) to you (4) in this situation."

Example: A schizophrenic disqualifies a relationship with someone by saying he is someone else who is speaking (the "I" element).

Haley, J. (1959). The family of the schizophrenic: A model system. *Journal of Nervous and Mental Disease, 129,* 357-374.

disruption in communication A major interactional domain characterized operationally by tension release, laughter, pauses, repetitions, incomplete phrases, or incomplete sentences.

Example: A daughter is telling her father about her school work and test grades and then pauses suddenly, as she thinks about getting caught cheating and whether her teacher will notify her parents.

Mishler, E., & Waxler, N. (1968). *Interaction in families: An experimental study of family process and schizophrenia.* New York: John Wiley.

disruptive behavior Any disturbance that tends to interfere, detour, or distract from the flow and pattern of ongoing behavior.

Example: The husband gets angry when confronted by his wife about staying out late. The real issue is neither the confrontation nor his getting angry, but rather the unsettled and unresolved distance between them. The wife is pursuing him to get closer. The husband's angry outburst (disruptive behavior) allows him to keep the distance unchanged and to take away attention from the real issue—the distance between them.

Singer, M., & Wynne, L. (1966). Principles of scoring communication defects and deviances in parents of schizophrenics: Rorschach and TAT scoring manuals. *Psychiatry, 29,* 260-288.

D

dissipative stage A stage of formation for a new system. In this stage, a high degree of information exchange occurs between and within systems. Also, tension occurs between the needs of the system and the needs of its individual members. This stage may be observed during couple formation and family formation, at the time children become school age, during adolescence, and when the children leave home.

Minuchin, S., & Fishman, H. (1981). *Family therapy techniques.* Cambridge, MA: Harvard University Press.

distantiation Discussion of experimental procedures or the expression of impersonal material in referring to persons outside the family, talking about an absent family member, or discussing a family member in the third person as if that person were not present.

Example: A mother and father talk about their son's irresponsibility and what they should do about his interest in obtaining a driver's license and use of their car. The son is in their company, but he is not included in the discussion; they refer to him as "he this" and "he that," rather than as "you."

McPherson, S. (1968). *A manual for multiple coding of family interaction.* Unpublished manuscript.

Riskin, J., & Faunce, E. (1972). An evaluative review of family interaction research. *Family Process, 11,* 365-455.

distance-sensitive families See **environment-sensitive families.**

distinction-clarifying question A type of reflexive question used to clarify attributions that different family members make about behaviors. The same question is asked of every family member to ascertain the kind of assumptions being made about a particular behavior.

Tomm, K. (1987). Interventive interviewing: Part II. Reflexive questioning as a means to enable self-healing. *Family Process, 26,* 167-184.

distraction techniques Techniques, subjective or objective, employed by a male partner to distract himself from his partner's demand for sexual fulfillment and to enhance ejaculatory control. These techniques are used frequently by premature ejaculators, although the methods are usually ineffective.

Example: Each time the husband is about to ejaculate before his wife is ready, he imagines sunbathing on a beach, feeling the heat of the sun, the sound of the waves, and the touch of the wind.

Masters, W., & Johnson, V. (1970). *Human sexual inadequacy.* Boston: Little, Brown.

distractor A pattern of communication in the family. The distractor says or does things that are irrelevant to what everyone else is doing. As a result, the family can avoid dealing with emotional issues and thus does not have to change. Distractors often use humor to distract. See also **mascot.**

Satir, V. (1972). *Peoplemaking.* Palo Alto, CA: Science & Behavior Books.

disturbances in communication (1) Communication deletions (removal of portions of an original experience); (2) communication distortions (change, exaggeration, or minimization of an experience); or (3) generalizations (e.g., "You never . . . ," or "You always . . ."). Deletions are equivalent to the psychoanalytic concept of *repression;* in most cases, they involve the elimination of painful emotional experiences or the minimization of them by giving more emphasis to rational processes (distortions), which then result in a process of generalization. Other disturbances of communication take place through the process of *externalization,* in which external targets are made responsible for one's behavior.

Bandler, R., & Grinder, J. (1975). *The structure of magic* (Vol. 1). Palo Alto, CA: Science & Behavior Books.

divided attention See **attention.**

divided custody An arrangement in which neither parent has primary custody, but each has equal legal access to the children. This arrangement also is called *shared custody.* Each parent generally has reciprocal visitation privileges. It is most workable when the two homes are in the same school district. Otherwise it involves twice yearly upheavals, from both school and neighborhood situations, that most people would consider educationally and psychologically detrimental.

Gardner, R. A. (1989). *Family evaluation in child custody, mediation, arbitration, and litigation.* Cresskill, NJ: Creative Therapeutics.

divorce An emotional and physical process of separation that begins with the first serious and sustained thoughts and discussion a couple have about dissolving their marital union. It continues throughout the resolution of the emotional, legal, economic, religious, and extended family and community/work aspects of their relationship. If they have children, parenting and visitation issues also need to be handled, as are explanations to the children of what has happened and what is likely to occur for them in the future. The unresolved issues often extend into the postdivorce period and need to be coped with so that psychic reequilibration and closure can occur.

Kaslow, F. W., & Schwartz, L. L. (1989). *Dynamics of divorce: A life cycle perspective.* New York: Brunner/Mazel.

D

divorce chain relationships   A "chain" of relationships that is formed among spouses and their former spouses. This complex of relationships typically is maintained because of the children from former marriages.

Example: The two women who are former wife and current wife and the two men who are former husband and current husband face the same problem of normal ambiguity. This situation is extended when the current wife has a former husband, and so on.

Goetting, A. (1980). Former spouse-current spouse relationships. *Journal of Family Issues, 1,* 58-80.

D

divorce counseling or therapy   A process whereby the therapist helps those in the decision-making phase of divorce assess their needs, strengths, and shortcomings and thus facilitates their arriving at a satisfactory decision (to stay married or to divorce). The therapist further helps couples and families who are facing divorce restructure their individual lives, present and future relationships, problems with their children, financial difficulties, and general adjustment to singlehood.

Kaslow, F. (1981). Divorce and divorce therapy. In A. S. Gurman & D. P. Kniskern (Eds.), *Handbook of family therapy* (pp. 662-698). New York: Brunner/Mazel.

divorce mediation   The process by which a couple meets with a trained mental health professional or an attorney educated in mediation and the psychology of conflict resolution. The differences and issues for the couple are mediated in a task-oriented manner until a settlement is reached. In this process, each person assumes responsibility for his or her actions, respect for each other's concerns is expressed, and the integrity of the family unit is maintained. Although the husband and wife separate and obtain a divorce, the family continues and the agreement is discussed in terms of the relationships among mother, father, and children. The advisory attorney rewrites the mediated settlement in legal terms and relates impartially to the "family as the client," not to two parties in conflict. The settlement task for mediation includes division of marital property, possible spousal maintenance or rehabilitative alimony, required child support, shared parenting responsibilities, and custodial or visitation arrangements for the children.

There are four basic models of divorce mediation: integrative (the newest), structural (the oldest), therapeutic, and labor negotiation.

Sauber, S. R., Beiner, S. F., & Meddoff, G. S. (in press). Divorce mediation: A new system for dealing with the family in transition. In R. H. Miskesell, D. D. Lusterman, and S. H. McDaniel (Eds.). *Family psychology and systems therapy: A handbook.* Washington, DC: American Psychological Association.

Sauber, S. R., & Panitz, D. R. (1982). Divorce counseling and mediation. In A. Gurman (Ed.), *Questions and answers in the practice of family therapy* (Vol. 2, pp. 207-213). New York: Brunner/Mazel.

doer A dysfunctional role in the family. The doer provides most or all of the maintenance functions of the family. For example, the doer makes sure the children are dressed and fed, the bills are paid, dinner is cooked, and all of the children get to afterschool activities. However, often the doer feels tired, lonely, taken advantage of, neglected, and empty. Doers have excessive unhealthy guilt and an overdeveloped sense of responsibility that keeps them doing.

Friel, J., & Friel, L. (1988). *Adult children: The secrets of dysfunctional families.* Deerfield Beach, FL: Health Communications.

D

doll's house marriage A marriage in which a competent, powerful, but actually dependent male is both mother and father to a helpless, childlike wife.

Pittman, F. S. (1970). Treating the doll's house marriage. *Family Process, 9,* 143.
Skynner, A. C. R. (1976). *Systems of family and marital psychotherapy.* New York: Brunner/Mazel.

domestic partners Two individuals who reside together. For example, a partnership ordinance in San Francisco stipulates that the partners of city employees (heterosexual or homosexual) who are unmarried would be entitled to health and insurance benefits previously limited to the legally wed. The partners would file a sworn statement that they share in the "common necessities of life as the principal domestic partner of the other and have been such for at least 6 months."

Sauber, S. R. (1988). *It's all in the name: A language guide for the single, his friends, and her family.* Hollywood, FL: Fredrick Fell.

dominance Variously defined operationally as the number of times one speaks, the percentage of time one speaks, the act of gaining attention, and speaking for a group.

Example: A wife tells her husband that he should not retire, even though he has reached the age of 65 and no longer desires to work. She makes the decision for him about what, seemingly, is in his best interests to do. She overpowers his timid objections, and he complies with her requests by continuing to work.

Riskin, J., & Faunce, E. (1972). An evaluative review of family interaction research. *Family Process, 11,* 365-455.

dominance-submission dimension A dimension that reflects the status position that a speaker attempts to establish in relation to another.

Example: As they meet together as a family unit, the husband tells his wife not to express her opinion until he decides what is best for their children.

Gottman, M. (1979). *Marital interaction.* New York: Academic Press.

dominant-submissive marriage   A marriage in which one spouse habitually lets the other take charge.

Ravich, R., & Wyden, B. (1974). *Predictable pairing.* New York: Wyden.

door knobbers   Those very crucial comments dropped by family members when their hand is on the doorknob, ready for flight. Such comments prove particularly troublesome when one member "hangs behind the others to share an anecdote with the therapist."

Luber, R. F., & Anderson, C. M. (1983). *Family intervention with psychiatric patients.* New York: Human Sciences Press.

double bind   An intense relationship in which a person thinks it is vitally important that he or she identify accurately the sort of message that is being communicated so that it can be responded to appropriately. The communicator is expressing two orders of messages, one of which denies the other. As a result, the recipient is unable to comment on the message being expressed in order to correct his or her discrimination of the order of message that should be responded to (he or she cannot make a metacommunicative statement). The conditions of a double bind situation are two or more persons; a repeated experience; a primary negative injunction; a secondary injunction that conflicts with the first at a more abstract level and, like the first, is enforced by punishments or signals that threaten survival; and a tertiary negative injunction prohibiting the victim from escaping from the field.

Example: The wife walks over to her husband and says to him, "Kiss me" (primary injunction). Then, if he attempts to do so, she moves away from him (secondary injunction) and berates him for not being a good husband (tertiary injunction). This interaction is repeated many times. The husband responds to a communication that has both overt and covert messages requiring mutually exclusive or incongruent responses.

Bateson, G., Jackson, D., Haley, J., & Weakland, J. (1956). Toward a theory of schizophrenia. *Behavioral Science, 1,* 251-264.

double description   A method used to introduce difference in therapy. The assumption is that the whole is greater than the sum of its parts. Two perspectives on the same event are juxtaposed, which then produces a third dimension on the relationship. An analogy is looking at the world through the left eye, then the right eye, then both eyes together, which produces the added dimension of depth.

Bateson, G. (1972). *Steps to an ecology of mind.* New York: Ballantine.

White, M. (1986). Negative explanation, restraint, and double description: A template for family therapy. *Family Process, 25,* 169-184.

double message A message that contains a contradiction between different aspects of the content or between the content level and the metacommunicative level.

Example: One person says to another, "You're really fun when you're stupid."

Bernard, C., & Corrales, R. (1979). *The theory and technique of family therapy.* Spring field, IL: Charles C Thomas.

drama technique A psychodramatic technique used in counseling to re-create a situation of conflict for the purpose of bringing painful experiences and affects of the past into the present situation. Once the real emotion is present in the context of the created situation, the problem and its dimensions can be seen more clearly than when merely talking about them, and an opportunity can be created for gaining understanding of the problem and for trying new behaviors.

Example: A family that has difficulty grieving the loss of a member re-creates some aspect of the death, such as the funeral, to bring the feelings to the surface.

D

Dodson, L., & Kurpuis, D. (1977). *Family counseling: A systems approach.* Muncie, IN: Accelerated Development.

drama triangle In transactional analysis, a pathological triangle consisting of three interlocking roles: persecutor, rescuer, and victim. The persecutor blames the victim; the rescuer tries to save the victim; and the victim assumes the role of a helpless, sick, or bad person.

Karpman, S. (1968). Script drama analysis. *Transactional Analysis Bulletin, 26,* 39-43.

drug-enhanced libido The idea that pharmacological agents may enhance sexual desire in humans. No well-documented support exists for this idea at this time. Some of the drugs that have been investigated are L-dopa, dopaminergic drugs, serotonin antagonists and precursors, and others, including antidepressants.

Seagraves, R. (1988). Drugs and desire. In S. Leiblum & R. Rosen (Eds.), *Sexual desire disorders* (pp. 313-347). New York: Guilford.

drug-suppressed libido The idea that pharmacological agents may suppress sexual desire in humans. Pharmacological agents that interfere with various aspects of sexual functioning form a large, diverse group, including some of the following: antihypertension agents, psychiatric drugs, anticonvulsant drugs, anticancer chemotherapy, and a number of drugs that are commonly abused, such as alcohol.

Seagraves, R. (1988). Drugs and desire. In S. Leiblum & R. Rosen (Eds.), *Sexual desire disorders* (pp. 313-347). New York: Guilford.

dry-bed procedure   A behavioral technique used to eliminate childhood enuresis. The procedure involves an all-night training session, with the parents awakening the child hourly to perform various tasks and providing immediate consequences if the child wets the bed during the night. The technique involves training the child to inhibit urination, positively reinforcing the child for correct urinations, training in rapid awakening, decreasing fluid intake before going to bed, self-corrections for accidents, and practice in toilet training.

Azrin, M. H., Sneed, T. J., & Foxx, R. M. (1974). Dry-bed training: Rapid elimination of childhood enuresis. *Behavior Research and Therapy, 12,* 147-156.

D

dry drunk   A person who exhibits the behavior, attitude, and thinking process associated with the addictive disease of alcoholism but who does not abuse the chemical. Thus an alcoholic may no longer drink but still not yet be fully recovered.

Schaef, A. W. (1986). *Co-dependence: Misunderstood-mistreated.* New York: Harper & Row.

dry ejaculation   Ejaculation in the absence of seminal fluid, possibly caused by the use of certain drugs that impair the adrenergic mechanism of the sympathetic nervous system that controls the emission phase of ejaculation.

Kaplan, H. S. (1974). *The new sex therapy.* New York: Brunner/Mazel.

dual-career family   A family in which the husband and wife each engage in a career involving a high degree of emotional commitment and time; used synonymously with *dual paycheck family.*

Johnson, C., & Johnson, F. (1977). Attitudes toward parenting in dual-career families. *American Journal of Psychiatry, 134,* 391-394.

dual sex therapy team   The use of a male therapist and a female therapist working jointly with a couple. This approach was developed by Masters and Johnson and is recommended for all cases involving sex therapy.

Masters, W., & Johnson, V. (1970). *Human sexual inadequacy.* Boston: Little, Brown.

duty to warn and protect   Based on the Tarasoff case, in which the California Supreme Court (1976) ruled that a mental health professional who knew, or by the standards of the profession should have known, that his or her client posed a threat to another has a duty to warn the intended victim. Three conditions apply to duty to warn: (a) a special relationship exists (e.g., the therapist-client relationship), (b) a determination that the patient's conduct needs to be controlled due to the patient being dangerous or violent, and (c) there is a foreseeable victim. Originally thought of as the duty to warn, the concept is now considered to be the *duty to protect*. Protecting includes conventional clinical intervention such as reassessment, medication changes, or hospitalization designed to relieve the patient's symptoms until they no longer pose a threat of dangerousness or violence. In cases in which the potentially violent patient refuses treatment, in most states the patient then may be committed to a treatment facility. Failure to fulfill one's professional duty could result in liability for negligence. Duty to warn and protect supersedes the client's right to confidentiality. Although most states and jurisdictions have laws requiring therapists to warn or protect, this varies from state to state.

Gehring, D. D. (1982). The counselor's "duty to warn." *Personnel and Guidance Journal, 61,* 208-210.

Koocher, G. P., & Keith-Spiegel, P. C. (1990). *Children, ethics, and the law.* Lincoln: University of Nebraska Press.

Tarasoff v. Regents of University of California, 529 P.2d 553 (Cal. 1974), *vacated, reheard, en banc, and aff'd,* 131 Cal. Rptr., 14, 551.P.2d 334 (1976).

dyadic interview An interview by a therapist with any dyad in the family. The kind of dyad can vary greatly, but the most common types are those that include the marital couple, a parent and a child, or two siblings.

Howells, J. (1975). *Principles of family psychiatry.* New York: Brunner/Mazel.

dyadic model A model in which psychological problems are assumed to be the result of two-person interactions. Thus the unit of treatment is the dyad. This concept has been replaced more recently with "triadic" concepts denoting a three-person interaction or coalition used in assessing family alliances.

Example: Jamal shoplifts to get his mother's attention. The treatment involves changing their interactional patterns.

Nichols, M. (1984). *Family therapy: Concepts and methods.* New York: Gardner.

dynamic imagery A hypnotherapy technique emphasizing ego-enhancing mental involvement through any or a combination of "the inner senses" (sight, hearing, etc.). It usually is combined with positive affirmations that become powerful self-suggestions.

Araoz, D. L. (1981). Negative self-hypnosis. *Journal of Contemporary Psychotherapy, 12,* 45-51.

dysfunctional communication A breakdown or impairment of communication in a family; its members neither give nor receive clear messages.

D

Example: One person says to another person: "You would like to see a movie, wouldn't you?" "It would do you good to see a movie," or "We might as well go to a movie."

Satir, V. (1983). *Conjoint family therapy* (3rd ed.). Palo Alto, CA: Science & Behavior Books.

D

dysfunctional family   Salvador Minuchin described the dysfunctional family as one that cannot fulfill its function of nurturing the growth of its members. He described several types of dysfunctional families: the disengaged family, the enmeshed family, the family with the peripheral male, the family with the noninvolved parents, and the family with juvenile parents. He described dysfunctional families as being too far on the continuum in either direction of disengagement versus enmeshment. More recently, the term has been used more generically as a family system that creates dysfunctional, maladaptive, and unhealthy behavior and emotions in one or more of the individual members of the family. Dysfunctional families exhibit one or more of the following characteristics: any problems in the family are denied, intimacy is lacking, shame is used to motivate individuals, family roles are rigid, individual identity is devalued for the sake of the family identity, individual needs are sacrificed for the needs of the dysfunctional family system, communication is very poor, and clear ego boundaries are lacking. Such dysfunctional family systems produce psychopathology in individual members. Addictions, obsessions, antisocial behavior, and other types of psychopathology are seen to stem from a dysfunctional family system. See also **functional family.**

Friel, J., & Friel, L. (1988). *Adult children: The secrets of dysfunctional families.* Deerfield Beach, FL: Health Communications.
Minuchin, S. (1974). *Families and family therapy.* Cambridge, MA: Harvard University Press.
Minuchin, S., Montalvo, B., Guerney, B. G. Jr., Rosman, B. L., & Schumer, F. (1967). *Families of the slums: An exploration of their structure and treatment.* New York: Basic Books.

dysfunctional marriage   A marriage marked by low self-esteem and trust. The partners attempt to use each other to ensure their self-esteem.
Example: Two persons marry solely on the basis of appearance. Each secretly feels unworthy of the other but uses the other to bolster self-esteem.

Satir, V. (1983). *Conjoint family therapy* (3rd ed.). Palo Alto, CA: Science & Behavior Books.

dysfunctional pattern   A situation in which a family responds to stress with rigid, unyielding behavior, rather than flexibility. A dysfunctional pattern is often the impetus that brings the family into therapy.

Example: A wife notices that her husband has become less affectionate. She asks him to show her more attention. He maintains a rigid stance, communicating that, "If I gave an inch, she would take a mile."

Minuchin, S. (1974). *Families and family therapy.* Cambridge, MA: Harvard University Press.

dyslexia An older term used to indicate a learning disability in reading. See also **learning disability.**

Barkley, R. A. (1990). *Attention deficit hyperactivity disorder: A handbook for diagnosis and treatment.* New York: Guilford.

dysorgasmia Any kind of ejaculatory dysfunction: premature, retarded, absent, or retrograde.

Araoz, D. L. (1982). *Hypnosis and sex therapy.* New York: Brunner/Mazel.

dyspareunia Difficult or painful coitus. This sexual dysfunction may have organic or psychogenic causes.

Masters, W., & Johnson, V. (1970). *Human sexual inadequacy.* Boston: Little, Brown.

D

D

ecological approach   An approach to family therapy in which the total field of a problem is included in any understanding of a problem, such as the neighborhood, extended family, community service providers, local citizens, and institutional or governmental bureaucrats. In short, the therapist takes a holistic approach to the problem.

Example: The father is injured in an automobile accident, and he spends his time going to doctors for rehabilitation and to lawyers to seek revenge from the drunk driver who caused the accident and consequent disability. The family has to go on welfare for financial support, sell their home in the suburbs, and move to a less desirable neighborhood. The children feel upset about their father's injury, embarrassed about being on welfare, ashamed and fearful of living in a rundown house in a high-risk crime area, and depressed about going to a school with poor academic records and without their old school friends. The mother has to give up her full-time job to take care of her husband and has to find part-time evening work so that he will have the children to take care of him when they come home from school.

Auerswald, E. (1968). Interdisciplinary versus ecological approach. *Family Process, 7,* 205-215.

Hoffman, L. (1981). *Foundations of family therapy.* New York: Basic Books.

ecological systems   Two or more co-evolving, self-organizing systems. Co-evolution is a necessary feature of the relationship between two or more self-organizing systems (e.g., living creatures and parts of their environment). It brings about the necessary reshaping of each and conserves and extends the systems' pattern match, on which their continued growth and development crucially depends.

Duhl, B. S. (1983). *From the inside out and other metaphors.* New York: Brunner/Mazel.

ecology   The science concerned with the nature of the interaction of organisms and populations with the embedding environment, which supports, influences, and determines the limits of the structures and functions of those organisms and populations. An ecological view of family intervention encompasses at least three types of analyses:

1. An analysis of the community, social system, or organizational network through the interrelationship of the various kinds of human services provided within a defined geographic and population area. The principle underlying this type of analysis is that any change in operation of one service unit will affect the operation of all other service units.

Example: An increase in admissions to one local human service agency is likely to be attributed either to a decrease in service opportunities at another facility or to a change in the social stress and tolerance patterns that may have produced more clients.

2. An ecological analysis that considers the relationship between the physical environment, the setting's physical characteristics, and the individual's behavior.

Example: Research on population density, local community action groups' responses to public housing, or the effects of urban renewal on life-styles.

3. An analysis of the interrelationships between individual behavior and the immediate social environment. Here attention is directed to studying individuals in specific behavioral settings and redefining the concept of *pathology of behavior* not viewed as sick or well but as transactional (as an outcome of reciprocal interactions between specific social situations and the individual).

Example: A child complained to his mother of headaches shortly after he was placed in a new special education class.

Sauber, S. R. (1983). *The human services delivery system.* New York: Columbia University Press.

ecomap   A diagrammatic assessment procedure that portrays the family's relationships to other systems—for example, work, school, social welfare, church. The term relates to the concept of *ecosystem,* in which the transactions between individuals, rather than the characteristics of each individual, are the primary data.

Sluzki, C. E. (1978). Marital therapy from a systems theory perspective. In T. Paolino & B. McCrady (Eds.), *Marriage and marital therapy* (pp. 366-394). New York: Brunner/Mazel.

ecostructural approach   The combination of an ecological approach with Salvador Minuchin's structural approach to family therapy. The ecostructural approach holds that the structure of the home situation is replicated in other settings.

Example: A boy who is misbehaving at home tends to replicate that situation at school.

Aponte, H. (1976). The family-school interview: An ecostructural approach. *Family Process, 15,* 303-311.
Hoffman, L. (1981). *Foundations of family therapy.* New York: Basic Books.

ecosystemic epistemology   An epistemological model that views symptomatic behavior or symptoms as the result of multiple system interaction. The symptom is seen as a metaphoric communication about the patient's relationships.

Example: A child refuses to sleep in her bed at night. She sleeps by her mother's bedside because she is aware of the difficulties her mother has when her father arrives at home late at night.

Keeney, B. (1979). Ecosystemic epistemology: An alternative paradigm for diagnosis. *Family Process, 18,* 117-129.

efficiency   An average or normal decision time for a family beyond which there is wastefulness in family functioning.

Ferreira, A., & Winter, W. (1968). Decision making in normal and abnormal two-child families. *Family Process, 7,* 17-36.
Riskin, J., & Faunce, E. (1972). An evaluative review of family interaction research. *Family Process, 11,* 365-455.

ego-dystonic homosexuality   In this homosexuality, individuals are not comfortable with their homosexual behavior or feelings, and they desire to acquire or increase heterosexual arousal. They describe their homosexuality as unwanted and as causing persistent distress.

Kaplan, H. (1983). *The evaluation of sexual disorders.* New York: Brunner/Mazel.

ego fusion   A condition in which the intrapsychic systems of involved family members are so intimately fused that differentiation of one from the other is impossible. The fusion involves the entire range of ego functioning. One ego can function for that of another; for example, one family member assumes she can accurately know the thoughts, fantasies, feelings, or dreams of another.

Example: In a psychotic family, one member becomes physically ill in response to the emotional stress of another.

Bowen, M. (1976). Theory in the practice of psychotherapy. In P. J. Guerin (Ed.), *Family therapy: Theory and practice* (pp. 42-90). New York: Gardner.

ego-state therapy   A hypnotherapeutic technique in which the therapist asks to talk with the fearful part of the patient.

Watkins, J., & Watkins, N. (1984). Ego-state therapy. In R. Corsini (Ed.), *Handbook of innovative psychotherapies* (pp. 252-270). New York: John Wiley.

Zilbergeld, B., & Hammond, D. (1988). The use of hypnosis in treating sexual disorders. In S. Leiblum & R. Rosen (Eds.), *Sexual desire disorders* (pp. 192-223). New York: Guilford.

ejaculatory control   The ability to control consciously the ejaculatory reflex.

Masters, W., & Johnson, V. (1970). *Human sexual inadequacy.* Boston: Little, Brown.

ejaculatory incompetence   A male sexual disorder in which ejaculation is difficult, if not impossible, to achieve intravaginally. *Retarded ejaculation* is one form of ejaculatory incompetence.

Masters, W., & Johnson, V. (1970). *Human sexual inadequacy.* Boston: Little, Brown.

ejaculatory inevitability   The point at which the male can no longer inhibit the ejaculatory reflex.

Kaplan, H. S. (1974). *The new sex therapy.* New York: Brunner/Mazel.

ejaculatory pain   Pain due to muscle spasms that occur immediately after ejaculation. This syndrome may be treated by systematic in vivo desensitization.

Kaplan, H. S. (1979). *Disorders of sexual desire.* New York: Brunner/Mazel.

elastic band syndrome   A syndrome in which families shift suddenly from disengagement to involvement.

   Example: A child progressively increases acting up behavior in an attempt to elicit a response from a disengaged parent. At some point, the irritated parent responds, often violently, to the child. The syndrome is analogous to stretching a rubber band until it breaks, with the child being hit as the band snaps back.

Levant, R. F. (1984). *Family therapy: A comprehensive overview.* Englewood Cliffs, NJ: Prentice-Hall.

Minuchin, S., Montalvo, B., Guerney, B. G., Jr., Rosman, B. L., & Schumer, F. (1967). *Families of the slums: An exploration of their structure and treatment.* New York: Basic Books.

emancipation of offspring   The normal separation of children from the parental family. Such emancipation is an evolutionary task in a nuclear family system and culture. The emancipation must occur physically and geographically, as well as psychologically and socially. The separation is the culmination of many forms of increasing psychosocial separateness between parent and child.

Example: The son leaves the family, gets a job, and is able to live separately and support himself; he feels more confident in social relationships and becomes a mature adult, no longer dependent on his parents.

Fleck, S. (1972). An approach to family pathology. In G. D. Erickson & T. P. Hogan (Eds.), *Family therapy: An introduction to theory and technique* (pp. 103-119). Belmont, CA: Wadsworth.

embedded-suggestion question A type of reflexive question in which a suggestion is embedded in the question.

Example: A therapist might embed an action by saying, "What would happen if you held your thought until you fully understood what your partner had to say first?"

Tomm, K. (1987). Interventive interviewing: Part II. Reflexive questioning as a means to enable self-healing. *Family Process, 26,* 167-184.

embittered-chaotic parent A parent in extreme and bitter opposition, such as in a divorce situation. Every aspect becomes an opportunity for the expression and consolidation of rage, particularly when the children are present as an audience.

Example: A wife whose husband has deserted her goes into a rage over the lack of money whenever her husband visits the children. The maneuver is intended to produce guilt in the husband.

Wallerstein, J., & Kelly, J. (1980). *Surviving the breakup: How children and parents cope with divorce.* New York: Basic Books.

emotional complementarity A fused relationship in which each partner plays out the opposite side of each manifestation of togetherness. The end result often gives the appearance of one partner's being more independent or differentiated than the other, when, in fact, both have equivalent needs for togetherness and equivalent capacities to be a self.

Example: One partner appears independent, cool, and unemotional, while the other is dependent and desires closeness in the relationship. In fact, they both have the same emotional needs, but the needs are played out in mirror-opposite ways.

Bowen, M. (1971). Family therapy and family group therapy. In H. Kaplan & B. Sadock (Eds.), *Comprehensive group psychotherapy* (pp. 384-421). Baltimore: Williams & Wilkins.

Kerr, M. (1981). Family systems theory and therapy. In A. S. Gurman & D. P. Kniskern (Eds.), *Handbook of family therapy* (pp. 226-264). New York: Brunner/Mazel.

emotional cutoff   A method of dealing with unresolved fusion with families of origin by insulating or cutting oneself off emotionally from the parental family. This process can be accomplished by physical distance, by keeping contacts with the parental family brief and infrequent, or through such internal mechanisms as withdrawal and avoidance of emotionally charged areas while in the presence of the family.

Example: A son who feels he must always defend his alcoholic mother from a persecuting father simply isolates himself from the family to escape the psychic pain of dealing with the issue.

Bowen, M. (1978). *Family therapy in clinical practice.* New York: Jason Aronson.

emotional distance   Distance between two people that is based on their emotional reactivity to each other, causing them to focus their togetherness needs elsewhere. The distance is a compromise that people make to reduce their anxiety or discomfort about too much closeness.

Example: A husband enjoys affection, hand holding, and tender expressions; his wife prefers sleeping alone to avoid being touched. In a nonverbal exercise, a husband walks toward his wife and stops at whatever distance he feels comfortable. Then the wife walks toward the husband and does the same. The physical distance between the spouses correlates positively with their emotional distance and depicts the difference in their comfort level.

Kerr, M. (1981). Family systems theory and therapy. In A. S. Gurman & D. P. Kniskern (Eds.), *Handbook of family therapy* (pp. 226-264). New York: Brunner/Mazel.

emotional divorce   A marked emotional distance and lack of any kind of bond between marital partners. Although the marriage appears to have the form and content of closeness, emotional divorce may arise in a relationship in which the marital partners seem to have few overt differences and live conforming lives but in which highly charged personal feelings are not shared; on the other hand, it may describe a marital relationship in which the partners appear congenial in ordinary social settings but cannot tolerate each other when alone together.

Example: The marriage partners are very polite and proper around others but, when alone, they spend their time emotionally isolated and resentful of one another.

Bowen, M. (1960). A family concept of schizophrenia. In D. D. Jackson (Ed.), *The etiology of schizophrenia* (pp. 346-372). New York: Basic Books.

emotionality   (1) Expressive behavior, including laughter and verbal and nonverbal expressions of feeling. (2) A tendency to use and rely on emotions and feelings rather than on rationality or activity.

L'Abate, L., & Frey, J. (1981). The E-R-A model. *Journal of Marital and Family Therapy, 9,* 143-150.

O'Connor, W., & Stachowiak, J. (1971). Patterns of interaction in families with high adjusted, low adjusted, and mentally retarded members. *Family Process, 10,* 229-241.

emotional process The process by which one family member emotionally responds automatically to the emotional state of another without being consciously aware of the process. This deep emotional process is related to the "being" of the person. It occurs silently, beneath the surface, between two people who have a very close relationship.

Example: Schizophrenic families may have little or no conflict, but the emotional process may be involved intimately in perpetuating the "silent" schizophrenia.

Bowen, M. (1960). A family concept of schizophrenia. In D. D. Jackson (Ed.), *The etiology of schizophrenia* (pp. 346-372). New York: Basic Books.

E

emotional room A family appears to be able to support only a certain amount of emotional disturbance among its members at any one time. Thus, following disaster, the family members may have to take turns being emotionally upset. When one finally improves, another may mysteriously fall ill.

Example: The mother undergoes brain surgery for a neurological condition. During her operation, her younger son wets his bed, and her daughter develops a school phobia. Once the mother shows signs of recovery, the father becomes agitated and expresses somatic complaints of stomach cramps and dizziness. The oldest sibling soon thereafter gets caught at school for taking the illegal drug called angel dust—a new occurrence since his mother's operation.

Hill, R., & Hensen, D. (1962). Families in disaster. In G. Baker & D. Chapman (Eds.), *Man and society in disaster* (pp. 185-221). New York: Basic Books.

emotional shock wave Underground aftershocks of serious life events that can occur anywhere in the extended family system in the months or years following serious emotional events in the family.

Example: Years after a family tragedy, members of the nuclear or extended family develop symptoms ranging from psychosomatic illness to phobias and psychotic conditions.

Bowen, M. (1976). Family reaction to death. In P. J. Guerin (Ed.), *Family therapy: Theory and practice* (pp. 335-348). New York: Gardner.

empathic involvement Deep caring among family members about each other's thoughts and feelings. This is characteristic of healthy families.

Example: When his mother became ill, the son flew to his hometown to provide emotional support to his father and to assist his mother. He was concerned about their welfare and understood their worries about growing older.

Epstein, N., & Bishop, D. (1981). Problem-centered systems therapy of the family. In A. S. Gurman & D. P. Kniskern (Eds.), *Handbook of family therapy* (pp. 444-482). New York: Brunner/Mazel.
Epstein, N. B., Bishop, D. S., & Levin, S. (1978). The McMaster model of family functioning. *Journal of Marriage and Family Counseling, 4,* 19-31.

empathic understanding   A category of communication that indicates empathy, respect, and worth for the listener. The speech is reassuring, showing that the listener identifies with the other's problem, shares feelings, and accepts the person at face value. Such communication indicates no preevaluations or prejudgments and serves to reduce defensiveness.

Alexander, J., Barton, C., Lindsey, D., Turner, C., & Warburton, J. (1988). Defensive and supportive communication interaction system. In D. Grotevant & C. Carlson (Eds.), *Handbook of family assessment* (pp. 182-187). New York: Guilford.

empathy   The accurate perception of the internal frame of reference of another person, including the emotional components and meanings that pertain thereto, as if one were that other person, but without ever losing the "as if" condition. If the "as if" quality is lost, the state is one of identification.

Rogers, C. P. (1959). A theory of therapy, personality, and interpersonal relationships, as developed in the client-centered framework. In S. Koch (Ed.), *Psychology: A study of a science, Vol. III. Formulation of the person and the social context* (pp. 184-256). New York: McGraw-Hill.
Thayer, L. (1982). A person-centered approach to family therapy. In A. M. Horne & M. M. Ohlsen (Eds.), *Family counseling and therapy* (pp. 175-213). Itasca, IL: F. E. Peacock.

empty chair technique   A technique in which the therapist sets up two chairs to illustrate the opposite pulls within the person, and then the therapist has that person perform a dialogue with the symbolized opposites as a means of reaching sufficient synthesis within the person to be able to communicate more clearly and increase awareness.

Example: The therapist sets up a situation in which a daughter is to play out two opposite feelings she has toward her mother (e.g., rejection vs. acceptance).

Perls, F. S. (1969). *Gestalt therapy verbatim.* Moab, UT: Real People Press.

empty nest syndrome   A situation in which the parents cannot cope with the separation of their children from the home because of their fear of being alone as husband and wife and being no longer able to fulfill their children's parenting needs.

Example: A mother becomes an evening volunteer at a training center for retarded children when her last child gets married and leaves home.

Glick, I. D. & Kessler, D. P. (1980). *Marital and family therapy* (2nd ed.). New York: Grune & Stratton.

enabler   A dysfunctional role in the family in which the enabler provides all of the nurturance and sense of belongingness in the family but, by so doing, allows a family member to continue to act irresponsibly or self-destructively. The enabler keeps everyone together, preserving the family unit at any cost and trying to smooth out ruffled feathers and avoid conflict. Fear of abandonment and fear that the other members cannot stand on their own two feet are what motivates the enabler.

Friel, J., & Friel, L. (1988). *Adult children: The secrets of dysfunctional families.* Deerfield Beach, FL: Health Communications.

E

enactment   The actualization of transactional patterns under the control of the therapist. This technique allows the therapist to observe how family members mutually regulate their behavior and to determine the place of the problem behavior in the sequence of transactions. Enactment is also the vehicle through which the therapist introduces disruption in the existent patterns, probing the system's ability to accommodate to different rules and ultimately forcing the experimentation of alternative, more functional rules.

Example: The therapist asks the mother whether she feels comfortable with the situation as it is—for example, the grownups trying to talk while two little girls run in circles screaming and demanding everybody's attention. When the mother replies that she feels tense, the therapist invites her to organize the situation in a way that will feel more comfortable and then asks her to "make it happen," which will be the motto for the following sequence. The purpose of this enactment is to facilitate an experience of success for the mother and the experience of a successful mother for the rest of the family. The therapist keeps the enactment going on until the mother eventually succeeds in organizing the girls to play by themselves in a corner of the room so that the adults can resume their talk.

Colapinto, J. (1982). Structural family therapy. In A. M. Horne & M. M. Ohlsen (Eds.), *Family counseling and therapy* (pp. 112-140). Itasca, IL: F. E. Peacock.
Minuchin, S. (1974). *Families and family therapy.* Cambridge, MA: Harvard University Press.

enactment inducement   The technique of encouraging family members to transact their habitual patterns of relating.

Example: The therapist raises a core issue in the family and then withdraws to allow the participants to demonstrate their usual way of relating.

Aponte, H., & van Deusen, J. (1981). Structural family therapy. In A. S. Gurman & D. P. Kniskern (Eds.), *Handbook of family therapy* (pp. 310-360). New York: Brunner/Mazel.

encouraging resistance   A situation in which the client's resistance is defined as cooperative behavior. This definition has a tendency to defuse or short circuit the effect the client's behavior normally has on those in the client's environment.

Example: A client is not sure he is ready to find a job yet. The therapist encourages his resistance by agreeing that it may be several years before he is ready to return to work. This technique defuses the power struggle that could occur between the therapist and the client over the issue of work.

Watzlawick, P., Weakland, J., & Fisch R. (1974). *Change: Principles of problem formation and problem resolution*. New York: Norton.

enculturating tasks   Tasks that help socialize a child (transmit cultural values to the child).

Example: Teaching a child to obey parents transmits the value of respect for parents and elders.

Fleck, S. (1972). An approach to family pathology. In G. D. Erickson & T. P. Hogan (Eds.), *Family therapy: An introduction to theory and technique* (pp. 103-119). Belmont, CA: Wadsworth.

energized family   A healthy family endowed with a fluid internal organization characterized by flexible role relationships and shared power; this type of organization promotes personal growth and member autonomy.

Example: When the father becomes ill, the ensuing family crisis is approached by the family members with a sense of unity and shared responsibility to perform the required tasks.

Pratt, L. (1976). *Family structure and effective health behavior: The energized family*. Boston: Houghton-Mifflin.

energy   A family characteristic that is both static and kinetic: static in that family members have supplies of stored energy available to them, and kinetic in that members actually expend those supplies. Although each family's use, deployment, and restoration of its energies will vary, a general pattern of charging and discharging energy is common in all families. In general, the more energy that is involved in a sequence, the more intense the sequence. The energy sphere interfaces with the time sphere, enabling the therapist to gauge the amount and intensity of energy present in the family in the beginning, the middle, and the termination of events. Some families (and persons) have high impetus but make little or no impact. They are forever starting, but they almost never finish things.

Kantor, D., & Lehr, W. (1975). *Inside the family: Toward a theory of family process.* San Francisco: Jossey-Bass.

engulfment   A situation in which a person lacks a clear and strong sense of autonomy. Because a firm sense of one's own autonomous identity is needed to be able to relate as one human being to another, the person with vague or weak ego boundaries is constantly afraid of being swallowed up by the other (of being engulfed). This person has only two options: absorption in the other (engulfment) or complete aloneness (isolation).

Example: A woman isolates herself from others to preserve a fragile sense of self.

Foley, V. (1974). *An introduction to family therapy.* New York: Grune & Stratton.
Laing, R. (1969). *The divided self.* New York: Penguin.

enmeshment   A transactional style in which family relationships tend to be undifferentiated, closed, and diffuse. The behavior of one family member as a subsystem spreads contagiously to every other member in the family, rather than remaining confined in the subsystem where it began. Any overprotectiveness or overinvolvement on the part of a parent with a child, in turn, affects both the parent's and the child's relationship with every other member of the family. The boundaries between members are blurred. A heightened sense of belonging is gained by sacrificing or discouraging autonomy. Enmeshment is at the opposite end of the continuum from disengagement. See also **diffuse boundaries.**

Example: A mother is overinvolved with her daughter to the point where she does not allow the daughter to accept any responsibilities for herself. This pattern excludes the father from assuming any parental responsibility and, by forcing him away, affects his relationship with his wife.

Minuchin, S. (1974). *Families and family therapy.* Cambridge, MA: Harvard University Press.

enrichment, structured   Most of the enrichment programs available in primary prevention for families vary in degree of structure. Very unstructured programs leave a great deal of responsibility to the leaders, as in the programs developed by the Association for Couples Marital Enrichment (ACME). At the other end of the continuum of structure are programs in which instructions to leaders (or trainers, enrichers, etc.) are given verbatim, as in the programs developed by L'Abate and his associates. These structured programs deal with issues ranging from man-woman relationships over the family life cycle to parent-child relationships involving the whole family, rather than just the parents alone. These programs also include lessons for single-parent families and families with depression, alcohol, and mental retardation. Among the areas covered by these programs are description, evaluation, negotiation, problem solving, touching, and playing.

Example: A couple learn that the local church is sponsoring Marital Enrichment Programs devoted to "Reciprocity in Marriage." They join a series of six classes in which reciprocity in marriage is broken down into its component parts, such as giving and receiving, complementarity, and so on.

E

L'Abate, L. (1990). *Building family competence: Primary and secondary prevention strategies.* Newbury Park, CA: Sage.

L'Abate, L., & Weinstein, S. (1987). *Structured enrichment programs for couples and families.* New York: Brunner/Mazel.

L'Abate, L., & Young, L. (1987). *Sourcebook of structured enrichment programs for couples and families.* New York: Brunner/Mazel.

entitlement   What one is due as a parent or child, or what one has come to merit.

Example: In return for giving loving support to a child, the parent is entitled to loyalty.

Boszormenyi-Nagy, I., & Ulrich, D. (1981). Contextual family therapy. In A. S. Gurman & D. P. Kniskern (Eds.), *Handbook of family therapy* (pp. 159-186). New York: Brunner/Mazel.

entropic family   A family that maintains rigid, unchanging patterns by being oblivious to input from other members.

Example: Parents who have a daughter late in life refuse to allow the daughter, as an adolescent, to behave as she claims her friends behave. They follow the rules and child-rearing practices as they were instructed by their parents.

Beavers, W. R. (1977). *Psychotherapy and growth: A family systems perspective.* New York: Brunner/Mazel.

entropy   The steady degradation of a system into a less organized, random state. When entropy occurs unimpeded, maximum disorganization or disorder is the result. For open systems to survive, therefore, they must acquire a steady state of negentropy (negative entropy). Negative entropy counterbalances the process of entropy, which is a constant process and therefore needs to be checked constantly. Organization represents the presence of information, and disorganization the absence of information. Thus the way to balance entropy is to introduce more organization. In this way, open systems restore their energy and repair breakdowns in their organization. There is a general trend in an open system, as long as it is alive, to maximize the ratio of imported to expended energy. Open systems typically seek to improve their survival position and to acquire in their reserves a comfortable level of organization. See also **negentropy.**

Bateson, G. (1972). *Steps to an ecology of mind.* New York: Ballantine.
Sauber, S. R. (1983). *The human services delivery system.* New York: Columbia University Press.

environmental acclimation   The task of creating and maintaining a safe environment for change, one in which people can risk to be different, try new behaviors, and express those thoughts and feelings they once considered to be inexpressible. This task calls for the application of growth-enhancing rules during sessions.

Example: The therapist enhances the safety of the therapy session by making a rule that members may not bring up the past.

Dodson, L., & Kurpuis, D. (1977). *Family counseling: A systems approach.* Muncie, IN: Accelerated Development.

environment-sensitive families   Families characterized by clarity in communication and flexibility in perception. When confronted with a problem, the family members perceive the problem as separate and apart from the family. Thus the problem has no symbolic value to the family, and the solution to the problem generally is governed by rules of logic. This logical approach to problem resolution requires a thorough consideration of all objective evidence. Information from other family members is evaluated on its own merit, with little contamination related to the informant's role in the family. Members of environment-sensitive families continually undergo change in their worldview to adjust their perceptions to changing external realities.

Example: The oldest son in a family explores a number of colleges during his senior year in high school. Although he considers his father's alma mater, he does not feel pressured to go there. He is not certain about his occupational choice, so he talks with family, friends, counselors, and workers in various fields. As the deadline for application approaches, he decides that it is premature to decide on an occupational field. Therefore he selects a school with a broad liberal education that includes his main areas of interest.

Reiss. D. (1981). *The family's construction of reality.* Cambridge, MA: Harvard University Press.

episodic dyscontrol   Episodes of violent behavior in a family member. Others in the family have difficulty transmitting values regarding the control of aggression.

Example: The adolescent daughter becomes enraged when her parents deny her. She breaks things and threatens to injure them; her siblings and parents are fearfully paralyzed, not knowing what to do.

Glick, I. D., & Kessler, D. P. (1980). *Marital and family therapy* (2nd ed.). New York: Grune & Stratton.

Harbin, H. (1977). Episodic dyscontrol and family dynamics. *American Journal of Psychiatry, 134,* 1113-1116.

E

episodic therapy   Therapy in which sessions are held at irregular intervals as needed.

Example: A multiproblem family calls the therapist for an appointment when a crisis occurs. The therapist is receptive to seeing the family, knowing they have limited coping skills, especially for the complex difficulties that seem to arise frequently in the family.

Hoffman, L. (1981). *Foundations of family therapy.* New York: Basic Books.

epistemological error   Any thought or action that fails to take into account the circular nature of living systems.

Bateson, G. (1972). *Steps to an ecology of mind.* New York: Ballantine.

epistemology   In family therapy, the term generally applies to the rules used to make sense of the world, a worldview, or belief system. It is how the individual organizes precepts of the world and ascribes meaning to experience. A common distinction is made between linear and nonlinear epistemology. In the first case, experience is organized into discrete elements, one of which is seen as acting on another (cause-effect relationships). Nonlinear (also called recursive, circular, reflexive, or systemic) categorizes experiences such that any behavior is simultaneously cause *and* effect in relation to all other behavior in that context.

Bateson, G. (1972). *Steps to an ecology of mind.* New York: Ballantine.

Campbell, D., & Draper, R. (1985). Creating a context for change. In D. Campbell & R. Draper (Eds.), *Applications of systemic family therapy* (pp. 1-8). New York: Grune & Stratton.

equifinality   The concept that, no matter where one enters the system, patterning in the family will be the same. As applied to systems-based therapy, the term means that the therapist studies patterns of behavior and interaction, not individual topics. This and related terms relate to causality: Different causes can produce the same results. This is in opposition to *equipotentiality,* where the same cause can produce different results.

Example: Family members exhibit a number of symptoms, but they all reflect an underlying dynamic. Wherever the therapist chooses to start, the interaction is basically the same; only the content differs.

Bertalanffy, L. von. (1968). The meaning of general systems theory. In L. von Bertalanffy (Ed.), *General systems theory* (pp. 30-53). New York: Braziller.

Foley, V. (1974). *An introduction to family therapy.* New York: Grune & Stratton.

equilibrium model   A model postulating that the family tries to maintain a steady state. This model is based on the second law of thermodynamics; that is, all entities tend toward entropy, a gray, random sameness without movement or change.

Example: When the "rebel and troublemaker" in the family is behaving well, the "goodie-goodie" sibling begins to fail in her school work.

E

Sauber, S. R. (1983). *The human services delivery system.* New York: Columbia University Press.

equipotentiality   One cause may produce different results in general systems theory. See also **equifinality.**

Example: Father-daughter incest may promote sexual promiscuity or sexual inhibition in the daughter later in life.

Bertalanffy, L. von. (1968). The meaning of general systems theory. In L. von Bertalanffy (Ed.), *General systems theory* (pp. 30-53). New York: Braziller.

equitability   A situation in which all are entitled to have their individual welfare interests considered in a way that is fair from a multilateral perspective. One who contributes to the balance by regarding and supporting the interests of another may be said to acquire merit. The term is basic to relational ethics.

Boszormenyi-Nagy, I., & Ulrich, D. (1981). Contextual family therapy. In A. S. Gurman & D. P. Kniskern (Eds.), *Handbook of family therapy* (pp. 159-186). New York: Brunner/Mazel.

equivalent   Reciprocally and correspondingly differentiated and valued, not necessarily equal: People can be equivalently new to different situations. The concept is based on respect and differentiation of individual skills, attributes, meanings, and experiences.

Example: A soccer ball for the son and a leotard for the daughter are equivalent gifts, given each one's interests. Similarly, for the child, "school" is equivalent to adult "work."

Duhl, B. S. (1983). *From the inside out and other metaphors.* New York: Brunner/Mazel.

Ericksonian hypnosis   Indirect suggestion and induction, as originated by Milton H. Erickson, M.D. See also **indirect suggestion.**

Lankton, S. R., & Lankton, C. H. (1983). *The answer within: A clinical framework of Ericksonian hypnotherapy.* New York: Brunner/Mazel.

erratic distancing   Highly unstable styles of relating to and establishing proper distance with other family members. At one moment, the members are remote and emotionally detached; at the next, they are intrusive or engulfing. The cognitive focal distance appropriate for a given task or communication shifts bewilderingly.

Example: At one moment, a wife is angry and distant from her husband; at the next moment, she tries to engulf him emotionally by demanding his attention and affection.

Singer, M., & Wynne, L. (1965). Thought disorders and family relations of schizophrenics: III. Methodology using projective techniques. *Archives of General Psychiatry, 12,* 187-200.

Wynne, L. (1965). Some indications and contraindications for exploratory family therapy. In I. Boszormenyi-Nagy & J. Framo (Eds.), *Intensive family therapy: Theoretical and practical aspects* (pp. 289-322). New York: Harper & Row.

error-amplifying feedback   A systems process in which an attempted solution to a problem adds to the problem.

Example: A couple with serious marital problems have a child, believing that having children will make their lives more enriched and thereby solve many of their problems.

Gerson, M., & Barsky, M. (1979). For the new family therapist: A glossary of terms. *American Journal of Family Therapy, 7,* 15-30.

Watzlawick, P., Weakland, J., & Fisch, R. (1974). *Change: Principles of problem formation and problem resolution.* New York: Norton.

escalating stress   A restructuring technique used to increase stress in the family, thereby helping the family experiment with alternative ways of interaction.

Example: The therapist stops the child from making jokes in the family session, thus forcing the parents to deal directly with each other without the "buffer" of humor provided by the child.

Minuchin, S. (1974). *Families and family therapy.* Cambridge, MA: Harvard University Press.

escalation   In a relationship of coercive interchange, a process in which one person increases in intensity and the other follows suit. Given the reciprocal increases in intensity, one person eventually does not reciprocate the increase, but rather terminates the exchange. In doing so, that person becomes the "victim." At this point, the mechanism of negative reinforcement operates to increase the likelihood that, in future exchanges, the winner will start at higher levels of intensity.

Example: A daughter begins a series of irritating behaviors. The parents deal with the problem by using punishment. However, the child responds by escalating her behavior, and the parents match her response by escalating their punishment.

Patterson, G. (1976). The aggressive child: Victim and architect of a coercive system. In E. Mash, L. Hamerlynck, & L. Handy (Eds.), *Behavior modification and families* (pp. 267-316). New York: Brunner/Mazel.

ethnicity A sense of commonality transmitted over generations by the family and reinforced by the surrounding community. Ethnicity is more than race, religion, or national and geographic origin; it involves conscious and unconscious processes that fulfill a deep psychological need for identity and historical continuity. It plays a major role in determining what we eat, how we work, how we relax, how we celebrate holidays and rituals, and how we feel about life, death, and illness. An interest in families inevitably leads to an interest in ethnicity.

Example: The dominant American (WASP) focuses on the intact nuclear family. Black families focus on a wide network of kin and community. Italians have strong, tightly knit, three- or four-generational families that include godparents and old friends. The Chinese go beyond this and include as family all of their ancestors and all of their descendants.

McGoldrick, M. (1982). Ethnicity and family therapy: An overview. In M. McGoldrick, J. K. Pearce, & S. Giordano (Eds.), *Ethnicity and family therapy* (pp. 3-30). New York: Guilford.

ethos (1) The fundamental character or spirit of a culture; the underlying sentiment that forms the beliefs, mores, or practices of a group or society; the dominant assumptions of a people or period. (2) The moral element that determines a person's action rather than his or her thought or emotion. Each family has its own feel, ambience, and ethos that create the bond of connection of each member to the whole.

Duhl, B. S. (1983). *From the inside out and other metaphors.* New York: Brunner/Mazel.

evasiveness A mechanism that effectively obscures its user's knowledge and, when pervasive and continuous, contributes to incoherence.

Example: An adolescent boy asks whether he may use the family car. His mother responds by talking about how much money his father has just spent on repairing the car.

Beavers, W. R. (1977). *Psychotherapy and growth: A family systems perspective*. New York: Brunner/Mazel.

exchange theory   A theory based on an economic analysis of the interaction between two actors. The interaction is viewed in terms of the rewards and costs the actors mediate for each other; it focuses on the exchange aspect of the mutual dispensation of rewards and punishments or costs. The general assumption is that individuals behave in a way that maximizes the differences between the rewards and costs they experience. Thus A has power over B and can influence B's behavior to the extent that A can determine or control the rewards and costs that B experiences.

Cromwell, R. E., & Olson, D. H. (1975). *Power in families*. New York: Halsted.

Thibault, J. W., & Kelly, H. H. (1959). *The social psychology of groups*. New York: John Wiley.

E

excitement phase   The first phase of the sexual response cycle. It is characterized generally by the appearance of the erection in the male and vaginal lubrication in the female.

Masters, W., & Johnson, V. (1970). *Human sexual inadequacy*. Boston: Little, Brown.

excuse   A statement that hides a reason or avoids stating a reason fully. *Example:* A wife kept making excuses for not following through on those marital matters to which she agreed with her husband to do.

Wahlroos, S. (1974). *Family communication: A guide to emotional health*. New York: Macmillan.

ex parte hearing   A court hearing when the divorcing couple has no disagreements over property or children to be resolved by the court. Any negotiations over these matters were settled previously by the couple and/or their lawyers. The purpose of the hearing is simply to dissolve the marriage. Usually only one marital partner—the one who filed the divorce petition—and his or her lawyer appear before the judge. The other partner defaults by not answering the petition and summons, which were sent to him or her at least 20 days prior to the hearing. Because the divorce is uncontested, there is no need for both parties to be present. During the hearing, the petitioner's lawyer asks him or her a short set of questions about residency, length of separation, and reasons for the marital breakup for the judge's information. The hearing usually lasts about 15 minutes.
Example: A couple were able to resolve their differences with their divorce mediator, avoiding the adversarial process of two opposing attorneys. Going to court then becomes a simple matter of procedure and formality, rather than conflict for the judge to resolve.

Glass, B. L. (1984). No-fault divorce law. *Journal of Family Issues, 5*, 47-69.

expelling   A transactional mode consisting of enduring neglect and/or outright rejection of an individual. The individual is left with a sense of being a creditor, definitely not a debtor, in the framework of loyalties and obligations. As a result, the expelled individual's behavior toward others may be characterized by a "the-world-owes-me" attitude. This mode is activating and demonstrative of the centrifugal forces in the family.

Example: A mother who has an unwanted child treats the child with neglect and rejection. The child runs away from home, with the idea that the world will give him what he never received at home.

Stierlin, H. (1974). *Separating parents and adolescents: A perspective on running away, schizophrenia and waywardness.* New York: Quadrangle.

expelling mode   A transactional pattern in which the parents contribute to distorted separation. In trying to deal with their own crisis, the parents begin to see their children as hindrances. They do not want their children, which results in neglect, rejection, and withdrawal of love.

Example: A young professional couple are striving to become successful in their careers, and they get caught up in competition and striving for superiority. The demands of their children (e.g., time, caring when sick and lonely) are perceived as obstacles to their vocational goal attainments.

Stierlin, H. (1974). *Separating parents and adolescents: A perspective on running away, schizophrenia and waywardness.* New York: Quadrangle.

experience   "All that is going on within the envelope of the organism at any given moment and that is potentially available to awareness." In a psychological sense, experience "includes events of which the individual is unaware, as well as all the phenomena which are in consciousness. . . . To experience means simply to receive in the organism the impact of the sensory or physiological events which are happening at the moment. . . . To experience in awareness means to symbolize in some accurate form at the conscious level the above sensory or visceral events. . . . To experience a feeling means that one has an emotionally tinged experience, together with its personal meaning." The "cognitive content of the meaning of that emotion in its experiential context" is included in the concept. An individual experiences a feeling fully when he or she is "congruent in his experience (of the feeling), his awareness (of it), and his expression (of it)[11] (Rogers, 1959, pp. 197-198).

Rogers, C. P. (1959). A theory of therapy, personality, and interpersonal relationships, as developed in the client-centered framework. In S. Koch (Ed.), *Psychology: A study of a science, Vol. III. Formulations of the person and the social context* (pp. 184-256). New York: McGraw-Hill.

Thayer, L. (1982). A person-centered approach to family therapy. In A. M. Horne & M. M. Ohlsen (Eds.), *Family counseling and therapy* (pp. 175-213). Itasca, IL: F. E. Peacock.

experiential family therapy   An approach to therapy that (a) gives attention to current emotionality of the family-therapist interaction as the pivotal point for all awareness and interventions and (b) requires the involvement of the therapist as a person. This approach was derived from Gestalt family therapy.

Kempler, W. (1981). *Experiential psychotherapy within families.* New York: Brunner/Mazel.

experiential psychopathology   Psychopathology arising from harmful experience (all of the harmful events the organism has been subject to or undergone in life).

Howells, J. (1975). *Principles of family psychiatry.* New York: Brunner/Mazel.

experimental isomorphism   A methodological assumption that a valid laboratory experiment with a family can be conducted as long as the experimentally produced variables are conceptually similar to those in the real world.

Riskin, J., & Faunce, E. (1972). An evaluative review of family interaction research. *Family Process, 11,* 365-455.

Straus, M. (1970). Methodology of a laboratory experimental study of families in three societies. In R. Hill & R. Konig (Eds.), *Families in east and west* (p. 184). New York: Norton.

exploitation   A process denoting a breakdown of trustworthiness in a relationship. Interactions become ethically stagnant or pathological, and there is no support for future acts of merit.

Example: A wife who shows her husband love and affection that is not reciprocated feels exploited.

Boszormenyi-Nagy, I., & Ulrich, D. (1981). Contextual family therapy. In A. S. Gurman & D. P. Kniskern (Eds.), *Handbook of family therapy* (pp. 159-186). New York: Brunner/Mazel.

exploration   A process in which clients examine existing relationships or alternative ways of interacting within those relationships.

Minuchin, S., & Fishman, H. (1981). *Family therapy techniques.* Cambridge, MA: Harvard University Press.

exploratory interaction   The establishment and maintenance of acquaintanceship and familiarity through sensory contact. When sensual contact is absent in a couple, sexual difficulties and dysfunctions may arise.

Verhulst, J., & Heiman, J. (1988). A system perspective on sexual desire. In S. Leiblum & R. Rosen (Eds.), *Sexual desire disorders* (pp. 243-270). New York: Guilford.

expressed emotion (EE)   A degree to which emotion is expressed in the family. The theory of expressed emotion, initiated by George Brown and his colleagues at the Institute for Social Psychiatry in London, England, suggests that affective factors might account for relapse. In the research, when EE was high, relapse occurred much more frequently. Expressed emotion has an attitudinal component (e.g., highly critical views of the patient) and a behavioral component (e.g., a tendency to be overinvolved with the patient such that the family member is highly protective, attentive, or reactive).

Brown, G. W., Monck, E. M., Carstairs, G. M., & Wing, J. K. (1962). Influence on family life in the course of schizophrenic illness. *British Journal of Psychiatry, 16,* 55-68.

E

expressive family function   A family task involving the maintenance of solidarity and the management of tensions, with primary responsibility for care and emotional support of children.
   Example: A family develops an internal conflict over the tasks of its children in the house. Traditionally the mother has led in the resolution of this type of conflict and acts accordingly.

Parsons, T. (1955). The American family: Its relation to personality and social structure. In T. Parsons & R. Bales (Eds.), *Family socialization and interaction process* (pp. 3-34). New York: Free Press.

expressive leader   The family member who is the mediator or conciliator of the family, the person who smoothes over disputes and resolves hostilities in the family. The expressive leader is solicitous, warm, affectionate, and emotional with the children (the comforter and consoler).

Parsons, T. (1955). The American family: Its relation to personality and social structure. In T. Parsons & R. Bales (Eds.), *Family socialization and interaction process* (pp. 3-34). New York: Free Press.

expressiveness   Marked manifestations of feelings, affect, and emotion that can be either positive or negative in tone.

Mishler, E., & Waxler, N. (1968). *Interaction in families: An experimental study of family processes and schizophrenia.* New York: John Wiley.
Riskin, J., & Faunce, E. (1972). An evaluative review of family interaction research. *Family Process, 11,* 365-455.

extended family   A group of individuals consisting of the nuclear family (husband, wife, and children), as well as individuals related by ties of consanguinity. Extension of ties exists among parents and their children, grandchildren, and between siblings. In America, the extended family has been common among rural and frontier societies and immigrants, as well as the very wealthy. Anthropologically, the term is restricted to two or more nuclear families affiliated by blood ties over at least three generations.

Murdock, G. (1949). *Social structure*. New York: Macmillan.

extended family systems therapy   Therapy that combines various strategies in a context involving all of the significant people in a person's life.

Example: The husband wants to save his marriage after he has an argument with his wife and she impulsively moves out of the house. The therapist encourages the husband to communicate with his wife's family and friends to persuade her that he loves her and that he wants to try again to work out their marital differences. The husband asks his mother-in-law to persuade her daughter that she should get marital counseling or at least try one more time to maintain her marriage before she decides to seek divorce.

Boszormenyi-Nagy, I., & Ulrich, D. (1981). Contextual family therapy. In A. S. Gurman & D. P. Kniskern (Eds.), *Handbook of family therapy* (pp. 159-186). New York: Brunner/Mazel.

extended kin network   The group of individuals relevant to a family's functioning, going beyond the nuclear family. The network includes grandparents, uncles, and aunts, as well as friends and neighbors.

Speck, R., & Attneave, C. (1973). *Family networks*. New York: Pantheon.

external frame of reference   A mode of perception that lacks empathy with the perceived object. To perceive from an external frame of reference is to perceive solely from one's own subjective internal frame of reference without empathizing with the observed person or object.

Example: A mother had her own idea of what was best for her son, regardless of his statements or actions.

Rogers, C. P. (1959). A theory of therapy, personality, and interpersonal relationships, as developed in the client-centered framework. In S. Koch (Ed.), *Psychology: A study of a science, Vol. III. Formulations of the person and the social context* (pp. 184-256). New York: McGraw-Hill.

Thayer, L. (1982). A person-centered approach to family therapy. In A. M. Horne & M. M. Ohlsen (Eds.), *Family counseling and therapy* (pp. 175-213). Itasca, IL: F. E. Peacock.

externalization of the problem   A technique used systematically to separate problematic attributes, ideas, assumptions, beliefs, habits, and so on from a person's sense of self-identity. It is used to counter the assumptions that the person who has the problem is the problem. This technique was developed first on children with encopresis. The label "Sneaky Poo" was developed and used in statements such as "What do you call that messy stuff that gets you in trouble?" or "Has it ever caught you when you weren't aware of it?"

Tomm, K. (1989). Externalizing the problem and internalizing personal agency. *Journal of Strategic and Systemic Therapies, 8,* 54-59.

White, M., & Epston, D. (1990). *Narrative means to therapeutic ends.* New York: Norton.

externalizing disorders   Childhood behavior disorders characterized by behaviors that are undercontrolled, noncompliant, defiant, and socially disruptive and that include the diagnostic categories of attention deficit hyperactivity disorder, conduct disorder, and oppositional defiant disorders. Typically others in the environment, such as parents, siblings, peers, and teachers, suffer more than the children with these disorders.

Breen, M. J., & Altepeter, T. S. (1990). *Disruptive behavior disorders in children.* New York: Guilford.

E

extinction   A process involving the discontinuation of the reinforcement that maintains the behavior in question, resulting in a decrease in the behavior as it returns to its operant level (the prereinforced rate of the behavior).

Example: The therapist advises the parent to ignore the child's symptomatic behavior until it becomes extinct.

LeBow, M. (1972). Behavior modification for the family. In G. D. Erickson & T. P. Hogan (Eds.), *Family therapy: An introduction to theory and technique* (pp. 347-376). Belmont, CA: Wadsworth.

extramarital sex (EMS)   Sex outside of marriage without the knowledge or consent of the partner. EMS is difficult to define because it occurs in a variety of patterns, dimensions, and constellations. Criteria on which to assess EMS include (a) the length of time (e.g. one-night stand vs. long term), (b) the degree of emotional involvement, (c) the presence or absence of intercourse, (d) secret or not, (e) whether single or bilateral (one partner or both having affairs), and (f) heterosexual or homosexual. The third criterion above refers to extramarital affairs rather than extramarital sex. Those relationships do not involve penetration but may have other forms of sex and high levels of emotional involvement.

Humphrey, F. (1987). Treating extramarital sexual relationships in sex and couples therapy. In G. Weeks & L. Hof (Eds.), *Integrating sex and marital therapy* (pp. 149-170). New York: Brunner/Mazel.

E

facilitating engagement   An involvement by the therapist that encourages the interaction between family members.

Example: The therapist encourages a discussion between father and son over the choice of a college. The therapist acts as observer, moderator, and facilitator.

Aponte, H., & van Deusen, J. (1981). Structural family therapy. In A. S. Gurman & D. P. Kniskern (Eds.), *Handbook of family therapy* (pp. 310-360). New York: Brunner/ Mazel.

fair fighting   Handling conflict and disagreement between two individuals in a healthful and functional manner. Fair fighting rules include being assertive instead of aggressive, staying in the now, avoiding score keeping, avoiding lecturing, avoiding judgment, using "I" messages, being honest, not assigning blame, using active listening, fighting over one thing at a time, and focusing on a solution as opposed to focusing on who is right.

Example: "When you do X, I feel hurt" is an example of a statement made by a person who is fighting fairly. "When you do X, you're just like your mother" is an example of a statement made by a person who is not fighting fairly.

Bach, G., & Goldberg, H. (1974). *Creative aggression.* Garden City, NY: Doubleday.

famcum   A family in which one member carries the symptoms and, in individual terms, could be described as schizophrenic or neurotic. This situation is referred to as a *famcum neurosis,* rather than as one in which one family member is "sick." In other words, the member carries the symptoms of the whole family.

Example: A family presents itself for therapy, requesting that the son be treated for depression. In fact, the whole family is depressed, but the son is the only member who exhibits the symptoms overtly.

Bloch, D. (1975). Notes and comments. *Family Process, 1,* 109-110.

family   A basic unit of society, characterized as one whose members are economically and emotionally dependent on one another and are responsible for each other's development, stability, and protection. The "nuclear" family includes two adults, one of each gender, who maintain a socially approved sexual relationship, with one or more children of their own or with adopted children. The family serves as the basic unit of socialization to teach cultural values and adaptation to society. Currently, in our society, the traditional definition of the family is undergoing transition because of the emerging prominence of alternative life-styles. For example, growing numbers of families are without children, or are single-parent families, homosexual families, and blended families.

Burr, W. R., Hill, R., Nye, F. I., & Reiss, I. L. (Eds.). (1979). *Contemporary theories about the family* (Vols. 1 & 2). New York: Free Press.

F

family actualization   The enhancement of personal growth, and that of other family members, and the pooling of knowledge, skill, feeling, intuition, and uniqueness to evolve a system of interaction that will facilitate and enrich each individual's process in a way that that individual could not accomplish alone. The system serves the individuals within the family unit.

Dodson, L., & Kurpuis, D. (1977). *Family counseling: A systems approach.* Muncie, IN: Accelerated Development.

family adaptability   The ability of a marital or family system to change its power structure, role relationships, and relationship rules in response to situational and developmental stress. Like cohesion, adaptability is a continuum on which the central levels are hypothesized as more conducive to marital and family functioning than the extremes. In family theory, adaptability originally was presented as *homeostasis,* or the ability of a system to maintain equilibrium. More recently, writers have stressed the dual concepts of *morphogenesis* (system altering or change) and *morphostasis* (system maintaining or stability) and the family's need for a dynamic balance between the two. On the one hand, families with too little adaptability (rigid systems) are unable to change even when it appears necessary. On the other hand, families with too much adaptability (chaotic systems) also have problems dealing with stress. Thus a balance of stability and change appears most functional to individual and family development.

Olson, D. H., Russell, C. S., & Sprenkle, D. H. (1980). Marital and family therapy: A decade review. *Journal of Marriage and the Family, 42,* 973-993.

family art therapy A form of therapy that employs art techniques conducted with the whole family to observe how the family unit operates. This activity can provide material for further discussion of how the members function together.

Example: The family members each draw a picture of their home and then discuss their drawings.

Kwiatkowska, H. Y. (1978). *Family therapy and evaluation through art.* Springfield, IL: Charles C Thomas.

family as a subsystem A perspective of the family as a subsystem of society with a degree of internal organization and a certain level of self-regulatory functioning but without the ability to be self-sufficient and enduringly independent of the larger societal system of which it is a part.

Parsons, T., & Bales, R. (1955). *Family, socialization, and interaction process.* New York: Free Press.
Wynne, L. (1965). Some indications and contraindications for exploratory family therapy. In I. Boszormenyi-Nagy & J. Framo (Eds.), *Intensive family therapy: Theoretical and practical aspects* (pp. 289-322). New York: Harper & Row.

F

family assessment Evaluation of a family takes place mostly through an interview, usually covering historical and situational factors. It may consist of just a subjective interview, or it could be implemented by a genogram (see **genogram**) plus a variety of objective, semiobjective, and projective instruments, depending on the interests and knowledge of the examiner and the needs of the family.

Example: The Watson family has been referred for evaluation by a judge in a child custody dispute to help the judge decide which parent should be given major responsibility of the children and how the children feel about and interact with each parent. The examiner interviews the family, including nonverbal interaction tasks such as sculpting (see **sculpting**), and allocation of loose change among family members, with a discussion of decision making ("Which TV show should you watch tonight?"). In addition to evaluating the family as a whole, the examiner (a clinical psychologist) administers the Minnesota Multiphasic Personality Inventory (MMPI) to both parents and a sentence completion test to the two children, aged 10 and 13.

Fredman, N., & Sherman, R. (1987). *Handbook of measurements for marriage and family therapy.* New York: Brunner/Mazel.
Grotevant, H. D., & Carlson, C. I. (1989). *Family assessment.* New York: Garner.

Jabob, T., & Tennebaum, D. L. (1988). *Family assessment: Rationale, methods, and future directions.* New York: Plenum.

Kerr, M. E., & Bowen, M. (1988). *Family evaluation: An approach based on Bowen theory.* New York: Norton.

L'Abate, L., & Bagarozzi, D. A. (1993). *Sourcebook of marriage and family evaluation.* New York: Brunner/Mazel.

Touliatos, J., Perlmutter, B. F., & Straus, M. A. (Eds.). (1990). *Handbook of family measurement techniques.* Newbury Park, CA: Sage.

family boundaries   The limits of a family's world of experience. These boundaries are more or less constraining and more or less permeable to relationships and experiences defined as extrafamilial. As each family maps its domain of acceptable and desirable experience, it raises signposts for goals and signals for danger. But these boundaries, which lie within persons as well as among them, are tested continually as new experiences occur, new feelings arise, and new actions are taken.

Example: Neighboring boys who are close in age know which toys and personal belongings they can use together in play and which ones they cannot share.

Hess, R., & Handel, G. (1959). *Family worlds: A psychological approach to family life.* Chicago: University of Chicago Press.

family boundary market   A therapeutic device by which the therapist joins with one subsystem of the family and excludes others during sessions of the entire family to differentiate boundaries.

Example: A mother and a son are overinvolved with one another. The therapist joins with the father and the son, excluding the mother from the interaction.

Minuchin, S. (1974). *Families and family therapy.* Cambridge, MA: Harvard University Press.

family-centered family   A family in which there is a strong emphasis on the importance of the whole family as a unit and in which individuals are subordinated to the needs and functions of the family group.

Example: Meal planning and food selection are based on the preferences of most of the family, rather than on a particular individual's favorites that may be disliked by the majority.

Reiss, D. (1981). *The family's construction of reality.* Cambridge, MA: Harvard University Press.

family choreography   A method of actively intervening in the nuclear and extended family by realigning family relationships. This realignment is done by exploring alternative transactional patterns in terms of physical movement and positioning. Family choreography is an outgrowth of family sculpture.

Example: A family with marital difficulties and conflicts between the parents and their two grown children presents for therapy. Each person is asked to mold the family in order to visualize the problem. Next the members are asked to mold the family as they would like it to be. The first set of sculptures indicates the type of problem the family is experiencing. During the second set of sculptures, members are asked to take responsibility for changing what is happening. Initially the wife places her husband outside the room. She is encouraged later to find a way of bringing him back into the family. She does so by extending her hand to him while at the same time letting go of the children.

Papp, P. (1976). Family choreography. In P. J. Guerin (Ed.), *Family therapy: Theory and practice* (pp. 465-479). New York: Gardner.

family climate   The general emotional atmosphere or tone in a family. At times, the emotional climate may be difficult to perceive as it truly exists, because of a facade created for others. To determine the family climate, the focus is on interpersonal relationships among family members, on the directions of personal growth emphasized in the family, and on the organization or structure of the family. The Family Environment Scale, developed by Moos and Moos, consists of 10 subscales that measure dimensions in three domains of the family climate: relationship dimensions (cohesion, expressiveness, conflict), personal growth or goal-orientation dimensions (independence, achievement, moral-religious, intellectual-cultural, and active-recreational), and systems maintenance and change dimensions (organization and control).

Fuhr, R., Moos, R., & Dishotsky, N. (1981). The use of family assessment and feedback in ongoing family therapy. *American Journal of Family Therapy, 9,* 24-36.
Moos, R. H., & Moos, B. S. (1981). *Family Environmental Scale manual.* Palo Alto, CA: Consulting Psychologists Press.

family coalition   A pattern of communicative, emotional, and physical interactions in a family. Graphic representations of some family coalitions are shown in Figure 2. A "typical" four-member family is taken as the unit, with the squares representing males and the circles representing females. The larger symbols stand for spouse/parent; the smaller symbols represent the offspring/siblings, respectively. The solid straight lines joining these symbols represent positive communicational, emotional, and activity bonds between the individuals involved; these bonds are semiquantitative, indicated by the number of straight lines used. Dashed lines represent the relative absence of such bonds or the relatively negatively tinged tone of the interactions.

Turning first to Example A, the functional family, the marital coalition here has the strongest pathway in the family, with all other channels

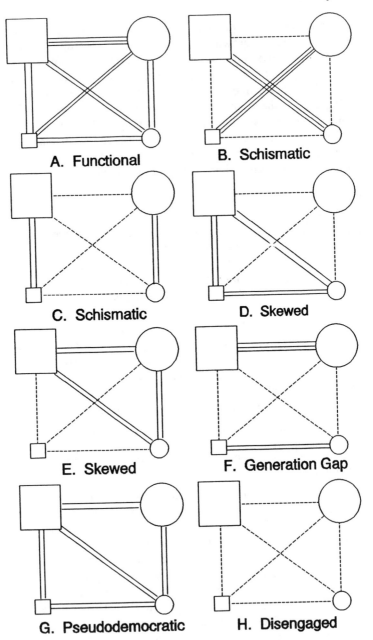

Figure 2. Types of Family Coalitions

SOURCE: From *From Marital and Family Therapy* (2nd ed.), (p. 78) by I. D. Glick and D. P. Kessler, 1980, New York: Grune & Stratton. Copyright 1987 by Grune & Stratton. Reprinted by permission.

open and about equal to each other in importance. In contrast, note the various types of dysfunctional families. In Example B, for example, the marital coalition is relatively weak or absent; instead, strong alliances occur across the generations and sexes, between father and daughter, and between mother and son. Other channels are relatively unavailable.

Glick, I. D., & Kessler, D. P. (1980). *Marital and family therapy* (2nd ed.). New York: Grune & Stratton.

family cohesion The emotional bonding that family members have vis-à-vis one another. At the extreme high end of the cohesion dimension (enmeshed systems) is overidentification with the family, which results in extreme emotional, intellectual, and/or physical closeness. At the extreme low end of cohesion (disengaged systems) is emotional, intellectual, and/or physical isolation from the family. It is hypothesized that the central area of this continuum is most viable for family functioning because the family members are able to experience and balance being independent from and being connected to their families. Adaptability is one of the two sides of Olson and his associates' complex model of family functioning.

Olson, D. H., Russell, C. S., & Sprenkle D. H. (1980). Marital and family therapy: A decade review. *Journal of Marriage and the Family, 42,* 973-993.

family conference or council A group of people who live together—whether or not they are related by blood or marriage—have regularly scheduled meetings, and operate under rules agreed on in advance. The meetings are open forums at which all members can speak without interruption, with freedom of expression, without fear of consequences, and without regard for age or status. The group's deliberations result in decisions only when all members present agree—that is, come to a common understanding. The group must adhere to the following basic criteria: equality of all members, mutual respect, open communication, regularity, agreed rules, joint deliberation, reciprocal responsibility, and mutual decisions.

Dreikurs, R., Gould, S., & Corsini, R. J. (1974). *Family council.* Chicago: Contemporary Books.
L'Abate, L. (1981). The role of family conferences in family therapy. *Family Therapy, 8,* 33-38.

family consensual experience The experience of perception held in common by family members concerning the family's environment and the family's relationship to the environment.

Example: All members of a family believe that other families in their neighborhood cannot be trusted.

Reiss, D. (1981). *The family's construction of reality.* Cambridge, MA: Harvard University Press.

family constellation   The sociopsychological configuration of a family group. The personality characteristics and emotional distance of each person, age differences, order of birth, dominance or submissiveness of each member, gender of the siblings, and size of the family are all factors in the family constellation and affect the development of the personality. The position of each child in the family constellation not only helps determine that child's personality development but also enables the therapist to understand the particular client's personality dynamics. Certain behavior types can be characterized by examining the individual's place in the constellation. Thus the first born, the second born, the third born, and the only child each have certain characteristics that render their personalities predictable in terms of attitudes, personality traits, and subsequent behavior.

Shulman, B. H., & Nikelly, A. G. (1971). Family constellation. In A. G. Nikelly (Ed.), *Techniques for behavior change: Applications of Adlerian theory* (pp. 35-40). Springfield, IL: Charles C Thomas.

family construct   The family's subjective estimate of its environment; one of the primary theoretical concepts of a theory of consensual experience. The family construct serves to relate individual thinking to family interaction.

Example: The individuals in a family see the world as a dangerous and unpredictable place. Collectively they see the world in the same way, which reinforces the family's construction of reality.

Reiss, D. (1981). *The family's construction of reality.* Cambridge, MA: Harvard University Press.

family developmental tasks   Norms sanctioned by society that, at each stage in the life cycle of the family, stipulate certain role expectations of the family's members. Successful adherence to these norms leads to personal satisfaction, equilibrium of the family, and success with later tasks. Unsuccessful adherence leads to distress in the family, disapproval and sanctions by society, and emotional problems with later developmental tasks.

Example: During her child's infancy, a mother seeks to fulfill her child's symbiotic needs for merging, but during the child's adolescence, the family needs to allow for individuation and separation.

Duvall, E. (1977). *Marriage and family development* (5th ed.). Philadelphia: J. B. Lippincott.

family diagnosis   Diagnosis of a family's roles, relationships, communications, expectations, and conflicts, with a view to resolving the family's presented problem(s). The diagnosis encompasses the following:

1. Presenting complaint. The specific reasons for referral as seen by the family and the referral source. Specifically the following children's functions are explored:

   adjustment to school

   adjustment to work

   adjustment to the family

   adjustment to the community and their peers

   significant personality disorders

2. Role functioning. The following areas in relation to the parents, as husband and wife and as father and mother, are explored.

   Disorders in functioning:

   (1) sexual functioning

   (2) capacity to give and receive affection

   (3) decision making

   (4) discipline and parental concern

   (5) economic and social functioning

   (6) basic patterns of interaction

   Nature of role expectations:

   (1) expectations of husband in own role

   (2) expectations of wife in own role

   (3) conflict or competition in role expectation

   (4) adaptation to role by each

   (5) breakdown in role performance

3. Family relationships:

   alignments and splits

   scapegoating

   dynamics of relationships

4. Communication process:

   use of silence

   disqualifications (evidence that one or more family members attempt to disqualify self or another family member to give information or to participate in communication)

   double bind

   digression (use of digression as a technique to obscure or avoid conflict, excessive attention to detail in recital of events, tendency toward "babbling," and reaction of family to babbling and digression)

5. Resolution of conflict:

   tolerance

F

unity (degree of solidity or rigidity imposed by the family when faced with conflict)

patterns of avoidance

patterns of resolution

Thorman, G. (1965). *Family therapy: A handbook*. Beverly Hills, CA: Western Psychological Services.

family dynamics   The intrapsychic, interpersonal, and family-as-a-whole patterns operating in the family system, such as the thoughts, feelings, and behavior, conscious or unconscious, that two or more members of the family consistently employ, as well as the attitudes and emotional climates that the whole family maintains as the framework for its relationships.

Example: Sibling rivalry for the mother's negative attention (to compensate for her lack of positive attention) dominates the family members' interactions.

Framo, J. (1965). Systematic research on family dynamics. In I. Boszormenyi-Nagy & J. Framo (Eds.), *Intensive family therapy: Theoretical and practical aspects* (pp. 407-462). New York: Harper & Row.

F

family ecology therapy   A therapeutic approach designed to place the correct interventions needed to help a client deal with a crisis. The approach deals with the forces that have converged to effect a condition of disorganization in the family system-condition that shows up as a crisis in one part of the system. In family therapy, the approach defines the therapeutic tool and modality used to put into effect the planned interventions within the parameters of the actual contacts with the client in therapy sessions.

Example: The therapist invites the acting-out adolescent to bring the leader of his peer group to the session.

Leonhard, E. (1977). Toward a new formulation of object relation-systems theory from analysis and family ecology theories. In T. J. Buckley, J. J. McCarthy, E. Norman, & M. A. Quaranta (Eds.), *New directions in family therapy* (pp. 42-56). Oceanside, NY: Dabor.

family ego mass   The whole constellation of attitudes, feelings, values, and beliefs that constitute a family's emotional system. See **undifferentiated family ego mass.**

Bowen, M. (1976). Theory in the practice of psychotherapy. In P. J. Guerin (Ed.), *Family therapy: Theory and practice* (pp. 42-90). New York: Gardner.

Gerson, M., & Barsky, M. (1979). For the new family therapist: A glossary of terms. *American Journal of Family Therapy, 7,* 15-30.

family enrichment   One of the many fields of prevention (Kahn & Kamerman, 1982; L'Abate, 1985, 1986), spawned in the past decade, that use a prearranged number of sessions on a specific topic for functional or semifunctional couples and families. *Family enrichment* covers approaches that vary in degree of structure, format, focus, length, and intensity (Hoopes, Fisher, & Barlow, 1984); for example: (a) marital enrichment, represented by, among many others, the Association of Couples in Marital Enrichment (Mace, 1983); (b) Bernard Guerney, Jr.'s relationship enhancement (Guerney, 1977); (c) L'Abate's structured enrichment (L'Abate, 1985); and (d) Minnesota Couples Communication Program (L'Abate & McHenry, 1983). See also **family facilitation** and **family life education.**

Guerney, B. G. (1977). *Relationship enhancement: Skill training programs for therapy, problem prevention, and enrichment.* San Francisco: Jossey-Bass.

Hoopes, M. H., Fisher, B. L., & Barlow, S. H. (1984). *Structured family facilitation programs: Enrichment, education, and treatment.* Rockville, MD: Aspen Systems.

Kahn, A. H., & Kamerman, S. B. (1982). *Helping America's families.* Philadelphia: Temple University Press.

L'Abate, L. (1985). Structured enrichment (SE) with couples and families. *Family Relations, 34,* 169-175.

L'Abate, L. (1986). Prevention of marital and family problems. In B. Edelstein & L. Michelson (Eds.), *Handbook of prevention* (pp. 177-193). New York: Plenum.

L'Abate, L., & McHenry, S. (1983). *Handbook of marital intervention.* New York: Grune & Stratton.

Mace, D. (Ed.). (1983). *Prevention in family services: Approaches to family wellness.* Beverly Hills, CA: Sage.

F

family facilitation   An approach to mental health that is designed to strengthen individuals and families by using the family context. Family facilitation covers a broad range of activities, from high school family life classes to family therapy that customizes treatment for pathological families. The process is designed to enhance a family's ability to reach desired goals. Therefore a *structured family facilitation program* may be defined as a formal plan with predetermined parameters that is designed to facilitate a family's achievement of goals. Structured family facilitation programs involve a group format, including several family units with one or more facilitators. Three basic approaches facilitate family change and growth: family life education, family enrichment, and family treatment (see Table 1). *Structured family life education programs* include programs that are primarily instructional in focus, with the intent of imparting information and skills to family members outside an educational setting (for example, in community-based parent education classes). *Structured family enrichment programs* are designed to enhance skills and health of family interactions through instructional

Table 1   Comparison of Elements of Family Life Education, Family Enrichment, and Family Treatment Approaches

	Family Life Education	Family Enrichment	Family Treatment
Function	Education/ Prevention	Prevention/ Enhancement	Remediation/ Education/ Enrichment
Goal	To provide information about a relevant content area	To prevent dysfunction and increase relationship skill and satisfaction	To correct dysfunction or assist in coping with a stressful situation
Change process	Occurs through assimilation of information/ knowledge; primarily a cognitive process	Occurs through exercises, activities, and practice of skill; primarily an experiential process	Occurs through discussion of issues; primary focus is on resolution of an area
Information flow and generation of energy	Moves from leader to participants	Moves within family, between families, leader to participant, participant to leader	Moves within family, between families, leader to participant, participant to leader
Participants	Usually includes individual members of a family wanting information	Usually includes whole families or couples wanting to enhance their relationships	Usually includes whole families or family subsystems experiencing specific problems
Facilitator role	To impart information and teach	To direct activities and discussions	To facilitate learning activities and discussions
Process	Uses lecture, discussion, question-and-answer activities	Uses family activities, discussion, homework assignments	Uses group and family activities and discussion

SOURCE: From *Structured Family Facilitation Programs: Enrichment, Education, and Treatment* (p. 13) by M. H. Hoopes, B. L. Fisher, & S. H. Barlow, 1984, Rockville, MD: Aspen Systems. Reprinted by permission.

and experiential activities. *Structured family treatment programs* are designed to resolve problems encountered or developed by a functional or semifunctional family. See also **family enrichment.**

Hoopes, M. H., Fisher, B. L., & Barlow, S. H. (1984). *Structured family facilitation programs: Enrichment, education, and treatment.* Rockville, MD: Aspen Systems.

family functioning The ability of a family to function in four critical areas: (a) *personal* functioning (e.g., satisfaction with self in the family), (b) *marital* functioning (e. g., giving and receiving attention or the gratification of sexual needs), (c) *parental* functioning (e.g., use of parental authority, socialization of children), and (d) *socioeconomic* functioning (e.g., family values or economic status).

L'Abate, L. (1976). *Understanding and helping the individual in the family.* New York: Grune & Stratton.

family group diagnosis A procedure by which all individuals who are meaningful in the family's situation at a particular time are interviewed together. This group may involve two or three generations, and it may include others living in the family household at the time. The procedure aims to get a firsthand picture of the dynamics of the family.

Howells, J. (1975). *Principles of family psychiatry.* New York: Brunner/Mazel.

family group therapy Short-term therapy designed to facilitate change in the family in sessions with one or more family members. Its basic theoretical formulations are derived from conventional individual theory and the practice of group therapy. The method is determined more by who attends the sessions than by the method employed.

Bowen, M. (1971). Family therapy and family group therapy. In H. Kaplan & B. Sadock (Eds.), *Comprehensive group psychotherapy* (pp. 384-421). Baltimore: Williams & Wilkins.

family growth framework A situation in which family members confront issues as they appear in the life process and deal with each incident without the need for precedents or established patterns for behavior. The family is involved in a process of interaction in which current data and feelings are considered in decision making.

Example: Winona does not receive the award in school that she expected to win and feels depressed over the situation. The family discusses Winona's expectations with her and how she feels about the situation. The family's unconditional love for her is reaffirmed and is differentiated from conditional love. The former says, "I love you regardless of how you perform"; the latter says, "I love you provided that you perform according to my expectations," and Winona becomes aware of her unrealistic expectations.

Dodson, L., & Kurpuis, D. (1977). *Family counseling: A systems approach.* Muncie, IN: Accelerated Development.

family healer The family member who takes on the role of peacemaker, protector, healer, or "family doctor" to rescue a "victim" from a punishing attack. To the degree to which the rescuing member holds the capacity to neutralize the destructive force of the prejudicial assault, that member offers to the victim some immunity against breakdown. At times, the member who starts out in the role of persecutor or destroyer may shift to the role of victim or even healer, and vice versa.

Example: When he drinks, an alcoholic father (persecutor) starts to belittle his son (victim). When this pattern begins, the oldest daughter (healer) steps in to placate the father and to direct his attention elsewhere.

Ackerman, N. W. (1966). *Treating the troubled family.* New York: Basic Books.

family homeostasis   A balance in family relationships. The family unit establishes an internal, ongoing, interactional process and rule structure that its members maintain overtly and covertly in relative balance and constancy. Repetitious, circular, and predictable communication patterns in the family provide evidence of the balance. When family homeostasis is precarious, the members exert much effort to maintain it.

Example: An alcoholic husband is trying to remain sober, but his wife, while saying she supports him in this effort, selects a restaurant in which he will see his old drinking buddies at the bar.

Jackson, D. (1968). The question of family homeostasis. In D. Jackson (Ed.), *Communication, family, and marriage* (pp. 1-11). Palo Alto, CA: Science & Behavior Books.

family indicators   Can be viewed as a subset under the larger heading of *social indicators* that measures the family's context of the social life of members of society. These are similar to other indicators of social concerns, such as health, income, and employment. But they also are unique in that the family domain crosscuts so many other social issues: Health, education, employment, income, housing, leisure and recreation, population, and public safety all have "family implications." However, the family includes the family structure, stability, composition, new activities performed by the family on behalf of individuals, and family accounting.

Example: The economic needs alter with the number and ages of the children. The relationship between income and financial requirements points to the "life-cycle squeeze" for families of blue-collar workers. Well-being can change as a result of either external events, such as inflation, or altered conditions within the family, such as the birth of a child. Family indicators, therefore, can illuminate the vulnerability of families at different stages of the life-cycle to significant life events and conditions such as unemployment or economic hardship.

Moen, P. (1980). Developing family indicators. *Journal of Family Issues, 1,* 5-30.

family interaction The systems-based, psychodynamic ways by which members of a family communicate and relate to each other and play their roles vis-à-vis one another.

Framo, J. (1965). Systematic research on family dynamics. In I. Boszormenyi-Nagy & J. Framo (Eds.), *Intensive family therapy: Theoretical and practical aspects* (pp. 407-462). New York: Harper & Row.

family interaction scales Scales designed to assess whole family interaction. The scales cover the following family characteristics:

clarity: Whether family members speak clearly to each other

topic continuity: Whether family members stay on the same topic with each other and how they shift topics

commitment: Whether family members take direct stands on issues and feelings with one another

agreement and disagreement: Whether family members explicitly agree or disagree with one another

affective intensity: Whether family members show variations in affect as they communicate with one another

relationships: Whether family members are friendly or attack one another

Riskin, J., & Faunce, E. (1972). An evaluative review of family interaction research. *Family Process, 11,* 365-455.

family leader A family member who assumes or is selected by the family to take on the role of peacemaker or protector in an attempt to rescue the victim from the scapegoating attack of the family or to turn the attack away from him or her.

Ackerman, N. W. (1958). *The psychodynamics of family life.* New York: Basic Books.
Luber, R. F., & Anderson, C. M. (1983). *Family intervention with psychiatric patients.* New York: Human Sciences Press.

family life cycle A longitudinal view of a family's development, comprising both expected and unexpected or traumatic phases. The development is cyclical in that the couple starts out as a single unit and then goes through a series of developmental stages until the family unit is again only the original couple. Stages of family life include separation from one's parents, marriage, having children, aging, retirement, and, finally, death. See Figure 3.

Carter, E. A., & McGoldrick, M. (Eds.). (1988). *The changing family life cycle: A framework for family therapy* (2nd ed.). New York: Gardner.
Glick, I. D., & Kessler, D. P. (1980). *Marital and family therapy* (2nd ed.). New York: Grune & Stratton.

F

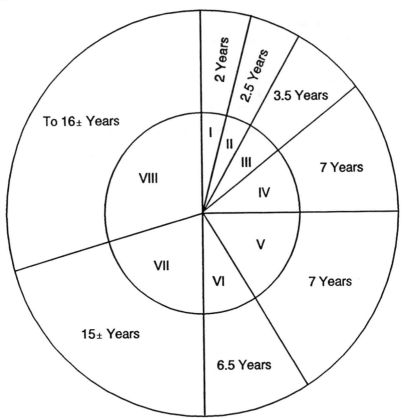

Figure 3. The Family Life Cycle
SOURCE: From *From Marital and Family Therapy* (3rd ed.), (p. 53) by I. D. Glick, J. P. Clarkin, and D. P. Kessler, 1987, New York: Grune & Stratton. Reprinted by permission.

family life education   A well-established and widely used educational process and method in teaching members of the local community new information and knowledge and in acquiring helpful skills related to family life and problem solving.

Example: Parent education programs, such as systematic training for effective parenting, are the most common types of courses in family life education.

Sauber, S. R. (1973). *Preventive educational intervention for mental health.* Cambridge, MA: Ballinger.

family life-style analysis   Analysis of the cognitive maps (the styles of acting, thinking, and perceiving) from which family members select the specific operations that enable them to cope with life tasks. Study of the family constellation and the family members' basic orientations toward life provides brief individual portraits of the members' early social worlds, the influential forces to which they reacted, and the raw material they selected to create an apperceptive framework to assist their survival and progress through life. The factors most frequently discussed in the analysis are birth order, comparative sibling characteristics and interactions, parental relationship (between the parents and with the children), adjustments to physical development, schooling, family values, socioeconomic status, achievements and deficiencies, and peer relationships.

The basic objective of a family life-style analysis is to extract the following central themes:

The individual family member's *roles* within the family (either alone or in comparison with the roles played by other members of the family)

Major areas of success and failure

Major influences that seem to have affected a member's decision to adopt a specific role

Each member's apparent major goals and/or conceptions of self and others, of life in general, or of some particular aspect of life

This analysis, when completed, provides a picture somewhat similar to that given by playwrights when introducing their characters: The family members have a clearer understanding of themselves and their interrelationships within the family.

Dinkmeyer, D., Pew, W., & Dinkmeyer, D. (1979). *Adlerian counseling and psychotherapy.* Belmont, CA: Wadsworth.

family loyalty system A system of positive affect and interaction in both normal and dysfunctional families. For all of its constrictingly pathologic aspects, a family loyalty system provides a nucleus of genuinely positive feeling that is, for all family members, including the patient, a cherished possession.

Searles, H. (1965). The contributions of family treatment to the psychotherapy of schizophrenia. In I. Boszormenyi-Nagy & J. Framo (Eds.), *Intensive family therapy: Theoretical and practical aspects* (pp. 463-496). New York: Harper & Row.

family map A diagrammatic representation of the family in the therapeutic process. The family map can provide new insights into how the family functions. Including both a family history and a diagramming of the organizational schema, it can help the therapist understand the complex material gathered from the family. The family may take into account the development of each member of the nuclear family, the families of origin of each parent in the extended kin network, and the origins and transmissions of power across generations.

Example: The therapist's family map shows the positions of family members in their coalitions and affiliations and in the way they group themselves in explicit and implicit conflict resolution.

Bowen, M. (1971). The use of family theory in clinical practice. In J. Haley (Ed.), *Changing families* (pp. 159-192). New York: Grune & Stratton.

Minuchin, S. (1974). *Families and family therapy.* Cambridge, MA: Harvard University Press.

family medicine   A specialty within medicine in which the physician specialist medically treats the individual across the entire life cycle. Thus family physicians are likely to treat everyone in the family. Basic tenets of family medicine are (a) the family is the primary social context for health care, (b) the patient's individual problems are also family problems, (c) the patient's family is potentially the physician's greatest ally in treatment, (d) a patient's family is present during every patient interview, (e) primary care family-oriented treatment can be an effective way to help patients and their families, and (f) family-oriented medical care requires sophistication beyond the normal training of physicians.

Doherty, W. J., & Baird, M. A. (1983). *Family therapy and family medicine.* New York: Guilford.

family myths   Well-integrated beliefs shared by all family members concerning each other and their relative positions in the family. These myths go unchallenged by everyone involved, despite the reality distortions they may conspicuously imply. Myths serve the homeostatic mechanisms in that their purpose is to maintain the "steady state" of the family. The family myths are to the relationship what the defense is to the individual.

Examples: All members of a family believe that partners should be totally honest with each other: "Nothing bothers Daddy," "I only want the best for you," "Mother is the sick one," and "Marriage should make one totally happy."

Anderson, S., & Bagarozzi, D. (1989). *Family myths: Psychotherapy implications.* New York: Haworth.

Ferreira, A. (1963). Family myths and homeostasis. *Archives of General Psychiatry, 9,* 457-463.

family of origin   The family into which a person is born or adopted. In family therapy, at least one session often is conducted with each marriage partner or with that partner's family of origin. This approach is based on the belief that current family problems are partial reenactments of previous or current problems with the families of origin.

Example: A woman was assigned the role of family healer in her family of origin. She continues to play this role in her marriage, which prevents her from getting her needs met in the marriage.

Framo, J. L. (1981). The integration of marital therapy with sessions with family of origin. In A. S. Gurman & D. P. Kniskern (Eds.), *Handbook of family therapy* (pp. 133-158). New York: Brunner/Mazel.

family of procreation The family that an individual establishes through marriage and reproduction.

Christensen, H. (1964). Development of the family field of study. In H. T. Christensen (Ed.), *Handbook of marriage and the family* (pp. 3-32). Chicago: Rand McNally.

family power structure The structure that determines who wields power and what the hierarchy or "pecking order" is in a family.

Beavers, W. R. (1976). A theoretical basis for family evaluation. In J. M. Lewis, W. R. Beavers, J. T. Gossett, & V. A. Phillips (Eds.), *No single thread: Psychological health in the family system* (pp. 46-82). New York: Brunner/Mazel.

family priorities The allocation of commitments, attachments, and allegiances to the various components of the family (self, marriage, children, work, in-laws, friends, leisure) and the various modalities of functioning (doing, having, being).
Example: A father's overinvolvement with work produces a parallel overinvolvement with the children on the mother's part.

L'Abate, L. (1983). *Family psychology: Theory, therapy, and training.* Washington, DC: University Press of America.

family problem-solving effectiveness The family's ability to work as a group in solving an individual family member's problem.

Reiss, D. (1981). *The family's construction of reality.* Cambridge, MA: Harvard University Press.

family process The pattern of interaction between family members. The *study* of the family process, as distinguished from *content,* requires insightful perception of the family members and of the significance of their transactions within the family. What a family argues about is content; how the family argues is process. To identify these processes and the purposes they serve, the therapist may construct a model of family interactions that takes into account (a) alignments and splits (Is any member usually isolated from the others?), (b) pseudomutuality (Are strong efforts made to overcome divergences?), and (c) scapegoating (Is one person singled out as being at fault, as the "black sheep"?).

Example: The therapist asks the family members to imagine they are planning an outing or picnic and to discuss who will do what. As the family plans the activity, the therapist watches the various interactions unfold. The therapist observes that the father is uninvolved in the process, which suggests that he is also uninvolved in family activities at home.

Thorman, G. (1965). *Family therapy: A handbook.* Beverly Hills, CA: Western Psychological Services.

family projection process The transmission of a parental (husband and/or wife) problem to one or more of the children or a spouse. The transmission occurs when parents focus on their child instead of dealing with their own difficulties. Such a process helps maintain the illusion of a harmonious marital relationship, but at the expense of transmitting symptoms to the child. Thus the child becomes the presenting patient.

Example: Two immature parents are not able to express their anger toward each other. Their child becomes hostile in response to the parents' suppression of anger and begins to act out. The parents direct their anger toward the child, rather than toward each other.

Bowen, M. (1978). *Family therapy in clinical practice.* New York: Jason Aronson.
Haley, J. (Ed.). (1971). *Changing families.* New York: Grune & Stratton.

family psychology An academic specialization within psychology devoted to the study of relationships between the individual and the family. As an academic specialization, family psychology is practically nonexistent: There are no academic programs in family psychology as a discipline. Most family psychologists are clinicians or psychotherapists (Kaslow, 1990). A great deal of confusion exists between family psychology as an academic discipline and family psychology as a profession (see the Introduction). Thus far, most academic training programs basically focused on the applied and clinical use of family therapy and ignore scientific aspects of the discipline, like assessment, or preventive approaches along the whole continuum of functionality/dysfunctionality with families (see primary, secondary, or tertiary **prevention**). Most training programs in this field take place in departments of child and family studies, rather than in departments of psychology. Training in these departments usually is limited to family therapy.

Kaslow, F. (Ed.). (1990). *Voices in family psychology.* Newbury Park, CA: Sage.
L'Abate, L. (1976). *Understanding and helping the individual in the family.* New York: Grune & Stratton.
L'Abate, L. (1983). *Family psychology: Theory, therapy, and training.* Washington, DC: University Press of America.
L'Abate, L. (1987). *Family psychology: Theory, therapy, enrichment, and training.* Washington, DC: University Press of America.

F

family psychotherapy Psychotherapy directed at the hypothesized emotional oneness within the family—that is, the "family ego," as opposed to individuals in the family. The therapy is directed at the family unit rather than at the individual, both conceptually and clinically. It deals with the "family" as a single organism, as a "unit of illness" or a "unit of treatment." The goal is to help the family members differentiate themselves from the "undifferentiated family ego mass" by meeting with two or more of them together.

Bowen, M. (1978). *Family therapy in clinical practice.* New York: Jason Aronson.

family reconstruction In-depth exploration of a family background. In the process, all family participants explore their life histories and learn about themselves and one another. Such techniques as role playing and psychodrama can be used to bring out significant past events in the lives of the members. A family map or genogram is used to diagram the family of origin.

Glick, I. D., & Kessler, D. P. (1980). *Marital and family therapy* (2nd ed.). New York: Grune & Stratton.
Nerin, W. F. (1986). *Family reconstruction: Long day's journey into light.* New York: Norton.

F

family relations indicator A picture projective technique designed to indicate relationships between individuals in the family. The subjects' responses are analyzed on a linguistic basis and thus may be interpreted by any school of psychopathology.
Example: A child is shown several pictures of family interactions. He is asked to tell a story about each picture. In one instance, the child is shown a picture of a family without a father. The boy remarks that this is like his family because his dad is rarely home.

Howells, J. (1975). *Principles of family psychiatry.* New York: Brunner/Mazel.

family rituals See **rituals.**

family roles A pattern of acts structured and learned in accordance with cultural values for the function a person has with his or her role partners in a social situation. Trouble can result from role conflicts that are not faced directly, negotiated, and modified, but are avoided or distorted so that it seems as if one person is dysfunctional. Role theorists see "complementarity" as a goal.

Kluckhohn, F. R., & Spiegel, J. P. (1954). *Integration and conflict in family behavior* (Report No. 27). Topeka, KS: Group for the Advancement of Psychiatry.
Luber, R. F., & Anderson, C. M. (Eds.). (1983). *Family intervention with psychiatric patients.* New York: Human Sciences Press.

family rules   The explicit and implicit agreements between members of a family. Some rules are totally unconscious. Such rules govern the transactional patterns of the family, including the mutual expectations that family members have developed about each other over a period of years. The concept was developed as an alternative to *family roles* to study family relationships for the purpose of detecting certain redundancies—typical and repetitive patterns of interaction that characterize the family as more than a collection of individuals.

   Example: A family has an implicit rule that conflict is not openly acknowledged.

Satir, V. (1983). *Conjoint family therapy* (3rd ed.). Palo Alto, CA: Science & Behavior Books.

family rule systems   A system of rules that family members establish to respond to each other and to govern their behavior. The family is thus a self-correcting, error-activating system. Should one family member break a family rule, the others become activated until the member conforms to the rule again or until a new rule is established successfully.

   Example: If a member breaks a family rule not to comment on certain behavior, all of the other members may respond by disqualifying the message.

Haley, J. (1972). The family of the schizophrenic. In G. D. Erickson & T. P. Hogan (Eds.), *Family therapy: An introduction to theory and technique* (pp. 51-75). Belmont, CA: Wadsworth.

family schizophrenia   Schizophrenia as a family process that requires three or more generations to develop.

   Example: The paternal grandparents (first generation) were relatively mature and highly respected members of the farming community in which they lived. Their eight children were also relatively mature, except for a son (second generation), who was the father of the patient and who was much less mature than his siblings. As a child, he was very dependent on his mother and distant from his father. In adolescence, he suddenly became very successful in business but was uncomfortable in close personal relationships. A similar pattern occurred on the mother's side of the family. Here were two people who had high levels of immaturity and loneliness and who were aloof in relationships with others. Once married, their relationship became covertly conflictual and one of "emotional divorce." Their child also had a high level of immaturity and developed schizophrenia in an attempt to adapt to the demands of growing up. Thus the combined immaturity of the grandparents was acquired by a child who was strongly attached to his mother. When married to a similar spouse, their child, in turn, became the patient in the third generation.

McFarlane, W. R. (1983). *Family therapy in schizophrenia.* New York: Guilford.

family sculpture   A nonverbal technique whereby each family member tries to create a physical representation of their relationships at one point in time by arranging their bodies in space. The goals are to reveal the way the person experiences the family in terms of space, attitudes, alliances, and underlying feelings and to recognize defenses, particularly of projection of blame and intellectualization.

Example: A daughter places herself in her mother's lap in a rocking position with her father by her side and asks her brother and sister to leave the room.

Duhl, F., Kantor, D., & Duhl, B. (1973). Learning, space and action in family therapy: A primer of sculpture. In D. Bloch (Ed.), *Techniques of family psychotherapy* (pp. 47-63). New York: Grune & Stratton.

family secrets   See **secrets in the family.**

family sets   Patterned sequence of interaction among family members.

Example: A wife invariably interrupts her husband whenever he tries to discipline their child. The husband simply withdraws from the family, allowing the wife to dominate. This sequence repeats itself over and over, making it a habitual family set.

Minuchin, S. (1974). *Families and family therapy.* Cambridge, MA: Harvard University Press.

family sociogram   The pattern that develops when family members are asked to locate themselves in the therapy room according to how they perceive themselves in relation to other family members. With this technique, the alliances, coalitions, triangles, boundaries, and other dimensions of the family become apparent.

Example: The youngest son places himself between his mother and father and then places his older brother, who picks on him, beside his father and his sister, with whom he relates well, behind him.

Bernard, C., & Corrales, R. (1979). *The theory and technique of family therapy.* Springfield, IL: Charles C Thomas.

family status quo   A situation in which family variables are maintained as they have been in the past—that is, the maintenance of sameness through avoidance of change and refection of new and different ideas, values, and behaviors. See also **family homeostasis.**

Example: A family begins to work out a behavioral contract for their child's poor school performance and problems at home. In the past, the father treated these problems by using only punishment. Just as the contractual system is ready to begin, the father rejects the process and drops out of therapy.

Zuk, G. (1971). *Family therapy: A triadic-based approach.* New York: Behavioral Publications.

family structure   The routinized characteristics of the family-as-a-whole that have become stabilized. These characteristics evolve with family development and serve to describe the family group at a given time. They are highly resistant to change. Therapeutic attempts to change them lead to overt calls for loyalties, covert fear, and guilt-inducing maneuvers.

Minuchin, S. (1974). *Families and family therapy.* Cambridge, MA: Harvard University Press.

family style   A way of defining intimate relationships in a family. Three styles can be distinguished: (a) an apathetic-abusive-atrophied style, (b) a reactive-repetitive-retaliatory style, and (c) a conductive change-oriented commitment to improve the relationship. The first pattern is characterized by physical coercion, giving up, powerlessness, hopelessness, and inadequacy (both emotional and interpersonal), which may result in physical and/or pharmacological abuse. In the second style, verbal coercion (rather than physical coercion) is used; this style defines one's behavior according to the behavior of the other (I did this because you did that!). Reactivity comes out of a context of apathy, while conductivity comes out of a context of self-knowledge and mature awareness of self.

L'Abate, L. (1983). Styles in intimate relationships: The A-R-C model. *Personnel and Guidance Journal, 61,* 277-283.

family support programs   One of the many types of primary prevention, consisting of self-help groups available to families to get together on a regular basis to find warm, nurturant relationships with other families who need the same kind of nurturance. These groups are designed to give members of these families a heightened sense of self-importance (empowerment). Usually these groups do not teach skills of any kind.
Example: The Wander family is new to town, is geographically distant from its families of origin, lacks friends, feels isolated, and feels lost in the new surroundings. Its members need to establish new relationships with

people they can trust. Although asymptomatic at the present time, their level of stress is so high that if no support is found, one or more members of this family may develop a physical or emotional problem.

Kagan, S., Powell, D. R., Weissbound, B., & Zigler, E. F. (1987). *America's family support programs*. New Haven, CT: Yale University Press.

family syntonic disorder   Bizarre or disturbed behavior that may appear as such to outside observers but is accepted by the family as being "normal" and therefore acceptable. In fact, the behavior could be considered as an asset or a strength that represents the family's closeness and functionality.

Example: Some families accept nudity as "normal." Other families consider not touching each other as "normal." Still other families consider criminal behavior as acceptable. In each case, the bizarre behavior is incorporated as representative of the family identity.

Wynne, L. (1965). Some indications and contraindications for exploratory family therapy. In I. Boszormenyi-Nagy & J. Framo (Eds.), *Intensive family therapy: Theoretical and practical aspects* (pp. 289-322), New York: Harper & Row.

F

family system   The family, viewed as a social system that operates through transactional patterns. The system consists of repeated interactions that establish patterns of how, when, and to whom to relate. Repeated operations build the patterns, and the patterns underpin the family system. The patterns that evolve become familiar and preferred. The system maintains itself in a preferred range; deviations that pass the system's threshold of tolerance usually elicit counterdeviation mechanisms that reestablish the accustomed range.

Minuchin, S. (1974). *Families and family therapy*. Cambridge, MA: Harvard University Press.

family systems medicine   A model in which a primary health care medical team is composed of collaboration between a family physician and a family therapist. It is based on the belief that the family is the primary social context for health care and that family dynamics influence an individual's medical condition. Family systems medicine takes into account the developmental stages of the family life cycle. Intervention is based on the analysis of several systemic levels and then the targeting of which level will be used for the most efficient intervention. Thus illness is viewed as a process of biological, psychological, and interpersonal systems.

Dym, B., & Berman, S. (1985). Family systems medicine: Family therapy's next frontier? *Family Therapy Networker, 9,* 20-29, 66.

family tasks   Tasks, focusing on behavioral change, that therapists assign for a family to perform during the session and between sessions. The tasks usually ask people to stop doing something, to start doing something, or to do things in a different way. A family task also may be an activity for which a family member assumes responsibility according to self-interest—that is, family-initiated sharing in daily life duties or roles. See also **tasks.**

Example: The therapist directs the parents to set aside 15 minutes a day to discuss a new program or behavior assigned to their children.

Haley, J. (1987). *Problem-solving therapy* (2nd ed.). San Francisco: Jossey-Bass.

family theme   A pattern of feelings, motives, fantasies, and conventionalized understandings that are grouped about some particular locus of concern in the personalities of individual family members. The pattern comprises some fundamental view of reality and some way or ways of dealing with it. In family themes are found the family's implicit direction, its notion of "who we are" and "what we do about it."

Example: A member of the family stops going to church, and the family pulls together to assert to the member that they are a Christian family and to imply that certain social sanctions will follow if the member does not conform to the family theme.

Hess, R., & Handel, G. (1959). *Family worlds: A psychological approach to family life.* Chicago: University of Chicago Press.

family therapy   Therapy in which the family is the unit of treatment and more than one member of the family is seen individually or conjointly during the course of the therapy. In this sense, when a therapist works with a mother and a child, the parents and the children, or any other combination of family members, the treatment would be regarded as family therapy. Family therapy operates generally in the following way:

- Because the family is considered to be the unit of treatment, no individual member of the family is singled out as the patient. Rather, the individual family member whom the family identifies as the patient reflects the disturbances of the family itself.
- The family members usually are seen conjointly, rather than individually.
- The diagnosis of an emotional or behavioral disorder is based on observations of the family as a unit.
- New diagnostic concepts are used; traditional concepts and theories that describe personality functioning to explain individual behavior are usually inappropriate to the diagnosis and treatment of family pathology.
- The therapist relates to the family, rather than to its individual members. If the therapist meets with the family as a unit but continues to relate to individual

members, the therapist is not engaged in family therapy. The therapist must see the family as a unit emotionally as well as physically.

- Therapeutic goals and methods are family centered. The therapist is concerned primarily with the outcome of treatment insofar as the total family's welfare is concerned.

Family therapy is more than a novel therapeutic technique; it is an entirely new approach to understanding human behavior. Prior to family therapy, behavior was considered to be a product of individual personalities as influenced by discrete events in the past. This "monadic" view based on "linear causality" was replaced by the idea that behavior is a product of "family systems," which operate according to "circular causality" (part of ongoing, circular causal loops). To contrast family therapy with individual therapy, see Table 2 (with **individual therapy** entry).

Nichols, M. P. (1984). *Family therapy: Concepts and methods.* New York: Gardner.
Thorman, G. (1965). *Family therapy: A handbook.* Beverly Hills, CA: Western Psychological Services.

family transference   The tendency of a hospital setting to evoke a familylike atmosphere for some patients.

Example: Hospitalized patients begin to respond to other patients as siblings, evoking the same type of hostility that usually is directed toward siblings at home.

Boszormenyi-Nagy, I., & Framo, J. (1962). Family concept of hospital treatment of schizophrenia. In J. Masserman (Ed.), *Current psychiatric therapies* (Vol. 2, pp. 159-166). New York: Grune & Stratton.
Zuk, G., & Rubinstein, D. (1965). A review of concepts in the study and treatment of families of schizophrenics. In I. Boszormenyi-Nagy & J. Framo (Eds.), *Intensive family therapy: Theoretical and practical aspects* (pp. 1-32). New York: Harper & Row.

family types   Structural and strategic patterns that distinguish families. The three basic family types are (a) the *closed family system,* which typically relies on stable structures (fixed space, regular time, and steady energy) as reference points for order and change; (b) the *open family system,* in which order and change are expected to result from the interaction of relatively stable, evolving, family structures (moveable space, variable time, and flexible energy); and (c) the *random family system,* in which unstable structures are experimented with as reference points for order and change (dispersed space, irregular time, and fluctuating energy).

Kantor, D., & Lehr, W. (1975). *Inside the family: Toward a theory of family process.* San Francisco: Jossey-Bass.

family typology   A way of classifying the complexity of marital and family life-styles. Currently families may be classified in several ways: by the rules for defining power, by parental stage, by level of intimacy, by personality style, and by a description of the family in treatment.

Glick, I. D., & Kessler, D. P. (1980). *Marital and family therapy* (2nd ed.). New York: Grune & Stratton.

family unit   A conceptualization of the family as though it were a single unit or organism. The focus is on "family oneness," rather than on the individual. The family is both the unit of illness and the unit of treatment. The three major levels of therapist awareness are (a) intellectual (conceptual understanding of the family unit), (b) clinical (treatment of the family), and (c) emotional (changing from emotional identification and involvement with the individual to an emotional awareness of the family unit).

Bowen, M. (1978). *Family therapy in clinical practice.* New York: Jason Aronson.

family violence   Acts by family members that result in or are likely to result in physical injury. A family is defined as violent if at least one such act has occurred within the year. Violent acts include acts of minor violence with the potential for causing serious injury—for example, pushing, shoving, slapping, and throwing things. Minor violence thus is distinguished from severe violence—for example, kicking, biting, punching, hitting with an object, "beating up," or attacking with a knife or gun—which has a high likelihood of causing serious injury.

Shapiro, R. J. (1984). Therapy with violent families. In S. Saunders, A. M. Anderson, C. A. Hart, & G. M. Rubenstein (Eds.), *Violent individuals and families* (pp. 112-136). Springfield, IL: Charles C Thomas.
Straus, M. (1980). Victims and aggressors in marital violence. *American Behavioral Scientific, 23,* 681-704.

fantasy break   A technique in which the individual is asked to spend 10 to 30 minutes a day generating a sexual fantasy. The purpose of this exercise is to increase the level of sexual desire. Prior to giving this assignment, the individual's attitudes and ability to fantasize should be examined, and the person should receive fantasy training.
Example: A woman who experienced low sexual desire reported never fantasizing and rarely thinking about sex until her husband approached her. She was asked to read several books of sexual fantasies and then to begin developing her own fantasies on a daily basis. As a result, her level of sexual awareness and desire increased.

LoPiccolo, J., & Friedman, J. (1988). Broad-spectrum treatment of low sexual desire. In S. Leiblum & R. Rosen (Eds.), *Sexual desire disorders* (pp. 107-144). New York: Guilford.

fear of performance   The major deterrent to effective sexual functioning because it distracts the individual from his or her sexual responsivity by blocking reception of sexual stimulation. The fear is that of not being able to perform according to one's expectation. The fear creates anxiety, which, in turn, increases the likelihood of failure. Failure escalates the fear of performance therapy, thereby creating a vicious cycle.

Masters, W., & Johnson, V. (1970). *Human sexual inadequacy*. Boston: Little, Brown.

feedback   The process by which the input of each family member leads to a more complex, systems-oriented output. The output of the family system is thus no longer individually determined and analyzed. Rather, the whole becomes more than the sum of its parts. Therapeutic feedback to a family is geared, not toward individuals, but toward the system and its alteration. The concept of *feedback* assumes that the malfunction of any one person is caused, not by a breakdown in the intrapsychic machinery, but by the failure of the family system itself to operate properly. Treatment, therefore, consists of correcting, changing, or altering the feedback mechanism. Two basic types of feedback occur in families:

1. *Negative:* Negative feedback attempts to correct a system in trouble and to reestablish its previous state of equilibrium. For example, a child is given the role of "acting sick" in order to reestablish harmony between her parents. Thus negative feedback is used to keep the status quo, or to maintain family homeostasis.

2. *Positive:* Positive feedback forces a family into new ways of behaving by making old behavior patterns untenable. It often is used to counteract negative feedback—that is, as a crisis-inducing mechanism to produce therapeutic movement and prevent the family from maintaining the status quo. For example, a maneuver by the therapist may prevent the family from using the identified patient to hide other family issues.

Watzlawick, P., Beavin, J. H., & Jackson, D. D. (1967). *Pragmatics of human communication*. New York: Norton.

feedback loop   The relation of two objects or events in a circular fashion. Instead of assuming that the objects or events are related only in a straight-line cause-and-effect fashion, they can, in certain circumstances, be assumed to be related in a circular pattern, in either a positive or a negative feedback loop. See also **positive feedback loop.**

Example: A wife tells her husband that she wants him to be more emotionally intimate with her. He responds, but she thinks he is doing it only to please her. Her response turns him away, and he becomes distant again. They become ensnared in a feedback loop in which things stay the same.

Bateson, G. (1987). *Steps to an ecology of mind*. New York: Ballantine.
Steinglass, P. (1978). The conceptualization of marriage from a systems theory perspective. In T. Paolino & B. McCrady (Eds.), *Marriage and marital therapy* (pp. 298-368). New York: Brunner/Mazel.
Weiner, N. (1962). *Cybernetics*. Cambridge: MIT Press.

female sexual dysfunctions   Female sexual disorders comprising general sexual dysfunction, primary and secondary orgasmic dysfunction, dyspareunia, and vaginismus.

1. *General sexual dysfunction* consists of the inhibition of the vasocongestive/arousal stage of the sexual response, so that vaginal lubrication and swelling develop minimally or not at all.
2. *Orgasmic dysfunction* consists of the inhibition of the orgasm phase of the female sexual response. It is subdivided into *primary orgasmic dysfunction,* which exists when the patient has never experienced an orgasm in any way, and *secondary orgasmic dysfunction,* a disorder in which the client has had an orgasm at least once through some form of sexual stimulation but currently experiences coital orgasms rarely or not at all. (The term *frigidity* often is used in the literature on sexual dysfunctions as a catchall category for orgasmic dysfunction and general sexual dysfunction. The term has, however, little utility.)
3. *Dyspareunia* is painful intercourse from postcoital vaginal irritation to severe pain during penile thrusting.
4. *Vaginismus* is a condition in which the vaginal introitus closes tightly when intercourse is attempted, thus preventing penetration. It is caused by an involuntary spastic contraction of the sphincter vaginae and the levator ani, the muscles surrounding the vagina.

LoPiccolo, J., & LoPiccolo, L. (Eds.). (1978). *Handbook of sex therapy*. New York: Plenum.

feminist family therapy   An approach to family therapy in which the therapist recognizes the impact of gender role socialization of men and women, the difference in access to economic and social resources for men and women, and the primary role women have been socialized to perform in family relations and childbearing. The therapist supports options for women beyond the roles in the family.

Walters, M., Carter, B., Papp, P., & Silverstein, O. (1988). *The invisible web: Gender patterns in family relationships*. New York: Guilford.

fetishism   The use of nonliving objects to satisfy recurrent and intense sexual urges and fantasies.

Example: A person might have an intense and compelling desire to hold an undergarment during masturbation or lovemaking.

American Psychiatric Association. (1987). *Diagnostic and statistical manual of mental disorders* (3rd ed., rev.). Washington, DC: Author.

F

filial therapy A therapeutic technique by which parents are trained to conduct Rogerian client-centered therapy with their emotionally disturbed children. Filial therapy usually is done in groups of six to eight parents. Three general stages are involved in the therapy: (a) explanation of the benefits of Rogerian techniques to the parent-child relationship and instruction in the techniques, (b) play therapy sessions at home with the child, and (c) termination. Filial therapy allows the parent both to be helped and to be of help. Negative patterns of interaction may be weakened, and there may be increased awareness of destructive aspects of the relationship that may continue to be worked through after the play therapy itself is discontinued.

Guerney, B. (1964). Filial therapy: Description and rationale. *Journal of Consulting Psychology, 28,* 304-310.

final hearing A court hearing in which a divorcing couple will resolve issues such as property, children, and alimony, as well as obtain a request for the dissolution of the marriage. Both marital partners and their lawyers attend the hearings. Through questioning of the husband, wife, and possibly other witnesses, the lawyers present testimony to the judge, which he or she uses to make decisions about the property, visitation rights, attorneys' fees, alimony, or whatever is in question. It is possible for the judge to dissolve the marriage at the time of the first final hearing but to "reserve jurisdiction" on the property settlement. When this occurs, the lawyers and clients do further preparation, such as drawing up lists of property and providing estimates of value, to be presented to the judge. Sometimes an out-of-court agreement is reached as a result of this procedure, and the judge does not see the couple again.

Example: A couple and their attorneys were unable to reach an agreement and had to go to court to have an independent authority make decisions about their private lives.

Glass, B. L. (1984). No-fault divorce law. *Journal of Family Issues, 5,* 47-69.

finger catalepsy A condition induced by a sex hypnotherapy technique to treat male vasocongestive dysfunction. The technique consists of associating a rigid finger with penile erection.

Araoz, D. L. (1982). *Hypnosis and sex therapy.* New York: Brunner/Mazel.

finger hypersensitivity A condition induced by a sex hypnotherapy technique to treat retarded ejaculation. The technique consists of associating or transferring hypersensitivity in a finger to the penis.

Araoz, D. L. (1982). *Hypnosis and sex therapy.* New York: Brunner/Mazel.

F

finger numbness   A condition induced by a sex hypnotherapy technique to treat premature ejaculation. The technique consists of associating or transferring numbness in the fingers to numbness in the penis.

Araoz, D. L. (1982). *Hypnosis and sex therapy.* New York: Brunner/Mazel.

first-order change   A temporary change in which the symptom is removed but the systemic interactions continue. See also **second-order change.**

Example: A couple agree not to argue anymore. However, the marital conflicts remain unresolved.

Watzlawick, P., Weakland, J., & Fisch, R. (1974). *Change: Principles of problem formation and problem resolution.* New York: Norton.

first-order cybernetics   Conceptualizing the treatment unit (family system) as a homeostatic machine. The symptom plays an important part in maintaining the homeostasis of the family. Thus the "system creates the problem"; that is, a dysfunctional family system creates the psychiatric disorder. Compare with **second-order cybernetics.**

F

Boscolo, L., Cecchin, G., Hoffman, L., & Penn, P. (1987). *Milan systemic family therapy: Conversations in theory and practice.* New York: Basic Books.

fixed distancing   A relentless, deadening fixity of distance in relationships and a rigid manner of organizing thoughts and perceptions. The family members are aware of the need for relatedness but feel blocked in their attempts to allow intimacy or affection.

Example: A son appears angry and restless in a session, as shown by his appearance and counting down to a shout of, "Blast off!" The family distances itself from the boy's anger by referring only to his obsession with counting.

Wynne, L. (1965). Some indications and contraindications for exploratory family therapy. In I. Boszormenyi-Nagy & J. Framo (Eds.), *Intensive family therapy: Theoretical and practical aspects* (pp. 289-322). New York: Harper & Row.

flexibility   A system's ability to shift its organization to achieve a goal and to create new structures for itself as required by circumstances.

Aponte, H., & van Deusen, J. (1981). Structural family therapy. In A. S. Gurman & D. P. Kniskern (Eds.), *Handbook of family therapy* (pp. 310-360). New York: Brunner/Mazel.

fluctuating families   Families that change in either locational or familial composition. For example, locational fluctuations occur in military families in which one spouse is transferred many times or in ghetto families that move from one place to another because of overdue rent.

Familial fluctuations occur most frequently when a single parent has serial love affairs.

Minuchin, S., & Fishman, H. (1981). *Family therapy techniques.* Cambridge, MA: Harvard University Press.

focus   The subject of a family interaction—that is, the content, rather than the style, of its communications.

Mishler, E., & Waxler, N. (1968). *Interaction in families: An experimental study of family processes and schizophrenia.* New York: John Wiley.

focused attention   See **attention.**

folie à deux   A mental disorder in two or more predisposed individuals who have been symbiotically associated. The disorder is characterized by delusional ideas of a persecutory nature that may be transferred from one to the other.

Example: A husband and a wife both have delusions that the world is coming to an end and that aliens will come to rescue them.

Tuke, D. (1982). *Dictionary of psychological medicine* (Vol. 1). Philadelphia: Blakiston.

F

forbidding change   A paradoxical intervention in which the family is told it should not attempt to change at the present time.

Example: A couple arrive for treatment for a sexual problem. The therapist asks them not to have intercourse. They respond to this request by doing just the opposite, and doing it successfully because their performance anxiety has been relieved.

Weeks, G., & L'Abate, L. (1982). *Paradoxical psychotherapy: Theory and practice with individuals, couples, and families.* New York: Brunner/Mazel.

force   In a therapeutic context, the relative influence strength and intensity of each family member on the outcome of an activity. In an underorganized family, force is not distributed in an orderly way.

Example: A mother holds all of the force in a family. Her children behave in her presence but do whatever they like in her absence.

Aponte, H. (1976). Underorganization in the poor family. In P. J. Guerin (Ed.), *Family therapy: Theory and practice* (pp. 432-448). New York: Gardner.

foster care placement and parenting   A substitute child-care arrangement for the child's natural parents that varies according to the length of time of placement (temporary vs. permanent), the developmental stage of the child (adolescent or infant), the disability of the child (e.g., mental retardation, emotional disturbance, visual impairment), and the acceptance of siblings in the same home. Foster parenting is a nonnormative parenting arrangement. When a child enters foster care, parental authority is shared by the natural parents, the agency, and the foster parents.

Eastman, K. S. (1982). Foster parenthood: A nonnormative parenting arrangement. In M. B. Sussman & H. Gross (Eds.), *Alternatives to traditional family living* (pp. 95-120). New York: Hawthorn Press.

fractured families   Families in which husbands avoid their wives and are verbally and perhaps physically abusive to them. The wives attempt to gain support for themselves through emotional appeals, but, as they increase their appeals, their husbands become more withdrawn and abusive. The women and children in such families eventually have problems requiring professional attention. Relationships in the home are fractured, not by a divorce, but by the destructive behaviors exhibited in daily living. The children generally perceive one parent as the loser. This noticeable imbalance in power in the husband-wife relationship impels a child into a protective alignment with the "losing" parent. The split-parenting pattern is reflected in a split within the child, who loves both parents but feels compelled to support one over the other.

Example: The son assumes the role of the caretaker for his mother, who is cast in the role of "loser" in the marital battle. In fact, she historically has set the stage to become the victim in order to secure her son's devotion.

Little, M. (1982). *Family break-up.* San Francisco: Jossey-Bass.

fragile bond   A marital relationship in which the husband and the wife both withdraw and move away from each other when they encounter problems. A deceptive tranquility is maintained by both avoiding confrontation on troublesome issues. Over the years, the two partners drift apart emotionally but cling to the shell of their marriage. One day, quite suddenly, the marriage ends when one partner simply walks away. The abrupt ending shocks the partner who is left in the home (Little, 1982). The term also is used to refer to the marital relationship in general and to the balance between equality, intimacy, and endurance in marriage, with this balance being rather fragile (Napier, 1988).

Example: A husband and a wife emotionally and behaviorally separate themselves from each other and create two different worlds: male and female.

Little, M. (1982). *Family break-up.* San Francisco: Jossey-Bass.
Napier, A. (1988). *The fragile bond.* New York: Harper & Row.

fragility syndrome   A situation in which the patient thinks, "If I ask, the other person will fall apart," or "If I ask, I will get an answer that will make me fall apart."

Satir, V. (1983). *Conjoint family therapy* (3rd ed.). Palo Alto, CA: Science & Behavior Books.

fragmentation   Disruptions in communication that are operationally defined as incomplete sentences, repetitions, fragments, or laughter.

    Example: A wife says, "How could you do that?" The husband says, "Well . . ." and then laughs, and the sequence is repeated.

Mishler, E., & Waxler, N. (1968). *Interaction in families: An experimental study of family processes and schizophrenia.* New York: John Wiley.

frames   Principles of organization that govern social events and people's subjective involvement in them. A frame can be compared with the rules of a game or with a "code" as a device that informs and patterns all events that fall within the boundaries of its application. Frames, in short, operate as if they are the rules that define situations. The family thinks and operates as though it has a certain set of rules, or overlapping sets of individual rules plus "unit rules," that define its situation. The rules may define what is serious versus what is not serious, what is good versus what is not good, and how to show love versus how not to show love. Identification of many other such rules (inferred by the observer) is necessary to have a full description of a family's frames.

    Example: Two spouses' unspoken frames stipulate different rules about which behaviors can be included in "how to show love versus how not to show love."

de Shazer, S. (1982). *Patterns of brief family therapy.* New York: Guilford.

fraternal polyandry   A family pattern in which several brothers are cohusbands.

Zelditch, M. (1964). Cross-cultural analyses of family structure. In H. T. Christensen (Ed.), *Handbook of marriage and the family* (pp. 462-500). Chicago: Rand McNally.

freeze frame   The result of arranging the bodies of the family members in terms of their positioning and posture (family sculpture), thus graphically portraying the hidden and poignant aspects of family life—that is, those private perceptions or invisible structures that come to light only very slowly through verbal techniques.

Levant, R. F. (1984). *Family therapy: A comprehensive overview.* Englewood Cliffs, NJ: Prentice-Hall.
Simon, R. M. (1972). Sculpting the family. *Family Process, 11,* 49-57.

frustrated dependency needs   Unfulfilled needs resulting from the failure of a marital union to meet lifelong narcissistic yearnings for all-absorbing, unconditional love. Alcohol abuse is a common consequence

F

of the frustration of dependency needs. Typically a husband will struggle with unacceptable, unmet dependency yearnings that usually are kept repressed because of the threat their recognition would constitute to his sense of masculinity but that are permitted expression through episodes of total alcoholic helplessness—that is, helplessness mercifully kept from clear representation in consciousness by the fact of his intoxication.

Blinder, M., & Kirschenbaum, M. (1969). The technique of married couple group therapy. In B. N. Ard & C. C. Ard (Eds.), *Handbook of marriage counseling* (pp. 233-246). Palo Alto, CA: Science & Behavior Books.

functional action   Observable acts within a family, including the manifestation of purposes or motivations evaluations, resolutions and decisions, interpersonal adjustments, rehearsals, and other elements of total action processes.

Example: Communications are generated within a family to help the family reach a goal: how to plan finances for a vacation.

Bell, J. (1976). A theoretical framework for family group therapy. In P. J. Guerin (Ed.), *Family therapy* (pp. 129-143). New York: Gardner.

F

functional analysis of behavior   The process in operant behavior therapy of determining what environmental and interpersonal contingencies are maintaining undesirable behavior or reducing the occurrence of desirable behavior.

Example: If a child is misbehaving, the therapist seeks a precise definition of the problem behavior and information about what happened before, during, and after the symptomatic behavior.

Liberman, R. (1972). Behavioral approaches to family and couple therapy. In G. D. Erickson & T. P. Hogan (Eds.), *Family therapy: An introduction to theory and technique* (pp. 120-134). Belmont, CA: Wadsworth.

functional coalition   A coalition in which the marital relationship is the strongest dyad, the generation boundary is intact, and other channels are open and coequal.

Glick, I. D., & Kessler, D. P. (1980). *Marital and family therapy* (2nd ed.). New York: Grune & Stratton.

functional family   A family characterized by:

a flexible power structure with shared authority, a clear family rule system, a strong parental coalition, intact generational boundaries, and an affiliative style

individuation of family members, characterized by both separateness and closeness, comfort with disagreement and uncertainty, freedom and

> spontaneous communication, respect for and sensitivity to differentness and the subject world of others, and little scapegoating or blaming
> strong marital and community relationships
> family myths attuned to reality
> humor, tenderness, caring, and hopefulness, with conflict out in the open and an absence of chronic resentments

See also **dysfunctional family.**

Glick, I. D., & Kessler, D. P. (1980). *Marital and family therapy* (2nd ed.). New York: Grune & Stratton.

functional family therapy Therapy using an interpersonally based model of behavior change that combines both behavioral and systems-based interventions. The central concept of function guides the therapist to a set of step-by-step decision rules regarding goals, therapist behavior, and treatment technologies for each phase of family intervention. The model emphasizes operationalization of systems theory concepts for assessing family interaction and planning intervention, applications of cognitive (attribution) change techniques prior to the application of behavior change technology, and the importance of therapist characteristics and nontechnical behaviors.

Alexander, J., & Parsons, B. V. (1982). *Functional family therapy.* Monterey, CA: Brooks/Cole.

functionality The suitability of behavior for achieving common goals while minimizing impasses and backlogs. Functionality is a component of stability/instability.

Bodin, A. (1981). The interactional view: Family therapy approaches of the Mental Research Institute. In A. S. Gurman & D. P. Kniskern (Eds.), *Handbook of family therapy* (pp. 267-309). New York: Brunner/Mazel.
Lederer, W., & Jackson, D. (1968). *The mirages of marriage.* New York: Norton.

functional level of differentiation The degree of fusion between intellectual and emotional systems, based on shifts in the level of anxiety a person experiences. A person acts more differentiated as a result of fusion with another; basic changes in personality do not result.

Example: A man enters therapy because of overriding anxiety. He fuses with the therapist and begins to act more appropriately, as long as the relationship with the therapist continues.

Kerr, M. (1981). Family systems theory and therapy. In A. S. Gurman & D. P. Kniskern (Eds.), *Handbook of family therapy* (pp. 226-264). New York: Brunner/Mazel.

funneling technique An interviewing strategy in which the initial aspects of the interview focus on broad, general topics and gradually proceed toward more sensitive topics.

Gelles, R. (1974). *The violent home: A study of physical aggression between husbands and wives.* Beverly Hills, CA: Sage.

Okun, B. F., & Rappaport, L. J. (1980). *Working with families: An introduction to family therapy.* Belmont, CA: Brooks/Cole.

fusion   The merging of the intellectual and emotional aspects of a person, paralleling the degree to which that person fuses into or loses self in relationships. Fusion undermines the person's ability to maintain individuality in relationships. Fusion can be both a source of relief and a source of anxiety.

Example: A man fuses with his wife. He cannot think for himself. He consults her over the smallest decision. He also mirrors her feelings. His ability to function independently is overshadowed by what he thinks his wife thinks and feels.

Bowen, M. (1976). Theory in the practice of psychotherapy. In P. J. Guerin (Ed.), *Family therapy* (pp. 42-90). New York: Gardner.

Kerr, M. (1981). Family systems theory and therapy. In A. S. Gurman & D. P. Kniskern (Eds.), *Handbook of family therapy* (pp. 226-264). New York: Brunner/Mazel.

F

future-oriented question   One type of reflexive question used to help families think about their future when they are stuck in the present or past. These questions can serve a variety of functions, including cultivating family goals, operationalizing values, exploring anticipated outcomes, highlighting consequences, exploring catastrophic expectations, suggesting future actions, and instilling hope and optimism.

Tomm, K. (1987). Interventive interviewing: Part II. Reflexive questioning as a means to enable self-healing. *Family Process, 26,* 167-184.

future pacing   The neurolinguistic process of ensuring that the changes accomplished during therapy become generalized and available in the appropriate outside contexts. Too often, changes that occur in therapy become anchored to the therapist's office or even to the therapist, rather than made available to the client in the specific situations that most need the new behaviors and responses. The primary method of future pacing new behaviors is to anchor the new behavior or response to a sensory stimulus that naturally occurs in the applicable context.

Example: The therapist asks the client, "What is the very first thing you will see, hear, or feel externally that will indicate that you need this resource?" When the specific experience is identified, the client is asked to generate it internally and then to anchor it to the appropriate resource. When the stimulus later occurs in external experience, it naturally or unconsciously triggers the appropriate feelings/behavior.

Dilts, R., & Green, J. D. (1982). Applications of neurolinguistic programming in family therapy. In A. M. Horne & M. M. Ohlsen (Eds.), *Family counseling and therapy* (pp. 214-244). Itasca, IL: F. E. Peacock.

future tense A diagnostic sex hypnotherapy technique in which the client is asked to visualize a double scene in the mind's eye. The person is encouraged to see self now with the problem and also in the future when the problem no longer exists.

Araoz, D. L. (1982). *Hypnosis and sex therapy.* New York: Brunner/Mazel.

F

F

gender identity   The inner conviction, established in the first 2 or 3 years of life, that one is male or female; the personal sense of maleness or femaleness.

Stoller, R. J. (1985). Gender identity disorders in children and adults. In H. I. Kaplan & B. J. Sadock (Eds.), *Comprehensive textbook of psychiatry* (4th ed., pp. 1034-1040). Baltimore: Williams & Wilkins.

gender roles   Socially prescribed roles that delineate different behaviors as appropriate for men and women.

Walters, M., Carter, B., Papp, P., & Silverstein, O. (1988). *The invisible web: Gender patterns in family relationships.* New York: Guilford.

gender sensitivity   The therapist's recognition of how gender issues and the differential socialization of each gender affect the therapeutic process. A gender-sensitive therapist seeks to provide opportunities for both partners to choose roles that differ from those prescribed by the larger social system.

Hoffman, L. (1990). Constructing realities: An art of lenses. *Family Process, 29,* 1-12.

general systems theory   Living organisms are seen as part of a sequence of larger systems—for example, family, group, community, nation. All living organisms, furthermore, are composed of a series of ever-smaller subsystems (for example, organs, tissues, cells). Each system has a measure of independence from the suprasystem of which it is a part (e.g., the individual from the family, the family from the community) but only within certain limits beyond which it must comply or suffer. The individuality of each system is maintained by its boundary, a region that contains and protects the part of the system and where

181

the transfer of information and matter/energy is restricted relative to regions internal and external to it. Just as the boundary maintains a degree of autonomy for the system despite a general control by the suprasystem for which it is a part, so feedback loops adjusting the functioning of the system according to its performance (like a thermostat in a heating system) maintain a general continuity of structure and function despite being "loose" enough to permit changing growth within permissible limits.

Bertalanffy, L. von. (1950). An outline of general systems therapy. *British Journal of the Philosophy of Science, 1,* 134-165.

Skynner, A. C. R. (1981). An open-systems, group-analytic approach to family therapy. In A. S. Gurman & D. P. Kniskern (Eds.), *Handbook of family therapy* (pp. 39-84). New York: Brunner/Mazel.

generalization/termination phase   The third and final phase of treatment in functional family therapy. The therapist's goal is to create change that will persist beyond treatment. The therapist must assess when the family is ready to function independently on the basis of problem cessation, changes in family structure, and/or the acquisition of problem-solving skills.

G

Alexander, J. (1988). Phases of family therapy process: A framework for clinicians and researchers. In L. Wynne (Ed.), *The state of the art in family therapy and research: Controversies and recommendations* (pp. 175-187). New York: Family Process Press.

generation   "(1) A body of living beings constituting a single step in the line of descent from an ancestor; (2) a group of individuals born and living contemporaneously; (3) a group of individuals having, contemporaneously, a status (as that of students in a school) that each one holds only for a limited period; (4) the average span of time between the birth of parents and the birth of their offspring; (5) the action or process of producing offspring (*Webster's new collegiate dictionary,* 1979, p. 474)." In families, a different order in the power hierarchy, on the basis of age and years, such as parent and child.

Haley, J. (1987). *Problem-solving therapy* (2nd ed.). San Francisco: Jossey-Bass.

Webster's new collegiate dictionary. (1979). Springfield, MA: Merriam-Webster.

generational boundaries   Reorganized generational limits on family member roles. In well-functioning families, invisible lines between parents and children are clearly demarcated and observed: Children remain in child roles, and parents remain in parental roles. Children do not take over parental roles or become parental figures, nor do they usurp the traditional roles belonging to the parents. Thus a child does not have to "mother" her own mother. The relationship of the parents, sometimes called the *marital coalition* or the *spouse subsystem,* is the unit within the family where the adults can meet their needs for sexual gratification and for companionship. This relationship is separate and private from their relationship with the children, yet enables them to provide support, limits, and privacy to the children.

Minuchin, S. (1974). *Families and family therapy.* Cambridge, MA: Harvard University Press.

generational inversion   A family situation in which an elderly parent is dependent on the younger generation for emotional, financial, physical, or mental support. Generationally inverted families are no longer unique; they are, in fact, increasing as a result of greater longevity and increasing numbers of physically and financially dependent elders. In these families, not only the roles are reversed but also the entire set of generationally linked rights, responsibilities, and obligations are reversed.

Thus today it is not uncommon for one or two brothers or sisters to bear the responsibility for four or five family members over 75 years of age who are no longer able to live independently. The existence of multiple generations in generationally inverse families is a growing phenomenon, and the impact of "parent caring" on the middle-aged offspring is increasingly apparent. The question of who takes care of the caretakers when the caretakers need taking care of needs to be raised. In short, the problems created by increased longevity are not confined to the elderly but encompass the whole family life cycle.

Example: The 34-year-old divorced mother of two children spends most of her time caring for her ill mother and attending to her father's postoperative recovery.

Steinmets, S. (1983). Dependency, stress, and violence between middle-aged caregivers and their elderly parents. In J. I. Kosbers (Ed.), *Abuse and maltreatment of the elderly* (pp. 134-149). Littleton, MA: John-Wright.

generation gap family   A family in which the marital unit and the offspring form cohesive subsystems, with little interaction across generational lines. A coalition takes place in the generation gap when the marital unit and the offspring each form a fairly cohesive duo, with little or no interaction across generational lines.

Example: The parents travel extensively and spend all of their time in an adult world, while the children form a cohesive unit to ensure their emotional survival.

Glick, I. D., & Kessler, D. P. (1980). *Marital and family therapy* (2nd ed.). New York: Grune & Stratton.

G

genogram   A schematic diagram of the family relationship system based on the genetic tree, usually involving several generations. Squares represent men; circles represent women. Horizontal lines indicate marriages; vertical lines drawn down from the horizontal, with the appropriate square or circle, indicate children and their gender. Ages of these individuals may be entered in the square or circle. Other important events may be listed, as well as indications of patterns of alliance and conflict.

Example: See Figure 4.

Guerin, P., & Pendergast, E. (1976). Evaluation of family system and genogram. In P. J. Guerin (Ed.), *Family therapy* (pp. 450-465). New York: Gardner.

McGoldrick, M., & Gerson, R. (1985). *Genograms in family assessment.* New York: Norton.

Pinney, E. L., & Slipp, S. (1982). *Glossary of group and family therapy.* New York: Brunner/Mazel.

G

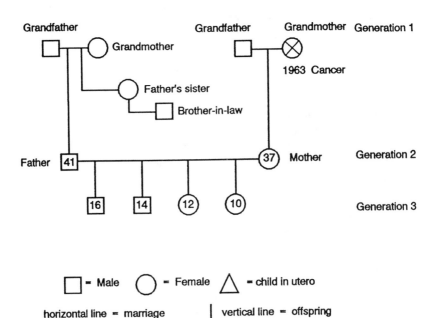

Figure 4. A Genogram

Gestalt family therapy An experientially oriented approach to marital and family therapy that is relational in nature but that uses the same techniques traditionally used in individual Gestalt therapy developed by Fritz Perls. The assumption is that awareness and congruence of thoughts and feelings are the primary requirements for change.

The goal of treatment is to help the clients achieve self-awareness and increased self-direction. By focusing on here-and-now experiences, the therapist attempts to remove blocks and entrenched patterns in the relationship. The ultimate goal of therapy is to promote individual and systemic growth by facilitating spontaneity and the creation of new experiences.

Kempler, W. (1981). *Experiential psychotherapy with families.* New York: Brunner/Mazel.
L'Abate, L., & McHenry, S. (1983). *Handbook of marital interventions.* New York: Grune & Stratton.
Perls, F. S. (1969). *Gestalt therapy verbatim.* Moab, UT: Real People Press.

ghost family A family that has lost a member through either death or desertion and is having difficulty coming to terms with the loss. Relegating the missing member's responsibilities and functions may be regarded as an act of disloyalty. Many times, the family will believe that if the missing person had lived, that person would have known what to do. Old mannerisms and restrictions may be enforced as if the member were still there.

Minuchin, S., & Fishman, H. (1981). *Family therapy techniques.* Cambridge, MA: Harvard University Press.

give-to-get principle A therapeutic stipulation that one marital partner approach the other with the intention of giving sensate pleasures while the other partner focuses on receiving the pleasures. After a reasonable time, the marital partners exchange roles of pleasuring (giving) and being pleasured (getting).

Masters, W., & Johnson, V. (1970). *Human sexual inadequacy.* Boston: Little, Brown.

giving in A paradoxical approach to treatment in which the client is told to surrender to a symptom.

Example: A man believes it is bad to feel depressed. He constantly fights depressed feelings. The therapist instructs him to give in to his depression to find out just how bad it really would be. "Allow yourself to be depressed. You've been fighting it for so long, and see what has happened. Stay with your depression."

Weeks, G., & L'Abate, L. (1982). *Paradoxical psychotherapy: Theory and practice with individuals, couples, and families.* New York: Brunner/Mazel.

goal discrepancy   A situation in which one partner in a dyad has goals that conflict with those of the other partner.

Example: A husband stresses the importance of making money and moving up socially, while his wife is oriented toward the internal emotional needs of the family.

Foley, V. (1974). *An introduction to family therapy.* New York: Grune & Stratton.
Spiegel, J. (1957). The resolution of role conflict within the family. *Psychiatry, 20,* 1-16.

goal-oriented performance   A concept, used in sex therapy, that refers to either the client or the therapist setting a goal for a particular sexual interaction. Setting a goal creates performance anxiety that is antitherapeutic.

Example: An inexperienced sex therapist told a couple to stimulate each other until the male partner reached orgasm manually. By emphasizing the goal, more performance anxiety was created in this client. The therapist should have said to stimulate each other and to focus on the pleasure for as long as it feels good.

Masters, W., & Johnson, V. (1970). *Human sexual inadequacy.* Boston: Little, Brown.

go-between process   A process in which the therapist attempts to unbalance a system by joining with one or more members on a conflictual point. The therapist probes issues in the family, establishes the existence of conflict, encourages open expression of disagreement, exposes and resists the family's efforts to deny or disguise disagreement, encourages the expression of recent or current disagreement rather than rehashes of the old, and encourages expression of conflict between members present at the session. The four steps in the process are as follows:

1. introduction of an issue on which there are at least two identifiable opponents
2. intensification of conflict and the beginning movement of a person into the role of go-between
3. attempts by the principals and go-between to define and delimit each other's roles or positions
4. a recession or cessation of conflict associated with a change in the principals' positions or redefinition of the conflict, or both

The intent is to apply leverage against "pathogenic relating" in families in order to break it up. The therapist positions him- or herself to take or trade the roles of mediator and side-taker during conflicts in family therapy.

Example: The therapist mediates between the narcissistic father and nuturant daughter who has taken on the mother-wife role. The father, in turn, is destructive to the real mother-wife.

Zuk, G. (1971). *Family therapy: A triadic-based approach.* New York: Behavioral Publications.

good faith contract   Contracts in which nonproblem behaviors are used as reinforcers; a reward (or penalty) is substituted for the behavior targeted for change. An example agreement would be if a spouse engages in a desired behavior, she receives a positive reinforcer that is independent of the change in her partner's behavior. In such a contract, there is no benefit in waiting for one's partner to change first. Each partner receives rewards for changing in the desired direction.

Example: Morgan would like Wynne to figure the household budget, and Wynne would like Morgan to play cards with her. A good faith contract between them might read: (a) If Morgan plays cards with Wynne for 1 hour, then he is entitled to choose the TV programming for that evening; or (b) if Wynne figures the household budget, then she gets private time for an evening while Morgan watches the children. In such a contract, there is no benefit in waiting for one's partner to change first. Each spouse receives rewards—from the partner, the external environment, or the therapist—for changing in the desired direction.

Weiss, R., Hops, H., & Patterson, G. (1973). A framework for conceptualizing marital conflict: A technique for altering it, some data for evaluating it. In L. A. Hamerlynck, L. C. Handy, & E. J. Marsh (Eds.), *Behavior change: Methodology, concepts and practice* (pp. 309-342). Champaign, IL: Research Press.

G

"good" mother   Refers to the concept of being a "good" mother in American culture, which is understood as making motherhood preeminent. This concept entails putting the role of mother above that of spouse. A separate, but related, rendering of preeminence encompasses doing what is best for one's child. Acting in the name of the best interest of the child, however, may be construed as a common standard for behaving as a good parent.

Example: The mother relinquishes custody to the father because she thinks he has more psychological resources for the best welfare of the children. This illustration is used as a contrast of what often is implied in the "good" mother—demanding custody even when it is not what she wants or is best for her children but rather what society expects.

Rosenblum, K. E. (1986). Leaving as a wife, leaving as a mother: Ways of relinquishing custody. *Journal of Family Issues, 7,* 197-213.

"good provider"   The general structure of the traditional "American family," in which the husband-father is the provider and the wife-mother is the "housewife," began to take shape early in the 19th century. The structure lasted about 150 years, from the 1830s to 1980, when the U.S.

Bureau of the Census no longer automatically named the male as the head of the household. As "providing" became increasingly mediated by cash derived from participation in the labor force or from commercial enterprises, the powers and prerogatives of the provider role augmented, and those of the housewife, who lacked income, declined. Gender identity became associated with the work site, as well as with work.

Example: A wife graduated from law school and earned more money than her husband did as a teacher.

Bernard, J. (1981). The good provider role: Its rise and fall. *American Psychologist, 36,* 1-12.

go slow directive   See **restraining.**

graded sexual assignments   A procedure for promoting sexual adequacy and responsiveness, in which the patient is instructed not to make any sexual responses that engender feelings of tension or anxiety but to proceed only to the point where pleasurable reactions predominate.

Wolpe, J. (1958). *Psychotherapy by reciprocal inhibition.* Stanford, CA: Stanford University Press.

group analytic family therapy   A systems approach to family and marital therapy developed by A. C. R. Skynner from the "group-as-a-whole" ideas of S. H. Foulkes (group-analysis) and the British object-relations school of psychoanalysis.

Skynner, A. C. R. (1976). *Systems of family and marital psychotherapy.* New York: Brunner/Mazel.

group analytic technique   An analytic technique that necessitates the involvement of the therapist as a person who interacts with the family to facilitate a process of growth and development on both sides. The key requirement for the therapist is a deep awareness of self-identity that can be sustained in the face of overwhelming emotional arousal engendered by encounters with profoundly disturbed family systems seeking to externalize their pathology.

Beels, C., & Ferber, A. (1969). Family therapy: A view. *Family Process, 8,* 280-318.
Skynner, A. C. R. (1981). An open-systems, group analytic approach to family therapy. In A. S. Gurman & D. P. Kniskern (Eds.), *Handbook of family therapy* (pp. 39-84). New York: Brunner/Mazel.

group dynamics   Interactions among group members that emerge as a result of properties and processes of the group, rather than individual personalities.

Slavson, S. R. (1943). *An introduction to group therapy.* New York: Commonwealth Fund.

group marriage A marriage involving multiple mates for both wife and husband.

Christensen, H. (1964). Development of the family field of study. In H. T. Christensen (Ed.), *Handbook of marriage and the family* (pp. 3-32). Chicago: Rand McNally.

group of meaning A coding category used with the Relations Rorschach that measures the accuracy and sensitivity of others' communications, the level of differentiation, and imaginativeness.

Loveland, N. (1967). The Relations Rorschach: A technique for studying interaction. *Journal of Nervous and Mental Disease, 142,* 93-105.
Riskin, J., & Faunce, E. (1972). An evaluative review of family interaction research. *Family Process, 11,* 365-455.

Groves Conference on the Family An association that meets annually, composed by selected (by nomination only) theory- and research-oriented professionals, mostly sociologists, with a sprinkling of other researchers from related disciplines in social science.

Dail, P. W., & Jewson, R. H. (1986). *In praise of fifty years: The Groves Conference on the conservation of marriage and the family.* Lake Mills, IA: Graphic Publishing.

growth orientation An approach to therapy in which the goal of therapy is the expansion of the life of the human being, as opposed to solving specific problems. The therapist's task is to help enrich the person's life through experiential means.

Haley, J. (1987). *Problem-solving therapy* (2nd ed.). San Francisco: Jossey-Bass.

G

growth vitality games Exercises in which each person includes self and others in interaction by expressing self and also permitting others to express their selves. This activity occurs on the content reality level, rather than on the survival level (as is also the case in rescue, coalition, and lethal games). A growth vitality game allows one to agree or disagree with one's own self in accord with one's own experience of reality.

Satir, V. (1983). *Conjoint family therapy* (3rd ed.). Palo Alto, CA: Science & Behavior Books.

guardian ad litem A court-appointed representative, usually an attorney, who serves as the guardian of the children in order to act on their behalf in litigation. Used frequently in custody litigation, the guardian ad litem is free to access all information pertinent to the custody litigation and can present the court with information that either party may be interested in withholding. The guardian ad litem can initiate investigations (including psychological evaluations) and introduce evidence but generally does not cross-examine witnesses with regard to the custodial decision. The guardian ad litem serves the children in a capacity similar to the way the parents' attorneys serve them, but their functions are not entirely parallel. The guardian ad litem does not have the right to appeal, whereas the attorneys of the parents do. The guardian ad litem is paid by one or both parents.

Gardner, R. A. (1986). *Child custody litigation: A guide for parents and mental health professionals.* Cresskill, NJ: Creative Therapeutics.

guided (sexual) fantasy   A technique in which the therapist guides the patient through a scene involving intense sexual interaction while noting the person's emotional and physical reactions.

LoPiccolo, J., & Friedman, J. (1988). Broad-spectrum treatment of low sexual desire. In S. Leiblum & R. Rosen (Eds.), *Sexual desire disorders* (pp. 107-144). New York: Guilford.

G

habituation (sexual habituation)   The loss of intensity in sexual arousal as a function of familiarity with one's partner. In such cases, sexual fantasies may help compensate for this phenomenon.

Lazarus, A. (1988). A multimodal perspective on problems of sexual desire. In S. Leiblum & R. Rosen (Eds.), *Sexual desire disorders* (pp. 145-167). New York: Guilford.

hero   A dysfunctional role in the family. The hero provides self-esteem for the family. The hero makes the family proud, often being an extremely high achiever, but often pays the terrible price in terms of his or her own well-being. The hero sacrifices individuality and uniqueness for the sake of the family.

Friel, J., & Friel, L. (1988). *Adult children: The secrets of dysfunctional families.* Deerfield Beach, FL: Health Communications.

heterogamy   (1) Sexual reproduction involving fusion of unlike gametes often differing in size, structure, and physiology. (2) The predisposition of people to choose partners with traits different, if not opposite, from their own.
   Example: A man who is shy marries a woman who is very outgoing.

Ard, B. (1969). Love and aggression: The perils of loving. In B. N. Ard & C. C. Ard (Eds.), *Handbook of marriage counseling* (pp. 50-60). Palo Alto, CA: Science & Behavior Books.
Webster's new collegiate dictionary. (1979). Springfield, MA: Merriam-Webster.

hierarchical structure   Family functioning based on clear generational boundaries, with the parents maintaining control and authority.

Nichols, M. (1984). *Family therapy: Concepts and methods.* New York: Gardner.

H

hierarchy   The organization of a system based on power and decision-making ability. The higher up in the hierarchy, the greater the power and the ability to make decisions that affect others. The parent subsystem in healthy systems makes decisions for the family and carries the power. In dysfunctional families, children have more power.

Example: In a healthy family, the parent decides where the child sleeps at night. In a dysfunctional family, a child is asked each night where he or she wants to sleep: at mother's house or at the grandmother's house.

Haley, J. (1987). *Problem-solving therapy* (2nd ed.). San Francisco: Jossey-Bass.

holism   The view that the whole structure of a family system determines the system's properties and functions. A clinician holding this view of family systems (a) examines the present context and structures within which a symptom manifests itself (e.g., an apparently socially disabled 27-year-old male still living at home is the last of three children to leave), (b) looks for the etiology and the sustaining dynamics of the particular problem within the present active functioning of the organism (the child's guilt about leaving and the parents' anxiety about having "no one" at home), and (c) diagnoses and treats the problem on the basis of these "holistic" observations.

Okun, B. F., & Rappaport, L. J. (1980). *Work with families: An introduction to family therapy.* Belmont, CA: Brooks/Cole.

H

holistic principle   The theoretic principle that a person or group has a totality or gestalt that is unique and cannot be understood by merely studying the individual elements or "atoms" comprising the whole.

Example: A child's behavior appears unusual when the child is interviewed alone, but makes sense when viewed within the context of the family.

Hinsie, L., & Campbell, B. (1970). *Psychiatric dictionary* (4th ed.). New York: Oxford University Press.

holons   The component parts of a system, each of which is considered to be a whole in its own right, as well as a part of the larger system. (The term was coined by Arthur Koestler to indicate systems of holons: the individual, the nuclear family, the extended family, and the community.) A holon exerts competitive energy for autonomy and for self-preservation as a whole in itself. It also carries integrative energy as a part of the larger whole. Thus the nuclear family is a holon of the extended family, the extended family is a holon of the community, and so forth.

Examples:

- *Parental holon:* The system of individuals whose responsibility is the care and management of a child or children. It may include grandmothers and aunts, a child who is given the responsibility for siblings, and so on.
- *Sibling holon:* The system in which children first learn to interact, support, give, take, and enjoy. In this holon, children establish patterns that continue into extrafamilial peer groups. The sibling holon is a subset of the family holon.
- *Family holon:* The system of individuals comprising the "family." Usually this means the nuclear family, but it also may include the extended family. The family holon comprises all family members who take an active part in maintaining the system.

Koestler, A. (1979). *Janus: A summing up.* New York: Vintage.

Minuchin, S., & Fishman, H. (1981). *Family therapy techniques.* Cambridge, MA: Harvard University Press.

Umbarger, C. C. (1984). *Structural family therapy.* New York: Grune & Stratton.

homeodynamics The dynamics of family interaction. A nearly constant condition, such as that resulting from the homeostatic control of temperature within the body, is impossible in the area of interpersonal relations. Homeodynamics functions not only to restore a preexisting equilibrium but also to make room for accommodation to new experience, for learning, change, and growth.

Example: A teenage son receives his driver's license. New rules are developed to deal with his driving, staying out, and dating.

Ackerman, N. W. (1966). *Treating the troubled family.* New York: Basic Books.

H

home observations Procedures involving the observation of family members interacting together in their home.

Hansen, C. (1969). An extended home visit with conjoint family therapy. *Family Process, 7,* 67-87.

homeostasis The tendency toward maintenance of a relatively stable internal environment through a series of interacting physiological processes. In psychodynamic theory, homeostasis is the maintenance of balances in the intrapsychic system. Family theorists use the term to mean the maintenance of balances within a family to keep a certain established equilibrium or to ensure a relatively stable family environment. Systematic attempts are made by the family to restore the equilibrium when it is threatened in any way. Usually all members of the family are engaged in this process. See also **negative feedback.**

Example: A schizophrenic daughter attempts to leave home. The parents say she cannot leave because of her illness. The solidarity of the family is protected by her illness.

Gerson, M., & Barsky, M. (1979). For the new family therapist: A glossary of terms. *American Journal of Family Therapy, 7,* 15-30.

Jackson, D. (1968). The question of family homeostasis. In D. Jackson (Ed.), *Communication, family, and marriage* (pp. 1-11). Palo Alto, CA: Science & Behavior Books.

home visits   Visits the therapist makes to the family's home to hold sessions. This procedure gives the therapist the opportunity to determine what effect the physical environment has on the interactions of family members.

Bloch, D. (1973). The clinical home visit. In D. Block (Ed.), *Techniques of family therapy: A primer* (pp. 39-45). New York: Grune & Stratton.

homework assignment   An assignment to be completed outside the session. These assignments are designed to educate, extend what has been discussed or practiced in the office, and provide more experience through practice. Homework is a part of many approaches to couples and family work and is a hallmark of sex therapy. In the treatment of all major sexual dysfunctions, homework is the key to successful treatment.

Example: In the early stages of sex therapy, a couple may need to improve their sexual communication. An assignment usually is given in which each partner takes turns caressing the other, with the receiving partner practicing verbalizing what feels good and what he or she would like.

Masters, W., & Johnson, V. (1970). *Human sexual inadequacy.* Boston: Little, Brown.

H

homogamy   A perceived tendency for husbands and wives in families to resemble one another in various physical, psychological, and social characteristics. *Endogamy* and *assortive mating* are other terms used to indicate the process of choosing a partner similar to oneself.

Burgess, E., & Wallin, P. (1953). *Engagement and marriage.* Philadelphia: J. B. Lippincott.

horizontal bookkeeping   In human relationships, the attempt to analyze and manifest one's behaviors with the view to balancing them against others in the same generation. In this orientation, behavior in relationships is understood in accordance with what individuals think they owe to, or have coming to them from, these various relationships.

Example: A single-parent mother feels guilty about depriving her former husband of his daughter, so she thinks she owes him special favors, while he thinks he deserves those favors.

Boszormenyi-Nagy, I., & Spark, G. L. (1973). *Invisible loyalties: Reciprocity in intergenerational family therapy.* New York: Harper & Row.

"how rule"   The assumption that the use of the word *how* to begin a question contributes to the development of a problem-solving orientation between partners. The corollary is that "why" questions create an accusatorial exchange.

Example: A couple fighting with each other might ask, "Why do we fight?" A more productive approach would be to ask, "How do our arguments begin?"

Baruth, L. G., & Huber, C. H. (1984). *An introduction to marital theory and therapy.* Belmont, CA: Brooks/Cole.

human services   The provision of comprehensive and coordinated services to people in need. Service delivery requires integrative approaches by the major help-giving systems of mental health, social welfare, health, education, and criminal justice. Other related services also frequently are classified under the human services rubric—for example, family planning, recreation, parole and probation, advocacy and legal services, industrial relations, protective and foster care services for children and the aged, employment counseling, vocational rehabilitation, youth services, education programs for formal training, alternative learning schools, and continuing education.

Example: An adolescent who has a drinking problem is likely to come to the attention of the traffic court for driving while intoxicated; of the school counselor for truancy and inability to concentrate; of his family physician for disturbed sugar metabolism with symptoms of dizziness, weakness, and blackouts; of the welfare worker for fighting and abuses in the home; and of the mental health center for alcoholism. Family treatment is indicated.

Sauber, S. R. (1977). The human services delivery system. *International Journal of Mental Health, 5,* 121-140.

Sauber, S. R. (1983). *The human services delivery system.* New York: Columbia University Press.

H

humor   A disposition or state of mind that allows a person to (a) relabel a situation and thus gain control over a situation in which the person previously had been caught or (b) reduce tension and thus restore a sense of commonality that was cut off by bitterness. Thus the therapist makes humorous comments to ease a tense moment or to make changes in the family. Carrying a situation to the point of absurdity often helps people to gain perspective on their overly intense involvement in a rigid position and to reduce to triviality what was threatening and serious.

Example: A mother who says she cannot get anything done and cannot stay focused on one thing for very long is viewed as seriously disturbed by members of the family. Saying that she has a "jumping bean" mind lightens the mood. It implies that the problem may not be as serious as the family thinks it is.

Carter, E. A., & McGoldrick-Orfanidis, M. (1976). Family therapy with one person and the family therapist's own family. In P. J. Guerin (Ed.), *Family therapy* (pp. 193-219). New York: Gardner.

hyperactive child syndrome   See attention deficit hyperactivity disorder.

hyperactivity   A class of heterogeneous behavior disorders in which a high level of activity is exhibited at inappropriate times and cannot be inhibited on command. A number of other symptoms are usually present with hyperactivity: short attention span, distractibility, impulsivity, emotional liability, low frustration tolerance, aggressiveness, destructiveness, poor school performance, and poor peer relationships. Hyperactivity usually is evidenced by difficulty remaining seated, excessive jumping about, running in the classroom, fidgeting, manipulating objects, twisting and giggling in one's seat, squirming, and difficulty sustaining attention. See also **attention deficit hyperactivity disorder.**

American Psychiatric Association. (1987). *Diagnostic and statistical manual of mental disorders* (3rd ed., rev.). Washington, DC: Author.

Connors, C. K., & Wells, K. C. (1986). *Hyperkinetic children: A psychological approach.* Beverly Hills, CA: Sage.

Ross, B. N., & Ross, S. A. (1982). *Hyperactivity: Current issues, research and theory* (2nd ed.). New York: John Wiley.

hyperkinesis   An older term previously used to denote the disorder that is now called *attention deficit hyperactivity disorder.* See also **attention deficit hyperactivity disorder.**

Barkley, R. A. (1990). *Attention deficit hyperactivity disorder: A handbook for diagnosis and treatment.* New York: Guilford.

hyperkinetic reactions of childhood   An older term previously used to denote the disorder that is now called *attention deficit hyperactivity disorder.* See also **attention deficit hyperactivity disorder.**

Barkley, R. A. (1990). *Attention deficit hyperactivity disorder: A handbook for diagnosis and treatment.* New York: Guilford.

hyperprolactinemia   An excessive blood level of prolactin, a pituitary hormone. In men, this condition may result in loss of libido and erectile difficulty. This condition may appear to be psychogenic, rather than organic.

Seagraves, R. (1988). Drugs and desire. In S. Leiblum & R. Rosen (Eds.), *Sexual desire disorders* (pp. 313-347). New York: Guilford.

hypersexuality   An exaggerated or excessive level of sexual desire. In general, an individual with this condition is obsessed with sexual thoughts and feelings and feels compelled toward sexual activity over and over again that produces only temporary gratification or that is devoid of any gratification.

Goldberg, M. (1987). Understanding hypersexuality in men and women. In G. Weeks & L. Hof (Eds.), *Integrating sex and marital therapy* (pp. 202-220). New York: Brunner/Mazel.

hypoactive sexual desire   A sexual dysfunction characterized by persistent and pervasive inhibition of sexual desire. This dysfunction also may be caused by a dysfunctional marital relationship. Primary causes are depression, stress, drugs, and hormone imbalances.
   Example: Over several years, a couple have grown apart; there is little intimacy and little time for each other. Time is taken up with career, children, yard work, and volunteer activities. One of the spouses has no interest in sex at all.

Kaplan, H. S. (1979). *Disorders of sexual desire.* New York: Brunner/Mazel.

hypogonadism   A reduction in libido and sexual activity resulting from failure of the gonads or from inappropriate stimulation of the gonads by the pituitary. The usual medical treatment is the administration of exogenous testosterone.

H

Money, J. (1961). Components of eroticism in man: The hormones in relation to sexual morphology and sexual desire. *Journal of Nervous and Mental Disease, 132,* 239-248.
Seagraves, R. (1988). Drugs and desire. In S. Leiblum & R. Rosen (Eds.), *Sexual desire disorders* (pp. 313-347). New York: Guilford.

hypothesis-introducing question   A type of reflexive question used to introduce the therapist's hypothesis to the family.
   Example: The therapist may develop a specific hypothesis that could be introduced as follows: "If he were to admit he is depressed, do you think you would actually be able to respond to him in spite of saying that is what you need?"

Tomm, K. (1987). Interventive interviewing: Part II. Reflexive questioning as a means to enable self-healing. *Family Process, 26,* 167-184.

hypothesizing   A term used by the Milan group to describe the therapist's conceptualization of the family and the subsystems. This conceptualization includes ideas about communication in the family, the meaning of symptoms in the family context, the organization of the family system, and what is necessary to achieve second-order change. Hypothesizing occurs throughout the entire process of therapy, and information is sought to confirm or refute the therapist's hypothesis. See also **strategizing.**

Example: During the first session of family therapy, the therapist notices that the 12-year-old child sits in the mother's lap, while the father sits on the other side of the room. The therapist hypothesizes that the mother and the child are overinvolved and that the father is underinvolved.

Boscolo, L., Cecchin, G., Hoffman, L., & Penn, P. (1987). *Milan systemic family therapy: Conversations in theory and practice.* New York: Basic Books.

hysteric-compulsive family   A family in which the father is a caricature of maleness, being strong and silent; the mother is a caricature of femaleness, being quite emotional and seemingly relatively powerless.

Lewis, J. M., Beavers, W. R., Gossett, J. T., & Phillips, V. A. (1976). *No single thread: Psychological health in the family system.* New York: Brunner/Mazel.

H

id binding   Parents' exploitation of the dependency needs of their children, with an emphasis on regressive gratification. The result is infantilization of the adolescent. See also **affective binding.**

Stierlin, H. (1974). *Separating parents and adolescents: A perspective on running away, schizophrenia and waywardness.* New York: Quadrangle.

identification   Any of a number of ways by which a person or family can be characterized. Identification has been defined variously by a number of writers, and the term has been applied to several broad classes of phenomena, sometimes by the same theorist—for example, identification as behavior (emphasizing overt action), identification as motive (disposition to act), identification as process (a mechanism by which behaviors and motives are acquired), and identification as a set of beliefs or cognitions about the self. Freud usually treated identification as a process—that is, as the sequential interplay of forces, internal and external, that impel a child to take on the characteristics of the parent (e.g., anaclitic and aggressive identification). But on at least one occasion, he used the term to describe the product or outcome of the process as the resultant similarity in the characteristics of the child and the model. Identification is used also in reference to one individual's similarity to another individual, to individuals belonging to a particular group, and to individuals falling within a single category. Finally, identification may be applied to a perceived similarity, a motive to become similar, a process of becoming similar, and a state of being similar.

Hall, C., & Lindzey, G. (1970). *Theories of personality.* New York: John Wiley.
L'Abate, L. (1976). *Understanding and helping the individual in the family.* New York: Grune & Stratton.

199

identified patient   The symptom bearer or official patient as identified by the family. For example, it may be the family member who is most obviously affected by a pained marital relationship or most subjected to dysfunctional parenting. The identified parent's (IP) symptoms signal the parent's pain and family imbalance. They also distort the IP's growth as a result of trying to absorb and alleviate the parent's pain.

> Satir, V. (1983). *Conjoint family therapy* (3rd ed.). Palo Alto, CA: Science & Behavior Books.

identity struggle   The manifest content of family verbal conflicts, often taking the form of an argument over what kind of person each of the participants is. Each person alternately plays the role of aggressor and defender, at times accusing the other of having an undesirable characteristic, at other times stoutly defending one's own character from criticism.

Example: A mother wants her daughter to be friendly and outgoing and to confide in her. She tries to force this behavior by accusing the daughter of being unfriendly. The daughter responds by accusing the mother of not being understanding.

> Wallace, A., & Fogelson, H. (1965). The identity struggle. In I. Boszormenyi-Nagy & J. Framo (Eds.), *Intensive family therapy: Theoretical and practical aspects* (pp. 365-406). New York: Harper & Row.

idiopanima   The perception of another's perception of one's self. Idiopanima is related to insight and empathy. *Empathy* refers to the understanding of another; *idiopanima* is one's understanding of another's concept of one's self.

> Corsini, R. J. (1966). *Role playing in psychotherapy: A manual.* Chicago: Aldine.

I

if-then assumption   In sex therapy, the term refers to the idea that one partner assumes that if one behavior is allowed, then others inevitably must follow. This type of thinking must be made known to the individual and challenged cognitively.

Example: A common example involves the female partner who assumes that if she allows her partner to touch her genitally, then he will demand, implicitly and explicitly, to have intercourse.

> Lazarus, A. (1988). A multimodal perspective on problems of sexual desire. In S. Leiblum & R. Rosen (Eds.), *Sexual desire disorders* (pp. 145-167). New York: Guilford.

illusion of no alternatives   A strategy in which the therapist limits the choices of the clients by presenting an illusion of no or limited alternatives. The purpose is to get the clients to exercise their own choices.

This technique is used with clients who have too many choices, according to their assessment, and cannot choose among them.

Madanes, C. (1984). *Behind the one-way mirror*. San Francisco: Jossey-Bass.

image relationship A relationship in which the inner image of the other person takes precedence. The emphasis is on changing reality to fit with expectation, rather than on changing expectation to fit reality.
Example: A husband is seen as cold and insensitive by his wife because of her history with men. In fact, he is quite warm and sensitive.

Brody, W. (1961). The family as the unit of study and treatment: Image, object, and narcissistic relationships. *American Journal of Orthopsychiatry, 31,* 69-73.
Searles, H. (1965). The contributions of family treatment to the psychotherapy of schizophrenia. In I. Boszormenyi-Nagy & J. Framo (Eds.), *Intensive family therapy: Theoretical and practical aspects* (pp. 463-496). New York: Harper & Row.

image thinking The development of imagination and the ability to think visually. As the therapist listens to family members talk, visualizations of what they are saying are created. The therapist then can "see" what is being discussed.

Dodson, L., & Kurpuis, D. (1977). *Family counseling: A systems approach.* Muncie, IN: Accelerated Development.

imago Derived from the Latin term for "image," the imago is a composite mental image of all of the people who influenced an individual at an early age (parents, siblings, relatives, teachers, etc.). Romantic interest and mate selection are largely an unconscious act of matching one's imago with another individual. The higher the degree of correlation, the greater the romantic attraction. *Mate selection* is the process of seeking and finding a partner on whom one projects imago traits. In *romantic love,* one projects the positive traits and denies the negative traits.

I

Hendrix, H. (1988). *Getting the love you want: A guide for couples.* New York: Harper & Row.

immovability Inflexible family patterns that the therapist tries to modify, change, or eliminate. The relevant therapeutic technique may be either a joining technique or a maneuver to initiate change. With a joining technique, the therapist enters the therapeutic relationship, demanding that the members of the system accommodate the therapist. This demand relays the message that there is a possibility for change. With a technique for initiating change, the therapist forces the family to change patterns that have been inflexible. They now must be modified to accommodate the inflexible therapist.

Example: A young student who recently had a psychotic break returns to his parents' home with his wife. On beginning therapy, he agrees to a date for him and his wife to move out of his family's house and into an apartment of their own. On that date, the son oversleeps, and they subsequently do not move out. In the next therapy session, the therapist deals with this issue intensively and confronts the son. The wife, backed by the therapist, decides to move alone. The son protests, but the wife and the therapist are adamant. Heretofore the family modified their behavior to allow for the son's behavior. The therapist (and his wife) then became immovable to force the son to move.

Minuchin, S., & Fishman, H. (1981). *Family therapy techniques.* Cambridge, MA: Harvard University Press.

impaired female excitement   In females, the consistent and persistent failure to attain or maintain the lubrication-swelling response during the sexual act. This condition also has been termed *frigidity* and *inhibited sexual excitement.*

Kaplan, H. S. (1983). *The evaluation of sexual disorders.* New York: Brunner/Mazel.

impartial evaluator, expert   Technically, any person who serves a court as an expert witness is assumed to be impartial, regardless of who hired this expert. The expert, by virtue of education or specialized experience, is to assist a trier-of-facts (judge, jury, court-appointed mediator) on matters where it is assumed the latter, without this help, would be incapable of forming accurate conclusions. In practice, greatest imparitality is assumed to exist in a custody evaluation when the evaluator has been court appointed or at least mutually agreed upon by both sides in the dispute rather than hired by one side or the other. While some experts may limit their participation to isolated aspects of the case (e.g., examining one or only a few of the critical participants, which is legitimate just so long as any proferred conclusions are also limited) the impartial evaluator conducts a comprehensive evaluation. This involves seeing all critical participants (parents, children) as well as many significant others (e.g., grandparents, live-in companions, full time babysitters, potential stepparents, etc.). Documents (e.g., psychological, medical, educational, financial, employment, etc.) may be reviewed. Psychological tests may be administered, and home and office observations made. The purpose is to optimize a child's exposure to available parental strengths, and minimize exposure to weaknesses. The evaluator attempts to create the best possible match-up between a given parent's resources and the psychological, developmental, educational, medical, and moral needs of a child. There is scientific controversy about whether expert witnesses should ever address the "ultimate" legal issue, in a custody case to name the parent assumed to be the better primary custodial parent (legally, this is permissable), but there is no controversy about the expert's offering information to assist the trier of fact in this matter.

Example: Mr. and Mrs. Frenski appear to be equally competent as parents and are equally available timewise. However, the evaluator decides, based on all of the data, that Mrs. Frenski's range of parenting styles is a better "fit" for the particular child involved and therefore would be the better bet for primary custodial parent.

Bricklin, B. (1994). *Custody evaluation problems and solutions.* New York: Brunner/Mazel.
Gardner, R. A. (1989). *Family evaluation in child custody mediation, arbitration, and litigation.* Cresskill, NJ: Creative Therapeutics.

implosion The empty feeling experienced by the ontologically insecure person, a feeling similar to the terrible fear that the world will crash in on one's self and wipe out all identity, like gas rushing in to fill up a vacuum. Consequently, because reality is necessarily implosive by nature, any contact with it is dreaded.

Example: A schizophrenic man has the feeling that he is totally alone in the world. He dreads his day-to-day life, fearing that only harm will come to him.

Foley, V. (1974). *An introduction to family therapy.* New York: Grune & Stratton.
Laing, R. (1969). *The divided self.* New York: Penguin.

implosive therapy Therapy designed to eliminate avoidance behavior through the process of extinction. The therapist floods the patient with anxiety-provoking stimuli without allowing any harm to come.

Example: A boy suffering from a school phobia is asked to imagine anxiety-rousing stimuli in their extremes without being allowed to leave the situation or to experience harm.

Stampl, T., & Lewis, D. (1967). Essentials of implosive therapy: A learning theory based on psychodynamic behavioral therapy. *Journal of Abnormal Psychology, 72,* 496-503.

impotence A condition that prevents the male from obtaining and/or maintaining an erection long enough to accomplish intercourse. *Primary impotence* refers to a male who has never had a successful coital experience; *secondary impotence* refers to a male who has had at least one successful experience but can no longer function. Impotence also is termed an *erectile dysfunction.*

Masters, W., & Johnson, V. (1970). *Human sexual inadequacy.* Boston: Little, Brown.

impulsive family   A family characterized by an adolescent or young adult acting out anger toward a parent onto the community or expressing the parent's difficulties in a socially unacceptable way.

Cuber, J., & Harroff, P. (1966). *Sex and the significant Americans.* New York: Penguin.
Glick, I. D., & Kessler, D. P. (1980). *Marital and family therapy* (2nd ed.). New York: Grune & Stratton.

incest   Incest encompasses sexual behavior with a variety of patterns, variations, types, relationships, and aftereffects. Incest is illegal in all U.S. states, although the degree of the relatedness varies across some states. In general, incest laws forbid marriage, cohabitation, and sexual relations between individuals who are closely related by blood, marriage, and/or adoption. The most common form of incest is parent-child. In this case, the child is unable to give consent, is more dependent, and is powerless. It should be noted that not all incest is abusive if it is consented between adults or exploratory sex play between peers. See also **nonabusive incest.**

Courtois, C. (1988). *Healing the incest wound.* New York: Norton.

incompatibility   A marital situation in which two people, usually husband and wife, have nothing in common or are conflictful and cannot get along because of different personality makeups, interests, or values. The two partners may use attributed or real differences between them to justify separation and divorce—that is, incompatibility is an excuse to avoid closeness. This is the process of "monsterizing" that some partners need to achieve what they cannot achieve otherwise—distance. By the same token, however, differences can be used to unite and enhance a relationship and to make it more vital and interesting. Hence the differences underlying incompatibility can justify breaking a relationship even though the same differences could be used to sustain the relationship.

Example: The husband is warm, affectionate, and sexually oriented; the wife is cold, distant, and lacks sexual desire. He values human sharing and intimacy as most important; she is interested in power through social recognition and career success.

Ellis, A., & Harper, R. (1961). *Creative marriage.* New York: Lyle Stuart.

incongruent manifestation   Communication in which a person's words and expression are disparate: The person says one thing but seems to mean another by voice or gestures. The person thus presents an incongruent communication, and the person to whom the person is talking receives a double-level message.

Example: A man tells his wife that he wants to go to the beach with her; but, as he speaks, he frowns and clenches his teeth.

I

Satir, V. (1983). *Conjoint family therapy* (3rd ed.). Palo Alto, CA: Science & Behavior Books.

independence   The process of denial of dependence, of being able to be alone and self-sufficient. Independence is a stage between the dependence of childhood and the autonomous interdependence of ideal adulthood. It usually is found most prominently in adolescence.

Erskine, R. G. (1982). Transactional analysis and family therapy. In A. M. Horne & M. M. Ohlsen (Eds.), *Family counseling and therapy* (pp. 245-275). Itasca, IL: F. E. Peacock.

index patient   The individual family member whose behavior is labeled as problematic. Sometimes the use of this label may lead to an incorrect labeling of the entire family, as in referring to "schizophrenic families" or "drug addiction families."

Umbarger, C. C. (1984). *Structural family therapy.* New York: Grune & Stratton.

indicator therapy   Treatment of a symptom that is so life-threatening, inconvenient, or painful that it deserves therapy in its own right.
   Example: A boy steals women's underclothes. This symptom has serious personal and social consequences. The initial treatment is aimed at stopping the stealing behavior.

Howells, J. (1975). *Principles of family psychiatry.* New York: Brunner/Mazel.

indifference   Verbal and nonverbal behavior that shows disregard for another person's welfare or value. This type of speech or behavior usually carries little affect and communicates rejection or disinterest.

Alexander, J., Barton, C., Lindsey, D., Turner, C., & Warburton, J. (1988). Defensive and supportive communication interaction system. In D. Grotevant & C. Carlson (Eds.), *Handbook of family assessment* (pp. 182-187). New York: Guilford.

indirect induction   See **indirect suggestion.**

indirect suggestion   Telling someone to do something in a roundabout way, without stating it directly. Includes the use of metaphor, implication, and nonverbal suggestions.

O'Hanlon, W. H., & Hexum, A. L. (1990). *An uncommon casebook: The complete clinical work of Milton H. Erickson, M.D.* New York: Norton.

individual therapy   Therapy in which the focus is on the individual patient and the cure of the individual is the treatment goal. Individual therapy can be contrasted with family therapy along the dimensions listed in Table 2.

Carroll, J. (1964). Family therapy: Some observations and comparisons. *Family Process, 1,* 180-182.

Table 2   Individual Therapy Contrasted With Family Therapy

Individual Therapy	Family Therapy
1. Focus: Illness of the individual patient. The primary interest is in the intrapsychic disturbances of the individual.	1. Focus: Illness of the family. The primary interest is in the processes that occur within the family as a group
2. Responsibility: The therapist is responsible to the individual; the cure of the individual is the treatment goal.	2. Responsibility: The family is the patient. The therapist is responsible for the total family's welfare, rather than that of any one individual.
3. Process: The therapist studies the individual in depth, often apart from the individual's social environment and family relationship.	3. Process: The therapist studies the individuals as members of the family group, relating behavior to interactions with other family members.
4. Content: • The therapist relates present material to past experiences of the patient. • Fantasy, dream materials, and their meanings are used, more or less, as the content of the treatment. • Fantasy and dream materials may be interpreted and related by the therapist to feelings, attitudes, and behavior. • Patient's identity often is clarified by examining the integrations the patient makes between conflicts of the super ego and id. • Transferences may be highly individualized, with distortion of the image of the therapist based on infantile emotional experiences. • Materials revealed by the patient are highly confidential.	4. Content: • Emphasis is on the "here and now" and on ways the family can achieve healthy functioning. • Interactions between family members and their meanings form the focus of treatment. • Family interactions and processes are pointed out by the therapist; their meanings are explored as they occur. • Patient's identity evolves from a clarification of the role the patient plays in the family, the patient's self-image in this role, and the patient's role expectations. • Transference is diluted; the therapist is a reality figure. • Materials are openly shared by the family with the therapist.
5. Goals: • Diagnosis, analysis, and cure of the individual's illness or disorder. • Understanding oneself as a unique individual. • Exploring, developing insights, and gaining relief from inhibiting conflicts.	5. Goals: • Attaining effective family functioning, regardless of individual pathology. • Understanding oneself and other family members in relation to each other. • Establishing healthy interactions between family members.

SOURCE: From "Family Therapy: Some Observations and Comparisons" by J. Carroll, 1964, *Family Process, 1*, pp. 180-182. Reprinted by permission.

induction   The unknowing compliance of the therapist to the transactional structures and communicational rules of the family system. Induction is unwitting accommodation to the family patterns and occurs frequently in the initial phases of therapy.

Example: The therapist joins the family by occasionally converting to its folkways.

Umbarger, C. C. (1984). *Structural family therapy.* New York: Grune & Stratton.

I-ness   The ability of individual family members to express themselves clearly as feeling, thinking, acting, valuable, and separate individuals and to take responsibility for thoughts, feelings, and actions.

Example: The therapist asks the wife to restate herself in a dispute with her husband regarding their children by using the pronoun *I* rather than *we.* Thus, "We should not get angry with each other if we really love each other" becomes "I should not get angry at you if I really love you." The therapist thereby diverts the wife's statement toward her husband and away from the children. The wife experiences the impact of her irrational belief.

Beavers, W. R. (1976). A theoretical basis for family evaluation. In J. M. Lewis, W. R. Beavers, J. T. Gossett, & V. A. Phillips (Eds.), *No single thread: Psychological health in the family system* (pp. 46-82). New York: Brunner/Mazel.

infertility   The inability to conceive following an appropriate period of time, usually 1 year. Approximately 17% of couples experience some kind of problem. The psychological consequences of this problem can be far-reaching for the couple's sexual relationship and have been underemphasized by the medical professions.

Mahlstedt, P. (1987). The crisis of infertility: An opportunity for growth. In G. Weeks & L. Hof (Eds.), *Integrating sex and marital therapy* (pp. 121-148). New York: Brunner/Mazel.

I

information   A type of energy that leads to a reduction in the level of uncertainty within a system. This information can be either verbal or nonverbal. Gregory Bateson defined *information* as "news of a difference" (Bateson, 1972, p. 315). The Milan team redefined *information* to mean "news of a relationship difference" (Boscolo, Cecchin, Hoffman, & Penn, 1987, p. 96). Information is not the same as data; data are facts that do not necessarily describe a relationship.

Example: A father is an alcoholic. The fact that he is an alcoholic is a datum; how his being an alcoholic organizes relationships within the family is information (e.g., the wife is codependent and keeps his alcoholism a "secret" from the youngest children and people outside the family).

Bateson, G. (1972). *Steps to an ecology of mind.* New York: Ballantine.

Boscolo, L., Cecchin, G., Hoffman, L., & Penn, P. (1987). *Milan systemic family therapy: Conversations in theory and practice.* New York: Basic Books.

Rappaport, L. (1953). What is information? *Syntheses, 9,* 157.

Steinglass, P. (1978). The conceptualization of marriage from a systems theory perspective. In T. Paolino & B. McCrady (Eds.), *Marriage and marital therapy* (pp. 298-368). New York: Brunner/Mazel.

information exchange   In operational terms, the number of times a family member explicitly states a choice, approval, disapproval, preference, and so on among the number of alternatives the family is asked to select on the Unrevealed Differences Questionnaire.

Ferreira, A., & Winter, W. (1968). Information exchange and science in normal and abnormal families. *Family Process, 7,* 251-276.

Riskin, J., & Faunce, E. (1972). An evaluative review of family interaction research. *Family Process, 11,* 365-455.

information-processing style   The individual approach to perceiving, giving meaning, organizing, storing, and outputting data and experience that each person has. It includes thinking in images, kinesthetically, or by nonlinguistic sounds, as well as in verbal modes.

Duhl, B. S. (1983). *From the inside out and other metaphors.* New York: Brunner/Mazel.

inhibited male orgasm   See **retarded ejaculation.**

inhibition of developmental potential   A situation in which a person, because of family organization, cannot act in ways appropriate to that person's age within the family.

   Example: An adolescent girl does not wear makeup and dress as her friends do because of sexual taboos and restrictions in the family.

Aponte, H., & van Deusen, J. (1981). Structural family therapy. In A. S. Gurman & D. P. Kniskern (Eds.), *Handbook of family therapy* (pp. 310-360). New York: Brunner/Mazel.

inner dials   The focus of a sex hypnotherapy technique in which the client imagines an inner dial of sexual desire. The client then adjusts the dial knob upward while imagining the good sexual feelings associated with it. This technique is used to treat sexual desire dysfunctions.

Araoz, D. L. (1982). *Hypnosis and sex therapy.* New York: Brunner/Mazel.

input   A form of energy received by an open system from its external environment. The pattern of activities or energy exchange in an open system is cyclical. An open system receives input of some form of energy from the external environment and then transforms or reorganizes it through the application of throughput processes. The outputs of the system then become available for use as inputs for another system. The conception of an open system as a cycle of input → conversion → output facilitates the analysis of living systems at a variety of levels, from cell to society.

Example: The son gets caught stealing, and his parents tighten the family rules for all members. The parents ask the school counselor to monitor their son's behavior.

Sauber, S. R. (1983). *The human services delivery system.* New York: Columbia University Press.

insight-awareness approach A therapeutic approach in which observation, clarification, and interpretation are used to foster understanding and, presumably, change.

Glick, I. D., & Kessler, D. P. (1980). *Marital and family therapy* (2nd ed.). New York: Grune & Stratton.

instrumental activity Behavior that is directed toward some goal and that helps the behaving person adapt to his or her environment. In traditional families, it is the husband's role in decision making and task functions.

Example: A husband finds that he has trouble standing up to his wife, so he enrolls in a course in assertiveness training.

Parsons, T., & Bales, R. (1955). *Family, socialization, and interaction process.* New York: Free Press.

instrumental discrepancy A situation in which one partner has something (e.g., money) that gives that partner leverage that the other partner does not have.

Foley, V. (1974). *An introduction to family therapy.* New York: Grune & Stratton.
Spiegel, J. (1957). The resolution of role conflict within the family. *Psychiatry, 20,* 1-6.

instrumental expression axis A continuum of differences in instrumental versus expressive functions of a system. Instrumental functions concern the system's relation to situations outside the system and aimed at maintaining equilibrium (material goods and money). Expressive functions concern the integrative relation between members and the regulation of the patterns and tension levels of the system's component units (feelings and emotions).

Parsons, T., & Bales, R. (1955). *Family, socialization, and interaction process.* New York: Free Press.

instrumental family functions The ways a family deals with the outside world in terms of attaining goals and maintaining its equilibrium.

Example: A father spends much of his time away from home, engaging in work activity, so that his family can maintain itself financially.

Parsons, T., & Bales, R. (1955). *Family, socialization, and interaction process.* New York: Free Press.

instrumental influence   The sum of giving opinions and suggestions in Bales's coding system.

Bales, R. (1950). *Interaction process analysis: A method for the study of small groups.* Reading, MA: Addison-Wesley.
Riskin, J., & Faunce, E. (1972). An evaluative review of family interaction research. *Family Process, 11,* 365-455.

instrumental leader   The person who is the judge, the final court of appeals, and the executor of punishment, discipline, and control in the family.

Bales, R. (1950). *Interaction process analysis: A method for the study of small groups.* Reading, MA: Addison-Wesley.

integrative family therapy   Therapy designed to integrate the awareness of the simultaneous existence of a variety of viewpoints or systems levels such as nonverbal modes of communication, felt meanings, information-processing styles, and core images of the past, present, and future. It is a broad-based approach to family therapy, based on the idea that the family has its subsystems and suprasystems in operation at the same time.

Duhl, B., & Duhl, F. (1981). Integrative family therapy. In A. S. Gurman & D. P. Kniskern (Eds.), *Handbook of family therapy* (pp. 483-513). New York: Brunner/Mazel.

intense relationship   A relationship in which both positive and negative responses of each person are exaggeratedly important.
Example: A mother attempts to deal with her child with a mixture of overaffection and exasperation.

Haley, J. (1987). *Problem-solving therapy* (2nd ed.). San Francisco: Jossey-Bass.

intensionality   Seeing the cause of behavior in absolute and unconditional terms; to overgeneralize, to be dominated by concept or belief, to fail to anchor reactions in space and time, to confuse fact and evaluation, or to rely on abstractions rather than on reality testing. The term is derived from general semantics and includes the concept of *rigidity.*

Horne, A. M., & Ohlsen, M. M. (1982). *Family counseling and therapy.* Itasca, IL: F. E. Peacock.
Rogers, C. P. (1959). A theory of therapy, personality, and interpersonal relationships, as developed in the client-centered framework. In S. Koch (Ed.), *Psychology: A study of a science, Vol. III. Formulations of the person and the social context* (pp. 184-256). New York: McGraw-Hill.

intensity (1) Changing maladaptive transactions by using story affect, repeated intervention, or prolonged pressure; (2) a quality of the therapist's message, correlated to the level at which the family "hears" and assimilates the message. Families often have a highly selective sense of hearing, and therapists have to increase intensity to go above the family's threshold of deafness. This may be done in various ways, from soft intervention with great drama to high levels of involvement on everyone's part.

Minuchin, S., & Fishman, H. (1981). *Family therapy techniques.* Cambridge, MA: Harvard University Press.

interaction An interpersonal activity in which one person acts on another; person is balanced against person in a causal interconnection.
Example: One person's behavior affects another, causing the second person to react in some predictable way.

Dewey, J., & Bentley, A. (1949). *Knowing and the known.* Boston: Beacon Hill.
Framo, J. (1965). Systematic research on family dynamics. In I. Boszormenyi-Nagy & J. Framo (Eds.), *Intensive family therapy: Theoretical and practical aspects* (pp. 407-462). New York: Harper & Row.

interactional approach of the Mental Research Institute A family interactional approach based on the theories of Harry Stack Sullivan, Franz Alexander, and Ludwig von Bertalanffy, as derived from the philosophies of Russell, Whitehead, Wittgenstein, and others. The goal is to change transactions and communication patterns in the dysfunctional family that affect the identified patient. Attention is paid to verbal and nonverbal behaviors, their timing, and their congruence. The focus is on modification and change of behavior, not on cognitive insight or emotional catharsis.
Example: A patient is asked not to change (a paradoxical instruction) or is pressured to change by making the change contingent on continuation of therapy.

Pinney, E. L., & Slipp, S. (1982). *Glossary of group and family therapy.* New York: Brunner/Mazel.

interactional contract The operational contract that describes how two mates try to achieve fulfillment of the terms of their separate contracts. It is the set of conventions and implicit rules of behaviors, maneuvers, strategies, and tactics that they have developed in their dealings with each other.
Example: A husband and a wife contract for one night a week to be with their own set of friends. The contract dictates how they will fulfill certain needs, but not necessarily what each will do.

Sager, C. (1981). Couples therapy and marriage contracts. In A. S. Gurman & D. P. Kniskern (Eds.), *Handbook of family therapy* (pp. 25-32). New York: Brunner/Mazel.

interactional sequences   Patterns of behavior within a family system that reflect the roles and hierarchical positions assigned to each family member.

Haley, J. (1987). *Problem-solving therapy* (2nd ed.). San Francisco: Jossey-Bass.
Levant, R. F. (1984). *Family therapy: A comprehensive overview.* Englewood Cliffs, NJ: Prentice-Hall.

interaction pattern   The rules, implied or explicit, concerning who does what, when, where, and to whom. The relevant interaction is virtually synonymous with communication. The term bridges abstract concepts of systems theory to specific behavior.

Bernard, C., & Corrales, R. (1979). *The theory and technique of family therapy.* Springfield, IL: Charles C Thomas.

interaction process analysis   An analytical method, devised by Bales, to quantify face-to-face, group interactive data. Probably the most widely used system for categorizing social interaction, the method relies on the interpretation of manifest level of activity. Based on the theoretical idea that the basic nature of social interaction is problem solving, the assumption is that groups are instrumentally task oriented, which, in turn, creates strains leading to emotional-integrative problems; the groups then attempt to deal with the resulting expressively positive and negative tensions to reintegrate back to the task. The flow back and forth between instrumental and expressive activities constitutes the essence of the Bales method. The content of Bales's 12 categories, their sequential and symmetrical relationships, and their ordering with respect to each other are empirically and theoretically based. The categories are (a) shows solidarity, (b) shows tension release, (c) agrees, (d) disagrees, (e) shows tension, (f) shows antagonism, (g) gives suggestion, (h) gives opinion, (i) gives orientation, (j) asks for orientation, (k) asks for opinions, and (l) asks for suggestions.

Bales, R. (1950). *Interaction process analysis: A method for the study of small groups.* Reading, MA: Addison-Wesley.

interaction testing technique   A procedure used to generate spouse or family interactions. First, each spouse (or family member) is asked to fill out separately a subtest form of the Wechsler-Bellevue Comprehension and Similarities Subtests. Second, the respondents are brought together and are asked to fill out the same form together and then to discuss each answer as they make their joint decisions.

Bauman, G., & Roman, M. (1966). Interaction testing in the study of marital dominance. *Family Process, 5,* 230-242.

interdependency   The combination of autonomy of independence and acknowledgment of responsibility and dependency that each person experiences in relation to others with whom that person is living, directed at the satisfaction of some emotional or physical need. The basic areas of interdependency are (a) the exchanges between the system and its environment, (b) the processes within the system, and (c) the processes through which parts of the environment are related to each other. Each of these sets of interdependencies (transactional, internal, and interdependencies within the environment itself) must be considered.

Example: A recently married man bought his bride a car that she could not afford to buy herself. He wanted her to be more mobile and less dependent on the use of his car.

Sauber, S. R. (1983). *The human services delivery system.* New York: Columbia University Press.

interdependent triad   The intense interdependence between father, mother, and patient in disturbed families. In such families, change among the members occurs slowly.

Example: Members of a family form intense dependencies on each other to avoid looking at their own unhappiness. Mother and father argue constantly but have such low self-esteem that they cannot split; the child believes he or she is no good to the outside world and so stays tied to the parents' problems.

Bowen, M. (1965). Family psychotherapy with schizophrenia in the hospital and in private practice. In I. Boszormenyi-Nagy & J. Framo (Eds.), *Intensive family therapy: Theoretical and practical aspects* (pp. 213-244). New York: Harper & Row.

interexperience   The experiential relationship that goes on between people: "Your behavior and mine as I experience it, and your behavior and mine as you experience it"—that is, a statement that indicates that self exists only in relation to others.

Foley, V. (1974). *An introduction to family therapy.* New York: Grune & Stratton.
Laing, R. (1967). *The politics of experience.* New York: Ballantine.

interface   The area of contact between one system and another. An organizational system engages in numerous transactions at the interface, including the transfer of matter, energy, information, and people. Drawing the boundaries of a system is the first step in defining its structure. The next step usually entails defining the relationship of the elements to each other. Most frequently, the elements are grouped together in a hierarchical arrangement to be either subordinate or superordinate to each other. Accordingly, groups of related elements may be classified as subsystems or suprasystems. Face-to-face interaction by family members across the family system interface can be conceptualized as interaction between the system and its environment.

Example: As a distinct systemic entity, a family service agency must maintain some discontinuity from its external environment to continue to exist as a separate system. Its boundaries may be rigid and closed, not permitting any interaction between the elements inside and outside the system; or they may be flexible and open, permitting interaction with elements outside the system. In the case of the family, a boundary may be difficult to detect in terms of physical factors but may be observed more readily in terms of the discontinuity in pattern clusterings of family interactions.

Sauber, S. R. (1983). *The human services delivery system.* New York: Columbia University Press.

intergenerational family therapy   Therapy that attempts to rebind family loyalties and relationships between generations by using family conflict as a growth ingredient, rather than as an obstacle with grandparents, parents, and children.

Boszormenyi-Nagy, I., & Spark G. L. (1973). *Invisible loyalties: Reciprocity in intergenerational family therapy.* New York: Harper & Row.

intergenerational loyalties   The understructure of emotional commitments and obligations both to one's family of origin and to broader dynamics that cross several generations. *Vertical loyalties* are those imbedded in early childhood dependency and parental attachments. At marriage, these loyalties are rebalanced with new *horizontal loyalties* to an adult peer.

Boszormenyi-Nagy, I., & Spark, G. L. (1973). *Invisible loyalties: Reciprocity in intergenerational family therapy.* New York: Harper & Row.

interlocking jealousy patterns   A complex system of interlocking neurotic needs and attitudes that binds many pathological families. A system of mutual projection such as this is difficult to understand or treat in intrapsychic terms.

Example: A wife suspects her husband of being unfaithful. The husband feeds her suspicions by frequently going out without telling her where he is going, because she, too, is fanning his jealous suspicions by making secret telephone calls.

Boszormenyi-Nagy, I. (1965). A theory of relationships: Experience and transaction. In I. Boszormenyi-Nagy & J. Framo (Eds.), *Intensive family therapy: Theoretical and practical aspects* (pp. 33-86). New York: Harper & Row.

interlocking need template   A pattern of spouses locked into a tightly overritualized relationship in which each serves as the "monstrous" part of the other—that is, substitutive victimization.

Example: A wife who complains that her husband is not intimate enough covertly frustrates his attempts to get closer, while her obsession with his distance allows her to disown her role in the problem.

Boszormenyi-Nagy, I. (1962). The concept of schizophrenia from the point of view of family treatment. *Family Process, 1,* 103-113.
Boszormenyi-Nagy, I., & Ulrich, D. (1981). Contextual family therapy. In A. S. Gurman & D. P. Kniskern (Eds.), *Handbook of family therapy* (pp. 159-186). New York: Brunner/Mazel.

interlocking pathology   A situation in which all members of the family are locked together psychologically and one or more of its members are not individuating. In this type of family, there is no allowance for differentiations of self.

Example: A woman who acts hysterically marries a man with obsessive-compulsive features. The two form an interlocking system, in that one is undercontrolled emotionally, while the other is overcontrolled emotionally.

Ackerman, N. (1982). Interlocking pathologies. In D. Bloch & R. Simon (Eds.), *The strength of family therapy: Selected papers of Nathan W. Ackerman* (pp. 174-184). New York: Brunner/Mazel.
Bernard, C., & Corrales, R. (1979). *The theory and technique of family therapy.* Springfield, IL: Charles C Thomas.

interlocking racket system   A dysfunctional family in which awareness of each person's needs and desires is avoided or concealed and family problems are met with rigidity and manipulation. The dynamics of an interlocking racket system are illustrated as various family members attempt to live out their scripts. Each person influences and is influenced by the behavior of others in the family, and the members provide reinforcing experiences that confirm their script beliefs. In family therapy, the therapist watches for the transactions (or lack of appropriate transactions) that are script reinforcing for someone in the family.

Example: A wife exhibits long periods of silence without initiating contact with her husband. The husband interprets his wife's avoidance behavior as "there is something wrong with me." The husband then angrily defends himself against his wife and son. The wife withdraws further.

Erskine, R. G. (1982). Transactional analysis and family therapy. In A. M. Horne & M. M. Ohlsen (Eds.), *Family counseling and therapy* (pp. 245-275). Itasca, IL: F. E. Peacock.

internal frame of reference   The portion of experience that is available to the awareness of the individual at a given moment. The subjective internal frame of reference includes all sensations, perceptions, meanings, and memories available to consciousness.

Rogers, C. P. (1959). A theory of therapy, personality, and interpersonal relationships, as developed in the client-centered framework. In S. Koch (Ed.), *Psychology: A study of a science, Vol. III. Formulations of the person and the social context* (pp. 184-256). New York: McGraw-Hill.

Thayer, L. (1982). A person-centered approach to family therapy. In A. M. Horne & M. M. Ohlsen (Eds.), *Family counseling and therapy* (pp. 175-213). Itasca, IL: F. E. Peacock.

internalized family   A family characterized by a fearful, pessimistic, hostile, threatening view of the world, leading to a constant state of vigilance. Such a family has a well-defined role structure, high family loyalty, and a pseudomutual bond between the parents. Also called an *enmeshed family.*

Cuber, J., & Harroff, P. (1966). *Sex and the significant Americans.* New York: Penguin.

Glick, I. D., & Kessler, D. P. (1980). *Marital and family therapy* (2nd ed.). New York: Grune & Stratton.

internalizing disorders   Behavior disorders in children in which the psychopathology is internalized. These include behaviors that are over-controlled, inhibited, anxious, and withdrawn, and diagnosis categories such as depressive, avoidant, and overanxious disorders. Typically children with these orders suffer more than others in their environment as a result of their difficulties.

Breen, M. J., & Altepeter, T. S. (1990). *Disruptive behavior disorders in children.* New York: Guilford.

I

interpersonal competence   Effectiveness in interpersonal relationships based on (a) *self-acceptance,* the degree to which the individual has self-confidence; (b) *confirmation,* the result of others experiencing the person as that person experiences self, thus leading to self-confidence; and (c) *essentiality,* the use of one's central abilities and the expression of one's central needs, leading to commitment. These conditions facilitate the behaviors of owning up to or accepting responsibility for one's ideas and feelings; being open to the ideas and feelings of others and those from within one's self; experimenting with new ideas and feelings; and helping others own up to and be open and experiment with their ideas or feelings. Facilitation of these behaviors leads to individuality (rather than conformity), concern, and trust.

Argyris, C. (1970). *Intervention: Theory and method.* Reading, MA: Addison-Wesley.

interpersonal distance-sensitive family   A family characterized by extreme independence of each member because neither the outside world nor the family is trustworthy. Each problem situation is viewed by each member as an individual challenge to be mastered alone. Feedback from others is considered to be either irrelevant information or unsolicited criticism. Therefore decisions usually are reached in isolation from the other members. Some members maintain their isolation by making impulsive decisions based on insufficient information, while others remain steadfastly independent by collecting information indefinitely without taking a position.

Example: A family with three children ranging in age from 10 to 17 receives a cash windfall that allows the family to plan its first vacation in 2 years. When presented with the prospect of planning a joint vacation that all would enjoy, family members begin talking about how each would spend a proportion of the money. The subject thus shifts from selecting a family vacation to how to split the money equitably. The oldest child clings to her suggestion to split the money evenly among the five, while the parents consider a number of elaborate plans for dividing the money. Discussion of a family vacation is abandoned.

Reiss, D. (1981). *The family's construction of reality.* Cambridge, MA: Harvard University Press.

interpersonal perceptivity   The ability of an individual to guess, nonverbally and more or less accurately, the mood, attitude, and behavior of another individual.

Example: A mother notices her daughter withdrawing in her behavior after school. She knows her daughter must be feeling depressed again over a boy she has been dating.

Ferreira, A. (1964). Interpersonal perceptivity among family members. *American Journal of Orthopsychiatry, 34,* 64-70.
Riskin, J., & Faunce, E. (1972). An evaluative review of family interresearch. *Family Process, 11,* 365-455.

interruption   Breaking into the speech of another so that the interrupted statement is left incomplete.

Mishler, E., & Waxler, N. (1968). *Interaction in families: An experimental study of family processes and schizophrenia.* New York: John Wiley.
Riskin, J., & Faunce, E. (1972). An evaluative review of family interaction research. *Family Process, 11,* 365-455.

interspersal   Nonverbally emphasizing certain words, phrases, or sentences to make an indirect suggestion.

I

O'Hanlon, W. H., & Hexum, A. L. (1990). *An uncommon casebook: The complete clinical work of Milton H. Erickson, M.D.* New York: Norton.

intersubjective continuum   A dimension defined by extreme consensus and agreement among family members at one end and complete disagreement and inability to share one's viewpoint or perception of reality at the other end. At the first extreme, family agreement may rob the members of individual choices and freedom of choice. At the second extreme, individual perceptions are allowed as the only basis for a "right" choice for each individual. The first extreme tends to produce conformity, while the second tends to develop individuality.

Kantor, D., & Lehr, W. (1975). *Inside the family: Toward a theory of family process.* San Francisco: Jossey-Bass.
Reiss, D. (1981). *The family's construction of reality.* Cambridge, MA: Harvard University Press.

intersystems approach   An integrative approach to marital and family therapy that stresses the simultaneous integration of the individual, interactional, and intergenerational components of the client system. The therapist assesses the client from all three of these perspectives in developing a case formulation and then intervenes sequentially or concurrently at these levels. This approach is comprehensive, integrative, and designed to fit the therapy to the client, not the client to the therapy.

Weeks, G. (Ed.). (1989). *Treating couples: The intersystem model of the Marriage Council of Philadelphia.* New York: Brunner/Mazel.

intervention   The process of entering into an ongoing system of relationships between or among persons, groups, or objects for the purpose of helping them. An important implicit assumption is that the system exists independently of the intervener. One might wish to intervene for many reasons, ranging from helping the clients make their own decisions about the kind of help they need to coercing the clients to do what the intervener wishes them to do. Intervention acknowledges interdependencies between the intervener and the client system. It focuses on how to maintain or increase the client system's autonomy, how to differentiate more clearly the boundaries between the client system and the intervener, and how to conceptualize and define the client system's health independently of the intervener's. The client system is valued as an ongoing, self-responsible unit that has an obligation to be in control of its own destiny. An intervener, accordingly, assists the system to become more effective in problem solving, decision making, and decision implementation so that it can be increasingly effective in such activities and have a decreasing need for the intervener.

Argyris, C. (1970). *Intervention: Theory and method.* Reading, MA: Addison-Wesley.
Sauber, S. R. (1973). *Preventive educational intervention for mental health.* Cambridge, MA: Ballinger.

intimacy   Physical, intellectual, and emotional closeness and self-disclosure with another person (Sloan & L'Abate, 1985). Intimacy means sharing our hurts and our fears of being hurt, the expression of our vulnerabilities, fallibilities, frailties, and needs to the ones we love and who love us (L'Abate, 1977). From this definition derive three paradoxes: (a) We need to be separate as individuals before we can be close to another person, (b) we hurt mainly the ones we love because hurt and love are intertwined (we love others to the extent that we hurt when they hurt), and (c) we need to receive comfort from and give comfort to those whom we have hurt and who have hurt us (L'Abate & L'Abate, 1979). Our inability, sometimes our unwillingness, to be intimate appears to be a basic cause of marital and family dysfunctionality (L'Abate, Weeks, & Weeks, 1979). Jessee and L'Abate (1982, 1983) suggested that intimacy in a couple's relationship is an antidote for depression. The ability to be intimate requires a certain degree of self-good (each of us must have a self before we can share it with another self).

Example: The wife cries and blames the husband for her hurt ("It's all your fault!"). Typically the husband responds in anger or simply leaves the room. In this case, no intimacy can be achieved. In contrast, the wife cries but says, "I feel very bad right now, and I need you to be close to me and to comfort me." The husband hugs her and responds, "I cannot stand it when you cry and hurt, because when you hurt, I hurt, too." In this case, intimacy is achieved.

Jessee, E., & L'Abate, L. (1982). The paradoxes of depression. *International Journal of Family Psychiatry, 3,* 175-187.
Jessee, E., & L'Abate, L. (1983). Intimacy and marital depression: Interactional partners. *International Journal of Family Therapy, 9,* 39-53.
L'Abate, L. (1977). Intimacy is sharing hurt feelings: A reply to David Mace. *Journal of Marriage and Family Counseling, 3,* 13-16.
L'Abate, L., & L'Abate, B. (1979). The paradoxes of intimacy. *Family Therapy, 6,* 175-184.
L'Abate L., Weeks, G., & Weeks, K. (1979). Of scapegoats, strawmen, and scarecrows. *International Journal of Family Counseling, 1,* 86-96.
Sloan, S. Z., & L'Abate, L. (1985). Intimacy. In L. L'Abate (Ed.), *Handbook of family psychology and therapy* (Vol 1., pp. 405-427). Homewood, IL: Dow Jones-Irwin.

I

intrafamilial alignment   A concept describing the perception by two or more people that they are joined together in a common interest or bond and in that experience they have positive feelings toward one another. This term is used to describe shifts and sequences in a family.

Example: A father was the coach for his son's Little League team.

Wynne, L. (1961). The study of intrafamilial alignments and splits in exploratory family therapy. In N. W. Ackerman, F. L. Beatman, & S. N. Sherman (Eds.), *Exploring the base of family therapy* (pp. 95-115). New York: Family Services Association.

intrafamilial split   The perception by two or more people that they are in opposition to or have differences from each other with associated negative feelings. The alignments and splits within a social system define the emotional organization of the system.

Example: Sisters were 1 year apart in age, but they made it clear to everyone that they were far apart in personality and preferences.

Wynne, L. (1961). The study of intrafamilial alignments and splits in exploratory family therapy. In N. W. Ackerman, F. L. Beatman, & S. N. Sherman (Eds.), *Exploring the base of family therapy* (pp. 95-115). New York: Family Services Association.

introduction/motivation phase   The first phase in working with a family system. During this phase, the therapist is trying to induct the family into the therapeutic process and to motivate the members toward change through the use of techniques such as relabeling and reframing.

Alexander, J. (1988). Phases of family therapy process: A framework for clinicians and researchers. In L. Wynne (Ed.), *The state of the art in family therapy and research: Controversies and recommendations* (pp. 175-187). New York: Family Process Press.

introjection   A primitive form of identification by taking in aspects of other people that then become part of self-image.

Example: A young girl admired her teacher and began to imitate the teacher's mannerisms.

Nichols, M. (1984). *Family therapy: Concepts and methods.* New York: Gardner.

I

intrusion   The process by which a family member diffuses the boundaries of another family member and thereby incorporates the first member into the other's role and place in the family.

Examples: Often in a family consisting of a mother and a child, the two rely heavily on one another. The child often spends much more time with adults than with peers and often has an intense symbiotic relationship with the mother, in which the two respond as one. Another kind of intrusion may be observed in a dyad of one "competent" member and one "helpless" one. The competent member may be intrusive to "help," protect, and handle events for the "helpless" one.

Minuchin, S., & Fishman, H. (1981). *Family therapy techniques.* Cambridge, MA: Harvard University Press.

intrusiveness   Any act or series of acts that perforates or is allowed to perforate the emotional boundaries defining the relationships among family members.

Example: In a single-parent family, the oldest child is required or reinforced to fulfill a parental role. This role taking breaks down the necessary generational boundaries between parent and child. Incest is an extreme act of intrusion, physical or otherwise.

Riskin, M., & Faunce, E. (1970). Family interaction order: I. Theoretical framework and method. *Archives of General Psychiatry, 22,* 504-512.

intrusive symptoms   In the case of incest survivors, those individuals with severe memory deficits often describe almost complete amnesia of childhood yet report jarring, recurrent symptoms such as flashbacks and body sensations.

Example: One adult woman experienced feelings of fear when her partner began making love to her. She would physically close off from him by placing her arms over her torso in an effort to force him away.

Courtois, C. (1988). *Healing the incest wound.* New York: Norton.

invalidation   A coercive disqualification of a dependent person's state-ments, as when parents ignore those views of their child that threaten the parents' authority and positive self-image.

Example: Laing refers to the first schizophrenic patient in psychiatric literature whose major "feature" was a hatred of his father. The psychia-trist, Dr. Morrel, acting as the father's agent, managed to invalidate the man's hatred by declaring it to be a symptom of mental illness.

Laing, R. D. (1965). Mystification, confusion, and conflict. In I. Boszormenyi-Nagy & J. Framo (Eds.), *Intensive family therapy* (pp. 343-364). New York: Harper & Row.

I

invariant prescription   This prescription was developed by Mara Selvini Palazzoli (Selvini Palazzoli, Cirillo, Selvini, & Sorrentino, 1989) to break up repetitively resistant patterns in intact families where generational boundaries are either weak or inconsistently contradictory, producing one severely disturbed member among the children. It con-sists of having both parents leave the children with a baby-sitter sud-denly and without explanations for an evening out. On coming back, the parents are to give no information or explanation of why they left and what they did when they were gone. They are to record what questions the children ask in reaction to the sudden leaving and to bring their notes to the next therapy session. In addition to strengthening generational boundaries, this prescription may help increase bonds among the children.

Example: The Smiths call their baby-sitter ahead of time and warn her about what they are going to do the next time she is to baby-sit for them. She will be given a phone number of a relative or friend to call in case of emergency. However, she is to answer all questions from the children by disclaiming (correctly) any knowledge of the parents' whereabouts. Otherwise she is to follow the usual routine followed on previous baby-sitting occasions with the children.

Selvini Palazzoli, M., Cirillo, S., Selvini, M., & Sorrentino, A. M. (1989). *Family games: General models of psychotic processes in the family.* New York: Norton.

invasiveness   The disqualification of another's experience; invading another's personal life space by speaking for that person.
Example: A child who is angry is told by the mother, "You don't really feel that way."

Beavers, W. R. (1977). *Psychotherapy and growth: A family systems perspective.* New York: Brunner/Mazel.

inventory of marital conflict   The generation of marital interactions with an emphasis on differences and how they are handled. Each spouse is given a list of 18 short vignettes concerning various types of marital conflict, such as conflict concerning a wife's lateness for dinner engagements and conflict about sexual relationships. For each vignette, there are two possible ways of resolving the conflict, which the spouses are asked to either accept or reject. They also are asked, "Who is primarily responsible for the problem?" "Have you had a similar problem?" and "Have you known other couples who have similar problems?" After the spouses individually have completed their answer sheets, they are brought together and asked to discuss each conflict and to decide jointly who is responsible for the problem.

Olson, D., & Ryder, R. (1970). Inventory of Marital Conflicts (IMC): An experimental interaction procedure. *Journal of Marriage and the Family, 31,* 443-448.

invisible loyalty   (1) The ethical base of expectations, the central motivating factor in families, the commitments to one's parents, spouse, and children; (2) accountability with an action orientation; (3) a child's belief that the debt to the parents is endless and that its payment takes priority over every other human concern. To be this type of loyal member, a person has to internalize a spirit of expectation and to have a set of specifiable attitudes to comply with the internalized injunctions.
Example: A son's area of study and occupational choice are the same as his father's because the father was paying the boy's college tuition.

Boszormenyi-Nagy, I., & Spark, G. L. (1973). *Invisible loyalties: Reciprocity in intergenerational family therapy.* New York: Harper & Row.

involvement   The process of having all family members involved in the therapy, starting from the point of scheduling for the initial interview—for example, family members discussing available times, continuing during the treatment and termination phases. Each family member needs to attend and to contribute his or her thoughts, feelings, and opinions. All members have some role in planning the action the family takes.

Example: The major focus for several sessions with a family may be for an adolescent boy and his parents to learn to communicate more effectively about household chores. The therapist might express appreciation of the younger sister's presence because she may have some ideas about how her brother and parents can get along better. She may want to communicate better with all three herself, and she will surely not want agreements negotiated in her absence about household chores that may affect her role.

Nelsen, J. C. (1983). *Family therapy: An integrative approach.* Englewood Cliffs, NJ: Prentice-Hall.

involvement devoid of feeling   Intellectual interest among family members, but no emotional ties.

Example: A husband admires his wife's intellect but shows no interest in sharing an emotional life with her.

Epstein, N., & Bishop, D. (1981). Problem-centered systems therapy of the family. In A. S. Gurman & D. P. Kniskern (Eds.), *Handbook of family therapy* (pp. 444-482). New York: Brunner/Mazel.
Epstein, N. B., Bishop, D. S., & Levin, S. (1978). The McMaster model of family functioning. *Journal of Marriage and Family Counseling, 4,* 19-31.

"I" position   An individual takes a position based on his or her thinking, and his or her feelings, and maintains this position despite emotional pressure from others. Taking the "I" position promotes differentiation within the family system by taking action and repsonsibility for happiness and well-being instead of defining one's self in terms of others. See **differentiation.**

Bowen, M. (1966). The use of family theory in clinical practice. *Comprehensive Psychiatry, 7,* 345-374.
Bowen, M. (1978). *Family therapy in clinical practice.* New York: Jason Aronson.

"I" rule   A rule of self-expression holding that self-statements should begin with the pronoun *I*. I statements are expressions of self-responsibility. They are clear, are based on personal awareness, leave room for the awareness of others, and encourage the disclosure of differences.

Barth, L. G., & Huber, C. H. (1984). *An introduction to marital theory and therapy.* Belmont, CA: Brooks/Cole.

Miller, S., Nunnally, E. W., & Wackman, D. B. (1976). *Couple workbook: Increasing awareness and communication skills.* Minneapolis: Interpersonal Communication.

isomorphic transactions   Messages, given by one subsystem of the family to another, that are not structurally, but rather dynamically, equivalent. *Isomorphic* literally means "the same shape."

Example: A mother insists that her 18-year-old son not date and not learn to drive. She wants, effectively, to control his life. The sum of these messages is "Don't grow up." Although the messages are not structurally equal, they convey the same message.

Bateson, G. (1987). *Steps to an ecology of mind.* New York: Ballantine.

Minuchin, S., & Fishman, H. (1981). *Family therapy techniques.* Cambridge, MA: Harvard University Press.

isomorphism   The relationship of two complex structures when they are mapped onto each other in such a way that, for each part of one structure, there is a corresponding part in the other structure (*corresponding* means that the two parts play similar roles in their respective structures). The term as used in family therapy is derived from a more precise notion in mathematics. It is the perceptions of isomorphism that create meanings in the minds of people. The meaning of the therapy situation can be described as "change." In general, the change process can be seen to start with an "idea" ("news of a difference") that is a "result" of reframing or changing the contextual meanings of a set of concrete "facts."

Thus the concept of *isomorphism* as applied to family therapy is the ability of the treatment team to describe the family's patterns (A) in such a way that their reframed description (A_1) can serve as a guide for designing an intervention that can be mapped onto the pattern (A) the family has described and shown. The elements of the team's description must correspond with the elements of the family's description and the patterns it has shown to the team in the therapy sessions. Furthermore the team's description (A_1) must be from a different angle so that the family (at least potentially) can receive the news of a difference, a perceptual shift, that promotes change in the family patterns. The resultant behavior change creates a different subjective experience. This isomorphic description enables the therapy team to design isomorphic interventions, in particular the "compliment subset" of the intervention set of "compliment and clue."

Bateson, G. (1987). *Steps to an ecology of mind.* New York: Ballantine.

de Shazer, S. (1982). *Patterns of brief family therapy.* New York: Guilford.

joining The process of forming an alliance and working relationship between the therapist and each family member, leading to the development of the therapeutic system. It includes the many ways therapeutic contact is embraced, resisted, and reciprocated by the family as a unit and by the individual family members. The therapist's data and diagnoses are achieved experientially in the process of joining the family. "Diagnosis in family therapy is achieved through the interactional process of joining" (Minuchin, 1974, p. 130). The therapist joins primarily through contact with individual family members, not with some abstraction called the "system"; although some properties of the superordinate entity (e.g., mood, tempo, language) soon will emerge, these will influence the therapist's joining style. The process of contact and response to contact is inevitable because to join a family is, of necessity, to interfere with its life. Joining is an effort to cross the family-knit boundary, gaining a foothold wherever possible and seeking alliances with any subgroup willing to make one. Joining as a diagnostic strategy requires one to attempt an alteration of the family's rules and then to observe how the family reacts.

Example: Instead of contacting the mother directly, the therapist addresses all communications to the maternal grandmother. The therapist asks the grandmother to speak to the mother. If the therapist wants to restructure this arrangement, he or she can challenge the communication pathway and speak directly to the mother, perhaps asking her to give the history of a child's difficulty. The accommodation intervention would allow for one kind of joining—probably an alliance with the grandmother and a temporary estrangement from the mother. The restructuring intervention would promote an alliance with the mother. The examples in Figure 5 illustrate the use of structural mapping symbols

J

and the assumption that the therapist's experience of joining the family offers diagnostic information.

Minuchin, S. (1974). *Families and family therapy.* Cambridge, MA: Harvard University Press.
Umbarger, C. C. (1984). *Structural family therapy.* New York: Grune & Stratton.

Accommodation	**Restructuring**

Figure 5. Two Kinds of Therapeutic Joining With a Family

SOURCE: From *Structural Family Therapy* (p. 49) by C. C. Umbarger, 1984, New York: Grune & Stratton. Reprinted by permission.

joint custodial parents   Divorced parents who agree to establish a cooperative relationship with each other regarding the exercise of their continuing responsibilities as parents of their children. They accept that each has an equal right to determine and share in the children's upbringing, including their education, health care, and religious training. They agree that the children's living arrangements between the two parents shall be in the best interests of the children. Even though joint custody reflects a cooperative attitude on the part of both parents, specific living arrangements are included in the settlement agreement.

Coogler, O. J. (1978). *Structured mediation in divorce settlement.* Lexington, MA: Lexington.

joint process   A therapeutic arrangement in which all of those involved with the family problem are in the same room with the therapist to work on their relationships with mutual awareness, consent, and effort. See also **conjoint family therapy.**

Aponte, H., & van Deusen, J. (1981). Structural family therapy. In A. S. Gurman & D. P. Kniskern (Eds.), *Handbook of family therapy* (pp. 310-360). New York: Brunner/Mazel.

judgmental-dogmatic communication   Evaluative statements that pass judgments on such things as a person's character, activities, thoughts, motives, work, and ambitions. Typical statements include blaming, classifying things as good or bad, accusing, complaining, and being critical.

Alexander, J., Barton, C., Lindsey, D., Turner, C., & Warburton, J. (1988). Defensive and supportive communication interaction system. In D. Grotevant & C. Carlson (Eds.), *Handbook of family assessment* (pp. 182-187). New York: Guilford.

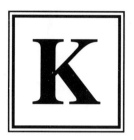

Kegel's exercises   Exercises developed by Kegel to strengthen muscu-
lature. These exercises have been used effectively in treatment programs
for inorgasmic women. The exercises consist of tightening and relaxing
the pubococcygeal muscle surrounding the vaginal outlet.

Kegel, A. H. (1952). Sexual functions of the pubococcygeal muscle. *Western Journal of
   Surgery, Obstetrics, and Gynecology, 60,* 521-524.
Kline-Graber, G., & Graber, B. (1978). Diagnosis and treatment procedures of pubococcygeal deficiencies in women. In J. LoPiccolo & L. LoPiccolo (Eds.), *Handbook of
   sex therapy* (pp. 227-240). New York: Plenum.

kinesics   The microstudy of human communication patterns and social
settings. Invented by Scheflen in the 1950s, videotapes were studied to
analyze family sessions as well as other behavior events.

Scheflen, A. E. (1960). Regression one-way relationships. *Psychiatric Quarterly, 23,*
   692-709.

kinship rating scheme   A scoring system for determining whether family members ascribe relationships to figures depicted on TAT cards. The
system includes six categories: (a) clearly defined nuclear family member, (b) vaguely mentioned nuclear family member, (c) extended family
member, (d) friend, business acquaintance, or social contact, (e) identified figure but with no specific role determination, and (f) total avoidance of a character never mentioned.

Goldstein, M., Gould, E., Alkire, A., Rodrick, E., & Judd, L. (1970). Interpersonal themes
   in the Thematic Apperception Test stories of families of disturbed adolescents.
   Journal of Nervous and Mental Disease, 100, 354-365.
Riskin, J., & Faunce, E. (1972). An evaluative review of family interaction research.
   Family Process, 11, 365-455.

K

K

labeling Attaching a linguistic symbol to a person's behavior. The label influences how the client behaves, as well as other people's perceptions of and reactions to the label bearer. Specific labels also have a way of generalizing to the whole person. In dysfunctional families, many labels are negative.

Example: A child who failed an exam labels herself a "failure" or calls herself "stupid."

Weeks, G., & L'Abate, L. (1982). *Paradoxical psychotherapy: Theory and practice with individuals, couples, and families.* New York: Brunner/Mazel.

lack of functional power A condition in which individuals are unable to exercise the force necessary to carry out the functions appropriate to themselves in the system in which they are operating.

Example: A mother is not able to carry out the executive function of directing her child's behavior. She fosters dependency by hindering the child from playing with friends, yet allows the child to stay up late with her.

Aponte, H., & van Deusen, J. (1981). Structural family therapy. In A. S. Gurman & D. P. Kniskern (Eds.), *Handbook of family therapy* (pp. 310-360). New York: Brunner/Mazel.

language muting The use of technical language to refer to traumatic events, particularly to sexually abusive experiences. The purpose is to avoid the emotional language associated with the trauma and, as such, to act as a defense against the reality of the event.

Courtois, C. (1988). *Healing the incest wound.* New York: Norton.

L

larger systems Viewing the family system in the context of the broader social context. Thus a truly "systemic" perspective looks at not only the family system but also all systems that affect the life of a family, including the school system, court system, church system, career system, mental health system, and hospital system. A systemic view also understands how these various systems interact with each other to produce and/or maintain an individual's behavior.

Imber-Black, E. (1988). *Families in larger systems.* New York: Guilford.

lateral coital position   A sexual position, used during sex therapy, in which the female assumes a superior (top) position, with her torso off to the side of her partner. This position gives the female pelvic freedom to move as needed. It allows the woman to tilt her pelvis to maximize clitoral stimulation.

Masters, W., & Johnson, V. (1970). *Human sexual inadequacy.* Boston: Little, Brown.

laughter   A spontaneous chuckle or explosive sound expressing a variety of emotions (e.g., joy, mirth, scorn). Laughter is used to express both positives and negatives. It can be used to disguise such feelings as anger, love, hostility, and shame; or it may reflect some general tension or anxiety. It may be a socially acceptable cloak for feelings that are unacceptable, or a mechanism for disguise.

Zuk, G. (1971). *Family therapy: A triadic-based approach.* New York: Behavioral Publications.

learning disability (LD)   A deficit in a learning process that causes children to achieve below expectation in school in the absence of any general intellectual deficit, emotional handicap, or inadequate opportunity to learn. A child with a learning disability exhibits a deficit in one more of the basic psychological processes involved in understanding or using spoken or written language. These deficits may be manifested by disorders of listening, thinking, talking, reading, writing, spelling, or arithmetic. The term *learning disability* is a generic term, as opposed to a specific diagnosis. The definition of *learning disability* is often defined by state law regarding placement of children in special education programs. A discrepancy between academic achievement and expected level of achievement based on age, grade, or IQ is required.

Example: A child receives a Full Scale IQ of 104 on the Wechsler Intelligence Scale for Children—Revised, and a Standard Score of 82 on the mathematics subtest of the Woodcock-Johnson Psychoeducational Battery—Revised. Because both assessment instruments have a mean of 100 and a standard deviation of 15, the child is considered to be achieving significantly less in mathematics than expected, based on his or her intelligence.

L

Taylor, H. G. (1988). Learning disabilities. In E. J. Mash & L. G. Terdel (Eds.), *Behavior assessment of childhood disorders* (2nd ed., pp. 402-450). New York: Guilford.

U.S. Office of Education. (1968). *First annual report. National advisory on handicapped children.* Washington, DC: U.S. Department of Health, Education and Welfare.

leaving the room An unexpected strategic action by the therapist to reduce escalating conflict. It is aimed at keeping spouses off balance and startling them into realizing how nonproductive their behavior has become. The action conveys a potent message to the sparring spouses; at the same time it serves as a self-preservation tactic for the mediator or therapist, who may welcome the short break from the argument.

Example: The therapist stands up and says to the couple: "I am not interested in hearing you two argue. That behavior is for the courtroom, not for mediation. Please continue your argument until you are finished. I will be in the waiting room. When you are done arguing and are ready to mediate, please let me know." The therapist then walks out of the room and closes the door. Usually, within 5 minutes or so, one of the spouses opens the door to announce that they have finished arguing and that they are ready to resume mediation.

Saposnek, D. T. (1983). Strategies in child custody mediation: A family systems approach. *Mediation Quarterly, 1,* 29-54.

ledger of merit and indebtedness An accumulation of the accounts of what has been given and what is owed in the family. The ledger has two ethical components. The first deals with the debts and entitlements dictated by legacy. These may vary greatly, even between two siblings (e.g., it may be imperative for the son to become a success, for the daughter to become a failure). According to the legacy of this family, the son may be entitled to approval, the daughter only to shame. Thus the legacy may fall with gross unfairness on the two. The second ethical component deals with the accumulation of merit through contributions to the welfare of the other. Thus "entitlement" may combine what is due as a parent or child and what one has come to merit. A natural mother who abandons her child may have earned no merit, yet the legacy of filial loyalty puts the child into a special ledger position vis-à-vis the mother, who still retains some entitlement.

Example: A woman took care of her sick mother during the latter's last few years. Now she expects her own daughter to take care of her whenever she is sick.

L.

Boszormenyi-Nagy, I., & Ulrich, D. (1981). Contextual family therapy. In A. S. Gurman and D. P. Kniskern (Eds.), *Handbook of family therapy* (pp. 159-186). New York: Brunner/Mazel.

legacy The specific configuration of expectations handed down from generation to generation. The legacy's origins are multigenerational.

Example: Women may be expected to be successes, while men may be expected to desert their families.

Boszormenyi-Nagy, I., & Spark G. L. (1973). *Invisible loyalties: Reciprocity in intergenerational family therapy.* New York: Harper & Row.
Boszormenyi-Nagy, I., & Ulrich D. (1981). Contextual family therapy. In A. S. Gurman and D. P. Kniskern (Eds.), *Handbook of family therapy* (pp. 159-186). New York: Brunner/Mazel.

lethal games A situation in which everyone agrees with everyone else, at the expense of one's own needs and satisfactions.

Satir, V. (1983). *Conjoint family therapy* (3rd ed.). Palo Alto, CA: Science & Behavior Books.

letter writing A therapeutic technique in which the client is instructed to write a letter to a family member even if that member is deceased. In the letter, the client expresses feelings about the relationship with that family member. The letter may be assigned as a project to be worked on daily over a week, or it may be written in one sitting. The act of writing can be so cathartic as to allow the past to be put to rest. The letter may or may not be mailed.

Example: A wife comes to therapy because of her preoccupation with what others think of her. When asked about her relationship with her parents, she says her parents never took her seriously and constantly belittled her, which has resulted in considerable resentment. The woman is instructed to write a letter to her parents in which she is to be completely honest about her feelings toward them. She is given the choice of mailing the letter or not. In the next session, the woman reports that although she decided not to mail the letter, writing it has allowed her to release a great deal of anger she felt toward her parents, resulting in a tremendous feeling of relief. As a result, she is able to develop a stronger sense of self-esteem, and her preoccupation with others' perceptions about her are diminished.

Anonymous. (1972). Toward the differentiation of the self in one's own family. In J. L. Framo (Ed.), *Family interactions* (pp. 111-173). New York: Springer.
Lange, A., & van der Hart, O. (1983). *Directive family therapy.* New York: Brunner/Mazel.

L

level of abstraction code A code used to measure the similarity of verbal information processing among family members.

Reiss, D. (1968). Individual thinking and family interaction: III. An experimental study of categorization performance in families of normals, those with character disorders, and schizophrenia. *Journal of Nervous and Mental Disease, 146,* 324-403.

Riskin, J., & Faunce, E. (1972). An evaluative review of family interaction research. *Family Process, 11*, 365-455.

levels of intervention Types of efforts to systematically introduce family change in individuals, social systems, populations, or networks of systems. The goal at each level is the improvement of the individual-family-environment fit. The family intervener is the person who assumes the greatest responsibility for initiating the change. The six levels of intervention are as follows:

1. *Individual interventions,* such as family life education and job training.
2. *Individual relocations,* such as placing a child in a foster home when her natural parents are incapable of caring for her.
3. *Population interventions,* the focus of which is to change, prepare, or provide added resources to a population that is or will be in an inharmonious relationship with its social systems. Prevention programs are good illustrations of this kind of intervention—that is, they try to prepare people for future crises, such as late-middle-aged people for retirement, or parents and children for initial entry of the child into school.
4. *Social systems interventions,* which influence the structure of the social system (e.g., rearranging the power hierarchy, changing the behavior of key personnel), rather than simply add new tasks or activities to the existing structure.
5. *Intersystem interventions,* such as intersystem assistance programs involving mothers with their children in the early stages of separation, on entering school, or on admission to a hospital; and intersystem coordination programs, such as suicide prevention centers or employment agency programs that are aimed at increasing employment opportunities for adolescents as a deterrent to juvenile delinquency.
6. *Family network interventions,* such as special reception systems for Vietnam immigrants to help them adapt to their new habitat.

Sauber, S. R. (1977). The human services delivery system. *International Journal of Mental Health, 5,* 121-140.
Sauber, S. R. (1983). *The human services delivery system.* New York: Columbia University Press.

life-style A personalized style of living that develops out of a person's special life plan and characterizes everything that person does. It refers to how the personality expresses itself in reaction to an external stimulus or to a stimulus that originates within the person.

Anshacher, H., & Anshacher R. (1956). *The individual psychology of Alfred Adler.* New York: Harper & Row.

L

likeness continuum A continuum displaying the process of dyadic differentiation and individuation of self or personality. The continuum encompasses ranges: symbiosis ("I am you"), sameness ("I am like you"), similarity ("I am almost [but not quite] like you"), differentness ("I am not like you"), oppositeness ("I am the opposite [or contrary] of you"), and autism or alienation ("I am not").

Example: A father and a son choose the same careers and share many personality characteristics and hobbies. They can be described as being like each other.

L'Abate, L. (1976). *Understanding and helping the individual in the family.* New York: Grune & Stratton.

limerence   An emotional state of intense arousal brought about by an association with a romantic love object. The limerence state is characterized by a set of features that include physiological changes, as well as subjective feelings. An individual experiencing limerence is obsessed with desire to be with the limerent object and is preoccupied with thoughts about that individual. Mood swings with respect to the state of the interpersonal relationship reflect changes in brain chemistry, as different neurotransmitters are produced in greater or lesser quantities. The limerent state lasts as long as there is instability in the relationship and is replaced by either long-term bonding or extinction of the feelings of attraction.

Example: A man meets a woman and is initially aroused by some aspect of her appearance or personality. Subsequent to the early encounters with her, he finds himself thinking more and more about her face, laugh, aroma, and other distinguishing characteristics that he believes are special about her. He counts the hours until he can see her again, and in her absence he desires to call and speak with her. Any indication that she is interested in him creates great euphoria, while her rejection of his attentions immediately causes unusual discomfort and even depression.

Silfen, R. (1980). *Biopsychology of love and lust.* Unpublished manuscript, New School for Social Research, New York.
Tennov, D. (1980). *Love and limerence: The experience of being in love.* New York: Stein & Day.

linear causality   A description of a part of a sequence that assumes one event or person causes another's behavior (A causes B). See also **circular causality.**

Watzlawick, P., Beavin, J. H., & Jackson, D. D. (1967). *Pragmatics of human communication.* New York: Norton.

L

linear statement   A straightforward, honest statement about a client's behavior that is accepted by the client at face value.

Weeks, G., & L'Abate, L. (1982). *Paradoxical psychotherapy: Theory and practice with individuals, couples, and families.* New York: Brunner/Mazel.

linguistic tyranny   A situation in which language locks a person into seeing reality in certain ways. Our language tends to be linear (simple cause-effect), digital (either/or), and content oriented (ignores nonverbal behavior), rather than process oriented.

Selvini Palazzoli, M., Boscolo, L., Cecchin, G., & Prata, G. (1978). *Paradox and counterparadox: A new model in the theory of the family in schizophrenic transaction.* New York: Jason Aronson.

Weeks, G., & L'Abate, L. (1982). *Paradoxical psychotherapy: Theory and practice with individuals, couples, and families.* New York: Brunner/Mazel.

linkage   A relationship that is considered to be temporary in its duration, usually less than 1 year in length. A link is the man and/or woman involved in a linkage relationship. In a linkage of one natural parent and one member not the biological parent, the child of the nonbiological parent is referred to as that parent's "linkette"; the child refers to the nonbiological parent as "Rex" for the man or "Regi" for the woman, both terms derived from the Latin translation for king and queen, respectively.

Examples: A man goes out of town on a 2-week business trip, and he and the woman in the link agree that they may engage in sexual relations with others until he returns from the trip. The man and the woman do not have open sexual relationships with others when their link is available to them. In another situation, a man or woman going through a postdivorce adjustment may have a convenient partner move in for social/sexual purposes. Finally a man and woman may have been linked for some time, intending to share their lives in the future, and they wish to have a "trial marriage," although their goal may not be to get married.

Sauber, S. R. (1988). *It's all in the name: A language guide for the single, his friends, and her family.* Hollywood, FL: Frederick Fell.

Sauber, S. R., & Weinstein, C. (1986). Terminology for male/female relationships for the 1980s. *Australian Journal of Sex, Marriage, and the Family, 7,* 99-108.

listening   A process that integrates physical, emotional, and intellectual inputs in a search for meaning and understanding. The listening process is more intricate and complicated than the physical process of hearing.

Example: A brother discerns and understands his sister's desire to buy something and gives her some money without question.

Gordon, T. (1982). *P. E. T. training in action.* New York: Bantam.

L

little princess/little man   Roles in a dysfunctional family in which a girl becomes Dad's little princess or a boy becomes Mom's little man. The child gets to be a "little spouse" to one of the parents. The child does not get to be a child, but rather is put into a position to meet the needs of an adult who is too dysfunctional to get his or her needs met by another adult.

Friel, J., & Friel, L. (1988). *Adult children: The secrets of dysfunctional families*. Deerfield Beach, FL: Health Communications.

live supervision   A method of education and training in which a family therapist sees a family, and the supervisor watches the session either on a television monitor or behind a one-way mirror. The supervisor or supervisory team made up of supervisors and colleagues offers feedback and guidance to the therapist during the therapy session by a "bug-in-the-ear" (earphone), telephone, or discussion with the therapist by asking the therapist to leave the consultation room. See also **reflecting team.**

Haley, J. (1987). *Problem-solving therapy* (2nd ed.). San Francisco: Jossey-Bass.
Montalvo, B. (1973). Aspects of live supervision. *Family Process, 12,* 343-359.

lockage   A committed relationship between a man and a woman, as in marriage. The man and the woman may or may not have children as a result of their relationship. The two reside together, making a commitment similar to that of marriage in that there is an intention of a permanent "lock" in which the man and the woman generally have been linked beyond 1 year in duration. A "lock" is the man and/or woman who is involved in a lockage relationship. In a lockage of one natural parent and one member not the biological parent, the child of the nonbiological parent is referred to as that parent's "lockette"; the child refers to the nonbiological parent as "Rex" for the man or "Regi" for the woman, terms derived from the Latin translation for king and queen, respectively.

Sauber, S. R. (1988). *It's all in the name: A language guide for the single, his friends, and her family*. Hollywood, FL: Frederick Fell.
Sauber, S. R., & Weinstein, C. (1986). Terminology for male/female relationships for the 1980s. *Australian Journal of Sex, Marriage, and the Family, 7,* 99-108.

locus   The system or person for whom a problem is currently an issue. The locus excludes the generating structure of the problem as it first occurred and focuses only on the here and now.

Example: The parents are locked in conflict. They have a son who is now old enough to understand their problem. The son decides always to side with his mother, which, in turn, makes the problem worse. The locus of the current problem is now three people.

Aponte, H., & van Deusen, J. (1981). Structural family therapy. In A. S. Gurman & D. P. Kniskern (Eds.), *Handbook of family therapy* (pp. 310-360). New York: Brunner/Mazel.

L

long-brief therapy Therapy consisting of a small number of sessions stretched over a long period of time.

Selvini Palazzoli, M. (1980). Why a long interval between sessions? In M. Andolfi & I. Zwerling (Eds.), *Dimensions of family therapy* (pp. 161-170). New York: Guilford.

lost child A dysfunctional role in the family also known as the *loner*. The lost child deals with family dysfunction by escaping. However, his or her leaving the family by escape often takes care of the family's needs for separateness and autonomy. Such a child may stay in his or her room a lot or move to a distant place.

Friel, J., & Friel, L. (1988). *Adult children: The secrets of dysfunctional families.* Deerfield Beach, FL: Health Communications.

low sexual desire A subjective complaint about the absence of sexual feelings, voiced by one or both partners and indicating unsatisfactory individual coordination and/or interpersonal synchronization. This definition emphasizes subjective dissatisfaction and an imbalance in sexual interaction. It generally indicates more complex interpersonal dissatisfaction for the couple.

Verhulst, J., & Heiman, J. (1988). A systems perspective on sexual desire. In S. Leiblum & R. Rosen (Eds.), *Sexual desire disorders* (pp. 243-270). New York: Guilford.

loyalty binding The act of inducing excessive breakaway guilt in the bound person and turning that person into a lifelong, self-sacrificing member of the relationship system.
Example: Every time a young adult son tries to learn how to lead his own life, his parents induce guilt in him by acting depressed over his gestures toward leaving.

Stierlin, H. (1974). *Separating parents and adolescents: A perspective on running away, schizophrenia and waywardness.* New York: Quadrangle.

loyalty system A powerful force operating on the behavior of individuals in a family, characterized as an uninterrupted bookkeeping of obligations through the generations, with alternating positive and negative balances.
Example: A showing of concern and caring adds to the positive balance, and any form of exploitation depletes it in marital or family relationships.

L

Boszormenyi-Nagy, I., & Framo, J. (Eds.). (1965). *Intensive family therapy: Theoretical and practical aspects.* New York: Harper & Row.

L

machismo In a very restricted sense, sexual prowess and aggressive behavior, equated with maleness; in a general sense, an ethos comprising traits and behaviors prized by and expected of men in Latin countries. The term is derived from *macho,* meaning "male." Machismo is the fusion of two distinct elements—sexism and self-respect (*respeto*); the former is "destructive and reactionary," and the latter is "benign and progressive." Among the macho ideals are courage, fearlessness, pride, honor, charisma, and the ability to be a leader of men. Whereas macho ideals are highly valued among Latin men, they frequently are ascribed negative values by others.

Example: If a man works and provides for his family, is a good role model for his children, protects and defends his family's interests, and keeps his feelings to himself, he is a "man." By fulfilling his part of the bargain, he is entitled to respect and obedience from his family and the right to do as he pleases. Correspondingly failure to fulfill his contract implies that he has failed as a man and as a person. Dignity and self-respect, so important in Hispanic culture, are lost if he becomes dependent on his wife's earnings or on social service payments for support.

Panitz, D. R., McChonchie, R. D., Sauber, S. R., & Fonseca, J. A. (1983). The role of machismo and the Hispanic family in the etiology and treatment of alcoholism in Hispanic American males. *American Journal of Family Therapy, 11,* 31-44.

madness mission Recruitment of a child to embody and externalize the parent's feelings of badness or craziness. The parent seeks the embodiment of those feelings in the child.

Example: A father feels trapped and angry in his marriage but cannot admit these feelings to himself. He fears what might happen to the

M

marriage if he lets the feelings out. His teenage son begins to get into trouble at school and with other boys on the weekend. The son is on a mission to act out his father's unacceptable feelings.

Stierlin, H. (1974). *Separating parents and adolescents: A perspective on running away, schizophrenia and waywardness.* New York: Quadrangle.

Madonna-prostitute theme   The traditional view of sex roles that dictates that males can be sexually permissive, while socially acceptable females cannot. This view leads to a perceived distinction between "good girls" (Madonnas) and "bad girls" (prostitutes). No such sexual distinction is perceived for men.

Abse, D. W., Nash, E. M., & Louden, L. M. R. (1974). Marital and sexual counseling in medical practice (2nd ed.). Hagerstown, MD: Harper & Row.
Leiblum, S., & Pervin, L. (1980). *Principles and practice of sex therapy.* New York: Guilford.

magnetic field   A field of psychological force in which, if a child is too close to the mother, the child is suddenly "pulled into the mother" and loses his or her own identity; if the child is too far away from the mother, he or she develops no self at all.

Example: A 15-year-old son, while still at home, uses denial and isolation to escape his mother. He experiences helplessness after he fails to function without his mother.

Bowen, M. (1978). *Family therapy in clinical practice.* New York: Jason Aronson.

maintenance   As a therapeutic technique, the therapist accommodates to the family to support the current family structure.

Example: The mother asks as the spokesperson for the family. The therapist then addresses all questions to her, thus maintaining and accommodating to the system's structure. See **accommodation** and **joining.**

Minuchin, S. (1974). *Families and family therapy.* Cambridge, MA: Harvard University Press.

male bridge maneuver   A treatment for retarded ejaculation in which, after the female manipulates her partner nearly to orgasm, she executes rapid intromission.

Masters, W., & Johnson, V. (1970). *Human sexual inadequacy.* Boston: Little, Brown.

male climacteric   The idea of a precipitous decline of testosterone levels to a loss of libido in middle-aged and elderly men. This concept is not supported by research. Instead there is a gradual decline of libido.

Seagraves, R. (1988). Drugs and desire. In S. Leiblum & R. Rosen (Eds.), *Sexual desire disorders* (pp. 313-347). New York: Guilford.

M

male sexual dysfunction A male sexual disorder that can be subdivided into erectile failure, retarded ejaculation, premature ejaculation, and dyspareunia. *Erectile failure* (termed *impotence* in the past) refers to the inability of the male to achieve or maintain an erection, and thus he is unable to engage in satisfactory intercourse. *Retarded ejaculation (RE),* also termed *ejaculatory incompetence* or *ejaculative impotence,* is a disorder in which the male suffers from delayed intravaginal ejaculation or the inability to ejaculate intravaginally. *Premature ejaculation (PE)* is topographically the opposite of RE: The patient suffering from PE ejaculates prior to or soon after inserting his penis into his partner's vagina. *Dyspareunia,* or painful intercourse, may be caused by organic factors.

LoPiccolo, J., & LoPiccolo, L., (Eds.). (1978). *Handbook of sex therapy.* New York: Plenum.

maneuverability The therapist's ability to take action despite obstacles and restrictions. As therapy progresses, the therapist may need to shift from one approach to another.
Example: The therapist begins by using a particular technique or approach but discovers it is not going to work. The therapist must be able to shift freely to another strategy.

Fisch, R., Weakland, J., & Segal, L. (1982). *Doing therapy briefly.* San Francisco: Jossey-Bass.

manipulation The act of successfully generating social reinforcement for one's maladaptive behavior. Individuals using manipulation get the message that, as long as they produce undesirable behaviors, others will show interest and concern. Manipulation may be a conscious or unconscious act.

Liberman, R. (1972). Behavioral approaches to family and couple therapy. In G. D. Erickson & T. P. Hogan (Eds.), *Family therapy: An introduction to theory and technique* (pp. 120-134). Belmont, CA: Wadsworth.

mapping strategy A technique that graphically describes how the family system is organized and which particular subunit is most involved in a problem. Structural maps are useful in helping to organize family process data into elementary guesses about the structural features of the family. The maps should be revised or discarded quickly as new data appear.
Example: The map in Figure 6 shows "an open-family-unit boundary, enclosing a parental subsystem characterized by the mother's overinvolvement with her own mother, who in turn is in conflict with her daughter's husband, perhaps related to the diffuse tie between the

M

spouses. The map also shows a normal open boundary between parents and children" (Umbarger, 1984, p. 37).

Umbarger, C. C. (1984). *Structural family therapy.* New York: Grune & Stratton.

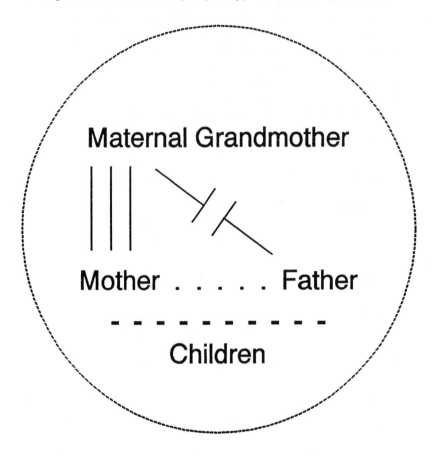

Figure 6. Structural Map of a Family
SOURCE: From *Structural Family Therapy* (p. 37) by C. C. Umbarger, 1984, New York: Grune & Stratton. Reprinted by permission.

marathon sex therapy   Sex therapy combined with the use of group modalities, conducted during an extended period of time without interruption.
   Example: A couple chose to experience continuous treatment for 2 days, rather than hourly sessions once a week for 2 months.

Kaplan, H. S. (1981). *The new sex therapy.* New York: Brunner/Mazel.

M

marital behavior modification   A therapeutic approach that employs social learning principles and operant conditioning with couples. Treatment is based on the assumption that each partner does not know how to produce enough rewarding behavior to gratify the other. See also **behavioral marital therapy.**

Liberman, R. (1970). Behavioral approaches in family and couple therapy. *American Journal of Orthopsychiatry, 40,* 106-118.

marital coalition   The interactional pattern that spouses initially evolve for their mutual needs and satisfaction. Later, in the evolving structure and the dynamics of the family, this coalition must serve the age-appropriate needs of the children and still maintain an area of exclusive relationship and mutuality between the parents.
Example: Parents form a sexual relationship that is exclusive of their relationship with their children.

Meck, S. (1972). An approach to family pathology. In G. D. Erickson & T. P. Hogan (Eds.), *Family therapy: An introduction to theory and technique* (pp. 103-119). Belmont, CA: Wadsworth.

marital contract   Spousal agreement as to each spouse's expressed and unexpressed, conscious and unconscious expectations of that spouse's obligations within the marital relationship and the benefits the spouse expects to derive in exchange. In therapy, an explicit contract is worked out.
Example: A wife says to her husband, "I will allow you to engage in activities that I personally dislike—religious, spiritual, and so on—and you will not complain when I engage in activities you don't like."

Sager, C. J. (1976). *Marriage contracts and couple therapy.* New York: Brunner/Mazel.

marital dyad   A relationship composed of a husband and a wife.

Glick, I. D., & Kessler, D. P. (1980). *Marital and family therapy* (2nd ed.). New York: Grune & Stratton.

marital endogamy   The selection of marriage partners within one's own social group.

Eshleman, J. R. (1974). *The family: An introduction.* Boston: Allyn & Bacon.

marital enrichment group   A therapeutic group designed to increase awareness and communication of the positive aspects in a marital relationship by use of a highly structured sequence of group procedures requiring a brief number of sessions. The group is developmental and preventive in nature. A marital enrichment group may be described as a

M

"growth experience"; that is, the group procedures are not intended primarily to help couples resolve problems. Therefore couples who are seeking marriage counseling or psychotherapy are discouraged from participating. However, husbands and wives who are concurrently in therapy may well find additional value in participating in a marital enrichment group.

Clarke, C. (1970). Group procedures for increasing positive feedback between married partners. *Family Coordinator, 19,* 324-328.

L'Abate, L., & Sloan, S. (1984). A workshop format to facilitate intimacy in married couples. *Family Relations, 33,* 245-250.

Sauber, S. R. (1974). Primary prevention and the marital enrichment group. *Journal of Family Counseling, 12,* 39-44.

marital group therapy   Therapy in which the husband and the wife are treated in a group with other couples.

Lebedun, M. (1970). Measuring movement in group marital counseling. *Social Case Work, 51,* 35-43.

marital maladjustment   *Marital maladjustment* may be the failure of the marital partners to prepare themselves adequately before marriage to cope with the current demands and the varied responsibilities they are assuming. *Marital discontent* is the difference between what couples want, what they expect, and what they get. The conventional concept of an innocent and a guilty party with relationship problems—the white sheep and the black sheep—does not stand up under close scrutiny. When marriage fails, it is usually because both spouses make mistakes, and the husband and the wife are caught in an emotional deadlock of circularity.

Real *incompatibilities* may be defined as those situations or conditions in which a marriage therapist literally cannot bring about any sort of change through acceptance, compromise, negotiation, or improved insight and communication. In such situations, there may be (a) wide differences in intelligence that lead to different tastes, interests, and ways of thinking; (b) wide differences in education that lead to feelings of growing apart; (c) wide differences in age, to the extent that they may affect habits, sex drives, choice of friends, and activities; and (d) physical disabilities of one partner that restrict that partner's activities, partially or completely, in one or more areas. In contrast, neurotic conflicts are subject to change through insight and therapy. These conflicts cause intelligent people to behave in confused, irrational, hostile, and marriage-defeating ways toward each other. The neurotic interactions block each other's needs for love and intimacy.

Example: A man gets married, expecting his spouse to love and respect him unconditionally, no matter how stupidly, boringly, or annoyingly he

M

behaves. If his wife does not respond to him with endless love in all of these situations, he decides that his wife does not love him at all.

Sauber, S. R. (1972). *An honest guide to marriage counseling.* West Palm Beach, FL: Mental Health Association Press.

marital quality The subjective evaluation of a married couple's relationship on a number of dimensions and evaluations. The range of evaluations constitutes a continuum reflecting numerous characteristics of marital interaction and functioning. High marital quality is associated with good adjustment, adequate communication, a high level of marital happiness, integration, and a high degree of satisfaction with the relationship. Marital quality is not a fixed picture of discrete categories (a high- vs. low-quality marriage), but rather a gradation of elements on a continuum ranging from high to low. See Figure 7.

Lewis, R. A., & Spanier, G. B. (1979). Theorizing about the quality and stability of marriage. In N. R. Burr, R. Hill, F. I. Nye, & I. L. Reiss (Eds.), *Contemporary theories about the family* (Vol. 2, pp. 268-291). New York: Free Press.
Spanier, G. B., & Lewis, R. A. (1980). Marital quality: A review of the seventies. *Journal of Marriage and the Family, 42,* 825-839.

marital quid pro quo (1) A contract in which spousal behavior changes are cross-linked; the contract is devised so that if one spouse engages in the desired behavior, the other spouse also will change in the requested manner. (2) A metaphorical statement of the marital relationship—that is, how the couple have agreed to define themselves within the relationship.

Example: Tom wants Megan to figure the household budget, and Megan wants Tom to play cards with her. A quid pro quo contract might be written as (a) If Megan figures the household budget, then Tom will play cards with her for 1 hour or (b) If Tom plays cards with Megan for 1 hour, then Megan will figure the household budget. The spouses' behavior changes are dependent on one another. If the first spouse does not honor the first part of the contract, the second spouse is under no obligation to change.

Jackson, D. (1965). Family rules: The marital quid pro quo. *Archives of General Psychiatry, 12,* 589-594.
Lederer, W., & Jackson, D. (1968). *The mirages of marriage.* New York: Norton.

marital satisfaction A state of satisfaction with one's marriage, defined by an intrapersonal conceptualization (subjectively experienced reaction) or an interpersonal conceptualization (marital satisfaction as the congruence between one's expectations and another's behavior). The focus of marital satisfaction may be satisfaction with leisure, decision making, income, life-style, communication, sex, or friends.

M

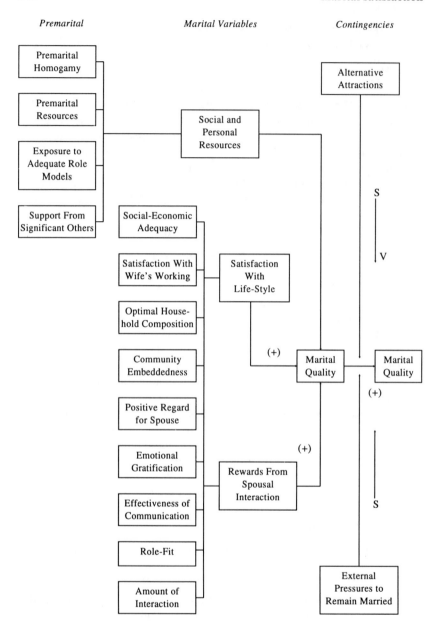

Figure 7. Graphic Depiction of Marital Quality

SOURCE: From "Theorizing About the Quality and Stability of Marriage" by R. A. Lewis & G. B. Spanier, 1979, in *Contemporary Theories About the Family* (Vol. 2) by N. R. Burr, R. Hill, F. I. Nye, & I. L. Reiss (Eds.), p. 239, New York: Free Press. Reprinted by permission.

M

Spanier, G. B., & Lewis R. A. (1980). Marital quality: A review of the seventies. *Journal of Marriage and the Family, 42,* 825-839.

marital schism/skew   A mutual failure of the marital partners to meet each other's deep dynamic needs. A *marital schism* refers to the division of the family into two antagonistic and competing factions. A *marital skew* exists when one partner dominates the family to a striking degree. The two terms characterize the disturbed marital relationship in schizophrenic families.

   Example: A family with a marital schism has the father and son aligned against the mother and daughter over household responsibilities.

Lidz, T., Cornelison, A., Fleck, S., & Terry, D. (1957). Schism and skew in families of schizophrenics. *American Journal of Psychiatry, 114,* 241-248.

marital sociogram   A device employing nonverbal methodologies to depict each spouse's experience of self in relation to the other in the relationship. The device demonstrates for the therapeutic system the amount of distance (symbolic of emotional distance) each spouse desires in the relationship.

   Example: One spouse is placed in a specific location and is instructed to remain stationary. The other spouse is placed directly across from the first and is told to move slowly toward the other until a comfortable distance is found.

Bernard, C., & Corrales, R. (1979). *The theory and technique of family therapy.* Springfield, IL: Charles C Thomas.

marital stability   (1) How long a couple remains married. (2) A state conceptualized as a function of the comparison between one's marital expectations and one's marital outcomes. Marital stability may be a function of the comparison between one's best available marital outcomes. An exchange typology of marital quality and stability is shown in Figure 8.

Spanier, G. B., & Lewis, R. A. (1980). Marital quality: A review of the seventies. *Journal of Marriage and the Family, 42,* 825-839.

marital therapy   A therapeutic approach in which the focus is on the marital relationship (the interactions and transactions that take place), in addition to the intrapsychic forces within the individual. Marital therapy usually involves the therapist meeting with the two spouses conjointly. See also **marriage counseling.**

Haley, J. (1963). Marriage therapy. *Archives of General Psychiatry, 8,* 213-234.

marking boundaries   A restructuring operation aimed at attaining clear boundaries. This procedure may include delineating individual boundaries,

M

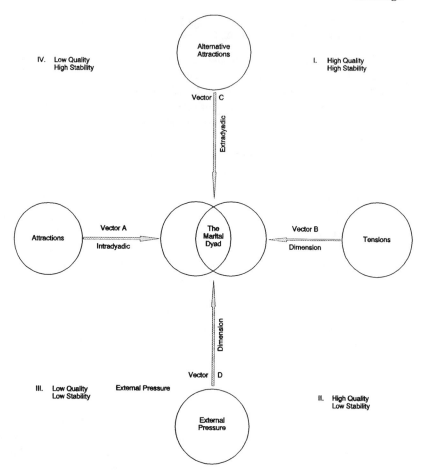

Figure 8. An Exchange Typology of Marital Quality and Stability

SOURCE: From "Marital Quality: A Review of the Seventies" by G. B. Spanier & R. A. Lewis, 1980, *Journal of Marriage and the Family, 42,* p. 833. Reprinted by permission.

strengthening subsystem boundaries, or increasing closeness or distance between family members.

Minuchin, S. (1974). *Families and family therapy.* Cambridge, MA: Harvard University Press.

marriage   A complex of customs centering on the relationship between a sexually associating pair of adults within the family. Marriage defines the manner of establishing and terminating such a relationship, the normative behavior and reciprocal obligations within it, and the locally accepted restrictions on the spouses.

Murdock, G. (1949). *Social structure.* New York: Macmillan.

marriage ability   The ability of individuals to engage in and maintain intimate relationships with their spouses on a scale ranging from high to low. As with terms such as *musical ability* and *athletic ability,* some individuals have the natural talent, some individuals can be trained to develop this ability, and some individuals will never learn to play the piano or throw a ball. Marriage may not be for everyone. Those with low marriage ability should consider singlehood. The variables comprising marriage ability, for example, include the desire to share one's time and interests versus the "loner"; the willingness to make a commitment to another person, which requires a long-term interdependence, versus "doing your thing" on a short-term basis; and assuming the responsibility to understand and express consideration for your partner versus being egocentric.

Sauber, S. R. (1972). *An honest guide to marriage counseling.* West Palm Beach, FL: Mental Health Association Press.

marriage counseling   The process whereby, within the context of an understanding and accepting face-to-face relationship, professional skills and experience are made available to spouses as they explore, evaluate, and clarify feelings and issues; as they seek to communicate verbally and emotionally; and as they learn to choose courses of action that will lead to some resolution of their problems. The goal of marriage counseling is the optimal development of the individual's potentialities and the enhancement of the marriage relationship. Its approaches include:

Individual: Only one mate participates in counseling.

Concurrent: Both the husband and the wife participate in counseling, but each spouse has separate sessions.

Conjoint: Both partners participate together in counseling.

Group: Counseling takes place when either a single mate joins a single mate's group or both mates join a couples group.

Combined: A combination of several of the above methods.

See also **marital therapy.**

L'Abate, L., & McHenry, S. (1983). *Handbook of marital interventions.* New York: Grune & Stratton.

Sauber, S. R. (1972). *An honest guide to marriage counseling.* West Palm Beach, FL: Mental Health Association Press.

M

martyr complex   A pattern of behavior in which the individual constantly communicates verbal or nonverbal messages designed to induce self-guilt.

Example: A woman says she does not mind doing things for another but, each time she is asked to do something, she responds in a tone of voice that says she does not want to do it.

Wahlroos, S. (1974). *Family communication: A guide to emotional health.* New York: Macmillan.

mascot   A dysfunctional role in the family in which the individual assuming the role provides humor and comic relief for the family. The mascot often gives the family a sense of fun and playfulness. The difficulty for the family is that this behavior allows the family to be distracted from emotional issues, and thus emotional issues are never dealt with. The difficulty for the mascot is that his or her negative feelings are never expressed.

Example: Every time the mother and the father begin an argument, the teenage son tells a funny story or joke.

Friel, J., & Friel, L. (1988) *Adult children: The secrets of dysfunctional families.* Deerfield Beach, FL: Health Communications.

masked sexual deviation   A covered-up sexual deviation in a relationship. In sex therapy, this phenomenon may lead to a loss of desire for one partner.

Example: A man exhibited less and less desire for his wife. He had not revealed his transvestism. Had he been able to cross-dress during sex, his level of desire would have been driven by his fetish.

LoPiccolo, J., & Friedman, J. (1988). Broad-spectrum treatment of low sexual desire. In S. Leiblum & R. Rosen (Eds.), *Sexual desire disorders* (pp. 107-144). New York: Guilford.

master control room technique   A hypnotherapeutic technique in which the individual is asked to enter the sexual center in the hypothalamus. A dial is visualized that sets the level of sexual arousal. The person learns to manipulate the dial to increase arousal.

Araoz, D. L. (1982). *Hypnosis and sex therapy.* New York: Brunner/Mazel.
Zilbergeld, B., & Hammond, D. (1988). The use of hypnosis in treating sexual disorders. In S. Leiblum & R. Rosen (Eds.), *Sexual desire disorders* (pp. 192-223). New York: Guilford.

masturbation   Self-stimulation and/or manipulation of the genital area, engaged in as a sexual outlet.

Masters, W., & Johnson, V. (1970). *Human sexual inadequacy.* Boston: Little, Brown.

M

masturbation therapy The treatment of erectile failure, premature ejaculation, retarded ejaculation, frigidity, general sexual dysfunction, primary orgasmic dysfunction, or secondary orgasmic dysfunction through masturbation techniques.

LoPiccolo, J., & LoPiccolo, L. (Eds.). (1978). *Handbook of sex therapy.* New York: Plenum.

material reinforcers Items such as stars, points, tokens, or money that are used to reward desirable behavior patterns.

Example: When Rajiv brings home a paper with a score above a certain point, he is awarded stars on a chart that he can display to the whole family.

LeBow, M. (1972). Behavior modification for the family. In G. D. Erickson & T. P. Hogan (Eds.), *Family therapy: An introduction to theory and technique* (pp. 347-376). Belmont, CA: Wadsworth.

mate selection The process by which people choose a partner for marriage. This process involves conscious, unconscious, sociological, and ecological factors.

Framo, J. L. (1982). *Explorations in marital and family therapy. Selected papers of James L. Framo.* New York: Springer.
Winch, R. (1954). The theory of complementary need in mate selection: An analytic and descriptive study. *American Sociological Review, 19,* 241-249.

matriarchy A family system in which authority is based on a female as the head of the family.

Christensen, H. (1964). Development of the family field of study. In H. T. Christensen (Ed.), *Handbook of marriage and the family* (pp. 3-32). Chicago: Rand McNally.

matrilocal residence A rule of residence requiring that a woman live with her mother and bring her husband to her mother's home to live.

Zelditch, M. (1964). Cross-cultural analyses of family structure. In H. T. Christensen (Ed.), *Handbook of marriage and the family* (pp. 462-500). Chicago: Rand McNally.

matrix of identity The sense of belonging that comes with a child's accommodation to the groups within the family and with the child's assumption of the transactional patterns that form the family structure. Families mold and program the child's sense of identity early in the socialization process. The matrix of identity develops through participation in different family subsystems in different contexts, as well as through participation in extrafamilial groups. The family, then, is the matrix of its members' sense of identity—of belonging and of being

M

different. Its chief task is to foster its members' psychosocial growth and well-being throughout their lives in common.

Minuchin, S. (1974). *Families and family therapy.* Cambridge, MA: Harvard University Press.

maturation   The state in which human beings are responsible and fully in charge of themselves. Mature people are able to make choices and decisions based on accurate perceptions about themselves, about others, and about the contexts in which they find themselves. They acknowledge those choices and decisions as their own, and they accept responsibility for their outcomes.

Satir, V. (1983). *Conjoint family therapy* (3rd ed.). Palo Alto, CA: Science & Behavior Books.

MBD   See **minimal brain damage** and **minimal brain dysfunction.**

mediation   The process by which disputants attempt to reach a consensual settlement of the issues in dispute, with the assistance and facilitation of a neutral resource person or persons. At minimum, the process consists of systematically isolating points of agreement and disagreement, developing options, and considering accommodations. Generically mediation is a goal-directed, problem-solving intervention. The goal is to help the parties resolve their dispute and reduce the conflict between them. Even if all elements of the dispute cannot be resolved, the conflict may be reduced to a manageable level. However, resolution of the dispute does not always eliminate the conflict. Thus some refer to mediation as a process, not of dispute resolution, but of conflict management. Mediation is also a time-limited process. It emphasizes the present and the future, not the past. Crisis and short-term therapies share some of mediation's parameters, but they differ from mediation in their goals, tasks, and issues and in the way each commences. To reach a negotiated settlement, the clients and the mediator must deal throughout the process with tasks that are concrete, and their focus must be predominantly on external data and issues, not on internal psychological reactions.

Example: To identify and seek values for their separate and common assets and liabilities, married couples must focus on the important changes they desire in life insurance policies or titles of jointly held property. If they have children, they need to develop workable plans for postdivorce parenting that will meet the needs of each family member. If they value college education for their children, they will have to develop methods of financing that education.

Kelly, J. B. (1983). Mediation and psychotherapy: Distinguishing the differences. *Mediation Quarterly, 1,* 33-44.
Sauber, S. R., Beiner, S. F., & Meddoff, G. S. (in press). Divorce mediation: A new system for dealing with the family in transition. In R. H. Miskesell, D. D. Lusterman, & S.

M

H. McDaniel (Eds.), *Family psychology and systems therapy: A handbook.* Washington, DC: American Psychological Association.

Mental Research Institute   A family therapy institute in Palo Alto, California. It grew out of the work in the early 1950s of Gregory Bateson, Jay Haley, Williams Fry, John Weakland, and Don D. Jackson. Originally this group of researchers was at the Palo Alto Veterans Administration Hospital and developed the double-bind therapy of schizophrenia. A variety of other therapists became associated with MRI in the 1960s and 1970s, including Virginia Satir, Jules Riskin, Paul Watzlawick, John E. Bell, Arthur Bodin, Diana Everstine, Carlos Sluzki, and Nick Cummings. MRI became associated with brief therapy and strategic therapy. See also **brief therapy** and **strategic family therapy.**

Bodin, A. (1981). The interactional view: Family therapy approaches of the Mental Research Institute. In A. S. Gurman & D. P. Kniskern (Eds.), *Handbook of family therapy* (pp. 267-309). New York: Brunner/Mazel.

merging   A behavioral pattern that involves the active, yet unconscious, collaboration of two partners, wherein the first partner does not merely choose the second but enters into an implicit agreement to choose the second partner on the basis of the first partner's own unfulfilled needs and to form an implicit contract. People attached to one another in this manner share each other's feelings and motivations, instead of recognizing their differences. See **fusion.**

Example: A couple merge to overcome their sense of emptiness. By sharing feelings about such things as family relationships and worldviews, they validate each other's existence.

Boszormenyi-Nagy, I. (1965). A theory of relationships: Experience and transaction. In I. Boszormenyi-Nagy & J. Framo (Eds.), *Intensive family therapy: Theoretical and practical aspects* (pp. 33-86). New York: Harper & Row.

message symptom   A symptom that a client imagines to be something concrete. The client then changes aspects of the image in order to eliminate the symptom. Message symptoms are a focus of sex hypnotherapy.

Araoz, D. L. (1982). *Hypnosis and sex therapy.* New York: Brunner/Mazel.

meta   Changed, transposed, or beyond something. In family systems therapy, *meta* (in recognition of Gregory Bateson's usage and influence) is used to mean "about," as in *metacommunication*—that is, a communication about communication—or as in *metalanguage*—that is, a language or symbolic system used to discuss, describe, or analyze another language or symbolic system. Bateson also used the prefix *meta-* to refer to a higher level of generalization.

M

Duhl, B. S. (1983). *From the inside out and other metaphors.* New York: Brunner/Mazel.

metacommunication   A message about a message. The second message qualifies what was said in the first message—for example, by commenting on the latent content of the message or on how the message was expressed. Metacommunication is conveyed by voice, inflection, or body language. It may convey the following:

> The sender's attitude toward the message: "The message I sent was a friendly one."
>
> The sender's attitude toward self: "I am friendly."
>
> The sender's attitude toward the receiver: "I see you as a friendly person."

Bateson, G. (1987). *Steps to an ecology of mind.* New York: Ballantine.
Watzlawick, P., Beavin, J. H., & Jackson, D. D. (1967). *Pragmatics of human communication.* New York: Norton.

metacomplementary relationship   A reciprocal relationship in which a person allows or forces a second person to be in charge.

Example: A husband says he is bored and wants to do something but then refuses to suggest any activities. He forces his wife to make all of the decisions regarding their entertainment.

Watzlawick, P., Beavin, J. H., & Jackson, D. D. (1967). *Pragmatics of human communication.* New York: Norton.

metaphor   A statement about one thing that resembles something else. It is based on an analogous relationship between two things. Metaphors sometimes are used by therapists in giving directives, because people often are more willing to follow the directive if they do not have to concede that they received one.

Examples: "I feel like I was run over by a train" is an example of a metaphor. In therapy, an example is discussing the family "adopting" a pet to explain that a child was adopted as an infant.

Haley, J. (1987). *Problem-solving therapy* (2nd ed.). San Francisco: Jossey-Bass.

metasymmetrical relationship   A mutual relationship in which one person allows or forces a second person to be equal.

Example: A husband says he is bored and would like to go to a dance. His wife agrees without expressing her opinion. Because he sees his wife as his coequal, the husband forces her to tell him whether she would really like to go and, if not, what she would really like to do.

Watzlawick, P. Beavin, J. H., & Jackson, D. D. (1967). *Pragmatics of human communication.* New York: Norton.

M

Milan family therapy group   The original Milan family therapy was created by Mara Selvini Palazzoli, Luigi Boscolo, Gianfranco Cecchin, and Giuliana Prata. This group broke up along gender lines because of the different interests of its members. The women were interested in theorizing, while the men were interested in training. Consequently this original group disbanded in 1980. See also **invariant prescription, strategic family therapy,** and **systemic.**

Boscolo, L., Cecchin, G., Hoffman, L., & Penn, P. (1987). *Milan systemic family therapy: Conversations in theory and practice.* New York: Basic Books.

Selvini Palazzoli, M., Boscolo, L., Cecchin, G., & Prata, G. (1978). *Paradox and counterparadox: A new model in the therapy of the family in schizophrenic transaction.* New York: Jason Aronson.

Milan method   This method of therapy was developed in Milan, Italy, by Mara Selvini Palazolli, Luigi Boscolo, Gianfranco Cecchin, and Guiliana Prata, a group of four clinicians who worked as a team with families. It is not just a collection of techniques, but rather represents an "epistemology," or a way of thinking about and acting in social systems. Therapists who use this approach can be seen as systemic, reflexive, and circular, in sharp contrast to most families' linear view of causality. See **Milan family therapy group.**

Cronen, W., & Pearce, W. (1985). Toward an explanation of how the Milan method works: An invitation to a systemic epistemology and the evolution of family systems. In D. Campbell & R. Draper (Eds.), *Applications of systemic family therapy* (pp. 69-84). New York: Grune & Stratton.

mimesis   A therapeutic skill used by the therapist to join with the family and become like the family members in the manner or content of their communications (e.g., joking with a jovial family or talking slowly and sparsely with a slow-talking family). The therapist also can join with the family mimetically by conveying personal experiences to its members.

Aponte, H., & van Deusen, J. (1981). Structural family therapy. In A. S. Gurman & D. P. Kniskern (Eds.), *Handbook of family therapy* (pp. 310-360). New York: Brunner/Mazel.

Minuchin, S. (1974). *Families and family therapy.* Cambridge, MA: Harvard University Press.

mind reading   Making assumptions about the thoughts, feelings, and motives of a partner and then telling that partner what he or she thinks or feels or ought to think or feel.

Example:

Wife	Why did you forget my book?
Husband	I had a lot to do and just forgot.
Wife	That's not it at all. You just don't care about me.

M.

Bach, G., & Deutsch, R. (1970). *Pairing*. New York: Avon.

minimal brain damage (MBD)   A term used in the 1950s and 1960s to refer to the underlying cause for the behavior of children with excessive activity level and poor attention span. The assumption was that the brain damage was too small to be detected by normal neurological measures and that it could only be detected through behavioral observation of the child. Thus the term was used to imply underlying brain impairment despite no medical evidence supporting the brain injury hypothesis. The term typically referred to children with attention deficit hyperactivity disorder and/or learning disabilities.

Barkley, R. A. (1990). *Attention deficit hyperactivity disorder: A handbook for diagnosis and treatment*. New York: Guilford.
Taylor, H. G. (1983). MBD: Meanings and misconceptions. *Journal of Clinical Neuropsychology, 5,* 271-287.
Wender, P. H. (1971). *Minimal brain dysfunction in children*. New York: Wiley-Interscience.

minimal brain dysfunction (MBD)   *Minimal brain dysfunction* replaced the term *minimal brain damage* because no actual brain damage could ever be demonstrated. The term is most often synonymous with *attention deficit hyperactivity disorder.* MBD is a disorder of behavioral and perceptual-cognitive functioning that, theoretically, involves some impairment of the central nervous system but in which no detectable organic pathology can be demonstrated.

Barkley, R. A. (1990). *Attention deficit hyperactivity disorder: A handbook for diagnosis and treatment*. New York: Guilford.
Taylor, H. G. (1983). MBD: Meanings and misconceptions. *Journal of Clinical Neuropsychology, 5,* 271-287.
Wender, P. H. (1971). *Minimal brain dysfunction in children*. New York: Wiley-Interscience.

mirror image disagreement   An arrangement that allows parents to express their differences indirectly regarding their child's behavior. If, in their conflict over the child, the parents begin to struggle with each other directly, their own relationship might be imperiled.

Haley, J., & Hoffman, L. (1967). *Techniques of family therapy*. New York: Basic Books.

model analysis   Attempts to discover the models that influenced family members in their early lives gave them messages about the presence and desirability of growth, gave them the blueprints from which they learned to evaluate and act on new experience, and showed them how to become close to others.

M

Satir, V. (1983). *Conjoint family therapy* (3rd ed.). Palo Alto, CA: Science & Behavior Books.

modern nuclear family   A broad kinship model in which the entirety of individuals, extended families, community, and neighborhood is seen as the family.

Glick, I. D., & Kessler, D. P. (1980). *Marital and family therapy* (2nd ed.). New York: Grune & Stratton.

modification hearing   This type of hearing may occur after the final hearing in which a marriage is dissolved. The parties request a "modification" of a final order due to circumstances that have changed since the final hearing. The modification often involves an increase or decrease in the amount of child support payments, a request for a change in primary custody of the children, or changes in child visitation rights.

Example: A husband lost his job due to a company layoff and asked the court to change his support payments until he obtained another job of equal salary.

Glass, B. L. (1984). No-fault divorce law. *Journal of Family Issues, 5,* 47-69.

monadic model   A model that assumes psychological problems are a result of intrapsychic disturbances. Thus the individual is the unit of treatment.

Nichols, M. P. (1984). *Family therapy: Concepts and methods.* New York: Gardner.

monitoring/boundary control activity   An intrasystem regulatory activity that involves checking an operating activity or taking action to institute a new or modified operating activity. Monitoring and boundary control regulatory activities are external to the operating activity of the system; they relate a system to its environment by controlling the input and output transitions across the system's boundary.

Example: A father who was previously weak and inefficient gains the strength in family therapy to assert himself and take control over the events that occur in his family.

Sauber, S. R. (1983). *The human services delivery system.* New York: Columbia University Press.

monogamy   The marriage of one man to one woman at one time.

Christensen, H. T. (Ed.). (1964). *Handbook of marriage and the family.* Chicago: Rand McNally.

moral codes   Rules developed by individuals or groups of individuals to sustain their philosophies or religious beliefs. If the rules are violated, the individuals lose their privileges or good standing.

M

Example: A couple may have a rule that extramarital sex is acceptable, provided that the other partner is told about the affair in advance. If one partner breaks the rule, the result is a lack of trust and withdrawal of affection.

Bedford, S. (1969). The "new morality" and marriage counseling. In B. N. Ard & C. C. Ard (Eds.), *Handbook of marriage counseling* (2nd ed., pp. 83-87). Palo Alto, CA: Science & Behavior Books.

morphogenesis   A process by which a living system changes its basic structure to adapt to environmental conditions. The process involves positive feedback, or sequences that serve to amplify deviation and functioning with a flexible structure that is open to growth and change and responsive to new stimulation.

Example: The family members come to therapy recognizing their problems and their need for help and for new ways to function.

Beavers, W. R. (1976). A theoretical basis for family evaluation. In J. M. Lewis, W. R. Beavers, J. T. Gossett, & V. A. Phillips (Eds.), *No single thread: Psychological health in the family system* (pp. 46-82). New York: Brunner/Mazel.

Speer, D. (1970). Family systems: Morphostasis and morphogenesis, or is homeostasis enough? *Family Process, 9,* 259-278.

morphostasis   The process by which a system maintains constancy through negative feedback in the face of environmental changes. It denotes a lack of change, or stagnation of the structure of the system.

Example: A child is referred for treatment, but the parents refuse to allow the child to go to the clinic. They thus deny the existence of any problems regarding the child, while blaming the child's school for not doing its job effectively.

Beavers, W. R. (1976). A theoretical basis for family evaluation. In J. M. Lewis, W. R. Beavers, J. T. Gossett, & V. A. Phillips (Eds.), *No single thread: Psychological health in the family system* (pp. 46-82). New York: Brunner/Mazel.

Speer, D. (1970). Family systems: Morphostasis or morphogenesis, or is homeostasis enough? *Family Process, 9,* 259-278.

mourning and empathy   A technique by which the therapist elicits unresolved grief to effect change. An attempt is made to release long-hidden feelings, expectations, and emotions.

Bernard, C., & Corrales, R. (1979). *The theory and technique of family therapy.* Springfield, IL: Charles C Thomas.

Paul, N. (1967). The use of empathy in the resolution of grief. *Perspectives in Biology and Medicine, 11,* 153-169.

M

movie directing   A sex hypnotherapy technique used to treat negative sexual processing. The client sees him- or herself in a situation that elicits all of his or her anxieties. The client then takes over the scene as a director in an effort to change it so that it is pleasant. The client switches back and forth until the anxious aspects disappear.

Araoz, D. L. (1982). *Hypnosis and sex therapy.* New York: Brunner/Mazel.

MRI   See **Mental Research Institute.**

multidirected partiality   The therapist's acknowledgment of each person's side. This recognition provides everyone with an opportunity to be heard so that her or his position on the issue is acknowledged. This acknowledgment is the cornerstone of rebuilding trust in relationships.

Boszormenyi-Nagy, I., & Spark, G. L. (1973). *Invisible loyalties: Reciprocity in intergenerational family therapy.* New York: Harper & Row.
Kaslow, F. W. (1987). Marital and family therapy. In M. B. Sussman & S. K. Steinmetz (Eds.), *Handbook of marriage and the family* (pp. 835-859). New York: Plenum.

multifamily group therapy   Therapy in which several families are brought together in weekly group sessions. This technique has the advantage of fostering wholeness of the family, rather than fragmentation. In this type of therapy, cross-influences and cross-interactions from family to family are more effective than techniques in individual family therapy in shaking up the rigid family systems that family members have a stake in maintaining and preserving.

Leichter, E., & Schulman, G. (1968). Emerging phenomena in multifamily group treatment. *International Journal of Group Psychotherapy, 18,* 56-69.
Leichter, E., & Schulman, G. (1972). Emerging phenomena in group treatment. In G. D. Erickson & T. P. Hogan (Eds.), *Family therapy: An introduction to theory and technique* (pp. 327-335). Belmont, CA: Wadsworth.

multigenerational family therapy   Family therapy in which the family of origin is brought into therapy. Adults then can deal directly with their mothers, fathers, brothers, and sisters about previously avoided issues. This reconstructive change is possible in the marital relationship and in the relationship between the adults and their children. See also **Bowenian family therapy.**

Framo, J. L. (1981). The integration of marital therapy with sessions with family of origin. In A. S. Gurman & D. P. Kniskern (Eds.), *Handbook of family therapy* (pp. 133-158). New York: Brunner/Mazel.

multigenerational therapy   A form of multiple family therapy using the presenting family and its two preceding families in a single large group therapeutic situation.

M

Howells, J. (1975). *Principles of family psychiatry.* New York: Brunner/Mazel.

multigenerational transmission   The emergence of severe psycho-pathology in an individual family member as the outcome of genera-tional influences. The principle of projection to different children in the family varies, depending on their levels of immaturity. The maximally involved child emerges with a lower level of self-differentiation.

Example: The mother of a schizophrenic child does not create the schizophrenia; she is seen as one involved person in a long line of involved persons down through the generations.

Boszormenyi-Nagy, I., & Spark, G. L. (1973). *Invisible loyalties: Reciprocity in intergen-erational family therapy.* New York: Harper & Row.

Bowen, M. (1978). *Family therapy in clinical practice.* New York: Jason Aronson.

Kerr, M. (1981). Family systems theory and therapy. In A. S. Gurman & D. P. Kniskern (Eds.), *Handbook of family therapy* (pp. 226-264). New York: Brunner/Mazel.

multilaterality   See **multidirected partiality.**

multilateral marriage   A voluntary group of three or more persons, each of whom is committed to and maintains a relationship with more than one person in the group in a manner regarded by the participants as being "married." Participants develop a structure for sharing eco-nomic and personal resources and tend to live together in one residence. This marital arrangement is also called a *group marriage.*

Constantine, L. L., Constantine, J. M., & Edelman, S. K. (1975). Counseling implications of alternative marriage styles. In A. S. Gurman & D. G. Rice (Eds.), *Couples in conflict* (pp. 124-134). New York: Jason Aronson.

multiorgasmic   Achievement of more than one orgasm by the female during coitus. New research suggests that males may also have multiple orgasms.

Masters, W., & Johnson, V. (1970). *Human sexual inadequacy.* Boston: Little, Brown.

multiple family group counseling   A form of family treatment in which several families are brought together in a weekly group session to assist families in developing a shared view of a client's difficulty and in evaluating a collaborative plan of changing maladaptive behaviors. Short-term, multiple family group counseling is an effective treatment for family problems of which a student is the "identified client." Such counseling is based on the premise that the worlds of the home and the school are inseparable; yet, with the family as the primary influence, school personnel are often powerless unless communication has been established with the parents. The place to attack the problem is with the people whom it involves and the setting in which it occurs. Working with the problem student in a school situation offers students and parents

M

the unique benefit of "sharing the responsibility" in an atmosphere of mutuality in which the concerns of the school and the family can be integrated, discussed, and dealt with in an efficacious manner.

Sauber, S. R. (1971). Multiple family group counseling. *Personnel and Guidance Journal, 49,* 459-465.

multiple family group sensitivity procedures   A set of group procedures used to stimulate awareness and communication of positive feelings between parents and adolescents. The procedure is used for families in which the generation gap has broken down communication lines between the members. It can involve as many as six families, or a total of 12 parents and 9 adolescents. To get the parents and adolescents to talk to each other, six different group formations are used during five 2-hour sessions. For example, the "simulated family group" may consist of an unrelated father, mother, and one or two adolescents. The "role group in concentric circles" may consist of all of the mothers talking among themselves in the inner circle while the fathers and adolescents sit observing in the outer circle. A number of topics may be discussed in the various groupings, within the context of all possible relationships.

Example: A son's perspective of a father-son relationship includes the following: (a) the father's and son's positive behavior, which makes the son feel loved, appreciated, valued, and understood; (b) the positive characteristics that his father likes, admires, and respects; (c) the commitment behavior and wished-for behaviors; and (d) the feedback from all participants revealing their feelings about the session, themselves, and other members.

Clarke, C. (1969, October). *Group procedures for stimulating awareness and communication of positive feelings between parents and young adults.* Paper presented at the meeting of the Family Life Council, Goldsboro, NC.

Sauber, S. R. (1971). Multiple group family counseling. *Personnel and Guidance Journal, 49,* 459-465.

multiple family group therapy   A form of therapy in which several families (or married couples) are seen in groups. This type of therapy is particularly effective in pathologically homogeneous families that have profound mental and emotional, sex, or generational differences. It affords a sense of camaraderie among the sexes (or generations), as well as an increased awareness and acceptance of differences among the participants.

Laqueur, H. P. (1976). Multiple family therapy. In P. J. Guerin (Ed.), *Family therapy: Theory and practice* (pp. 405-416). New York: Gardner.

multiple family therapy   Therapy for multiple members of multiple families who meet together for discussion of individual and joint problems.

M

The therapy is designed to help the individual family members achieve higher levels of functioning. The therapist works with each family separately, dividing the time between the several families, but avoiding communication exchanges between them. Emotional exchanges between the families would encourage a group process, which would overshadow the family process and impair or block individuation. The two advantages of this type of therapy are faster progress in each family due to observing others and a net saving in time. The two disadvantages are the additional work in scheduling and the energy required of the therapist in maintaining structure.

Bowen, M. (1975). Family therapy after twenty-five years. In J. Dyrud & D. Freedman (Eds.), *American handbook of psychiatry* (2nd ed., Vol. 5, pp. 367-392). New York: Basic Books.

Laqueur, H. P. (1972). Mechanisms of change in multiple family therapy. In C. J. Sager & H. S. Kaplan (Eds.), *Progress in group and family therapy* (pp. 400-415). New York: Brunner/Mazel.

multiple impact therapy   Therapy in which families are seen on an intensive basis and in different combinations over a 2- or 3-day period by members of a therapy team that includes a psychiatrist, a psychologist, a social worker, and a vocational counselor. The techniques focus on bringing about rapid change. This approach generally has been used with families in crisis.

MacGregor, R., Ritchie, A., Serrano, A., & Schuster, F. (1964). *Multiple impact therapy with families.* New York: McGraw-Hill.

multiple incest   A situation in which the incest victim has been abused by more that one perpetrator either concurrently (e.g., group incest) or sequentially, as well as in situations in which the perpetrator abuses more than one victim.

Courtois, C. (1988). *Healing the incest wound.* New York: Norton.

mutuality   A relationship characterized by convergence of self-interests and a willingness to accommodate to one another without fear of criticism or loss of individuality.

Example: The spouses' interactive patterns on implicit and explicit levels resulted in the sharing of feelings and the conveying of respect and appreciation for one another, as well as to other people.

Fleck, S. (1972). Family pathology. In G. D. Erickson & T. P. Hogan (Eds.), *Family therapy: An introduction to theory and technique* (pp. 103-119). Belmont, CA: Wadsworth.

Foley, V. (1974). *An introduction to family therapy.* New York: Grune & Stratton.

Wynne, L., Ryckoff, I., Day, J., & Hirsch, S. (1958). Pseudomutuality in the family relations of schizophrenics. *Psychiatry, 21,* 205-220.

M

mystification   Misdefinition of the issue of who is doing what to whom. Mystification is accomplished in three steps:

1. *Attribution:* Attributing to an individual a characteristic or role that is functional to or for the attributor
2. *Invalidation:* Disqualifying any action that is manifested by the individual who is being mystified
3. *Induction:* Actively recruiting and seducing the person into accepting the attribution, or at least part of it

Example: A child is playing noisily in the evening. His mother is tired and wants him to go to bed. A straight statement by the mother would be: "I am tired. I want you to go to bed," or, "Go to bed because I say so," or, "Go to bed because it's your bedtime." A mystifying way to induce the child to go to bed would be: "I'm sure you feel tired, darling, and you want to go to bed now, don't you?" Mystification occurs here in different ways. What is ostensibly an attribution about how the child feels ("You are tired") is really a command ("Go to bed"). The child is told how he feels (he may or may not feel tired), and what he is told he feels is what mother feels herself (projective identification). If we suppose he does not feel tired, he may contradict his mother's statement. He then may become liable to a further mystifying ploy, such as: "Mother knows best."

Laing, R. (1965). Mystification, confusion, and conflict. In I. Boszormenyi-Nagy & J. Framo (Eds.), *Intensive family therapy* (pp. 343-364). New York: Harper & Row.

M

narcissistic involvement   An investment in others that is egocentric or self-centered; the person so invested has no feeling of the meaning a particular situation holds for others.

Example: A man is interested in his wife only to the extent that she bolsters his ego by being attractive and attentive and by praising his accomplishments.

Epstein, N., & Bishop, D. (1981). Problem-centered systems therapy of the family. In A. S. Gurman & D. P. Kniskern (Eds.), *Handbook of family therapy* (pp. 444-482). New York: Brunner/Mazel.

Epstein, N. B., Bishop, D. S., & Levin, S. (1978). The McMaster model of family functioning. *Journal of Marriage and Family Counseling, 4,* 19-31.

narcissistic relationship   A relationship in which each person acts to validate an image-derived expectation of the other—that is, each person serves to validate and bolster the image projected by the other.

Example: A wife puts her husband on a pedestal, referring to him as handsome, intelligent, social, kind, and successful in everything. The higher in esteem she places her husband, the higher becomes her own self-image (much like the "doctor's wife" syndrome), in which the husband's status is used as an expression of the wife's own status. The husband constantly tells his wife how beautiful she is to him. The more beautiful she is to him, the higher his self-esteem.

Brody, W. (1961). The family as the unit of study and treatment: Image, object, and narcissistic relationship. *American Journal of Orthopsychiatry, 31,* 69-73.

Searles, H. (1965). The contributions of family treatment to the psychotherapy of schizophrenia. In I. Boszormenyi-Nagy & J. Framo (Eds.), *Intensive family therapy: Theoretical and practical aspects* (pp. 463-496). New York: Harper & Row.

National Council on Family Relations   One of the major associations of professionals interested in marriage and the family. It is made up mostly of sociologists and other academicians interested in family theory, research, and practice, as well as advocacy, enrichment, and family life education. It publishes three of the major journals in the field: *Journal of Marriage and the Family* (mostly research and theory), *Family Relations* (mostly applications, advocacy, family life education, and enrichment), and formerly, *Journal of Family History.*

natural and logical consequences   Consequences to a child's misbehavior that are natural and/or logical. Natural and logical consequences allow a child to be responsible for his or her behavior and teach responsibility and independence. They build on the common sense approach of letting children "suffer the consequences" of their actions. Consequences must have a logical connection to the misbehavior, the severity of the consequences must be appropriate to the misbehavior, and rules must relate to and stem from the generally accepted social order and not from the capricious whims of adults.

Example: A child is late to the dinner table. Instead of repeatedly calling the child, lecturing the child, or feeding the child after everyone else is finished, the child is served cold food. If the child misses the meal, the child goes hungry until the next meal.

Bullard, M. L. (1973). Logical and natural consequences. In H. H. Mosak (Ed.), *Alfred Adler: His influence on psychology today* (pp. 171-174). Park Ridge, NJ: Noyes.
Dreikurs, R. (1964). *Children: The challenge.* New York: Hawthorn/Dutton.

negation/retraction code   A code to measure the amount of negating words (*no, don't, not*) or retractors (*although, except, nevertheless*) present in verbal interaction.

Mishler, E., & Waxler, N. (1968). *Interaction in families: An experimental study of family processes and schizophrenia.* New York: John Wiley.
Riskin, J., & Faunce, E. (1972). An evaluative review of family interaction research. *Family Process, 11,* 365-455.

negative complementarity   See **neurotic complementary.**

negative consequence of change   A client's ambivalence about change by which positive consequences are framed negatively. The technique used to resolve this condition increases the client's motivation to change.

Example: A client who has been withdrawn and depressed for many years says he wants to change. The therapist points out that if he becomes stronger, he would demand more of his wife, which, in turn, could lead to arguments—that is, a negative consequence stems from a positive one. The client actively fights this view of what would happen.

Weeks, G., & L'Abate, L. (1982). *Paradoxical psychotherapy: Theory and practice with individuals, couples, and families.* New York: Brunnel/Mazel.

negative entropy   See **negentropy.**

negative feedback   The family system continually receives information from the environment that helps it adjust and take corrective actions on deviations from a prescribed course. In feedback, a portion of the output (e.g., behavior of a family member) is returned to the system as input, which functions to modify succeeding outputs of the system. *Negative feedback* is informational input looping back to the family system in such a way that it decreases the deviation of output from the family's steady state. In contrast to positive feedback, signals are fed back over a feedback channel in such a way that they increase the deviation of the output from a steady state. Negative feedback maintains the status quo. See also **homeostasis.**

Example: The mother observed her son at nursery school and told him that certain actions should be done differently.

Sauber, S. R. (1983). *The human services delivery system.* New York: Columbia University Press.

negative processing   A mental activity connected with any aspect of behavior that leads to guilt, anxiety, anger, or any other negative feeling. The processing is a continuum with the following range: (a) detection or awareness of a situation, (b) the labeling of it, (c) attribution or the interpretation of it, and (d) evaluation. Sexual negative processing is this mental process in the area of sex.

Example: A man thinks, "She (detection) turns me off (labeling) by being seductive (attribution). I don't like to be manipulated by a woman (evaluation)."

Araoz, D. L. (1982). *Hypnosis and sex therapy.* New York: Brunner/Mazel.

negative projection   The projection of one's own feared identity onto another group, which can lead to extensive intergroup fear and hostility.

Example: A man believes he is going crazy. Rather than deal with this belief, he begins to say it is his family that is crazy.

Wallace, A., & Fogelson, H. (1965). The identity struggle. In I. Boszormenyi-Nagy & J. Framo (Eds.), *Intensive family therapy: Theoretical and practical aspects* (pp. 365-406). New York: Harper & Row.

negative reinforcement trap   The use of reinforcement to terminate an aversive event, which, in turn, reinforces the behavior leading to the event.

N

Example: A child wants a candy bar in a store, but the mother refuses. The child has a tantrum. The mother does not want the child to have the candy, but neither does she want the tantrum. She decides to give the child the candy. This action reinforces the probability that the child will have other tantrums.

Wahler, R. (1976). Deviant child behaviors within the family. In H. Leitenberg (Ed.), *Handbook of behavior modification and therapy* (pp. 516-546). Englewood Cliffs, NJ: Prentice-Hall.

negative self-hypnosis Negative thoughts, both affirmations and imagery, that lie outside of awareness and become part of one's belief system. These thoughts act as powerful hypnotic suggestions because (a) they have been accepted by the inner mind without critical evaluation or rational analysis, (b) they activate negative imagery, and (c) they affect mood, motivation, and behavior in such a way that a person cannot break through.

Araoz, D. L. (1982). *Hypnosis and sex therapy.* New York: Brunner/Mazel.

negativistic A person's resistance to participate in family communication and interaction. This resistance is often seen as an attitude marked by skepticism about nearly everything affirmed by others in the family.

Riskin, J., & Faunce, E. (1972). An evaluative review of family interaction research. *Family Process, 11,* 365-455.
Singer, M., & Wynne, L. (1966). Communication styles in parents of normals, neurotics, and schizophrenics. *Psychiatric Research Reports, 20,* 25-38.

negentropic family A family in which members combine intimacy and individuality.

Beavers, W. R. (1977). *Psychotherapy and growth: A family systems perspective.* New York: Brunner/Mazel.

negentropy (negative entropy) The opposite of entropy—that is, the emergence of the organization and structure of a system. The perception of these patterns is called *information.* Thus negentropy leads to knowledge. However, excessive structure and complexity to any living system ultimately causes the death of the organism. All living systems, to survive, must have a balance of entropy and negentropy. See also **entropy.**

Bateson, G. (1972). *Steps to an ecology of mind.* New York: Ballantine.
Schroedinger, E. (1945). *What is life?* Cambridge, UK: Cambridge University Press.

neglect The degree to which a parent fails to provide minimal standards of care and nurturance. Thus neglect is a form of child abuse but is viewed more as omission of appropriate parenting toward children, rather than commission of inappropriate and destructive behavior toward children. In many states, *neglect* is a legal term. See also **child abuse.**

Example: A single mother goes out on dates three or four nights a week, leaving the 12-year-old daughter to baby-sit the 7-year-old brother. Neither child gets the parental attention, discipline, or appropriate parenting needed, and both are left in potentially dangerous situations being by themselves at night.

Azar, S. T., & Wolfe, D. A. (1989). Child abuse and neglect. In E. J. Mash & R. A. Barkley (Eds.), *Treatment of childhood disorders* (pp. 451-489). New York: Guilford.

neolocal residence A residence in which a nuclear family lives independently of either the husband's or wife's parents.

Zelditch, M. (1964). Cross-cultural analyses of family structure. In H. T. Christensen (Ed.), *Handbook of marriage and the family* (pp. 462-500). Chicago: Rand McNally.

neomarital programs Marital enrichment programs designed to help newly married couples preview their upcoming developmental tasks, as well as a wide range of behavioral skills.

Levant, R. F. (1984). *Family therapy: A comprehensive overview.* Englewood Cliffs, NJ: Prentice-Hall.

neoparental program A program consisting of various forms of childbirth education classes. Such programs are offered by prenatal clinics, maternity hospitals, the Red Cross, and the Childbirth Education Association. Their content typically encompasses the health needs of the expectant mother, her labor and delivery, and the care of the newborn infant. Some programs also attempt to prepare the expectant parents for the developmental transition to parenthood.

Levant, R. F. (1984). *Family therapy: A comprehensive overview.* Englewood Cliffs, NJ: Prentice-Hall.

network therapy Therapy in which not only family members but also resources beyond the family, such as members of the kinship system, friends, and significant others, work together on the patient's problem. The network of individuals is described as a *tribe.* Often the therapy session will include 20 to 100 participants.

Speck, R., & Attneave, C. (1973). *Family networks.* New York: Pantheon.

neurogenic disorders Neurological disorders primarily affect the sex centers of the brain and the lower neural structures that serve the genital reflexes. In some way, they impair or affect certain phases of the sexual response.

N

Kaplan, H. S. (1979). *Disorders of sexual desire.* New York: Brunner/Mazel.

neurolinguistic programming   The neurological process of organizing the structure of subjective experience in humans. The human system's neural processes are represented, ordered, and sequenced into models and strategies through language and communications systems.

Dilts, R., Grinder, J., Bandler, R., Cameron-Bandier, L., & DeLozier, I. (1980). *Neurolinguistic programming* (Vol. 1). Cupertino, CA: Meta Publications.

neurotic complementarity   A relationship in which each partner satisfies a neurotic need in the other. Also referred to as *negative complementarity.*

Example: A woman with strong, repressed sexual needs chooses a man who becomes an alcoholic, has affairs, or is sexually perverted.

Rutledge, A. (1969). Male and female roles in marriage counseling. In B. N. Ard & C. C. Ard (Eds.), *Handbook of marriage counseling* (pp. 120-127). Palo Alto, CA: Science & Behavior Books.

White, S. G., & Hatcher, C. (1984). Couple complementarity and similarity: A review of the literature. *American Journal of Family Therapy, 12,* 15-25.

neurotic marital interaction   The expression of neurotic needs in the marriage. The interaction may involve an individual subconsciously seeking a parental figure, trying to prove something about the individual, or replicating an old conflictual relationship.

Example: A daughter feels that she was never fully loved and accepted by her father. In her marriage, she makes every effort to please her husband in order not to lose his affection.

Framo, J. (1965). Rationale and technique of intensive family therapy. In I. Boszormenyi-Nagy & J. Framo (Eds.), *Intensive family therapy: Theoretical and practical aspects* (pp. 143-212). New York: Harper & Row.

Kubie, L. (1956). Psychoanalysis and marriage: Practical and theoretical issues. In V. Eisenstein (Ed.), *Neurotic interaction in marriage* (pp. 10-43). New York: Basic Books.

neutrality   A term used by the Milan team to describe the metaposition taken by the therapist and the team. Neutrality is achieved by siding with each member of the family as that person renders his or her perception of the relationships. The end result is that the family is unable to say the therapist has sided with anyone. The therapist thus avoids becoming part of the family alliance in the face of pressure to do so.

Selvini Palazzoli, M., Boscolo, L., Cecchin, G., & Prata, G. (1980). Hypothesizing-circularity-neutrality: Three guidelines for the conductor of the session. *Family Process, 19,* 3-12.

Tomm, K. (1985). Circular interviewing. In D. Campbell & R. Draper (Eds.), *Applications of systemic family therapy* (pp. 33-45). New York: Grune & Stratton.

new hypnosis   An approach in hypnosis that deemphasizes the ritual of induction. It induces a state in which the person lets him- or herself go into goal-directed daydreams to the extent that the person dissociates from the surrounding reality and becomes engrossed in inner reality.

Araoz, D. L. (1982). *Hypnosis and sex therapy.* New York: Brunner/Mazel.

nocturnal penile tumescence   Erectile episodes typically occurring in healthy boys and men every 90 to 100 minutes during sleep. The absence of these episodes is often used to aid the diagnosis of the etiology of impotence.

Karacan, I. (1978). Advances in the psychophysiological evaluation of male erectile impotence. In J. LoPiccolo & L. LoPiccolo (Eds.), *Handbook of sex therapy* (pp. 137-146). New York: Plenum.

no-fault divorce   A form of divorce granted without the establishment of blame. In 1970, California was the first state to abandon traditional grounds for divorce (adultery, desertion, cruelty, drunkenness) and to substitute one comprehensive basis: the breakdown of the marriage. In a no-fault divorce, it is not necessary to find blame for the marital failure. Emphasis is placed on an equitable determination of financial rights and child care responsibilities. In the past decade, all but two states have enacted some form of no-fault divorce procedure.

Marlow, L., & Sauber, S. R. (1990). *Handbook of divorce mediation.* New York: Plenum.

no-gossip principle   The principle underlying the behavioral pattern in which persons with problems in their relationships either fail to communicate or communicate through a third party. Despite the clients' initial resistance, the therapist must disrupt the pattern by forcing them to address each other directly, not through the therapist.

Example: A young woman complains to her therapist that she cannot discuss with her mother certain important subjects. When the therapist suggests that she try to discuss these subjects with her mother, she insists that she cannot. The therapist then asks her to go to her mother and tell her that she finds it difficult to discuss the subjects with her. The result is a highly significant and mutually rewarding conversation between the young woman and her mother.

Kempler, W. (1974). *Principles of Gestalt family therapy.* Oslo, Norway: A. S. John Nordahl Trykkery.
Lange, A., & van der Hart, O. (1983). *Directive family therapy.* New York: Brunner/Mazel.

nonabusive incest   Sexual acts between brothers, sisters, cousins, or other relatives, including adults who are age peers, when it is mutually desired and without coercion. Nonabusive incest is still illegal. Also see **incest.**

Courtois, C. (1988). *Healing the incest wound.* New York: Norton.

noncompliance   One of three categories of child behavior: (a) A child fails to initiate requested behaviors within a reasonable time after a command is given by an adult, (b) a child fails to sustain compliance until the requirements stipulated and an adult's command have been fulfilled, and (c) a child fails to follow previously taught rules of conduct in a given situation.

Barkley, R. A. (1987). *Defiant children: A clinician's manual for parent training.* New York: Guilford.

nondemand ambience   A condition induced by therapeutic treatment that structures a couple's interactions around sensual pleasure instead of performance goals and orgasm.
   Example: A couple is told simply to enjoy the sensation of intercourse without trying to achieve orgasm.

Kaplan, H. S. (1974). *The new sex therapy.* New York: Brunner/Mazel.

nontherapeutic coalition   An alliance between two or more family members, usually with the exclusion of the other family members.
   Example: The mother and the son are united in keeping the father excluded from their emotional involvement. As a result, the father becomes more punitive, and the mother more permissive, toward the son.

Minuchin, S., & Fishman, H. (1981). *Family therapy techniques.* Cambridge, MA: Harvard University Press.

nonverbal communication   Communication through physical movement or gesture of a portion of the body: facial expressions, glances of the eyes, hand and arm movements, or the manner of sitting or walking.

Ard, C. (1969). The role of nonverbal communication in marriage counseling. In B. N. Ard & C. C. Ard (Eds.), *Handbook of marriage counseling* (pp. 128-138). Palo Alto, CA: Science & Behavior Books.

normative-comparison question   A type of reflexive question in which family members are asked to compare themselves with other families along the lines of what would be socially/developmentally normal.
   Example: To a family with an adolescent, "What do you think are the main struggles and conflicts of other families with 13-year-olds?"

Tomm, K. (1987). Interventive interviewing: Part II. Reflexive questioning as a means to enable self-healing. *Family Process, 26,* 167-184.

norms Societal controls to enforce certain attitudes and behaviors that would not normally exist. Normative controls require (a) an initial definition of the attitudes and behaviors in question (e.g., dinner is at 6 p.m.), (b) some way of monitoring those members who conform and those who do not (Dad sees who is 15 minutes late), and (c) rewards or punishment for conformity or nonconformity (those who are late go without dinner). Normative controls exist in families whose members have come to depend on the family for need satisfaction. The family members abide by the normative structure because of their mutually satisfying contract, and they disapprove of interference with their satisfaction. Family researchers refer to this phenomenon as *homeostasis.* Initially each family is likely to have a firm or cohesive normative structure.

Thibault, J. W., & Kelly, H. H. (1959). *The social psychology of groups.* New York: John Wiley.

now rule A therapeutic rule stipulating that self-expressions should be made in the present tense. The use of past or future tenses can create a distance in verbal communication—a situation in which a person divests at least part of the responsibility for the words he or she speaks. Staying in the present tense increases openness and reduces potential defensiveness on the part of the listener.

Baruth, L. G., & Huber, C. H. (1984). *An introduction to marital theory and therapy.* Belmont, CA: Brooks/Cole.
Nierenberg, G. I., & Calero, H. (1973). *Meta-talk: Guide to hidden meanings on conversations.* New York: Simon & Schuster.

nuclear family A family consisting of a husband, a wife, and their immediate children. The nuclear family sometimes is referred to as the *conjugal family.*

Christensen, H. (1964). Development of the family field of study. In H. T. Christensen (Ed.), *Handbook of marriage and the family* (pp. 3-32). Chicago: Rand McNally.

nuclear family emotional system The patterns of emotional functioning in a family in a single generation. These patterns are replicas of past generations and are repeated in future generations.
   Example: The fathers in a vertical family system are all distant emotionally from others in their respective families.

Bowen, M. (1976). Theory in the practice of psychotherapy. In P. J. Guerin (Ed.), *Family therapy: Theory and practice* (pp. 42-90). New York: Gardner.

numbing symptoms Symptoms that help withdraw from or numb against the anxiety associated with incest. These symptoms may include

N

depersonalization, derealization, or dissociation. They range from short lapses, as when the client has "blanked," to long-term trancelike states and amnesia. Amnesia of some or all of the incest is common among incest survivors.

Courtois, C. (1988). *Healing the incest wound.* New York: Norton.

nupercainal cream   A cream used by males who suffer from premature ejaculation. The cream helps deaden the sensations of the penis.

Perelman, M. (1980). Treatment of premature ejaculation. In S. Leiblum & L. Pervin (Eds.), *Principles and practice of sex therapy* (pp. 199-234). New York: Guilford.

nurturant functions   Functions encompassing, in addition to the ingestion of food and the psychological aspects of feeding, the early nurturance of the child (helping the child learn how to manage and control the body and to observe, distinguish, and communicate about inner and external experiences), the provision of appropriate experiences and learning opportunities, and the establishment of basic trust.

Fleck, S. (1972). An approach to family pathology. In G. D. Erickson & T. P. Hogan (Eds.), *Family therapy: An introduction to theory and technique* (pp. 103-119). Belmont, CA: Wadsworth.

object-focused family A family characterized by overemphasis on the children (child centered), the outside community, or the self (narcissistic). The motivation for treatment depends on the willingness of the marital couple to form an effective coalition.

Cuber, J., & Harroff, P. (1966). *Sex and the significant Americans*. New York: Penguin.
Glick, I. D., & Kessler, D. P. (1980). *Marital and family therapy* (2nd ed.). New York: Grune & Stratton.

objectification The process of taking a thoroughly and completely rational, nonemotional stance in which a logical analysis of cost-rewards is made without attention or recourse to personal, emotional, or interpersonal factors.

Example: A father makes a global assessment that his son is lazy. In fact, the son is seen as lazy because a particular behavior occurs at a low frequency. It is logical to the father that if his son is lazy in one area, he will be lazy in all areas.

Weiss, R. (1978). The conceptualization of marriage from a behavioral perspective. In T. Paolino & B. McCrady (Eds.), *Marriage and marital therapy* (pp. 165-239). New York: Brunner/Mazel.

object relations family therapy An integration of psychodynamic object relations theory with family systems therapy. It is an attempt by psychoanalytic therapists to apply their theories to the family and for family therapists to rediscover the self in the system. Believing that insight is essential for change, object relations family therapists help each family member experience the family unconscious on a personal level. In theory, this experience results in interpretations that are more likely to be effective because the family will feel more thoroughly related to and understood.

Framo, J. L. (1982). *Explorations in marital and family therapy.* New York: Springer.
Scharff, J. S. (Ed.). (1989). *Foundations of object relations family therapy.* New York: Jason Aronson.

O

object relations theory   The psychodynamic theory that the mind and the psychic structures that comprise it evolve out of human interactions, rather than out of biologically derived tensions (Freudian theory). Instead of being motivated by tension reduction, human beings are motivated by the need to establish and maintain human relationships. In the broadest terms, object relations theory represents the psychoanalytic study of the nature and origin of interpersonal relations and of the nature and origin of intrapsychic structures derived from fixating, modifying, and reactivating past internalized relations with others in the context of present interpersonal relations. Object relations theory focuses on the internalization of interpersonal relations and the contribution to normal and pathological personality development. People react to and interact with not only an actual other but also an internal other, a psychic representation of a person that in itself has the power to influence both the individual's affective state and his or her covert behavioral reactions. These mental representations of others have various names in the psychoanalytic literature. In different theoretical systems they are called *internal objects, illusory others, introjects, personifications,* and the *constituents of a representational world.* These internal mental images constitute the residue within the mind of relationships of important people in the individual's life. In some way, crucial exchanges with others leave their mark such that they are "internalized" and thus shape subsequent attitudes, reactions, perceptions, and so on. *Object relations* refers to an individual's interactions with both external and internal (real and imagined) other people and to the relationship between their internal and external object worlds.

Cashdan, S. (1988). *Object relation therapy: Using the relationship.* New York: Norton.
Greenberg, J. R., & Mitchell, S. A. (1983). *Object relations and psychoanalytic theory.* Cambridge, MA: Harvard University Press.
Kernberg, O. (1976). *Object relations theory and pathological narcissism.* New York: Jason Aronson.

object-sorting task   A task, in a standard psychological test, used by some researchers to generate interaction between the subject and the tester for the purpose of measuring disordered styles of thinking.

Reiss, D. (1981). *The family's construction of reality.* Cambridge, MA: Harvard University Press.

obligatory relationship   A tradition-controlled, role-structured form of commitment in which success and satisfaction are measured by living up to external standards of excellence or the appearance of excellence. Doing what is correct is more important than the expression of self.

Example: Going to church and presenting a facade of togetherness is more important to a family than each member's individuality.

Weiss, R. (1978). The conceptualization of marriage from a behavioral perspective. In T. Paolino & B. McCrady (Eds.), *Marriage and marital therapy* (pp. 165-239). New York: Brunner/Mazel.

O

observational blindness   The therapist or patient fails to see the obvious unless it fits into the therapist's or patient's theoretical frame of reference.

Example: The therapist's theoretical background is based on the individual orientation of psychoanalysis, which does not recognize the possibilities of family dynamics and family system intervention.

Bowen, M. (1978). *Family therapy in clinical practice.* New York: Jason Aronson.

observer-perspective question   One type of reflexive question in which the goal is to help family members distinguish behaviors, events, or patterns. These questions may be used to enhance self-awareness and awareness of others and to explore interpersonal perception and interpersonal interaction.

Tomm, K. (1987). Interventive interviewing: Part II. Reflexive questioning as a means to enable self-healing. *Family Process, 26,* 167-184.

observing family mealtimes   The technique of monitoring the family mealtime as a microcosm of the family in sociological and dynamic terms. The clinician observes the mealtime to assess the family's way of relating.

Example: In one family, the members do not eat together. The members eat separately as they come home, and then they go their separate ways.

Glick, I. D., & Kessler, D. P. (1980). *Marital and family therapy* (2nd ed.). New York: Grune & Stratton.

White, S. (1976). Family dinner time: A focus for life space diagrams. *Journal of Clinical Social Work, 4,* 93-101.

odd/even day   A paradoxical prescription in which the patient or family is told to engage in a certain behavior only on odd days and not on even days (or vice versa).

Example: A couple in which the man has difficulty initiating sex is told that the man can only initiate sex on even days of the month and that the woman can only initiate sex on the odd days of the month.

Selvini Palazzoli, M., Boscolo, L., Cecchin, G., & Prata, G. (1978). A ritualized prescription in family therapy: Odd days and even days. *Journal of Marriage and Family Counseling, 4,* 3-9.

one-way mirror   A device by which researchers, therapists in training, or family members can observe family interaction. One-way mirrors have been used in child guidance clinics and have been adopted by the family therapy movement.

Example: A family is given a specific task to work on while one member of the family observes from behind a mirror. The mother believes that the father cannot discipline their son. By giving the father a task involving discipline, the mother can see his behavior objectively.

Minuchin, S., Montalvo, D., Guerney, B. G., Jr., Rosman, B., & Schumer, F. (1967). *Families of the slums: An exploration of their structure and treatment.* New York: Basic Books.

open family system   (1) A family system permitting honest self-expression by the participating members. In such a family, differences are viewed as natural, and open negotiation occurs to resolve the differences before they are allowed to develop without limits in the family. (2) The relationship between the family and the outside world; boundaries are permeable and not rigid.

Kantor, D., & Lehr, W. (1975). *Inside the family: Toward a theory of family process.* San Francisco: Jossey-Bass.

open system   A system in which material, energy, and information are exchanged with the environment. Open systems have three properties: wholeness, relationship, and equifinality. *Wholeness* implies that the whole is greater than the sum of the parts. *Relationship* refers to the fact that one must understand connections and interactions between the parts in order to understand the system. *Equifinality* means that no matter where one begins, the conclusions will be the same. Thus, in family theory, if a systems view is taken of an ongoing interrelationship such as marriage, the pattern of behavior will be the same regardless of the specific subject matter (e.g., money, in-laws, sex, children). Thus, in family systems work, the therapist looks for wholeness, interrelationships between individuals, and patterns of behavior.

Example: The parents did everything possible to raise their daughter in a healthy way, but her adolescent peer group influenced her values to the extent that she became drug addicted. Her parents continued to be supportive in hopes of her learning from the difficult experiences she is now going through.

Dell, P. (1985). Understanding Bateson and Maturana: Toward a biological foundation for the social sciences. *Journal of Marital and Family Therapy, 11,* 1-20.

Sauber, S. R. (1983). *The human services delivery system.* New York: Columbia University Press.

operant behavior Behavior that has a statistical frequency of occurrence over time when an eliciting stimulus is either unknown or not present. Operant behavior can be reinforced independently of the intention of others.

Example: A person cries frequently but does not know why. It could be that each time the person cries, a great deal of attention is given, which reinforces the behavior.

Weiss, R. (1978). The conceptualization of marriage from a behavioral perspective. In T. Paolino & B. McCrady (Eds.), *Marriage and marital therapy* (pp. 165-239). New York: Brunner/Mazel.

oppositional defiant disorder A childhood behavioral disorder of less severity than a conduct disorder. Children who have oppositional defiant disorder typically have a behavior pattern that is negativistic, hostile, and defiant but without the more serious violations of the basic rights of others that are seen in a conduct disorder. These children typically are seen as argumentative, frequently throw temper tantrums, and are often angry, resentful, and easily annoyed. They frequently show a good deal of noncompliance and may deliberately do things to annoy other people.

American Psychiatric Association. (1987). *Diagnostic and statistical manual of mental disorders* (3rd ed., rev.). Washington, DC: Author.

optimal balance theory The theory that, for effective group functioning, agreements must outnumber disagreements and that answers must outweigh questions.

Lennard, H., & Bernstein, A. (1969). *Patterns in human interaction.* San Francisco: Jossey-Bass.

Riskin, J., & Faunce, E. (1972). An evaluative review of family interaction research. *Family Process, 11,* 365-455.

optimal functioning A pattern of adapting to circumstances in a way that reaches toward change, intrasystem determinism, and innovation. Optimal functioning is characterized by flexible marital and parental coalitions, clear boundaries, spontaneous and free interchange, and respect for the individuality of family members.

Lewis, J. M., Beavers, W. R., Gossett, J. T., & Phillips, V. A. (1976). *No single thread: Psychological health in the family system.* New York: Brunner/Mazel.

Orbon's erect-aid system   An external vacuum pump device and ring used to help men with erection problems achieve and maintain an erection.

Althof, S. (1989). Psychogenic impotence: Treatment of men and women. In S. Leiblum & R. Rosen (Eds.), *Principles and practice of sex therapy* (2nd ed., pp. 237-265). New York: Guilford.

ordeal technique   Having someone perform some burdensome action when a symptom occurs or to stave off the symptom. The ordeal is more severe than the problem. It works best if it is something good for the person and is something the person can do, but is not something the person can easily object to. Ordeals are of several types:

1. *Straightforward tasks:* The therapist clarifies the problem and requires that each time it occurs, the person go through a specific ordeal. For example, a man who felt anxious was required to exercise for X minutes.

2. *Paradoxical ordeals:* The symptomatic behavior is the ordeal. The client is asked to do so much more of the same that it is experienced as too great an ordeal to continue.

3. *Therapist as ordeal:* The therapist may use the relationship to create an ordeal. The therapist may reframe behavior, confront, or increase the fee when the symptom increases.

Haley, J. (1984). *Ordeal therapy.* San Francisco: Jossey-Bass.
O'Hanlon, W. H., & Hexum, A. L. (1990). *An uncommon casebook: The complete clinical work of Milton H. Erickson, M.D.* New York: Norton.

ordinal position   According to the theory of Alfred Adler, a rank that a person holds in the family determines the situation in which that person finds him- or herself. The ordinal position is not a "cause" of behavior disturbances, but rather a fact of life to which the family member responds. Five ordinal positions can be considered as basic; all other positions can be seen as variations, combinations, or permutations of these five: (a) an only child, (b) the eldest child, (c) the second child, (d) the middle child, and (e) the youngest child. A child may occupy two positions (second and youngest child), or a child may be several years in one position and then move to another (a youngest child becomes a middle child, or a middle child becomes the youngest child when a younger sibling dies). Finally a child may be overrun by a younger sibling who is more intelligent.

Hoopes, M., & Harper, J. (1987). *Birth order roles and sibling positions in individual, marital and family therapy.* Rockville, MD: Aspen Systems.
Shulman, B. H., & Nikelly, A. G. (1971). Family constellation. In A. G. Nikelly (Ed.), *Techniques for behavior change: Applications of Adlerian theory* (pp. 35-40). Springfield, IL: Charles C Thomas.

organization (in systems therapy) Wholeness, structure, and hierarchies in a system. The relationship among the components of a system that are both necessary and sufficient for defining the system.

Maturana, H. R. (1978). Biology of language: The epistemology of reality. In G. A. Miller & E. Lenneberg (Eds.), *Psychology and biology of language and thought* (pp. 27-63). New York: Academic Press.

Miller, J. G. (1965). Living systems: Basic concepts. *Behavioral Science, 10,* 193-245.

orgasmic phase The third stage of the sexual response cycle, usually referred to as the *climax*. This stage is marked by pleasurable rhythmic contractions localized in the pelvic area.

Masters, W., & Johnson, V. (1970). *Human sexual inadequacy.* Boston: Little, Brown.

orgasm of the female Sexual release, reached at an increment peak of pelvic tissue vasocongestion and myotonia, in which the orgasmic platform in the outer third of the vagina and the uterus contract with a regularly recurring rhythmicity.

Masters, W., & Johnson, V. (1970). *Human sexual inadequacy.* Boston: Little, Brown.

orgastic threshold The amount of stimulation required to elicit the female orgasm. This threshold varies widely from woman to woman.

Kaplan, H. S. (1974). *The new sex therapy.* New York: Brunner/Mazel.

out-of-control families Families characterized by issues of control that are usually systemic, not individual, in nature. The developmental stages of family members tend to define the types of problems encountered. For example, in families with young children, the controlling youngster often elicits support from one of the adults. The adults are "disqualified," which leaves the position of control to the child. In families with adolescents, a major issue of control is the "inability of the parents to move from the stage of concerned parents of young children to respectful parents of young adolescents" (Minuchin & Fishman, 1981, pp. 58-59). Problems with control also are found in families with delinquent children, in which the parent's control is dependent on their presence. Families in which child abuse occurs have a great deal of difficulty with control issues. In such cases, the family is the only place where the abusive parent feels in control, and subsequently that control becomes aggression. Out-of-control families are characterized by chaotic communication patterns. Contact becomes unimportant because the family members do not expect to be heard and only relationship messages are apparent. Communication is limited to "small, disconnected, affect-carrying bits or transactions" (Minuchin & Fishman, 1981, p. 59).

Minuchin, S., & Fishman, H. (1981). *Family therapy techniques.* Cambridge, MA: Harvard University Press.

outsight   The act of understanding the motives of others, of comprehending them in depth. Outsight differs from empathy in that it is more intellectual than emotional. It also differs from *idiopanima,* which refers to A's perception of B's perception of A. Outsight is the analogue of insight.

Corsini, R. J. (1966). *Role playing in psychotherapy: A manual.* Chicago: Aldine.

overadequate-inadequate reciprocity   A relational pattern in which both parents are equally immature. The one who makes the decisions for the two of them becomes the overadequate parent, and the other one becomes the inadequate parent. Neither is able to find a midground between the two extremes (domineering, authoritative, and stubborn vs. helpless, compliant, and submissive).

Example: A father has no problem making important decisions at work, but he ends up in an emotional, paralyzing deadlock when he and his wife (the "mother") try to decide which movie the family should see together.

Bowen, M. (1978). *Family therapy in clinical practice.* New York: Jason Aronson.

overfocusing   A narrowing of a family's experience of reality due to focusing on a specific problem. The intensity of the family's experiences around the symptom and the symptom's bearer causes the family members to ignore other significant aspects of their transactions.

Minuchin, S., & Fishman, H. (1981). *Family therapy techniques.* Cambridge, MA: Harvard University Press.

overfunctioning   When an individual in a family assumes the feeling of responsibility for the emotional well-being of other family members and acts to compensate for real or perceived deficits in functioning in the others.

Kerr, M. E., & Bowen, M. (1988). *Family evaluation: An approach based on Bowen theory.* New York: Norton.

overinvolvement   An intrusive, overly warm, dependently affective engagement with another person.

Example: A husband constantly attends to his wife's moods, for example, by asking her, "Is everything OK now?" He cannot operate as a separate emotional entity.

Epstein, N., & Bishop, D. (1981). Problem-centered systems therapy of the family. In A. S. Gurman & D. P. Kniskern (Eds.), *Handbook of family therapy* (pp. 444-482). New York: Brunner/Mazel.

Epstein, N. B., Bishop, D. S., & Levin, S. (1978). The McMaster model of family functioning. *Journal of Marriage and Family Counseling, 4,* 19-31.

overprotection   An extreme degree of concern for somebody's welfare. In children, overprotection produces dependency, submissiveness, shyness, and possibly disobedience.

Example: A mother does not let her child assume any age-appropriate activities; she keeps the child at a level appropriate for a much younger age by limiting the child's play with neighborhood children ("They are too rough") or by controlling food intake ("It's no good for you"), appearances ("You may catch a cold"), or behavior ("You cannot go because it is dangerous for you").

Parker, G. (1983). *Parental overprotection: A risk factor in psychosocial development.* New York: Grune & Stratton.

overt fusion   The condition of being overly trapped in the family's emotional system. The person involved stresses belongingness, relatedness, and togetherness. Although an adult, the person is unable to assume the adult tasks of dealing with marriage, career options, care of parents, or the assumption of a different role in the family.

Barnard, C., & Corrales, R. (1979). *The theory and technique of family therapy.* Springfield, IL: Charles C Thomas.
Minuchin, S. (1974). *Families and family therapy.* Cambridge, MA: Harvard University Press.

overwhelmed mother   A mother who is in charge of everyone, with no hierarchy established among the children. In her role as the hub of the family, the mother must settle all issues with her children, individually and collectively.

Example: A mother asks her child to do a simple task, such as play with some toys. The child constantly interrupts his mother to ask her something, show her something, and check out her next activity. If another child tries to become involved in the play, the boy returns to his mother to ask questions about the situation, rather than deal himself with the other child.

Haley, J. (1987). *Problem-solving therapy* (2nd ed.). San Francisco: Jossey-Bass.

ownership   The act of being responsible for one's own perceptions, feelings, thoughts, and deeds.

Example: The assertion, "You make me angry," is not a statement of ownership. However, if a person says, "When you don't act as I expect, I become angry," the person is asserting ownership because he or she is

O

making a statement about his or her own feeling and assuming responsibility for it.

Duhl, B., & Duhl, F. (1981). Integrative family therapy. In A. S. Gurman & D. P. Kniskern (Eds.), *Handbook of family therapy* (pp. 483-513). New York: Brunner/Mazel.

Palo Alto group   Often used to describe the Mental Research Institute. Jay Haley notes, however, that there were actually two Palo Alto groups. The first group was the project, directed by Gregory Bateson, that developed the double-bind theory of schizophrenia. This group of clinicians and researchers included Gregory Bateson, Jay Haley, John Weakland, Don D. Jackson, and William Fry and was part of the Palo Alto Veterans Administration. Later Jackson formed the Mental Research Institute in Palo Alto. Bateson declined to be a member of the Mental Research Institute and disliked his project being confused with that group. See also **Mental Research Institute.**

Haley, J. (1987). *Problem-solving therapy* (2nd ed.). San Francisco: Jossey-Bass.

papaverine   A drug that is injected directly into the penis to produce an erection. This treatment is used for men with organic erectile problems.

Tiefer, L., & Melman, A. (1989). Comprehensive evaluation of erectile dysfunction and medical treatments. In S. Leiblum & R. Rosen (Eds.), *Principles and practice of sex therapy* (2nd ed., pp. 207-326). New York: Guilford.

paradigm   A frame of reference used to organize perceptions. Different paradigms produce different perceptions. Levenson suggests three paradigms in therapy: the work machine model, the communication model, and the organismic model. In the *work machine model,* cure involves undoing the past; in the *communication model,* cure occurs by staying in the present; and in the *organismic model,* the emphasis is on organization. This concept is used to distinguish the "family" concept from the "individual" conceptualization.

Foley, V. (1974). *An introduction to family therapy.* New York: Grune & Stratton.

Levenson, E. (1972). *The fallacy of understanding.* New York: Basic Books.

paradox   A contradiction that follows correct deduction from consistent premises. Paradoxes are of three types: logico-mathematical antinomies, paradoxical definitions (semantical antinomies), and pragmatic paradoxes (paradoxical injunctions and paradoxical predictions).

Watzlawick, P., Bevin, J. H., & Jackson, D. D. (1967). *Pragmatics of human communication.* New York: Norton.

paradoxical contract   Tying together two problem behaviors in two different family members so that if one person has the symptom, the other is encouraged to have his or her own symptom. This strategy is based on the assumption that the person with the presenting problem is trying to help the other person with his or her symptom by becoming sympathetic.

Example: After an assessment with a family, it was clear the daughter was starving herself in order to deal with her father's alcoholism, which, in turn, placed the daughter in serious medical jeopardy. An overt deal was made: The daughter agreed to starve herself for the day if her father drank, but to eat if he was abstinent. Because each partner was concerned about the other, the strategy worked.

Madanes, C. (1984). *Behind the one-way mirror.* San Francisco: Jossey-Bass.

paradoxical definition   A definition in which the same concept is used to refer both to a member of a class and to the class itself, thus creating an illusion of identity.

Example: The statement, "I am lying," is a paradoxical definition of self. The statement is true only if it is not true, and vice versa.

Watzlawick, P., Bevin, J. H., & Jackson, D. D. (1967). *Pragmatics of human communication.* New York: Norton.

paradoxical injunction   A communication that must be obeyed but that must be disobeyed to be obeyed. Two conditions are required for a paradoxical injunction: (a) There must be a strong complementary relationship (e.g., father-son), and (b) the person who receives the injunction cannot step outside the frame of reference or metacommunicate.

Example: A father advises his daughter, "Be yourself," but then qualifies the injunction by limiting the kind of friends she can make, the places she can visit, and the curfews she must keep. Consequently there is no way she can be herself. If she is herself, she may make choices that go counter to her father's wishes. If she does what her father wants her to do, she may not have a will or personality of her own. Thus she is offered a digital choice (being either what her father wants her to be or the opposite of what her father wants). Being herself would be tantamount to being the opposite of her father. If she does what he wants, she cannot be herself. The same kind of logic is present in therapeutic situations where the therapist obtains change by asking for sameness—that is, no change. For example, a prescription of the symptom may put a family in the same situation. If the family members follow the prescription, they are under the control of the therapist; if they start, rather than stop, the symptom, they learn to acquire control. Either way, they win.

Watzlawick, P., Bevin, J. H., & Jackson, D. D. (1967). *Pragmatics of human communication.* New York: Norton.

Weeks, G., & L'Abate, L. (1982). *Paradoxical psychotherapy: Theory and practice with individuals, couples, and families.* New York: Brunner/Mazel.

paradoxical intention   A special technique of logotherapy used when a client is concerned about the frequency of an undesired response. When the client wants to reduce the frequency of a behavior, the therapist requires that the client attempt to increase its occurrence.

Example: A man perspires excessively when he meets authority figures. He wants to eliminate this response. The therapist asks him to sweat out as much as he can when he meets an authority figure. This tactic removes the anticipatory anxiety and, hence, the problem.

Ascher, L. (1980). Paradoxical intention. In A. Goldstein & E. Foa (Eds.), *Handbook of behavioral interventions* (pp. 266-321). New York: John Wiley.

Frankl, V. (1955). *The doctor and the soul: From psychotherapy to logotherapy.* New York: Knopf.

paradoxical letter   A written paradoxical intervention given directly or mailed to a client. Such letters are used after verbal paradoxical interventions have failed.

Example: The following is a typical paradoxical letter, with a subsequent analysis keyed to specific statements:

Dear Norma, Sara, Ann, and Dave:

I was very impressed with the sadness and hurt in your family in our last session. I am glad the two of you were able to express your sadness.[1] It is important when you are sad and hurt to be able to share your feelings with other family members. Family members who share their hurts really love one another.[2]

However, I have grave misgivings about how much you should share at this time. I think it is much too soon for you to communicate these feelings to each other.[3] Instead each of you should continue to protect the family from its sadness by distracting or keeping each other busy.[4] You might even select one family member on whom you can focus all of your attention, or maybe someone in the family has already decided to take this role. This person could be responsible for starting fights and misbehavings.[5] The person selected should be a very responsible and local member of the family; this should make the choice easy because one of you already is acting in an overtly responsible manner (but enjoying it).[6]

Your family is also in a silent crisis.[7] Someone has changed recently, which has the family confused and uncertain about the future. The confusion and chaos in the family are actually part of the preparation for the family's forthcoming growth and change.[8] *Warning:* The family should be prepared for a big fight on Wednesday night.[9]

1. *Cryptic statement:* Raises the question of who expressed sadness, is designed to unite the family in guessing who it was.

2. *Relabeling:* Sharing hurt is equated to love.

3. *Restraining:* Previous statement tells the family members it is good to share hurt, but now they are warned that it may be risky.

4. *Positive connotation:* Distraction is said to protect the family, which puts them all on the same level.

5. *Prescription:* The fighting is prescribed.

6. *Relabeling:* The most distracting member of the family is relabeled as the one who is responsible and loyal.

7. *Cryptic statement:* What is a "silent crisis"?

8. *Relabeling:* Remember, this is a chaotic family; there is no predictability or certainty; the confusion is relabeled as preparation for growth.

9. *Paradoxical question:* Our next session is scheduled for Thursday; the oldest daughter said she would not return; hence we expect a fight about her attendance on Wednesday night, if not earlier.

Weeks, G., & L'Abate, L. (1982). *Paradoxical psychotherapy: Theory and practice with individuals, couples, and families.* New York: Brunner/Mazel.

paradoxical prescription   A statement to the family that overtly strengthens or promotes the family's homeostatic defenses and does not arouse resistance. The prescription reveals the secondary gain of the patient's symptomatic behavior for the family; thus, covertly, change is expected. Paradoxical prescriptions (also called *therapeutic double binds*) are used in strategic family therapy. See also **symptom prescription.**

Example: The therapist tells the son to continue to fail because in that way he is helping his father feel good about himself.

Watzlawick, P., Beavin, J. H., & Jackson, D. D. (1967). *Pragmatics of human communication.* New York: Norton.

Weeks, G., & L'Abate, L. (1982). *Paradoxical psychotherapy: Theory and practice with individuals, couples, and families.* New York: Brunner/Mazel.

parallel relationship   A relationship in which the spouses alternate comfortably between symmetrical and complementary relationships as they adapt to changing situations. At times, one partner assumes a one-up relationship vis-à-vis the other; at other times, they are on equal terms.

Example: The husband decides which model car to buy, but the decision to buy the car is reached mutually with his wife.

Bodin, A. (1981). The interactional view: Family therapy approaches of the Mental Research Institute. In A. S. Gurman & D. P. Kniskern (Eds.), *Handbook of family therapy* (pp. 267-309). New York: Brunner/Mazel.
Lederer, W., & Jackson, D. (1968). *The mirages of marriage.* New York: Norton.

parallel treatment   Treatment given to one person to indirectly treat another.

O'Hanlon, W. H., & Hexum, A. L. (1990). *An uncommon casebook: The complete clinical work of Milton H. Erickson, M.D.* New York: Norton.

paraphilias   A class of disorders also known as *perversions, deviations,* and *variations.* For all of the disorders, unusual or bizarre imagery or acts are needed to produce sexual excitement. There are eight specific paraphilias: (a) fetishism—using nonliving objects, (b) transvestism—cross-dressing, (c) zoophilia—engaging in sex with animals, (d) pedophilia—fantasizing about or engaging in sex with children, (e) exhibitionism—exposing oneself to others, (f) voyeurism—observing others naked or engaging in sex, (g) masochism—being humiliated, bound, beaten, or made to suffer, and (h) sadism—infliction of pain or psychological suffering on another. A ninth category includes a myriad of other behaviors.

Kaplan, H. S. (1983). *The evaluation of sexual disorders.* New York: Brunner/Mazel.

parataxic distortion   Projections, stemming from early life experiences, that are placed on another person. Such distortions generally occur in new relationships.
Example: A woman claims her husband is rejecting her because she was rejected by her father.

Beavers, W. R. (1977). *Psychotherapy and growth: A family systems perspective.* New York: Brunner/Mazel.
Sullivan, H. S. (1956). *Clinical studies in psychiatry.* New York: Norton.

parental alienation syndrome   A disorder primarily in children who have been involved in protracted custody litigation. A child with this disorder is preoccupied with deprecation and criticism of a parent. Often the degradation is unjustified and/or exaggerated. The concept of *parental alienation syndrome* includes a brainwashing component but is much more inclusive. A parent will unconsciously "program" a child to denigrate the other, thus contributing to the child's alienation from the other parent.
Example: A 7-year-old boy, living with his mother since his parents separated, kicks, screams, and yells when his father comes to pick him

up for a weekend visit. The child "hates" the father and says he should not go because the father never pays his mother any child support.

Gardner, R. A. (1987). *The parental alienation syndrome and the differentiation between fabricated and genuine child sex abuse.* Cresskill, NJ: Creative Therapeutics.

parental child   An older child who functions as parent for the younger children. Although not yet an adult and lacking the relevant power, the parental child assumes responsibility for the younger children. The child thus is caught between misbehaving children and a mother who has failed to delegate the requisite power.

Haley, J. (1987). *Problem-solving therapy* (2nd ed.). San Francisco: Jossey-Bass.
Minuchin, S., Montalvo, B., Guerney, B. G., Jr., Rosman, B. L., & Schumer, F. (1967). *Families of the slums: An exploration of their structure and treatment.* New York: Basic Books.

parental coalition   A clearly defined husband-wife subsystem within the family. The parents are able to create well-defined generational boundaries that help the children maintain their own identities within the sibling subsystem. See also **marital schism/skew.**

Example: The parents in a family are careful not to discuss such issues as sex, money, and parental conflict with their children. They have established a strong bond between themselves, and this bond serves to keep such issues at their generational level.

Bernard, C., & Corrales, R. (1979). *The theory and technique of family therapy.* Springfield, IL: Charles C Thomas.
Lidz, T., Fleck, S., & Cornelison, A. (Eds.). (1965). *Schizophrenia and the family.* New York: International Universities Press.

parental dyad   A relationship composed of a father and a mother.

Glick, I. D., & Kessler, D. P. (1980). *Marital and family therapy* (2nd ed.). New York: Grune & Stratton.

parental group therapy   A form of therapy in which each parent is seen in a group with other same-sex parents. This type of therapy often is conducted with parents of severely disturbed children who simultaneously receive either individual or group psychotherapy. Parental group therapy affords emotional support to the parents; within the group, the parents often become aware of their own dependency needs and feelings of isolation.

Speers, R. W., & Lansing, C. (1964). Group psychotherapy with preschool psychotic children and collateral group therapy of their parents: A preliminary report of the first two years. *American Journal of Orthopsychiatry, 34,* 659-666.

parental identification   Internalization of the personality characteristics of a given parent. The person who does this makes unconscious reactions similar to those of that parent.

Example: A son becomes hostile and sarcastic toward his mother because he identifies with his father's similar behavior.

Lynn, D. (1969). *Parental and sex role identification: A theoretical formulation.* Berkeley, CA: McCutchan.

parental loading   The tendency of parental standards to be more rigid for the eldest child in the family.

Glick, I. D., & Kessler, D. P. (1974). *Marital and family therapy.* New York: Grune & Stratton.

parental preference   The child's desire to adopt behavior characteristics of a particular parent.

Example: A child prefers to adopt her mother's emotional approach to other people, rather than her father's cold and aloof stance.

Lynn, D. (1969). *Parental and sex role identification: A theoretical formulation.* Berkeley, CA: McCutchan.

parent effectiveness training (P.E.T.)   A communications method to assist parents in getting along with and in better disciplining their children. The training develops parental guidelines from theories of client-centered behavioral and communication models. The approach is similar to that used in systematic training for effective parenting (STEP), developed by Dinkmeyer and McKay and based on the writings of Alfred Adler and Rudolph Dreikurs.

Dinkmeyer, D., & McKay, G. (1976). *Systematic training for effective parenting (STEP).* Circle Pines, MN: American Guidance Service.

Gordon, T. (1970). *Parent effectiveness training.* New York: Peter H. Wyden.

L'Abate, L. (1981). Skill training programs for couples and families. In A. S. Gurman & D. P. Kniskern (Eds.), *Handbook of family therapy* (pp. 631-662). New York: Brunner/Mazel.

parentification   Fantasizing or behaving as if one's partner or child were one's parent. This process typically puts the partner or child in a caretaking role and so puts excessive responsibility on the parentified individual. This subjective distortion, the result of wishful fantasy or dependent behavior, can be either a pathological condition or a component of the regressive core of an evenly balanced, reciprocal relationship.

Example: A single parent asks the oldest child to assume parental duties and responsibilities, such as sharing the parent's anxieties and financial problems, taking care of the younger siblings, and acting, in general, as a confidant and friend, without generational boundaries. These duties and responsibilities are beyond the age and maturity level of the child; but, as a result of assuming them, the child displays adultlike behavior much earlier than expected.

Boszormenyi-Nagy, I., & Spark, G. L. (1973). *Invisible loyalties: Reciprocity in intergenerational family therapy.* New York: Harper & Row.

parentification of a child   Unconscious attempts by parents who have been deprived of their own parents through loss or separation to transform their own children into parentlike figures. Such identification is especially likely if the marital partner fails to gratify the need to recover the lost parents. Parentification of a child normally occurs in large families or in families where the parents work and an older child is given authority over the younger children. It occurs abnormally when a parent abdicates a position of authority or assigns an adult role to a child, thereby breaching generational boundaries.

Example: Alanna's mother is alcoholic. In the evening, Alanna cooks dinner for the family, puts mother to bed, and makes sure her younger brother does his homework.

Boszormenyi-Nagy, I., & Spark, G. L. (1973). *Invisible loyalties: Reciprocity in intergenerational family therapy.* New York: Harper & Row.

parent surrogate   An adult who fills the role of an absent parent in the development of the child.

Example: The husband's sister assumes the role of the mother after the wife leaves the husband and fails to return to the family.

Glick, I. D., & Kessler, D. P. (1980). *Marital and family therapy* (2nd ed.). New York: Grune & Stratton.

participation rate   The relative amount of communication contributed by each family member to the family's total interaction.

Mishler, E., & Waxler, N. (1968). *Interaction in families: An experimental study of family processes and schizophrenia.* New York: John Wiley.

parts technique   A technique in which family members are asked to visualize and define parts of themselves.

Example: A mother feels that one part of her, her household self, is inefficient. She is asked to sculpt one of her children to represent her felt inefficiency. The sculpting leads to a discussion of her feelings.

Dodson, L., & Kurpuis, D. (1977). *Family counseling: A systems approach.* Muncie, IN: Accelerated Development.

passive-congenial marriage   A marital relationship in which one member is passive and somewhat withdrawn and the other member is gregarious and happy-go-lucky.

Example: The wife practices as a Jehovah's Witness; the husband excludes himself by choice from all of the religious activities of his wife and children. He spends most of his time drinking with his friends.

Glick, I. D., & Kessler, D. P. (1980). *Marital and family therapy* (2nd ed.). New York: Grune & Stratton.

P

past-present switch   A device in which, in answer to a question, present and past difficulties are connected in a very illogical fashion.

Example: A school-age girl is brought into therapy because she has been acting strangely and talking in riddles. When the mother is asked, "When did you notice that your child was not developing as she should?" she replies, "Well, she was a 7-month-old baby, and she was in an incubator for 6 weeks." The child's present and past difficulties thus are connected illogically.

Satir, V. (1983). *Conjoint family therapy* (3rd ed.). Palo Alto, CA: Science & Behavior Books.
Watzlawick, P. (1963). *An anthology of human communication.* Palo Alto, CA: Science & Behavior Books.

paternal rejection   A pattern of paternal behaviors ranging from physical abuse, distancing, lack of interest and concern, to uninvolvement vis-à-vis a child.

L'Abate, L. (1975). Pathogenic role rigidity in fathers: Some observations. *Journal of Marriage and Family Counseling, 1,* 69-79.

pathogenic family   A family whose adaptive and coping mechanisms have been exhausted. The family members are trapped chronically in stereotyped patterns of interaction that severely limit their range of choice, but no alternatives seem possible. This situation produces extremely dysfunctional behavior in the offspring.

Minuchin, S., Rosman, B. L., & Baker, L. (1978). *Psychosomatic families: Anorexia nervosa in context.* Cambridge, MA: Harvard University Press.

pathogenic relating   A destructive behavioral process between family members. A pervasive form of this type of relating is silence.

Example: A son is acting out. Every time the parents raise the issue of their son's misbehavior, he becomes sullen, withdrawn, and silent.

Zuk, G. (1971). *Family therapy: A triadic-based approach.* New York: Behavioral Publications.

pathologic need complementarity   Unconscious needs of the parent to shape the psychic structure of the child. The parent's unconscious needs are transferred to the child as rigid superego demands that the child accepts passively. By accepting such demands, the child's dependent needs are gratified. The parent and child feed each other's narcissistic demands, thus helping to overcome loneliness, helplessness, and isolation.

Boszormenyi-Nagy, I. (1962). The concept of schizophrenia from the point of view of family treatment. *Family Process, 1,* 103-113.

Zuk, G., & Rubenstein, D. (1965). A review of concepts in the study and treatment of families of schizophrenics. In I. Boszormenyi-Nagy & J. Framo (Eds.), *Intensive family therapy: Theoretical and practical aspects* (pp. 1-32). New York: Harper & Row.

patriarchal family   A family or clan marked by the supremacy of the father.

Garrett, W. (1982). *Seasons of marriage and family life.* New York: Holt, Rinehart & Winston.

patrilineal descent group   A group based on parent-child genealogical relationships in which membership is determined solely through male genealogical relationships.

Zelditch, M. (1964). Cross-cultural analyses of family structure. In H. T. Christensen (Ed.), *Handbook of marriage and the family* (pp. 462-500). Chicago: Rand McNally.

patrilocal residence   A rule of residence requiring that a man live with his father and that when he is married, he bring his wife home with him.

Zelditch, M. (1964). Cross-cultural analyses of family structure. In H. T. Christensen (Ed.), *Handbook of marriage and the family* (pp. 462-500). Chicago: Rand McNally.

pattern of alignment   The distribution of ties among members of a family. It refers to any basis on which family members line up with each other—unconsciously or consciously, in fantasy or in action, for reasons of comfort, affection, or power—to enhance or defeat each other.

Example: A child aligns himself with his father to get what he wants because he believes his father will override his mother's prohibitions.

Hess, R., & Handel, G. (1959). *Family worlds: A psychological approach to family life.* Chicago: University of Chicago Press.

pattern recognition task   A task used by Reiss to test family problem-solving effectiveness. In the task, each family member is given a sample card with a sequence of letters on it; the children are given one type of sequence, and the parents another type. Each person then is asked to conceptualize and identify the correct sequences without any verbal communication. A variation of this task is to give each family member a series of 15 cards with sequences on them and to ask each member to sort the cards into patterns. The family then is asked to sort the same 15 cards as a group, discussing the sort as they do it. Finally each member is asked to sort the cards separately a second time.

Reiss, D. (1981). *The family's construction of reality.* Cambridge, MA: Harvard University Press.

pattern regulators   Nonsymbolic, routinized sequences of behavior that determine space and distance among family members and between the family and the outside world. These sequences of behavior are manifested by all family members. However, they occur continuously and are beyond the members' awareness.

Example: In a family with a disabled child, certain remedial motor exercises are performed with the child. These exercises are conducted only by the parents or by the oldest child, thus determining a clear hierarchy within the family. No one outside the family helps the disabled child with daily exercises, which defines the family's boundary with the outside world.

Reiss, D. (1981). *The family's construction of reality.* Cambridge, MA: Harvard University Press.

patterns of interaction   Redundant sequences of behavior or interaction patterns in the family that define who talks to whom, when, about what, and in what manner.

Example: At the dinner table, the oldest child, Rob, begins to talk about an experience he had at school. Mom listens attentively while Dad continues eating and Rob's two sisters begin to whisper about a boy they like. Rob gets upset and complains that Dad and his sisters are not paying attention. Mom fusses at the girls and gives Dad a warning glance. Everyone then listens more carefully to Rob's story. This fairly simple interaction pattern is repeated over and over in the family.

Hoopes, M. H., Fisher, B. L., & Barlow, S. H. (1984). *Structured family facilitation programs: Enrichment, education, and treatment.* Rockville, MD: Aspen Systems.

pause   (1) A break between sentences spoken by the same speaker or a break between two or more speakers. (2) Any silence in which it is felt that some one "should" be speaking.

Mishler, E., & Waxler, N. (1968). *Interaction in families: An experimental study of family processes and schizophrenia.* New York: John Wiley.

peak experience   A personal and private experience of great emotional significance that may lead to rapid changes in personality (e.g., a religious conversion).

Maslow, A. H. (1959). *New knowledge in human values.* New York: Harper & Row.

peculiar forms of verbalization   A code used by Singer and Wynne to denote statements with odd grammatical constructions, mispronunciations, slips of the tongue, or violations of conventional usage and logic.

Singer, M., & Wynne, L. (1966). Principles of scoring communication defects and deviances in parents of schizophrenics: Rorschach and TAT scoring manuals. *Psychiatry, 29,* 260-288.

pediatric psychology   A term used to describe activities of psychologists working in service capacities in pediatric medical settings. These settings include children's hospitals, developmental clinics, and private pediatric practices. The activities of psychologists working in such places are quite diverse and overlap considerably with those of individuals in related specialty areas, such as clinical child psychology, developmental psychology, school psychology, and family psychology. Thus pediatric psychologists often work with children who have life-threatening conditions and chronic diseases (e.g., diabetes, failure to thrive, accidental injuries, childhood cancer, childhood asthma, hemophilia, spina bifida, infectious diseases, brain injury), medically related behaviors (e.g., adherence, enuresis, encopresis, anorexia, bulimia, obesity), and the management of pain and discomfort (e.g., dental treatment, burns, preparation for hospitalization, somatization disorder).

Routh, D. K. (Ed.). (1988). *Handbook of pediatric psychology.* New York: Guilford.

pejorative communication   A category of verbal communication that is person devaluing. These statements are intended to control others by asserting superiority or blame. Statements that fall into this category are overt superiority, overt control, overblame, and sarcasm.

Alexander, J., Barton, C., Lindsey, D., Turner, C., & Warburton, J. (1988). Defensive and supportive communication interaction system. In D. Grotevant & C. Carlson (Eds.), *Handbook of family assessment* (pp. 182-187). New York: Guilford.

penalty deposit system   A system that maintains patient compliance in treatment by requiring patients to pay the therapist a deposit that is refunded in full if they comply with, but is forfeited if they violate, a therapeutic prescription.

Lobitz, W., & LoPiccolo, J. (1972). New methods in the behavioral treatment of sexual dysfunctions. *Journal of Behavior Therapy and Experimental Psychiatry, 3,* 265-271.

LoPiccolo, J. (1978). Direct treatment of sexual dysfunction. In J. LoPiccolo & L. LoPiccolo (Eds.), *Handbook of sex therapy* (pp. 1-18). New York: Plenum.

penchant for closure A family's proclivity to suspend or apply ordered and coherent concepts to raw sensory experience. A penchant for closure is a dimension of family consensual experience.

Reiss, D. (1981). *The family's construction of reality.* Cambridge, MA: Harvard University Press.

P

penile containment A technique of sex therapy in which the male is asked to experience intravaginal containment with little if any thrusting. This technique usually is used in treating premature ejaculation.

Masters, W., & Johnson, V. (1970). *Human sexual inadequacy.* Boston: Little, Brown.

penile implant A prosthetic device, implanted inside the penis, that enables the male to achieve intercourse. Two types of implants are available. One type is semirigid and malleable, consisting of two rods. The other is an inflatable device that simulates tumescence and detumescence. Implants are indicated only in cases of organic erectile dysfunction.

Tiefer, L., & Melman, A. (1989). Comprehensive evaluation of erectile dysfunction and medical treatments. In S. Leiblum & R. Rosen (Eds.), *Principles and practice of sex therapy* (2nd ed., pp. 207-236). New York: Guilford.

peoplemaking An attempt to explicate the procedures by which a family might extricate itself from a dysfunctional system. This explication is not easily accomplished and may require an outside intention by one who is not part of the family system.
Example: The wife was advised to move out of her parents' home, to stop following her mother's dictates, and to begin to relate to her husband as a capable man instead of as her son.

Satir, V. (1972). *Peoplemaking.* Palo Alto, CA: Science & Behavior Books.

perceived parental similarity Perception of oneself as being similar to a particular parent whether or not an actual similarity exists.

White, S. G., & Hatcher, C. (1984). Couple complementarity and similarity: A review of the literature. *American Journal of Family Therapy, 12,* 15-25.

perceived sex role similarity Perception of oneself as being similar to others of a given sex whether or not an actual similarity exists.
Example: The husband and the wife are equally responsible for financial decisions; the wife is in charge of spending the money, and the husband earns it.

Lynn, D. (1969). *Parental and sex role identification: A theoretical formulation.* Berkeley, CA: McCutchan.

perceptual distortion A condition in which the mates in dysfunctional marital pairs see their spouses as they expect them to be, rather than as they really are, and treat them accordingly.

Example: A wife sees her husband as cold and reflecting and thus does not have to confront her lack of sexual desire for him.

Satir, V. (1965). Conjoint marital therapy. In B. Green (Ed.), *The psychotherapies of marital disharmony* (pp. 121-134). New York: Free Press.

performance anxiety The fear that one will not be able to perform sexually. A cycle of anxiety is established such that anxiety creates failure and the failure perpetuates the anxiety.

Example: A man failed to have an erection due to excessive alcohol intake. This failure led him to believe he would fail in the future, thus creating anxiety every time he approached a sexual experience. This type of anxiety escalated, with failure trapping the man in a vicious cycle.

Masters, W., & Johnson, V. (1970). *Human sexual inadequacy.* Boston: Little, Brown.

perineometer A cylindrical instrument inserted into the vagina to provide a simple means of exercising the pubococcygeal muscle against resistance.

Kegel, A. H. (1952). Sexual functions of the pubococcygeal muscle. *Western Journal of Surgery, Obstetrics, and Gynecology, 60,* 521-524.
Kline-Graber, G., & Graber, B. (1978). Diagnosis and treatment procedures of pubococcygeal deficiencies in women. In J. LoPiccolo & L. LoPiccolo (Eds.), *Handbook of sex therapy* (pp. 227-240). New York: Plenum.

peripheral person A relatively uninvolved or less involved outside person whom a therapist uses to achieve an objective.

Example: A therapist interviews a whole family presenting a child problem and sees the mother and the child as overinvolved and the father as more peripheral. The therapist tells the family that the child needs to identify more with the father by structuring father-son activities that exclude the mother.

Haley, J. (1987). *Problem-solving therapy* (2nd ed.). San Francisco: Jossey-Bass.

permeability The extent to which family members and nonmembers can move freely into and out of the family. Family boundaries necessarily vary, both across family systems and within families over time. Across family systems, permeability relates to the degree of system organization; overorganized systems have relatively impermeable boundaries (with reference to nonfamily members), and underorganized systems have extremely permeable boundaries. These boundaries are determined, in part, by the environment—particularly cultural, ethnic, and occupational systems. Family boundaries tend to ebb and flow through time, expanding and becoming more permeable with the addition of members and becoming more impermeable with the loss of members. A family system that is relatively permeable at the level of interaction may be equally "open" at the level of meaning, affect, and communication. But such covariation does not always occur; at times, permeability at the level of interaction and communication may be associated with impermeability at the level of meaning and affect.

Example: The husband is not open to any kind of influence from his in-laws when they want to give him advice on childbearing, because he knows the kinds of parents they were with his wife, their daughter.

Benjamin, M. (1982). General systems theory, family system theories, and family therapy. In A. Bross (Ed.), *Family therapy: Principles of strategic practice* (pp. 34-88). New York: Guilford.

permeability to others   The ability to hear and respond to others within the family system.

Beavers, W. R. (1976). A theoretical basis for family evaluation. In J. M. Lewis, W. R. Beavers, J. T. Gossett, & V. A. Phillips (Eds.), *No single thread: Psychological health in the family system* (pp. 46-82). New York: Brunner/Mazel.

permeable boundaries   Ambiguity regarding stepfamily boundaries when an emotionally or legally important adult is living elsewhere as a result of a previous marriage relationship. When a family system has permeable boundaries, flexibility exists with respect to individuals and events of influence entering and existing within the system.

Example: A child lives with his mother, who usually exercises parental control over him. However, this boundary may shift from time to time when the father reenters the system to assume responsibility.

Visher, E., & Visher, J. (1979). *Stepfamilies: A guide to working with stepparents and stepchildren.* New York: Brunner/Mazel.

person control strategy   The use of successful interruptions (direct control) and questions (indirect control) to influence others.

Example: A person is talking about a serious subject when another person, to change the subject, interrupts to ask about the time.

Mishler, E., & Waxler, N. (1968). *Interaction in families: An experimental study of family processes and schizophrenia.* New York: John Wiley.

perturbation   A therapeutic intervention that accommodates to, but does not alter, the organization of the system. Such an intervention is designed to unbalance the system, therefore setting up the system for later change.

Example: The therapist tells an overprotective mother to take better care of her child. Exaggerating the symptom, the family is in a position to make a change.

Maturana, H. R. (1978). Biology of language: The epistemology of reality. In G. A. Miller & E. Lenneberg (Eds.), *Psychology and the biology of language and thought* (pp. 27-63). New York: Academic Press.

perverse triangle   A family relationship triangle in which the separation between the generations is blocked in a covert way. The presence of the triangle coincides with undesirable manifestations of violence, symptomatic behavior, or dissolution of the system. A perverse triangle has the following characteristics: (a) It comprises two members from one generation and one from another, (b) two members from different generations form a coalition excluding the third party, and (c) the coalition is kept hidden or denied.

Example: Two parents (same generation) and a child (different generation) go to the maternal grandparents' home for a special Sunday dinner. The child becomes restless during dinner and starts to complain. The father does not like his in-laws but is too polite to reveal his feeling. As the meal proceeds, the father supports the child's complaints indirectly by attending closely to every word the child says and failing to set any limits (hidden coalition). The mother becomes increasingly frustrated and angry. Her attempts to discipline the child are undermined by the father (different generation in coalition).

Haley, J. (1977). Toward a theory of pathological systems. In P. Watzlawick & J. Weakland (Eds.), *The interactional view* (pp. 11-27). New York: Norton.
Hoffman, L. (1981). *Foundations of family therapy.* New York: Basic Books.

petrification   The process of mentally turning oneself or another person into a stone, a robot, a thing, without subjectivity. The act of petrifying a person negates that person's autonomy and ignores the person's feelings.

Example: A psychotic patient dreams that members of her family had turned into inanimate objects.

Laing, R. (1969). *The divided self.* New York: Penguin.

phantom orgasm   An orgasm or orgasmlike response, in an individual with spinal cord injury, that is assumed to be purely cerebrocognitional and that serves intrapsychic functions.

Higgins, G. (1978). Aspects of several responses in adults with spinal cord injury: A review of the literature. In J. LoPiccolo & L. LoPiccolo (Eds.), *Handbook of sex therapy* (pp. 387-410). New York: Plenum.

Money, J. (1960). Phantom orgasm in dreams of paraplegic men and women. *Archives of General Psychiatry, 3,* 373-382.

phase differentiation   Sequential changes that two people or a group go through in a given time period.

Example: The first phase in a group's development is one in which the members get to know one another and then set some tasks for the group.

Lennard, H., & Bernstein, A. (1969). *Patterns in human interaction.* San Francisco: Jossey-Bass.

Riskin, J., & Faunce, E. (1972). An evaluative review of family interaction research. *Family Process, 11,* 365-455.

phasic relational process   A process in which all relationships go through phases of unrelatedness (autistic phase), affiliative overinvolvement (symbiotic phase), growth of autonomy in members (individuation phase), and dissolution (separation phase), leading to reinvolvement in new groups.

Boszormenyi-Nagy, I. (1965). A theory of relationships: Experience and transactions. In I. Boszormenyi-Nagy & J. Framo (Eds.), *Intensive family therapy; Theoretical and practical aspects* (pp. 33-86). New York: Harper & Row.

physical symptoms   An adaptive mechanism for a current life situation.

Example: A woman complains that she has difficulty swallowing. Her family members call her every day to unload their problems. She can no longer "swallow" their problems or express her feelings toward them.

Haley, J. (1987). *Problem-solving therapy* (2nd ed.). San Francisco: Jossey-Bass.

placater   A pattern of communication in the family in which one person is always trying to please, apologize, or do whatever is necessary to prevent disagreements and conflicts.

Satir, V. (1972). *Peoplemaking.* Palo Alto, CA: Science & Behavior Book.

planning   An activity in which the therapist makes initial hypotheses on the basis of a minimum awareness of the family structure. Clues that may lead to information about the family may be the age of the family members, the number of family members, where they live, and the composition of the family.

Minuchin, S., & Fishman, H. (1981). *Family therapy techniques.* Cambridge, MA: Harvard University Press.

plan-something-together task   The first task of the Structured Family Interview (developed at the Mental Research Institute for therapy and research purposes), in which the family members are seated around a table in the interview room and are asked by the interviewer to "plan something you could all do together as a family; all of you please participate in the planning." The interviewer then leaves the room, and the family is given 10 minutes to deal with the task.

Riskin, M., & Faunce, E. (1970). Family interaction scales: I. Theoretical framework and method. *Archives of General Psychiatry, 22,* 504-512.

plateau phase   The second stage of the sexual response cycle, generally characterized by high level of sexual arousal.

Masters, W., & Johnson, V. (1970). *Human sexual inadequacy.* Boston: Little, Brown.

pleasure anxiety   The fear of being able to feel pleasure. This type of anxiety can lead to sexual difficulties and dysfunctions.
   Example: A woman reported she could not experience sexual pleasure and was afraid to let go in order to feel pleasure. As an incest survivor, she felt guilty over pleasure because of the pleasurable sensations she had experienced during the incest.

Appelbaum, B. (1988). An ego-analytic perspective on desire disorders. In S. Leiblum & R. Rosen (Eds.), *Sexual desire disorders* (pp. 75-106). New York: Guilford.

pleasuring exercise   A sex therapy exercise designed to facilitate sexual communication, sensual awareness, and permission to ask for what feels good.

Kaplan, H. S. (1981). *The new sex therapy.* New York: Brunner/Mazel.

p-li-ss-it model   A treatment model that provides four levels of approach with suggested methods for handling sexual concerns: (a) *p*ermission, (b) *li*mited information, (c) *s*pecific *s*uggestion, and (d) *i*ntensive *t*herapy. The first three levels constitute brief therapy.

Annon, J., & Robinson, C. (1978). The use of vicarious learnings in the treatment of sexual concerns. In J. LoPiccolo & L. LoPiccolo (Eds.), *Handbook of sex therapy* (pp. 35-56). New York: Plenum.

polyandry   A type of polygamous marriage in which a woman is simultaneously married to two or more husbands.

Christensen, H. (1964). Development of the family field of study. In H. T. Christensen (Ed.), *Handbook of marriage and the family* (pp. 3-32). Chicago: Rand McNally.

polygamy   The joining of nuclear families into larger social units. A polygamous relationship exists if the joining is at the point of the marriage relationship so that one person has two or more spouses and hence membership in two or more nuclear families.

Christensen, H. (1964). Development of the family field of study. In H. T. Christensen (Ed.), *Handbook of marriage and the family* (pp. 3-32). Chicago: Rand McNally.

positioning   A paradoxical strategy in which the therapist accepts and exaggerates the clients' position or self-assertion.

Example: A woman who says all of her friends hate her is told by the therapist that perhaps they do. The therapist then suggests that she list all of the ways people have expressed their hate toward her.

Rohrbaugh, M., Tennen, H., Press, S., White, L., Raskin, P., & Pickering, M. (1977, August). *Paradoxical strategies in psychotherapy.* Paper presented at the American Psychological Association, San Francisco, CA.
Weeks, G., & L'Abate, L. (1982). *Paradoxical psychotherapy: Theory and practice with individuals, couples, and families.* New York: Brunner/Mazel.

positive connotation   Reframing of the family's problem in a way to indicate that the problem is logical and meaningful in its context. *Positive connotation* was developed by the Milan group and evolved out of paradoxical interventions. The behavior of the identified patient is positively connoted, as is the symptomatic behavior of other family members.

Example: An 8-year-old boy stopped doing well in school after the death of his grandfather. He also started talking and acting like a caricature of a little old man. The boy insisted that his grandfather was following him when he took walks with his father. The therapist stated to the boy, "I understand that you considered your grandfather to be the central pillar of your family. Without your grandfather's presence, you are afraid something would change, so you thought of assuming his role, perhaps because you're afraid the balance in the family would change. For now, I think you should continue in this role and not change anything until our next session."

Boscolo, L., Cecchin, G., Hoffman, L., & Penn, P. (1987). *Milan systemic family therapy: Conversations in theory and practice.* New York: Basic Books.
Selvini Palazzoli, M., Boscolo, L., Cecchin, G., & Prata, G. (1978). *Paradox and counterparadox: A new model in the therapy of the family in schizophrenic transaction.* New York: Jason Aronson.

positive feedback   Feedback that leads to change or loss of stability. As a crisis-inducing mechanism, it counteracts negative feedback. See also **negative feedback.**

Example: Two married partners who are constantly fighting somehow find that this behavior protects their marriage from change. When a

therapist tells them how well they are fighting and that they should continue, this prescription creates a crisis in the couple, leading to change.

Watzlawick, P., Bevin, J. H., & Jackson, D. D. (1967). *Pragmatics of human communication.* New York: Norton.

positive feedback loop   A mechanism that relates two events in a
circular, amplifying manner. An increase in any component part of the
circular sequence increases, in turn, the next event in the sequence. In
this deviation-mollifying situation, the positive feedback loop is primarily a self-destruction mechanism. It sets up a runaway situation that
eventually drives the system beyond the limits or range within which it
can function. See **positive feedback.**

Maruyama, M. (1963). The second cybernetics: Deviation-exemplifying mutual causal
processes. *American Scientist, 51,* 164-179.
Steinglass, P. (1978). The conceptualization of marriage from a systems theory perspective. In T. Paolino & B. McCrady (Eds.), *Marriage and marital therapy* (pp.
292-368). New York: Brunner/Mazel.

positive reinforcement   Material reinforcers (e.g., tokens, stars, points,
money) or social reinforcers (e.g., praise, smiles) to increase desired
behavior.
   Example: Henry's parents want him to study more. They begin systematically to praise him for doing his homework and for engaging in
other school-related activities.

LeBow, M. (1972). Behavior modification for the family. In G. D. Erickson & T. P. Hogan
(Eds.), *Family therapy: An introduction to theory and technique* (pp. 347-376).
Belmont, CA: Wadsworth.

positive statement procedure   A procedure requiring that the client
make a positive statement for every negative statement he or she makes.

Azrin, N. H., Master, B. J., & Jones, R. (1973). Reciprocity counseling: A rapid learning-
based procedure for marital counseling. *Behavior Research and Therapy, 11,* 365-382.
O'Leary, K., & Turkewitz, H. (1978). Marital therapy from a behavioral perspective. In
T. Paolino & B. McCrady (Eds.), *Marriage and marital therapy* (pp. 240-297). New
York: Brunner/Mazel.

postmodernism   A philosophical system, emerging in the 1970s and
1980s, that focuses on elaboration, eclecticism, ornamentation, and
inclusiveness. Modernism, as seen in family therapy, ignored issues
such as gender, ethnicity, and the impact of larger systems such as
political and economic forces. Modernism also promoted allegiance to
a single model of therapy. Postmodernism, however, focuses on eclecticism and integration of theories.

Doherty, W. J. (1991). Family therapy goes postmodern. *Family Therapy Networker, 15,* 36-42.

power A concept that has been fraught with confusion and controversy over its existence, as well over its definition. One structural definition of *power* refers to the use of resources exchanged in the family (services, information, goods, and money), in contrast to presence, where love and status are exchanged. A process definition refers to who makes decisions (authority) and to who carries them out (responsibility) in the family. Decisions may be classified into routine, everyday ones (instrumental) and one-time, important ones, such as where should we live and what house should we buy (orchestration). Most functional families spread power evenly among their members, while most dysfunctional families have either no sense of power or power concentrated mainly in one or two members in a punitive or inconsistent fashion.

Foa, U. G., & Foa, E. B. (1974). *Societal structures of the mind.* Springfield, IL: Charles C Thomas.
L'Abate, L. (1986). *Systematic family therapy.* New York: Brunner/Mazel.

pragmatics The behavioral effects of communication. All behavior is considered to be communication. The data of romantics are words; their configurations and meanings are their nonverbal concomitants and body language. See also **aesthetics.**

Keeney, B. P. (1983). *Aesthetics of change.* New York: Guilford.
Keeney, B. P., & Sprenkle, D. H. (1982). Ecosystemic epistemology: Critical implications for the aesthetics and pragmatics of family therapy. *Family Process, 21,* 1-19.
Watzlawick, P., Bevin, J. H., & Jackson, D. D. (1967). *Pragmatics of human communication.* New York: Norton.

praxis The intentions of a person or a group of persons (e.g., a family) toward another person or group on the basis of the experiences the first person or group has had regarding that other person or group.

Example: Every time the daughter says something about her feelings, the mother changes the topic. The mother's experience of her daughter is that she will raise painful issues, as she did some time ago.

Esterson, A. (1970). *The leaves of spring.* London: Pelican.

preempting A strategy in which the client's thoughts, feelings, attitudes, and positions are anticipated and stated by the therapist or mediator in a neutralizing context before the client has a chance to state them. The best strategy for dealing with undesirable conflict is to prevent it in the first place. Preempting is useful not only for structuring the context of mediation in a general way but also for preventing conflict by removing the stingers before antagonizing words can be uttered. Thus the technique minimizes the client's opportunity to develop and manifest resistance to change or compromise.

Example: The mediator begins the mediation by informing both spouses, in an informed and authoritative manner, of the current understandings of the children's needs in the divorce situation and of the irrelevance of the various negative and incriminating comments and interpretations the spouses have made about each other. In this way, the spouses' resistance is minimized. Alternatively the mediator presents to the parents the assumption that their children need regular and continuing contact with both parents. It then becomes very difficult for the mother to state that the children do not need their father. In effect, that statement has been preempted.

Marlow, L., & Sauber, S. R. (1990). *Handbook of divorce mediation.* New York: Plenum.
Saposnek, D. T. (1983). Strategies in child custody mediation: A family systems approach. *Mediation Quarterly, 1,* 29-54.

premarital counseling   Counseling to help a couple prepare for marriage. Such counseling may be problem focused (remedial) or prevention oriented.

L'Abate, L. (1981). Skill training programs for couples and families. In A. S. Gurman & D. P. Kniskern (Eds.), *Handbook of family therapy* (pp. 631-662). New York: Brunner/Mazel.
L'Abate, L., & McHenry, S. (1983). *Handbook of marital intervention.* New York: Grune & Stratton.

premature ejaculation   The most common male sexual dysfunction involving the inability to control the ejaculatory reflex. This dysfunction occurs along a continuum ranging from those men who ejaculate during intromission to those who occasionally experience a loss of control.

Masters, W., & Johnson, V. (1970). *Human sexual inadequacy.* Boston: Little, Brown.

premonitory sensations   The sensations that occur just before ejaculation and serve as feedback to the man to indicate that ejaculation is near.

Masters, W., & Johnson, V. (1970). *Human sexual inadequacy.* Boston: Little, Brown.

prescribing the defense   Recognition of a defense and requesting the patient to maintain his or her "line of defense."

Example: A withdrawn husband shuts off his feelings, and his frantic wife tries to get through to him by constantly expressing her feelings, much as his mother used to do. The therapist acknowledges the importance of controlling feelings: "It takes independence and courage not to allow your wife to infringe on you."

Papp, P. (1980). The use of fantasy in a couples group. In M. Andolfi & I. Zwerling (Eds.), *Dimensions of family therapy* (pp. 73-90). New York: Guilford.

prescribing the role If the therapist senses a high degree of rigidity in the roles, it is better to define one aspect of the roles positively and to ask the client to act it out, rather than attempt to modify them directly.

Example: The husband was proud of protecting his wife, "shepherding" her all of these years. The therapist said he had not gone far enough in his shepherding: He had only shepherded one side of her, her moral side, and had neglected to shepherd the other side, her desire for pleasure.

Papp, P. (1980). The use of fantasy in a couples group. In M. Andolfi & I. Zwerling (Eds.), *Dimensions of family therapy* (pp. 73-90). New York: Guilford.

prescribing the symptom Directing the client to engage voluntarily in the symptomatic behavior. The behavior is then no longer spontaneous because the client has stepped outside the client's frame of the symptomatic game-without-end. See also **paradoxical prescription.**

Example: A woman complains about worrying off and on throughout the day. These worries interfere with her daily activities, and she enters therapy to eliminate them. She already has tried to put her worries aside, but with no success. The therapist tells her that these worries are trying to tell her something important about her life. Rather than attempt to get rid of them, however, she is told to worry more. In fact, she is to concentrate on her worrisome thoughts completely and exclusively whenever they occur. She is to worry about as many things as possible. In fact, in the hope that she will get the message sooner, she is instructed to amplify her worries.

Watzlawick, P., Beavin, J. H., & Jackson, D. D. (1967). *Pragmatics of human communication.* New York: Norton.

Weeks, G., & L'Abate, L. (1982). *Paradoxical psychotherapy: Theory and practice with individuals, couples, and families.* New York: Brunner/Mazel.

pretending A therapeutic method in which the therapist directs the identified patient to pretend, or practice, having the problem or directs the family members to enact the pattern of interaction that usually occurs around the symptom. The problem then is conducted in a voluntary, controlled context; as a result, the problem or interactions take new meaning. This method can produce a corresponding change in the family's interaction patterns.

Example: A father who is constantly worried about having a heart attack is to told by the therapist to pretend having a heart attack in the session.

Madanes, C. (1981). *Strategic family therapy*. San Francisco: Jossey-Bass.

pretense of problems   A therapeutic situation created by a paradoxical strategy in which an individual, usually a child, is asked to pretend to have a problem. The strategy is based on the assumption that the child's problem is helping to protect the family. Pretense of problems may be created in three ways:

1. The parents request that the child have the problem; that is, the parents ask the child to consciously and voluntarily enact the problem behavior. For example, a child who is bed-wetting might be asked to urinate and sleep in a wet bed.
2. The parents request that the child pretend to have the problem. A child who has stomachaches might be asked to fake stomachaches at particular times.
3. The parents request that the child pretend to help the parent. This method involves making an overt shift in the family hierarchy. The strategy makes the child superior, while the parent takes a one-down position. For example, a young boy develops chronic headaches, which take attention away from the father's unhappiness. The father is instructed to pretend to have a headache every evening so that his son can be helpful to him.

Madanes, C. (1981). *Strategic family therapy*. San Francisco: Jossey-Bass.

pretherapy training   Training procedures (e.g., role induction interview, videotaped recordings for vicarious learning and modeling, and/or therapeutic reading) for the purpose of maximizing the initial stage of the therapeutic relationship. With these procedures, the therapist prepares the patient to attend to, react to, and concern him- or herself with therapeutic issues.

Example: A resistant spouse views a videotape of a marital therapist describing what to expect in there and conducting a therapeutic and positive session.

Sauber, S. R. (1974). Approaches to pretherapy training. *Journal of Contemporary Psychotherapy, 6,* 190-197.

prevention, primary   Any intervention designed to improve the functioning of a couple or family and, therefore, to decrease the *risk* of future breakdown. It consists of two types of interventions. One type is made up of *support groups* (see **family support programs**) designed to empower individuals, couples, or families with a sense of importance and requiring no skills, like Alcoholic Anonymous (AA) for individuals, or cluster families. The second type of primary prevention is made up of groups especially designed to teach skills in its members. Most of these skills are listed under **psychoeducational programs** or **enrichment, structured.**

Example: In addition to AA, various support groups for homeless people, various addictions, and victims of sexual and physical abuse exist in most major cities. Skill training programs designed to teach marital and parental skills would fall within this type of prevention.

Bond, L. A., & Wagner, B. M. (1988). *Families in transition: Primary prevention programs that work.* Newbury Park, CA: Sage.
L'Abate, L. (1990). *Building family competence: Primary and secondary prevention strategies.* Newbury Park, CA: Sage.

P

prevention, secondary Any type of intervention designed to decrease the probability of breakdown in populations in *need* of help even though they may not need therapy or crisis intervention, such as children of alcoholics, rape victims, juvenile delinquents, children from single-parent families, and the like.

Example: A group of families that include children of alcoholics, who are at high risk for a possible repetition of the same self-destructive behavior as one or both of their parents, meets in a group format in the local mental health clinic under the direction of a professional or semiprofessional leader to learn how to avoid repeating some of the same addictive behaviors from their families of origin.

L'Abate, L. (1990). *Building family competence: Primary and secondary prevention with families.* Newbury Park, CA: Sage.

prevention, tertiary Another term for *psychotherapy,* a method of intervention designed to help individuals, couples, and families in *crisis.* They meet on a regular basis, usually weekly, with a professional helper who listens to them and may help them through active listening, suggestions, prescriptions, and interpretations.

Example: The Ramirez family has asked initially for help with a problem of bed-wetting in one of the children. During the first interview, however, a great deal of sibling rivalry is found among the three children in this family. Father is absent most of the week because of his work, and mother is 50 pounds overweight and has high blood pressure. They asked for help because their physician told them that unless they receive "family counseling," their problems would get worse and mother's condition may become lethal.

Lubin, B., Lubin, A. W., Whiteford, M. G., & Whitlock, R. V. (1988). *Family therapy: A bibliography, 1937-1989.* New York: Greenwood.

priapism A pathologic erection unassociated with sexual desire.

Kaplan, H. S. (1979). *Disorders of sexual desire.* New York: Brunner/Mazel.

primary family tasks   Tasks that involve socialization of the children and the stabilization of adult personalities.

Example: A primary task of the family is to teach the child to be independent.

Lewis, J. M., Beavers, W. R., Gossett, J. T., & Phillips, V. A. (1976). *No single thread: Psychological health in the family system.* New York: Brunner/Mazel.

Parsons, T., & Bales, R. (1955). *Family socialization, and interaction process.* New York: Free Press.

primary impotence   The male sexual dysfunction of being unable to achieve coitus because of an inability to obtain or maintain an erection.

Masters, W., & Johnson, V. (1970). *Human sexual inadequacy.* Boston: Little, Brown.

primary locus   The status of being structurally engaged in the essential and habitual generation and maintenance of a problem. The primary locus locks systems in relationships that generate the problem for all or some of those systems.

Example: The grandparents and parents in a family are locked in a struggle over who has ultimate control and authority over the children. This struggle produces confusion in the family's hierarchy, which, in turn, leads the children to develop symptoms.

Aponte, H., & van Deusen, J. (1981). Structural family therapy. In A. S. Gurman & D. P. Kniskern (Eds.), *Handbook of family therapy* (pp. 310-360). New York: Brunner/Mazel.

primary reinforcement   Reinforcement provided by stimuli that initially reinforce an organism. These stimuli, which reinforce without any prior learning taking place, satisfy such basic needs as food, water, and sex.

LeBow, M. (1972). Behavior modification for the family. In G. D. Erickson & T. P. Hogan (Eds.), *Family therapy: An introduction to therapy and technique* (pp. 347-376). Belmont, CA: Wadsworth.

primary relationships   Relationships in which intimacy, love, and services are exchanged and in which everyday activities involve marital or other close physical relationships of an intimate and prolonged nature.

Cooley, C. (1909). *Social organization.* New York: Scribner.

Garrett, W. (1982). *Seasons of marriage and family life.* New York: Holt, Rinehart & Winston.

primary versus secondary sexual phobia and aversion   Patients with primary disorders will have always found sex frightening and repulsive, while those experiencing secondary disorders will have enjoyed sex for some period of time. A history of sexual functioning leads to making a differential diagnosis.

Kaplan, H. S. (1987). *Sexual aversion, sexual phobia, and panic disorder.* New York: Brunner/Mazel.

privacy   The basic rights guaranteed by the Fourth Amendment and other sections of the U.S. Constitution. It is chiefly the right of the individual to make decisions about how much of his or her thoughts, feelings, and personal information should be shared with others.

Koocher, J. P., & Keith-Spiegel, P. C. (1990). *Children, ethics, and the law.* Lincoln: University of Nebraska Press.

privilege   A legal term used to describe the protection of certain specific types of relationships from being subject to forced disclosure in court or other legal proceedings. Privilege ordinarily belongs to the client. In the case of a child, privilege usually belongs to the parent. Traditionally privilege has been extended to attorney-client, husband-wife, physician-patient, and penitent-priest relationships. Most states have extended privilege to psychologist-client relationships.

Koocher, G. P., & Keith-Spiegel, P. C. (1990). *Children, ethics, and the law.* Lincoln: University of Nebraska Press.

privileged voyeurism   An attraction to and an excessive inquisitiveness about incest on the part of the therapist. Usually this reaction involves excessive interest in sexual details. The therapist may regard the patient as an object of curiosity. This pattern of behavior on the part of the therapist further adds to the sense of exploitation felt by the incest survivor.

Courtois, C. (1988). *Healing the incest wound.* New York: Norton.

problem behavior   Behavior that is part of a sequence of acts between several people. The repeating sequence of behavior is the focus of the therapy. The problem is not viewed as existing in a social vacuum.

Haley, J. (1987). *Problem-solving therapy* (2nd ed.). San Francisco: Jossey-Bass.

problem-centered systems therapy of the family   Therapy that focuses on assessing, contracting, treating, and establishing closure with respect to a presented family problem. The first stage, *assessment,* involves investigation of not only the presenting problem of the family but also a wide range of aspects of family functioning as described in the McMaster model of family functioning. In the assessment stage, areas of strength and deficit are examined in detail and highlighted. Comprehensive evaluations are made of as many levels of the family system as possible. At the end of the assessment, the family and the therapist construct and agree on a problem list. The second stage, *contracting,* deals with establishing the therapy's goals, expectations, and commitments, to which both the family and the therapist agree. *Treatment,* the third stage, makes use of the strengths identified in the assessment and focuses on shoring up the weak areas identified in the problem list. In *closure,* the fourth stage, the family sets long-term goals and procedures for self-monitoring. A distinctive feature of this model is that the therapy involves an active collaboration between the family and the therapist. The therapist ties the role of mediator and facilitator. At each stage, the therapist explains what is being done and why. Assessment and diagnostic impressions are clearly spelled out and agreed on before treatment proceeds.

Epstein, N., & Bishop, D. (1981). Problem-centered systems therapy of the family. In A. S. Gurman & D. P. Kniskern (Eds.), *Handbook of family therapy* (pp. 444-482). New York: Brunner/Mazel.

problem-determined system   The membership of the problem system to be diagnosed and treated are those members in active communication regarding the problem. The problem is not seen as residing in an individual, couple, or family system per se. Systems overlap in ways that create problems. For example, a family may have a problem that involves a school and a social service system not providing appropriate services for their child. The problem-determined system consists of members from these social systems.

Anderson, H., Goolishian, H., & Windermand, L. (1986). Problem-determined systems. *Journal of Strategic and Systemic Therapies, 5,* 1-13.

problem formation   Defining the problem such that it is solvable. Often patients define problems in such a manner that their definition of the problem *is* the problem. As such, the problem cannot be solved. Thus patients attempt a solution to an unsolvable problem and persist with their solution despite the fact that their solution is not working. The tendency to use "more of the same" contributes to the problem worsening. In an effort to redefine the problem, the therapist uses reframing, paradoxical interventions, and Socratic questioning. Thus the focus is on current, ongoing behavior that maintains the defined problem. See also **problem resolution.**

Watzlawick, P., Weakland, J., & Fisch, R. (1974). *Change: Principles of problem formation and problem resolution.* New York: Norton.

problem list   An inventory of a family's problems and strengths that is generated at the outset of therapy and agreed on by the family members.

Barker, P. (1981). *Basic family therapy.* Baltimore: University Park Press.

problem resolution   Based on the Mental Research Institute (MRI) assumptions that regardless of their origins or etiology, the problems people bring to a therapist persist only if they are maintained by ongoing current behavior. Therefore, if such problem-maintaining behavior is appropriately changed or eliminated, the problem will be resolved, regardless of its nature, origin, or duration. See also **problem formation.**

Watzlawick, P., Weakland, J., & Fisch, R. (1974). *Change: Principles of problem formation and problem resolution.* New York: Norton.

problem-solving dimension   The level of a family's ability to resolve problems in order to maintain effective family functioning. The problems may be either instrumental problems (mechanical problems of everyday life) or affective problems (problems related to feelings).

Epstein, N., & Bishop, D. (1981). Problem-centered systems therapy of the family. In A. S. Gurman & D. P. Kniskern (Eds.), *Handbook of family therapy* (pp. 444-482). New York: Brunner/Mazel.

process   (1) The dynamics of the relationship between individuals who are interacting with one another. In contrast to content, process looks at the "how" of communication; content looks at the "what" of communication between two people. (2) A discrete, time-limited sequence of behaviors that constitute particular transactions among system components. A process consists of linked behavioral exchanges. In contrast to structure, which has the qualities of repetition and duration, a process is a sequence of single behavioral temporal transactions.

Example: A family decision process is seen to consist of several linked behaviors: The father makes some opening statement, the oldest son opposes him, and the mother comes to the support of the son; the mother-son arrangement has enough force to determine an outcome. When a temporal dimension is added, a distinction may be made between structure and process and between process and content.

Satir, V. (1983). *Conjoint family therapy* (3rd ed.). Palo Alto, CA: Science & Behavior Books.

Umbarger, C. C. (1984). *Structural family therapy.* New York: Grune & Stratton.

Watzlawick, P., Beavin, J. H., & Jackson, D. D. (1967). *Pragmatics of human communication.* New York: Norton.

process imagery   A hypnotherapeutic technique in which the person imagines doing whatever is necessary to reach his or her goals.

Example: A male with an erection problem might imagine such things as what he needs to say, to hear, and how to be touched in order to achieve an erection.

Zilbergeld, B., & Hammond, D. (1988). The use of hypnosis in treating sexual disorders. In S. Leiblum & R. Rosen (Eds.), *Sexual desire disorders* (pp. 192-223). New York: Guilford.

process-interruption question   A type of reflexive question designed to raise awareness about process. These questions may be used to expose the current process, to reflect on the therapeutic relationship, or to facilitate readiness for termination.

Example: With a family fighting in the session, the therapist might ask the children, "When your parents are at home, do they fight as much as they do here?"

Tomm, K. (1987). Interventive interviewing: Part II. Reflexive questioning as a means to enable self-healing. *Family Process, 26,* 167-184.

process model   A model of the interactions and transactions (translated into methods and procedures) that move the individuals in the family and the family system from a symptomatic base toward one of wellness.

Satir, V. (1982). The therapist and family therapy: Process model. In A. M. Horne & M. M. Ohlsen (Eds.), *Family counseling and therapy* (pp. 12-42). Itasca, IL: F. E. Peacock.

process-oriented marriage counseling   Counseling that directs its attention to the quality and direction of the changing activity, the dynamic behavior, and the life-styles of the individuals who make up a marriage relationship.

Harper, R. (1969). Marriage counseling as rational process-oriented psychotherapy. In B. N. Ard & C. C. Ard (Eds.), *Handbook of marriage counseling* (pp. 115-119). Palo Alto, CA: Science & Behavior Books.

process research   An investigation that uses, totally or in part, data from direct or indirect measurement of patient, therapist, or dyadic (patient-therapist interaction) behavior in the therapy interview.

Kiesler, D. (1973). *The process of psychotherapy: Empirical foundations and systems of analysis.* Chicago: Aldine.
Pinsof, W. (1981). Family therapy process research. In A. S. Gurman & D. P. Kniskern (Eds.), *Handbook of family therapy* (pp. 699-741). New York: Brunner/Mazel.

process variables   Variables that focus on the process of intrafamilial or interpersonal transaction (e.g., who speaks to whom, who interrupts whom, who agrees with whom).

Pinsof, W. (1981). Family therapy process research. In A. S. Gurman & D. P. Kniskern (Eds.), *Handbook of family therapy* (pp. 699-741). New York: Brunner/Mazel.

product variables The outcome or end result of interaction (outcome variables, such as participation rate, total number of questions, and who wins in arguments).

Riskin, J., & Faunce, E. (1972). An evaluative review of family interaction research. *Family Process, 11,* 365-455.

P

projective identification Marital partners' projection of certain aspects of themselves onto their mates. The first partner thus views the mate as an embodiment of the projected characteristic. This projection is often part of self-object representation based on early family relationships (one's own family of origin). Through the process of projective identification, one or both partners misperceive important aspects of the other's character. Because the misperceptions serve to meet certain denied needs, the partners are strongly motivated to sustain them, regardless of the actual behavior manifested.

Example: A 32-year-old wife, married for 8 years, was reared by an overprotective mother. She perceives her husband as being like her mother and in anger often describes him as a "mother hen" or as a person who would have made a "good wife." No matter how masculine the husband's pursuits are, the wife's perception blinds her to those aspects of his character that do not fit her projected image of him. Their interactions take on a pseudorealistic quality as the wife undermines the husband's confidence and encourages him to behave in ways similar to her projected image.

Everett, C. A., Halperin, S., Volgy, S., & Wissler, A. (1989). *Treating the borderline family: A systemic approach.* Boston: Allyn & Bacon.
Greenspan, S., & Mannino, M. (1974). A model for brief intervention with couples based on projective identification. *American Journal of Psychiatry, 131,* 1103-1106.

protection A positive reframe that involves the therapist suggesting the identified patient's symptom serves as a way of protecting other family members in some manner.

Example: When the parents argue, their 9-year-old son complains of having a stomachache. This behavior is framed as a loving act, sacrificing himself so that the parents will not continue arguing.

Madanes, C. (1981). *Strategic family therapy.* San Francisco: Jossey-Bass.

protectiveness Behavior based on the need to protect an intimate other from hurt. Protectiveness can be a positive antecedent of pathology.

When protectiveness is carried to an extreme, the relationship cannot be negotiated.

Weeks, G., & L'Abate. L. (1982). *Paradoxical psychotherapy: Theory and practice with individuals, couples, and families.* New York: Brunner/Mazel.

proverb   One of the tasks of the structured family interview. The parents are asked to discuss by themselves the meaning of a proverb such as "A rolling stone gathers no moss." They then are asked to call in their children and teach the agreed-upon meaning to them. Although other proverbs have been used, the "rolling stone" proverb is the most commonly used because it has two valid but mutually exclusive meanings. These introduce the possibility of disagreement, which then has to be dealt with in some way.

Watzlawick, P. (1966). A structured family interview. *Family Process, 5,* 256-271.

pseudodemocratic family   A family in which all channels of communication seem to be of about equal importance, with the marital coalition and the parental role not particularly well differentiated.

Glick, I. D., & Kessler, D. P. (1980). *Marital and family therapy* (2nd ed.). New York: Grune & Stratton.

pseudodyspareunia   The female use of "pain during sex" as an excuse to avoid frequent or further contact with a husband or lover.

Lazarus, A. (1980). Psychological treatment of dyspareunia. In S. Leiblum & L. Pervin (Eds.), *Principles and practice of sex therapy* (pp. 147-166). New York: Guilford.

pseudohostility   Continuous bickering and turmoil to maintain relatedness. Quarreling and disruption can maintain a relationship without opening the possibility of genuinely expressing the tender, deep relationship feelings involved. Pseudohostility actually serves to cover up the need for intimacy and affection that family members cannot deal with easily.

Wynne, L., Ryckoff, I., Day, J., & Hirsch, S. (1958). Pseudomutuality in the family relations of schizophrenics. *Psychiatry, 21,* 205-220.

pseudoidentification   A phenomenological shift in a close, intimately interdependent relationship by a partner who begins to function with a facade of exaggerated strength and assertion, while the other partner seems to lose identity and become a relative nonentity.

Example: A wife is overshadowed by her husband, who suddenly has become flirtatious with other women, and she feels increasingly insecure.

Nadelson, C. (1976). Marital therapy from a psychoanalytic perspective. In T. Paolino & B. McCrady (Eds.), *Marriage and marital therapy* (pp. 89-164). New York: Brunner/Mazel.

pseudomarriage A marriage in which the couple's relationship is void of intimacy and the marriage is maintained either for convenience or for appearance.

Okun, B. F., & Rappaport, L. J. (1980). *Working with families: An introduction to family therapy.* Belmont, CA: Brooks/Cole.

Stahman, R. F., & Hiebert, W. I. (1977). Commonly recurring couple interaction patterns. In R. F. Stahman & W. I. Hiebert (Eds.), *Klemer's counseling in marital and sexual problems: A clinical handbook* (2nd ed., pp. 17-33). Baltimore: Williams & Wilkins.

pseudomutuality A process by which families seek to maintain a form of homeostasis. Pseudomutuality is a type of surface alignment that blurs and obscures from recognition and conscious experience both underlying splits and divergences and deeper affection and alignment. Through this mechanism, the family wards off real or imagined threats to its unity, thus avoiding the discomforts of intimate relations, which often are highly loaded with emotional positive or negative forces.

Example: In the following illustration, the father seeks to avoid disagreement between himself and his wife. The mother seeks to avoid open conflict with her daughter. The underlying disagreement between the parents and the daughter is disguised so that the real issue—which boyfriends are acceptable—is avoided. Discussion of this issue would create an open conflict whose impact on their relationships all the family members fear.

Mother	I think Rasheeta is old enough to have dates if the boyfriends are of a high-class type.
Rasheeta	But, Mother, you told me I couldn't date Juwan, and I don't see anything wrong with him.
Mother	Your father was the one who objected.
Father	Well, I don't really object. I think I said she would have to ask you. I really think your mother knows best.
Rasheeta	But she always says to ask you.
Mother	Well, I think your father and I agree on what kind of boys you can date. You wouldn't want to go out with Antonio, would you?
Rasheeta	Gee, no. He's a geek.
Mother	Well, I think you'd agree with Dad most of the time anyway.

Wynne, L., Ryckoff, I., Day, J., & Hirsch, S. (1958). Pseudomutuality in the family relations of schizophrenics. *Psychiatry, 1,* 205-220.

pseudoself A very low level of differentiation of self. Individuals with pseudoselves manage to function fairly well in their life adjustments. As children, they do not "grow away" from the family ego mass, as do their more differentiated siblings. They remain emotionally attached and dependent on their parents. After adolescence, they "tear themselves away" to attain a "pseudoseparation" from the family ego mass.

Example: A husband and a wife with equally poor differentiations of self become deeply involved emotionally and "fuse together" into a new undifferentiated family ego mass. Their separation from their parents is maintained only by finding new dependent attachments.

Bowen, M. (1978). *Family therapy in clinical practice.* New York: Jason Aronson.

pseudotherapeutic marriage   A reform-based marital relationship in which one partner tries to change the other's habits.

Example: A professional man brings his wife to therapy, complaining that he wanted an intellectual companion but ended up with an empty-headed emotional cripple. He requests that the therapist help him reform her so that she will be what he wanted.

Rutledge, A. (1969). Male and female roles in marriage counseling. In B. N. Ard & C. C. Ard (Eds.), *Handbook of marriage counseling* (pp. 120-127). Palo Alto, CA: Science & Behavior Books.

psychoanalytic family therapy   Family therapy concerned with the social and cultural aspects of personality development and functioning. This form of therapy is derived from the psychoanalytic theories of Alfred Adler, Carl Jung, Franz Alexander, Eric Fromm, Karen Horney, Abram Kardiner, Clara Thompson, and Harry Stack Sullivan. Influenced by these culturalists and neo-Freudian thinkers, many early analysts started working therapeutically with both spouses. (It is reported that Freud himself did concurrent marital therapy.) Nathan W. Ackerman, Don D. Jackson, Theodore Lidz, and Murray Bowen, who pioneered family therapy, were trained in psychoanalysis.

The aim of *psychoanalytic family therapy* is to establish a collaborative working alliance with the family members to explore the relationship of individual and interpersonal factors in current relationships, to provide insight into genetic and unconscious factors from past conflicts, and to help the members function more freely and authentically in terms of emotions and thoughts. Change occurs internally by working through old conflicts that influence current relationships. In *directive family therapy,* in contrast, change is imparted from the outside by providing solutions to problems, teaching skills, manipulating power, and communication structures or by applying paradoxical prescriptions. It is assumed that the changes resulting from the growth in the family members will result in greater and more permanent personality strengths and individualism.

Meissner, W. W. (1978). The conceptualization of marriage and family dynamics from a psychoanalytic perspective. In T. Paolino & B. McCrady (Eds.), *Marriage and marital therapy* (pp. 000-000). New York: Brunner/Mazel.

psychoeducational programs   This field is one type of primary preventive approach that includes various interpersonal skill training approaches for individuals, couples, and families. Skills may consist of active listening, negotiation training, problem solving, role playing, and empathy sensitization. See also **prevention, primary** and **enrichment, structured.**

Example: Family members realize, or are lead to realize after crisis therapy, that they need to learn to negotiate and to problem-solve together. They do not spend time together, and they have very few interactions among themselves. They realize they need to learn to talk with, rather than shout at, each other. They enroll in a course offered from a local church about "family learning."

L'Abate, L. (1986). Prevention of marital and family problems. In B. A. Edelstein & L. Michelson (Eds.), *Handbook of prevention* (pp. 177-193). New York: Plenum.

L'Abate, L. (1990). *Building family competence: Primary and secondary prevention strategies.* Newbury Park, CA.: Sage.

Levant, R. F. (Ed.). (1986). *Psychoeducational approaches to family therapy and counseling.* New York: Springer.

psychological contagion   Individual psychopathology that affects others in the family system.

Examples: The presence of maladjustment in the parents can increase the probability of disorders or maladjustments in their children. In other cases, if one family member in treatment improves, another member may develop symptoms of pathology; or improvement in a sick member may bring shifts in family alignments. The family members may resist changes because of their unconscious needs to keep a patient member ill. Thus parents sometimes use a child's symptoms as a defense against their own anxiety, shifting their problems to the child and resisting the therapist's attempts to clarify their emotional conflicts.

Two types of marital situations, through psychological contagion, can lead to disorders in children: (a) *marital schism,* the failure to work out complementary role relationships, which results in open conflict; and (b) skewed relationships between husband and wife, with one partner very dependent or masochistic and the other independent and supportive. In the latter case, overt conflict seldom appears.

Ehrenwald, J. (1958). Neurosis in the family: A study of psychiatric epidemiology. *American Journal of Psychiatry, 115,* 134-142.

Lidz, T., Cornelison, A., Terru, D., & Fleck, S. (1958). Intrafamilial environment of the schizophrenic patient: VI. Parental personalities and family interaction. *American Journal of Orthopsychiatry, 28,* 764-776.

psychosomatic family   A family in which emotional conflicts are transformed into somatic symptoms. Characteristics of a psychosomatic family are enmeshment, overprotectiveness, rigidity, and lack of conflict resolution.

Example: The parents in a family experience covert conflict but are overtly pleasant and conflict free. Their daughter develops anorexia, which diverts the parents' attention. They now fight with her over not eating.

Minuchin, S., Rosman, B. L., & Baker, L. (1978). *Psychosomatic families: Anorexia nervosa in context.* Cambridge, MA: Harvard University Press.

psychotic family   A type of family with these commonly cited characteristics: failure to form a nuclear family; family schism and skew; blurring of generational lines; pervasion of the entire atmosphere with irrational, usually paranoid, ideation; persistence of unconscious incestuous preoccupation; and sociocultural isolation.

Example: A family in which the grandparents are crossing generation lines, the parents are in conflict over a child, and a parental child is saving the child from the parents.

Fleck, S. (1960). Family dynamics and origin of schizophrenia. *Psychosomatic Medicine, 22,* 333-344.
Haley, J. (1987). *Problem-solving therapy* (2nd ed.). San Francisco: Jossey-Bass.

pubococcygeal muscle hypothesis   The hypothesis that the poor tone of the pubococcygeal muscle accounts for a substantial number of cases of female sexual inadequacy.

Kaplan, H. S. (1974). *The new sex therapy.* New York: Brunner/Mazel.

punching-bag marriage   A marriage based on the idea that one gender is superior and has special rights. If the rights of the partner of that gender are not respected, the other partner is physically or verbally beaten.

Rutledge, A. (1969). Male and female in marriage counseling. In B. N. Ard & C. C. Ard (Eds.), *Handbook of marriage counseling* (pp. 120-127). Palo Alto, CA: Science & Behavior Books.

punctuation   What one defines as stimulus and response when the two are not clearly distinguishable. *Punctuation* is a concept in family communication that labels cause and effect.

Example: A wife nags her husband because he comes home late, but he says he comes home late because she nags. They punctuate this sequence differently, each blaming the other; the husband punctuates the interaction as, "She nags, so I withdraw," whereas the wife punctuates the interaction as, "He withdraws, so I nag him."

Watzlawick, P., Bevin, J. H., & Jackson, D. D. (1967). *Pragmatics of human communication.* New York: Norton.

punisher   A stimulus that decreases the probability of a behavior occurring.

Example: When a husband approaches his wife sexually, she becomes hostile, telling him that the only time he approaches her is when he wants sex. Her behavior decreases the chances that he will approach her, except to meet overriding needs.

Weiss, R. (1978). The conceptualization of marriage from a behavioral perspective. In T. Paolino & B. McCrady (Eds.), *Marriage and marital therapy* (pp. 165-239). New York: Brunner/Mazel.

P

pursuer distancer   A relational system based on a pursuer-distancer polarity. The pursuer believes the solution to anxiety lies in external action or in moving toward another for comfort. The distancer tries to avoid anxiety by withdrawing and moving away from others.

Example: In a marriage, one spouse moves toward the other, while the other moves away. They may alter the roles they play, but the pattern of interaction remains stable.

Fogarty, T. (1976). Marital crisis. In P. J. Guerin (Ed.), *Family therapy: Theory and practice* (pp. 335-350). New York: Gardner.
L'Abate, L., & McHenry, S. (1983). *Handbook of marital interventions.* New York: Grune & Stratton.

P

quantity of speech   The amount of speaking each individual contributes to the family discussion.

Ferreira, A., Winter, W., & Poindexter, E. (1966). Some interaction variables in normal and abnormal families. *Family Process, 5,* 65-70.
Riskin, J., & Faunce, E. (1972). An evaluative review of family interaction research. *Family Process, 11,* 365-455.

quid pro quo   Something that is given or received for something else. When applied to family systems, it refers to the interactional patterns in which something is given to one person in exchange for something in return. The quid pro quo specifies in very general terms the rules, implicit or explicit, of the relationship. After the rules are formalized, the couple is said to have a marital contract.

Example: A husband agrees to help with the children if his wife agrees to help with the family budgeting.

Gerson, M., & Barsky, M. (1979). For the new family therapist: A glossary of terms. *American Journal of Family Therapy, 7,* 15-30.
Jackson, D. (1965). Family rules: The marital quid pro quo. *Archives of General Psychiatry, 12,* 589-594.

racket system In transactional analysis, a self-reinforcing, distorted system of feelings, thoughts, and actions that is maintained by individuals who are functioning in a script or longitudinal life plan. A racket system has three interrelated and interdependent components: a script beliefs and feelings, the rackety display, and the reinforcing experiences. The racket system stipulates how the script is lived out day by day. It shows how the script plot is reinforced and how others are manipulated into the roles the script requires. Identification of a client's racket system can provide useful guideposts for therapeutic intervention.

Example: A person acts in a way defined by the script beliefs—for example, saying, "I don't know," when believing, "I'm stupid"; or the person acts in a way that socially defends against the script beliefs—for example, by excelling in school and acquiring numerous degrees.

Erskine, R. G. (1982). Transactional analysis and family therapy. In A. M. Horne & M. M. Ohlsen (Eds.), *Family counseling and therapy* (pp. 245-275). Itasca, IL: F. E. Peacock.

Erskine, R. G., & Falcman, M. (1979). The racket system: A model for racket analysis. *Transactional Analysis Journal, 9,* 1.

random-type family A family structural arrangement in which space is dispersed—that is, the members separately develop their individual boundary patterns in defending their own and their family's territory. Because the random-type family's territorial pattern is an aggregate of individual styles, including the effect of each on each other, there may be as many territorial guidelines as there are members of the family.

Example: The family den contains papers, books, unopened letters, gardening and carpentry tools, a movie projector, several dead plants, and other seemingly unconnected items, some of which are swept by the wind into messy confusion every time the children pass through the room on their way to the backyard.

Kantor, D., & Lehr, W. (1975). *Inside the family: Toward a theory of family process.* San Francisco: Jossey-Bass.

rank-order interactions   The acquisition and defense of social position or status. When these interaction are in conflict, sexual dysfunction may occur. The conflict would stem from unresolved issues of dominance, whether relational or sexual.

Example: One man did not like the female superior position. This position symbolized his mother's dominance over him as a child. To compensate for this unresolved issue, he attempted to dominate in many areas of the current relationship.

Rapoport, A. (1974). *Conflict in man-made environment.* New York: Penguin.
Verhulst, J., & Heiman, J. (1988). A systems perspective on sexual desire. In S. Leiblum & R. Rosen (Eds.), *Sexual desire disorders* (pp. 243-270). New York: Guilford.

R

rape trauma syndrome   The constellation of psychological effects that typically follow rape. The individual goes through two stages of recovery: a disorganization phase and then the long-term reorganization phase. Individual reactions to rape may vary from hyperemotionality to denial and calmness.

Burgess, A., & Holmstrom, L. (1974). *Rape: Victims of crisis.* Bowie, MD: Brady.
Miller, W. (1987). Effects of rape on the marital relationship. In G. Weeks & L. Hof (Eds.), *Integrating sex and marital therapy* (pp. 171-182). New York: Brunner/Mazel.

rapid-treatment format   An approach used at the Masters and Johnson Institute in which couples are seen for sex therapy over a period of 14 days. The couple are isolated from family and work to focus on their relationship intensively.

Schwartz, M., & Masters, W. (1988). The Masters and Johnson Institute treatment model. In S. Leiblum & R. Rosen (Eds.), *Sexual desire disorders* (pp. 229-242). New York: Guilford.

rational emotive family therapy   A comprehensive system of therapy that consciously and actively employs cognitive, emotive, and behavioral methods. The intent is not to effect symptom removal, but rather to bring about profound philosophic changes in all involved family members. In rational emotive family therapy (RET), the husband and the wife are shown how they usually create their own disturbances and are not (as they often erroneously believe) emotionally upset by other family members. Their children, if old enough, are shown how they upset themselves *about,* rather than get disturbed *by,* their parents' and siblings' actions and verbalizations. All participants in the therapy are taught how to recognize clearly and dispute their own irrational beliefs about themselves, about others, and about the world. In particular, they are shown that their emotional disturbances almost always arise from their self-defeating way of turning their desires and preferences into absolutistic shoulds, oughts, and musts.

Ellis, A., & Grieger, R. (1977). *Handbook of rational emotive therapy.* New York: Springer.

rational sex ethics   A humanistic, empirical, and scientific approach to the resolution of ethical dilemmas having to do with sex. Rather than look at revelations, intuition, religion, or feelings, rational sex ethics looks to the basic sciences relevant to sex—for example, psychology, sociology, psychiatry, sexology, and anthropology. With these basic resources at hand, rational sex ethics then applies rigorous logic and clear thinking to arrive at humanistic, empirical conclusions.

Example: Masturbation was long considered to be a sin, an affront to God, and the cause of all sorts of illnesses, from acne to blindness to insanity. Rational sex ethics examines all of the scientific evidence and concludes that masturbation is not a sin and is neither harmful nor a causative factor in illness or disease, but is rather a normal, natural phenomenon.

Ard, B. N. (1978). *Rational sex ethics.* Washington, DC: University Press of America.

reactance   The need to maintain one's freedom. The degree of reactance is a function of three variables that can be manipulated by the therapist: (a) the importance of free behavior to the individual, (b) the number of freedoms threatened, and (c) the magnitude of threat.

Rohrbaugh, M., Tennen, H., Press, S., & White, L. (1981). Compliance, defiance, and therapeutic paradox. *American Journal of Orthopsychiatry, 51,* 454-467.

Weeks, G., & L'Abate, L. (1982). *Paradoxical psychotherapy: Theory and practice with individuals, couples, and families.* New York: Brunner/Mazel.

reality impairment   Distortions in family attitudes toward or perceptions of reality. Frequently parental unrealities can be imposed on the child. Powerful guilt pressures and implications of treason or disloyalty can be brought to bear on the child if he or she persists in pursuing reality. These pressures can not only force the child to renounce reality but also block off the higher levels of reasoning associated with abstract thinking.

Example: A girl who has always allowed her mother to set her hair now refuses to let her do so. The mother perceives this as a threat to her symbiotic tie to her daughter. The mother deals with her daughter's refusal by stating that the daughter must be getting sick again because stubbornness and rebelliousness are signs that something is happening. The daughter accepts the reality of her mother's statements, feeling that something is wrong with her because her mother said it was true.

Framo, J. (1965). Rationale and technique of intensive family therapy. In I. Boszormenyi-Nagy & J. Framo (Eds.), *Intensive family therapy: Theoretical and practical aspects* (pp. 143-212). New York: Harper & Row.

reciprocal   A systemic term describing the interaction between family members when the interaction of two family members are complementary.
   Example: When the husband is angry, the wife becomes submissive. However, the wife may show passive-aggressive behavior, which provokes anger in the husband.

Everett, C. A., Russell, C. S., & Keller, J. (Eds.). (1992). *Family therapy glossary.* Washington, DC: American Association for Marriage and Family Therapy.

reciprocal structural coupling   The organizational closure that is obtained when circularity is achieved; the result is an organized, stable system. See **circular causality.**
   Example: The husband spends beyond his means; the wife works a second job to cover her husband's debt.

Dell, P. (1982). Beyond homeostasis: Toward a concept of coherence. *Family Process, 21,* 21-41.

reciprocity awareness procedure   A procedure in which each spouse is asked to make a list of behaviors of that spouse's partner that are satisfying. The spouses read their lists in subsequent sessions with the therapist. The procedure is designed to facilitate positive interaction between the spouses.

Azrin, N. H., Naster, B. J., & Jones, R. (1973). Reciprocity counseling: A rapid learning-based procedure for marital counseling. *Behavior Research and Therapy, 11,* 365-382.
O'Leary, D., & Turkewitz, H. (1978). Marital therapy from a behavioral perspective. In T. Paolino & B. McCrady (Eds.), *Marriage and marital therapy* (pp. 240-297). New York: Brunner/Mazel.

reconstituted family   A family in which the spouses have custody of their children from previous marriages. Structurally these families are characterized by a relatively open system regarding the inclusion of members. The family members are not clearly defined because there may not be a consensus about who is in the family. The family is influenced by a network of people and relationships created through the prior divorce(s) and the formalization of the remarriage. This family network is called the *rem supra system,* a system comprising the different individuals and functionally related people (subsystems) who impinge on the reconstituted family. Some of these subsystems may cross two or more households.

Example: Reconstituted families must frequently solve problems that result directly from the "ghosts" of past relationships, from inadequate or incomplete mourning of the lost relationship, or from the complexities of stepkin relationships.

Baptiste, D. A. (1983). Family therapy with reconstituted families: A crisis-induction approach. *American Journal of Family Therapy, 11,* 3-9.
Sager C. J., Brown, H. S., Crohn, H., Engel, T., Rodstein, E., & Walker, L. (1983). *Treating the remarried family.* New York: Brunner/Mazel.

recovery   Originally thought of as abstinence from the substance (e.g., alcohol or drugs) that one was addicted to or abused. However, recovery now is thought to include rebuilding one's life such that the individual has healthy, adult relationships, is not co-dependent, no longer lives in a state of denial, and has self-awareness.

R

Larsen, E. (1985). *Stage II recovery: Life beyond addiction.* New York: Harper & Row.

recursive language   Language that describes relationships in terms of other relationships. Recursive language is contextual, multicausal, and reciprocal or circular.

Example: A husband yells at his wife, who yells back in response. Each influences and is influenced by the other.

Bateson, G. (1978). The birth of a double bind. In M. Berger (Ed.), *Beyond the double bind* (p. 53). New York: Brunner/Mazel.
Hoffman, L. (1981). *Foundations of family therapy.* New York: Basic Books.

redefinition   In clinical theory, a shift of perspective from the individual patient to the family system, resulting in a new meaning of the individual symptom. In clinical practice, redefinition may be shared with the family as a reframing of the presenting problem so that individual behaviors may be seen as linked to a meaningful family pattern.

Example: The 6-year-old daughter refuses to eat most of the food her mother prepares for her. The therapist redefines her eating difficulty in terms of her older sister excelling in school and gaining all of her mother's positive attention.

Umbarger, C. C. (1984). *Structural family therapy.* New York: Grune & Stratton.

reeducating the inner child   A sex hypnotherapy technique used to treat negative sexual processing. The client imagines that he or she is a child and that the adult self is bringing him or her up free of sexual guilt and anxiety.

Araoz, D. L. (1982). *Hypnosis and sex therapy.* New York: Brunner/Mazel.

referee system A system in which all family members are subjugated to standards of thought, behavior, and feelings that are pathetically insensitive to their needs. The system does not limit itself to behavioral control; it also disciplines feelings and thoughts, continually trying to bring everyone's inner life into agreement with the rules. In such a family, feelings are rarely expressed spontaneously.

Beavers, W. R. (1977). *Psychotherapy and growth: A family systems perspective.* New York: Brunner/Mazel.

R

reflected appraisal The perception of self as shaped by the parts of one's behavior to which others respond, positively or negatively. The child grows in response to shifting social situations as he or she matures.

Example: In a family, the siblings and parents observe how the oldest son takes charge. The son's friends also see him as a natural leader.

Broderick, C., & Schrader, S. (1981). The history of professional marriage and family therapy. In A. S. Gurman & D. P. Kniskern (Eds.), *Handbook of family therapy* (pp. 5-35). New York: Brunner/Mazel.
Sullivan, H. S. (1953). *The interpersonal theory of psychiatry.* New York: Norton.

reflecting team In training and consultation, a team of professionals who observe live therapy, either on videotape or behind a one-way mirror, and give suggestions to the therapist conducting the therapy while the therapy is occurring. See also **live supervision.**

Anderson, T. (Ed.). (1990). *The reflecting team.* Kent, UK: Borgmann.
Papp, P. (1980). The Greek chorus and other techniques of family therapy. *Family Process, 19,* 45-57.

reflexive questioning Questions the therapist asks members of a family that are designed to challenge the family's or individual's construction of reality or views about a relationship or event. These include hypothetical questions, questions about the future, and triadic questioning. See also **triadic questioning.**

Tomm, K. (1988). Interventive interviewing: III. Intending to ask linear, circular, strategic, or reflexive questions? *Family Process, 27,* 1-16.

reframing Relabeling or redefining a concept or reality to give it a slightly different and more constructive perspective. The process by which we label feelings, thoughts, attitudes, behaviors, and events has, in recent years, been recognized by cognitive psychologists as having an extraordinarily significant influence on the way we perceive reality. It appears that, to a large extent, we construct our own reality on the basis of the frames or points of view that we impose on our experiences.

Example: If, in talking with a couple about the couple's child-sharing plans in a divorce situation, one spouse says, "I want to keep custody of my children!" the therapist can reframe the statement as, "You would like the children to share a significant amount of time with you." When one spouse says to the other, "You can visit the children every other weekend," the therapist can reframe it, "The children will be able to share time with their dad for two weekends every month."

Marlow, L., & Sauber, S. R. (1990). *Handbook of divorce mediation.* New York: Plenum.
Watzlawick, P. (1978). *The language of change: Elements of therapeutic communication.* New York: Basic Books.

reification   The process by which an idea is thought to exist in reality.

Examples: In Freudian psychology, regarding the unconscious, id, ego, and superego as real things rather than a process. In family psychology, regarding family boundaries as existing in reality, rather than being a process.

Bateson, G. (1972). *Steps to an ecology of mind.* New York: Ballantine.

reinforcement schedule   The relationship (either temporal or as determined by response frequency) between responding and the occurrence of consequences.

Example: Each time the husband takes his wife shopping, she initiates sexual advances toward him that evening.

Weiss, R. (1978). Marriage from a behavioral perspective. In T. Paolino & B. McCrady (Eds.), *Marriage and marital therapy* (pp. 165-239). New York: Brunner/Mazel.

rejunction   Movement toward trustworthy relatedness. In contextual family therapy, trustworthiness is seen as the basic dynamic among family members.

Example: A husband who strives to enhance his wife's trust in her parents also improves her trust in his familial relationships.

Boszormenyi-Nagy, I., & Ulrich, D. (1981). Contextual family therapy. In A. S. Gurman & D. P. Kniskern (Eds.), *Handbook of family therapy* (pp. 159-186). New York: Brunner/Mazel.

relabeling   Changing the label attached to a person or problem without necessarily changing the frame of reference. Relabeling usually involves changing the label from a negative to a positive.

Example: A man who is upset because he is confused is told that confusion is part of the preparation required for new growth.

Minuchin, S. (1974). *Families and family therapy.* Cambridge, MA: Harvard University Press.
Weeks, G., & L'Abate, L. (1982). *Paradoxical psychotherapy: Theory and practice with individuals, couples, and families.* New York: Brunner/Mazel.

relapse prediction   A paradoxical intervention in which a client is told that a problem will reappear, thereby reducing the likelihood of its reappearance or of placing it under the therapist's control if it does. This intervention is made only after a successful paradoxical prescription has been given.

Example: A couple stop fighting in response to an intervention. The two partners then are told they may experience a relapse, fighting even more because they have saved up some fights.

Weeks, G., & L'Abate, L. (1982). *Paradoxical psychotherapy: Theory and practice with individuals, couples, and families.* New York: Brunner/Mazel.

R

relatedness, expressive   Having meaningful feelings—that is, relating on a feeling level.

Wynne, L. (1970, March). *Communication disorders and the quest for relatedness in families of schizophrenics.* Paper presented at the Association for the Advancement of Psychoanalysis, New York.

relatedness, instrumental   Interaction that emphasizes the nonpersonal aspects of a task.

Wynne, L. (1970, March). *Communication disorders and the quest for relatedness in families of schizophrenics.* Paper presented at the Association for the Advancement of Psychoanalysis, New York.

relation   A coding category, devised by Loveland to analyze the Relation Rorschach, which measures the affective stand a speaker takes in relation to other participants and the task.

Loveland, N. (1967). The Relation Rorschach: A technique for studying interaction. *Journal of Nervous and Mental Disease, 142,* 93-105.
Riskin, J., & Faunce, E. (1972). An evaluative review of family interaction research. *Family Process, 11,* 365-455.

relational corruption   A situation in which a person is so bound to a legacy of familial corruption that he or she feels entitled to be unfair to everybody else. In a contextual family therapy session, a person may give a caring response, only to be cut down by another who feels entitled to be unfair.

Boszormenyi-Nagy, I., & Ulrich, D. (1981). Contextual family therapy. In A. S. Gurman & D. P. Kniskern (Eds.), *Handbook of family therapy* (pp. 159-186). New York: Brunner/Mazel.

relational ethics   Long-term preservation of an oscillating balance of equitable fairness among family members, whereby the basic interests of each member are taken into account by the others. Relational ethics is a focus in contextual family therapy.

Boszormenyi-Nagy, I., & Ulrich, D. (1981). Contextual family therapy. In A. S. Gurman & D. P. Kniskern (Eds.), *Handbook of family therapy* (pp. 159-186). New York: Brunner/Mazel.

relational needs template   Projecting the inner need onto a relationship. A real (interpersonal) relationship passes through a period of adjustment—on the one hand, between each person's relational need templates and, on the other hand, between each person's internal and real demands. The internal relational need template (or its fitting object) may or may not be consciously represented in a patient's mind.

Example: Paranoid hallucinations may be projected onto real others in the process of trying to relate to them.

Boszormenyi-Nagy, I. (1965). A theory of relationships: Experience and transaction. In I. Boszormenyi-Nagy & J. Framo (Eds.), *Intensive family therapy: Theoretical and practical aspects* (pp. 33-86). New York: Harper & Row.

relational stagnation   In contextual family therapy, familial disengagement from concern about fairness, thereby blocking out moves toward greater trust.

Example: The husband demands that his wife contribute to the family equally in financial terms, although it is impossible for her to do so.

Boszormenyi-Nagy, I., & Ulrich, D. (1981). Contextual family therapy. In A. S. Gurman & D. P. Kniskern (Eds.), *Handbook of family therapy* (pp. 159-186). New York: Brunner/Mazel.

relationship enhancement (RE)   A method used for problem prevention, enrichment, and therapy. It is used to help couples and families deal with problems more effectively. Participants are taught to (a) express clearly their feelings and thoughts, (b) accept the expressions of others, (c) critique and facilitate their own communication skills, (d) reach constructive resolutions of conflicts, (e) achieve self-change, (f) help others change, (g) generalize the skills to a variety of settings, and (h) maintain these skills in daily life within family, peer, and work situations.

Guerney, B. G. (1977). *Relationship enhancement: Skill training programs for therapy, problem prevention, and enrichment.* San Francisco: Jossey-Bass.

L'Abate, L., & McHenry, S. (1983). *Handbook of marital interventions.* New York: Grune & Stratton.

relationship skills   The stylistic form of the therapeutic relationship that is created by the therapist. These skills are a part of the therapist's training and are one of the best predictors of success with a family. The skills include such behaviors as helping the client system integrate affect and behavior, being nonblaming and warm, using humor, and using self, such as through self-disclosure.

Barton, C., & Alexander, J. (1981). Functional family therapy. In A. S. Gurman & D. P. Kniskern (Eds.), *Handbook of family therapy* (pp. 403-443). New York: Brunner/Mazel.

remarried (REM) family   A blended or reconstituted family or a step-family that is formed by the marriage or living together of two adults—one or both widowed or divorced—with their custodial or visiting children.

Sager, C., Brown, H., Crohn, H., Engel, T., Rodstein, E., & Walker, L. (1983). *Treating the remarried family.* New York: Brunner/Mazel.

R

replacement partner   The partner of choice brought by a sexually inadequate unmarried man or woman to share the experiences and the education of a sex therapy program.

Masters, W., & Johnson, V. (1970). *Human sexual inadequacy.* Boston: Little, Brown.

replay   A scenario in which a couple present a frustrating discussion or hostile argument they had during the week and are asked to replay the sequence. The therapist interrupts the interaction to help the spouses pinpoint the destructive behaviors that contributed to the negative chain, and the couple are asked to generate alternative responses that would be more productive.

O'Leary, K., & Turkewitz, H. (1978). Marital therapy from a behavioral perspective. In T. Paolino & B. McCrady (Eds.), *Marriage and marital therapy* (pp. 240-297). New York: Brunner/Mazel.

report level   The verbal message of a communication, especially the dictionary meaning of the words—that is, a message that means what it says. See also **command level.**
   Example: A wife asks her husband to tell their daughter to complete her homework.

Haley, J. (1959). An interactional description of schizophrenia. *Psychiatry, 22,* 321-332.
Watzlawick, P., Beavin, J. H., & Jackson, D. D. (1967). *Pragmatics of human communication.* New York: Norton.

representational system   The manner in which a person typically represents or interprets his or her input into a system. Input may be interpreted kinesthetically, visually, or auditorily. To increase rapport with a client, the therapist tries to match the client's dominant representational system.

Example: A client says, "I see," repeatedly and is thus visually oriented. The therapist decides to use visual verbs in talking with this person—for example, "Let's get a clear picture of this problem."

Grinder, J., & Bandler, R. (1976). *The structure of magic* (Vol. 2). Palo Alto, CA: Science & Behavior Books.
Weeks, G., & L'Abate, L. (1982). *Paradoxical psychotherapy: Theory and practice with individuals, couples, and families.* New York: Brunner/Mazel.

rescue games Situations in which one member of the original family triad always agrees, a second member always disagrees, and a third's statements are always irrelevant. In most interactional systems, the same person plays the same role most of the time.

Satir, V. (1983). *Conjoint family therapy* (3rd ed.). Palo Alto, CA: Science & Behavior Books.

resistance Any block to change. Resistance has been seen as "located" in the client; it also has been described as something the client is doing, rather than as a product of client-therapist interaction. Psychoanalytically oriented therapists see resistance as a transference reaction; systemic therapists view it as the therapist's poor choice of an intervention.

Examples: In more than one sense, this form of problem resolution is similar to the philosophy and technique of judo, in which the opponent's thrust is not opposed by a counterthrust of at least the same force, but rather is accepted and amplified by yielding to and going with it. This the opponents do not expect; they are playing the game of force against force, of more of the same, and by the rules of their game they anticipate a counterthrust and not a different game altogether.

In a therapeutic context, resistance can be illustrated by a situation in which a patient explains how busy he is at work and says he cannot do something suggested by the therapist even though he thinks the therapist's suggestion is a good one.

de Shazer, S. (1982). *Patterns of brief family therapy.* New York: Guilford.
Erickson, M. H., & Rossi, E. (1979). *Hypnotherapy: An exploratory casebook.* New York: Irvington.

resolution phase The fourth and final stage of the sexual response cycle, characterized by the body returning to its normal, unstimulated state. During this phase, no amount of sexual stimulation can initiate sexual excitement in the male. The length of the resolution phase varies greatly and extends with age.

Masters, W., & Johnson, V. (1970). *Human sexual inadequacy.* Boston: Little, Brown.

resonance   The system's sensitivity to its members' actions and information flow. In diffuse families, information flow occurs very easily, and thus resonance is high. Conversely, in rigid families, information flow is difficult, and thus resonance is low.

Minuchin, S. (1974). *Families and family therapy.* Cambridge, MA: Harvard University Press.

resource exchange theory   A theory, developed by Foa and Foa, stipulating six categories or classes of resources that are exchanged between and among people: love, status, money, possessions, services, and information. L'Abate, Sloan, Wagner, and Malone reduced these to three: being (love and status), having (money and possessions), and doing (information and services). Most interpersonal and family dysfunctions derive from deficits and disturbances in being.

Foa, U. G., & Foa, E. B. (1974). *Societal structures of the mind.* Springfield, IL: Charles C Thomas.

L'Abate, L., Sloan, S. Z., Wagner, V., & Malone, K. (1980). The differentiation of resources. *Family Therapy, 7,* 237-246.

resource theory   A theory based on three major assumptions: (a) Every individual is continually attempting to satisfy his needs and desires to attain goals; (b) Most of the individual's needs are satisfied through social interaction with other persons or groups; and (c) During this interaction, there is a continual exchange of resources which contribute to the satisfaction of individual need; and to the attainment of individual or group goals. The theory asserts that the balance of power (in decision-making) will be on the side of the partner who contributes the greatest resources to the marriage. The family member with the greatest command of resources to meet another's needs and goals is defined as having the greater power. The basic idea is that one person possesses resources that are instrumental to the attainment of another person's goals, needs, desires, or interests.

Example: In desiring the economic resources that the husband provides, but lacking the opportunities to gain those resources in other ways, the wife relinquishes power to her husband in order to fulfill her needs.

Cromwell, E., & Olson, D. H. (1975). *Power in families.* New York: Halsted.

respondent   A person who is responding under the control of an eliciting stimulus and therefore responds "on call"—that is, the frequency of the stimulus equals the frequency of the response.

Example: Whenever the wife looks depressed, the husband becomes angry and wants to know what he has done wrong. His response has become conditioned to her depressions.

Weiss, R. (1978). Marriage from a behavioral perspective. In T. Paolino & B. McCrady (Eds.), *Marriage and marital therapy* (pp. 165-239). New York: Brunner/Mazel.

response anxiety   The pressure that arises out of the fear to engage in and enjoy a sexual exchange. This type of anxiety has been proposed to be one, if not the primary, cause of inhibited sexual desire.

Example: A woman had lost her desire for sexual exchange. She was fully aware of the fact that her lack of desire was troubling to her partner. When her partner approached her sexually, her fear was of disappointing him because she did not believe she would be able to respond emotionally the way he would like her to respond.

Appelbaum, B. (1988). An ego-analytic perspective on sexual desire. In S. Leiblum & R. Rosen (Eds.), *Sexual desire disorders* (pp. 75-106). New York: Guilford.

R

response cost   The taking away of positive reinforcers from an individual's pool of available reinforcers when a specific undesirable behavior occurs.

Example: To try to cure a boy of playing with matches, each time the boy strikes a match, one penny is removed from a stack of pennies he had been given previously.

LeBow, M. (1972). Behavior modification for the family. In G. D. Erickson & T. P. Hogan (Eds.), *Family therapy: An introduction to theory and technique* (pp. 347-376). Belmont, CA: Wadsworth.

restraining   A paradoxical intervention in which the therapist keeps the client from change. Change may be restrained in several ways. The therapist may (a) point out the negative consequences of change, even though the client might define them as positive, (b) inhibit and forbid change, (c) predict and prescribe a relapse, or (d) declare that change is hopeless. The underlying message in a restraining statement is, "In order to change, stay the same or give up." This type of intervention may be used at any point in therapy, but it is recommended after the use of symptom prescription.

Example: A client enters therapy, stating that her main problem is doing the opposite of what everyone else tells her to do. She acts as though she wants to stop this pattern immediately and completely. The therapist forbids her to change, by stating that an abrupt change would be too painful. Hence, she is permitted to cooperate with another on only one small request. By implication, her spontaneous opposition to another's request is prescribed, which places it under voluntary control.

Rohrbaugh, M., Tennen, H., Press, S., White, L., Raskin, P., & Pickering, M. (1977, August). *Paradoxical strategies in psychotherapy.* Paper presented at the American Psychological Association, San Francisco, CA.
Weeks, G., & L'Abate, L. (1982). *Paradoxical psychotherapy: Theory and practice with individuals, couples, and families.* New York: Brunner/Mazel.

restraint   A belief that prevents the system from changing.
Example: The wife believes that her husband is incapable of change, and, even if he could change, he does not care.

Bateson, G. (1972). *Steps to an ecology of mind.* New York: Ballantine.
White, M. (1986). Negative explanation, restraint, and double description: A template for family therapy. *Family Process, 25,* 169-184.

restructuring   A therapeutic task in which the therapist's interventions alter the family's interactions such that boundaries, hierarchies, communication patterns, and power within the family are changed.

Minuchin, S. (1974). *Families and family therapy.* Cambridge, MA: Harvard University Press.

retarded ejaculation   A condition in which the male has absence of or difficulty in reaching ejaculation following sufficient sexual excitement.

Masters, W., & Johnson, V. (1970). *Human sexual inadequacy.* Boston: Little, Brown.

retribalization   A basic strategy of network therapy in which a large number of people who have some connection to a troubled family are brought together to help reestablish network ties.

Speck, R., & Attneave, C. (1973). *Family networks.* New York: Pantheon.

revealed differences   The result of a technique by which subjects who have shared experiences are asked to make individual evaluations of them and then to reconcile any differences in interpretations that may have occurred.

Strodtbeck, F. (1954). The family as a three-person group. *American Sociological Review, 19,* 23-29.

revictimization   One of the social effects sometimes resulting from incest. The victim of incest/child abuse is more likely than a nonvictim to be a sexual victim again, either inside or outside the family. This effect may be due to the survivor's impaired ability to choose partners who are trustworthy.

Courtois, C. (1988). *Healing the incest wound.* New York: Norton.

revivification   A sex hypnotherapy technique used to treat sexual desire dysfunction. The client is requested to replay an old sexual experience that was very pleasant.

Araoz, D. L. (1982). *Hypnosis and sex therapy.* New York: Brunner/Mazel.

revolving slate A legacy of patterns repeated from one generation to the next. From the viewpoint of contextual family therapy, the revolving slate is a chief factor in marital and familial dysfunction.

Example: A father abandons his children because he, too, was abandoned.

Boszormenyi-Nagy, I., & Ulrich, D. (1982). Contextual family therapy. In A. S. Gurman & D. P. Kniskern (Eds.), *Handbook of family therapy* (pp. 159-186). New York: Brunner/Mazel.

rigid boundaries Boundaries that are relatively impermeable, so it is difficult for information to flow between subsystems in a family. This difficulty leads to disengagement. See also **disengaged family.**

Minuchin, S. (1974). *Families and family therapy.* Cambridge, MA: Harvard University Press.

R

rigid complementarity A relationship based on inequality—for example, doctor-patient, well one-sick one. This type of relationship usually is based on the traditions of the culture. The relationship is defined by assigned roles, not by equality. See also **neurotic complementarity.**

Watzlawick, P., Bevin, J. H., & Jackson, D. D. (1967). *Pragmatics of human communication.* New York: Norton.

rigid family A family that permits only very stereotyped and limited interactions, in which the patient's personality is usually an extension of one of the parents'.

Alanen, Y. (1958). The mothers of schizophrenic patients. *Acta Psychiatry Neurological Scandinavian Supplement, 12,* 124.
Fleck, S. (1972). An approach to family pathology. In G. D. Erickson & T. P. Hogan (Eds.), *Family therapy: An introduction to theory and technique* (pp. 103-119). Belmont, CA: Wadsworth.

rigid triad A family triangle in which members are locked into pathogenic roles. In structural family therapy, triads include triangulations, parent-child coalitions, detouring attacking coalitions, and detouring supportive coalitions.

Minuchin, S., Rosman, B. L., & Baker, L. (1978). *Psychosomatic families: Anorexia nervosa in context.* Cambridge, MA: Harvard University Press.

rituals Rituals are co-evolved, symbolic acts that include not only the ceremonial aspect of the actual presentation of the ritual but also the process of preparing for it. A ritual may or may not include words, but it does have both open and closed parts that are "held" together by a guiding metaphor. Repetition can be part of a ritual through the content, the form, or the occasion. Therapeutic rituals should have enough space for the incorporation of multiple meanings by various family members and clinicians, as well as a variety of levels of participation.

Robert, J. (1988). Setting the frame: Definition, functions, and topologies of rituals. In E. Imber-Black, J. Roberts, & R. Whiting (Eds.), *Rituals in families and family therapy* (pp. 3-46). New York: Norton.

Selvini Palazzoli, M., Boscolo, L., Cecchin, G., & Prata, G. (1980). *Paradox and counterparadox: A new model in the therapy of the family in schizophrenic transaction.* New York: Jason Aronson.

role complementarity   The assumption that a role does not exist in isolation, but rather is always patterned to gear with the complementary, or reciprocal, role of a role partner. John Spiegel notes that role complementarity is chiefly responsible for the degree of harmony and stability that exists in interpersonal relations. He cites five causes for the failure to develop complementarity in role systems within the family: (a) cognitive discrepancy, (b) discrepancy of goals, (c) allocative discrepancy, (d) instrumental discrepancy, and (e) discrepancy in cultural value orientations.

Spiegel, J. (1971). *Transactions.* New York: Science House.

role conflict   Conflict arising from disparities between family members' perceptions of each other's roles. Each member has a conception of his or her role in the family. A father may follow his father's example and be a strict disciplinarian. He may consider his role in the context of his assets and competencies. For example, he may regard his wife as a more efficient manager than he is and may delegate to her the tasks of budgeting the family income. He still may regard budgeting as his function, but he delegates those tasks to her because of a realistic consideration of his own limitations.

Each family member also has a conception of the roles of the other members. Such conceptions are based on factors similar to those affecting one's conception of one's own role (family of origin, sexual identification, sense of personal identity, and social expectations). However, one's conception of one's own role and the conceptions of other members of that role may differ. In some families, the roles are complementary and the family functions adequately. But, if the family lacks complementarity, conflict becomes highly probable.

Families deal with conflict in one or more ways. The conflict may be

- expressed openly and resolved through normal channels of communication
- recognized but obscured through patterns of communication that conceal or evade conflict

- expressed by acting-out problems, rather than through a rational consideration of solutions
- projected on a member in the form of a neurotic or psychotic disorder
- evaded by limiting or avoiding physical or psychological contact with members

Stuart, R. B. (1980). *Helping couples change: A social learning approach to marital therapy.* New York: Guilford.

Thorman, G. (1965). *Family therapy: A handbook.* Beverly Hills, CA: Western Psychological Services.

role cycling Attempts by couples to mesh the blend of their individual careers with the changing responsibilities of the family. Couples avoid additional strain by staggering their career and family cycles so that peak career and family stress times do not occur simultaneously.

Example: The husband tries to cycle his role due to responsibilities stemming from the birth of his second child.

McCubbin, H. I., & Figley, C. R. (1983). *Stress and the family: Coping with normative transitions* (Vol. 1). New York: Brunner/Mazel.

role equilibrium The family is a small-scale system constantly shifting its equilibrium. When there is role equilibrium, decision making takes place at a low level, events tend to occur in automatic fashion, and there is considerable spontaneity in family members interacting with each other. When complementarity fails through role conflict, the interpersonal relations move toward disequilibrium. The failure of complementarity is so disruptive that it is almost always accompanied by processes of restoration or reequilibrium, such as role reversal, coercion, coaxing, or postponement.

Spiegel, J. (1971). *Transactions.* New York: Science House.

role induction The changing of another's concept of a role (e.g., by coaxing, coercing, masking, evaluating, or postponing) to induce complementarity.

Spiegel, J. (1971). *Transactions.* New York: Science House.

role induction interview This pretherapy training procedure is used to prepare couples for conjoint therapy by providing a general explanation of the process, as well as a description and exposition of the behavior expected of the patient and the therapist and by preparing them for such typical therapeutic phenomena as resistance and induction expectancies or improvement within several months. The session may take place with one couple or with as many as five couples.

Example: The husband did not want to participate in therapy because he believed that his wife had the problem. His wife said they could overcome their difficulties if he would attend one or two sessions. The therapist requested that the couple attend a group role induction interview to learn to be more realistic about marital and individual therapy and to find out what other couples are questioning and wish to achieve.

Sauber, S. R. (1972). Patient training prior to entering psychotherapy. *Social Psychiatry, 7*, 139-143.

role model   An individual whose behavior in a particular role provides a pattern or model on which another individual bases behavior in performing the same role.

Example: A recovering alcoholic who has been abstinent for many years is a role model for a newly recovering alcoholic.

Amaranto, E. (1971). Glossary. In H. Kaplan & B. Sadock (Eds.), *Comprehensive group psychotherapy* (pp. 823-872). Baltimore: Williams & Wilkins.

role modification   A therapeutic technique to produce a change that will induce complementarity—for example, by exploring, compromising, or consolidating or by referral to a third party.

Example: The husband believes that he has fulfilled his marital role simply by bringing home the paycheck. He and his wife consult a therapist, who helps them reach a compromise over how much and what kind of housework the husband can or should do.

Foley, V. (1974). *An introduction to family therapy.* New York: Grune & Stratton.
Spiegel, J. (1957). The resolution of role conflict within the family. *Psychiatry, 20,* 1-16.

role playing   An action technique in which family members act out a problem. The essence of role playing is "making believe" that the situation is real—that is, acting in a spontaneous manner. Role playing is useful when other techniques have been ineffective in families that operate on an intellectual level.

Example: A couple have an argument every day when the husband arrives home from work. The couple play this scene in the therapist's office so that the therapist can observe the patterns of interaction.

Satir, V. (1983). *Conjoint family therapy* (3rd ed.). Palo Alto, CA: Science & Behavior Books.

role reversal   The exchange of roles with another family member to facilitate seeing the other member's viewpoint and to increase empathy between the members. Role reversal enables the individual who has played one role to move into the other's role and to demonstrate how that individual would like to have been treated. If the role reversal takes place during the enactment, it is known as *switching.* Role reversal also may occur when a passive partner is allowed to assume the role of the dominant partner.

Example: There is an exchange of roles when the parents and the children interact and the children take on parental roles in the family. In some family scenes, members may switch roles several times. For example, the daughter may say that the vacation was too expensive.

Corsini, R. J. (1966). *Role playing in psychotherapy: A manual.* Chicago: Aldine.

role reversal theory A theory postulating that, in schizophrenogenic families, the mother usurps the father's role as the authority figure in the household. Role reversal theory derives from the clinical tradition of working with families with a schizophrenic member.

Lidz, T., Fleck, S., & Cornelison, A. (1965). Family studies and a theory of schizophrenia. In T. Lidz, S. Fleck, & A. Cornelison (Eds.), *Schizophrenia and the family* (pp. 362-376). New York: International Universities Press.

roles The expected behaviors of family members. For example, Mom is the caretaker, Dad is the breadwinner, daughter Cindy is the clown, and daughter Julie is the peacemaker. Sociologists divide roles into two basic types: ascribed and achieved. *Ascribed roles* are assigned on the basis of factors over which the individual has no control—for example, gender and race. *Achieved roles* are earned on the basis of individual achievement—for example, becoming a boss, peacemaker, breadwinner, or scapegoat. The two kinds of roles overlap in families. However, family role structure is often so obscured in its early development that the family members may not know the origins of their roles and may feel trapped in them.

Role differentiation is important as a defensive effort to restore a sense of self in families. The cost of such differentiation to both the individual and the family is that, to remain a part of the family yet still have individually unique qualities, the individual may distort or simplify personal emotions. Each member experiences pressure to be both a unique individual and a valued member of the family.

Ackerman, N. (1958). *The psychodynamics of family life.* New York: Basic Books.
Hoopes, M. H., Fisher, B. L., & Barlow, S. H. (1984). *Structured family facilitation programs: Enrichment, education, and treatment.* Rockville, MD: Aspen Systems.

role strain Stress produced by confronting a task that has not been a part of one's normal role.

Example: A new single-parent mother takes her son to baseball practice, where all of the other boys have been brought by their fathers.

Blechman, E. A., & Manning, M. (1976). A reward-cost analysis of the single-parent family. In E. L. Mash, L. Hamerlynck, & L. Handy (Eds.), *Behavior modification and families* (pp. 61-90). New York: Brunner/Mazel.
Goode, W. (1960). A theory of role. *American Sociological Review, 25,* 423-496.

role theory   A theory that focuses on role functioning in the study and analysis of family disorders. The following concepts of role theory often are incorporated by most models of family therapy.

- An individual has a fairly well defined role in the family. This role involves obligations to be met and expectations to be fulfilled.
- There may be confusion in identifying, accepting, or enacting roles.
- Conflict in roles may result. For example, the wife may assume responsibility for disciplining the children, while the husband may regard this function as part of his role as father.
- Roles may be complementary.
- Roles may be stereotyped and inflexible.
- Family therapy aims at the modification of role functioning. The achievement of complementarity helps the family achieve a balance of role functioning to maximize the mutual gratification of needs and opportunities for growth.

Glick, I. D., & Kessler, D. P. (1980). *Marital and family therapy* (2nd ed.). New York: Grune & Stratton.

Thorman, G. (1965). *Family therapy: A handbook.* Beverly Hills, CA: Western Psychological Services.

romantic concepts   Concepts that lead to unrealistic and false expectations and thus to subsequent disillusionment.

Crosby, J. (1976). *Illusion and disillusion in marriage* (2nd ed.). Belmont, CA: Wadsworth.

romantic success   A problem symbolically equated with the dangerous competition for sex and power that the patient experienced with the same-gender parent in the Oedipal problem situation. Most persons who suffer from success problems show evidence of unresolved Oedipal problems.

Kaplan, H. S. (1979). *Disorders of sexual desire.* New York: Brunner/Mazel.

rosaphrenia   A psychosexual disorder of women, characterized by inadequate sexual psychological development, exaggeration of sexual tendencies, and inability to achieve orgasm. Self-worth exists in the woman's sexuality, and she reacts passively or aggressively to that perception by adopting attitudes and behaviors typical of frigidity or nymphomania. Her manner of dress and behavior usually either exaggerates or masks feminine attributes. The rosaphrenian woman can be identified by her stereotypical female roles, such as the ultimately feminine secretarial type who dresses to provoke male admiration, or the matronly type who looks and acts as if she has nothing to do with sex or men.

Examples: A woman who promises sexual favors for economic or social gain. A woman who withholds sex as punishment to her mate.

Baisden, M. (1971). *The world of rosaphrenia: The sexual psychology of the female.* Sacramento, CA: Allied Research Society.

Baisden, M., & Baisden, J. (1979). A profile of women who seek counseling for sexual dysfunctions. *American Journal of Family Therapy, 7,* 62-76.

rotary depression Feelings of dysphoria that seem to rotate among family members in a way that may be used to predict which family member other than the nominal patient may become either an identified patient requiring special help or a particularly strong resource in the family. Rotary depression is viewed as a part of a natural self-rehabilitation process by which a family rids itself of obsolete mechanisms and its members return to accessibility to outside stimuli. It is a cooperative process that serves as a natural model from depression through grief.

MacGregor, R., Ritchie, A., Serrano, A., & Schuster, F. (1964). *Multiple impact therapy with families.* New York: McGraw-Hill.

R

roundtable discussion A therapeutic technique used to summarize the facts that have been obtained in separate interviews involving both marital partners and the co-therapists.

Masters, W., & Johnson, V. (1970). *Human sexual inadequacy.* Boston: Little, Brown.

rubber fence Lyman Wynne's term for the family's collective and unconscious dynamic equilibrium between the intense need to maintain a collective ego (symbiotic ego) and the members' strivings for individuality. In schizophrenic families, the members act as if they are a self-sufficient social system with completely encircling boundaries. In a rubber fence situation, the persons who do not follow family rules (myths) are experienced as psychologically excluded. The specific location of the family's boundaries may shift as if made of rubber, always encircling but without clearly defined gates for entry or exit.

Searles, H. (1965). The contribution of family treatment to the psychotherapy of schizophrenia. In I. Boszormenyi-Nagy & J. Framo (Eds.), *Intensive family therapy: Theoretical and practical aspects* (pp. 463-496). New York: Harper & Row.

Wynne, L., Ryckoff, I., Day, J., & Hirsch, S. (1958). Pseudomutuality in the family relations of schizophrenics. *Psychiatry, 21,* 205-220.

rule A persistent pattern of family interactions, deviation from which evokes awareness that something new has occurred. Some rules are intentionally announced and followed, as in a family that describes itself as "close-knit and without fighting." The more important rules, however, are often outside the family's awareness and are composed of the repetitive behaviors that make up the routines of daily family life.

Example: A conscious rule is that the children are not allowed to watch TV until they have completed their homework. An unconscious rule is that when mother cries, the youngest child has an asthma attack.

Umbarger, C. C. (1984). *Structural family therapy*. New York: Grune & Stratton.

runaway   A system that is "off track" because of responding to positive feedback, which reinforces errors, instead of being self-correcting through negative feedback. See also **deviation amplification.**

Watzlawick, P., Beavin, J. H., & Jackson, D. D. (1967). *Pragmatics of human communication*. New York: Norton.

runaway technique   A crisis-inducing therapeutic maneuver that brings about a positive feedback process. The family symptom is so escalated that its breakdown or blowup results, and the family is then ready for change.

Example: The wife is suspicious every time her husband leaves the house. She does not tell her husband directly about her suspicions, but she expresses them indirectly. The therapist directs her to be overtly suspicious and, to precipitate a crisis, to ask "20 questions" when he returns home.

Haley, J. (1963). *Strategies of psychotherapy*. New York: Grune & Stratton.

sabotage   A marital partner's subtle reinforcement of a spouse's dysfunction in ways not apparent to the sabotaging partner, due to the latter's unconscious fears or underlying conflicts.

Example: A husband tells his wife he wants her to initiate sex, but when she tries, he finds a reason for not being interested.

Kaplan, H. S. (1974). *The new sex therapy.* New York: Brunner/Mazel.

saint   A dysfunctional role in a family also known as *priest, nun,* or *rabbi.* A child in the family expresses the family's spirituality and often is expected to become a priest, nun, rabbi, monk, or minister, but is not expected to be sexual, and is expected to be perfect. Often the expectation is never spoken.

Friel, J., & Friel, L. (1988). *Adult children: The secrets of dysfunctional families.* Deerfield Beach, FL: Health Communications.

saint syndrome   A situation in which the entire family agrees that a particular family member is more gracious, more loving, more generous, and more self-sacrificing than any ordinary mortal. The family member is assumed to possess no negative traits and to be capable of an even better performance if the member were not surrounded by less worthy people.

Example: The father is a physician who is worshipped by his patients. At home, he is greatly admired by his family members, who assume the roles of either children or sinners.

Beavers, W. R. (1977). *Psychotherapy and growth: A family systems perspective.* New York: Brunner/Mazel.

satisfaction phase   A concept used by Lazarus to extend the phases of sexual excitement developed by Masters and Johnson and by Kaplan. In the model, the sexual response cycle includes desire, arousal, stimulation, orgasm, resolution, and satisfaction. *Satisfaction* refers to the subjective evaluation of the sexual experience.

Lazarus, A. (1988). A multimodal perspective on problems of sexual desire. In S. Leiblum & R. Rosen (Eds.), *Sexual desire disorders* (pp. 145-167). New York: Guilford.

satyriasis   A male sexual disorder characterized by insatiable sexual desire. This condition is believed to be psychogenic in nature and stems from such factors as a need to prove potency, to compensate for failures and other personal shortcomings, to distract oneself from anxiety, and to deny homosexual tendencies.

Goldenson, R. (Ed.). (1924). *Longman dictionary of psychology and psychiatry.* New York: Longman.
Lazarus, A. (1988). A multimodal perspective on problems of sexual desire. In S. Leiblum & R. Rosen (Eds.), *Sexual desire disorders* (pp. 145-167). New York: Guilford.

S

say-ask rule   The principle that, when a question must be asked, it is best for it to be preceded by a self-statement. This behavior increases the level of responsibility the speaker assumes for the messages he or she sends and thus lowers the need for defensiveness on the part of the listener.

Example: The husband says to his wife, "I have the feeling you don't want to go. What would you like to do?"

Baruth, L. G., & Huber, C. H. (1984). *An introduction to marital theory and therapy.* Belmont, CA: Brooks/Cole.

scapegoat   A role in a dysfunctional family in which one member takes the blame and/or is given the blame for all of the problems within the family. The scapegoat is often the "black sheep" who often becomes addicted to drugs, gets into fights, acts out sexually, or has trouble with the law as a way to express family dysfunction.

Friel, J., & Friel, L. (1988). *Adult children: The secrets of dysfunctional families.* Deerfield Beach, FL: Health Communications.

scapegoating   A process in which an external target (e.g., spouse, child, parent) is chosen by members of a family system to assume responsibility for whatever is wrong in the system. The scapegoat not only assumes and accepts this role but also often becomes so entrenched as to be unable to behave otherwise.

Example: A mother and a father cannot deal with the anger they experience toward each other in their marriage. They begin to blame their child for all kinds of misconduct in order to ventilate their anger. They project their blame onto the child as a maneuver to avoid having to face the marital conflict.

Ackerman, N. (1966). *Treating the troubled family.* New York: Basic Books.

L'Abate, L., Weeks, G., & Weeks, K. (1979). Of scapegoats, strawmen, and scarecrows. *International Journal of Family Counseling, 1,* 86-96.

Vogel, S. E., & Bell, N. (1960). The emotionally disturbed child as family scapegoat. In N. Bell & S. E. Vogel (Eds.), *A modern introduction to the family* (pp. 382-397). New York: Free Press.

schism (1) A relationship marked by failure to achieve mutuality, with a consequent outbreak of unresolved conflict and a chronic state of marital separation at the emotional level. This situation eventually is transmitted to or projected on the children. The spouses' status and worth are undercut, and there is a tendency to compete for and form alliances with the children, thereby breaching generational boundaries. (2) A relationship marked by chronic failure to achieve complementarity of purpose or role reciprocity or by excessive attachment of the children to the parental home. In the latter case, the attachment is used to delay or prevent the threatened breakup of the marriage. It thus becomes a rescue maneuver on the part of the children.

Lidz, T., Fleck, S., & Cornelison, A. (Eds.). (1965). *Schizophrenia and the family.* New York: International Universities Press.

schismatic coalition A family pattern in which the marital coalition is absent or relatively weak and in which strong alliances exist across the generations and sexes.

Example: The marital partners have an emotionally distant relationship but feel close to their opposite-sex children.

Glick, I. D., & Kessler, D. P. (1980). *Marital and family therapy* (2nd ed.). New York: Grune & Stratton.

schismatic family A family in which the parents fill complementary roles, undercut each other, and compete for the children. The family is in two camps, and the identified patient cannot use one parent as a model for identification or as a love object without losing the support of the other parent. There are two types of schismatic families: In one, the marital coalition is weak or absent, and there are strong alliances across the generations and sexes. In the other, there are cross-generational alliances between same-sex parent and child.

Lidz, T., Fleck, S., & Cornelison, A. (Eds.). (1965). *Schizophrenia and the family.* New York: International Universities Press.

schizogenic A pathologic process that occurs in the family and that is associated with psychotic symptoms. In contrast, *schizophrenia* denotes a psychotic disorder in the individual.

Rubinstein, D. (1960, January). *The family of the schizophrenic.* Paper presented at the Second Cuban Congress of Neurology and Psychiatry, Havana.

Zuk, G., & Rubinstein, D. (1965). A review of concepts in the study and treatment of families of schizophrenics. In I. Boszormenyi-Nagy & J. Framo (Eds.), *Intensive family therapy: Theoretical and practical aspects* (pp. 1-32). New York: Harper & Row.

schizomogensis See **symmetrical schizogensis.**

schizophrenic omnipotence Assumption by the identified patient of the exalted position, power, and privileges accorded a superparent. The price paid by the patient is a burden of guilt so overwhelming that it helps bring about ego disruption.

Example: The schizophrenic assumes the position of master decision maker in the family.

Framo, J. (1965). Systematic research on family dynamics. In I. Boszormenyi-Nagy & J. Framo (Eds.), *Intensive family therapy: Theoretical and practical aspects* (pp. 407-462). New York: Harper & Row.

schizophrenogenic mother A mother in a family with a schizophrenic member as viewed from psychoanalytic theory. The mother is viewed as being aggressive, domineering, insecure, and rejecting. This type of mother was seen as an important causal factor in the development of schizophrenia. In a family with a schizophrenogenic mother, the father is seen as inadequate, passive, and indifferent.

Fromm-Reichmann, F. (1948). Notes on the development of schizophrenia by psychoanalytic psychotherapy. *Psychiatry, 11,* 267-277.

Zuk, G., & Rubinstein, D. (1965). A review of concepts in the study and treatment of families of schizophrenics. In I. Boszormenyi-Nagy & J. Framo (Eds.), *Intensive family therapy: Theoretical and practical aspects* (pp. 1-32). New York: Harper & Row.

school phobia A reluctance or refusal to go to school on the part of a child because of intense anxiety and fear about being there. It involves a dread of the school setting that is out of proportion to any real danger and cannot be relieved by explanations or reassurances that there is nothing to fear. Typically, school-phobic children express their reluctance to attend school through physical complaints that convince their parents to keep them home or the school nurse to excuse them from the classroom. Often the school-phobic child has an intense desire to watch and guard one or more of his or her parents. Either the child and/or one parent may have serious anxieties regarding separation.

Weiner, I. (1982). *Child and adolescence psychopathology*. New York: John Wiley.

script From a transactional analysis framework, a script is a life plan formulated from what one experiences as a child and from decisions made under stress. A script limits spontaneity and flexibility in problem solving and in relating to people because the story, including all of the major events and the ending, has already been written in early childhood. In essence, the script answers the question, "What does a person like me do in a family like this with people like you?"

Examples: The mother says to the child, "You don't need anything," and the child accepts it literally, developing a life plan of denying wants and needs. Or the message may be inferred, as when a boy whose father continually ignores him concludes that the father is saying to him, "Don't exist."

Erskine, R. G. (1982). Transactional analysis and family therapy. In A. M. Horne & M. M. Ohlsen (Eds.), *Family counseling and therapy* (pp. 245-275). Itasca, IL: F. E. Peacock.

sculpting A technique in which family members are physically molded, by a family member during a therapy session, into positions symbolizing their actual relationships. Through the sculpting process, past events and attitudes as they affect the present are perceived and experienced immediately and directly. The sculpting inevitably provides new meanings and new imagery of family relations in a way that verbal sharing alone cannot.

Example: A fragmented family is sculpted in such a way that the members are placed in different parts of a room facing different directions, or even in different rooms.

Duhl, K., Kantor, D., & Duhl, B. (1973). Learning, space and action in family therapy. A primer of sculpture. In D. Bloch (Ed.), *Techniques of family psychotherapy* (pp. 47-63). New York: Grune & Stratton.
Gerson, M., & Barsky, M. (1979). For the new family therapist: A glossary of terms. *American Journal of Family Therapy, 7*, 15-30.
Papp, P., Silverstein, O., & Carter, E. (1973). Family sculpting in preventive work with families. *Family Process, 12*, 197-212.

secondary gain A secondary advantage that arises from an illness or symptom presentation, such as gratification of dependent yearnings or attention seeking. A secondary gain offers a way of obtaining some particular intrafamilial benefit.

Example: When the husband comes home from work, his wife complains of chronic back pain in order to get him to assist her in household chores and, thereby, to pay attention to her.

Framo, J. (1965). Rationale and technique of intensive family therapy. In I. Boszormenyi-Nagy & J. Framo (Eds.), *Intensive family therapy: Theoretical and practical aspects* (pp. 143-212). New York: Harper & Row.

secondary locus   The part of a system that supports, but is not essential to, the generation and maintenance of a problem. The actions of the systems in the secondary locus may reinforce the problematic structure through an accommodation that supports the structure.

Example: Each time the husband and the wife engage in an upsetting disagreement, the wife confides in her neighbor, who provides the wife support and reassurance of her correct position. The actions of the systems in the secondary locus may reinforce the problematic structure through an accommodation that supports the structure.

Aponte, H., & van Deusen, J. (1981). Structural family therapy. In A. S. Gurman & D. P. Kniskern (Eds.), *Handbook of family therapy* (pp. 310-360). New York: Brunner/Mazel.

second career   Any line of activity entered into with a high commitment after a significant time in a prior occupation. Such changes can occur more than once, so the term *second career* might signify a third or fourth career. The considerations include some form of monetary reward, although the earnings are usually smaller than in the prior career and the number of second careers is relatively unstructured and must be created and defined in most cases. A typology of the mode of entry into second careers includes mid-life career change, early retirement by choice, forced early retirement, normal retirement, postchild-rearing, combining artistic interests with ongoing careers, and continuing in a career but in a new setting.

Example: A wife decides to go back to school to prepare for a second career as a viable alternative to the stress she experiences associated with the "empty nest syndrome."

Lieberman, L., & Lieberman, L. (1986). Husband-wife interaction in second careers. *Journal of Family Issues, 7,* 215-229.

second-order change   A change in the frame of reference or system itself. This is change that not only removes the symptom but also alters the systemic interaction, producing permanent change. See also **first-order change.**

Example: Moving from a dream state to a working state; in therapy, defining a symptom as something that is "good," rather than "sick" or "bad."

Watzlawick, P., Bevin, J. H., & Jackson, D. D. (1967). *Pragmatics of human communication.* New York: Norton.

Weeks, L., & L'Abate, L. (1982). *Paradoxical psychotherapy: Theory and practice with individuals, couples, and families.* New York: Brunner/Mazel.

second-order cybernetics   Conceptualizing the treatment unit as consisting of both the observer and the observed as one unit. The "problem creates the system"—that is, the problem does not exist independently of the observing systems that are reciprocally and collectively defining the problem. Thus an intervention is designed to reframe the problem such that the problem has a positive connotation, rather than a negative connotation, and once the problem is redefined, a different family interactional pattern will emerge. Compare with **first-order cybernetics.**

Boscolo, L., Cecchin, G., Hoffman, L., & Penn, P. (1987). *Milan systemic family therapy: Conversations in theory and practice.* New York: Basic Books.

secrets in the family   Those events that are acknowledged as actual events by one family member but kept secret from others, and those events that have no such factual foundation. The latter arise from fantasies that cannot be expressed due to feelings from a time when jealousy, rivalry, love, and hate within one family were faced. Such secrets may be shared unconsciously by parents and children for generations and are sometimes difficult to distinguish from family myths. Open and closed secrets in the family determine group behavior. Secrets may be between family members or between the family and the outside world.

Karpel, M. (1980). Family secrets: I. Conceptual and ethical issues in the relational context. II. Ethical and practical considerations in therapeutic management. *Family Process, 19,* 295-306.

Pincus, L., & Dare, C. (1978). *Secrets in the family.* New York: Pantheon.

selective attention   See **attention.**

self-blamer   One who accepts the blame for something without being able to look outside one's self.

Example: Two people are equally responsible for an embarrassing situation. The self-blamer thinks, "If I had not been so awkward, this would not have happened."

Bowen, M. (1965). Family psychotherapy with schizophrenia in the hospital and in private practice. In I. Boszormenyi-Nagy & J. Framo (Eds.), *Intensive family therapy: Theoretical and practical aspects* (pp. 213-244). New York: Harper & Row.

self-concept   The organized, consistent, conceptual gestalt composed of perceptions of the characteristics of the "I" or "me" and the perceptions of the relationships of the "I" or "me" to others and to various aspects of life, together with the values attached to these perceptions. Thus the self-concept involves a changing and fluid process. In general, self-experiences are the raw material from which the organized self-concept is formed. The ideal self is the self-concept that the individual would most like to possess.

Rogers, C. P. (1959). A theory of therapy, personality, and interpersonal relationships, as developed in the client-centered framework. In S. Koch (Ed.), *Psychology: A study of a science. Vol. 3. Formulations of the person and the social context* (pp. 184-256). New York: McGraw-Hill.

Thayer, L. (1982). A person-centered approach to family therapy. In A. M. Horne & M. M. Ohlsen (Eds.), *Family counseling and therapy* (pp. 175-213). Itasca, IL: F. E. Peacock.

self-confrontation   A technique that provides a person with a means to observe the supportive or maladaptive impact he or she makes on others.
    Example: A wife who constantly interrupts her husband is unaware of her behavior. Audio playback is used to enhance her awareness.

Paul, N. (1972). Effects of playback on family members of their own previously recorded conjoint therapy material. In G. D. Erickson & T. P. Hogan (Eds.), *Family therapy: An introduction to theory and technique* (pp. 251-264). Belmont, CA: Wadsworth.

self-control   A psychological process that, in cases of conflict between possible behavioral choices, involves behavioral shifts in which external influences are supplemented by self-generated cues and reinforcers. The outcome of the process is either (a) the probability of a response with initial high likelihood of occurrence is decreased or (b) the probability of a response with initially low likelihood is increased by the execution of self-generated behaviors. Usually the initial behaviors are well established by prior learning, have been supported for a long time by immediate reinforcement, or have been maintained by socially or physiologically determined contingencies. Self-control (also called *self-management*) methods are used to train individuals to become better problem solvers and behavior analysts by becoming more independent of their immediate environment and other persons.
    Example: An alcohol-prone man passes up a drink so that he can later boast to his wife about his major feat of self-management. However, he thereby demonstrates, not self-control, but a choice between a lesser (alcohol) and a major (attention by a significant other) reinforcement.

Kanfer, F. H. (1977). The many faces of self-control, or behavior modification changes its focus. In R. B. Stuart (Ed.), *Behavioral self-management* (pp. 1-48). New York: Brunner/Mazel.

self-destruction (continuum of)   Addicts show high death rates, shorter than average life expectancies, and greater than normal incidences of sudden deaths. Addicts view death as more positive and potent than pain and are more likely to express a wish for it than do other psychiatric patients. Family members state that they would rather see the addict dead than lost to people outside the family. There seems to be a contract within these families in which the addict's part is to die or to come close to death. The addict becomes the martyr who sacrifices him- or herself at the family's behest. The addict's behavior may be viewed as part of an unresolved family mourning process.

Stanton, M. D., & Todd, T. C. (1982). *The family therapy of drug abuse and addiction.* New York: Guilford.

self-differentiation   The process of becoming a clearly defined individual with well-defined ego boundaries. A self-differentiated person is a mature person who is a contained emotional unit. Once differentiated, the person can be emotionally close to family members and other people without fusing into a new emotional oneness.

Example: Although the 20-year-old son still resides with his parents while attending a local college, he is able to assert himself emotionally, financially, and socially in an independent way with his parents.

Bowen, M. (1976). Theory in the practice of psychotherapy. In P. J. Guerin (Ed.), *Family therapy: Theory and practice* (pp. 42-90). New York: Gardner.

S

self-disclosure   The process of verbally revealing personal information to another person, particularly information of an intimate nature that is not generally known. Such information may be about traumatic events, current feelings, moments of happiness and pride, sexual urges, fears, weaknesses, feelings of inadequacy and personal goals, and wishes and plans.

Example: After 11 years of marriage, the wife revealed some of her childhood fears that helped her husband understand why she would not walk around her own home or outside her home without wearing makeup. She had never told these feelings to anyone else.

Jourard, S. M. (1971). *The transparent self* (2nd ed.). New York: Van Nostrand.

self in the system   In family therapy, the idea that regardless of how a family system is coordinated, family members remain separate individuals. Originally family systems therapy reacted against seeing people uniquely as individuals, but rather saw individuals in the context of the family system. Currently there is a movement within family systems theorists not to forget the individual. It is the belief that family therapy has moved too far from the psychology of the individual.

Nichols, M. P. (1987). *The self in the system.* New York: Brunner/Mazel.

sensate focus   A sex therapy technique that involves touching experiences. Each partner takes a turn touching the other in a way that the other wants and feels comfortable with. The partner being touched communicates whether he or she needs the partner to stop a given type of touching experience. At first, all touching will be nongenital. Over several sessions, the touching gradually will progress to genital touching.

Masters, W., & Johnson, V. (1970). *Human sexual inadequacy.* Boston: Little, Brown.

separateness and connectedness   Separateness and connectedness are issues that underlie a family's life. The process of attempting to achieve a satisfactory pattern of separateness and connectedness is basic to the family's functioning. As each member of a family develops a unique personality, adapts to changes through the life cycle, and creates an individual life space, he or she also is involved in more or less binding ties with other family members. Healthy individuals are both separate (well differentiated) and connected (intimate).

Hess, R., & Handel, G. (1959). *Family worlds: A psychological approach to family life.* Chicago: University of Chicago Press.

S

separation anxiety   Traumatic tension resulting from time apart from the parent, particularly the mother or the "mother substitute." The separation poses a threat or creates a fear or neurotic belief that loss or abandonment will occur. As a developing biological and social organism, a child normally sees separation as a process, rather than an event. However, in the case of a premature removal of the child from the biological mother (e.g., through death, chronic illness, desertion, emotional inadequacy, temporary admission to a hospital), separation anxiety can develop.

Bowlby, J. (1951). Maternal care and mental health. *Bulletin of the World Health Organization, 3,* 355-384.

separation anxiety disorder   A disorder of childhood in which the child shows an excessive amount of anxiety concerning separation from those to whom the child is attached. The reaction is beyond what is expected for the child's developmental level. Separation anxiety disorder is the *DSM-III-R* term that subsumes *school phobia.* Children with separation anxiety disorder have at least three of the following: (a) unrealistic or persistent worry that possible harm will befall a major attachment figure or fear that the attachment figure will leave and not return, or the unrealistic or persistent worry that a calamitous event will separate the child from a major attachment figure; (b) refusal to go to school in order to stay with the major attachment figure or to stay home; (c) refusal to go to sleep without being near the major attachment figure; (d) persistent avoidance of being alone and showing clinging behavior;

(e) repeated nightmares with the theme of separation, physical symptoms; (f) recurrent signs or complaints of excessive distress in anticipation of separation from the major attachment figure (e.g., temper tantrums, crying, pleading); and (g) recurrent excessive distress when separated from the major attachment figure.

American Psychiatric Association. (1987). *Diagnostic and statistical manual of mental disorders* (3rd ed., rev.). Washington, DC: Author.

separation counseling   Crisis intervention counseling using a time-limited approach that deals specifically with the immediate crisis of marital separation. The purpose is to help separating individuals understand their relationship, resolve their conflicts, decide whether their future relationship will be together or apart, and grow through the separation process. A structured separation is a model for distressed families with children. In such cases, the children are presented with parental behavior that displays honesty, choice, and respect as primary values. The damage caused by the suddenness and emotional uproar common to most divorce situations is thereby mitigated. The children have the time and an open interpersonal situation in which to adapt to the major change in their lives.

S.

Toomin, M. K. (1975). Structured separation for couples in conflict. In A. S. Gurman & D. G. Rice (Eds.), *Couples in conflict* (pp. 353-362). New York: Jason Aronson.

separation response   The total experience stemming from a marital separation. The first response is a shock reaction, particularly when the separation is sudden and unexpected. The most frequent expressions of this shock reaction are denial and somatic symptoms. The shock reaction generally is followed by an 8-to-12-week affective cycle. The first phase of this cycle is characterized by a 4-to-6-week period of either depression and withdrawal or euphoria and activity. In the following 4 to 6 weeks, those who have been depressed and withdrawn usually begin to feel more open and become more active. They seldom go as "high" as those who were initially euphoric. On the other hand, those who have been at first euphoric and active tend to withdraw and become somewhat depressed. The "low" tends to be less intense than that experienced by those who were initially depressed. In both groups, the counterreaction gradually shifts and stabilizes in an intermediate affective and activity level.

Example: Joel has difficulty living alone and moves in with the first woman he dates after separating from his wife.

Toomin, M. K. (1975). Structured separation for couples in conflict. In A. S. Gurman & D. G. Rice (Eds.), *Couples in conflict* (pp. 353-362). New York: Jason Aronson.

separation structure　The structure of personal and family relationships developed by a separating couple. The separating partners are
asked to make a 3-month commitment to explore themselves and the
relationship. During this time, both see the therapist individually and
conjointly. They are asked not to live in the same house, not to see a
lawyer, and not to make any permanent financial, property, or child
custody arrangements. The children remain in the family's home, with
whichever parent is best able to care for them. Their lives are disrupted
as little as possible. It is important that they maintain contact with such
environmental supports as friends and school. As the partners communicate with each other, they realistically assess their needs and resolve
practical issues. They are both free to initiate and end social contacts as
they wish and for whatever reason. They may have sex together only if
both want it. Freedom to explore other relationships is encouraged, on
the theory that such exploration maximizes choice. A variety of social,
emotional, and sexual encounters gives each a more realistic view of
self interacting with others. These contacts serve to eliminate "If-it-
weren't-for-you" games. The process of seeing each other only by
choice requires that they examine themselves and each other often to
decide whether they want to be together and, if so, when, or how to reject
each other. In this process of repeatedly accepting and rejecting, each
has an extraordinary opportunity to learn to be honest with the other in
communicating love, appreciation, need, hurt, fear, and anger in a
responsible way.

Toomin, M. K. (1975). Structured separation for couples in conflict. In A. S. Gurman &
D. G. Rice (Eds.), *Couples in conflict* (pp. 353-362). New York: Jason Aronson.

sequence　A repeating cycle of linked behaviors. A sequence often is
analyzed as a linear event, in that each step in the cycle is followed by
another. But because the final step in the progression is always the
occasion to return to the beginning of the cycle, a sequence, in fact,
describes a circular and repetitive unfolding of linked behaviors. A
behavior-exchange sequence involves the transformation of psychological content into observable behaviors that are exchanged across subsystem boundaries. Content events occurring totally within a subsystem are
usually unobservable and can only be inferred. When these events result
in interpersonal contact, however, the behaviors occur in sequence,
among the subsystems, and these exchanges may be observed.

Example: A brother and his older sister engage in a sequence of
thoughts that helps the mother stay firmly allied with her daughter and
estranged from her husband. The larger systems goal (the maintenance
of strict subunit boundaries between men and women) is well served by

the repetitive fights. The sequence of fight activity is used by the family to achieve that larger systems goal.

Umbarger, C. C. (1984). *Structural family therapy*. New York: Grune & Stratton.

sequential process   A process in which the therapist resolves an issue with a subsystem of the family before continuing with the whole or another subsystem of the family on the same or another matter.

Example: A couple enter therapy for help with a teenage daughter. The couple are also in the midst of a marital crisis. The therapist recommends that they either separate or work on their relationship before trying to deal with their daughter's problem.

Aponte, H., & van Deusen, J. (1981). Structural family therapy. In A. S. Gurman & D. P. Kniskern (Eds.), *Handbook of family therapy* (pp. 310-360). New York: Brunner/ Mazel.

serial monogamy   A succession of monogamous relationships of varying duration that is terminated by mutual agreement and/or divorce. Also referred to as *progressive monogamy*.

S

Constantine, L. L., & Constantine, J. M. (1971). Group and multilateral marriage: Definitional notes, glossary and annotated bibliography. *Family Process, 10,* 157-176.

sex manuals   Books that discuss human sexual functioning. Historically these manuals have addressed techniques and goal-oriented behavior such as how to have simultaneous orgasms.

Appelbaum, B. (1988). An ego-analytic perspective on desire disorders. In S. Leiblum & R. Rosen (Eds.), *Sexual desire disorders* (pp. 75-106). New York: Guilford.

sex role adoption   Acting out the behavior characteristics of one gender or the other.

Lynn, D. (1969). *Parental and sex role identification: A theoretical formulation*. Berkeley, CA: McCutchan.

sex role identification   Internalization of aspects of the role appropriate to a given gender and of the unconscious reactions characteristic of that role.

Lynn, D. (1969). *Parental and sex role identification: A theoretical formulation*. Berkeley, CA: McCutchan.

sex role preference   A desire to adopt behavior associated with one gender or the other.

Lynn, D. (1969). *Parental and sex role identification: A theoretical formulation*. Berkeley, CA: McCutchan.

sex therapist   A therapist who uses dynamic psychotherapeutic principles, marital counseling, and behavioral methods in the treatment of
specific sexual problems. A sex therapist needs an understanding of
psychopathology and the dynamics of marital interaction, as well as
clinical skills in both individual and conjoint therapy. The sex therapist
must understand male/female sexuality and the dynamics of marital
discord and should have extensive knowledge of learning theory and the
theory and practice of dynamic psychotherapy. Standards for practice
and certification are provided by the American Association of Sex
Educators, Counselors, and Therapists (AASECT) and the American
Board of Sexology.

LoPiccolo, J. (1978). The professionalization of sex therapy: Issues and problems. In J.
   LoPiccolo & L. LoPiccolo (Eds.), *Handbook of sex therapy* (pp. 511-526). New
   York: Plenum.

sex therapy   A type of therapy, focused on the resolution of sexual
problems, that (a) emphasizes the mutual responsibility of the couple
for the sexual dysfunction, (b) stresses information and education in
treatment, (c) is concerned with attitudinal change and performance
anxiety, (d) increases communication skills and the effectiveness of
sexual techniques, (e) prescribes changes in behavior, and (f) frees
individuals from destructive life-styles and sex roles. Sex therapy also
recognizes the pervasive interaction between sexual dysfunction and the
marital relationship.

Kaplan, H. S. (1981). *The new sex therapy.* New York: Brunner/Mazel.

sexual abuse   Any sort of sexual act between a child and an adult or
between two adults when one individual has sexual behavior forced on
him or her. Definitions of sexual abuse are very difficult because they
are imprecise and unreliable and often lack taxonomic delineation. In
1980, 34 states included sexual abuse in their child abuse statutes but
did not attempt to define what sexual abuse meant. In general, legal and
medical definitions are thought to be too restrictive. However, sexual
abuse most often includes sexual intercourse, oral or anal intercourse,
mutual masturbation, fondling, or sexual touching that is forced on one
individual by another.

Waterman, J., & Lusk, R. (1986). Scope of the problem. In K. MacFarlane, J. Waterman,
   S. Conerly, L. Damon, N. Durfee, & S. Long (Eds.), *Sexual abuse of young children*
   (pp. 3-12). New York: Guilford.

sexual addiction   Refers to an individual who uses sex addictively
despite serious negative consequences. The sexual behavior is out of the

person's control, interferes with his or her life, and has compulsive and addictive elements. The addict goes through a predictable cycle of (a) *preoccupation*—the individual is in a trancelike mood regarding sex, obsessively searching for stimulation, (b) *ritualization*—the individual goes through a ritual leading up to the sexual acting out, (c) *compulsive behavior*—the individual is unable to stop the sexual acting out, and (d) *despair*—the addict feels a sense of hopelessness and powerlessness vis-à-vis his or her sexual behavior. The cycle repeats over and over with the sexual acting out becoming more serious in some cases.

Carnes, P. (1983). *Out of the shadows: Understanding sexual addiction.* Minneapolis: Compcare.

sexual anesthesia   A disorder in which a female "feels nothing" from sexual stimulation or penile intromission. Sexual anesthesia is not considered to be a true sexual dysfunction, but rather a symptom of psychological conflict.

Kaplan, H. S. (1974). *The new sex therapy.* New York: Brunner/Mazel.

sexual aversion   A persistent or recurrent extreme discomfort with or avoidance of genital contact with a sexual partner. Sexual aversions are a significant source of distress and may restrict seriously the person's ability to function sexually.

Kaplan, H. S. (1987). *Sexual aversion, sexual phobia, and panic disorder.* New York: Brunner/Mazel.

sexual dysfunction   Cognitive, affective, and/or behavioral problems that prevent an individual or couple from engaging in and/or enjoying satisfactory intercourse and orgasm. A sexual dysfunction is distinguished from a *sexual variation,* in which an individual may engage successfully in intercourse in an unconventional way or with an unconventional object choice.

LoPiccolo, J. (1978). The professionalization of sex therapy: Issues and problems. In J. LoPiccolo & L. LoPiccolo (Eds.), *Handbook of sex therapy* (pp. 511-526). New York: Plenum.

sexual enhancement   Enhancing the total sexual relationship, including performance, along with attitudes, expectations, myths, and general emotional closeness or intimacy. This approach involves using both in-office and homework assignments.

Treat, S. (1987). Enhancing a couple's sexual relationship. In G. Weeks & L. Hof (Eds.), *Integrating sex and marital therapy* (pp. 57-81). New York: Brunner/Mazel.

sexual genogram   A traditional family therapy assessment device used to explore issues of sexuality in the structure and belief system of the client's family of origin. The genogram includes the sexual thoughts, feelings, and behaviors that were transmitted both overtly and covertly.

Example: In a case involving a male client with a sexual aversion, it was learned that his mother was the all-powerful figure in his family and that she had been sexually seductive. The client saw his mother, and later all women, as threatening and wanting to manipulate him by using sex.

Berman, E., & Hof, L. (1987). The sexual genogram: Assessing family-of-origin factors in the treatment of sexual dysfunction. In G. Weeks & L. Hof (Eds.), *Integrating sex and marital therapy* (pp. 37-56). New York: Brunner/Mazel.

Hof, L., & Berman, E. (1986). The sexual genogram. *Journal of Marital and Family Therapy, 12,* 39-47.

sexual identity   A combination of several concepts: gender identity, sexual orientation, and sexual intention. *Gender identity* is the sense of oneself as masculine, feminine, ambiguous, or androgenous. *Sexual orientation* refers to the sex and gender characteristics of images that elicit arousal; this term is more commonly thought of as the biological sex of one's partner. *Sexual intention* comprises those behaviors the person wishes to engage in with his or her partner.

Levine, S. (1988). Intrapsychic and individual aspects of sexual desire. In S. Leiblum & R. Rosen (Eds.), *Sexual desire disorders* (pp. 21-44). New York: Guilford.

sexuality assessment inventories   A group of inventories used to measure sexual function and global sexual satisfaction and/or psychological symptoms that affect sexual function.

Talmadge, L., & Talmadge, W. (1990). Sexuality assessment measures for clinical use: A review. *American Journal of Family Therapy, 18,* 80-105.

sexuality education   In sex therapy, a technique used to increase knowledge about sexuality, to increase awareness of the individual's attitude and values and those in the culture, and to promote effective communication in discussing sex.

Roger, M. (1987). Dealing with sexual concerns of children. In G. Weeks & L. Hof (Eds.), *Integrating sex and marital therapy* (pp. 82-99). New York: Brunner/Mazel.

sexual panic state   An extreme and irrational fear of sex, accompanied by a strong desire to avoid sexual situation. This state has been called *phobic avoidance* of sex, *sexual aversion,* and *sexual phobia.*

Kaplan, H. S. (1987). *Sexual aversion, sexual phobia, and panic disorder.* New York: Brunner/Mazel.

sexual phobia   A persistent, irrational fear of and compelling desire to avoid sexual experiences and feelings. The individual recognizes the fear as excessive and unreasonable, relative to the dangerousness of the situation. The phobic response may be general or may be limited to specific aspects of sex, such as genital touching, penetration, kissing, or orgasm.

Kaplan, H. S. (1987). *Sexual aversion, sexual phobia, and panic disorder.* New York: Brunner/Mazel.

sexual scapegoating   A situation set up by one partner in which, because of fear of exposure of his or her own sexual inadequacy, the other partner is blamed for an unsatisfactory sex life. Usually the blaming partner makes only hurried, halfway attempts to improve the sexual situation.

Example: An inorgasmic wife blames her husband for her problems, but she refuses to allow him to engage in extended foreplay with her.

Kaplan, H. S. (1974). *The new sex therapy.* New York: Brunner/Mazel.

sexual script   In adulthood, the ability to appropriately identify partners and situations for sexual interactions. The sexual script contains performative and cognitive dimensions. The *performative script* refers to the overt sequence of behaviors characterizing a sexual encounter. The *cognitive script* is comprised of the covert aspects, including thoughts, fantasies, beliefs, and attitudes.

S

Rosen, R., & Leiblum, S. (1988). A sexual scripting approach to problems of desire. In S. Leiblum & R. Rosen (Eds.), *Sexual desire disorders* (pp. 168-191). New York: Guilford.

sexual script assessment   A technique for assessing the differences in sexual desire in a couple. The clinician examines several dimensions of sexual functioning, including complexity, rigidity, satisfaction, and conventionality. The overt behavior of the couple is assessed, followed by the ideal for both partners.

Example: On the dimensions of rigidity, the clinician might find little variety in the couple's sexual interaction. The husband might ideally prefer a rigid script and behavior, while the wife would like greater variety and spontaneity.

Rosen, R., & Leiblum, S. (1988). A sexual scripting approach to problems of desire. In S. Leiblum & R. Rosen (Eds.), *Sexual desire disorders* (pp. 168-191). New York: Guilford.

sexual self-talk   An individual's internalized self-statements based on beliefs that person holds about his or her own sexuality and that of others. Both positive and negative self-talk may exist. An individual with negative sexual self-talk usually experiences a lack of sexual desire or some form of sexual dysfunction. Sexual self-talk is used to assess the sexual relationship at the outset of treatment and then therapeutically to counter and create new positive self-statements.

Example: The husband would think frequently about his wife being a few pounds overweight during sex. This thought turned him off. He was asked to focus on thoughts about pleasing parts of his wife's body in order to generate some positive sexual feeling toward her.

Weeks, G. (1987). Systematic treatments of inhibited sexual desire. In G. Weeks & L. Hof (Eds.), *Integrating sex and marital therapy* (pp. 183-201). New York: Brunner/Mazel.

sexual status examination   A method of assessment in which a detailed description of the couple's current sexual behavior is acquired. This description includes an analysis of the couple's sexual interactions, as well as their other erotic interactions. The purpose of this method is to identify the psychological components of the problem. The analysis would include such data as thoughts and feelings, physical responses, what they do, how each feels and reacts, level of sensitivity and responsivity, communication, whether and/or when anxiety occurs, fantasies, disappointment and anger, self-defeating patterns, and how they deal with sexual difficulties.

Kaplan, H. S. (1983). *The evaluation of sexual disorders.* New York: Brunner/Mazel.

sexual task   An exercise used as a therapeutic tool to shift a couple's objective away from the achievement of a specific sexual response (e.g., organism) to the giving and receiving of pleasure. After this goal has been achieved, sexual exercises designed to relieve specific problems are prescribed.

Masters, W., & Johnson, V. (1970). *Human sexual inadequacy.* Boston: Little, Brown.

shadow reality   Integrated alterative realities not now in the relationship reality but, at times, available to those in the relationship. Shadow realities include unacceptable and threatening information and interpretations that fit the relationship and that could undermine the negotiated relationship reality. Carl Jung used the term *shadow* to describe a well-organized part of the individual's unconscious that can be either dangerous or valuable. Jung's analysis indicated that this individual shadow cannot be avoided; it is always there. To have a marital reality necessitates having a shadow reality. A couple cannot, for example, function as a "good" couple without putting out of sight aspects of their "bad" couplehood, or vice versa.

Example: A couple's marriage reality includes a belief (reflecting societal standards and images of what relationships should be) that they are open with each other. However, they still retain "in the shadows" their awareness of withholding and the ways in which they are not open (the feelings, events, and beliefs that each keeps from the other).

Jung, C. (1964). *Man and his symbols.* Garden City, NY: Doubleday.

Rosenblatt, P. C., & Wright, S. E. (1984). Shadow realities in close relationships. *American Journal of Family Therapy, 12,* 45-54.

Zuk, G. (1971). *Family therapy: A triadic-based approach.* New York: Behavioral Publications.

shaping   The process of reinforcing smaller approximations to the target behavior.

Example: A young retarded boy must wear glasses. He is reinforced initially for just wearing the frames, then the frames and lenses during selected reinforcing activities, and finally for longer and longer periods.

Bandura, A. (1969). *Principles of behavior modification.* New York: Holt, Rinehart & Winston.

S

shared meaning   A situation in which the message being sent coincides with the message being received. The sender sends the message briefly and clearly, and the receiver rephrases the message in different words and feeds it back to the sender. The sender then can confirm the message or clarify it.

Example: The husband conveyed to his wife that he wanted to be more than a sexual athlete to please her, and his wife responded that she would be more attentive to his need to give and receive affection and tenderness in their lovemaking. The husband expressed his appreciation to his wife for her interest in trying to be more understanding to his needs for sexual intimacy.

Bernard, C., & Corrales, R. (1979). *The theory and technique of family therapy.* Springfield, IL: Charles C Thomas.

shift   The transition from a statement of a person's personal, subjective view to a statement of an opposite position, without any of the necessary indicators to acknowledge ambivalence.

Example: A client is talking about wanting his wife to return to the marriage, but then he begins to discuss the advantages he had when single. He seems unaware of the fact that he has shifted his stance.

Beavers, W. R. (1977). *Psychotherapy and growth: A family systems perspective.* New York: Brunner/Mazel.

sibling functioning position   A characteristic of people who are born into the same sibling position in different families and grow up with many personality characteristics in common.

Example: The middle child in a family is often more similar to another middle child in another family in the neighborhood than to older and younger siblings raised in the same family.

Toman, W. (1976). *Family constellation* (3rd ed.). New York: Springer Verlag.

sibling position profile   A technique in which a diagram of siblings is made to provide insight into why a certain child has been chosen to present the undesirable behavioral symptom for the whole family. The profile includes the birth orders and genders of all children.

Bowen, M. (1971). The use of family theory in clinical practice. In J. Haley (Ed.), *Changing families* (pp. 159-192). New York: Grune & Stratton.

sibling rivalry   The jealous desire of a child to usurp a sibling's place in the affection and attention of one or both parents. The overt characteristics of sibling rivalry take many forms, from a direct attack on a brother or a sister to withdrawal or regressive behavior.

Schaefer, C., & Millman, H. (1977). *Therapies for children.* San Francisco: Jossey-Bass.
Smart, M., & Smart, R. (1953). *An introduction to family relationships.* Philadelphia: W. B. Saunders.

sibling subsystem   The grouping of children in a family in which they interact as peers, negotiating issues of competition, defeat, accommodation, cooperation, and protection.

Bank, S., & Kahn, M. (1982). *The sibling bond.* New York: Basic Books.
Lamb, M., & Sutton-Smith, B. (Eds.). (1982). *Sibling relationship.* Hillsdale, NJ: Lawrence Erlbaum.

side-taking   A structural technique to support a particular subsystem in the family. The therapist may side with the mother against the father, with the father against the mother, or with nonverbal, reticent children against the parents in an effort to help the family members verbalize and share thoughts, perceptions, and feelings.

Minuchin, S. (1974). *Families and family therapy.* Cambridge, MA: Harvard University Press.

significant others   (1) Nonrelated people who may have an impact on the individuals in treatment, although not necessarily the same type of emotional impact and influence that the natural family unit has. (2) The person with whom one is intimately involved.

Glick, I. D., & Kessler, D. P. (1980). *Marital and family therapy* (2nd ed.). New York: Grune & Stratton.

silencing strategies Maneuvers designed to punish a person for some transgression by isolating the person in silence to induce compliance or conformity at the public level.

Example: The wife asks her husband to spend more time with her. He responds by becoming silent, and then he attempts to change the subject by criticizing her for always being busy.

Zuk, G. (1971). *Family therapy: A triadic-based approach.* New York: Behavioral Publications.

silent treatment A maneuver in which family members agree not to speak to the victim, as punishment for violation of a code.

Zuk, G. (1971). *Family therapy: A triadic-based approach.* New York: Behavioral Publications.

SIMFAM A game-playing situation adapted by Straus and Talman to elicit family interaction data. Family triads are asked to discover the rules of the SIMFAM game by playing it and then analyzing what they did correctly or incorrectly, as signaled by lights. The interaction generated by the game's tasks can be analyzed by different types of coding systems.

Aldous, T., Condon, T., Hill, R., Straus, M., & Talman, I. (1971). *Family problem solving.* Hinsdale, IL: Dryclere.

simplicity-speaks-the-truth rule The injunction that self-statements should be made directly, openly, honestly, and free from any verbal excess. Manipulations that maneuver the listener into expressing the reaction desired by the speaker—regardless of the message's true impact—should be avoided.

Example: The therapist avoids such statements as, "You're going to like what I tell you," "Don't worry, but . . . ," "You haven't heard this yet, but . . ."

Baruth, L. G., & Huber, C. H. (1984). *An introduction to marital theory and therapy.* Belmont, CA: Brooks/Cole.
Wierenberg, G. I., & Calero, H. H. (1973). *Meta-talk: Guide to hidden meanings on conversations.* New York: Simon & Schuster.

simulated family Members of an audience who role-play family members as a training technique.

Satir, V. (1983). *Conjoint family therapy* (3rd ed.). Palo Alto, CA: Science & Behavior Books.

simultaneous bilateral identity delineation The process of relating to both good and bad objects at the same time. The need to assign dichotomous roles of goodness and badness to others is based on a frame of reference of good and bad archetypes.

Boszormenyi-Nagy, I. (1965). A theory of relationships: Experience and transaction. In I. Boszormenyi-Nagy & J. Framo (Eds.), *Intensive family therapy: Theoretical and practical aspects* (pp. 33-86). New York: Harper & Row.

single parent   Someone who raises a child or children alone, without the presence of a second parent figure. This situation may be the result of marital separation, widowhood, parenthood without marriage, or, less frequently, adoption of a child by an unmarried individual or informal adoption of a child by a child's grandparent, older sibling, or other relative. Married men and women whose partners are away indefinitely in the armed forces, are working in another community, or are hospitalized with a chronic illness may also function as single parents, even though they may not identify themselves as such.

Weiss, R. S. (1977). *Going it alone.* New York: Basic Books.

single-parent family   A family that contains only one parent. Divorce creates new households with single parents, but it results in a single-parent family only when one of the parents, usually the father, has no further contact with the family and does not continue to perform a parental function. (More appropriate terminology would distinguish between these two circumstances and would describe the former as a one-parent household.)

Ahrons, C. R., & Perlmutter, N. S. (1982). The relationship between former spouses: A fundamental subsystem in the remarriage family. In J. C. Hansen & L. Messinger (Eds.), *Therapy with remarriage families* (pp. 31-46). Rockville, MD: Aspen.

situational idiosyncracies   Events in particular geographic or social milieus that impinge on the family.

Example: Repairing the city drainage system requires digging up the streets in such a way that the children have no place to play, the parents have no place to park, and the inconvenience results in increased family tensions and frustration.

Bernard, C., & Corrales, R. (1979). *The theory and technique of family therapy.* Springfield, IL: Charles C Thomas.

situational orgasmic dysfunction   To make this diagnosis, the patient must have had at least one orgasmic experience but is unable to achieve orgasm through one of several means. Three types of situational inorgasmia exist: masturbatory, coital, and random. A woman with masturbatory inadequacy cannot achieve an orgasm through masturbation; a coitally inorgasmic woman is unable to do so via intercourse. The random type has had at least one orgasm through both masturbation and coitus but is rarely orgasmic through any means of stimulation.

Masters, W., & Johnson, V. (1970). *Human sexual inadequacy.* Boston: Little, Brown.

skewed family A pathological family situation in which one parent is strong and the other is weak. The situation imposed by the pathologically dominant mate is accepted or shared by the other mate, without any attempt to change it. The serious psychopathology of the dominant mate is indeed supported by the spouse, resulting in the distorted ideation being accepted in the family (folie á famille). There is considerable masking of conflict, creating an unreal atmosphere that makes it difficult for a child to trust self-perceptions and self-judgments or to learn social adaptive skills.

Lidz, T., Fleck, S., & Cornelison, A. (Eds.). (1965). *Schizophrenia and the family.* New York: International Universities Press.

skewed marriage A marital relationship in which one member is strong, overfunctioning, and therefore dominant, and the other member is weak, underfunctioning, and generally submissive. A skewed marriage may be one in which there is a schism, a failure to achieve mutuality, and in which, as a result, the children have difficulty maintaining their own identity (the children need same-sex family members with whom to identify and opposite-sex members who are seen as desirable). In either of these marital structures, the environment is characterized by irrationality and the lack of a logical, rational basis for communication. In both contexts, the children cannot make sense of their environments and thus of their own identities.

Example: The father is a physician and a workaholic. The son decides he does not want that kind of slavery and thus evolves pathologically in his professional choice or escalates to a failure in medical school.

Bernard, C., & Corrales, R. (1979). *The theory and technique of family therapy.* Springfield, IL: Charles C Thomas.
Lidz, T., Fleck, S., & Cornelison, A. (Eds.). (1965). *Schizophrenia and the family.* New York: International Universities Press.

skill training program Educational training or enrichment for couples and families, alone or in groups, that facilitates functioning but does not attempt to change structure therapeutically. Existing skill training programs include systemic training for effective parenting and teaching couples how to fight nondestructively. A skill training program encompasses issues facing couples or families before marriage, during marriage (as in marriage encounters), in parenting, in the family, and during divorce.

L'Abate, L., & Rupp, G. (1981). *Enrichment: Skill training for family life.* Washington, DC: University Press of America.

social genes   Qualities of intimacy and separateness at various levels in a family. In a healthy family, a wide range of intimacy and separateness levels is found, and the levels can be moved without inducing panic in the family. The size of the family "space bubble" and that of each individual's space bubble is determined by the experiences and historical perspective the family members inherited via their social genes. Neither of the social genes of intimacy and separateness in the family can increase without an increase in the other; one can only be as close as one can be separate, and one can only be as separate as one can be close. Dependency and autonomy are similarly linked.

Grinker, R. R. (1971). Biomedical education on a system. *Archives of General Psychiatry, 24,* 291-297.

Keith, D. V., & Whitaker, C. A. (1982). Experiential/symbolic family therapy. In A. M. Horne & M. M. Ohlsen (Eds.), *Family counseling and therapy* (pp. 43-74). Itasca, IL: F. E. Peacock.

S

social influence   Influence that family members use to move each other or to avoid being moved themselves in certain directions. Social influence may take the form of (a) private dependent power—the use of certain personalized dimensions implicit in the parent-child relationship to justify one's position or to demand a change in another's behavior; (b) information giving—the use of facts or opinions designed to provide a rational basis for behavior change in the listener; or (c) information seeking—includes both requests for information or permission and seeking explanations, opinions, or feelings.

Goldstein, M., Judd, L., Rodnick, E., Alkire, A., & Gould, E. (1968). A method for studying social influence and coping patterns within families of disturbed adolescents. *Journal of Nervous and Mental Disorders, 148,* 233-251.

social learning   Learning that takes place within a social environment as a person observes, reacts to, and interacts with other people. It is a result of teaching people how to relate interpersonally. In short, it is education in human relations. Within a social matrix, children learn ways of behaving (behavior patterns) by receiving support for some actions and punishment for others. The result of this selective social reinforcement is the behavior that we characteristically exhibit (our personalities).

Horne, A. M. (1982). Counseling families—Social learning family therapy. In A. M. Horne & M. M. Ohlsen (Eds.), *Family counseling and therapy* (pp. 360-388). Itasca, IL: F. E. Peacock.

social learning approach An assembly of several social learning models, most important, those based on operant learning, social exchange, general systems, and attribution theories. In this approach, the emphasis is on observational assessment methods, behavioral specifics, and the interplay of data, theory, and clinical application. Its basic tenets are readily translatable into treatment modalities and techniques that can be tested empirically. The treatment approach attempts to provide an environment in which effective learning may occur. Behavioral alternatives are expanded, and new options are presented so that families and couples may remedy deficits and develop new skills for dealing with the problems of living in close human relationships. The treatment occurs in a systematic teaching-modeling program that emphasizes learning procedures.

Jacobson, N. S., & Margolin, G. (1979). *Marital therapy: Strategies based on social learning and behavior exchange principles.* New York: Brunner/Mazel.

social network A societal pattern in which each individual is linked to several others by social bonds that partly reinforce and partly conflict with one another; the orderliness or disorderliness of social life results from the constraints these bonds impose on the actions of individuals.

Collins, A. H., & Pancoast, D. L. (1976). *Natural helping network: A strategy for prevention.* Washington, DC: National Association of Social Workers.

social reinforcement Verbal and nonverbal means of giving attention and recognition. Social reinforcement is the most important source of motivation for human behavior.

Example: A caregiver smiling and saying, "Good, you're using your fork," reinforces a child's eating behavior.

Liberman, R. (1972). Behavioral approaches to family and couple therapy. In G. D. Erickson & T. P. Hogan (Eds.), *Family therapy: An introduction to theory and technique* (pp. 120-134). Belmont, CA: Wadsworth.

social role The adaptational unit of personality in action. The social role is a bridge between the intrapsychic and social life. It has semipermeable boundaries in that it permits a limited penetration in both directions—that is, between the environment and the self.

Ackerman, N. (1958). *The psychodynamics of family life.* New York: Basic Books.
Foley, V. (1974). *An introduction to family therapy.* New York: Grune & Stratton.

social work   One of the helping professions whose distinctive clinical or casework features has been its historic concern with the family, as well as the specialists of social group work and community organization. The primary emphasis of study has been multiperson unit(s). Social workers have been involved in family problems since the inception of the profession.

Sherman, S. N. (1981). A social work frame for family therapy. In E. R. Tolson & W. J. Reid (Eds.), *Models of family treatment* (pp. 7-32). New York: Columbia University Press.

societal emotional processes   A process in which the forces tending toward individuality on the one hand, and togetherness on the other, operate to counterbalance each other on a societal level in a manner similar to that in individual families.

Kerr, M. (1981). Family systems theory and therapy. In A. S. Gurman & D. P. Kniskern (Eds.), *Handbook of family therapy* (pp. 226-264). New York: Brunner/Mazel.

sociogram   A pictorial representation of the configuration of members of a group, indicating their sociometric relationship to each other. See Figure 9.

Dodson, L., & Kurpuis, D. (1977). *Family counseling: A systems approach.* Muncie, IN: Accelerated Development.
Moreno, J. (1953). *Who shall survive? Foundations of sociometry, group psychotherapy, and sociodrama.* New York: Beacon House.

sociometry   A method for measuring the patterns of an individual's feeling interaction with other members of a group. The patterns are depicted on a sociometric map that consists of lines of preferred relationships between individuals. From such maps, one can determine the central figure, cliques, and isolates in a group.

Corsini, R. J. (1966). *Role playing in psychotherapy: A manual.* Chicago: Aldine.
Moreno, J. (1953). *Who shall survive? Foundations of sociometry, group psychotherapy, and sociodrama.* New York: Beacon House.

sole custody   The most common type of custodial arrangement in which one parent has custody and the other has visitation privileges. The parent with whom the child lives makes most of the decisions regarding the child's life, although both parents usually participate in major decisions regarding education, religious training, and vacations. Usually a fairly specific schedule of visitation is included in the separation agreement and divorce decree. Ideally, however, this schedule should serve mainly as a guideline for parents who are flexible enough to agree to alter it as conditions warrant. Such flexibility requires a certain degree of cooperation between the

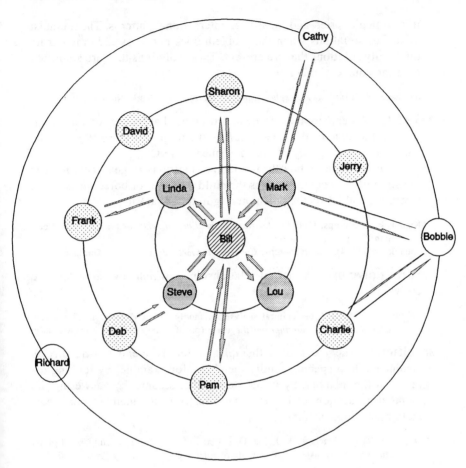

Figure 9. A Sociogram

parents. The traditional visitation schedule is basically unnatural because it cannot take into consideration the unpredictability of life situations or the vicissitudes and desires of all individuals involved. Ideally
the sole custodial arrangement blends into a joint custodial pattern, in
which both parents are involved actively in the child's life.

Gardner, R. A. (1989). *Family evaluation in child custody mediation, arbitration, and
litigation.* Cresskill, NJ: Creative Therapeutics.

solution-focused therapy   A model of therapy developed by de Shazer.
It was derived from the Mental Research Institute (MRI) school in that

it is strategic, brief, and focuses on interactional patterns. The therapist identifies situations when the problem does not exist and draws from the family solutions that are present. These solutions then are amplified over the course of therapy.

de Shazer, S. (1985). *Keys to solution in brief therapy.* New York: Norton.

SORKC   A behavioral assessment procedure that focuses on the stimulus (S), the state of the organism (O), the target response (R), and the nature and contingency of the consequences (KC).

Example: When a boy throws temper tantrums to get a cookie, S is the sight of the cookie jar, O is the child's hunger or boredom, R is the tantrums, and KC is the parent giving in to the tantrums.

Kanfer, F., & Phillips, J. (1970). *Learning foundations of behavior therapy.* New York: John Wiley.

Nichols, M. (1984). *Family therapy: Concepts and methods.* New York: Gardner.

sororal polygyny   A marital relationship in which several sisters are co-wives.

Zelditch, M. (1964). Cross-cultural analyses of family structure. In H. T. Christensen (Ed.), *Handbook of marriage and the family* (pp. 462-500). Chicago: Rand McNally.

specificity   The focus of a therapist or family member who directs statements to a specific family member—for example, by looking directly at the member, by using the member's name, by answering the member's question, or by referring directly to the member's immediately preceding statement.

O'Connor, W., & Stachowiak, J. (1971). Patterns of interaction in families with high adjusted, low adjusted, and mentally retarded members. *Family Process, 10,* 229-241.

Riskin, J., & Faunce, E. (1972). An evaluative review of family interaction research. *Family Process, 11,* 365-455.

spectator role   A role assumed involuntarily by members of a sexually dysfunctional marital unit in which they become psychologically trapped into observing the physical aspects of the sexual exchange, rather than involved in relaxing, enjoying the sensual stimulation, and becoming physiologically involved in the experience.

Masters, W., & Johnson, V. (1970). *Human sexual inadequacy.* Boston: Little, Brown.

spectator therapy   (1) Treatment based on vicarious reinforcement and modeling. By watching others (in role playing or therapy), the spectator is able to benefit by the experience. (2) Treatment in which a person observes the behavior of another person, such as in a role-playing situation.

Corsini, R. J. (1966). *Role playing in psychotherapy: A manual.* Chicago: Aldine.

spiral effect   In sex therapy, the phenomena that occur when one partner begins to withdraw sexually. The withdrawal of one leads to pursuit by the other, which, in turn, leads to further withdrawal. The partner who withdraws experiences heightened levels of performance anxiety, while the other feels unloved, undesirable, and rejected.

Schwartz, M., & Masters, W. (1988). The Masters and Johnson Institute treatment model. In S. Leiblum & R. Rosen (Eds.), *Sexual desire disorders* (pp. 229-242). New York: Guilford.

split   The experience of opposition, alienation, or estrangement that occurs between the members or subsystems of a family. It is the opposite of alliance or coalition.

Example: A daughter feels hostile toward her mother and so splits off from other family members. She actually opposes what her mother expects of her.

Wynne, L. (1961). The study of intrafamilial alignments and splits in exploratory family therapy. In N. W. Ackerman, F. L. Beatman, & S. N. Sherman (Eds.), *Exploring the base of family therapy* (pp. 95-115). New York: Family Service Association.

split custody   A custody arrangement in which the children are divided between the two parents. One or more children live permanently with the mother, and one or more live with the father. Most experts agree with the arguments for attempting to keep the children together. In this way, the children can provide support for one another and can develop a sense of family continuity despite the parental breakup.

Gardner, R. A. (1989). *Family evaluation in child custody mediation, arbitration, and litigation.* Cresskill, NJ: Creative Therapeutics.

split double bind   A situation in which the expectations of one parent with respect to a child conflict with the expectations of the other parent. The child who loves both parents equally is unable to satisfy one without frustrating the other.

Example: One parent expects an adolescent child to stay at home and never go out. The other parent expects age-appropriate behavior. Whatever the child does frustrates one of the parents.

Ferreira, A. (1960). The double bind and delinquent behavior. *Archives of General Psychiatry, 3,* 359-367.

split loyalty   A situation in which the parents set up conflicting claims so that a child can offer loyalty to only one parent, at the cost of the child's loyalty to the other parent.

Example: A son chooses to support his mother's position in the postdivorce war because he resides with her. His father, whom he loves more, is only a weekend visitor.

Boszormenyi-Nagy, I., & Ulrich, D. (1981). Contextual family therapy. In A. S. Gurman & D. P. Kniskern (Eds.), *Handbook of family therapy* (pp. 159-186). New York: Brunner/Mazel.

Stierlin, H. (1974). *Separating parents and adolescents: A perspective on running away, schizophrenia and waywardness.* New York: Quadrangle.

splitting   In object relations therapy, a primitive defense mechanism in which an individual splits the good from the bad in an external object and then internalizes this split perception. Thus individuals experience perceptions, thoughts, and feelings in terms of "black and white," without regard to the complexities of reality. In the family, this interactive style perpetuates diffusion of personal boundaries, rigid roles within the family, and rigid external boundaries of the family.

Example: An adult views her mother as being "all good" and her father as being "all bad," thus blaming the father for most of life's problems.

Everett, C. A., Halperin, S., Volgy, S., & Wissler, A. (1989). *Treating the borderline family: A systemic approach.* Boston: Allyn & Bacon.

spontaneous agreement   The agreement of two or more family members on the same choice(s) as indicated in their answers on the Unrevealed Differences Questionnaire.

Ferreira, A., & Winter, W. (1965). Family interaction and decision making. *Archives of General Psychiatry, 13,* 214-223.

Riskin, J., & Faunce, E. (1972). An evaluative review of family interaction research. *Family Process, 11,* 365-455.

spontaneous recovery   The processes that lead to recovery in untreated individuals.

Example: The husband and the wife finally had made the decision to enter marital therapy, agreeing that they were ready and receptive to making changes as individuals as well as in their relationship. The family psychologist they chose was going on vacation during the summer, so they decided to begin couples therapy in the fall. After the psychologist's return, they realized that they were getting along better, their relationship had become more stable, and they were satisfied with how they were feeling about themselves.

Bergin, A. E. (1967). Some implications of psychotherapy research for therapeutic practice. *International Journal of Psychiatry, 3,* 136-150.

Levant, R. F. (1984). *Family therapy: A comprehensive overview.* Englewood Cliffs, NJ: Prentice-Hall.

spouse-aided therapy   Therapy that involves the patient's spouse as a co-agent of change. This approach is based on the recognition of marital problems that contribute to the creation and/or continuation of persisting psychological problems.

Example: A man seeks therapy because of depression. He wants individual therapy because he believes that most of his problems are internal and based on his extreme deprivation and abuse as a child. It is apparent, however, that his marriage has numerous other problems (e.g., his wife blames him for his lack of willpower in overcoming his depression).

Badenoch, A., Fisher, J., Hafner, J., & Swift, H. (1984). Predicting the outcome of spouse-aided therapy for persisting psychiatric disorders. *American Journal of Family Therapy, 12,* 59-72.

Hafner, R. (1981). Spouse-aided therapy in psychiatry: An introduction. *Australian and New Zealand Journal of Psychiatry, 15,* 329-337.

squeeze technique   A technique employed by the female to deter premature ejaculation in the male. The women places her thumb on the frenulum (located on the ventral surface) and her first and second fingers on the superior (dorsal) surface of the penis in a position immediately adjacent to one another on either side of the coronal ridge. Pressure is then applied by squeezing the thumb and first two fingers together for an elapsed time of 3 to 4 seconds.

Masters, W., & Johnson, V. (1970). *Human sexual inadequacy.* Boston: Little, Brown.

stable coalition   A coalition in which a child is allied with one parent, most commonly the mother. Such a coalition may exist in cases of spouse conflict. The excluded parent either keeps asking for the child's loyalties with no result or gives up relating to the child and steps out of the situation.

Example: When the mother "bad-mouths" her ex-husband, the son and the daughter go along with their mother's assertions. When the father is critical of his ex-wife, the children resent his comments and defend their mother.

Aponte, H., & van Deusen, J. (1981). Structural family therapy. In A. S. Gurman & D. P. Kniskern (Eds.), *Handbook of family therapy* (pp. 310-360). New York: Brunner/Mazel.

Minuchin, S. (1974). *Families and family therapy.* Cambridge, MA: Harvard University Press.

stable-unsatisfactory marriage   A marriage characterized by a couple profile described as the "spare-time battlers" or the "pawnbrokers." This profile determines the design of the therapeutic intervention. Other couple profiles are the *stable-satisfactory,* a marriage that is stable and provides a mutually supportive environment, with two subgroups: the "heavenly twins" and the "collaborative geniuses"; the *unstable-unsatisfactory,* characterized by the "weary wranglers" and the "psychosomatic avoiders"; and the *unstable-satisfactory,* characterized by the "gruesome twosome" and the "paranoid predators."

Example: "Spare-time battlers" usually do not seek professional help because they fight and get enough out of the family aspects of the marriage to keep them going and because they are less apt to have problems with sex.

Lederer, W., & Jackson, D. (1968). *Mirages of marriage.* New York: Norton.

stability   The least change in unit structure over time—that is, in the patterns of "who speaks to whom" or in the way coalitions in the family are organized.

Example: The son misbehaves, the father reprimands the son, the mother chastises the father, the father defends his action, and the mother is exasperated with him. This process occurs repeatedly, with no change.

Haley, J. (1963). *Strategy of psychotherapy.* New York: Grune & Stratton.

staging   The division of a therapeutic intervention into separate, self-contained units that are, in turn, arranged in some sort of logical progression.

Example: In staging the entire treatment plan, the therapist begins with the entire family and then moves to progressively smaller family units. In staging a single intervention, the therapist asks some central family members first to sit next to each other and then to begin a dialogue without interruptions from the other family members.

Umbarger, C. C. (1984). *Structural family therapy.* New York: Grune & Stratton.

stagnation   A condition produced by ethically invalid attempts to solve life's problems, without awareness of what one's basic life interests might be. It represents a selfish attempt to live in the world.

Example: A father provides his family with an income but refuses to invest anything else in the family because he feels he has fulfilled his responsibilities to it.

Boszormenyi-Nagy, I., & Spark, G. L. (1973). *Invisible loyalties: Reciprocity in intergenerational families.* New York: Harper & Row.
Boszormenyi-Nagy, I., & Ulrich, D. (1981). Contextual family therapy. In A. S. Gurman & D. P. Kniskern (Eds.), *Handbook of family therapy* (pp. 159-186). New York: Brunner/Mazel.

statement rule   The rule that, whenever possible, self-expressions should be in the form of statements, rather than questions.

Example: A woman who feels ambivalent about going to a party says, "I'm not sure I want to go out," rather than, "Do I really want to go out tonight?"

Baruth, L. G., & Huber, C. H. (1984). *An introduction to marital theory and therapy.* Belmont, CA: Brooks/Cole.

Stuart, R. B. (1980). *Helping couples change: A social learning approach to marital therapy.* New York: Guilford.

staying with negative feelings   A therapeutic process in which specially structured interactions are employed to expose the patient to personal feelings and aspects that previously were avoided. Patients are placed in anxiety-reducing situations that they previously managed to avoid and in which they are encouraged and helped to stay with their negative feelings.

Example: A woman denies her sexual feelings because they are equated with sin. In an exercise, she is supported in experiencing herself sensually and sexually.

Kaplan, H. S. (1974). *The new sex therapy.* New York: Brunner/Mazel.

S

stepfamily   (1) A family in which children live with a remarried parent and a stepparent. (2) A family in which children from a previous marriage visit with their remarried parent and stepparent. (3) A family in which the couple is not married, and children from a previous marriage either live with or visit the couple.

Visher, E., & Visher, J. (1979). *Stepfamilies: A guide to working with stepparents and stepchildren.* New York: Brunner/Mazel.

Stepfamily Association of America   Originally conceived by John and Emily Visher in 1979, this association provides educational services for stepfamilies and the larger community that interacts with them. The local chapters of this nonprofit educational organization supply a support network and advocacy group for stepfamilies. Its national and state divisions have assisted in starting a wide variety of services, including self-help groups, lectures, meetings, community education programs, and workshops for members and professionals. Their newsletter includes a regular column addressing issues concerning stepchildren that is written by the children themselves.

Sager, C. J., Brown, H. S., Crohn, H., Engel, T., Rodstein, E., & Walker, L. (1983). *Treating the remarried family.* New York: Brunner/Mazel.

step-function   A change in calibration. A step-function has a stabilizing effect in that it recalibrates the system and makes it more adaptive.

Example: Psychosis in the family represents a sharp change that recalibrates the system.

Watzlawick, P., Beavin, J. H., & Jackson, D. D. (1967). *Pragmatics of human communication.* New York: Norton.

stereotyping   (1) A strategy that isolates an offending person by caricaturing certain of that person's physical or mental traits. (2) The process whereby a characteristic is generalized to a whole population.

Examples: A husband who works with computers is accused of being a "computer" when he does not respond to his wife in the way she expects. Another example is the notion that all workaholics are poor husbands.

Zuk, G. (1971). *Family therapy.* New York: Behavioral Publications.

stimulus control strategies   Strategies in which spouses are instructed to bring their problem-solving attempts under control at particular times and in particular settings, such as during "administrative time." Specifically, regular times are scheduled during the week, such as after dinner with coffee, when the spouses can engage in problem-solving discussions.

Weiss, R., Hops, H., & Patterson, G. (1973). A framework for conceptualizing marital conflict: A technique for attaining it, some data for evaluating it. In L. A. Hamerlynck, L. C. Handy, & E. J. Marsh (Eds.), *Behavior change: Methodology, concepts and practice* (pp. 309-342). Champaign, IL: Research Press.

stochastic process   As a result of trial-and-error attempts at new behavior, change occurs in a random, discontinuous fashion, causing the system to develop a new organization and level of functioning.

Example: After working with a child in developing better self-control, the family begins to set limits in a more functional manner.

Bateson, G. (1972). *Steps to an ecology of mind.* New York: Ballantine.

stop-start technique   A treatment devised by Semans for premature ejaculation. The female extravaginally stimulates her partner's penis to erection until the sensation premonitory to ejaculation is experienced. The stimulation then is interrupted until the sensation has disappeared. Penile stimulation is resumed until the premonitory sensation returns, and then it is again discontinued. The amount of time involved is variable, designed to increase the length of time between stops and starts.

Kaplan, H. S. (1974). *The new sex therapy.* New York: Brunner/Mazel.
Semans, J. (1956). Premature ejaculation: A new approach. *Southern Medical Journal, 49,* 353-361.

strategic family therapy Therapy in which the clinician actively designs interventions to fit a problem. Three specific strategic therapeutic approaches are as follows:

1. *Haley's approach:* This approach blends Salvador Minuchin's structural work with formal ideas of communication theory. Although Jay Haley strives for a clear generational hierarchy, he describes his diagnostic and intervention work in terms of communication, rather than "structural engineering." He focuses on the presenting problem (e.g., symptomatic behavior) and tries to see what communicative function the problem has in the sequence of family events that embody it. The task is then to change the sequence, which, if effectively done, will change the outcome (e.g., alleviation of the symptomatic behavior).

2. *Mental Research Institute (MRI) communicational approach:* If one eliminated the parts of Haley's work related to structural family therapy, one would come close to the MRI communication approach. The MRI approach attends strictly to a "chess game" approach to solving problems. Thus the context of the problem is perceived first and then altered. A change is tagged metaphorically as a second-order change when the target of change is the system, not just the symptom. This approach gives particular attention to the therapeutic paradox and the use of therapeutic language that addresses the right (nonrational) hemisphere of the brain. The work of Gregory Bateson and Milton Erickson has significantly influenced the MRI orientation.

3. *The strategic group approach:* Mara Selvini Palazzoli's strategic group model in the treatment of schizophrenic transaction is based on a blending of the work of Gregory Bateson, Jay Haley, and Paul Watzlawick. At the heart of this approach is a paradoxical relabeling maneuver called *positive connotation,* in which the family's homeostatic, yet dysfunctional, organizational pattern is respected. The injunction not to change, paradoxically, gives the family freedom to change. The strategic group approach uses a wide variety of other paradoxical maneuvers, including family rituals, to achieve the desired end.

S

Haley, J. (1987). *Problem-solving therapy* (2nd ed.). San Francisco: Jossey-Bass.

Olson, D. H., Russell, C. S., & Sprenkle, D. H. (1980). Marital and family therapy: A decade review. *Journal of Marriage and the Family, 42,* 973-993.

Selvini Palazzoli, M., Boscolo, L., Cecchin, G., & Prata, G. (1978). *Paradox and counterparadox: A new model in the therapy of the family in schizophrenic transaction.* New York: Jason Aronson.

Watzlawick, P., Weakland, J., & Fisch, R. (1974). *Change: Principles of problem formation and problem resolution.* New York: Norton.

strategic questions Questions based on linear assumptions about the nature of the therapeutic process. The intent of these questions is to have a corrective effect on the family. Although framed as questions, these statements imply what members of the family ought to do.

Example: In a family where the mother talks to her daughter about her problems, the therapist says, "Why don't you talk to your husband about these things, rather than your children?"

Tomm, K. (1988). Interventive interviewing: Part III. Intending to ask linear, circular, strategic, or reflexive questions? *Family Process, 27,* 1-16.

strategizing   The therapist's cognitive activity in constructing interventions, in evaluating consequences, and in how to proceed at a particular moment. See also **hypothesizing.**

Tomm, K. (1988). Interventive interviewing: Part III. Intending to ask linear, circular, strategic, or reflexive questions? *Family Process, 27,* 1-16.

structural balance theory   A theory postulating that triads in a family attempt to balance themselves—that is, when all three relationships are positive or when two form a stable alliance against the third.

Hoffman, L. (1981). *Foundations of family therapy.* New York: Basic Books.

S

structural determinism   The structure of a system determines the degree to which a system can change.

Efran, J. S., Lukens, R. J., & Lukens, M. D. (1988). Constructivism: What's in it for you? *Family Therapy Networker, 12,* 27-35.

structural family therapy   A form of therapy developed by Salvador Minuchin that focuses on changing the communication, functioning, and power structures of the family so as to alter symptomatic behavior in the identified patient. A change in familial interaction is considered to bring about changes in the individual behavior of family members. The focus is ahistoric (in the here and now), with the therapist playing an active role, such as in monitoring communication or even rearranging the seating to change the structure and functioning of the family. For instance, the marital and parental subsystems are given clear boundaries to protect the privacy of the spouses and the parents, respectively. The focus is on the realignment of the structural relationships within the family or on a change of rules that will allow the system to maximize its potential for conflict resolution and individual growth.

Example: The mother and the daughter are acting like siblings. The therapist puts the mother in charge of the daughter's activities for the week.

Levant, R. F. (1984). *Family therapy: A comprehensive overview.* New York: Harper & Row.

Minuchin, S. (1974). *Families and family therapy.* Cambridge, MA: Harvard University Press.

Minuchin, S., & Fishman, H. (1981). *Family therapy techniques.* Cambridge, MA: Harvard University Press.

structural insufficiency A lack of the structural resources in a family or other social system that are needed to meet the functional demands of the system.

Example: A single-parent mother living in the slums with several children lacks the financial, social, and emotional resources to rear her children.

Aponte, H., & van Deusen, J. (1981). Structural family therapy. In A. S. Gurman & D. P. Kniskern (Eds.), *Handbook of family therapy* (pp. 310-360). New York: Brunner/ Mazel.

structural intervention In structural family therapy, an attempt to change the organization of a family system. A structural intervention frequently is aimed at delineating or creating subsystem boundaries, shifting power systems, or redefining family coalitions or alliances.

Example: The therapist gives the parents a task to do at home that excludes the children, such as leaving home suddenly. Usually the children would be involved in the parental system. The task is designed to establish a boundary between the parents and the children. For example, the children are not to disturb the parents in the mornings before a certain time.

L'Abate, L., Baggett, M. S., & Anderson, J. S. (1983). Linear and circular interventions with families of children with school related problems. In B. F. Okun (Ed.), *Family therapy with school related problems* (pp. 13-27). Rockville, MD: Aspen Systems.

structuralism A theoretical perspective that sees social behavior and cultural products as a communicative code. Not only verbal and nonverbal activity but also the entire range of what humans produce culturally is in a communication code context. The codes are rule governed; the rules define the formation and transformation of the relationships of the elements in the code in a given system. The rules of formation and transformation are related to fundamental cognitive characteristics and capabilities of the human organism. Structuralism assumes that these rules can be represented by a relatively general, abstract, and, in some degree, formal calculus—that is, the rules may be formalized for the system.

Cromwell, R. E., & Olson, D. H. (1975). *Power in families.* New York: Halsted.

structural-strategic therapy The integration of two different approaches to family therapy. Although it originally was conceived as a model in which the therapist might switch back and forth between the two approaches, later clinicians tried different theoretical/technological ways of integrating the two, which has led to debate about the pros and cons of this approach.

Liddle, H. (1984). Toward a dialectical-contextual-coevolutionary translation of struc-
    tural-strategic family therapy. *Journal of Strategic and Systemic Therapies, 4,*
    66-79.
Stanton, M. (1981). An integrated structural/strategic approach to family therapy. *Journal
    of Marital and Family Therapy, 7,* 427-439.

structure   The interactional patterns that arrange or organize a family's component subsystems into relatively constant relationships. These constant relationships endure through time but are less enduring than the continuous activity of the superordinate, total system—that is, the system, as an entity, continues throughout the family's entire lifetime, while various structures, or organizational arrangements of the components, shift and change from time to time. Structures are seen in the relatively stable subsystems, alliances, and hierarchies that characterize a family's organizational map. Structures may be thought of as slow processes of long duration. The expression of a process over time gives that process the status of a structure.

Example: The mother and the son repeatedly, over time, join forces against the father's effort to direct a decision. This pairing represents a mother-son coalitional structure. If this arrangement does not persist over time, it may be viewed as a transitional process in the evolving movement of family life, not as an enduring structure.

Maturana, H. R. (1978). Biology of language: The epistemology of reality. In G. A. Miller
    & E. Lenneberg (Eds.), *Psychology and biology of language and thought* (pp. 28-63).
    New York: Academic Press.
Minuchin, S. (1974). *Families and family therapy.* Cambridge, MA: Harvard University
    Press.
Umbarger, C. C. (1984). *Structural family therapy.* New York: Grune & Stratton.

structured family interview   A series of interactional tasks that involve either the whole family or various subgroups of the family. The structured family interview was developed at the Mental Research Institute both as a clinical interview technique and as a family research tool.

Watzlawick, P. (1966). A structured family interview. *Family Process, 5,* 256-271.

structured interview technique   A technique that focuses on assessing family dysfunction through such tasks as identifying the main problem, planning something together, and discussing the meaning of a proverb. The technique has the advantage of shortening the time needed to gain information necessary for unveiling the family system.

Watzlawick, P. (1972). A structured family interview. In G. D. Erickson & T. P. Hogan
    (Eds.), *Family therapy: An introduction to theory and technique* (pp. 265-278).
    Belmont, CA: Wadsworth.

structured mediation   A process in which a husband and a wife agree to reach a divorce settlement based on marital mediation rules. Non-structured mediation is conducted without advance agreement on the rules of procedure and the guidelines to be followed by the parties and the mediator. The advantages of structured mediation are as follows:

The issues to be decided are clearly defined.

The issues are limited to those whose resolution is needed for reaching settlement.

Procedural methods are established for collecting and examining factual information.

All options for the settlement of each issue are systematically examined.

Options are selected within socially acceptable guidelines.

The consequences likely to follow selection of each option are examined.

Uninterrupted time is regularly allocated for working toward resolution.

Impasses are resolved promptly by arbitration.

Coogler, O. J. (1978). *Structured mediation in divorce settlement.* Lexington, MA: Lexington.

S

structured sexual experiences   The integrated use of systematically structured sexual experiences with conjoint therapeutic sessions. Structured sexual experiences are the main innovation and distinctive feature of sex therapy.

Examples: The wife informs her husband each time he touches her in a way that pleases her; otherwise, she says nothing. Or a therapist directs a couple to engage in bodily massage for 30 minutes, 15 minutes each, without touching the genital areas. Coitus is not permitted. This experience is designed for establishing a sensual bond between the couple.

LoPiccolo, J. (1978). Direct treatment of sexual dysfunction. In J. LoPiccolo & L. LoPiccolo (Eds.), *Handbook of sex therapy* (pp. 1-18). New York: Plenum.

structuring behaviors   A category of therapeutic behaviors designed to control implicitly what occurs in a session. Behaviors in this category are direct requests, directing the flow, asking process questions, asking specific or directed questions, and asking for a reduction or elimination of a negative behavior.

Alexander, J., Barton, C., Lindsey, D., Turner, C., & Warburton, J. (1988). Defensive and supportive communication interaction system. In D. Grotevant & C. Carlson (Eds.), *Handbook of family assessment* (pp. 182-187). New York: Guilford.

subconscious wisdom   A hypnotic technique in which the patient imagines viewing a problem through a crystal ball, a TV series, or a dream.

Araoz, D. L. (1982). *Hypnosis and sex therapy.* New York: Brunner/Mazel.

subgroup   A subset of a larger group. Breaking into small subgroups and then reassembling can help focus resistances and provide new possibilities for moving in different directions.

Alger, I. (1976). Multiple couple therapy. In P. J. Guerin (Ed.), *Family therapy* (pp. 364-387). New York: Gardner.

subject/object   A code designed by Mishler and Waxler to classify the subjects and objects of all acts in terms of whether they refer to someone within or outside the interacting family group.

Mishler, E., & Waxler, N. (1968). *Interaction in families: An experimental study of family processes and schizophrenia.* New York: John Wiley.

subsystem   An element or functional component that is itself a system but that also plays a specialized role in the operation of a larger system. A subsystem is the totality of all structures in a particular living system that carry out a particular process. At least three types of subsystems can be identified as parts of an open system: an input subsystem, a conversion or operating subsystem, and an output subsystem. Family systems are differentiated by generation, gender, interest, or function, such as the dyads of husband-wife, mother-father, mother-child, and child-child. An individual can belong to a number of subsystems.
   Example: A child and his dog (the family pet) are subsystems of the family.

Minuchin, S. (1974). *Families and family therapy.* Cambridge, MA: Harvard University Press.

superego binding   A type of binding created through the exploitation of loyalty. The parents attempt to instill repressive breakaway guilt. They convey, overtly or covertly, that they have totally sacrificed themselves for their children and that they can live only through them. The children typically become hospitalized as psychiatric patients, remaining targets of their parents' intrusive and ambivalent concern.

Stierlin, H. (1974). *Separating parents and adolescents: A perspective on running away, schizophrenia and waywardness.* New York: Quadrangle.

superperson   A person who expects to manage a career, home, and family with complete ease. Such a person expects to have a perfect job, a perfect marriage, and a perfect house and to be in perfect control of the children.
   Example: A woman feeds her children and husband a nutritional breakfast; goes off to her $35,000-a-year job; spends an hour of quality time after school with her children; feeds the family a healthy, well-

balanced meal; cleans the house; and spends time with her husband, talking and loving, before they go to sleep.

McCubbin, H. I., & Figley, C. R. (1983). *Stress and the family: Coping with normative transitions* (Vol. 1). New York: Brunner/Mazel.

support   A category of verbal communication that is person enhancing. These types of statements are positive, facilitative, respectful, and communicate worth for another person. Statements in this category are empathy, information seeking, positive interpretation, requests for action, and restatements.

Alexander, J., Barton, C., Lindsey, D., Turner, C., & Warburton, J. (1988). Defensive and supportive communication interaction system. In D. Grotevant & C. Carlson (Eds.), *Handbook of family assessment* (pp. 182-187). New York: Guilford.

supportive separation system   The four major components are (a) a foundation that would provide an opportunity for strong tripartite collaboration and cooperation of the marriage counseling profession, the legal profession, and the couple; (b) a means whereby the couple would assume greater responsibility and control over the resolution of the separation issue; (c) an alternative offering greater trust between the marital partners and between both professions; and (d) a written contract or agreement clarifying the respective responsibilities and benefits for both partners.

A key tenet of this approach is the ongoing involvement of the marital therapist beyond the point at which reconciliation counseling has come to an end. Traditionally, once marital counseling has been perceived as being unsuccessful in continuing the marital arrangement, the therapist has stepped aside and the couple has sought legal assistance to arrange a separation. In effect, the traditional approach removes a trusted and knowledgeable support when both partners are most vulnerable to anxiety, suspicion, and anger.

The couple then become involved with the legal and judicial systems, providing a determined adversarial stance that effectively dissolves whatever emotional support the two parties could offer each other; that is, separate legal representation often ruptures the couple's positive interpersonal communicating and relating processes. Mutual concerns must include the emotional and economic survival of both partners and the preservation of a life-style for the children that is conducive to their intellectual and emotional development.

Bartoletti, M. D., Bourke, P., & McDonald, E. M. (1982). The supportive separation system: A joint legal and marital counseling alternative. In J. C. Hansen & L. Messinger (Eds.), *Therapy with remarriage families* (pp. 79-91). Rockville, MD: Aspen.

S

suprasystem   A high-level system in which other systems play subsystem roles. A living system may be analyzed in terms of its components or subsystems, or it may be viewed as part of a larger system. The suprasystem of an individual is the group of which that individual is a member.

Example: Family therapy is a subsystem of the suprasystem of psychotherapy; it is, at the same time, the suprasystem of the subsystem of multiple family group therapy.

Sauber, S. R. (1983). *The human services delivery system.* New York: Columbia University Press.

surrogate partner   A sexual partner provided by the therapist when a patient does not have an available partner. For a fee, the surrogate partner participates in prescribed sexual tasks during the treatment.

Kaplan, H. S. (1974). *The new sex therapy.* New York: Brunner/Mazel.

sustained attention   See **attention.**

symbiosis   A psychological state in which the involvement of two or more individuals is so intense that their boundaries become blurred. The individuals respond as one. Schizophrenia has been conceptualized as an unresolved symbiotic attachment between child and mother. The attachment is initiated by the emotional immaturity of the mother, who uses the child to fulfill her own emotional needs.

Example: A mother feels guilty because, while she covertly does things to block the child's development, she simultaneously tries to force the child to achievement. The child, once entangled, tries to perpetuate the symbiosis, along with an opposite effort to grow up. The father passively permits himself to be excluded from the intense twosome and marries his business and other outside interests.

Bowen, M. (1978). *Family therapy in clinical practice.* New York: Jason Aronson.
L'Abate, L. (1976). *Understanding and helping the individual in the family.* New York: Grune & Stratton.

symbiotic involvement   A family situation in which the boundaries between two or more individuals are blurred or fused. This situation is characteristic of very disturbed families.

Example: Whatever the mother feels, the oldest daughter feels too; for example, the mother is full of rage toward the father, and so is the oldest daughter.

Epstein, N., & Bishop, D. (1981). Problem-centered systems therapy of the family. In A. S. Gurman & D. P. Kniskern (Eds.), *Handbook of family therapy* (pp. 444-482). New York: Brunner/Mazel.

symbolic-experiential family therapy   A form of family therapy, developed by Carl A. Whitaker, that considers change as coming primarily from experiential learning and self-evaluation. Insight into genetic factors is not considered to be necessary to change; however, interactional insights related to the here and now of treatment are valued. Co-therapy is encouraged because it provides an additional model or "metaexperience" for the family. Interpretations are most valuable when they are metaphorical and made symbolically about family relationships—for example, using humor, teasing, fantasy, or free association to challenge the family's method of resolving stressful situations. For example, Whitaker employs "acting crazy" as a therapeutic tool, using irrelevant phrases or free associative fantasy during the session. This action is seen to work in the same way as regression in the service of the ego; that is, it is controllable and reversible. In the process, the family is forced to assume the "sane" component. The therapist serves as an example, giving the patient or the family permission to remain crazy under controlled circumstances.

Keith, D. V., & Whitaker, C. A. (1982). Experiential/symbolic family therapy. In A. M. Horne & M. M. Ohlsen (Eds.), *Family counseling and therapy* (pp. 43-74). Itasca, IL: F. E. Peacock.

Neil, J. F., & Kniskern, D. P. (Eds.). (1982). *From psyche to system: The evolving therapy of Carl Whitaker.* New York: Guilford.

Pinney, E. L., & Slipp, S. (1982). *Glossary of group and family therapy.* New York: Brunner/Mazel.

symbolic interaction theory   A theory assuming that valid principles of human behavior can be derived from the study of social interaction, defined as a form of communication characteristic of human social life and involving either language or symbolic gestures. The theory assumes that these principles cannot be derived or inferred from the study of nonhuman forms.

Stryker, S. (1964). The interactional and situational approaches. In H. T. Christensen (Ed.), *Handbook of marriage and the family* (pp. 125-170). Chicago: Rand McNally.

symmetrical escalation   Runaway competitiveness to remain on at least an equal footing with a partner. The partners go through an escalating pattern of frustration until they eventually stop from sheer physical or emotional exhaustion.

Watzlawick, P., Beavin, J. H., & Jackson, D. D. (1967). *Pragmatics of human communication.* New York: Norton.

symmetrical relationship   A relationship based on equality or sameness. Statements indicating this type of relationship are either balanced

(A: "I like bowling"; B: "I like golf") or competitive (A: "I have a new bike"; B: "So what, I have a new camera"). A symmetrical marital relationship is one in which the spouses continually need to state to each other behaviorally, "I am as good as you are." Differences are minimized, role definitions are similar, and problems seem to stem from competition.

Watzlawick, P., Beavin, J. H., & Jackson, D. D. (1967). *Pragmatics of human communication*. New York: Norton.

symmetrical schizogenesis   An interaction characterized by a tendency for its participants to remain even with one another, no matter how casual or intense the competition.

Example: When members of one group begin to boast, members of the other group reply with boasting, thereby setting up a vicious circle.

Bateson, G. (1958). *Naven* (2nd ed.). Stanford, CA: Stanford University Press.
Watzlawick, P., Beavin, J. H., & Jackson, D. D. (1967). *Pragmatics of human communication*. New York: Norton.

symmetry   In relationships, equality or parallelism. *Symmetrical behavior* is behavior in which the protagonists are equal and behavior can escalate, thereby resulting in a disruption of the relationship. In contrast, *complimentary behavior* is behavior in which one person assumes a position opposite the other's submissive or assertive stance, thereby stabilizing the relationship.

Bateson, G. (1936). *Naven*. Cambridge, UK: Cambridge University Press.

symptom   A behavior that signals dysfunction in an individual or family. It is usually the problem that a family presents initially for therapy.

Example: Whenever the husband returns home, he complains of headaches that begin when he greets his wife. The headache functions as a symptom of marital dysfunction.

Umbarger, C. C. (1984). *Structural family therapy*. New York: Grune & Stratton.

symptom bearer   A family member who, by malfunctioning in the community, in the school, and/or at home, signals pain in the family.

Example: Every morning following a parental fight at home, the 7-year-old daughter keeps complaining to the school nurse that her stomach is upset.

Minuchin, S. (1974). *Families and family therapy*. Cambridge, MA: Harvard University Press.

symptom decontextualization   An integrative concept used to account for the efficacy of paradoxical interventions. This concept refers to changing both the form and context of the symptom. *Form* deals with requesting that the client exaggerate the symptom or express it in a different social environment; *context* deals with actively and deliberately enacting the symptom.

Omer, H. (1981). Paradoxical treatments: A unified concept. *Psychotherapy: Theory, Research, and Practice, 18,* 320-324.

symptom exchange A relationship in which the two parties experience the same problem, but their defenses against it are opposite. The one who resents the problem gets vicarious satisfaction from the one who expresses it. The danger in oneself is dealt with by dealing with it in another.

Example: Two individuals have a problem centered in sexuality. One acts out sexually, while the other acts inhibited and accuses the first person of being immoral. The inhibited person vicariously enjoys the acting-out behavior of the other person and deals with personal feelings through the other's misconduct.

Framo, J. (1965). Systematic research on family dynamics. In I. Boszormenyi-Nagy & J. Framo (Eds.), *Intensive family therapy: Theoretical and practical aspects* (pp. 407-463). New York: Harper & Row.

symptom focusing A restructuring technique, developed by Salvador Minuchin, to approach change directly through the symptom by exaggerating, deemphasizing, relabeling, or moving to a new symptom.

Example: A man who has withdrawn from his family by sitting at home in the corner is told to do more of the same on a prescribed basis.

Aponte, H., & van Deusen, J. (1981). Structural family therapy. In A. S. Gurman & D. P. Kniskern (Eds.), *Handbook of family therapy* (pp. 310-360). New York: Brunner/Mazel.

Minuchin, S. (1974). *Families and family therapy.* Cambridge, MA: Harvard University Press.

symptom-oriented treatment An approach to treatment in which the therapist focuses on the presenting problem or symptom, rather than searches for underlying causes and psychodynamic processes. This approach is in sharp contrast to psychoanalytic and psychodynamic therapies and is related more to behavioral approaches. However, the family therapist realizes that the symptoms may represent a problem in the system, not just in an isolated individual.

Nichols, M. P. (1984). *Family therapy: Concepts and methods.* New York: Gardner.

symptom prescription Directing the person to perform a symptom deliberately. See also **paradoxical prescription.**

Example: A man who has anxiety attacks is directed by the therapist to have an anxiety attack at the present moment in a therapy session.

Watzlawick, P., Beavin, J. H., & Jackson, D. D. (1967). *Pragmatics of human communication.* New York: Norton.

Weeks, G., & L'Abate, L. (1982). *Paradoxical psychotherapy: Theory and practice with individuals, couples, and families.* New York: Brunner/Mazel.

symptom scheduling   Directing the person to perform a symptom at specific times only.

Example: A man who has anxiety attacks is directed by the therapist to have anxiety attacks twice during the next week at designated times.

O'Hanlon, W. H., & Hexum, A. L. (1990). *An uncommon casebook: The complete clinical work of Milton H. Erickson, M.D.* New York: Norton.

symptom transformation   Taking the underlying energy of the symptom and changing its direction or application.

Example: A man who is attempting to quit smoking begins playing racquetball and doing other rigorous exercise.

O'Hanlon, W. H., & Hexum, A. L. (1990). *An uncommon casebook: The complete clinical work of Milton H. Erickson, M.D.* New York: Norton.

synchronizing   A mechanism through which a family develops and maintains a program for regulating the family's total use of time, including the ways its members clock and orient their movements. Synchronizing is the temporal equivalent of the spatial mechanism of centering. It includes the creation and execution of temporal guidelines, much as centering includes the creation and execution of spatial guidelines. For example: How do we spend our time so that we can get the maximal amount of what we want out of life? Which targets are we going to devote our time to pursuing? How much time do we want to spend together?

Example: The eldest son notices that his father seems grumpy every morning, and the son passes this information on to his mother. That evening, she approaches her husband and asks him whether he thinks he is working too hard.

Kantor, D., & Lehr, W. (1975). *Inside the family: Toward a theory of family process.* San Francisco: Jossey-Bass.

syntax   The way information is transmitted (e.g., means of encoding); channels of communication; the capacity, variability, noise, and redundancy inherent in the communicational transmitting system; and the patterns of speech over time. In marriages, *syntax* refers to such qualities as who-to-whom speech, the percentage of speaking time, the parsimony of speech, and the ratio of information to noise.

Steinglass, P. (1978). The conceptualization of marriage from a systems theory perspective. In T. Paolino & B. McCrady (Eds.), *Marriage and marital therapy* (pp. 298-368). New York: Brunner/Mazel.

system   A set of interrelated variables. A family is a system of interrelated individuals: the totality of family members in interaction with each other. *General systems theory* is a body of organized theoretical constructs that can be used to discuss general relationships. In a system, the focus is on the relationship between elements, rather than on the elements themselves. General systems theory was introduced into family therapy by the Palo Alto group (Gregory Bateson, Don D. Jackson, et al.) as a way of relating the interaction of the family and the individual and of determining how the homeostasis of the family system is maintained through negative feedback loops (morphostasis).

Bertalanffy, L. von. (1950). An outline of general systems therapy. *British Journal of the Philosophy of Science, 1,* 134-165.

systematic desensitization   A process by which an individual's incompatible behavior is conditioned to inhibit neurotic anxiety through a system of progressive muscle relaxation paired with a graded exposure to anxiety-eliciting cues.

LeBow, M. (1972). Behavior modification for the family. In G. D. Erickson & T. P. Hogan (Eds.), *Family therapy: An introduction to theory and technique* (pp. 347-376). Belmont, CA: Wadsworth.
Wolpe, J. (1969). *The practice of behavior therapy.* Elmsford, NY: Pergamon.

systematic training for effective parenting (STEP)   A parent education program, designed and developed by Dinkmeyer and McKay, that is based on the democratic principles of child-rearing of Alfred Adler and Rudolph Dreikurs. Emphasis is placed on encouragement (acting positively, rather than negatively) and responsibility as learned from the consequences of one's own behavior.

Dinkmeyer, D., & McKay, G. D. (1976). *Systematic training for effective parenting.* Circle Pines, MN: American Guidance Service.

system conflict   In structured family therapy, conflict that develops from the competing needs of the components of the family system.
   Example: A depressed husband with an alienated wife desires emotional support from his adolescent son, who, in time, wants more distance from the family. Each individual is trying to meet a different need, one that conflicts with those of the other members.

Aponte, H., & van Deusen, J. (1981). Structural family therapy. In A. S. Gurman & D. P. Kniskern (Eds.), *Handbook of family therapy* (pp. 310-360). New York: Brunner/Mazel.

Minuchin, S., Rosman, B. L., & Baker, L. (1978). *Psychosomatic families: Anorexia nervosa in context.* Cambridge, MA: Harvard University Press.

systemic An approach to family therapy often considered to be synonymous with the Milan model. The systemic therapist is interested primarily in the relationship between the individual and the system. Systems family therapists adhere to several basic premises: (a) All systems family therapists are systems thinkers, (b) an action must be seen as a response at one point in an evolving system, (c) meaning and actions are two sides of the same coin, (d) being in different contexts can simultaneously impede and restrain change, (e) behavior is recursive (a behavior is both cause and effect), and (f) creating a therapeutic context involves identifying redundant behavior and the confused message.

Campbell, D., & Draper, R. (1985). Creating a context for change. In D. Campbell & R. Draper (Eds.), *Applications of systemic family therapy* (pp. 1-8). New York: Grune & Stratton.

S

systemic intensity Intense emotional behavior, often resulting from a systemic void and reflecting boundary dysfunction. Systemic intensity has been described as the "crowded elevator" syndrome: When emotional intensity in a subsystem exceeds a tolerable level, distancing behavior results in the form of seepage, escape, or symptomatology.

Example: People in a crowded elevator do not look at each other. Instead they look for ways of reclaiming their personal space through some form of distancing behavior.

Hoffman, L. (1981). *Foundations of family therapy.* New York: Basic Books.

systemic rocking The dynamic reaction of a subsystem to an increase in tension, with no available outlet for the tension. Once a subsystem begins to rock, a stabilizer enters the subsystem, with the objective of restoring equilibrium. Systemic rocking, operating in the presentation of acting out, most often reflects a lack of tension outlet or lack of resolution in the marital subsystem, with the acting-out child functioning as the stabilizer. In most therapy with disturbed children, it can be assumed that if the parents could conceal their marital difficulties, the child would not be expressing the problems.

Example: A child with a problem stabilizes a marital dyad.

Haley, J. (1987). *Problem-solving therapy* (2nd ed.). San Francisco: Jossey-Bass.

systemic void The systemic condition that results from the absence, obstruction, or inadequate functioning of a subsystem, with a consequent effect on the members of interrelated subsystems and overall systemic functioning. The notion of *void* or *emptiness* often has been noted in the literature with reference to illness and death and to the intrapsychic or internal system of individuals who are experiencing emotional pain.

Example: Children are used to fill an emptiness in the lives of the parents, who have lost their own parents or who, by choice or by failure, do not participate in the nondomestic sphere of life. Clinically this circumstance emerges as the child-focused family, in which the child becomes the replacement for an unrealized achievement, for a "place in the world," or for a family member who is dead or out of contact.

Bowen, M. (1978). *Family therapy in clinical practice.* New York: Jason Aronson.
Bradt, J. O. (1980). The family with young children. In E. A. Carter & M. McGoldrick (Eds.), *The family life cycle* (pp. 121-146). New York: Gardner.

system prescription   Prescribing the dynamics of the family that have resulted in the symptoms of a family member. The prescription consists of a positive connotation of the family behavior, with a prescriptive statement to continue their behavior.

Example: In a conflict avoidance family with an identified patient, the members might be told that not fighting is a good thing because it serves to protect the family from their greater problem and that when they do feel angry, they should turn to the identified patient for help.

Selvini Palazzoli, M., Boscolo, L., Cecchin, G., & Prata, G. (1978). *Paradox and counterparadox: A new model in the therapy of the family in schizophrenic transaction.* New York: Jason Aronson.

system purist   A therapist who seeks to establish control with the family by perceiving how the family tries to influence the therapist to accept a relationship that, in effect, is an extension of the family system and that would maintain its homeostasis. Once this is perceived by the therapist, the rules of the therapeutic relationship are so arranged as to make it impossible.

Skynner, A. C. R. (1976). *Systems of family and marital psychotherapy.* New York: Brunner/Mazel.
Watzlawick, P., Beavin, J. H., & Jackson, D. D. (1967). *Pragmatics of human communication.* New York: Norton.

system recomposition   A restructuring technique that addresses structural change by adding to or taking away systems from those systems that are involved in the creation or maintenance of the problem.

Example: A mother and a son have problems because of the exclusiveness of their relationship. Adding a spouse, and thereby a father, to the household enriches the family structure and takes some of the pressure off of the mother-son system.

Minuchin, S., & Fishman, H. (1981). *Family therapy techniques.* Cambridge, MA: Harvard University Press.

system suction   Maneuvering by the family to entice the therapist to join the family system in such a way as to limit the therapist's objectivity and helpfulness. System suction is a way a family resists change.

   Example: The parents of an adolescent son see him as bad. The parents want the therapist too to see the son as bad, in order to fix only the son. They resist the idea that they too need help.

Rabkin, R. (1970). *Inner and outer space.* New York: Norton.

Riskin, J., & Faunce, E. (1972). An evaluative review of family interaction research. *Family Process, 11,* 365-455.

systems consultation   The application of systems theory to contexts other than the family (e.g., organizations, the workplace). The consultant's task is to interject new information into the system so that change occurs.

   Example: A therapist consults with an intensive care unit when the staff is divided about how to deal with the mother of a patient in the ICU. The therapist helps the staff work together by reframing the problem as a "split staff," as opposed to an "annoying family member."

Campbell, D., Draper, R., & Huffington, C. (1989). *A systemic approach to consultation.* London: Karnac.

Wynne, L., McDaniel, S., & Weber, T. (1987). *Systems consultation.* New York: Guilford.

systems orientation   In family therapy, a focus on comprehending the sources of leverage and power in the immediate field of action. A systems orientation explains change in terms of positive and negative feedback, rather than linear, cause-effect sequences.

Zuk, G. (1971). *Family therapy: A triadic-based approach.* New York: Behavioral Publications.

systems theory   Applied to families, a theory that delineates the interrelatedness of the family members to each other. Systems therapists believe that change in one family member necessitates change(s) in other members. Family systems psychotherapy is oriented to structural interventions even though it deals with individual processes.

Bowen, M. (1971). The use of family theory in clinical practice. In J. Haley (Ed.), *Changing families* (pp. 159-192). New York: Grune & Stratton.

Hansen, J. C., & L'Abate, L. (1982). *Approaches to family therapy.* New York: Macmillan.

systems wholeness   The tendency of a system—its elements and the interrelationship of its parts—to take on the character of the system's gestalt.

Example: A family is much more than the sum of its members' individual personalities; it is, in a sense, a totality, having an inner life and existence of its own.

Bowen, M. (1971). The use of family theory in clinical practice. In J. Haley (Ed.), *Changing families* (pp. 159-192). New York: Grune & Stratton.

S

S

Tarasoff duty   See **duty to warn and protect.**

task accomplishment   The interplay of forces affecting the outcome of critical transition points in a process. Task accomplishment is a product of factors antecedent to the situation in which the tasks arise.

Example: In a marriage, the way the partners accomplish the tasks presented to them on their honeymoon (e.g., developing a competence to participate in an appropriate sexual relationship, developing a competence to live in close association with one another) is related to the couple's potential for growth or disturbance.

Rapoport, R., & Rapoport, R. (1964). New light on the honeymoon. *Human Relations, 17,* 33-56.

Stuart, R. B. (1980). *Helping couples change: A social learning approach to marital therapy.* New York: Guilford.

task-centered family therapy   A short-term, structured, problem-solving practice model. Specific target problems are identified, and a plan is set with a defined number of sessions during a specified period of time. Tasks are described as individual, reciprocal, or shared, and conversation or enjoyable activity tasks.

Example: Mother and son agreed to the task objective of increased independence by being together less and respecting self-made decisions. The operational tasks called for specific action, such as not stating where the son was going and what time he would return home.

Reid, W. J. (1981). Family treatment within a task-centered framework. In E. R. Tolson & W. J. Reid (Eds.), *Models of family treatment* (pp. 306-331). New York: Columbia University Press.

tasks   A directive given by a therapist to a family member. Typically family members are told what to do, when to do it, and the goal the task is to achieve. Tasks also may be paradoxical.

Example: A single mother is instructed how to implement a time-out procedure and is told to begin using it with her child at home.

Haley, J. (1987). *Problem-solving therapy* (2nd ed.). San Francisco: Jossey-Bass.

task setting   In structural family therapy, the assignment to family members to carry out among themselves an operation within prescribed transactional parameters.

Example: The therapist asks that the father be totally responsible for his son's behavior in order to break up a pattern of overinvolvement between the mother and the son.

Aponte, H., & van Deusen, J. (1981). Structural family therapy. In A. S. Gurman & D. P. Kniskern (Eds.), *Handbook of family therapy* (pp. 310-360). New York: Brunner/Mazel.

TAT   See **Thematic Apperception Test.**

TEAM   Trust (T), expectation (E), attitudes (A), and motivation (M). The elements in the acronym (introduced by Araoz) are those that make hypnosis possible in sex hypnotherapy.

Araoz, D. L. (1982). *Hypnosis and sex therapy.* New York: Brunner/Mazel.

teasing technique   A sex therapy technique in which the female stimulates the male to erection and then stops and resumes stimulation after the penis has resumed to a flaccid state.

Masters, W., & Johnson, V. (1970). *Human sexual inadequacy.* Boston: Little, Brown.

telephone chart   A method of collecting information over the telephone prior to the first therapy session. The chart contains information about the relationships among family members. The purpose of the chart is to (a) formulate individual hypotheses, (b) decide who should come to the first meeting, and (c) help the therapist understand the repetitive dysfunctional patterns that they should avoid reinforcing.

Blasis, P., Fischer, J., & Prata, G. (1986). The telephone chart. *Journal of Strategic and Systemic Therapies, 5,* 31-44.

temporal compatibility   Being on acceptably similar wavelengths regarding short- and long-term goals. Temporal compatibility is a component of stability/instability.

Example: A couple agrees on the timing and spacing in having children.

Bodin, A. (1981). The interactional view: Family therapy approaches of the Mental Research Institute. In A. S. Gurman & D. P. Kniskern (Eds.), *Handbook of family therapy* (pp. 267-309). New York: Brunner/Mazel.

Lederer, W., & Jackson, D. (1968). *The mirages of marriage.* New York: Norton.

temporary relief hearing   A hearing that may occur before the final hearing is set, when disagreements over property or children must be decided immediately. For example, if both partners of a separated couple need the family car to go to work but cannot reach an agreement between themselves, a temporary relief hearing is held. The judge hears testimony only on the matter in question and makes a decision on that matter. The marriage is not dissolved, nor are other disagreements addressed.

Example: The husband and wife disagreed about the amount of money and who was going to continue to reside in the marital home, tensions increased to the threat of violence, and finances became increasingly limited.

Glass, B. L. (1984). No-fault divorce law. *Journal of Family Issues, 5,* 47-69.

tension   A state produced by problematic events, transitions, and related hardships. When tension is not overcome, stress or distress emerges. Family stress is produced by an actual or perceived imbalance between demand (e.g., challenge, threat) and capability (e.g., resources, coping) in the family's functioning. Family distress is a negative state produced by a family's defining the demands-resources imbalance as unpleasant. In contrast, stress may be construed as a positive state that results from the family's defining the demands-resources imbalance as desirable, as a challenge that family members enjoy.

Example: The husband's overcommitment to work to make financial ends meet has contributed to family imbalance and marital tension between the spouses. The tension is reduced when the wife returns to work and the husband has more time to be with his wife and children.

McCubbin, H. I., & Figley, C. R. (Eds.). (1983). *Stress and the family: Coping with normative transitions* (Vol. 1). New York: Brunner/Mazel.

territorial interactions   The acquisition, maintenance, and defense of ownership rights over one's body, food, and other possessions.

Example: A woman who had been severely traumatized became highly sensitive to men entering her bodily space without her feeling in full control of the way they approached her.

Bakker, C., & Bakker-Rabdau, M. (1973). *No trespassing: Explorations in human territoriality.* San Francisco: Chandler & Sharp.

Verhulst, J., & Heiman, J. (1988). A system perspective on sexual desire. In S. Leiblum & R. Rosen (Eds.), *Sexual desire disorders* (pp. 243-270). New York: Guilford.

tertiary locus   In structural family therapy, the passive environment of a problem. The tertiary locus is part of the context in which the problem occurs, but it is only incidental to the problem.

Example: A couple with a son fights chronically. The son manages not to get caught up in the fighting. However, he is an onlooker and, hence, part of the problem's passive environment.

Aponte, H., & van Deusen, J. (1981). Structural family therapy. In A. S. Gurman & D. P. Kniskern (Eds.), *Handbook of family therapy* (pp. 310-360). New York: Brunner/ Mazel.

Thematic Apperception Test (TAT)   A projective technique adapted for use in eliciting family interaction data. Two or more family members are asked to make up a story about a TAT card or a series of TAT cards. The cards often depict scenes that are commonly described as "family" scenes.

Walsh, F. (Ed.). (1982). *Normal family processes.* New York: Guilford.

theoretical-therapeutic system   A system in which theory determines therapy and in which observations from therapy can, in turn, modify the theory.

Bowen, M. (1969). The use of family theory in clinical practice. In B. N. Ard & C. C. Ard (Eds.), *Handbook of marriage counseling* (pp. 139-168). Palo Alto, CA: Science & Behavior Books.

therapeutic contract   A contract, used in therapy, in which a family member agrees to fulfill a negotiated behavior. Therapeutic contracts can be either verbal or written. Behavioral therapists have focused more on written contracts related to specific, concrete behaviors. Sager's method focuses on emotional, as well as behavioral, components of interaction.

Sager, C. J. (1976). *Marriage contracts and couples therapy.* New York: Brunner/Mazel.
Stuart, R. B. (1969). Operant-interpersonal treatment for marital discord. *Journal of Consulting and Clinical Psychology, 33,* 675-682.

therapeutic paradox   A therapeutic situation in which the psychotherapist (a) sets up a benevolent framework in which change is to take place, (b) permits or encourages the client to continue with an unchanged behavior, and (c) provides an ordeal that will continue as long as the client continues with the unchanged behavior. Typically it takes the form of "prescribing the symptom."

Example: A therapist tells a chronically depressed patient, "What surprises me is that you're not even more depressed than you are now. Actually, it's good you're depressed now, because if you weren't depressed, you'd be angry, and I don't know if you're ready to be angry yet. If you got angry, you'd have to deal with your wife and your relationship with her. Because you're not ready to get angry or to deal with your relationship with your wife, I think it's important that you continue to be depressed for now."

Haley, J. (1963). *Strategies of psychotherapy*. New York: Grune & Stratton.

therapeutic rituals A symbolic act used as an intervention in some form of psychological therapy. This symbolic act must have multiple meanings on behavioral, cognitive, and affective levels. Therapeutic rituals often focus on one of six themes: membership, healing, identity, belief, expression and negotiation, and celebration. A therapeutic ritual may have more than one theme. The meaning of these themes should never be imposed on families; rather, the family ultimately must determine both the form and meaning of the ritual.

Example: After the death of her favorite grandson, a grandmother no longer decorated her home for Christmas. Furthermore the family never spoke openly of the death of the grandson. A therapeutic task was prescribed in which two Sundays before Christmas the family ate Sunday dinner together at grandmother's. Prior to eating, the family read a poem written by the dead grandson and then said a prayer acknowledging everyone's loss and grief. Following dinner, the grandchildren decorated grandmother's home. Participating in this therapeutic ritual enabled the family to openingly acknowledge their grief, help the grandmother overcome her depression, and provide an opportunity for new interaction within the family.

Imber-Black, E. (1988). Ritual themes in families and family therapy. In E. Imber-Black, J. Roberts, & R. Whiting (Eds.), *Rituals in families and family therapy* (pp. 47-83). New York: Norton.

therapist-family fit The similarity of the therapist's race, ethnic background, social class, and value system with those of the family. It is hypothesized that the greater the therapist-family fit, the more likely that mutual understanding and sensitivity will ensue.

Glick, I. D., & Kessler, D. P. (1980). *Marital and family therapy* (2nd ed.). New York: Grune & Stratton.

therapy team (1) In sex therapy, a team composed of a male and a female co-therapist, each trained to treat the problems of sexual and family dysfunction. (2) In family therapy, a team frequently watching behind a one-way mirror and consulting to the therapist in the consulting room with the family. The team approach is used often as a strategic intervention.

Boscolo, L., Cecchin, G., Hoffman, L., & Penn, P. (1987). *Milan systemic family therapy: Conversations in theory and practice.* New York: Basic Books.
Masters, W., & Johnson, V. (1970). *Human sexual inadequacy.* Boston: Little, Brown.

threat to adaptive defenses   Threats that arise when partners in a dysfunctional marriage inadvertently fail to support each other's defenses against anxiety. The partners' self-esteems are so low that each seeks only self-relief and hence does not notice the anxiety of the other.

Example: A husband whose self-esteem has been lowered due to a setback at work fails to notice his wife's increased anxiety level over problems with one of their children.

Blinder, M., & Kirschenbaum, M. (1969). The technique of married couple group therapy. In B. N. Ard & C. C. Ard (Eds.), *Handbook of marriage counseling* (pp. 233-246). Palo Alto, CA: Science & Behavior Books.

three generation hypothesis   The hypothesis that schizophrenia is the result of an intergenerational process. It asserts that the grandparents' combined immaturities were acquired by the one child who was most attached to the mother. When this child marries a spouse with an equal degree of immaturity, and when the same process repeats itself in the third generation, it results in one child (the patient) with a high degree of immaturity, with the other siblings more mature.

Bowen, M. (1960). A family concept of schizophrenia. In D. D. Jackson (Ed.), *The etiology of schizophrenia* (pp. 346-372). New York: Basic Books.

tickling the defenses   The use of surprise and humor to keep from arousing unmanageable defensiveness in the family during a therapeutic session. A technique to expose dramatic discrepancies between family members self-justifying rationalizations and other nonverbal attitudes.

Ackerman, N. W. (1966). *Treating the troubled family.* New York: Basic Books.
Levant, R. F. (1984). *Family therapy: A comprehensive overview.* Englewood Cliffs, NJ: Prentice-Hall.

timebinding   The condition in which each generation of humans starts, at least potentially, where the previous generation left off.

Korzybski, A. (1933). *Science and sanity.* Lancaster, PA: International Non-Aristotelian Library.
Lewis, J. M., Beavers, W. R., Gossett, J. T., & Phillips, V. A. (1976). *No single thread: Psychological health in the family system.* New York: Brunner/Mazel.

time-designated therapy   An approach to determine the length of therapy that is deemed the best way to balance the advantages and disadvantages of open-ended and time-designated formats. The therapist estimates the probable length of the therapy in light of the therapeutic objectives and the family's strengths and limitations, and attempts to secure a commitment from the couple/family for that amount of therapy. Failing that, some shorter trial period is agreed to. In either case, when that time comes (or earlier, if anyone believes the objectives of therapy already have been met), both the couple/family and the therapist evaluate whether more time is needed; if so, a new designated number of sessions is agreed to, and the process is repeated.

Example: The therapist judges that the accomplishment of the therapeutic objectives will take 20 sessions. One member of the family objects to the whole idea of therapy and agrees to a trial of only 4 sessions. At the fourth session, the therapist and family evaluate progress, what still remains to be accomplished, if anything, and negotiate a new time designation.

Guerney, B. G. (1977). *Relationship enhancement: Skill training programs for therapy, problem prevention, and enrichment.* San Francisco: Jossey-Bass.

time out Removal of a person from a reinforcing environment for a brief time (isolation), or having the person physically remain in the situation but with a cessation of reinforcement.

Example: When the siblings argued, the mother sent each to a corner.

Green, D. R., Budd, K., Johnson, M., Larg, S., Pinkston, E., & Rudd, S. (1976). Training parents to modify problem child behaviors. In E. J. Marsh, L. C. Handy, & L. A. Hamerlynck (Eds.), *Behavior modification approach to parenting* (pp. 3-18). New York: Brunner/Mazel.

Reese, R. (1966). *The analysis of human operant behavior.* Dubuque, IA: William C. Brown.

time squeeze Family member(s) demanding a response or solution in advance of the optimal therapeutic time frame. When the time frame is compromised, the therapeutic or mediation efforts can be sabotaged.

Example: A spouse stated, "I want your decision right now so I can sell the house and get a loan, accept a new job offer, move out of the house and find a rental." The other spouse froze. The spouse was pushing to get things settled because of pain suffered in the divorce.

Saposnek, D. T. (1983). *Mediating child custody disputes.* San Francisco: Jossey-Bass.

timing and pacing A procedure by which the therapist checks the client's view before taking a firm stance. Throughout treatment, the therapist takes small steps and evaluates how each step is received before proceeding.

Example: The therapist does not believe that history taking is important, but the client believes that it is essential. Before making a firm statement about the role of history or skipping history taking altogether, the therapist assesses the client's view so that the therapeutic process can move forward without causing a rift in the relationship.

Fisch, R., Weakland, J., & Segal, L. (1982). *The tactics of change.* San Francisco: Jossey-Bass.

token economy   A program in which tokens (e.g., points, gold stars) are earned by completing certain designated behaviors. A contingency is established between completing a task and earning an agreed-upon number of tokens. The tokens can be traded later for money or privileges.

Ayllon, T., & Azrin, N. H. (1968). *The token economy: A motivation system for therapy and rehabilitation.* New York: Appleton.

topic continuity   A category of Riskin and Faunce's Topic Scale, which measures whether family members stay on the same topic as that of the immediately preceding speech.

Riskin, J., & Faunce, E. (1972). An evaluative review of family interaction research. *Family Process, 11,* 365-455.

toxic parent   A parent whose negative and dysfunctional behavior consistently dominates a child's life. As a result, great psychological harm befalls the child. The emotional damage inflicted by these parents is thought to be "toxic"—that is, it spreads throughout the child's being and affects most aspects of the child's life, even as the child becomes an adult. Examples of toxic parents are physical abusers, sexual abusers, verbal abusers, controllers, and inadequate parents.

Forward, S. (1989). *Toxic parents.* New York: Bantam Books.

tracking   A procedure by which the therapist helps the family elaborate the details of behavioral routes so that a coherent picture emerges of the particular complaint. Tracking the content of family life promotes such elaboration. Tracking also involves a therapeutic possibility—namely, that the extended inquiry into facets of family life will subtly guide the family to a new and expanded version of reality, thereby taking the focus off of the index patient.

Example: The mother complains that her oldest daughter hates being a child and wants to be a teenager and work in a store in the neighborhood. The mother says, "She should enjoy being a child as the best time in her life." The therapist asks the 9-year-old to describe what her responsibilities are around the house, including the ways she is supposed to take care of her younger sister.

Minuchin, S. (1974). *Families and family therapy.* Cambridge, MA: Harvard University Press.
Umbarger, C. C. (1984). *Structural family therapy.* New York: Grune & Stratton.

trading of dissociations An interlocking network of perceptions about others, based on dissociations about oneself. Each person projects the totality of a particular quality or feeling onto another family member and, in exchange, allows the other member to project unacceptable qualities onto the first person.

Example: In a family, all of the members have dissociated into unawareness of their hostile feelings toward the others, but each is keenly perceptive of that same feeling in the other members.

Wynne, L. (1965). Some indications and contraindications for exploratory family therapy. In I. Boszormenyi-Nagy & J. Framo (Eds.), *Intensive family therapy: Theoretical and practical aspects* (pp. 289-322). New York: Harper & Row.

transaction A unit of social intercourse when two people contact each other. Complementary transactions occur when we address an ego state in another person and the response is from the same ego state. As long as transactions are complementary, communication can continue indefinitely, with the response of each person serving as the stimulus for the next transaction. When transactions are crossed, communication stops or the subject changes. The most common crossed transactions involve a child-to-parent response or a parent-to-child response.

Erskine, R. G. (1982). Transactional analysis and family therapy. In A. M. Horne, & M. M. Ohlsen (Eds.), *Family counseling and therapy* (pp. 245-275). Itasca, IL: F. E. Peacock.
Spiegel, J. (1971). *Transactions.* New York: Science House.

transactional analysis Analysis based on Berne's theory of personality that focuses on communication. Each personality is viewed as being composed of three ego states: parent, child, adult. Each ego state organizes external and internal stimuli in a specific way, resulting in unique communication. The analysis of the transactional patterns provides a tool to understand and change the interpersonal and intrapersonal dynamics that may be blocking effective communication.

The tendency of a person to favor a particular ego state as a basis for communication is determined, in part, by the life script, a plan decided on in childhood as a way to fit into the family. It is formulated out of what the child hears, experiences, and perceives as possible options. Transactional analysis provides family members with a cognitive understanding of the dynamics of family scripts, of the functions of personality, and of transactional patterns. The counseling methodology encourages each person to take responsibility for self, consistent with the person's developmental age, to express the emotions that are often held back or are ineffectively communicated, and to focus on specific behavioral changes that can improve family life.

Berne, E. (1961). *Transactional analysis in psychotherapy.* New York: Grove.
Erskine, R. G. (1982). Transactional analysis and family therapy. In A. M. Horne & M. M. Ohlsen (Eds.), *Family counseling and therapy* (245-275). Itasca, IL: F. E. Peacock.

transactional patterns of enacting   Scenarios that a therapist deliberately creates so that conflicts and other family problems can be acted out, rather than just described, in the family session. In essence, the task of the therapist is to help the family members demonstrate in the "here and now" how they deal with life situations.

Example: In the session, the therapist requests the family to act out an argument over how their son is disciplined.

Gerson, M., & Barsky, M. (1979). For the new family therapist: A glossary of terms. *American Journal of Family Therapy, 7,* 15-30.
Minuchin, S. (1974). *Families and family therapy.* Cambridge, MA: Harvard University Press.

transactional thought disorder   The chaotic communication that frequently occurs in schizophrenic families. In such families, each person's statements, apart from the transactional context, may appear sufficiently normal so that one would not ordinarily question the rationality of specific, isolated statements. The overall transactional sequence, however, is bizarre, disjointed, and fragmented. Even if the parents are psychotic to some degree, the overall transactional disorder in these families often exceeds the severity of the individual parental disorder. Transactional thought disorder is referred to by Wynne as "collective cognitive chaos."

Wynne, L. (1965). Some indications and contraindications for exploratory family therapy. In I. Boszormenyi-Nagy & J. Framo (Eds.), *Intensive family therapy: Theoretical and practical aspects* (pp. 289-322). New York: Harper & Row.
Wynne, L., & Singer, M. (1963). Thought disorder and family relations of schizophrenics. I: A research strategy. *Archives of General Psychiatry, 9,* 191-198.

transference   A psychoanalytic term for distorted emotional reactions to present relationships often based on unresolved family situations. Because family relationships are embedded most often in a transference context, the family therapist can enter the ongoing transference relationship system, rather than have to recreate it in the privacy of an exclusive therapist-patient work relationship.

Example: Marital conflict may be viewed as the result of mutual projection by each partner of early internalized objects and thus may become the battleground for past conflicts. The therapist must be aware of each spouse's transference projection onto the partner, as well as onto the therapist.

Boszormenyi-Nagy, I. (1972). Loyalty implications of the transference model in psychotherapy. *Archives of General Psychiatry, 27,* 374-380.
Nichols, M. P. (1984). *Family therapy: Concepts and methods.* New York: Gardner.

transference distortions   In family therapy, a behavioral pattern in which members of the family not only react to the therapist as a grandparent, parent, or sibling but also respond in accordance with one another without being aware of their postinfantile relationships. This situation creates a very complex array of transferences.

Framo, J. (1965). Rationale and technique of intensive family therapy. In I. Boszormenyi-Nagy & J. Framo (Eds.), *Intensive family therapy: Theoretical and practical aspects* (pp. 143-212). New York: Harper & Row.

transference neurosis   A neurosis that occurs when a patient reacts in the treatment relationship with a variety of neurotic conflicts, including many rooted in the patient's childhood experience. The cumulative transference reactions become so pervasive as to make therapy and the therapist the central concerns in the patient's life.

Gurman, A. (1978). Contemporary marital therapies. In T. Paolino & B. McCrady (Eds.), *Marriage and marital therapy* (pp. 445-566). New York: Brunner/Mazel.
Weiner, I. (1975). *Principles of psychotherapy.* New York: John Wiley.

transfer of blame   A defense against accepting responsibility for one's behavior. The transfer can be achieved by (a) qualifying a behavior as not having been done or as not done in a particular way, (b) indicating that it is someone else's fault, or (c) accepting the blame but claiming that one has been falsely accused.

Haley, J. (1972). The family of the schizophrenic. In G. D. Erickson & T. P. Hogan (Eds.), *Family therapy: An introduction to theory and technique* (pp. 51-75). Belmont, CA: Wadsworth.

transpersonal unconscious   The unconscious involved in cross-communication between one person and another, without the involvement of the conscious of either person.
   Example: An adolescent daughter sexually acts out her mother's unconscious wishes to be sexually free.

Framo, J. (1965). Systematic research on family dynamics. In I. Boszormenyi-Nagy & J. Framo (Eds.), *Intensive family therapy: Theoretical and practical aspects* (pp. 407-463). New York: Harper & Row.
Freud, S. (1957). The unconscious. In J. Strachey (Ed.), *The standard edition of the complete psychological works of Sigmund Freud* (Vol. 14, pp. 166-204). London: Hogarth.

transvestic fetishism   A disorder in which a person has acted on, but is distressed by, recurrent sexual urges and sexually arousing fantasies involving cross-dressing.

American Psychiatric Association. (1987). *Diagnostic and statistical manual of mental disorders* (3rd ed., rev.). Washington, DC: Author.

triad   A group of three family members, frequently viewed as inherently unstable as a unit.

Bowen, M. (1978). *Family theory in clinical practice.* New York: Jason Aronson.

triadic-based technique   In family therapy, the use of mediation and side taking judiciously to break up and replace pathogenic relating. The technique is composed of a series of negotiations in which the therapist and the family vie for control. The therapist is not only a releaser, but also a fashioner, of change.

Zuk, G. (1971). *Family therapy: A triadic-based approach.* New York: Behavioral Publications.

triadic model   A model assuming that psychological problems are the result of multiperson interactions. Thus the system must be the target of intervention.
   Example: Pablo shoplifts because his father covertly encourages him to defy his mother.

Nichols, M. (1984). *Family therapy: Concepts and methods.* New York: Gardner.

triadic one   In the schizophrenic family, the child who functions as a stabilizer for the parents, converting the unstable father-mother ego mass into a more stable triad.

Bowen, M. (1960). A family concept of schizophrenia. In D. D. Jackson (Ed.), *The etiology of schizophrenia* (pp. 346-372). New York: Basic Books.
Bowen, M. (1965). Family psychotherapy with schizophrenia in the hospital and in private practice. In I. Boszormenyi-Nagy & J. Framo (Eds.), *Intensive family therapy: Theoretical and practical aspects* (pp. 213-244). New York: Harper & Row.

triadic questioning   A type of circular questioning, used by the Milan group, in which a third member is asked to comment on the relationship of a dyad, or a fourth person is asked to comment on the relationship of a triad, and so on. Also known as *gossiping in the presence.* See also **reflexive questioning.**

Tomm, K. (1988). Interventive interviewing: Part III. Intending to ask linear, circular, strategic, or reflexive questions? *Family Process, 27,* 1-16.

trial marriage   A premarital relationship established with the avowed aim of eventual legal marital union. It usually is restricted to adult partners without plans for the birth or nurturance of children.

Bowman, H. (1974). *Marriage for moderns.* New York: McGraw-Hill.

triangle   A three-person subsystem that is the molecule of an emotional system. This term is contrasted with *triad,* which has come to have fixed connotations. The triangle has definite relationship patterns that predictably repeat in periods of calm and stress. In periods of calm, the triangle is made up of a comfortably close twosome and a less comfortable outsider. The twosome works to preserve the togetherness. In stress, each works to get the outside position to escape tension in the twosome. The outside position is the most comfortable and desired one.

Example: In a father-mother-child triangle, tensions exist between the parents. The father (regarded as passive, weak, and distant) gains the outside position, leaving the conflict between the mother and the child. The mother (regarded as aggressive and domineering) wins over the child, who moves another step toward chronic functional impairment. Thus the family projection process unfolds.

Bowen, M. (1978). *Family theory in clinical practice.* New York: Jason Aronson.

triangles, interlocking   A way in which members of a family fit together in interlocking relationships. The therapist must consider all of the triangles and how they interlock before attempting to differentiate or, in Bowen's words, "de-triangulate," the family in the therapeutic process.

Bowen, M. (1966). The use of family theory in clinical practice. *Comprehensive Psychiatry, 7,* 345-374.
Hoffman, L. (1981). *Foundations of family therapy.* New York: Basic Books.

triangulation   Detouring conflict between two people by involving a third person, thus stabilizing the relationship of the first two people. When this involves parents and a child, the parents, who are in conflict, ask for the child's loyalty, making it impossible for the child to get close to one of them without betraying the other.

Example: A 12-year-old son depends on and protects his mother against his father during and after the divorce.

Bowen, M. (1971). The use of family theory in clinical practice. In J. Haley (Ed.), *Changing families* (pp. 159-192). New York: Grune & Stratton.
Minuchin, S. (1974). *Families and family therapy.* Cambridge, MA: Harvard University Press.

troubleshooting   A particular sequenced series of therapeutic responses used in relationship enhancement therapy to overcome problems created by strong feelings, objections, resistance, and emotional blocks.

Example: The therapist troubleshoots when a wife breaks down in tears because her husband has said he is not sure whether he loves her anymore.

Guerney, B. G. (1977). *Relationship enhancement: Skill training programs for therapy, problem prevention, and enrichment.* San Francisco: Jossey-Bass.

true statements   In sex hypnotherapy, statements that treat negative sexual processing. Some clients have accepted untrue statements about sex. Clients are asked to formulate the statements before being placed in a hypnotic state. Then, in the hypnotic state, they are asked to imagine that an important authority figure is lecturing and directing the same statements to them. This technique is used to treat negative sexual processing.

Araoz, D. L. (1982). *Hypnosis and sex therapy.* New York: Brunner/Mazel.

two-question rule   The rule that the asker should always have a second question, seeking amplification of the answer to the first question. This technique avoids the possibility that the answer will be used by the asker for an immediate attack on the answerer. It also conveys the asker's interest in the answerer's response.

Baruth, L. G., & Huber, C. H. (1984). *An introduction to marital theory and therapy.* Belmont, CA: Brooks/Cole.

T

unbalancing A technique used to change the hierarchical relationship of the members of a system. Family members are encouraged to experiment with differing and expanded roles and functions. This experience may provide new understanding and new perspective to the family and its relationships. The therapist forms a coalition and supports one family member or subsystem at the expense of the others. The therapist usually joins with an underdog in the hierarchy, thus ignoring the family's preexisting patterns. This action often prevents the family from noticing and responding to cues given by the upper part of the hierarchy, and the affiliated member begins to respond in daring and unfamiliar ways, highlighting possibilities that previously were ignored.

Minuchin, S., & Fishman, H. (1981). *Family therapy techniques.* Cambridge, MA: Harvard University Press.

unclarity The situation when the content and tonal aspects of a speech do not fit with each other—that is, are incongruent and/or are unintelligible to the observer.

Riskin, J., & Faunce, E. (1972). An evaluative review of family interaction research. *Family Process, 11,* 365-455.

unconscious collusion Acting collusively on an unconscious level in order to reciprocally serve another's needs. In some problem families, two or more members may have narcissistically regressive attitudes that are complementary with one another. These complementarities are collusive in that they may contribute to an endless postponement of growth or of the resolution of mourning among the participants.

Example: The parents constantly fight over their son's problems and overtly agree on a way of solving the problem. However, they want to retain him in the symptom-bearer role at the unconscious level, which results in the parents sabotaging their own efforts.

Boszormenyi-Nagy, I. (1965). Intensive family therapy as process. In I. Boszormenyi-Nagy & J. Framo (Eds.), *Intensive family therapy: Theoretical and practical aspects* (pp. 87-142). New York: Harper & Row.

unconscious interpersonal conflict   Conflict resulting from incompletely experiencing a forbidden desire to relate in a certain way to oneself and others.

Example: The parents feel inhibited about expressing themselves sexually. Their daughter begins to act out sexually. The parents cannot relate to her behavior in an appropriate way because part of them receives vicarious gratification from her behavior, while the other part of them finds the behavior abhorrent.

Esterson, A. (1970). *The leaves of spring.* London: Tavistock.

unconsummated marriage   A marriage in which the couple have never been able to complete intercourse successfully. Sex may not have occurred for organic and/or psychological reasons.

Kaplan, H. S. (1983). *The evaluation of sexual disorders.* New York: Brunner/Mazel.

U

underachievement   When a student receives lower grades then he or she is intellectually capable of earning. Typically these students have average or better intelligence yet show unexpectably poor performance in school work. These students may have a learning disability. If the discrepancy between academic achievement and intelligence is severe enough, the student is considered to be learning disabled. However, some underachievers have no cognitive processing difficulty, but rather underachieve for a variety of other reasons, including low motivation, dysfunctional family, peer/group influences, school influences, emotional immaturity, fear of failure, or passive aggressive behavior. Also see **learning disabilities.**

Weiner, I. (1982). *Child and adolescence psychopathology.* New York: John Wiley.

underdog fallacy   The fallacy that a younger or weaker child is less skillful than an older child in getting someone else into trouble.

Wahlroos, S. (1974). *Family communication: A guide to emotional health.* New York: Macmillan.

underfunctioning   When an individual in a family has given up too much self-control and depends on another to do the things he or she feels unable to do or does not want to do. See also **overfunctioning.**

Kerr, M. E., & Bowen, M. (1988). *Family evaluation: An approach based on Bowen theory.* New York: Norton.

underorganization A deficiency in the degree of constancy differentiation and flexibility of the structural organization of the family system, accompanied by a lack of organizational continuity in the family.

Example: A mother is the controlling force in her family. When she is absent, the family becomes chaotic, due to the lack of other structures and supports to keep it working.

Aponte, H. (1976). Underorganization in the poor family. In P. J. Guerin (Ed.), *Family therapy: Theory and practice* (pp. 432-448). New York: Gardner.

undifferentiated family ego mass Bowen's theory that the egos of individual family members become fused with a common ego boundary. The ego fusion is most intense in the least mature families. In a family with a schizophrenic member, the fusion between father, mother, and child approaches maximum intensity. Theoretically the fusion is present to some degree in all families, but least so in those in which the family members have attained relatively complete emotional maturity. Clinically the undifferentiated family ego mass is considered to be equivalent to a single ego.

Bowen, M. (1978). *Family therapy in clinical practice.* New York: Jason Aronson.

unexpected context-change questions A type of reflexive question based on the assumption that for every quality, meaning, and context, there exists an opposite or a complementary. These questions may explore opposite content, context, and meaning and the need to maintain the status quo, introduce confusion, and join with the feared impulse.

Example: An example of an opposite context question might be, "Who in the family enjoys fighting the most?"

Tomm, K. (1987). Interventive interviewing: Part II. Reflexive questioning as a means to enable self-healing. *Family Process, 26,* 167-184.

U

unfreezing (and refreezing) In the quasi-stationary social equilibrium of individuals, groups, and families, something must be shaken up to unsettle accustomed beliefs and behaviors. Only then will the person or family member be prepared to accept change. Examples include Minuchin's promotion of crisis in family lunch sessions, Paul's use of cross-confrontations, and Papp's family choreography.

Lewin, K. (1951). *Field theory in social science.* New York: Harper & Row.
Minachin, S. (1974). *Families and family therapy.* Cambridge, MA: Harvard University Press.
Nichols, M. P. (1984). *Family therapy: Concepts and methods.* New York: Gardner.
Papp, P. (1980). The Greek Chorus and other techniques of family therapy. *Family Process, 19,* 45-57.

Paul, N. (1976). Cross-confrontation. In P. J. Guerin (Ed.), *Family therapy* (pp. 520-529). New York: Gardner.

Rosman, B., Minuchin, S., & Liebman, R. (1975). Family lunch session: An introduction to family therapy in anorexia nervosa. *American Journal of Orthopsychiatry, 45,* 846-853.

unique outcome   An exceptional situation where the individual or family have attained their goals or found solutions. The therapist amplifies these situations in the course of treatment.

Example: A anorexic understands that she no longer needs to isolate herself socially, which was part of her eating disorder for the last decade. Recognizing this, she feels encouraged about her ability to overcome her eating disorder and have healthy relationships.

White, M., & Epston, D. (1990). *Narrative means to therapeutic ends.* New York: Norton.

unit of analysis   The part of interaction that is coded and analyzed. The unit of analysis varies greatly among researchers.

Mishler, E., & Waxler, N. (1968). *Interaction in families: An experimental study of family processes and schizophrenia.* New York: John Wiley.

unrelatedness   The situation in which nothing a family member does, is, or becomes matters to anyone else in the family. Thus detachment and separateness occur.

Framo, J. (1965). Rationale and technique of intensive family therapy. In I. Boszormenyi-Nagy & J. Framo (Eds.), *Intensive family therapy: Theoretical and practical aspects* (pp. 143-212). New York: Harper & Row.

U

unrevealed differences questionnaire   A questionnaire based on Strodtbeck's revealed differences technique, in which family members are asked to indicate their personal preferences on 7 items by choosing the 3 choices they like best and the 3 they like least out of a list of 10 possible choices for each item. After the family members have each made their choices in private, the family is brought together and is asked to come to a joint decision on the three choices the whole family likes best and the three choices the whole family likes least. What each individual privately chose is not revealed to the whole family.

Ferreira, A., & Winter, W. (1965). Family interaction and decision making. *Archives of General Psychiatry, 13,* 214-223.

Riskin, J., & Faunce, E. (1972). An evaluative review of family interaction research. *Family Process, 11,* 365-455.

Strodtbeck, F. (1954). The family as a three-person group. *American Sociological Review, 19,* 23-29.

untensing   A sex hypnotherapy technique used to treat female vasocongestive dysfunction. The technique emphasizes the healthy forces within the body. The woman relaxes herself and her pelvic area and then explores all of her sexual parts in her imagination.

Araoz, D. L. (1982). *Hypnosis and sex therapy.* New York: Brunner/Mazel.

use of self   The therapist's feeling in response to family members. This is a basic cue to the therapist in interaction with the family. Knowing oneself and one's own family system provides a safeguard to assist the therapist in responding to the family, rather than to a projection of the therapist's own personal conflicts. The use of self in family therapy is closely parallel to the psychoanalyst's concept of countertransference. Early family therapists feared that the therapist's use of self could induct the therapist into the family system to such a degree that the therapist would lose therapeutic maneuverability. Whitaker's solution for maintaining therapeutic leverage was to have a co-therapist. The Milano group avoid induction by having the therapist use a therapeutic team. Bowen maintained objectivity and control over his use of self by acting as a coach and maintaining the position of being an expert, thus channeling all communication within a session. Minuchin maintains that the therapist's use of self will differ from therapist to therapist and from family to family. The therapist must be comfortable with different levels of involvement, sometimes being very engaged, at other times still being a coach, and at other times prescribing behavioral interventions.

Bowen, M. (1976). Theory in the practice of psychotherapy. In P. J. Guerin (Ed.), *Family therapy: Theory and practice* (pp. 42-90). New York: Gardner.

Minuchin, S., & Fishman, H. (1981). *Family therapy techniques.* Cambridge, MA: Harvard University Press.

Napier, A., & Whitaker, C. (1978). *The family crucible.* New York: Jason Aronson.

Selvini Palazzoli, M. Boscolo, L., Cecchin, G., & Prata, G. (1978). *Paradox and counterparadox: A new model in the therapy of the family in schizophrenic transaction.* New York: Jason Aronson.

U

utilizing symptoms   A restructuring operation that involves focusing on the symptom to change the family interactional patterns. The therapist may exaggerate the symptom to increase its intensity and to force the family into action. The therapist could, conversely, deemphasize the symptom, relabel the symptom, or relabel its effects on family interactions.

Example: A teenage anorexic is described by the therapist as being disobedient. The therapist then directs the parents to take control and not allow their child to be disobedient to them.

Minuchin, S. (1974). *Families and family therapy.* Cambridge, MA: Harvard University Press.

utopia syndrome   Extremism in the solving of human problems. This syndrome, cited by Watzlawick, seems to occur most frequently as a result of the belief that one has found the ultimate, all-embracing answer. It may take three forms: (a) blame of oneself for the inability to attain the unattainable, (b) devotion to an endless quest and hence to experience of fulfillment as a loss, and (c) self-righteous mission to encourage or embrace one's own answers.

Watzlawick, P. (1977). The utopia syndrome. In P. Watzlawick & J. Weakland (Eds.), *The interactional view: Studies at the Mental Research Institute, Palo Alto, 1965-1974.* New York: Norton.

U

vaginal photoplethysmograph A tamponlike acrylic tube that uses a photocell and light source to measure blood volume and pressure pulse changes in the vagina in order to treat vaginismus.

Heiman, J. (1978). Uses of psychophysiology in assessment and treatment of sexual dysfunction. In J. LoPiccolo & L. LoPiccolo (Eds.), *Handbook of sex therapy* (pp. 123-136). New York: Plenum.

vaginismus A sexual dysfunction that makes coitus difficult or impossible. The outer part of the vaginal outlet involuntarily closes, making attempts at penetration painful, if not impossible.

Masters, W., & Johnson, V. (1970). *Human sexual inadequacy.* Boston: Little, Brown.

value orientation discrepancy A situation in which the values of one partner conflict with the values of the other.

Example: The husband values most his wife being at home taking care of the family; his wife values most her extra part-time job to bring in more money for the family.

Foley, V. (1974). *An introduction to family therapy.* New York: Grune & Stratton.
Spiegel, I. (1971). *Transactions.* New York: Science House.

values Worth or merit of an idea or item that gives meaning to life and explains why family members make specific selections from alternative courses of action. Values are inclusive, deeply internalized, personal feelings about behavior and expectations of life that direct action. Because values cannot be seen, they must be recognized in behavior; freedom, love, honesty, prestige, and leisure are intangibles. Values can be verbalized and held at the conscious level (explicit) or held subconsciously and recognized only in behavior (implicit). Intrinsic values are desirable for their own sake, whereas instrumental values are important means of achieving higher level values.

Nickell, P., Rice, A. S., & Tucker, S. P. (1976). *Management in family living* (5th ed.). New York: John Wiley.

vasocongestion   The reflex dilation of penile and circumvaginal blood vessels in response to sexual stimuli, causing the genitals to become engorged and distended with blood. This process produces erection in the male and lubrication and swelling of the female genitals.

Kaplan, H. S. (1981). *The new sex therapy.* New York: Brunner/Mazel.

vasocongestive dysfunction   Inadequate physiological arousal of the sexual system. In the male, vasocongestion dysfunction (VCD) refers to the lack of an erection; in the female, it refers to little or no vaginal lubrication.

John, D. (1979). *Sexual dysfunctions.* New York: John Wiley.

vector relations   Synchrony in being able to handle marital change by heading toward a collaborative relationship, rather than taking a collision course. Vector relations are components of stability/instability.

Lederer, W., & Jackson, D. (1968). *The mirages of marriage.* New York: Norton.

vector therapy   A form of family therapy based on Lewin's "field," where the aim is the readjustment of the pattern of emotional forces within the life space to bring improvement to individual family members. Vector therapy involves (a) a change in the magnitude of the emotional forces, (b) a change in the direction of emotional force with no change in magnitude, (c) a change in the length of time during which the emotional force operates, and (d) a change in the quality of the emotional force when one force replaces another.

Howells, J. (1975). *Principles of family psychiatry.* New York: Brunner/Mazel.
Lewin, K. (1963). *Field theory in social sciences: Selected theretical papers.* London: Tavistock.

vertical bookkeeping   A one-way system of relationships that does not provide for reciprocation.

Example: The parents provide a positive and conducive environment without allowing for the opportunity of repayment, and the child becomes a debtor. The child's indebtedness prevents him from committing himself to other relationships because of his feelings of disloyalty to his family. As an adult, he becomes oversolicitous of his own children as a way of ridding himself of the debt.

Boszormenyi-Nagy, I., & Spark, G. L. (1973). *Invisible loyalties: Reciprocity in intergenerational family therapy.* New York: Harper & Row.

victim-victimizer couple A couple in a marital relationship in which one partner blames and the other accepts the blaming.

Example: A wife blames her husband for being lazy, while he agrees by saying "I am what I am and you are what you are."

Sluzki, C. E. (1978). Marital therapy from a systems theory perspective. In T. Paolino & B. McCrady (Eds.), *Marriage and marital therapy* (pp. 366-394). New York: Brunner/Mazel.

videotape/audiotape playback Devices used in therapy sessions to help family members become more self-aware and to correct distortions in their communications. Such playback also reveals nonverbal aspects of the communications. The technique may be used in treatment, for diagnosis, for therapist self-monitoring, or for training.

Alger, I. (1976). Integrating immediate video playback in family therapy. In P. J. Guerin (Ed.), *Family therapy* (pp. 530-548). New York: Gardner.

vigilance See **attention.**

violation of function boundaries Inappropriate intrusion of family members into functions that are in the domains of other members.

Example: A child tries to decide where the parents should live and thereby crosses over a boundary into the parents' decision area.

Aponte, G., & van Deusen, J. (1981). Structural family therapy. In A. S. Gurman & D. P. Kniskern (Eds.), *Handbook of family therapy* (pp. 310-360). New York: Brunner/Mazel.

Minuchin, S. (1974). *Families and family therapy.* Cambridge, MA: Harvard University Press.

V

violent behavior Acts that involve great force and are capable of and intended to injure, damage, destroy, or intimidate. The study of domestic violence includes marital rape, incest, child abuse, partner abuse, and parent abuse; other acts include gang warfare, victimization, aggressive behavior within institutions, and other crimes. Aggressive behaviors can become family norms and are distributed across all of the interacting family members. Physical violence occurs at home between family members more often than it occurs between any other individuals or in any other setting except for wars and riots.

Stuart, R. B. (1981). Violence in perspective. In R. B. Stuart (Ed.), *Violent behavior: Social learning approaches to prediction, management, and treatment* (pp. 3-30). New York: Brunner/Mazel.

vital marriage   A marriage in which the partners are able to work together and find their relationship intensely satisfying.

Glick, I. D., & Kessler, D. P. (1980). *Marital and family therapy* (2nd ed.). New York: Grune & Stratton.

voice technique   A technique in which the individual is encouraged to talk about a feeling in order to get emotional distance from it. A discrepancy may be produced between the feeling and the words used to describe it. An opportunity thus is provided for experiencing the feelings as they happen. This technique is especially effective when a discrepancy exists between the content of what one says and one's body messages.

Example: As a woman talks about the loss of a relationship, she begins to shed some tears, but she says that it is better that the relationship is ended. She does not appear to be in touch with her sadness. Using the voice technique, the therapist asks her to give her tears a voice so that she can experience the feelings associated with the event.

Dodson, L., & Kurpuis, D. (1977). *Family counseling: A systems approach.* Muncie, IN: Accelerated Development.

volume of communication   The median number of statements made during an interview by the individual family members and by the whole family.

Lennard, H., & Bernstein, A. (1969). *Patterns in human interaction.* San Francisco: Jossey-Bass.

V

walking on egg shells Using the other person's sensitivities as an excuse for not being open and sincere. The term connotes contempt for the other person's feelings and tension in the relationship.

Example: A woman avoids bringing up problems she has with her husband because she believes that, if she does, he will criticize her severely.

Wahlroos, S. (1974). *Family communication: A guide to emotional health.* New York: Macmillan.

weak executive functioning A condition in which parents lack the leverage required to direct their children.

Example: The parents in a family believe they have no way to control what time their son comes home at night. They do not know how to execute their roles as parental figures.

Aponte, H., & van Deusen, J. (1981). Structural family therapy. In A. S. Gurman & D. P. Kniskern (Eds.), *Handbook of family therapy* (pp. 310-360). New York: Brunner/Mazel.

W

weekend family marathon An arrangement in which the family unit comes together for extended periods of time, with facilitators or leaders conducting a variety of intensive encounters.

Bosco, A. (1977). *Marriage encounter: Rediscovery of love.* St. Meinrad, IN: Abby Press.
L'Abate, L. (1981). Skill training programs for couples and families. In A. S. Gurman & D. P. Kniskern (Eds.), *Handbook of family therapy* (pp. 631-662). New York: Brunner/Mazel.

whom spoken to A variable denoting the target of the speech in family interaction research.

Mishler, E., & Waxler, N. (1968). *Interaction in families: An experimental study of family processes and schizophrenia.* New York: John Wiley.

Riskin, J., & Faunce, E. (1972). An evaluative review of family interaction research. *Family Process, 11,* 365-455.

who-speaks   A variable indicating the number of times each family member speaks in family interaction research. It usually is involved in the analysis of the variables of dominance, control, and power.

Lennard, H., & Bernstein, A. (1969). *Patterns in human interaction.* San Francisco: Jossey-Bass.

Riskin, J., & Faunce, E. (1972). An evaluative review of family interaction research. *Family Process, 11,* 365-455.

who-speaks-to-whom   A pattern of interpersonal communication analyzed in family interaction research.

Mishler, E., & Waxler, N. (1968). *Interaction in families: An experimental study of family processes and schizophrenia.* New York: John Wiley.

Riskin, J., & Faunce, E. (1972). An evaluative review of family interaction research. *Family Process, 11,* 365-455.

widower's syndrome   A man, following the death of his wife, is unable to perform sexually with a new partner. This phenomenon may be due to not enough time having elapsed, and the man is still mourning; consequently he is unable to function sexually.

LoPiccolo, J., & Friedman, J. (1988). Broad-spectrum treatment of low sexual desire. In S. Leiblum & R. Rosen (Eds.), *Sexual desire disorders* (pp. 107-144). New York: Guilford.

wife abuse   See **spouse abuse.**

withdrawal of positive reinforcement   A behavioral therapy technique in which a pleasant event is removed, denied, or terminated, contingent on the emission of undesirable behavior. Its major effect is to decelerate the behavior it follows.

Example: When a child is disobedient, swimming in the backyard pool is denied for that day.

Patterson, G. (1971). *Families: Application of social learning theory to family life.* Champaign, IL: Research Press.

writing   Written assignments used as a supplemental adjunct to verbal therapy and, in some cases, such as inmates in jail, as the only method of therapy available. Writing can be used together with either primary or secondary prevention, becoming, therefore, either a paratherapeutic or a parapreventive approach. Written assignments consist of at least four types of writing, depending on the degree of structure, varying from little structure, as in *open* writing ("Write whatever comes to your mind."), *focused* ("Write about your depression."), to *guided* ("Answer the following questions about depression."), to the most structured, such as *programmed* writing ("Answer the questions in the first lesson of a series of lessons to help you deal with depression.").

Example: The Bickerson family is referred for therapy because of the frequent fighting and fierce arguments that go on, seemingly continuously. From the first to the second session of therapy, they are asked to set up a time at home for having an argument for an hour, recording it on an audiotape. They are to bring the tape of the argument the next time they are seen for "evaluation" of whether they can be helped or not. After they bring in the tape, they are given the task of making a content analysis of their tape by listening to it and counting how many "You" statements were made, how often the partner's mind was "read," how often the past was brought up, and how many threats, ultimatums, and blackmails were uttered by each partner. After they come back with their count, each of them is given a written lesson dealing with the category highest in its frequency count. Each family member gains insight into his or her own behavior. In addition, they discuss their written lessons with each other during the session and gain more understanding of how their family members interact.

L'Abate, L. (1986). *Systematic family therapy.* New York: Brunner/Mazel.

L'Abate, L. (1992). *Programmed writing: Self-administered approach for interventions with individuals, couples, and families.* Belmont, CA: Brooks/Cole.

L'Abate, L., & Platzman, K. (1991). The practice of programmed writing in therapy and prevention with families. *American Journal of Family Therapy, 19,* 1-10.

W

W

yielding Giving in to someone else's demand or request.

Example: A wife asks her husband to make a behavioral change. The husband responds to her request by saying, "Whatever you say, dear."

Goldstein, M., Judd, L., Rodnick, E., Alkire, A., & Gould, E. (1968). A method for studying social influence and coping patterns within families of disturbed adolescents. *Journal of Nervous and Mental Disease, 148,* 233-251.

yo-yo syndrome A relationship in which a child is pulled toward the parents when they need the child and is pushed away or ignored when the child's own needs come to the fore. Outright parental rejection is never expressed, however; the child simply is teased with love that is never quite delivered or sustained.

Framo, J. (1965). Rationale and techniques of intensive family therapy. In I. Boszormenyi-Nagy & J. Framo (Eds.), *Intensive family therapy: Theoretical and practical aspects* (pp. 143-212). New York: Harper & Row.

Y

zero-sum game   In marital conflicts, both the "winner" and the "loser" of any game are losers because the conflict issues are seldom resolved and the relationship becomes less unified and more individuated. The "win-lose trap" seeks gain at the other's expense. When the loser does not accept defeat (commonplace in marital disagreements), the victory is only an illusion, safe for a time, but sure to be overthrown. This concept has been expressed as a "one-winner," as opposed to a "two-winner," tactic. The former is based on the incorrect assumption that marriage is a zero-sum game; the latter is based on the more accurate assumption that marriage is the essential non-zero-sum game. The issue must be resolved "equitably," rather than intending to "win the battle."

Example: The couple argued about the wife cooking dinner for the husband's friend. Although she would have to work a full day, she complied under pressure to prepare dinner at home, as opposed to her preference to dine out. Following that dinner, she politely excused herself, explaining to her guest that she was tired from a long day at the office; she kindly asked her husband to clean up the dishes. An alternative solution would be for the couple to bring in Chinese food to entertain at home (husband's preference or win) and avoid all cooking and cleaning (wife's preference or win).

Patterson, G. P. (1971). *Families: Application of social learning to family life.* Champaign, IL: Research Press.
Watzlawick, P. (1988). *Ultra-solutions: How to fail most successfully.* New York: Norton.

Z

Z

Professional Organizations and Publications

Mental health professionals have access to professional associations, such as the American Psychological Association, the American Psychiatric Association, the National Association of Social Workers, the American Association for Counseling and Development, and the Division of Psychiatric Mental Health Nursing Practice of the American Nurses Association. These associations require certain educational and training backgrounds and a level of current professional functioning. The associations are involved in the credentialing process, including accreditation and designation of educational programs and, in some cases, nonstatutory certification of individuals. In addition, the associations are usually active in promoting statutory certification and licensure. The associations are involved in setting standards for professional behavior, particularly ethical behavior, and all of these associations have codes of ethics. Continued membership in each association requires a commitment to its code. Ethical violations are dealt with by select committees, which generally try to educate the professional and remedy the situation, rather than punish the individual.

FAMILY PSYCHOLOGY ORGANIZATIONS

For psychologists who are also marriage and family therapists, the Academy of Psychologists in Marital, Sex, and Family Therapy (APMSFT) was founded in 1958. The organization recognized that training in professional psychology does not always provide adequate preparation in marital and family therapy. The organization set professional standards and conducted continuing education programs. APMSFT was associated with the

American Journal of Family Therapy, which originally was called the *Journal of Family Counseling* by its founding editor, Dr. Daniel Araoz, in 1972. He established an association with the then -called National Alliance for Family Life, Inc. In 1976, Dr. Richard Sauber renamed the journal, becoming the founding editor of the *American Journal of Family Therapy,* changed publishers from Rutgers Press to Brunner/Mazel, and changed the organizational association to the Academy of Psychologists in Marital, Sex, and Family Therapy. Sauber continues to serve as editor-in-chief.

In 1981, the American Board of Family Psychology, Inc. (ABFamP) officially was established for the purpose of setting standards of practice and to recognize master practitioners at the Diplomate level. More than 200 individuals received their Diplomate status from ABFamP. Under the leadership of Drs. George F. Nixon, Jr., Executive Director, and Gerald R. Weeks, President, ABFamP applied to and was accepted into the American Board of Professional Psychology (ABPP). Thus now all Diplomates in Family Psychology are granted by ABPP. The address of the American Board of Professional Psychology is 2100 East Broadway, Suite 313, Columbia, Missouri 65201-6082.

In 1992, the American Board of Professional Psychology reorganized the structure of the specialty boards and the academies. The American Board of Professional Psychology had grown to nine specialties, including family psychology. The Specialty Board of Family Psychology is now responsible for establishing specialty standards; evaluating credentials; designing, administering, and evaluating examinations; and managing credentialing appeals. The document on specialization that first outlined the knowledge base and set the standards for training was written by Drs. Weeks, Nixon, Sauber, Kaslow, and others as a panel of consultants and has been published in the *Family Psychologist* (1991, 7(4)). This document was intended to be an evolving statement that would change as the field continued to grow. Under the new structure, the Academy of Family Psychology became the membership organization for all Diplomates.

The creation of Division 43 (Family Psychology) in 1984 was a major development for the field. (Information about Division 43 can be obtained from the American Psychological Association, Office of Division Affairs, 750 First Street, NW, Washington, DC 20002.) The inclusion of Family Psychology in the official structure of the American Psychological Association serviced to legitimize the field, give it greater visibility, create opportunities to present papers through the annual meeting, led to the development of new journal publications, and gave family psychology a political presence in APA. (For a complete history, the reader may wish to review an unpublished history of family psychology, written by George F. Nixon, Jr., P.O. Box 7977, Waco, Texas, 76714.) In 1987, the first issue of the *Journal of Family Psychology* was published under the editorship of Howard Liddle. By 1992, the *Journal of Family Psychology* officially became the Division 43 journal, thus making it an APA journal. The division also began publishing its own bulletin, called the *Family Psychologist*. This publication presents news items from the division, short articles, book reviews, and so on. Another recent development has been the creation of the journal *Topics in Family Psychology and Counseling* (Aspen Press). As the field continues to expand, there is reason to believe that new journals on family psychology will appear that are further specialized.

In 1990, the International Academy of Family Psychology (IAFP) was established. IAFP serves as the international academic-professional association for researchers and therapists interested in the field of family psychology. IAFP fosters the scientist-practitioner model and promotes cross-cultural research and interventions. Its first president was Dr. Luciano L'Abate. Its U.S. representative is Dr. Florence W. Kaslow. Membership information can be obtained from Kaslow at 2601 North Flagler Drive, Suite 103, West Palm Beach, FL 33407.

FAMILY THERAPY ORGANIZATIONS

The largest organization for marital and family therapists is the American Association of Marriage and Family Therapy (AAMFT). Founded in 1942 as the American Association of Marriage Counselors, and for many years representing the specific discipline of marriage counseling, this organization recently has become recognized as the primary affiliation for family therapists. An interdisciplinary group of leaders established the organization, including Dr. Robert Latou Dickinson, one of the United States' most distinguished gynecologists; Dr. Ernest R. Groves, a pioneer in family life education; psychiatrist Dr. Robert Laidlaw; Dr. Emily Mudd, a social worker and for many years director of the Marriage Council of Philadelphia; and Lester Dearborn, long-time counselor in Boston. Later the group was joined by Dr. Alfred Kinsey, whose research was strongly supported and greatly assisted by a number of AAMFT members.

AAMFT has authority to accredit graduate programs and training centers in marriage and family therapy. In addition, it offers credentials of its own for those who meet certain qualifications of a clinical member, fellow, and approved supervisor. The AAMFT has published an ethical code that includes eight principles: responsibility to clients, competence, integrity, confidentiality, professional responsibility, professional development, research responsibility, and social responsibility. AAMFT has been active in pursuing state certification and licensure for marriage and family therapists.

AAMFT publishes the *Journal of Marital and Family Therapy,* whose current editor is Dr. Douglas Sprenkle; former editors were Drs. Alan Gurman, Florence W. Kaslow, and William C. Nichols. Its association newsletter, *Family Therapy News,* is edited by Nichols. Association information is available at its headquarters: 1100 Seventeenth Street, NW, 10th Floor, Washington, DC 20036.

Another important organization is the American Family Therapy Academy (AFTA). Founded in 1978 and representing the interests of systemic family therapists as distinct from psychodynamic marriage counselors, AFTA has been viewed by some as a rival organization to AAMFT. A joint liaison committee was established between the two organizations, which met for a year from spring 1981. Through the process, the respective roles of the two organizations was clarified, with AAMFT retaining credentialing responsibilities. AFTA was founded under the leadership of Dr. Murray Bowen, following a discussion of the editorial board of *Family Process* (edited by Dr. Donald Bloch) in 1977. Its first officers were Dr. Murray Bowen, president; Dr. Gerald Berenson, executive vice-president; Dr. John Spiegel, vice-president; Dr. James Framo, secretary; and Dr. Geraldine Spark, treasurer. Association objectives are as follows:

1. Advancing family therapy as a science, which regards the entire family as a unit of study
2. Promoting research and professional education in family therapy and allied fields
3. Making information about family therapy available to practitioners in other fields of knowledge and to the public
4. Fostering cooperation among those concerned with medical, psychological, social, legal, and other aspects of the family and those involved in the science and practice of family therapy.

Members of AFTA often are identified as family therapy teachers and researchers, as well as practitioners. Requirements for membership include serving as a teacher of family therapy for at least 5 years and making important contributions to the field. The address of the American Family Therapy Academy is: AFTA, 2020 Pennsylvania Avenue, NW, Suite 273, Washington, DC 20006.

The International Family Therapy Association (IFTA) was founded by Dr. Florence Kaslow in June, 1987, at the International Congress of Family Therapy in Prague, Czechoslovakia, under her leadership and her initial presidency. Since its inception, the membership has grown to more than 1,000 members. It now publishes a semiannual bulletin and co-sponsors international conferences. For more information, contact Dr. Florence

Kaslow, 2601 North Flagler Drive, Suite 103, West Palm Beach, FL 33407.

OTHER ORGANIZATIONS WITH A FAMILY EMPHASIS

The National Council on Family Relations (NCFR) is concerned with a wide variety of issues affecting the family, from basic research and theory to political action. The council has sections on family therapy and on education and enrichment. NCFR sponsors several of the primary journals in the field of family studies, including the *Journal of Marriage and the Family,* the *Journal of Family Issues, Family Relations,* and the *Journal of Family History.* Its headquarters are located at 3989 Central Avenue NE, Suite 550, Minneapolis, Minnesota 55421.

The American Association of Sex Educators, Counselors, and Therapists (AASECT) was founded in 1967 and provides nonstatutory certification for sex educators, counselors, and therapists. AASECT was recognized as the only national interdisciplinary interest group whose charter and central purpose are training, education, and research in sex education and therapy. Standards of training and competency for certification were established in 1972 for sex educators, in 1973 for sex therapists, and in 1977 for sex counselors. AASECT offers publications, tapes, and educational materials for interested professionals. The *Journal of Sex Education and Therapy* is the official publication of AASECT. The association also maintains a national registry of certified health service providers in specialties such as sex education, sex counseling, and sex therapy. Certification also is given for supervisory status. Its central office is located at 11 Dupont Circle, NW, Suite 220, Washington, DC 20036.

A more recent organization committed to standards of training and practice at the Diplomate level is the American Board of Sexology, founded in 1989. Certification is restricted to those holding doctoral degrees in fields related to sexology, with rigorous criteria for set forth in subspecialty areas to achieve Diplomate status and/or Supervisor status. The organization publishes the newsletter *Diplomate.* Its headquarters are located at 2113 S Street, NW, Suite 300, Washington, DC 20008.

Still other family-oriented, interdisciplinary organizations offer a variety of opportunities for professionals to become involved with research, education, and therapy. These groups include:

Academy of Family Mediators
P. O. Box 246
Claremont, CA 91711

American Orthopsychiatric Association
1775 Broadway
New York, NY 10019

Association of Sexologists
1523 Franklin Street
San Francisco, CA 94109

Children's Rights Council
(formerly the National Council for Children's Rights)
220 Eye Street, NE, Suite 230
Washington, DC 20002-4362

Family Resource Coalition
230 N. Michigan Avenue, Suite 1625
Chicago, IL 60601

Family Services Association of America
44 E. 23rd Street
New York, NY 10010

National Academy of Counselors and Family Therapists
(formerly the National Alliance for Family Life, Inc.)
5885 Warner Avenue
Huntington Beach, CA 92649

National Family Life Education Network
1700 Mission Street, Suite 203
P.O. Box 8506
Santa Cruz, CA 95061-8506

Sex Information and Education Council of the United States
84 Fifth Avenue
New York, NY 10011

The Society for the Scientific Study of Sex
P. O. Box 29795
Philadelphia, PA 19117

Washington Coalition of Family Organizations
Cardinal Station
Washington, DC 20064

References

Ackerman, N. W. (1958). *The psychodynamics of family life*. New York: Basic Books.

Ackerman, N. W. (1966). *Treating the troubled family*. New York: Basic Books.

Ackerman, N. W. (1982). Interlocking pathologies. In D. Bloch & R. Simon (Eds.), *The strength of family therapy: Selected papers of Nathan W. Ackerman* (pp. 174-184). New York: Brunner/Mazel.

Ahrons, C. R. (1979). The binuclear family: Two households, one family. *Alternative Lifestyles, 2*, 499-515.

Ahrons, C. R., & Perlmutter, N. S. (1982). The relationship between former spouses: A fundamental subsystem in the remarriage family. In J. C. Hansen & L. Messinger (Eds.), *Therapy with remarriage families* (pp. 31-46). Rockville, MD: Aspen.

Alanen, Y. (1958). The mothers of schizophrenic patients. *Acta Psychiatry Neurological Scandinavian Supplement, 12*, 124.

Alberti, R., & Emmons, M. (1974). *Your perfect right: A guide to assertive behavior*. San Luis Obispo, CA: Impact.

Aldous, T., Condon, T., Hill, R., Straus, M., & Talman, I. (1971). *Family problem solving*. Hinsdale, IL: Dryclere.

Alexander, J. (1988). Phases of family therapy process: A framework for clinicians and researchers. In L. Wynne (Ed.), *The state of the art in family therapy and research: Controversies and recommendations* (pp. 175-187). New York: Family Process Press.

Alexander, J., Barton, C., Lindsey, D., Turner, C., & Warburton, J. (1988). Defensive and supportive communication interaction system. In D. Grotevant & C. Carlson (Eds.), *Handbook of family assessment* (pp. 182-187). New York: Guilford.

Alexander, J., & Parsons, B. V. (1982). *Functional family therapy*. Belmont, CA: Brooks/Cole.

Alger, I. (1976). Integrating immediate video playback in family therapy. In P. J. Guerin (Ed.), *Family therapy: Theory and practice* (pp. 530-548). New York: Gardner.

Alger, I. (1976). Multiple couple therapy. In P. J. Guerin (Ed.), *Family therapy: Theory and practice* (pp. 364-387). New York: Gardner.

Althof, S. (1989). Psychogenic impotence: Treatment of men and women. In S. Leiblum & R. Rosen (Eds.), *Principles and practice of sex therapy* (2nd ed., pp. 237-265). New York: Guilford.

Amaranto, E. (1971). Glossary. In H. Kaplan & B. Sadock (Eds.), *Comprehensive group psychotherapy* (pp. 823-872). Baltimore: Williams & Wilkins.

American Psychiatric Association. (1980). *Diagnostic and statistical manual of mental disorders* (3rd ed.). Washington, DC: Author.

American Psychiatric Association. (1987). *Diagnostic and statistical manual of mental disorders* (3rd ed., rev.). Washington, DC: Author.

Anderson, H., Goolishian, H., & Windermand, L. (1986). Problem-determined systems. *Journal of Strategic and Systemic Therapies, 5,* 1-13.

Anderson, S., & Bagarozzi, D. (1989). *Family myths: Psychotherapy implications.* New York: Haworth.

Anderson, T. (Ed.), (1990). *The reflecting team.* Kent, UK: Borgmann.

Annon, J., & Robinson, C. (1978). The use of vicarious learnings in the treatment of sexual concerns. In J. LoPiccolo & L. LoPiccolo (Eds.), *Handbook of sex therapy* (pp. 35-56). New York: Plenum.

Anonymous. (1972). Toward the differentiation of the self in one's own family. In J. L. Framo (Ed.), *Family interactions* (pp. 111-173). New York: Springer.

Anshacher, H., & Anshacher, R. (1956). *The individual psychology of Alfred Adler.* New York: Harper & Row.

Aponte, H. (1976). The family-school interview: An ecostructural approach. *Family Process, 15,* 303-311.

Aponte, H. (1976). Underorganization in the poor family. In P. J. Guerin (Ed.), *Family therapy: Theory and practice* (pp. 432-448). New York: Gardner.

Aponte, H., & van Deusen, J. (1981). Structural family therapy. In A. S. Gurman & D. P. Kniskern (Eds.), *Handbook of family therapy* (pp. 310-360). New York: Brunner/Mazel.

Appelbaum, B. (1988). An ego-analytic perspective on desire disorders. In S. Leiblum & R. Rosen (Eds.), *Sexual desire disorders* (pp. 75-106). New York: Guilford.

Araoz, D. L. (1981). Negative self-hypnosis. *Journal of Contemporary Psychotherapy, 12,* 45-51.

Araoz, D. L. (1982). *Hypnosis and sex therapy.* New York: Brunner/Mazel.

Ard, B. (1969). Love and aggression: The perils of loving. In B. N. Ard & C. C. Ard (Eds.), *Handbook of marriage counseling* (pp. 50-60). Palo Alto, CA: Science & Behavior Books.

Ard, B. N. (1978). *Rational sex ethics.* Washington, DC: University Press of America.

Ard, C. (1969). The role of nonverbal communication in marriage counseling. In B. N. Ard & C. C. Ard (Eds.), *Handbook of marriage counseling* (pp. 128-138). Palo Alto, CA: Science & Behavior Books.

Argyris, C. (1970). *Intervention: Theory and method.* Reading, MA: Addison-Wesley.

Ascher, L. (1980). Paradoxical intention. In A. Goldstein & E. Foa (Eds.), *Handbook of behavioral interventions* (pp. 266-321). New York: John Wiley.

Auerswald, E. (1968). Interdisciplinary versus ecological approach. *Family Process, 7,* 205-215.

Ayllon, T., & Azrin, N. H. (1968). *The token economy: A motivation system for therapy and rehabilitation.* New York: Appleton.

Azar, S. T., & Wolfe, D. A. (1989). Child abuse and neglect. In E. J. Mash & R. A. Barkley (Eds.), *Treatment of childhood disorders* (pp. 451-489). New York: Guilford.

Azrin, N. H., Master, B. J., & Jones, R. (1973). Reciprocity counseling: A rapid learning-based procedure for marital counseling. *Behavior Research and Therapy, 11,* 365-382.

Azrin, M. H., Sneed, T. J., & Foxx, R. M. (1974). Dry-bed training: Rapid elimination of childhood enuresis. *Behavior Research and Therapy, 12,* 147-156.

Bach, G., & Deutsch, R. (1970). *Pairing.* New York: Avon.

Bach, G., & Goldberg, H. (1974). *Creative aggression.* Garden City, NY: Doubleday.

Bach, G., & Wyden, P. (1968). *The intimate enemy.* New York: William Morrow.

Badenoch, A., Fisher, J., Hafner, J., & Swift, H. (1984). Predicting the outcome of spouse-aided therapy for persisting psychiatric disorders. *American Journal of Family Therapy, 12,* 59-72.

Baisden, M. (1971). *The world of rosaphrenia: The sexual psychology of the female.* Sacramento, CA: Allied Research Society.

Baisden, M., & Baisden, J. (1979). A profile of women who seek counseling for sexual dysfunctions. *American Journal of Family Therapy, 7,* 62-76.

Bakker, C., & Bakker-Rabdau, M. (1973). *No trespassing: Explorations in human territoriality.* San Francisco: Chandler & Sharp.

Bales, R. (1950). *Interaction process analysis: A method for the study of small groups.* Reading, MA: Addison-Wesley.

Bandler, R., & Grinder, J. (1975). *The structure of magic* (Vol. 1). Palo Alto, CA: Science & Behavior Books.

Bandura, A. (1969). *Principles of behavior modification.* New York: Holt, Rinehart & Winston.

Bank, S., & Kahn, M. (1982). *The sibling bond.* New York: Basic Books.

Baptiste, D. A. (1983). Family therapy with reconstituted families: A crisis-induction approach. *American Journal of Family Therapy, 11,* 3-9.

Barker, P. (1981). *Basic family therapy.* Baltimore: University Park Press.

Barkley, R. A. (1987). *Defiant children: A clinician's manual for parent training.* New York: Guilford.

Barkley, R. A. (1990). *Attention deficit hyperactivity disorder: A handbook for diagnosis and treatment.* New York: Guilford.

Barlow, D., & Wincze, J. (1980). Treatment of sexual deviations. In S. Leiblum & L. Pervin (Eds.), *Principles and practice of sex therapy* (pp. 367-376). New York: Guilford.

Barragan, M. (1976). The child-centered family. In P. J. Guerin (Ed.), *Family therapy: Theory and practice* (pp. 232-248). New York: Gardner.

Barth, L. G., & Huber, C. H. (1984). *An introduction to marital theory and therapy.* Belmont, CA: Brooks/Cole.

Bartoletti, M. D., Bourke, P., & McDonald, E. M. (1982). The supportive separation system: A joint legal and marital counseling alternative. In J. C. Hansen & L. Messinger (Eds.), *Therapy with remarriage families* (pp. 79-91). Rockville, MD: Aspen.

Barton, C., & Alexander, J. (1981). Functional family therapy. In A. S. Gurman & D. P. Kniskern (Eds.), *Handbook of family therapy* (pp. 403-443). New York: Brunner/Mazel.

Baruth, L. G., & Huber, C. H. (1984). *An introduction to marital theory and therapy.* Belmont, CA: Brooks/Cole.

Bateson, G. (1936). *Naven.* Cambridge, UK: Cambridge University Press.

Bateson, G. (1958). *Naven* (2nd ed.). Stanford, CA: Stanford University Press.

Bateson, G. (1972). *Steps to an ecology of mind.* New York: Ballantine.

Bateson, G. (1978). The birth of a double bind. In M. Berger (Ed.), *Beyond the double bind* (p. 53). New York: Brunner/Mazel.

Bateson, G. (1987). *Steps to an ecology of mind* (2nd. ed.). New York: Ballantine.

Bateson, G., & Jackson, D. (Eds.). (1968). *Some varieties of pathogenic organization in communication, family, and marriage.* Palo Alto, CA: Science & Behavior Books.

Bateson, G., Jackson, D., Haley, J., & Weakland, J. (1956). Toward a theory of schizophrenia. *Behavioral Science, 1,* 251-264.

Bauman, G., & Roman, M. (1966). Interaction testing in the study of marital dominance. *Family Process, 5,* 230-242.

Beattie, M. (1987). *Co-dependent no more.* New York: Harper/Hazeldon.

Beavers, W. R. (1976). A theoretical basis for family evaluation. In J. M. Lewis, W. R. Beavers, J. T. Gossett, & V. A. Phillips (Eds.), *No single thread: Psychological health in the family system* (pp. 46-82). New York: Brunner/Mazel.

Beavers, W. R. (1977). *Psychotherapy and growth: A family systems perspective*. New York: Brunner/Mazel.

Beck, A. T. (1988). *Love is never enough*. New York: Harper & Row.

Bedford, S. (1969). The "new morality" and marriage counseling. In B. N. Ard & C. C. Ard (Eds.), *Handbook of marriage counseling* (2nd ed., pp. 83-87). Palo Alto, CA: Science & Behavior Books.

Beels, C., & Ferber, A. (1969). Family therapy: A view. *Family Process, 8,* 280-318.

Belkin, G., & Goodman, N. (1980). *Marriage, family, and intimate relationships*. Chicago: Rand McNally.

Bell, J. (1976). A theoretical framework for family group therapy. In P. J. Guerin (Ed.), *Family therapy: Theory and practice* (pp. 129-143). New York: Gardner.

Benjamin, M. (1982). General systems theory, family system theories, and family therapy. In A. Bross (Ed.), *Family therapy: Principles of strategic practice* (pp. 34-88). New York: Guilford.

Bergin, A. E. (1967). Some implications of psychotherapy research for therapeutic practice. *International Journal of Psychiatry, 3,* 136-150.

Berman, E., & Hof, L. (1987). The sexual genogram: Assessing family-of-origin factors in the treatment of sexual dysfunction. In G. Weeks & L. Hof (Eds.), *Integrating sex and marital therapy* (pp. 37-56). New York: Brunner/Mazel.

Bern, S. (1974). The measurements of psychological androgyny. *Journal of Consulting and Clinical Psychology, 42,* 155-162.

Bernard, C., & Corrales, R. (1979). *The theory and technique of family therapy*. Springfield, IL: Charles C Thomas.

Bernard, J. (1981). The good provider role: It's rise and fall. *American Psychologist, 36,* 1-12.

Berne, E. (1961). *Transactional analysis in psychotherapy*. New York: Grove.

Berne, E. (1967). *Games people play*. New York: Grove.

Berscheid, E., & Walster, E. (1978). *Interpersonal attraction* (2nd ed.). Reading, MA: Addison-Wesley.

Bertalanffy, L. von. (1950). An outline of general systems theory. *British Journal of the Philosophy of Science, 1,* 134-165.

Bertalanffy, L. von. (Ed.) (1968). *General systems theory*. New York: Braziller.

Bertalanffy, L. von. (1968). The meaning of general systems theory. In L. von Bertalanffy (Ed.), *General systems theory* (pp. 1095-1120). New York: Braziller.

Bertalanffy, L. von. (1974). General systems therapy and psychiatry. In S. Arieti (Ed.), *American handbook of psychiatry* (Vol. 1, 2nd ed., pp. 1095-1120). New York: Basic Books.

Bion, W. (1960). *Experience in groups*. New York: Basic Books.

Blasis, P., Fischer, J., & Prata, G. (1986). The telephone chart. *Journal of Strategic and Systemic Therapies, 5,* 31-44.

Blechman, E. A., & Manning, M. (1976). A reward-cost analysis of the single-parent family. In E. L. Mash, L. Hamerlynck, & L. Handy (Eds.), *Behavior modification and families* (pp. 61-90). New York: Brunner/Mazel.

Blinder, M., & Kirschenbaum, M. (1969). The technique of married couple group therapy. In B. N. Ard & C. C. Ard (Eds.), *Handbook of marriage counseling* (pp. 233-246). Palo Alto, CA: Science & Behavior Books.

Bloch, D. (1973). The clinical home visit. In D. Block (Ed.), *Techniques of family therapy: A primer* (pp. 39-45). New York: Grune & Stratton.

Bloch, D. (1975). Notes and comments. *Family Process, 1,* 109-110.

Blood, R. (1969). Resolving family conflicts. In B. N. Ard & C. C. Ard (Eds.), *Handbook of marriage counseling* (pp. 329-341). Palo Alto, CA: Science & Behavior Books.

Boat, B. W., & Everson, M. D. (1986). *Using anatomical dolls: Guidelines for interviewing young children in sexual abuse investigations.* Unpublished manuscript, University of North Carolina, Department of Psychiatry, Chapel Hill.

Bodin, A. (1981). The interactional view: Family therapy approaches of the Mental Research Institute. In A. S. Gurman & D. P. Kniskern (Eds.), *Handbook of family therapy* (pp. 267-309). New York: Brunner/Mazel.

Bond, L. A., & Wagner, B. M. (1988). *Families in transition: Primary prevention programs that work.* Newbury Park, CA: Sage.

Bosco, A. (1977). *Marriage encounter: Rediscovery of love.* St. Meinrad, IN: Abby Press.

Boscolo, L., Cecchin, G., Campbell, D., & Draper, R. (1988). Twenty more questions—Selections from a discussion between the Milan associates and the editors. In D. Campbell & R. Draper (Eds.), *Applications of systemic family therapy* (pp. 225-293). New York: Grune & Stratton.

Boscolo, L., Cecchin, G., Hoffman, L., & Penn, P. (1987). *Milan systemic family therapy: Conversations in theory and practice.* New York: Basic Books.

Boszormenyi-Nagy, I. (1962). The concept of schizophrenia from the point of view of family treatment. *Family Process, 1,* 103-113.

Boszormenyi-Nagy, I. (1965). Intensive family therapy as process. In I. Boszormenyi-Nagy & J. Framo (Eds.), *Intensive family therapy: Theoretical and practical aspects* (pp. 87-142). New York: Harper & Row.

Boszormenyi-Nagy, I. (1965). A theory of relationships: Experience and transaction. In I. Boszormenyi & J. Framo (Eds.), *Intensive family therapy: Theoretical and practical aspects* (pp. 33-86). New York: Harper & Row.

Boszormenyi-Nagy, I. (1972). Loyalty implications of the transference model in psychotherapy. *Archives of General Psychiatry, 27,* 374-380.

Boszormenyi-Nagy, I., & Framo, J. (1962). Family concept of hospital treatment of schizophrenia. In J. Masserman (Ed.), *Current psychiatric therapies* (Vol. 2, pp. 159-166). New York: Grune & Stratton.

Boszormenyi-Nagy, I., & Framo, J. (Eds.). (1965). *Intensive family therapy: Theoretical and practical aspects.* New York: Harper & Row.

Boszormenyi-Nagy, I., & Spark, G. L. (1973). *Invisible loyalties: Reciprocity in intergenerational family therapy.* New York: Harper & Row.

Boszormenyi-Nagy, I., & Ulrich, D. (1981). Contextual family therapy. In A. S. Gurman & D. P. Kniskern (Eds.), *Handbook of family therapy* (pp. 159-186). New York: Brunner/Mazel.

Bowen, M. (1960). A family concept of schizophrenia. In D. D. Jackson (Ed.), *The etiology of schizophrenia* (pp. 346-372). New York: Basic Books.

Bowen, M. (1965). Family psychotherapy with schizophrenia in the hospital and in private practice. In I. Boszormenyi-Nagy & J. Framo (Eds.), *Intensive family therapy: Theoretical and practical aspects* (pp. 213-244). New York: Harper & Row.

Bowen, M. (1966). The use of family theory in clinical practice. *Comprehensive Psychiatry, 7,* 345-374.

Bowen, M. (1969). The use of family theory in clinical practice. In B. N. Ard & C. C. Ard (Eds.), *Handbook of marriage counseling* (pp. 139-168). Palo Alto, CA: Science & Behavior Books.

Bowen, M. (1971). Family therapy and family group therapy. In H. Kaplan & B. Sadock (Eds.), *Comprehensive group psychotherapy* (pp. 384-421). Baltimore: Williams & Wilkins.

Bowen, M. (1971). The use of family theory in clinical practice. In J. Haley (Ed.), *Changing families* (pp. 159-192). New York: Grune & Stratton.

Bowen, M. (1975). Family therapy after twenty-five years. In J. Dyrud & D. Freedman (Eds.), *American handbook of psychiatry* (2nd ed., Vol. 5, pp. 367-392). New York: Basic Books.

Bowen, M. (1976). Family reaction to death. In P. J. Guerin (Ed.), *Family therapy: Theory and practice* (pp. 335-348). New York: Gardner.

Bowen, M. (1976). Theory in the practice of psychotherapy. In P. J. Guerin (Ed.), *Family therapy: Theory and practice* (pp. 42-90). New York: Gardner.

Bowen, M. (1978). *Family therapy in clinical practice.* New York: Jason Aronson.

Bowlby, J. (1951). Maternal care and mental health. *Bulletin of the World Health Organization, 3,* 355-384.

Bowlby, J. (1969). *Attachment and loss: Vol. 1 Attachment.* New York: Basic Books.

Bowman, H. (1974). *Marriage for moderns.* New York: McGraw-Hill.

Bradt, J. O. (1980). The family with young children. In E. A. Carter & M. McGoldrick (Eds.), *The family life cycle* (pp. 121-146). New York: Gardner.

Breen, M. J., & Altepeter, T. S. (1990). *Disruptive behavior disorders in children.* New York: Guilford.

Bricklin, B. (1994). *Custom evaluation problems and solutions.* New York: Brunner/Mazel.

Broderick, C., & Schrader, S. (1981). The history of professional marriage and family therapy. In A. S. Gurman & D. P. Kniskern (Eds.), *Handbook of family therapy* (pp. 5-35). New York: Brunner/Mazel.

Brody, W. (1961). The family as the unit of study and treatment: Image, object, and narcissistic relationship. *American Journal of Orthopsychiatry, 31,* 69-73.

Brown, G. W., Monck, E. M., Carstairs, G. M., & Wing, J. K. (1962). Influence on family life in the course of schizophrenic illness. *British Journal of Psychiatry, 16,* 55-68.

Bullard, M. L. (1973). Logical and natural consequences. In H. H. Mosak (Ed.), *Alfred Adler: His influence on psychology today* (pp. 171-174). Park Ridge, NJ: Noyes.

Burgess, A., & Holmstrom, L. (1974). *Rape: Victims of crisis.* Bowie, MD: Brady.

Burgess, E., & Wallin, P. (1953). *Engagement and marriage.* Philadelphia: J. B. Lippincott.

Burns, D. (1980). *Feeling good: The new mood therapy.* New York: New American Library.

Burr, W. R., Hill, R., Nye, F. I., & Reiss, I. L. (Eds.). (1979). *Contemporary theories about the family* (Vols. 1-2). New York: Free Press.

Callahan, E., & Leitenberg, H. (1973). Aversion therapy for sexual deviation: Contingent shock and covert sensitization. *Journal of Abnormal Psychology, 21,* 60-73.

Campbell, D., & Draper, R. (1985). Creating a context for change. In D. Campbell & R. Draper (Eds.), *Applications of systemic family therapy* (pp. 1-8). New York: Grune & Stratton.

Campbell, D., Draper, R., & Huffington, C. (1989). *A systemic approach to consultation.* London: Karnac.

Carnes, P. (1983). *Out of the shadows: Understanding sexual addiction.* Minneapolis: Compcare.

Carroll, J. (1964). Family therapy: Some observations and comparisons. *Family Process, 1,* 180-182.

Carter, E. A., & McGoldrick, M. (1980). The family life cycle and family therapy: An overview. In E. A. Carter & M. McGoldrick (Eds.), *The family life cycle* (pp. 3-20). New York: Gardner.

Carter, E. A., & McGoldrick, M. (Eds.). (1988). *The changing family life cycle: A framework for family therapy* (2nd ed.). New York: Gardner.

Carter, E. A., & McGoldrick-Orfanidis, M. (1976). Family therapy with one person and the family therapist's own family. In P. J. Guerin (Ed.), *Family therapy: Theory and practice* (pp. 193-219). New York: Gardner.

Cashdan, S. (1988). *Object relations therapy: Using the relationship.* New York: Norton.

Christensen, H. T. (1964). Development of the family field of study. In H. T. Christensen (Ed.), *Handbook of marriage and the family* (pp. 3-32). Chicago: Rand McNally.

Christensen, H. T. (Ed.). (1964). *Handbook of marriage and the family.* Chicago: Rand McNally.

Clarke, C. (1969, October). *Group procedures for stimulating awareness and communication of positive feelings between parents and young adults.* Paper presented at the meeting of the Family Life Council, Goldsboro, NC.

Clarke, C. (1970). Group procedures for increasing positive feedback between married partners. *Family Coordinator, 19,* 324-328.

Cochran, S., & Mays, N. (1989). Women and AIDS-related concerns. *American Psychologist, 44,* 529-535.

Colapinto, J. (1982). Structural family therapy. In A. M. Horne & M. M. Ohlsen (Eds.), *Family counseling and therapy* (pp. 112-140). Itasca, IL: F. E. Peacock.

Collins, A. H., & Pancoast, D. L. (1976). *Natural helping network: A strategy for prevention.* Washington, DC: National Association of Social Workers.

Connors, C. K., & Wells, K. C. (1986). *Hyperkinetic children: A psychological approach.* Beverly Hills, CA: Sage.

Constantine, L. L., & Constantine, J. M. (1971). Group and multilateral marriage: Definitional notes, glossary and annotated bibliography. *Family Process, 10,* 157-176.

Constantine, L. L., Constantine, J. M., & Edelman, S. K. (1975). Counseling implications of alternative marriage styles. In A. S. Gurman & D. G. Rice (Eds.), *Couples in conflict* (pp. 124-134). New York: Jason Aronson.

Coogler, O. J. (1978). *Structured mediation in divorce settlement.* Lexington, MA: Lexington.

Cooklin, A. (1974). *Family preoccupation and role in conjoint therapy.* Paper presented to the Royal College of Psychiatrists, London.

Cooley, C. (1909). *Social organization.* New York: Scribner.

Cooper, A. (1969). A clinical study of "coital anxiety" in male potency disorders. *Journal of Psychosomatic Research, 13,* 143.

Corsini, R. J. (1966). *Role playing in psychotherapy: A manual.* Chicago: Aldine.

Courtois, C. (1988). *Healing the incest wound.* New York: Norton.

Cromwell, R. E., & Olson, D. H. (1975). *Power in families.* New York: Halsted.

Cronen, W., & Pearce, W. (1985). Toward an explanation of how the Milan method works: An invitation to a systemic epistemology and the evolution of family systems. In D. Campbell & R. Draper (Eds.), *Applications of systemic family therapy* (pp. 69-84). New York: Grune & Stratton.

Crosby, J. (1976). *Illusion and disillusion in marriage* (2nd ed.). Belmont, CA: Wadsworth.

Cuber, J., & Harroff, P. (1965). *The significant Americans.* New York: Random House.

Cuber, J., & Harroff, P. (1966). *Sex and the significant Americans.* New York: Penguin.

Dail, P. W., & Jewson, R. H. (1986). *In praise of fifty years: The Groves Conference on the conservations of marriage and the family.* Lake Mills, IA: Graphic Publishing.

Davison, G. C. (1966). Differential relaxation and cognitive restructuring in therapy with a "paranoid schizophrenia" or "paranoid state." *Proceedings of the 74th Annual Convention of the American Psychological Association.* Washington, DC: American Psychological Association.

Dell, P. (1982). Beyond homeostasis: Toward a concept of coherence. *Family Process, 21,* 21-41.

Dell, P. (1985). Understanding Bateson and Maturana: Toward a biological foundation for the social sciences. *Journal of Marital and Family Therapy, 11,* 1-20.

de Shazer, S. (1982). *Patterns of brief family therapy.* New York: Guilford.

de Shazer, S. (1985). *Keys to solution in brief therapy.* New York: Norton.

Dewey, J., & Bentley, A. (1949). *Knowing and the known.* Boston: Beacon Hill.

Deykin, E. Y., Patti, P., & Ryan, J. (1988). The fathers of adopted children: A study of the impact of the child surrender on birth fathers. *American Journal of Orthopsychiatry, 58,* 240-248.

Dicks, H. (1964). Concepts of marital diagnosis and therapy as developed at the Tavistock Family Psychiatric Units, London, England. In E. M. Nash, L. Jessner, & D. W. Abse (Eds.), *Marriage counseling in medical practice.* Chapel Hill: University of North Carolina Press.

Dicks, H. V. (1967). *Marital tensions.* London: Routledge & Kegan Paul.

Dilts, R., & Green, J. D. (1982). Applications of neurolinguistic programming in family therapy. In A. M. Horne & M. M. Ohlsen (Eds.), *Family counseling and therapy* (pp. 214-244). Itasca, IL: F. E. Peacock.

Dilts, R., Grinder, J., Bandler, R., Cameron-Bandier, L., & DeLozier, I. (1980). *Neurolinguistic programming* (Vol. 1). Cupertino, CA: Meta Publications.

Dinkmeyer, D., & McKay, G. D. (1976). *Systematic training for effective parenting.* Circle Pines, MN: American Guidance Service.

Dinkmeyer, D., Pew, W., & Dinkmeyer, D. (1979). *Adlerian counseling and psychotherapy.* Belmont, CA: Wadsworth.

Dodson, L., & Kurpuis, D. (1977). *Family counseling: A systems approach.* Muncie, IN: Accelerated Development.

Doherty, W. J. (1991). Family therapy goes postmodern. *Family Therapy Networker, 15,* 36-42.

Doherty, W. J., & Baird, M. A. (1983). *Family therapy and family medicine.* New York: Guilford.

Dollard, J., & Miller, N. (1950). *Personality and psychotherapy.* New York: McGraw-Hill.

Douglas, V. I. (1983). Attention and cognitive problems. In M. Rutter (Ed.), *Developmental neuropsychiatry* (pp. 280-329). New York: Guilford.

Dreikurs, R. (1964). *Children: The challenge.* New York: Hawthorn/Dutton.

Dreikurs, R., Gould, S., & Corsini, R. J. (1974). *Family council.* Chicago: Contemporary Books.

Drever, J. (1952). *A dictionary of psychology.* New York: Penguin.

Duhl, B., & Duhl, F. (1981). Integrative family therapy. In A. S. Gurman & D. P. Kniskern (Eds.), *Handbook of family therapy* (pp. 483-513). New York: Brunner/Mazel.

Duhl, B. S. (1983). *From the inside out and other metaphors.* New York: Brunner/Mazel.

Duhl, F., Kantor, D., & Duhl, B. (1973). Learning, space and action in family therapy: A primer of sculpture. In D. Bloch (Ed.), *Techniques of family psychotherapy* (pp. 47-63). New York: Grune & Stratton.

Duvall, E. (1977). *Marriage and family development* (5th ed.). Philadelphia: J. B. Lippincott.

Dym, B., & Berman, S. (1985). Family systems medicine: Family therapy's next frontier? *Family Therapy Networker, 9,* 20-29, 66.

Eastman, K. S. (1982). Foster parenthood: A nonnormative parenting agreement. In M. B. Sussman & H. Gross (Eds.), *Alternative to traditional family living* (pp. 95-120). New York: Hawthorn Press.

Edleson, J. L., Eisikobits, Z., & Guttman, N. E. (1985). Men who batter women. *Journal of Family Issues, 6,* 229-247.

Efran, J. S., Lukens, R. J., & Lukens, M. D. (1988). Constructivism: What's in it for you. *Family Therapy Networker, 12,* 27-35.

Ehrenwald, J. (1958). Neurosis in the family: A study of psychiatric epidemiology. *American Journal of Psychiatry, 115,* 134-142.

Eichel, E., Eichel, Q., & Kule, S. (1988). The technique of coital alignment and its relation to female orgasmic response and simultaneous orgasm. *Journal of Sex and Marital Therapy, 14,* 129-141.

Eliot, T. D. (1948). Handling family strains and shocks. In H. Becker & R. Hill (Eds.), *Family, marriage, and parenthood* (pp. 616-640). Lexington, MA: D. C. Heath.

Ellis, A., & Grieger, R. (1977). *Handbook of rational emotive therapy.* New York: Springer.

Ellis, A., & Harper, R. (1961). *Creative marriage.* New York: Lyle Stuart.

English, H., & English, A. (1958). *A comprehensive dictionary of psychological and psychoanalytic terms.* New York: David McKay.

Epstein, N., & Bishop, D. (1981). Problem-centered systems therapy of the family. In A. S. Gurman & D. P. Kniskern (Eds.), *Handbook of family therapy* (pp. 444-482). New York: Brunner/Mazel.

Epstein, N. B., Bishop, D. S., & Levin, S. (1978). The McMaster model of family functioning. *Journal of Marriage and Family Counseling, 4,* 19-31.

Erickson, M. H., & Rossi, E. (1979). *Hypnotherapy: An exploratory casebook.* New York: Irvington.

Erskine, R. G. (1982). Transactional analysis and family therapy. In A. M. Horne & M. M. Ohlsen (Eds.), *Family counseling and therapy* (pp. 245-275). Itasca, IL: F. E. Peacock.

Erskine, R. G., & Falcman, M. (1979). The racket system: A model for racket analysis. *Transactional Analysis Journal, 9,* 1.

Eshleman, J. R. (1974). *The family: An introduction.* Boston: Allyn & Bacon.

Esterson, A. (1970). *The leaves of spring.* London: Tavostock.

Everett, C. A., Halperin, S., Volgy, S., & Wissler, A. (1989). *Treating the borderline family: A systemic approach.* Boston: Allyn & Bacon.

Everett, C. A., Russell, C. S., & Keller, J. (Eds.). (1992). *Family therapy glossary.* Washington, DC: American Association for Marriage and Family Therapy.

Ferreira, A. (1960). The double bind and delinquent behavior. *Archives of General Psychiatry, 3, 359-367.*

Ferreira, A. (1963). Family myths and homeostasis. *Archives of General Psychiatry, 9,* 457-463.

Ferreira, A. (1964). Interpersonal perceptivity among family members. *American Journal of Orthopsychiatry, 34,* 64-70.

Ferreira, A., & Winter, W. (1965). Family interaction and decision making. *Archives of General Psychiatry, 13,* 214-223.

Ferreira, A., & Winter, W. (1968). Decision-making in normal and abnormal two-child families. *Family Process, 7,* 17-36.

Ferreira, A., & Winter, W. (1968). Information exchange and science in normal and abnormal families. *Family Process, 7,* 251-276.

Ferreira, A., Winter, W., & Poindexter, E. (1966). Some interaction variables in normal and abnormal families. *Family Process, 5,* 65-70.

Fisch, R., Weakland, J., & Segal, L. (1982). *Doing therapy briefly.* San Francisco: Jossey-Bass.

Fisch, R., Weakland, J., & Segal, L. (1982). *The tactics of change.* San Francisco: Jossey-Bass.

Fleck, S. (1960). Family dynamics and origin of schizophrenia. *Psychosomatic Medicine, 22,* 333-344.

Fleck, S. (1972). An approach to family pathology. In G. D. Erickson & T. P. Hogan (Eds.), *Family therapy: An introduction to theory and technique* (pp. 103-119). Belmont, CA: Wadsworth.

Fleck, S. (1972). Family pathology. In G. D. Erickson & T. P. Hogan (Eds.), *Family therapy: An introduction to theory and technique* (pp. 103-119). Belmont, CA: Wadsworth.

Foa, U. G., & Foa, E. B. (1974). *Societal structures of the mind.* Springfield, IL: Charles C Thomas.

Foerster, H. von (1979). Cybernetics of cybernetics. In K. Krippendorff (Ed.), *Communication and control in society* (pp. 5-8). New York: Gordon & Breach.

Fogarty, T. (1976). Marital crisis. In P. J. Guerin (Ed.), *Family therapy: Theory and practice* (pp. 335-350). New York: Gardner.

Foley, V. (1974). *An introduction to family therapy.* New York: Grune & Stratton.

Forward, S. (1989). *Toxic parents.* New York: Bantam.

Framo, J. (1965). Rationale and technique of intensive family therapy. In I. Boszormenyi-Nagy & J. Framo (Eds.), *Intensive family therapy: Theoretical and practical aspects* (pp. 143-212). New York: Harper & Row.

Framo, J. (1965). Systematic research on family dynamics. In I. Boszormenyi-Nagy & J. Framo (Eds.), *Intensive family therapy: Theoretical and practical aspects* (pp. 407-463). New York: Harper & Row.

Framo, J. L. (1981). The integration of marital therapy with sessions with family of origin. In A. S. Gurman & D. P. Kniskern (Eds.), *Handbook of family therapy* (pp. 133-158). New York: Brunner/Mazel.

Framo, J. L. (1982). *Explorations in marital and family therapy. Selected papers of James L. Framo.* New York: Springer.

Frankl, V. (1955). *The doctor and the soul: From psychotherapy to logotherapy.* New York: Knopf.

Fredman, N., & Sherman, R. (1987). *Handbook of measurements for marriage and family therapy.* New York: Brunner/Mazel.

Freud, S. (1957). The unconscious. In J. Strachey (Ed.), *The standard edition of the complete psychological works of Sigmund Freud* (Vol. 14, pp. 166-204). London: Hogarth.

Fried, E. (1971). Basic concepts in group psychotherapy. In H. Kaplan & B. Sadock (Eds.), *Comprehensive group psychotherapy* (pp. 47-71). Baltimore: Williams & Wilkins.

Friel, J., & Friel, L. (1988). *Adult children: The secrets of dysfunctional families.* Deerfield Beach, FL: Health Communications.

Fromm-Reichmann, F. (1948). Notes on the development of schizophrenia by psychoanalytic psychotherapy. *Psychiatry, 11,* 267-277.

Fuhr, R., Moos, R., & Dishotsky, N. (1981). The use of family assessment and feedback in ongoing family therapy. *American Journal of Family Therapy, 9,* 24-36.

Gardner, R. A. (1986). *Child custody litigation: A guide for parents and mental health professionals.* Cresskill, NJ: Creative Therapeutics.

Gardner, R. A. (1987). *The parental alienation syndrome and the differentiation between fabricated and genuine child sex abuse.* Cresskill, NJ: Creative Therapeutics.

Gardner, R. A. (1989). *Family evaluation in child custody mediation, arbitration, and litigation.* Cresskill, NJ: Creative Therapeutics.

Garrett, W. (1982). *Seasons of marriage and family life.* New York: Holt, Rinehart & Winston.

Gehring, D. D. (1982). The counselor's "duty to warn." *Personnel and Guidance Journal, 61,* 208-210.

Gelles, R. (1974). *The violent home: A study of physical aggression between husbands and wives.* Beverly Hills, CA: Sage.

Gerson, M., & Barsky, M. (1979). For the new family therapist: A glossary of terms. *American Journal of Family Therapy, 7,* 15-30.

Gerstel, N., & Gross, H. E. (1983). Commuter marriage: Couples who live apart. In E. Macklin & R. Rubin (Eds.), *Contemporary families and alternate lifestyles* (pp. 180-193). Beverly Hills, CA: Sage.

Ginker, R. R. (1971). Biomedical education on a system. *Archives of General Psychiatry, 24,* 291-297.

Glass, B. L. (1984). No-fault divorce law. *Journal of Family Issues, 5,* 47-69.

Gleitman, H. (1981). *Psychology.* New York: Norton.

Glick, I. D., Clarkin, J. P., & Kessler, D. P. (1987). *Marital and family therapy* (3rd ed.). New York: Grune & Stratton.

Goetting, A. (1980). Former spouse-current spouse relationships. *Journal of Family Issues, 1,* 58-80.

Goldberg, M. (1987). Understanding hypersexuality in men and women. In G. Weeks & L. Hof (Eds.), *Integrating sex and marital therapy* (pp. 202-220). New York: Brunner/Mazel.

Goldenson, R. (Ed.). (1924). *Longman dictionary of psychology and psychiatry.* New York: Longman.

Goldschmidt, W. (1971). Areta-motivation and models for behavior. In I. Galdston (Ed.), *The interface between psychiatry and anthropology* (pp. 55-87). New York: Brunner/Mazel.

Goldstein, M., Gould, E., Alkire, A., Rodrick, E., & Judd, L. (1970). Interpersonal themes in the Thematic Apperception Test stories of families of disturbed adolescents. *Journal of Nervous and Mental Disease, 100,* 354-365.

Goldstein, M., Judd, L., Rodnick, E., Alkire, A., & Gould, E. (1968). A method for studying social influence and coping patterns within families of disturbed adolescents. *Journal of Nervous and Mental Disorders, 148,* 233-251.

Goldstein, S., & Goldstein, M. (1990). *Managing attention disorders in children.* New York: John Wiley.

Goode, W. (1960). A theory of role. *American Sociological Review, 25,* 423-496.

Goodrich, D., & Boomer, D. (1963). Experimental assessment of modes of conflict resolution. *Family Process, 2,* 15-24.

Goodwin, H. M., & Mudd, E. H. (1969). Marriage counseling: Methods and goals. In B. N. Ard & C. C. Ard (Eds.), *Handbook of marriage counseling* (pp. 93-105). Palo Alto, CA: Science & Behavior Books.

Gordon, T. (1970). *Parent effectiveness training.* New York: Peter H. Wyden.

Gordon, T. (1982). *P.E.T. in action.* New York: Bantam.

Gottman, M. (1979). *Marital interaction.* New York: Academic Press.

Gottschalk, L., & Davidson, R. (1971). Sensitivity groups, encounter groups, training groups, marathon groups, and the laboratory movement. In H. Kaplan & B. Sadock (Eds.), *Comprehensive group psychotherapy* (pp. 422-459). Baltimore: Williams & Wilkins.

Green, D. R., Budd, K., Johnson, M., Larg, S., Pinkston, E., & Rudd, S. (1976). Training parents to modify problem child behaviors. In E. J. Marsh, L. C. Handy, & L. A. Hamerlynck (Eds.), *Behavior modification approach to parenting* (pp. 3-18). New York: Brunner/Mazel.

Greenberg, J. R., & Mitchell, S. A. (1983). *Object relations and psychoanalytic theory.* Cambridge, MA: Harvard University Press.

Greene, B., & Solomon, A. (1963). Marital disharmony: Concurrent psychoanalytic therapy of husband and wife by the same psychiatrist. *American Journal of Psychiatry, 17,* 443-450.

Greenspan, S., & Mannino, M. (1974). A model for brief intervention with couples based on projective identification. *American Journal of Psychiatry, 131,* 1103-1106.

Grinder, J., & Bandler, R. (1976). *The structure of magic* (Vol. 2). Palo Alto, CA: Science & Behavior Books.

Grotevant, H. D., & Carlson, C. I. (1989). *Family assessment.* New York: Garner.

Guerin, P., & Pendergast, E. (1976). Evaluation of family system and genogram. In P. J. Guerin (Ed.), *Family therapy: Theory and practice* (pp. 450-465). New York: Gardner.

Guerney, B. (1964). Filial therapy: Description and rationale. *Journal of Consulting Psychology, 28,* 304-310.

Guerney, B. G. (1977). *Relationship enhancement: Skill training programs for therapy, problem prevention and enrichment.* San Francisco: Jossey-Bass.

Gurman, A. (1978). Contemporary marital therapies. In T. Paolino & B. McCrady (Eds.), *Marriage and marital therapy* (pp. 445-566). New York: Brunner/Mazel.

Gurman, A., & Kniskern D. (1978). Research on marital and family therapy: Progress, perspective, and prospect. In S. Garfield & A. Bergin (Eds.), *Handbook of psychotherapy and behavior change* (pp. 817-901). New York: John Wiley.

Hafner, R. (1981). Spouse-aided therapy in psychiatry: An introduction. *Australian and New Zealand Journal of Psychiatry, 15,* 329-337.

Haley, J. (1959). The family of the schizophrenic: A model system. *Journal of Nervous and Mental Disease, 129,* 357-374.

Haley, J. (1959). An interactional description of schizophrenia. *Psychiatry, 22,* 321-332.

Haley, J. (1963). Marriage therapy. *Archives of General Psychiatry, 8,* 213-234.

Haley, J. (1963). *Strategies of psychotherapy.* New York: Grune & Stratton.

Haley, J. (Ed.). (1971). *Changing families.* New York: Grune & Stratton.

Haley, J. (1972). The family of the schizophrenic. In G. D. Erickson & T. P. Hogan (Eds.), *Family therapy: An introduction to theory and technique* (pp. 51-75). Belmont, CA: Wadsworth.

Haley, J. (1977). Toward a theory of pathological systems. In P. Watzlawick & J. Weakland (Eds.), *The interactional view* (pp. 11-27). New York: Norton.

Haley, J. (1984). *Ordeal therapy.* San Francisco: Jossey-Bass.

Haley, J. (1987). *Problem-solving therapy* (2nd ed.). San Francisco: Jossey-Bass.

Haley, J., & Hoffman, L. (1967). *Techniques of family therapy.* New York: Basic Books.

Hall, C., & Lindzey, G. (1970). *Theories of personality.* New York: John Wiley.

Handel, G. (1967). Analysis of correlative meaning: The TAT in the study of whole families. In G. Handel (Ed.), *The psychosocial interior of the family: A source book for the study of whole families* (pp. 104-124). Chicago: Aldine.

Hansen, C. (1969). An extended home visit with conjoint family therapy. *Family Process, 7,* 67-87.

Hansen, J. C., & L'Abate, L. (1982). *Approaches to family therapy.* New York: Macmillan.

Harbin, H. (1977). Episodic dyscontrol and family dynamics. *American Journal of Psychiatry, 134,* 1113-1116.

Harlow, H. (1958). The nature of love. *American Psychologist, 13,* 673-685.

Harper, R. (1969). Marriage counseling as rational process-oriented psychotherapy. In B. N. Ard & C. C. Ard (Eds.), *Handbook of marriage counseling* (pp. 115-119). Palo Alto, CA: Science & Behavior Books.

Heiman, J. (1978). Uses of psychophysiology in assessment and treatment of sexual dysfunction. In J. LoPiccolo & L. LoPiccolo (Eds.), *Handbook of sex therapy* (pp. 123-136). New York: Plenum.

Held, B. (1990). What's in a name? Some confusion and concerns about constructivism. *Journal of Marital and Family Therapy, 16,* 179-189.

Hendrix, H. (1988). *Getting the love you want: A guide for couples.* New York: Harper & Row.

Hess, R., & Handel, G. (1959). *Family worlds: A psychological approach to family life.* Chicago: University of Chicago Press.

Higgins, G. (1978). Aspects of several responses in adults with spinal cord injury: A review of the literature. In J. LoPiccolo & L. LoPiccolo (Eds.), *Handbook of sex therapy* (pp. 387-410). New York: Plenum.

Hill, R., & Hensen, D. (1962). Families in disaster. In G. Baker and D. Chapman (Eds.), *Man and society in disaster* (pp. 185-221). New York: Basic Books.

Hinsie, L., & Campbell, B. (1970). *Psychiatric dictionary* (4th ed.). New York: Oxford University Press.

Hof, L. (1987). Evaluating the marital relationship of clients with sexual complaints. In G. Weeks & L. Hof (Eds.), *Integrating sex and marital therapy* (pp. 5-22). New York: Brunner/Mazel.

Hof, L., & Berman, E. (1986). The sexual genogram. *Journal of Marital and Family Therapy, 12,* 39-47.

Hoffman, L. (1973). Deviation-amplifying processes in natural groups. In J. Haley (Ed.), *Changing families* (pp. 285-311). New York: Grune & Stratton.

Hoffman, L. (1981). *Foundations of family therapy.* New York: Basic Books.

Hoffman, L. (1982). A co-evolutionary framework for systemic family therapy. *Australian Journal of Family Therapy, 4,* 9-21.

Hoffman, L. (1990). Constructing realities: An art of lenses. *Family Process, 29,* 1-12.

Hogan, P. (1963). The content-context syndrome. *Newsletter, Society for Medical Psychoanalysts, 4,* 1-6.

Homme, L., & Tosti, D. (1969). Contingency management and motivation. In D. Gelfand (Ed.), *Social learning in childhood: Readings in theory and application* (pp. 000-000). Belmont, CA: Brooks/Cole.

Hoopes, M., & Harper, J. (1987). *Birth order roles and sibling positions in individual, marital and family therapy.* Rockville, MD: Aspen Systems.

Hoopes, M. H., Fisher, B. L., & Barlow, S. H. (Eds.). (1984). *Structured family facilitation programs: Enrichment, education, and treatment.* Rockville, MD: Aspen Systems.

Horne, A. M. (1982). Counseling families—Social learning family therapy. In A. M. Horne & M. M. Ohlsen (Eds.), *Family counseling and therapy* (pp. 360-388). Itasca, IL: F. E. Peacock.

Horne, A. M., & Ohlsen, M. M. (Eds.). (1982). *Family counseling and therapy.* Itasca, IL: F. E. Peacock.

Howells, J. (1975). *Principles of family psychiatry.* New York: Brunner/Mazel.

Humphrey, F. (1987). Treating extramarital sexual relationships in sex and couples therapy. In G. Weeks & L. Hof (Eds.), *Integrating sex and marital therapy* (pp. 149-170). New York: Brunner/Mazel.

Huntington, D. S. (1982). Attachment loss and divorce: A reconsideration of the concepts. In J. C. Hansen & L. Messinger (Eds.), *Therapy with remarriage families* (pp. 17-28). Rockville, MD: Aspen.

Imber-Black, E. (1988). *Families in larger systems.* New York: Guilford.

Imber-Black, E. (1988). Ritual themes in families and family therapy. In E. Imber-Black, J. Roberts, & R. Whiting (Eds.), *Rituals in families and family therapy* (pp. 47-83). New York: Norton.

Isaacs, M. B. (1982). Facilitating family restructuring and re-linkage. In J. C. Hansen & L. Messinger (Eds.) *Therapy with remarriage families* (pp. 121-144). Rockville, MD: Aspen.

Jabob, T., & Tennebaum, D. L. (1988). *Family assessment: Rationale, methods, and future directions.* New York: Plenum.

Jackson, D. (1965). Family rules: The marital quid pro quo. *Archives of General Psychiatry, 12,* 589-594.

Jackson, D. (1968). The question of family homeostasis. In D. Jackson (Ed.), *Communication, family, and marriage* (pp. 1-11). Palo Alto, CA: Science & Behavior Books.

Jackson, D., & Lederer, W. (1968). *The mirages of marriage.* New York: Norton.

Jackson, D., & Weakland, J. (1961). Conjoint family therapy. *Psychiatry, 24,* 30-45.

Jacobson, N. (1978). A review of the research on the effectiveness of marital therapy. In T. Paolino & B. McCrady (Eds.), *Marriage and marital therapy* (pp. 395-444). New York: Brunner/Mazel.

Jacobson, N. S., & Margolin, G. (1979). *Marital therapy: Strategies based on social learning and behavior exchange principles.* New York: Brunner/Mazel.

Jessee, E., & L'Abate, L. (1982). The paradoxes of depression. *International Journal of Family Psychiatry, 3,* 175-187.

Jessee, E., & L'Abate, L. (1983). Intimacy and marital depression: Interactional partners. *International Journal of Family Therapy, 9,* 39-53.

John, D. (1979). *Sexual dysfunctions.* New York: John Wiley.

Johnson, A. M., & Fishback, D. (1944). Analysis of a disturbed adolescent girl and the collaborative psychiatric treatment of the mother. *American Journal of Orthopsychiatry, 14,* 195-203.

Johnson, C., & Johnson, F. (1977). Attitudes toward parenting in dual-career families. *American Journal of Psychiatry, 134,* 391-394.

Jourard, S. M. (1971). *The transparent self* (2nd ed.). New York: Van Nostrand.

Jung, C. (1964). *Man and his symbols.* Garden City, NY: Doubleday.

Kagan, S., Powell, D. R., Weissbound, B., & Zigler, E. F. (1987). *America's family support programs.* New Haven, CT: Yale University Press.

Kahn, A. H., & Kamerman, S. B. (1982). *Helping America's families.* Philadelphia: Temple University Press.

Kanfer, F., & Phillips, J. (1970). *Learning foundations of behavior therapy.* New York: John Wiley.

Kanfer, F. H. (1977). The many faces of self-control, or behavior modification changes its focus. In R. B. Stuart (Ed.), *Behavioral self-management* (pp. 1-48). New York: Brunner/Mazel.

Kantor, D., & Lehr, W. (1975). *Inside the family: Toward a theory of family process.* San Francisco: Jossey-Bass.

Kaplan, A., & Sidney, M. (1980). *Psychology and sex roles: An androgynous perspective.* Boston: Little, Brown.

Kaplan, H. S. (1974). *The new sex therapy.* New York: Brunner/Mazel.

Kaplan, H. S. (1979). *Disorders of sexual desire.* New York: Brunner/Mazel.

Kaplan, H. S. (1983). *The evaluation of sexual disorders.* New York: Brunner/Mazel.

Kaplan, H. S. (1987). *Sexual aversion, sexual phobia, and panic disorder.* New York: Brunner/Mazel.

Kaplan, H., & Sadock, B. (Eds.). (1971). *Comprehensive group psychotherapy.* Baltimore: Williams & Wilkins.

Karacan, I. (1978). Advances in the psychophysiological evaluation of male erectile impotence. In J. LoPiccolo & L. LoPiccolo (Eds.), *Handbook of sex therapy* (pp. 137-146). New York: Plenum.

Karpel, M. (1980). Family Secrets: I. Conceptual and ethical issues in the relational context. II. Ethical and practical considerations in therapeutic management. *Family Process, 19,* 295-306.

Karpman, S. (1968). Script drama analysis. *Transactional Analysis Bulletin, 26,* 39-43.

Kaslow, F. (1981). Divorce and divorce therapy. In A. S. Gurman & D. P. Kniskern (Eds.), *Handbook of family therapy* (pp. 662-698). New York: Brunner/Mazel.

Kaslow, F. (1991). *Voices in family psychology.* Newbury Park, CA: Sage.

Kaslow, F. W. (1987). Marital and family therapy. In M. B. Sussman and S. K. Steinmetz (Eds.), *Handbook of marriage and the family* (pp. 835-859). New York: Plenum.

Kaslow, F. W., & Schwartz, L. L. (1989). *Dynamics of divorce: A life cycle perspective.* New York: Brunner/Mazel.

Katkins, S. (1978). Charting as a multi-purpose treatment intervention in family therapy. *Family Process, 17,* 465-468.

Kazdin, A. E. (1989). Childhood depression. In E. G. Mash & R. A. Barkley (Eds.), *Treatment of childhood disorders* (pp. 135-166). New York: Guilford.

Keeney, B. (1979). Ecosystemic epistemology: An alternative paradigm for diagnosis. *Family Process, 18,* 117-129.

Keeney, B. P. (1983). *Aesthetics of change.* New York: Guilford.

Keeney, B. P., & Sprenkle, D. H. (1982). Ecosystemic epistemology: Critical implications for the aesthetics and pragmatics of family therapy. *Family Process, 21,* 1-19.

Kegel, A. H. (1952). Sexual functions of the pubococcygeal muscle. *Western Journal of Surgery, Obstetrics and Gynecology, 60,* 521-524.

Keith, D. V., & Whitaker, C. A. (1982). Experiential/symbolic family therapy. In A. M. Horne & M. M. Ohlsen (Eds.), *Family counseling and therapy* (pp. 43-74). Itasca, IL: F. E. Peacock.

Kelly, J. B. (1983). Mediation and psychotherapy: Distinguishing the differences. *Mediation Quarterly, 1,* 33-44.

Kempler, W. (1974). *Principles of Gestalt family therapy.* Oslo, Norway: A. S. John Nordahl Trykkery.

Kempler, W. (1981). *Experiential psychotherapy within families.* New York: Brunner/Mazel.

Kendall, P. C., & Braswell, L. (1985). *Cognitive-behavioral therapy for impulsive children.* New York: Guilford.

Kernberg, O. (1976). *Object relations theory and pathological narcissism.* New York: Jason Aronson.

Kerr, M. (1981). Family systems theory and therapy. In A. S. Gurman & D. P. Kniskern (Eds.), *Handbook of family therapy* (pp. 226-264), New York: Brunner/Mazel.

Kerr, M. E., & Bowen, M. (1988). *Family evaluation: A approach based on Bowen theory.* New York: Norton.

Kiesler, D. (1973). *The process of psychotherapy: Empirical foundations and systems of analysis.* Chicago: Aldine.

Kline-Graber, G., & Graber, B. (1978). Diagnosis and treatment procedures of pubococcygeal deficiencies in women. In J. LoPiccolo & L. LoPiccolo (Eds.), *Handbook of sex therapy* (pp. 227-240). New York: Plenum.

Kluckhohn, F. R., & Spiegel, J. P. (1954). *Integration and conflict in family behavior* (Report No. 27). Topeka, KS: Group for the Advancement of Psychiatry.

Knopf, I. (1979). *Childhood psychopathology: A developmental approach.* Englewood Cliffs, NJ: Prentice-Hall.

Koestler, A. (1979). *Janus: A summing up.* New York: Vintage.

Koocher, G. P., & Keith-Spiegel, P. C. (1990). *Children, ethics, and the law.* Lincoln: University of Nebraska Press.

Korzybski, A. (1933). *Science and sanity.* Lancaster, PA: International Non-Aristotelian Library.

Kovacs, M., & Beck, A. T. (1977). An empirical clinical approach towards a definition of childhood depression. In J. G. Schulterbrandt & A. Raskin (Eds.), *Depression in children: Diagnosis, treatment, and conceptual models* (pp. 1-25). New York: Raven.

Kubie, L. (1956). Psychoanalysis and marriage: Practical and theoretical issues. In V. Eisenstein (Ed.), *Neurotic interaction in marriage* (pp. 10-43). New York: Basic Books.

Kubler-Ross, E. (1969). *On death and dying.* New York: Macmillan.

Kwiatkowska, H. Y. (1978). *Family therapy and evaluation through art.* Springfield, IL: Charles C Thomas.

L'Abate, L. (1975). Pathogenic role rigidity in fathers: Some observations. *Journal of Marriage and Family Counseling, 1,* 69-79.

L'Abate, L. (1976). *Understanding and helping the individual in the family.* New York: Grune & Stratton.

L'Abate, L. (1977). Intimacy is sharing hurt feelings: A reply to David Mace. *Journal of Marriage and Family Counseling, 3,* 13-16.

L'Abate, L. (1981). The role of family conferences in family therapy. *Family Therapy, 8,* 33-38.

L'Abate, L. (1981). Skill training programs for couples and families. In A. S. Gurman & D. P. Kniskern (Eds.), *Handbook of family therapy* (pp. 631-662). New York: Brunner/Mazel.

L'Abate, L. (1983). *Family psychology: Theory, therapy, and training.* Washington, DC: University Press of America.

L'Abate, L. (1983). Styles in intimate relationships: The A-R-C model. *Personnel and Guidance Journal, 61,* 277-283.

L'Abate, L. (1985). Descriptive and explanatory concepts in family therapy: Distance, defeats, and dependency. In L. L'Abate (Ed.), *Handbook of family psychology and therapy* (Vols. 1 & 2, pp. 1218-1248). Homewood, IL: Dow Jones-Irwin.

L'Abate, L. (1985). Structured enrichment (SE) with couples and families. *Family Relations, 34,* 169-175.

L'Abate, L. (1986). Prevention of marital and family problems. In B. A. Edelstein & L. Michelson (Eds.), *Handbook of prevention* (pp. 177-193). New York: Plenum.

L'Abate, L. (1986). *Systematic family therapy.* New York: Brunner/Mazel.

L'Abate, L. (1987). *Family psychology: Theory, therapy, enrichment, and training.* Washington, DC: University Press of America.

L'Abate, L. (1990). *Building family competence: Primary and secondary prevention strategies.* Newbury Park, CA: Sage.

L'Abate, L. (1992). *Programmed writing: Self-administered approach for interventions with individuals, couples, and families.* Belmont, CA: Brooks/Cole.

L'Abate, L., & Bagarozzi, D. A. (1993). *Sourcebook of marriage and family evaluation.* New York: Brunner/Mazel.

L'Abate, L., Baggett, M. S., & Anderson, J. S. (1983). Linear and circular interventions with families of children with school related problems. In B. F. Okun (Ed.), *Family therapy with school related problems* (pp. 13-27). Rockville, MD: Aspen Systems.

L'Abate, L., & Frey, J. (1981). The E-R-A model. *Journal of Marital and Family Therapy, 9,* 143-150.

L'Abate, L., & L'Abate, B. (1979). The paradoxes of intimacy. *Family therapy, 6,* 175-184.

L'Abate, L., & McHenry, S. (1983). *Handbook of marital intervention.* New York: Grune & Stratton.

L'Abate, L., & Platzman, K. (1991). The practice of programmed writing in therapy and prevention with families. *American Journal of Family Therapy, 19,* 1-10.

L'Abate, L., & Rupp, G. (1981). *Enrichment: Skill training for family life.* Washington, DC: University Press of America.

L'Abate, L., & Sloan, S. (1984). A workshop format to facilitate intimacy in married couples. *Family Relations, 33,* 245-250.

L'Abate, L., Sloan, S. Z., Wagner, V., & Malone, K. (1980). The differentiation of resources. *Family Therapy, 7,* 237-246.

L'Abate L., Weeks, G., & Weeks, K. (1979). Of scapegoats, strawmen, and scarecrows. *International Journal of Family Counseling, 1,* 86-96.

L'Abate, L., & Weinstein, S. (1987). *Structured enrichment programs for couples and families.* New York: Brunner/Mazel.

L'Abate, L., & Young, L. (1987). *Sourcebook of structured enrichment programs for couples and families.* New York: Brunner/Mazel.

Laing, R. D. (1965). Mystification, confusion, and conflict. In I. Boszormenyi-Nagy & J. Framo (Eds.), *Intensive family therapy* (pp. 343-364). New York: Harper & Row.

Laing, R. D. (1967). *The politics of experience.* New York: Ballantine.

Laing, R. D. (1969). *The divided self.* New York: Penguin.

Lamb, M., & Sutton-Smith, B. (Eds.). (1982). *Sibling relationship.* Hillsdale, NJ: Lawrence Erlbaum.

Lange, A., & van der Hart, O. (1983). *Directive family therapy.* New York: Brunner/Mazel.

Lankton, S. R., & Lankton, C. H. (1983). *The answer within: A clinical framework of Ericksonian hypnotherapy.* New York: Brunner/Mazel.

Laqueur, H. P. (1972). Mechanisms of change in multiple family therapy. In C. J. Sager & H. S. Kaplan (Eds.), *Progress in group and family therapy* (pp. 400-415). New York: Brunner/Mazel.

Laqueur, H. P. (1976). Multiple family therapy. In P. J. Guerin (Ed.), *Family therapy: Theory and practice* (pp. 405-416). New York: Gardner.

Larsen, E. (1985). *Stage II recovery: Life beyond addiction.* New York: Harper & Row.

Laschet, U., & Laschet, L. (1975). Antiandrogen in the treatment of sexual deviation of men. *Journal of Steroid Biochemistry, 6,* 821-826.

Lazarus, A. (1968). Behavior therapy and marriage counseling. *Journal of the American Society of Psychosomatic Dentistry and Medicine, 15,* 49-56.

Lazarus, A. (1968). Behavior therapy in groups. In G. Gazda (Ed.), *Basic approaches to group psychotherapy and group counseling* (pp. 149-175). Springfield, IL: Charles C Thomas.

Lazarus, A. (1980). Psychological treatment of dyspareunia. In S. Leiblum & L. Pervin (Eds.), *Principles and practice of sex therapy* (pp. 147-166). New York: Guilford.

Lazarus, A. (1988). A multimodal perspective on problems of sexual desire. In S. Leiblum & R. Rosen (Eds.), *Sexual desire disorders* (pp. 145-167). New York: Guilford.

Lebedun, M. (1970). Measuring movement in group marital counseling. *Social Case Work, 51,* 35-43.

LeBow, M. (1972). Behavior modification for the family. In G. D. Erickson & T. P. Hogan (Eds.), *Family therapy: An introduction to theory and technique* (pp. 347-376). Belmont, CA: Wadsworth.

Lederer, W., & Jackson, D. (1968). *The mirages of marriage.* New York: Norton.

Leiblum, S., & Pervin, L. (1980). *Principles and practice of sex therapy.* New York: Guilford.

Leiblum, S., & Rosen, R. (1988). Introduction: Changing perspectives on sexual desire. In S. Leiblum & R. Rosen (Eds.), *Sexual desire disorders* (pp. 1-20) New York: Guilford.

Leichter, E., & Schulman, G. (1968). Emerging phenomena in multifamily group treatment. *International Journal of Group Psychotherapy, 18,* 56-69.

Leichter, E., & Schulman, G. (1972). Emerging phenomena in group treatment. In G. D. Erickson & T. P. Hogan (Eds.), *Family therapy: An introduction to theory and technique* (pp. 327-335). Belmont, CA: Wadsworth.

Lennard, H., & Bernstein, A. (1969). *Patterns in human interaction.* San Francisco: Jossey-Bass.

Leonhard, E. (1977). Toward a new formulation of object relation-systems theory from analysis and family ecology theories. In T. J. Buckley, J. J. McCarthy, E. Norman, & M. A. Quaranta (Eds.), *New directions in family therapy* (pp. 42-56). Oceanside, NY: Dabor.

Levant, R. F. (1984). *Family therapy: A comprehensive overview.* Englewood Cliffs, NJ: Prentice-Hall.

Levant, R. F. (Ed.). (1986). *Psychoeducational approaches to family therapy and counseling.* New York: Springer.

Levenson, E. (1972). *The fallacy of understanding.* New York: Basic Books.

Levine, S. (1988). Intrapsychic and individual aspects of sexual desire. In S. Leiblum & R. Rosen (Eds.), *Sexual desire disorders* (pp. 21-44). New York: Guilford.

Lewin, K. (1951). *Field theory in social science.* New York: Harper & Row.

Lewin, K. (1963). *Field theory in social sciences: Selected theoretical papers* (2nd. ed.). London: Tavistock.

Lewis, J. M., Beavers, W. R., Gossett, J. T., & Phillips, V. A. (1976). *No single thread: Psychological health in the family system.* New York: Brunner/Mazel.

Lewis, R. A., & Spanier, G. B. (1979). Theorizing about the quality and stability of marriage. In N. R. Burr, R. Hill, F. I. Nye, & I. L. Reiss (Eds.), *Contemporary theories about the family* (Vol. 2, pp. 268-291). New York: Free Press.

Liberman, R. (1970). Behavioral approaches to family and couple therapy. *American Journal of Orthopsychiatry, 40,* 106-118.

Liberman, R. (1972). Behavioral approaches to family and couple therapy. In G. D. Erickson & T. P. Hogan (Eds.), *Family therapy: An introduction to theory and technique* (pp. 120-134). Belmont, CA: Wadsworth.

Liddle, H. (1984). Toward a dialectical-contextual-coevolutionary translation of structural-strategic family therapy. *Journal of Strategic and Systemic Therapies, 4,* 66-79.

Lidz, T., Cornelison, A., Fleck, S., & Terru, D. (1957). Schism and skew in families of schizophrenics. *American Journal of Psychiatry, 114,* 241-248.

Lidz, T., Cornelison, A., Terru, D., & Fleck, S. (1958). Intrafamilial environment of the schizophrenic patient. VI: Parental personalities and family interaction. *American Journal of Orthopsychiatry, 28,* 764-776.

Lidz, T., Fleck, S., & Cornelison, A. (1965). Family studies and a theory of schizophrenia. In T. Lidz, S. Fleck, & A. Cornelison (Eds.), *Schizophrenia and the family* (pp. 362-376). New York: International Universities Press.

Lidz, T., Fleck, S., & Cornelison, A. (Eds.). (1965). *Schizophrenia and the family.* New York: International Universities Press.

Lieberman, L., & Lieberman, L. (1986). Husband-wife interaction in second careers. *Journal of Family Issues, 7,* 215-229.

Lipchik, E., & deShazer, S. (1986). The purposeful interview. *Journal of Strategic and Systemic Therapies, 5,* 88-99.

Little, M. (1982). *Family break-up.* San Francisco: Jossey-Bass.

Lobitz, W., & LoPiccolo, J. (1972). New methods in the behavioral treatment of sexual dysfunctions. *Journal of Behavior Therapy and Experimental Psychiatry, 3,* 265-271.

LoPiccolo, J. (1978). Direct treatment of sexual dysfunction. In J. LoPiccolo & L. LoPiccolo (Eds.), *Handbook of sex therapy* (pp. 1-18). New York: Plenum.

LoPiccolo, J. (1978). The professionalization of sex therapy: Issues and problems. In J. LoPiccolo & L. LoPiccolo (Eds.), *Handbook of sex therapy* (pp. 511-526). New York: Plenum.

LoPiccolo, J., & Friedman, J. (1988). Broad-spectrum treatment of low sexual desire. In S. Leiblum & R. Rosen (Eds.), *Sexual desire disorders* (pp. 107-144). New York: Guilford.

LoPiccolo, J., & LoPiccolo, L. (Eds.). (1978). *Handbook of sex therapy.* New York: Plenum.

Loveland, N. (1967). The Relations Rorschach: A technique for studying interaction. *Journal of Nervous and Mental Disease, 142,* 93-105.

Lowen, A. (1975). *Bioenergetics.* New York: Penguin.

Luber, R. F., & Anderson, C. M. (1983). *Family intervention with psychiatric patients.* New York: Human Sciences Press.

Lubin, B., Lubin, A. W., Whiteford, M. G., & Whitlock, R. V. (1988). *Family therapy: A bibliography, 1937-1989.* New York: Greenwood.

Lusk, R., & Waterman, J. (1986). Effects of sexual abuse on children. In K. MacFarland & J. Waterman (Eds.), *Sexual abuse of young children* (pp. 101-118). New York: Guilford.

Lynn, D. (1969). *Parental and sex role identification: A theoretical formulation.* Berkeley, CA: McCutchan.

Mace, D. (Ed.). (1983). *Prevention in family services: Approaches to family wellness.* Beverly Hills, CA: Sage.

MacGregor, R. (1962). Multiple impact psychotherapy with families. *Family Process, 1,* 15-19.

MacGregor, R. (1972). Multiple impact psychotherapy. In G. D. Erickson & T. P. Hogan (Eds.), *Family therapy: An introduction to theory and technique* (pp. 150-163). Belmont, CA: Wadsworth.

MacGregor, R., Ritchie, A., Serrano, A., & Schuster, F. (1964). *Multiple impact therapy with families.* New York: McGraw-Hill.

Macklin, E. (1972). Heterosexual cohabitation among unmarried college students. *Family Coordinator, 11,* 463-472.

Madanes, C. (1981). *Strategic family therapy.* San Francisco: Jossey-Bass.

Madanes, C. (1984). *Behind the one-way mirror.* San Francisco: Jossey-Bass.

Mahlstedt, P. (1987). The crisis of infertility: An opportunity for growth. In G. Weeks & L. Hof (Eds.), *Integrating sex and marital therapy* (pp. 121-148). New York: Brunner/Mazel.

Maltz, W., & Holman, B. (1987). *Incest and sexuality: A guide to understanding and healing.* Lexington, MA: Lexington.

Margolin, G. (1982). Ethical and legal considerations and marital and family therapy. *American Psychologist, 37,* 788-801.

Marlow, L., & Sauber, S. R. (1990). *Handbook of divorce mediation.* New York: Plenum.

Martin, P. (1976). *A marital therapy manual.* New York: Brunner/Mazel.

Martin, P. A., & Bird, M. W. (1953). An approach to the psychotherapy of marriage partners: The stereoscopic technique. *Psychiatry, 16,* 123-127.

Maruyama, M. (1963). The second cybernetics: Deviation-exemplifying mutual causal processes. *American Scientist, 51,* 164-179.

Maslow, A. (1954). *Motivation and personality.* New York: Harper & Row.

Maslow, A. H. (1959). *New knowledge in human values.* New York: Harper & Row.

Masters, W., & Johnson, V. (1970). *Human sexual inadequacy.* Boston: Little, Brown.

Maturana, H. R. (1978). Biology of language: The epistemology of reality. In G. A. Miller & E. Lenneberg (Eds.), *Psychology and biology of language and thought* (pp. 27-63). New York: Academic Press.

McCubbin, H. I., & Figley, C. R. (Eds.). (1983). *Stress and the family: Coping with normative transitions* (Vol. 1). New York: Brunner/Mazel.

McFarlane, W. R. (1983). *Family therapy in schizophrenia.* New York: Guilford.

McGoldrick, M. (1982). Ethnicity and family therapy: An overview. In M. McGoldrick, J. K. Pearce, & S. Giordano (Eds.), *Ethnicity and family therapy* (pp. 3-30). New York: Guilford.

McGoldrick, M., & Gerson, R. (1985). *Genograms in family assessment.* New York: Norton.

McMahon, R. J., & Wells, K. C. (1989). Conduct disorders. In E. J. Mash & R. A. Barkley (Eds.), *Treatment of childhood disorders* (pp. 73-132). New York: Guilford.

McPherson, S. (1968). *A manual for multiple coding of family interaction.* Unpublished manuscript.

Meck, S. (1972). An approach to family pathology. In G. D. Erickson & T. P. Hogan (Eds.), *Family therapy: An introduction to theory and technique* (pp. 103-119). Belmont, CA: Wadsworth.

Meissner, W. W. (1978). The conceptualization of marriage and family dynamics from a psychoanalytic perspective. In T. Paolino & B. McCrady (Eds.), *Marriage and marital therapy* (pp. 25-88). New York: Brunner/Mazel.

Miller, J. G. (1965). Living systems: Basic concepts. *Behavioral Science, 10,* 193-245.

Miller, S., Nunnally, E., & Wackman, D. (1975). *Alive and aware: Improving communications in relationships.* Minneapolis: Interpersonal Communications.

Miller, S., Nunnally, E. W., & Wackman, D. B. (1976). *Couple workbook: Increasing awareness and communication skills.* Minneapolis: Interpersonal Communication.

Miller, W. (1987). Effects of rape on the marital relationship. In G. Weeks & L. Hof (Eds.), *Integrating sex and marital therapy* (pp. 171-182). New York: Brunner/Mazel.

Minuchin, S. (1965). Conflict-resolution family therapy. *Psychiatry, 28,* 278-286.

Minuchin, S. (1972). Conflict-resolution family therapy. In G. D. Erickson & T. P. Hogan (Eds.), *Family therapy: An introduction to theory and technique* (pp. 293-305). Belmont, CA: Wadsworth.

Minuchin, S. (1974). *Families and family therapy.* Cambridge, MA: Harvard University Press.

Minuchin, S., & Fishman, H. (1981). *Family therapy techniques.* Cambridge, MA: Harvard University Press.

Minuchin, S., Montalvo, B., Guerney, B. G., Jr., Rosman, B. L., & Schumer, F. (1967). *Families of the slums: An exploration of their structure and treatment.* New York: Basic Books.

Minuchin, S., Rosman, B. L., & Baker, L. (1978). *Psychosomatic families: Anorexia nervosa in context.* Cambridge, MA: Harvard University Press.

Mishler, E., & Waxler, N. (1968). *Interaction in families: An experimental study of family processes and schizophrenia.* New York: John Wiley.

Mittleman, B. (1944). The concurrent analysis of marital couples. *Psychoanalytic Quarterly, 13,* 479-491.

Moen, P. (1980). Developing family indicators. *Journal of Family Issues, 1,* 5-30.

Money, J. (1960). Phantom orgasm in dreams of paraplegic men and women. *Archives of General Psychiatry, 3,* 373-382.

Money, J. (1961). Components of eroticism in man: The hormones in relation to sexual morphology and sexual desire. *Journal of Nervous and Mental Disease, 132,* 239-248.

Montalvo, B. (1973). Aspects of live supervision. *Family Process, 12,* 343-359.

Moos, R. H., & Moos, B. S. (1981). *Family Environmental Scale manual.* Palo Alto, CA: Consulting Psychologists Press.

Moreno, J. (1953). *Who shall survive? Foundations of sociometry, group psychotherapy, and sociodrama.* New York: Beacon House.

Moreno, J. (1971). Psychodrama. In H. Kaplan & B. Sadock (Eds.), *Comprehensive group psychotherapy* (pp. 460-500). Baltimore: Williams & Wilkins.

Murdock, G. (1949). *Social structure.* New York: Macmillan.

Nadelson, C. (1976). Marital therapy from a psychoanalytic perspective. In T. Paolino & B. McCrady (Eds.), *Marriage and marital therapy* (pp. 89-164). New York: Brunner/Mazel.

Napier, A. (1988). *The fragile bond.* New York: Harper & Row.

Napier, A., & Whitaker, C. (1978). *The family crucible.* New York: Jason Aronson.

Neil, J. F., & Kniskern, D. P. (1982). (Eds.). *From psyche to system: The evolving therapy of Carl Whitaker.* New York: Guilford.

Nelsen, J. C. (1983). *Family therapy: An integrative approach.* Englewood Cliffs, NJ: Prentice-Hall.

Nerin, W. F. (1986). *Family reconstruction: Long day's journey into light.* New York: Norton.

Nichols, M. P. (1984). *Family therapy: Concepts and methods.* New York: Gardner.

Nichols, M. P. (1987). *The self in the system.* New York: Brunner/Mazel.

Nickell, P., Rice, A. S., & Tucker, S. P. (1976). *Management in family living* (5th ed.). New York: John Wiley.

Nicol, A. R. (Ed.). (1985). *Longitudinal studies in child psychology and psychiatry.* New York: John Wiley.

Nierenberg, G. I., & Calero, H. (1973). *Meta-talk: Guide to hidden meanings on conversations.* New York: Simon & Schuster.

O'Connor, W., & Stachowiak, J. (1971). Patterns of interaction in families with high adjusted, low adjusted, and mentally retarded members. *Family Process, 10,* 229-241.

O'Hanlon, W. H., & Hexum, A. L. (1990). *An uncommon casebook: The complete clinical work of Milton H. Erickson, M.D.* New York: Norton.

Okun, B. F., & Rappaport, L. J. (1980). *Working with families: An introduction to family therapy.* Belmont, CA: Brooks/Cole.

O'Leary, K., & Turkewitz, H. (1978). Marital therapy from a behavioral perspective. In T. Paolino & B. McCrady (Eds.), *Marriage and marital therapy* (pp. 240-297). New York: Brunner/Mazel.

Olson, D., & Ryder, R. (1970). Inventory of Marital Conflicts (IMC): An experimental interaction procedure. *Journal of Marriage and the Family, 31,* 443-448.

Olson, D. H., Russell, C. S., & Sprenkle, D. H. (1980). Marital and family therapy: A decade review. *Journal of Marriage and the Family, 42,* 973-993.

Omer, H. (1981). Paradoxical treatments: A unified concept. *Psychotherapy: Theory, Research, and Practice, 18,* 320-324.

O'Rourke, J. (1973). Field and lab: The decision-making behavior of family groups in two experimental conditions. *Sociometry, 26,* 422-435.

Palmer, C. E., & Noble, D. N. (1984). Child snatching: Motivations, mechanisms, and melodrama. *Journal of Family Issues, 5,* 27-46.

Panitz, D. R., McChonchie, R. D., Sauber, S. R., & Fonseca, J. A. (1983). The role of machismo and the Hispanic family in the etiology and treatment of alcoholism in Hispanic American males. *American Journal of Family Therapy, 11,* 31-44.

Papp, P. (1976). Brief therapy with couples groups. In P. J. Guerin (Ed.), *Family therapy: Theory and practice* (pp. 350-363). New York: Gardner.

Papp, P. (1976). Family choreography. In P. J. Guerin (Ed.), *Family therapy: Theory and practice* (pp. 465-479). New York: Gardner.

Papp, P. (1980). The Greek chorus and other techniques of family therapy. *Family Process, 19,* 45-57.

Papp, P. (1980). The use of fantasy in a couples group. In M. Andolfi & I. Zwerling (Eds.), *Dimensions of family therapy* (pp. 73-90). New York: Guilford.

Papp, P., Silverstein, O., & Carter, E. (1973). Family sculpting in preventive work with families. *Family Process, 12,* 197-212.

Parker, G. (1983). *Parental overprotection: A risk factor in psychosocial development.* New York: Grune & Stratton.

Parsons, T. (1955). The American family: Its relation to personality and social structure. In T. Parsons & R. Bales (Eds.), *Family socialization and interaction process* (pp. 3-34). New York: Free Press.

Parsons, T., & Bales, R. (1955). *Family, socialization, and interaction process.* New York: Free Press.

Patterson, G. (1971). *Families: Applications of social learning to family life.* Champaign, IL: Research Press.

Patterson, G. (1976). The aggressive child: Victim and architect of a coercive system. In E. Mash, L. Hamerlynck, & L. Handy (Eds.), *Behavior modification and families* (pp. 267-316). New York: Brunner/Mazel.

Patterson, G., & Reid, J. (1970). Reciprocity and coercion: Two facets of social systems. In C. Neuringer & J. Michael (Eds.), *Behavior modification in clinical psychology* (pp. 133-177). New York: Appleton-Century-Crofts.

Paul, N. (1967). The use of empathy in the resolution of grief. *Perspectives in Biology and Medicine, 11,* 153-169.

Paul, N. (1972). Effects of playback on family members of their own previously recorded conjoint therapy material. In G. D. Erickson & T. P. Hogan (Eds.), *Family therapy: An introduction to theory and technique* (pp. 251-264). Belmont, CA: Wadsworth.

Paul, N. (1976). Cross-confrontation. In P. J. Guerin (Ed.), *Family therapy: Theory and practice* (pp. 520-529). New York: Gardner.

Perelman, M. (1980). Treatment of premature ejaculation. In S. Leiblum & L. Pervin (Eds.), *Principles and practice of sex therapy* (pp. 199-234). New York: Guilford.

Perls, F. S. (1969). *Gestalt therapy verbatim.* Moab, UT: Real People Press.

Pike, K. (1954). *Language, Part I.* Glendale, CA: Summer Institute of Linguistics.

Pincus, L., & Dare, C. (1978). *Secrets in the family.* New York: Pantheon.

Pinney, E. L., & Slipp, S. (1982). *Glossary of group and family therapy.* New York: Brunner/Mazel.

Pinsof, W. (1981). Family therapy process research. In A. S. Gurman & D. P. Kniskern (Eds.), *Handbook of family therapy* (pp. 699-741). New York: Brunner/Mazel.

Pittman, F. S. (1970). Treating the doll's house marriage. *Family Process, 9,* 143.

Prata, G. (1987). The absent family member maneuver at the first sessions of concentration. *Journal of Strategic and Systemic Therapies, 6,* 24-41.

Pratt, L. (1976). *Family structure and effective health behavior: The energized family.* Boston: Houghton-Mifflin.

Prochaska, J., & Prochaska, J. (1978). Twentieth century trends in marriage and marital therapy. In T. Paolino & B. McCrady (Eds.), *Marriage and marital therapy* (pp. 1-24). New York: Brunner/Mazel.

Purdy, F., & Nickle, N. (1981). Practice principles for working with groups of men who batter. *Social Work With Groups, 4,* 111-122.

Quay, H. C., & Werry, J. S. (Eds.). (1986). *Psychopathological disorders of childhood.* New York: John Wiley.

Rabkin, R. (1970). *Inner and outer space.* New York: Norton.

Rapoport, A. (1974). *Conflict in man-made environments.* New York: Penguin.

Rapoport, R., & Rapoport, R. (1964). New light on the honeymoon. *Human Relations, 17,* 33-56.

Rappaport, L. (1953). What is information? *Syntheses, 9,* 157.

Ravich, R., & Wyden, B. (1974). *Predictable pairing.* New York: Wyden.

Reckless, J., & Geigger, N. (1978). Impotence as a practical problem. In J. LoPiccolo & L. LoPiccolo (Eds.), *Handbook of sex therapy* (pp. 295-322). New York: Plenum.

Reese, R. (1966). *The analysis of human operant behavior.* Dubuque, IA: William C. Brown.

Reid, W. J. (1981). Family treatment within a task-centered framework. In E. R. Tolson & W. J. Reid (Eds.), *Models of family treatment* (pp. 306-331). New York: Columbia University Press.

Reiss, D. (1968). Individual thinking and family interaction, III: An experimental study of categorization performance in families of normals, those with character disorders, and schizophrenia. *Journal of Nervous and Mental Disease, 146,* 324-403.

Reiss, D. (1971). Intimacy and problem solving: An automated procedure for testing a theory of consensual experience in families. *Archives of General Psychiatry, 25,* 442-455.

Reiss, D. (1980). Pathways to assessing the family. In C. Hofling & I. Lewis (Eds.), *The family: Evaluation and treatment* (pp. 86-92). New York: Brunner/Mazel.

Reiss, D. (1981). *The family's construction of reality.* Cambridge, MA: Harvard University Press.

Riskin, J., & Faunce, E. (1968). *Family interaction sides scoring manual.* Unpublished manuscript.

Riskin, J., & Faunce, E. (1970). Family interaction scales. I. Theoretical framework and method. *Archives of General Psychiatry, 22,* 504-512.

Riskin, J., & Faunce, E. (1972). An evaluative review of family interaction research. *Family Process, 11,* 365-455.

Robert, J. (1988). Setting the frame: Definition, functions, and topologies of rituals. In E. Imber-Black, J. Roberts, & R. Whiting (Eds.), *Rituals in families and family therapy* (pp. 3-46). New York: Norton.

Roger, M. (1987). Dealing with sexual concerns of children. In G. Weeks & L. Hof (Eds.), *Integrating sex and marital therapy* (pp. 82-99). New York: Brunner/Mazel.

Rogers, C. P. (1959). A theory of therapy, personality, and interpersonal relationships, as developed in the client-centered framework. In S. Koch (Ed.), *Psychology: A study of a science, Vol. III, Formulations of the person and the social context* (pp. 184-256). New York: McGraw-Hill.

Rohrbaugh, M., Tennen, H., Press, S., & White, L. (1981). Compliance, defiance, and therapeutic paradox. *American Journal of Orthopsychiatry, 51,* 454-467.

Rohrbaugh, M., Tennen, H., Press, S., White, L., Raskin, P., & Pickering, M. (1977, August). *Paradoxical strategies in psychotherapy.* Paper presented at the American Psychological Association, San Francisco, CA.

Rolfe, D. (1977). Pre-marriage contracts: An aid to couples living with parents. *Family Coordinator, 26,* 281-285.

Rosen, R., & Leiblum, S. (1988). A sexual scripting approach to problems of desire. In S. Leiblum & R. Rosen (Eds.), *Sexual desire disorders* (pp. 168-191). New York: Guilford.

Rosenblatt, P. C., & Wright, S. E. (1984). Shadow realities in close relationships. *American Journal of Family Therapy, 12,* 45-54.

Rosenblum, K. E. (1986). Leaving as a wife, leaving as a mother: Ways of relinquishing custody. *Journal of Family Issues, 7,* 197-213.

Rosman, B., Minuichin, S., & Liebman, R. (1975). Family lunch session: An introduction to family therapy in anorexia nervosa. *American Journal of Orthopsychiatry, 45,* 846-853.

Ross, B. N., & Ross, S. A. (1982). *Hyperactivity: Current issues, research and theory* (2nd ed.). New York: John Wiley.

Routh, D. K. (Ed.). (1988). *Handbook of pediatric psychology.* New York: Guilford.

Rubin, Z. (1973). *Liking and loving: An invitation to social psychology.* New York: Holt, Rinehart & Winston.

Rubinstein, D. (1960, January). *The family of the schizophrenic.* Paper presented at the Second Cuban Congress of Neurology and Psychiatry, Havana.

Rutledge, A. (1969). Male and female roles in marriage counseling. In B. N. Ard & C. C. Ard (Eds.), *Handbook of marriage counseling* (pp. 120-127). Palo Alto, CA: Science & Behavior Books.

Ryder, R., & Goodrich, D. (1966). Married couples' responses to disagreement. *Family Process, 5,* 30-42.

Sager, C. (1981). Couples therapy and marriage contracts. In A. S. Gurman & D. P. Kniskern (Eds.), *Handbook of family therapy* (pp. 25-32). New York: Brunner/Mazel.

Sager, C. J. (1976). *Marriage contracts and couple therapy.* New York: Brunner/Mazel.

Sager, C. J., Brown, H. S., Crohn, H., Engel, T., Rodstein, E., & Walker, L. (1983). *Treating the remarried family.* New York: Brunner/Mazel.

Saposnek, D. T. (1983). *Mediating child custody disputes.* San Francisco: Jossey-Bass.

Saposnek, D. T. (1983). Strategies in child custody mediation: A family systems approach. *Mediation Quarterly, 1,* 29-54.

Satir, V. (1965). Conjoint marital therapy. In B. Green (Ed.), *The psychotherapies of marital disharmony* (pp. 121-134). New York: Free Press.

Satir, V. (1972). *Peoplemaking.* Palo Alto, CA: Science & Behavior Books.

Satir, V. (1982). The therapist and family therapy: Process model. In A. M. Horne & M. M. Ohlsen (Eds.), *Family counseling and therapy* (pp. 12-42). Itasca, IL: F. E. Peacock.

Satir, V. (1983). *Conjoint family therapy* (3rd ed.). Palo Alto, CA: Science & Behavior Books.

Sauber, S. R. (1971). Multiple family group counseling. *Personnel and Guidance Journal, 49,* 459-465.

Sauber, S. R. (1972). *An honest guide to marriage counseling.* West Palm Beach, FL: Mental Health Association Press.

Sauber, S. R. (1972). Patient training prior to entering psychotherapy. *Social Psychiatry, 7,* 139-143.

Sauber, S. R. (1973). *Preventive educational intervention for mental health.* Cambridge, MA: Ballinger.

Sauber, S. R. (1974). Approaches to pretherapy training. *Journal of Contemporary Psychotherapy, 6,* 190-197.

Sauber, S. R. (1974). Primary prevention and the marital enrichment group. *Journal of Family Counseling, 12,* 39-44.

Sauber, S. R. (1977). The human services delivery system. *International Journal of Mental Health, 5,* 121-140.

Sauber, S. R. (1983). *The human services delivery system.* New York: Columbia University Press.

Sauber, S. R. (1988). *It's all in the name: A language guide for the single, his friends, and her family.* Hollywood, FL: Frederick Fell.

Sauber, S. R., Beiner, S. F., & Meddoff, G. S. (in press). Divorce mediation: A new system for dealing with the family in transition. In R. H. Miskesell, D. D. Lusterman, & S. H. McDaniel (Eds.), *Family psychology and systems therapy: A handbook.* Washington, DC: American Psychological Association.

Sauber, S. R., L'Abate, L., & Weeks, G. (1985). *Family therapy: Basic concepts and terms.* Rockville, MD: Aspen Systems.

Sauber, S. R., & Panitz, D. R. (1982). Divorce counseling and mediation. In A. Gurman (Ed.), *Questions and answers in the practice of family therapy* (Vol. 2, pp. 207-213). New York: Brunner/Mazel.

Sauber, S. R., & Weinstein, C. (1986). Terminology for male/female relationships for the 1980s. *Australian Journal of Sex, Marriage, and the Family, 7,* 99-108.

Schaef, A. W. (1986). *Co-dependence: Misunderstood-mistreated.* New York: Harper & Row.

Schaefer, C., & Millman, H. (1977). *Therapies for children.* San Francisco: Jossey-Bass.

Scharff, D. (1988). An object relations approach to inhibited sexual desire. In S. Leiblum & R. Rosen (Eds.), *Sexual desire disorders* (pp. 45-74). New York: Guilford.

Scharff, J. S. (Ed.). (1989). *Foundations of object relations family therapy.* New York: Jason Aronson.

Scheflen, A. (1972). Human communication: Behavioral programs and their integration in interaction. In G. D. Erickson & T. P. Hogan (Eds.), *Family therapy: An introduction to theory and technique* (pp. 86-102). Belmont, CA: Wadsworth.

Scheflen, A. E. (1960). Regression one-way relationships. *Psychiatric Quarterly, 23,* 692-709.

Schroedinger, E. (1945). *What is life?* Cambridge, UK: Cambridge University Press.

Schwartz, M., & Masters, W. (1988). The Masters and Johnson Institute treatment model. In S. Leiblum & R. Rosen (Eds.), *Sexual desire disorders* (pp. 229-242). New York: Guilford.

Seagraves, R. (1988). Drugs and desire. In S. Leiblum & R. Rosen (Eds.), *Sexual desire disorders* (pp. 313-347). New York: Guilford.

Seagraves, R. (1988). Hormones and libido. In S. Leiblum & R. Rosen (Eds.), *Sexual desire disorders* (pp. 271-312). New York: Guilford.

Searles, H. (1965). The contributions of family treatment to the psychotherapy of schizophrenia. In I. Boszormenyi-Nagy & J. Framo (Eds.), *Intensive family therapy: Theoretical and practical aspects* (pp. 463-496). New York: Harper & Row.

Selvini Palazzoli, M. (1980). Why a long interval between sessions? In M. Andolfi & I. Zwerling (Eds.), *Dimensions of family therapy* (pp. 161-170). New York: Guilford.

Selvini Palazzoli, M., Boscolo, L., Cecchin, G., & Prata, G. (1978). *Paradox and counterparadox: A new model in the therapy of the family in schizophrenic transaction.* New York: Jason Aronson.

Selvini Palazzoli, M., Boscolo, L., Cecchin, G., & Prata, G. (1978). A ritualized prescription in family therapy: Odd days and even days. *Journal of Marriage and Family Counseling, 4,* 3-9.

Selvini Palazzoli, M., Boscolo, L., Cecchin, G., & Prata, G. (1980). Hypothesizing-circularity-neutrality: Three guidelines for the conductor of the session. *Family Process, 19,* 3-12.

Selvini Palazzoli, M., Cirillo, S., Selvini, M., & Sorrentino, A. M. (1989). *Family games: General models of psychotic processes in the family.* New York: Norton.

Semans, J. (1956). Premature ejaculation: A new approach. *Southern Medical Journal, 49,* 353-361.

Shapiro, R. J. (1984). Therapy with violent families. In S. Saunders, A. M. Anderson, C. A. Hart, & G. M. Rubenstein (Eds.), *Violent individuals and families* (pp. 112-136). Springfield, IL: Charles C Thomas.

Sherman, S. N. (1981). A social work frame for family therapy. In E. R. Tolson & W. J. Reid (Eds.), *Models of family treatment* (pp. 7-32). New York: Columbia University Press.

Shulman, B. H., & Nikelly, A. G. (1971). Family constellation. In A. G. Nikelly (Ed.), *Techniques for behavior change: Applications of Adlerian theory* (pp. 35-40). Springfield, IL: Charles C Thomas.

Silfen, R. (1980). *Biopsychology of love and lust.* Unpublished manuscript, New School for Social Research, New York.

Simon, R. M. (1972). Sculpting the family. *Family Process, 11,* 49-57.

Singer, J. (1976). *Androgyny: Toward a new theory of sexuality.* Garden City, NY: Anchor/Doubleday.

Singer, J., & Singer, I. (1978). Types of female orgasm. In J. LoPiccolo & L. LoPiccolo (Eds.), *Handbook of sex therapy* (pp. 175-186). New York: Plenum.

Singer, M., & Wynne, L. (1963). Thought disorder and family relations of schizophrenics. I. A research strategy. *Archives of General Psychiatry, 9,* 191-198.

Singer, M., & Wynne, L. (1965). Thought disorders and family relations of schizophrenics, III. Methodology using projective techniques. *Archives of General Psychiatry, 12,* 187-200.

Singer, M., & Wynne, L. (1966). Communication styles in parents of normals, neurotics, and schizophrenics. *Psychiatric Research Reports, 20,* 25-38.

Singer, M., & Wynne, L. (1966). Principles of scoring communication defects and deviances in parents of schizophrenics: Rorschach and TAT scoring manuals. *Psychiatry, 29,* 260-288.

Skinner, B. F. (1953). *Science and human behavior.* New York: Macmillan.

Skynner, A. C. R. (1976). *Systems of family and marital psychotherapy.* New York: Brunner/Mazel.

Skynner, A. C. R. (1981). An open-systems, group-analytic approach to family therapy. In A. S. Gurman & D. P. Kniskern (Eds.), *Handbook of family therapy* (pp. 39-84). New York: Brunner/Mazel.

Slavson, S. R. (1943). *An introduction to group therapy.* New York: Commonwealth Fund.

Sloan, S. Z., & L'Abate, L. (1985). Intimacy. In L. L'Abate (Ed.), *Handbook of family psychology and therapy* (Vol. 1, pp. 405-427). Homewood, IL: Dow Jones-Irwin.

Sluzki, C. E. (1978). Marital therapy from a systems theory perspective. In T. Paolino & B. McCrady (Eds.), *Marriage and marital therapy* (pp. 366-394). New York: Brunner/Mazel.

Smart, M., & Smart, R. (1953). *An introduction to family relationships.* Philadelphia: W. B. Saunders.

Sojit, C. (1969). Dyadic interaction in a double bind situation. *Family Process, 8,* 235-260.

Sojit, C. (1971). The double bind hypothesis and the parents of schizophrenics. *Family Process, 10,* 53-74.

Spanier, G. B., & Lewis, R. A. (1980). Marital quality: A review of the seventies. *Journal of Marriage and the Family, 42,* 835.

Speck, R., & Attneave, C. (1973). *Family networks.* New York: Pantheon.

Speer, D. (1970). Family systems: Morphostasis and morphogenesis, or is homeostasis enough? *Family Process, 9,* 259-278.

Speers, R. W., & Lansing, C. (1964). Group psychotherapy with preschool psychotic children and collateral group therapy of their parents: A preliminary report of the first two years. *American Journal of Orthopsychiatry, 34,* 659-666.

Spiegel, J. (1957). The resolution of role conflict within the family. *Psychiatry, 20,* 1-16.

Spiegel, J. (1971). *Transactions.* New York: Science House.

Spotnitz, H. (1971). Comparison of different types of group psychotherapy. In H. Kaplan & B. Sadock (Eds.), *Comprehensive group psychotherapy* (pp. 72-103). Baltimore: Williams & Wilkins.

Stahman, R. F., & Hiebert, W. I. (1977). Commonly recurring couple interaction patterns. In R. F. Stahman & W. I. Hiebert (Eds.), *Klemer's counseling in marital and sexual problems: A clinical handbook* (2nd ed., pp. 17-33). Baltimore: Williams & Wilkins.

Stampl, T., & Lewis, D. (1967). Essentials of implosive therapy: A learning theory based on psychodynamic behavioral therapy. *Journal of Abnormal Psychology, 72,* 496-503.

Stanton, M. (1981). An integrated structural/strategic approach to family therapy. *Journal of Marital and Family Therapy, 7,* 427-439.

Stanton, M. (1981). Strategic approaches to family therapy. In A. S. Gurman & D. P. Kniskern (Eds.), *Handbook of family therapy* (pp. 361-402). New York: Brunner/Mazel.

Stanton, M., & Todd, T. (1979). Structural family therapy with drug addicts. In E. Kaufman & P. Kaufman (Eds.), *The family therapy of drug and alcohol abuse* (pp. 55-69). New York: Gardner.

Stanton, M. D., & Todd, T. C. (1982). *The family therapy of drug abuse and addiction.* New York: Guilford.

Steinglass, P. (1978). The conceptualization of marriage from a systems theory perspective. In T. Paolino & B. McCrady (Eds.), *Marriage and marital therapy* (pp. 298-368). New York: Brunner/Mazel.

Steinhauer, P. D., & Rae-Grant, Q. (Eds.). (1983). *Psychological problems of the child in the family.* New York: Basic Books.

Steinmets, S. (1983). Dependency, stress, and violence between middle-aged caregivers and their elderly parents. In J. I. Kosbers (Ed.), *Abuse and maltreatment of the elderly* (pp. 134-149). Littleton, MA: John-Wright.

Stierlin, H. (1974). *Separating parents and adolescents: A perspective on running away, schizophrenia and waywardness.* New York: Quadrangle.

Stierlin, H. (1976). The dynamics of owning and disowning: Psychoanalytic and family perspectives. *Family Process, 15,* 277-288.

Stoller, R. J. (1985). Gender identity disorders in children and adults. In H. I. Kaplan & B. J. Sadock (Eds.), *Comprehensive textbook of psychiatry* (4th ed., pp. 1034-1040). Baltimore: Williams & Wilkins.

Straus, M. (1970). Methodology of a laboratory experimental study of families in three societies. In R. Hill & R. Konig (Eds.), *Families in east and west* (p. 184). New York: Norton.

Straus, M. (1980). Victims and aggressors in marital violence. *American Behavioral Scientific, 23,* 681-704.

Strodtbeck, F. (1954). The family as a three-person group. *American Sociological Review, 19,* 23-29.

Stryker, S. (1964). The interactional and situational approaches. In H. T. Christensen (Ed.), *Handbook of marriage and the family* (pp. 125-170). Chicago: Rand McNally.

Stuart, R. B. (1969). Operant-interpersonal treatment for marital discord. *Journal of Consulting and Clinical Psychology, 33,* 675-682.

Stuart, R. B. (1976). An operant interpersonal program for couples. In D. H. L. Olson (Ed.), *Treating relationships* (pp. 119-132). Lake Mills, IA: Graphic Publishing.

Stuart, R. B. (1980). *Helping couples change: A social learning approach to marital therapy.* New York: Guilford.

Stuart, R. B. (1981). Violence in perspective. In R. B. Stuart (Ed.), *Violent behavior: Social learning approaches to prediction, management, and treatment* (pp. 3-30). New York: Brunner/Mazel.

Sullivan, H. (1948). The meaning of anxiety in psychiatry and life. *Psychiatry, 11,* 1-13.

Sullivan, H. S. (1953). *The interpersonal theory of psychiatry.* New York: Norton.

Sullivan, H. S. (1956). *Clinical studies in psychiatry.* New York: Norton.

Summit, R. (1983). The child sexual abuse accommodation syndrome. *Child Abuse and Neglect, 7,* 177-193.

Talmadge, L., & Talmadge, W. (1990). Sexuality assessment measures for clinical use: A review. *American Journal of Family Therapy, 18,* 80-105.

Tarasoff v. Regents of University of California, 529 P.2d 553 (Cal. 1974), *vacated, reheard, en banc, and aff'd,* 133 Cal. Rptr., 14, 551.P.2d 334 (1976).

Taylor, H. G. (1983). MBD: Meanings and misconceptions. *Journal of Clinical Neuropsychology, 5,* 271-287.

Taylor, H. G. (1988). Learning disabilities. In E. J. Mash & L. G. Terdel (Eds.) *Behavior assessment of childhood disorders* (2nd ed., pp. 402-450). New York: Guilford.

Tennov, D. (1980). *Love and limerence: The experience of being in love.* New York: Stein & Day.

Thayer, L. (1982). A person-centered approach to family therapy. In A. M. Horne & M. M. Ohlsen (Eds.), *Family counseling and therapy* (pp. 175-213). Itasca, IL: F. E. Peacock.

Thibault, J., & Kelly, H. (1959). *The social psychology of groups.* New York: John Wiley.

Thorman, G. (1965). *Family therapy: A handbook.* Beverly Hills, CA: Western Psychological Services.

Tiefer, L., & Melman, A. (1989). Comprehensive evaluation of erectile dysfunction and medical treatments. In S. Leiblum & R. Rosen (Eds.), *Principles and practice of sex therapy* (2nd ed., pp. 207-236). New York: Guilford.

Titchner, J., Risking, J., & Emerson, R. (1960). The family in psychosomatic medicine. *Psychosomatic Medicine, 22,* 127-142.

Toman, W. (1969). *Family constellation.* New York: Springer.

Toman, W. (1976). *Family constellation* (3rd ed.). New York: Springer Verlag.

Tomm, K. (1985). Circular interviewing. In D. Campbell & R. Draper (Eds.), *Applications of systemic family therapy* (pp. 33-45). New York: Grune & Stratton.

Tomm, K. (1987). Interventive interviewing: Part II. Reflexive questioning as a means to enable self-healing. *Family Process, 26,* 167-184.

Tomm, K. (1988). Interventive interviewing: Part III. Intending to ask linear, circular, strategic, or reflexive questions? *Family Process, 27,* 1-16.

Tomm, K. (1989). Externalizing the problem and internalizing personal agency. *Journal of Strategic and Systemic Therapies, 8,* 54-59.

Toomin, M. K. (1975). Structured separation for couples in conflict. In A. S. Gurman & D. G. Rice (Eds.), *Couples in conflict* (pp. 353-362). New York: Jason Aronson.

Touliatos, J., Perlmutter, B. F., & Straus, M. A. (Eds.). (1990). *Handbook of family measurement techniques.* Newbury Park, CA: Sage.

Treat, S. (1987). Enhancing a couple's sexual relationship. In G. Weeks & L. Hof (Eds.), *Integrating sex and marital therapy* (pp. 57-81). New York: Brunner/Mazel.

Tuke, D. (1982). *Dictionary of psychological medicine* (Vol. 1). Philadelphia: Blakiston.

Umbarger, C. C. (1984). *Structural family therapy.* New York: Grune & Stratton.

U.S. Office of Education. (1968). *First annual report. National advisory on handicapped children.* Washington, DC: U.S. Department of Health, Education and Welfare.

Verhulst, J., & Heiman, J. (1988). A systems perspective on sexual desire. In S. Leiblum & R. Rosen (Eds.), *Sexual desire disorders* (pp. 243-270). New York: Guilford.

Visher, E., & Visher, J. (1979). *Stepfamilies: A guide to working with stepfamilies and stepchildren.* New York: Brunner/Mazel.

Vogel, S. E., & Bell, N. (1960). The emotionally disturbed child as family scapegoat. In N. Bell & S. E. Vogel (Eds.), *A modern introduction to the family* (pp. 382-397). New York: Free Press.

Wahler, R. (1976). Deviant child behaviors within the family. In H. Leitenberg (Ed.), *Handbook of behavior modification and therapy* (pp. 516-546). Englewood Cliffs, NJ: Prentice-Hall.

Wahlroos, S. (1974). *Family communication: A guide to emotional health.* New York: Macmillan.

Walen, S., Hauserman, N., & Lavin, P. (1977). *Clinical guide to behavior therapy.* Baltimore: Williams & Wilkins.

Walker, L. E. (1979). *The battered woman.* New York: Harper & Row.

Walker, L. E. (1984). *The battered woman syndrome.* New York: Springer.

Wallace, A., & Fogelson, H. (1965). The identity struggle. In I. Boszormenyi-Nagy & J. Framo (Eds.), *Intensive family therapy: Theoretical and practical aspects* (pp. 365-406). New York: Harper & Row.

Wallerstein, J., & Kelly, J. (1980). *Surviving the breakup: How children and parents cope with divorce.* New York: Basic Books.

Walsh, F. (Ed.). (1982). *Normal family processes.* New York: Guilford.

Walters, M., Carter, B., Papp, P., & Silverstein, O. (1988). *The invisible web: Gender patterns in family relationships.* New York: Guilford.

Waring, E. M., & Russell, L. (1982). Cognitive family therapy. In F. W. Kaslow (Ed.), *The international handbook of family therapy* (pp. 186-195). New York: Brunner/Mazel.

Waterman, J., & Lusk, R. (1986). Scope of the problem. In K. MacFarlane, J. Waterman, S. Conerly, L. Damon, N. Durfee, and S. Long (Eds.), *Sexual abuse of young children* (pp. 3-12). New York: Guilford.

Watkins, J. (1971). The affect bridge: A hypnotherapeutic technique. *International Journal of Clinical and Experimental Hypnosis, 19,* 10-12.

Watkins, J., & Watkins, N. (1984). Ego-state therapy. In R. Corsini (Ed.), *Handbook of innovative psychotherapies* (pp. 252-270). New York: John Wiley.

Watzlawick, P. (1963). *An anthology of human communication.* Palo Alto, CA: Science & Behavior Books.

Watzlawick, P. (1966). A structured family interview. *Family Process, 5,* 256-271.

Watzlawick, P. (1972). A structured family interview. In G. D. Erickson & T. P. Hogan (Eds.), *Family therapy: An introduction to theory and technique* (pp. 265-278). Belmont, CA: Wadsworth.

Watzlawick, P. (1977). The utopia syndrome. In P. Watzlawick & J. Weakland (Eds.), *The interactional view: Studies at the Mental Research Institute, Palo Alto, 1965-1974.* New York: Norton.

Watzlawick, P. (1978). *The language of change: Elements of therapeutic communication.* New York: Basic Books.

Watzlawick, P. (Ed.). (1984). *The invented reality.* New York: Norton.

Watzlawick, P. (1988). *Ultra-solutions: How to fail most successfully.* New York: Norton.

Watzlawick, P., Beavin, J. H., & Jackson, D. D. (1967). *Pragmatics of human communication.* New York: Norton.

Watzlawick, P., Weakland, J., & Fisch R. (1974). *Change: Principles of problem formation and problem resolution.* New York: Norton.

Weakland, J., Fisch, R., Watzlawick, P., & Bodin, A. (1974). Brief therapy: Focused problem resolution. *Family Process, 13,* 141-168.

Webster's new collegiate dictionary. (1979). Springfield, MA: Merriam-Webster.

Weeks, G. (1986). Individual-system dialectic. *American Journal of Family Therapy, 14,* 5-12.

Weeks, G. (1987). Systematic treatments of inhibited sexual desire. In G. Weeks & L. Hof (Eds.), *Integrating sex and marital therapy* (pp. 183-201). New York: Brunner/Mazel.

Weeks, G. (Ed.). (1989). *Treating couples: The intersystem model of the Marriage Council of Philadelphia.* New York: Brunner/Mazel.

Weeks, G., & L'Abate, L. (1982). *Paradoxical psychotherapy: Theory and practice with individuals, couples, and families.* New York: Brunner/Mazel.

Weeks, G., & Nixon, G. (1991). Family psychology: The specialty statement of an evolving field. *Family Psychologist, 7*(4), 9-18.

Weiner, I. (1975). *Principles of psychotherapy.* New York: John Wiley.

Weiner, I. (1982). *Child and adolescence psychopathology.* New York: John Wiley.

Weiner, N. (1954). *The human use of human beings: Cybernetics and society.* Garden City, NY: Doubleday.

Weiner, N. (1962). *Cybernetics.* Cambridge: MIT Press.

Weiss, R. (1978). The conceptualization of marriage from a behavioral perspective. In T. Paolino & B. McCrady (Eds.), *Marriage and marital therapy* (pp. 165-239). New York: Brunner/Mazel.

Weiss, R., Hops, H., & Patterson, G. (1973). A framework for conceptualizing marital conflict: A technique for altering it, some data for evaluating it. In L. A. Hamerlynck, L. C. Handy, & E. J. Marsh (Eds.), *Behavior change: Methodology, concepts and practice* (pp. 309-342). Champaign, IL: Research Press.

Weiss, R. S. (1977). *Going it alone.* New York: Basic Books.

Wender, P. H. (1971). *Minimal brain dysfunction in children.* New York: Wiley-Interscience.

Wender, P. H. (1987). *The hyperactive child, adolescent and adult.* New York: Oxford University Press.

Wertheim, E. S. (1959). A joint interview technique with mother and child. *Children, 6,* 23-29.

Westley, W., & Epstein, N. (1969). *The silent majority.* San Francisco: Jossey-Bass.

Whitaker, C. (1970). *Marital and family therapy* [Cassette audiotapes]. Chicago: Instructional Dynamics.

Whitaker, C., & Keith, D. (1981). Symbolic-experiential family therapy. In A. S. Gurman & D. P. Kniskern (Eds.), *Handbook of family therapy* (pp. 187-225). New York: Brunner/Mazel.

White, M. (1986). Negative explanation, restraint, and double description: A template for family therapy. *Family Process, 25,* 169-184.

White, M., & Epston, D. (1990). *Narrative means to therapeutic ends.* New York: Norton.

White, S. (1976). Family dinner time: A focus for life space diagrams. *Journal of Clinical Social Work, 4,* 93-101.

White, S. (1986). Uses and abuses of sexually anatomically correct dolls. *Division of Child, Youth and Family Services Newsletter, 9,* 3, 6.

White, S., Strom, G., & Santilli, G. (1985). *Clinical protocol for interviewing preschoolers with sexually anatomically correct dolls.* Unpublished manuscript, Case Western Reserve University, School of Medicine, Cleveland Metropolitan General Hospital.

White, S. G., & Hatcher, C. (1984). Couple complementarity and similarity: A review of the literature. *American Journal of Family Therapy, 12,* 15-25.

Whitfield, C. L. (1987). *Healing the child within.* Deerfield Beach, FL: Health Communications.

Wierenberg, G. I., & Calero, H. H. (1973). *Meta-talk: Guide to hidden meanings on conversations.* New York: Simon & Schuster.

Winch, R. (1954). The theory of complementary need in mate selection: An analytic and descriptive study. *American Sociological Review, 19,* 241-249.

Woititz, J. G. (1990). *Adult children of alcoholics* (Expanded ed.). Pompano Beach, FL: Health Communications.

Wolpe, J. (1958). *Psychotherapy by reciprocal inhibition.* Stanford, CA: Stanford University Press.

Wolpe, J. (1969). *The practice of behavior therapy.* Elmsford, NY: Pergamon.

Wynne, L. (1961). The study of intrafamilial alignments and splits in exploratory family therapy. In N. W. Ackerman, F. L. Beatman, & S. N. Sherman (Eds.), *Exploring the base of family therapy* (pp. 95-115). New York: Family Services Association.

Wynne, L. (1965). Some indications and contraindications for exploratory family therapy. In I. Boszormenyi-Nagy & J. Framo (Eds.), *Intensive family therapy: Theoretical and practical aspects* (pp. 289-322). New York: Harper & Row.

Wynne, L. (1970, March). *Communication disorders and the quest for relatedness in families of schizophrenics.* Paper presented at the Association for the Advancement of Psychoanalysis, New York.

Wynne, L., McDaniel, S., & Weber, T. (1987). *Systems consultation.* New York: Guilford.

Wynne, L., Ryckoff, I., Day, J., & Hirsch, S. (1958). Pseudomutuality in the family relations of schizophrenics. *Psychiatry, 21,* 205-220.

Wynne, L., & Singer, M. (1963). Thought disorder and family relations of schizophrenics. I: A research strategy. *Archives of General Psychiatry, 9,* 191-198.

Zelditch, M. (1964). Cross-cultural analyses of family structure. In H. T. Christensen (Ed.), *Handbook of marriage and the family* (pp. 462-500). Chicago: Rand McNally.

Zilbergeld, B., & Hammond, D. (1988). The use of hypnosis in treating sexual disorders. In S. Leiblum & R. Rosen (Eds.), *Sexual desire disorders* (pp. 192-223). New York: Guilford.

Zuk, G. (1971). *Family therapy: A triadic-based approach.* New York: Behavioral Publications.

Zuk, G., & Rubinstein, D. (1965). A review of concepts in the study and treatment of families of schizophrenics. In I. Boszormenyi-Nagy & J. Framo (Eds.), *Intensive family therapy: Theoretical and practical aspects* (pp. 1-32). New York: Harper & Row.

About the Authors

S. Richard Sauber, Ph.D., has been in the practice of family psychology since 1971 and was formerly a Professor at Brown and Columbia Universities. He is a Diplomate in Clinical and Family Psychology, American Board of Professional Psychology; a Diplomate in Marital and Family Therapy, American Board of Family Psychology (and served as a member on this latter board); and a Diplomate and Supervisor in Sexology, American Board of Sexology. He has been editor-in-chief of *American Journal of Family Therapy* for the past 16 years and the author of six books in the field. His most recent book is *The Handbook of Divorce Mediation.* Dr. Sauber also is the Series Editor for 12 books on *Mental Health Practice Under Managed Care: Survival Sourcebooks for Providers* (Brunner/Mazel).

Luciano L'Abate, Ph.D., serves on numerous family therapy editorial boards and has written 15 textbooks in the field of family therapy. He is the editor of *Family Psychology: Theory, Therapy, and Training* and *The Handbook of Family Psychology and Therapy* (Vols. 1 and 2). He is a Consultant to Cross Keys Counseling Center in Atlanta and is Professor Emeritus of Psychology at Georgia State University.

Gerald R. Weeks, Ph.D., is Director of Training with the Marriage Council of Philadelphia and the Division of Family Study in the Department of Psychiatry at the University of Pennsylvania School of Medicine. He is the senior author of *Paradoxical Psychotherapy: Theory and Practice With Individuals, Couples, and Families,* editor of *Promoting Change Through Paradox Therapy* and *Treating Couples: The Intersystem Model of the Marriage Council of Philadelphia,* and co-editor of *Integrating Sex and Marital Therapy.* His most recent text is *Couples in Treatment.*

William L. Buchanan, Ph.D., is currently in independent practice in Gainesville, GA. Previously he was Assistant Director of the Department of Clinical Psychology and Neuropsychology at Northeast Georgia Medical Center in Gainesville. He is a graduate of the Family Psychology program of Georgia State University and specializes in psychological assessment, ADHD, family therapy, eating disorders, and weight control. He is on the editorial board of the *American Journal of Family Therapy* and is a clinical member of AAMFT and the Supervisor of Family Therapy and consultant to Eagle Ranch for Boys. He is actively involved in the Georgia Psychological Association, where he serves as Chair of the Legal and Legislative Aspects Committee.